survey of | # Operating Systems

Fifth Edition

Jane Holcombe
Charles Holcombe

SURVEY OF OPERATING SYSTEMS, FIFTH EDITION

Published by McGraw-Hill Education, 2 Penn Plaza, New York, NY 10121. Copyright © 2017 by McGraw-Hill Education. All rights reserved. Printed in the United States of America. Previous editions © 2015, 2012, and 2006. No part of this publication may be reproduced or distributed in any form or by any means, or stored in a database or retrieval system, without the prior written consent of McGraw-Hill Education, including, but not limited to, in any network or other electronic storage or transmission, or broadcast for distance learning.

Some ancillaries, including electronic and print components, may not be available to customers outside the United States.

This book is printed on acid-free paper.

2 3 4 5 6 7 8 9 RMN 21 20 19 18 17 16

ISBN 978-1-259-61863-5
MHID 1-259-61863-3

Senior Vice President, Products & Markets: *Kurt L. Strand*
Vice President, General Manager, Products & Markets: *Michael Ryan*
Vice President, Content Design & Delivery: *Kimberly Meriwether David*
Managing Director: *Scott Davidson*
Executive Brand Manager: *Wyatt Morris*
Senior Product Developer: *Alan Palmer*
Executive Marketing Managers: *Debbie Clare/Tiffany Russell*
Director, Content Design & Delivery: *Terri Schiesl*
Executive Program Manager: *Faye M. Herrig*
Content Project Manager: *Mary Jane Lampe*
Buyer: *Laura M. Fuller*
Cover Design: *Studio Montage*
Content Licensing Specialist: *Deanna Dausener*
Cover Image: © *Dave Cutler Studio, LLC*
Compositor: *SPI Global Technolgies*
Printer: *R. R. Donnelley*

All credits appearing on page or at the end of the book are considered to be an extension of the copyright page.

Library of Congress Cataloging-in-Publication Data

Cataloging-in-Publication Data has been requested from the Library of Congress.

The Internet addresses listed in the text were accurate at the time of publication. The inclusion of a website does not indicate an endorsement by the authors or McGraw-Hill Education, and McGraw-Hill Education does not guarantee the accuracy of the information presented at these sites.

mheducation.com/highered

About the Authors

JANE HOLCOMBE (MCSE, MCT, A+, Network+, CTT+, and Novell CNA) was a pioneer in the field of PC support training. In 1983, while working for a financial planning company, she moved the accounting and client-management operations to IBM PCs. This project included using three different operating systems to run the selected software and installing a local area network for sharing the accounting system and data. Although the network was not completely successful, this project showed the potential of networked PCs in business. Between 1984 and the mid-1990s she was an independent trainer, consultant, and course-content author, creating and presenting courses on PC operating systems nationwide and coauthoring a set of networking courses for the consulting staff of a large network vendor. In the early 1990s she worked with both Novell and Microsoft server operating systems, finally focusing on Microsoft operating systems. She achieved her Microsoft Certified Systems Engineer certification early, recertifying for new versions of Windows. Since 2000 she has worked primarily as a technical writer and technical editor.

CHARLES HOLCOMBE has a high-tech background in computing in the nuclear and aerospace fields. In his 15 years at Control Data Corporation, he was successively a programmer, technical sales analyst, salesman, and sales manager in the field marketing force. At corporate headquarters, he ran Control Data's Executive Seminar program, headed sales training for the corporation, was liaison to the worldwide university community, and was market development manager for the Plato computer-based education system. For the past 30 years, he has been an independent trainer and consultant. He has authored and delivered many training courses and is a skilled editor. Currently he is an independent editor for various clients and collaborates with Jane on writing projects. For a while, he claimed he was semi-retired, but, with his consulting and editing work, he cannot say that anymore.

Together the Holcombes have authored 12 books, beginning with the *MCSE Guide to Designing a Microsoft Windows 2000 Network Infrastructure* (Course Technology), and both the *A+ Certification Press Lab Manual* and the *MCSE Certification Press Windows 2000 Professional Lab Manual* (McGraw-Hill/Osborne). They wrote *Using Windows 8* (McGraw-Hill) and the sixth, seventh, and eighth editions of the *CompTIA A+ Certification Study Guide* (McGraw-Hill). The book you are holding is their fifth edition of *Survey of Operating Systems*. The Holcombes also contributed chapters to four other technical books published by McGraw-Hill.

About the Contributors

This book was greatly influenced by the comments, suggestions, and feedback from the following group of dedicated instructors. To them we give our heartfelt thanks.

Technical Editors

Gerlinde Brady	*Cabrillo College*
Brenda Nielsen	*Mesa Community College*
Manzurul Khan	*Houston Community College*
Tom Trevethan	*ECPI College of Technology*
Ralph Argiento	*Guilford Technical Community College*

Reviewers

Ralph Argiento	*Guilford Technical Community College*
David Barnes	*Penn State Altoona*
Gerlinde Brady	*Cabrillo College*
Trey Cherry	*Edgecombe Community College*
Randy Gambill	*Wilkes Community College*

Jeremy Gammill	*Northwest Arkansas Community College*
Amy Giddens	*Central Alabama Community College*
Hillard Holland	*Los Angeles Southwest College and Pasadena City College*
Annette Kerwin	*College of DuPage*
Manzurul Khan	*Houston Community College*
Kevin Eugene Lee	*Guilford Technical Community College*
Carmen Montanez-Rodriguez	*Allan Hancock Community College*
Ruth Neal	*Navarro College*
Brenda Nielsen	*Mesa Community College*
Ruth Parker	*Rowan-Cabarrus Community College*
Terry Partridge	*Emily Griffith Technical College*
Kathy Ruggieri	*Lansdale School of Business*
Theresa Savarese	*San Diego City College*
Ted Tedmon	*North Idaho College*
Thomas Trevethan	*ECPI University*
Charulata Trivedi	*Quinsigamond Community College*
Paul Weaver	*Bossier Parish Community College*
Casey Wilhelm	*North Idaho College*
Kevin Wyzkiewicz	*Delta College*

Acknowledgments

After completing work on the fourth edition of our *Survey of Operating Systems*, Jane took some time off from the intense pressure of meeting deadlines while Chuck continued his other editing work. Then, after realizing that she wasn't spending all that free time wisely or creatively (the urban fantasy novel never materialized and her oil paintings were "meh"), she went in search of a little work-for-hire project. She called Alan Palmer, our product developer at McGraw-Hill, who asked if we wanted to write the fifth edition of our *Survey of Operating Systems* book. Because much has happened with operating systems and with personal computing since we wrote the first four editions, we knew it would require a nearly complete rethinking of the content. Along with brand manager Wyatt Morris and Alan, we wrote a suggested Table of Contents that they sent to instructors—some of whom were still using the fourth edition. The results of this survey helped us create the outline for the fifth edition.

As with previous editions, knowledgeable peer reviewers scrutinized each chapter, giving us invaluable feedback on the relevancy and accuracy of the content. We can't imagine writing a book like this without these technical reviews.

We thank every member of the talented team of people at McGraw-Hill who ensured the book's integrity. They include Wyatt Morris, Alan Palmer, Mary Jane Lampe, and Ruma Khurana and Vivek Khandelwal from MPS Limited. We particularly want to thank Wyatt and Alan for their unstinting support, professionalism, and patience. We love the design of this edition, and we greatly appreciate the expertise of the members of the production group who all worked hard to make the book look wonderful. Creating and laying out the many elements of this complex book design was a huge task, and they handled it skillfully. We particularly offer thanks to our friend Walt, a retired master electrician. When Jane called him in a panic after her Android tablet was "really and truly dead," Walt showed up within minutes, Android smartphone in hand, and they spent the afternoon experimenting with settings and taking screen shots. Deadline salvation can come in many forms, and now we know it can look like Walt.

We appreciate all who worked so hard to make this book what it is.

Thank you!

About This Book

Important Technology Skills

Information technology (IT) offers many career paths, leading to occupations in such fields as PC repair, network administration, telecommunications, Web development, graphic design, and desktop support. To become competent in any IT field, however, you need certain basic computer skills. This book will help you build a foundation for success in the IT field by introducing you to fundamental information about desktop operating systems, a needed basis for working with computers at any level.

Try This!
exercises reinforce the concepts.

Notes and Warnings
create a road map for success.

Makes Learning Fun!
Rich, colorful text and enhanced illustrations bring technical subjects to life.

Engaging and Motivational!
Using a conversational style and proven instructional approach, the authors explain technical concepts in a clear, interesting way using real-world examples.

Effective Learning Tools

The design of this colorful, pedagogically rich book will make learning easy and enjoyable and help you develop the skills and critical thinking abilities that will enable you to adapt to different job situations and troubleshoot problems. Jane and Charles Holcombe's proven ability to explain concepts in a clear, direct, even humorous way makes this book interesting and motivational, and fun.

Step-by-Step exercises put concepts into practice.

Chapter Review sections provide concept summaries, key terms lists, and a variety of questions and projects for students.

Offers Practical Experience!
Step-by-Step tutorials and lab assignments develop essential hands-on skills and put concepts in real-world contexts.

Robust Learning Tools!
Summaries, key terms lists, quizzes, essay questions, and lab projects help you practice skills and measure progress.

Each chapter includes:

- **Learning Outcomes** that set measurable goals for chapter-by-chapter progress.
- **Four-Color Illustrations** that give you a clear picture of the technologies.
- **Step-by-Step Tutorials** that teach you to perform essential tasks and procedures hands-on.
- **Try This!** sidebars that encourage you to practice and apply the concepts in real-world settings.

- **Notes** and **Warnings** that guide you through difficult areas.
- **Chapter Summaries** and **Key Terms Lists** that provide you with an easy way to review important concepts and vocabulary.
- **Challenging End-of-Chapter Tests** that include vocabulary-building exercises, multiple-choice questions, essay questions, and on-the-job lab projects.

New to *Survey of Operating Systems*, Fifth Edition

General changes in this Fifth Edition:

- We removed *The Command-Line Interface*, the Fourth Edition's Chapter 9, and moved appropriate content into the Windows and OS X chapters.
- We added a new chapter, Chapter 6: *Windows 10*. This required renumbering the Fourth Edition Chapters 6, 7, and 8 to 7, 8, and 9. Because we also removed the Fourth Edition's Chapter 9, the next two chapters, 10 and 11, still have the same numbers and titles, although we updated them.
- In addition to reviewing and updating the content from the Fourth Edition, we worked to tighten the text throughout, improve the flow, and remove topics that are no longer relevant.
- Finally, you will find updated exercises, figures, and illustrations to support learning.

Chapter 1 Introduction to Operating Systems

- We added a short description of the Internet of Things (IoT) and system-on-a-chip (SoC).
- We updated content and images in the section titled *Today's Desktop Operating Systems* to include Windows 10.
- We updated text and images under *Mobile Operating System Features*.

Chapter 2 Computer Security Basics

- We updated chapter content and images, as appropriate.

Chapter 3 Desktop Virtualization

- We updated chapter content and images, and removed out-of-date content concerning *Microsoft Virtual PC 2007*.

Chapter 4 Windows 7

- This is now a leaner, more targeted chapter. In the Fourth Edition this chapter included some coverage of *Windows Vista*, which we removed in this Fifth Edition. We updated the text and appropriate images.

Chapter 5 Windows 8.1

- Because Windows 8 is no longer a new operating system, we removed, moved, updated, and scaled down content about the features of Windows 8 and Windows 8.1, and focused on the latter version. This reduced the Learning Outcomes from five to four, making the chapter more digestible.

Chapter 6 Windows 10 (New Chapter)

- This chapter introduces the latest version of Windows, beginning with selecting an edition, installing or updating it, and using the new desktop, universal apps, and other features.

Chapter 7 Under the Windows Desktop: Supporting and Troubleshooting Windows

- This chapter is an update to the Fourth Edition's Chapter 6, with coverage of Windows 10 added where appropriate. We moved the *Windows Command Prompt, PowerShell, Safe Mode with Command Prompt,* and *System Recovery Command Prompt* discussions into this chapter from the former *Command-Line Interface* chapter.

Chapter 8 Apple OS X on the Desktop

- This chapter is an update to the Fourth Edition's Chapter 7. The content and images in this chapter now include coverage of new features in the latest version of OS X: El Capitan (10.11).

Chapter 9 Linux on the Desktop

- This chapter is an update to the Fourth Edition's Chapter 8. After doing a major revision for the Fourth Edition, we only needed to update the content in this chapter.

Chapter 10 Connecting Desktops and Laptops to Networks

- This is an update to the Fourth Edition's Chapter 10. We updated content and images, where appropriate.

Chapter 11 Mobile Operating Systems

- This is a revision of the Fourth Edition's Chapter 11. We updated content and images to include new mobile OS features in Android, Apple iOS, and Windows.

Appendix: Windows Mouse and Keyboard Shortcuts

- We updated this revision of the Fourth Edition's Appendix B to include Windows 10.

Chapter 12 File Management in the Cloud (found at www .mhhe.com/holcombe5)

- This bonus chapter is an introduction to file management of personal data in the cloud.

Contents

1 | Introduction to Operating Systems   1

2 | Computer Security Basics   39

3 | Desktop Virtualization   85

4 | Windows 7   115

8 | Apple OS X on the Desktop   305

9 | Linux on the Desktop   349

10 | Connecting Desktops and Laptops to Networks   387

Introduction

What Will You Learn?

The first four editions of this book were well received by instructors and students. This fifth edition updates the material and presents new information that is relevant to the topic of desktop operating systems, including Windows, Apple OS X, and Linux. In addition to these operating systems, this edition includes new information on mobile operating systems, as well as chapters on subjects peripheral to operating systems, such as computer security, desktop virtualization, and connecting computers and mobile devices to networks. We carefully revised every chapter as needed, with more illustrations and plenty of hands-on opportunities. We have added content throughout, while working to streamline the book in response to feedback we received from instructors.

How Will You Learn?

We don't want to simply give you an encyclopedia of information because it can feel like you're standing in front of an information fire hose, and we've been there ourselves many times in the past decades. Rather, keeping in mind that "less is more," we present just the key points about operating systems, and guide you in your own exploration of the specifics of the technology. One book simply can't give you everything you need to know about operating systems, but we do hope to empower you and to increase your ability to use widely available tools and resources to figure out the answers to your questions. Such tools as the Internet and the help program in your OS are aids you should turn to when you need to learn more about a topic, and when you want to enhance your skills in working with each of these operating systems—and with computers in general.

Each chapter uses many techniques to help you learn. We start by listing learning outcomes, follow that up with a lucid explanation of each topic, and support it with real-world experience and a liberal use of graphics and tables. To give you hands-on experience and to help you "walk the walk," each chapter contains detailed Step-by-Step tutorials and short Try This! exercises to reinforce the concepts. To build vocabulary to help you "talk the talk," each chapter contains computer term definitions, highlighted in a Key Terms List and compiled into a Glossary at the end of the book.

We've also included notes, which provide handy pieces of knowledge to use with your desktop OS. Warnings will help you prevent mishaps.

You can measure what you've learned with end-of-chapter Key Terms, Multiple-Choice, and Essay quizzes. In addition, Lab Projects challenge you to independently complete tasks related to what you've just learned.

Let's Get Down to Work

OK, enough of this introductory stuff. This is the last time in this book that you'll see so many words without illustrations. From now on it's downright exciting. Learn a lot and *have fun*!

Supplements

For teachers using this book in the classroom, a powerful collection of teaching tools written by the authors is available online at www.mhhe.com/holcombe5:

- An Instructor's Manual that maps to the organization of the textbook and provides additional instructor tips and activities to use with the book.
- A test bank for each chapter available online in either Word or EZ Test format.
- Engaging PowerPoint slides on the lecture topics, including key points and illustrations from the chapters.
- A bonus chapter entitled "File Management in the Cloud" with an overview of cloud services as well as the basics of using cloud storage for personal data.

Jane Holcombe

Charles Holcombe

1

Introduction to Operating Systems

Learning Outcomes

In this chapter, you will learn how to:

LO **1.1** Describe the purpose and functions of operating systems.

LO **1.2** Describe major events in the evolution of operating systems.

LO **1.3** List and compare the common desktop operating systems in use today.

LO **1.4** List the most common mobile OSs, the devices associated with them, and the features found in most of these devices.

Understanding operating systems (OSs) is critical to your future success in life. It is. Just believe us. You don't? You say you drive a car just fine, but you don't understand its engine, transmission, or other systems? So why can't you just use your computer? Why do you have to even know it has an OS? If you can successfully operate a car, you actually know more about its internal workings than you realize. You turn on the ignition, shift to the correct gear, press the accelerator, and drive down the street without hitting anything. You stop it (in time, usually). You use your car to go somewhere, thus making the car your transportation tool. Having only superficial knowledge of the workings of your car is adequate if you never intend to repair your car or to explain to a mechanic the symptoms of a problem. And just as you can use a car without in-depth knowledge of how it works, you can use your computer to write a letter, send email, create a report, surf the Internet, participate in social networking, and much more without understanding operating systems. You only have to know how to turn it on, call up the application program you wish to use, perform tasks, and turn it off.

But if you ever want to understand how your car actually works, you need to spend time studying it. And if you want to get the most out of the computers you use in your work, school, and private life, you need to understand how the most critical software component, the computer's operating system, works.

This chapter provides an overview of microcomputer operating systems—specifically, those commonly found on desktop and laptop computers and the personal mobile devices we use today. We'll begin with a brief look at microcomputers—their components and their general types. Then we'll explore the functions that operating systems perform, as well as describe the classic categories of operating systems. Finally, we introduce you to the OSs in all types of microcomputers including those in home and office computers as well as tablets and smartphones. 🏵

LO 1.1 | An Overview of Microcomputer Operating Systems

Note: The OS is an interpretor between the user and the hardware.

An operating system (OS) is a collection of programs that controls all of the interactions among the various system components, freeing application programmers from needing to include such functions in their programs. An application is software that allows a user to perform useful functions, such as writing a report, picking up email, editing graphics, calculating a budget, and much more. Microsoft Word and Adobe Photoshop are applications. Applications send commands to the OS to interact with the hardware. This book explores the common operating systems used in microcomputers, but before we explore, let's answer a few general questions you may have: What is a microcomputer? What microcomputers are you using today?

About Microcomputers

Our friend Brianna uses a PC at work and an Apple iMac at home, and she always has her smartphone handy. She will soon take night classes in which she will use either a tablet or laptop that she will carry to and from school. She wants to learn more about the computers she uses each day, beginning with the hardware.

A typical PC with components.

Hardware Components

To understand microcomputers, you need to learn a few technical terms. A computer is a device that performs calculations. Early computers had many mechanical components, but a typical modern computer is an electronic device that can perform a huge number of useful tasks for its owner. Any computer, small or large, has a central processing unit (CPU) that performs the calculations, or processing for the computer.

A microcomputer is a computer small enough and cheap enough for the use of one person. The CPU in a microcomputer is a microprocessor, although many still refer to it simply as a CPU or processor. This miniaturization of computer components became possible through the invention and development of many technologies. One of the most important of those inventions was the integrated circuit (IC), a small electronic component made up of transistors (tiny switches) and other miniaturized parts. These replaced the bulky vacuum tubes in early TVs and in mid-twentieth century mainframe computers.

Note: Common slang for an integrated circuit is "chip."

Each computer that Brianna uses consists of many components, some of which allow her to interact with it. In techie talk, we call interaction with a computer input/output (I/O). When we send something into the computer we call it input. You are inputting through input devices when you type on the keyboard, tap on a touch screen, or talk to a computer through a microphone. Output is processed information of many types: sounds sent through the speakers, visual output to the display screen or printer and data files saved or sent over a network.

In a microcomputer the internal components include at least one micro-processor, random-access memory (RAM) that acts as the main memory for holding active programs and associated data, firmware (software resident in integrated circuits), and various other supporting circuitry, all installed onto a motherboard. The typical microcomputer also has some form of storage, such as a hard drive, and it has at least one means each for input and output.

System firmware contains program code that informs the processor of the devices present and how to communicate with them. Firmware is an interface between the hardware and the operating system. The system firm-ware in PCs for most of the last three decades has been read only memory basic input output system (ROM BIOS), which has been replaced by a new standard for system firmware called Unified Extensible Firmware Interface (UEFI). UEFI supports modern computers, while ROM BIOS had many techni-cal limits because it was designed to work with the original IBM PC. UEFI is faster and includes security features that protect the computer during that vulnerable time while an operating system is just starting up and not entirely in control.

Additionally, most components and peripheral devices that connect to a computer (such as the video and network adapters, USB ports, and digital cameras) have their own firmware, which is often limited to small programs for providing basic communication between the operating sys-tem and the component. Supplementing or replacing the firmware—even parts of the central system firmware—are device drivers. A device driver is a special program installed into an operating system. Each device driver contains code for controlling a component; it is an extension of the firm-ware, usually allowing much more control of a device than the device's firmware.

Although you may never be aware of the firmware on a mobile device, on an older PC or laptop you may see evidence of the system and other firmware as they perform tests of the hardware. The traditional system firmware test is known as the power on self-test (POST). Carefully watch the screen as you power up the computer, as shown in Figure 1–1. If status and error messages display in plain text on a black background during startup, they are the result of the POST and the tests of additional firmware on the computer's compo-nents. More recent computers may show a message only if there is a serious problem with the computer.

Note: Random-access memory (RAM) is volatile: when you turn off the computer the contents in RAM disappear.

Note: Fortunately, you may never need to be concerned about device drivers because they install automatically in most operating systems.

```
Phoenix — Award BIOS v6.00PC
Copyright (C) 1984-2003, Phoenix Technologies, LTD


Main Processor : AMD Athlon (tm) 64 X2 Dual Core Processor 3000+
Memory Testing : 1720000K OK
```

FIGURE 1–1 An example of a firmware start-up message on an old PC.

In general, consumers encountered their first microcomputers in 1977 with the introduction of Apple's Apple II, Radio Shack's TRS-80, and Commodore's PET. It was the Apple II that best combined the critical elements that defined a microcomputer at the time; these included a keyboard, a monitor, available peripherals, an operating system, desirable and useful applications, and a reasonable price tag.

Today's Microcomputers

What microcomputers do you use? The answer will include several, depending on your activities. The miniaturization of computers led to computers being built into all types of machinery, including vehicles, aircraft, and appliances. And that is just the short list. Computers touch our lives 24/7, and each has some form of operating system. For our purposes, we will concentrate on the operating systems in desktops, laptops, and mobile devices. We will limit the mobile device OSs to those in tablets and smartphones. Another type of computer that you use less directly is a server. Servers also use microcomputer technology, but on a larger scale. We describe these types of microcomputers next.

A PC laptop.

A MacBook laptop.

Desktops and Laptops. A desktop computer is a computer designed to spend its useful life in one location—on a desk. A laptop computer has a flat screen and a keyboard, each integrated into a panel with a hinge holding the two together and allowing you to close the laptop and slip it into a case for easy portability. There are many sizes and types of laptop computers. Laptops are often used as portable replacements for desktop PCs. The common operating systems for these computers are Microsoft Windows and Linux for PCs and laptops, and Apple's OS X, which runs on Apple's Mac desktop and laptop computers. The same version of the Windows OS will run on a desktop, a compatible laptop computer, or a compatible tablet.

In the decades since the introduction of the IBM PC in 1981, the majority of desktop and laptop computers used in private and public organizations have used Microsoft operating systems, with computers running versions of Apple's operating systems a distant second. In recent years however, Apple desktop and laptop computers have made great gains in market share, but Apple's real advances have been in their mobile products.

Mobile Devices. Microcomputers today include a long list of devices that don't have *computer* in their name, including mobile devices. A mobile device has all or most of its electronic circuitry, such as the microprocessor, controllers, and memory, on a single microchip. This is known as system-on-a-chip (SoC). Mobile devices use wireless technologies and include a wide variety of products ranging from single-purpose computers to multifunction mobile devices. Some mobile devices run proprietary OSs, while others run scaled-down versions of desktop OSs. A mobile device commonly stores its OS in firmware, as an embedded OS.

The most popular mobile devices are smartphones. Worldwide use of smartphones continues to grow significantly. Market research firm GfK reported 309.7 million smartphones sold in the first quarter of 2015, an increase of 7 percent over the first quarter of 2014. A smartphone works as a cell phone, but also lets you connect to the Internet, view your email, and install and run a variety of apps for entertainment, education, and work. Modern smartphones have high-quality touch screens. Examples of smartphones are Apple's iPhones and various models by Motorola, Nokia, HTC, Samsung, LG, and others. Examples of operating systems designed specifically for use on smartphones

Note: In this book we use the term **personal computer (PC)** for a desktop computer running Windows or Linux and **Mac** for the Apple iMac desktop computers as well as the MacBook laptop computers. Both types of Apple computers run OS X.

include Google's Android, Apple iOS, Windows Phone (versions 7, 8, and 8.1), and Windows 10 Mobile.

Another very popular type of mobile device is a tablet. A tablet has a touch screen, no integrated keyboard (usually), is larger than a smartphone, and is much more portable than a laptop. There are many lines of tablet products, such as the Apple iPad, Microsoft Surface, Samsung Galaxy, Google Nexus Sony Xperia, and Kindle Fire. The tablet operating systems we will study in this book are Apple iOS, Google Android, Microsoft Windows 8.1, and Windows 10.

try this!

More About Tablets

The tablet market changes quickly. Check out what is happening with tablets. Try this:

1. Using your PC, laptop, tablet, or smartphone, open a browser and (using a search engine such as Google, Bing, or Yahoo) search on the key words "tablet reviews."

2. Browse through the sites you find in the list of results, selecting recent reviews.

3. Read a few of the reviews to learn about the latest tablet features and comparative pricing.

4. Describe to a classmate how you would (or do) use a tablet at school or work.

Servers. A server is a computer that provides one or more services to other computers over a network. What services do servers provide? A file server stores data files for network-connected users. If a server has one or more printers connected to it that it shares with users on the network, it is a print server. We call a server doing both tasks a file and print server; even though it sounds like two services, they combine into one service.

Other services include messaging services (email and fax), Web services, and many others. It takes specialized software to provide each type of server service, and complementary client software to request each type of service over a network. A computer on the user end of these services is a client. Today's client computers include the PCs, laptops, tablets, and smartphones discussed in this book. A server can offer multiple services at the same time while also being a client to other servers.

A desktop or laptop computer can act as a server for a few network clients. However, a server to which hundreds or thousands of clients must connect requires much more capable hardware to provide more storage, faster processing, and faster network access. It also requires specialized software, beginning with the operating systems. There are versions of Windows, Apple Mac OS X, Linux, and UNIX especially designed as servers. The hardware for a high-quality server can run into the tens of thousands of dollars and upward, versus the much lower cost of a consumer-grade PC at a few hundred dollars.

Note: In the spring of 2014 Microsoft purchased Nokia Corporation's devices business, including the Lumia line of smartphones.

Note: The focus of this book is on using common desktop, laptop, and mobile operating systems. Therefore, it does not include details of server operating systems. Nor does it discuss the operating systems in the various devices included in the Internet of Things (IoT).

Internet of Things. And lastly, microcomputers exist in devices belonging to the Internet of things (IoT). These are devices we don't normally think of as computing devices. They include kitchen appliances, thermostats, utility meters, components in automobiles, light bulbs, and industrial control devices. They are not necessarily mobile, but they communicate on networks, often the Internet. IoT devices are increasingly used in industrial automation, connecting wirelessly, or via Ethernet, to automation networks.

Functions of Microcomputer Operating Systems

When using her PC at work or her Mac at home our friend Brianna spends much of her time in a specific application, such as a word processor, a graphical drawing program, or a Web browser. However, she must also perform tasks outside of these applications, beginning with the simple task of logging onto the computer, launching an application, and managing files. Since each type of computer requires different skills to complete tasks, she wants to gain

The functions of an operating system.

a better understanding of the OSs to perform better on the job and be more comfortable working with the different computers. She wants to learn what an OS is and what functions it performs, which we describe in the following sections.

When a computer is turned on an operating system starts up (or "boots up," a derivation of the expression "lifting yourself by your own bootstraps"). Its main component, the kernel, remains in memory while the computer is running, managing low-level (close-to-the-hardware) OS tasks.

When a programmer, also known as a "developer," writes an application, he or she designs the application to interact with the operating system and to make requests for hardware services through the operating system. To do this, a programmer must write the program to use the correct commands to request operating system services. The operating system, in turn, interacts with the hardware on behalf of the application and fulfills the requests the application made. An operating system performs several functions. We'll study them next.

User Interface

The user interface (UI) is the software layer, sometimes called the shell, through which the user interacts with the OS. The UI includes the command processor, which loads programs into memory, as well as the many visual components of the operating system (what you see when you look at the display). On a computer running Linux (without a graphical shell), this visual component consists of a character-based command line that requires text input. This is the command-line interface (CLI). Windows and OS X both also have an optional CLI that runs in a window. Figure 1–2 shows the Windows 10 Command Prompt for the user Jane: white characters against a black screen, with a blinking cursor waiting for you to type a command at the keyboard. A cursor in a CLI is merely a marker for the current position where what you type on the keyboard will appear. Only a limited set of characters can display on the screen.

To become proficient at working in a CLI, you must memorize the commands and their modifiers and subcommands. On the other hand, Apple's OS X, Microsoft's Windows, and even mobile operating systems each provides an information-rich graphical user interface (GUI), fully integrated into the operating system. It is through this GUI that you communicate with the OS and the computer. The GUI offers menus and small graphical icons that allow you to use a pointing device to select programs to run and to perform many other tasks, such as opening a word processor file.

Although you do not have to memorize commands, working within a GUI does require learning the meaning of the various graphical pieces that make up the GUI and how to navigate among them to access your programs and data. In addition, you must learn how to activate a program (start it running) so that you can get your work or play done. Figure 1–3 shows the Apple OS X GUI. Notice the icons and other graphical components, such as the bar at the bottom containing icons for starting apps. Three windows are open on the desktop. In a GUI you move a graphical pointer around using a pointing device—usually a mouse, trackball, touch pad, or touch screen. The pointer allows you to select or manipulate objects in the GUI to accomplish tasks. For example, to delete an item in OS X, drag it into the Trash, shown on the

FIGURE 1–2 The Windows Command Prompt.

Note: Although Linux traditionally had a CLI, most current versions of Linux for the desktop come with both CLIs and GUIs.

FIGURE 1–3 The OS X GUI.

bottom right of Figure 1–3. By contrast, in a CLI, you would type a command such as "delete report.txt."

Job Management

Job management, also known as process scheduler, is an operating system function that controls the order and time in which programs run. Two examples of programs that may take advantage of this function are a scheduling program that schedules other programs to run on a certain day and time, and a print program that manages and prioritizes multiple print jobs.

Task Management

Task management is an operating system function found in multitasking operating systems. Multitasking implies that a computer is running two or more programs (tasks) at the same time. In reality, a computer cannot simultaneously run more tasks than the number of processors that exist within the computer. Until recently, most microcomputers had only a single processor, so they accomplish multitasking through a scheme that makes order out of chaos by determining which program responds to the keystrokes and mouse movements. New processors can have multiple CPUs within a single chip, so they have true multitasking coexisting with task switching.

Task management controls the focus (where the system's attention is at any given moment). It allows the user to switch between tasks by giving the focus to the application the user brings to the foreground. In graphical operating systems, the foreground application runs in the current window, the window that is on top of other windows on the screen. This window receives input from the keyboard, mouse, and/or touch screen when

try this!

View Active Tasks in Windows or OS X

You can see what tasks are running on your Windows or OS X computer. Try this:

1. On a Windows computer with a keyboard, press CTRL-SHIFT-ESC to open Task Manager, a utility that lets you view tasks as running applications and their processes. Select the Processes tab and notice the large number of active processes.

2. On an OS X computer press COMMAND+SPACEBAR to open the Spotlight search box, and then type "activity" and select Activity Monitor from the results list. Notice the list of processes in the column labeled Process Name.

the user types. While active in memory, a program runs as one or more small components called processes. The OS's task management function manages these processes.

File Management

File management, also referred to as data management, is an operating system function that allows the operating system to read, write, and modify data, while managing the logical storage of the data. Each operating system has at least one scheme of logical organization, called a file system. A file system is the logical structure used on a storage device (hard disk, optical disc, thumb drive, etc.) for managing and storing files. The file system also includes the program code that performs these tasks. An operating system uses a technique called formatting to write the logical structure to a storage device. The operating system maps the logical organization of the file system to physical locations on the storage device, most often a conventional hard disk drive or solid-state drive (SSD), so that it can store and retrieve the data. The logical structure of a file system stores metadata, which summarizes data to facilitate searches.

Solid-state drives (SSDs) use integrated circuits, which the computer can write to and read from much faster than conventional hard disk drives and optical drives. We also call such storage solid-state storage. SSDs come in many forms, such as a tiny card installed inside the case of your tablet or smartphone, or a flat device, measuring about ¾ inch by 2 inches (or smaller) that you plug into a computer's USB connector. This type of SSD is called a thumb drive, jump drive, or flash drive.

> **Note:** As a rule, the term *folder* is used in a GUI, while the term *directory* is used in a non-GUI operating system.

Normally, a single storage device will have only a single file system, residing in an area defined as a partition, but some operating systems allow a storage device to have more than one partition. A partition may be an entire drive volume or just a portion of a drive, and an operating system automatically assigns some identifier, such as C for the first hard drive recognized by Windows. Windows follows the drive letter with a colon, so that a complete drive name is C:. We call this a logical drive.

Within the logical structure of a file system, data is organized into entities called files that are saved to storage devices. File management also allows users to organize their files, using other special files that act as containers. One of these special files, called a folder or directory, can contain lists of files as well as other folders, along with the physical location of the files and folders.

Device Management

The device management function controls hardware devices by using special software called device drivers that are installed in the operating system. Device drivers are unique to the device, and the manufacturer of the device creates them to work with a specific operating system. For instance, a printer or video adapter may come with drivers for Windows, OS X, and Linux. The device driver contains the commands understood by the device and uses these commands to control the device in response to requests it receives from the operating system. An operating system needs a component-specific device driver for each unique hardware component with which it interacts. OSs today are plug and play (PNP)—they are intelligent enough to detect a device connected by an external port and automatically install the needed device driver.

Memory Management

Memory management is an operating system function that manages the placement of programs and data in memory, while keeping track of where it put them.

Virtual Memory. Modern operating systems use a scheme for making optimal use of memory, even allowing more code and data to be in memory than what the actual physical system memory can hold. Using a memory management OS component called the virtual memory manager, operating systems move code and data, as necessary, to a portion of the disk defined as virtual memory, meaning that this disk space is used as if it were memory, not just disk storage space. The OS performs this transfer for code and data that are part of any program that currently does not have the user's attention because this information does not have to be kept in RAM for immediate use, so other programs that do need to use the memory can do so.

Operating System Memory Limits. We call an operating system that can take advantage of the addressing and processing features of a processor an *x*-bit OS, referring to the number of bits the OS (using the processor) can manipulate at once. The PC operating systems of the 1980s and 1990s, PC DOS and MS-DOS were 16-bit OSs, as was Windows 3.0. Windows 95, Windows 98, and Windows Millennium edition were really hybrids, with mostly 32-bit pieces but some 16-bit pieces for downward compatibility. Windows XP had a 64-bit version, but it was not widely used, and you are unlikely to encounter it. The Windows versions, OS X, and Linux OSs we discuss in this book are available in both 32-bit and 64-bit versions.

All things being equal, the 64-bit version of an operating system will be faster than its 32-bit counterpart, but the biggest difference between the 32-bit and 64-bit versions of Windows is in the number of unique locations (the address space) a CPU can assign to both system RAM and other RAM and ROM in your computer. A 64-bit CPU can have a theoretical address space of 2^{64}, or 9.2 quintillion (nine followed by 18 digits). Windows does not use the maximum theoretical address space of a CPU, as shown in Table 1–1.

A 64-bit operating system requires 64-bit drivers, and some 32-bit applications may not run, although Microsoft supports older applications in each upgrade of Windows. If you purchase a new computer today with either Windows or the Mac OS preinstalled, it is most likely to be a 64-bit OS. Figure 1–4 shows the System type information for 64-bit Windows 10.

try this!

Are You Running 32-bit or 64-bit Windows?

If you have a Windows computer handy, see if it is running a 32-bit or 64-bit version. Try this:

1. In the Windows 7 or Windows 10 Start menu Search box (or in the Windows 8.*x* Start screen) type "system."
2. In the search results list select "System." Do *not* select "System Information."
3. This opens Control Panel to the System page.
4. The System Type field will say "32-bit Operating System" or "64-bit Operating System."

TABLE 1–1 Windows Memory Limits

Edition	RAM Limit in 32-Bit Version	RAM Limit in 64-Bit Version
Windows 7 Home Premium	4 GB	16 GB
Windows 7 Ultimate/Enterprise/Professional	4 GB	192 GB
Windows 8.*x* and Windows 10 Home	4 GB	128 GB
Windows 8.*x* Pro/Enterprise	4 GB	512 GB
Windows 10 Pro/Enterprise/Education	4 GB	2 TB

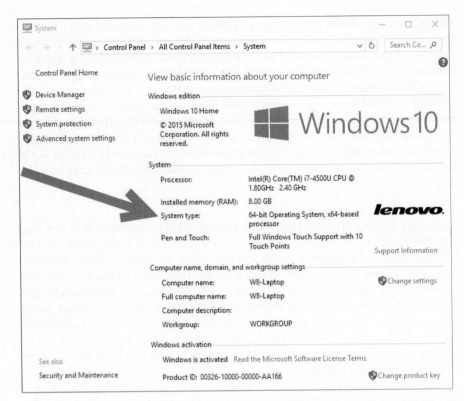

Note: The timeline running along the bottom of the next several pages shows highlights of computing history. Some are described in this chapter. Many are not.

FIGURE 1–4 Find the operating system type in the System page of Control Panel.

Security

Security

The built-in security features of an operating system provide password-protected authentication of the user before allowing access to the local computer and may restrict what someone can do on a computer. This

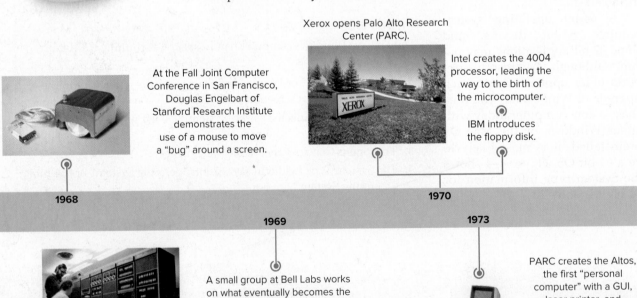

Xerox opens Palo Alto Research Center (PARC).

At the Fall Joint Computer Conference in San Francisco, Douglas Engelbart of Stanford Research Institute demonstrates the use of a mouse to move a "bug" around a screen.

Intel creates the 4004 processor, leading the way to the birth of the microcomputer.

IBM introduces the floppy disk.

1968

1970

1969

1973

Reprinted with permission of Alcatel-Lucent USA Inc.

A small group at Bell Labs works on what eventually becomes the UNIX operating system.

ARPANET is created, the first step in the building of the Internet.

PARC creates the Altos, the first "personal computer" with a GUI, laser printer, and a connection to the first Ethernet network.

The first portable telephone handset is invented at Motorola by Dr. Martin Cooper.

protects the computer and the data it contains from unauthorized access. For example, Rachel is the accounting clerk in a small company. She has confidential information on her computer, and she doesn't want just anyone to be able to walk up to her computer and access the information stored there. Rachel can set up her computer so that anyone getting into it must log on with a user name and password from a user account. A user account includes, at minimum, a name and an associated password stored inside the PC. Security is a large topic—one that would take many books and weeks of your time to really master—but to go much farther in this book without addressing computer security would be foolish, so Chapter 2 is devoted to computer security basics. There you will learn about threats to computers, what security is built in to the operating systems discussed in this book, and the steps you can take to protect yourself from threats.

LO 1.2 | Yesterday's Operating Systems

Sometimes people think that they can simply take the newest and best computer or other gadget and make it work without understanding anything about how it came to be. Well, they probably can. But they probably can't fix it, modify it, or use it effectively without understanding how and why it came to be in the form it's in now. One really can't understand current PC technology without having a grasp of older PC technology. In other words, studying history is important to understand how we arrived at today. We'll begin with UNIX, arguably the oldest OS still in use today, with beginnings that predate microcomputers. Then we'll explore the history of computers leading to today's PCs and Mac desktop computers and the operating systems that evolved for each of these hardware platforms.

> **Note:** The MITS Altair 8800 was an important predecessor to the Apple II, TRS-80, and PET computers. Although featured in a cover article of the January 1975 issue of *Popular Mechanics*, it was not for everyday use. Whether you bought the $395 kit or the fully assembled $495 version, the input method was switches that you flipped to program it, and the result of these efforts (the output) was a pattern of blinking lights. As a portent of the future, the Altair 8800 gave Bill Gates and Paul Allen their very first sale of a ROM-based interpreter for the BASIC programming language.

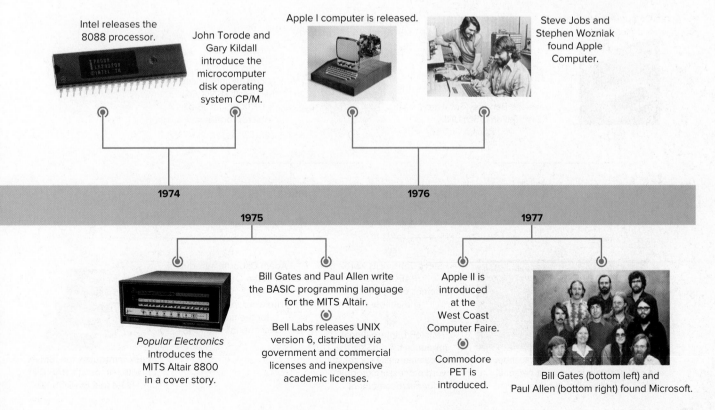

Intel releases the 8088 processor.

John Torode and Gary Kildall introduce the microcomputer disk operating system CP/M.

Apple I computer is released.

Steve Jobs and Stephen Wozniak found Apple Computer.

1974

1976

1975

1977

Popular Electronics introduces the MITS Altair 8800 in a cover story.

Bill Gates and Paul Allen write the BASIC programming language for the MITS Altair.

Bell Labs releases UNIX version 6, distributed via government and commercial licenses and inexpensive academic licenses.

Apple II is introduced at the West Coast Computer Faire.

Commodore PET is introduced.

Bill Gates (bottom left) and Paul Allen (bottom right) found Microsoft.

UNIX—The Operating System for All Platforms

UNIX has a longer history than any other popular operating system, and it is still in use today. In fact, Apple's Mac OS X is a certified UNIX operating system. UNIX grew out of an operating system developed for an early Digital Equipment Corporation (DEC) computer and went through several generations of changes before it emerged from the Bell Labs Computing Science Research Center (Bell Labs) as UNIX version 6 in 1975, a portable operating system for minicomputers and mainframe computers. A portable operating system is one that you can use on a variety of computer system platforms, with only minor alterations required to be compatible with the underlying architecture. Minicomputers and mainframe computers allowed multiple remote users to connect and use the computer's resources, and UNIX supported the time-sharing and multitasking features that made this possible.

The University of California at Berkeley licensed UNIX, modified it, and distributed it to other schools as Berkeley Software Distribution (BSD) version 4.2. Later versions followed. The schools paid licensing fees to Bell Labs. Students and others improved on and added to UNIX, freely sharing their code with each other. This tradition still prevails today with such versions of UNIX as FreeBSD, NetBSD, OpenBSD, and OpenSolaris. Commercial versions of UNIX today include AIX, OpenServer (derived from SCO UNIX), and HP/UX.

Today UNIX is still used on very large computer systems (referred to as mainframes) and less commonly on Intel desktop systems, as well as on a variety of midsize computers. Versions of UNIX run on many of

try this!

Research the History of UNIX

Learn more about the UNIX operating system.
Try this:

1. Point your browser to www.unix.org.
2. Explore the links on this page to learn more about the history of UNIX.
3. Select the *What is UNIX* link and then select the *History and Timeline* link to read a more complete history of this OS.
4. Look in the timeline for a current OS, featured in this book, that is certified to UNIX 03.

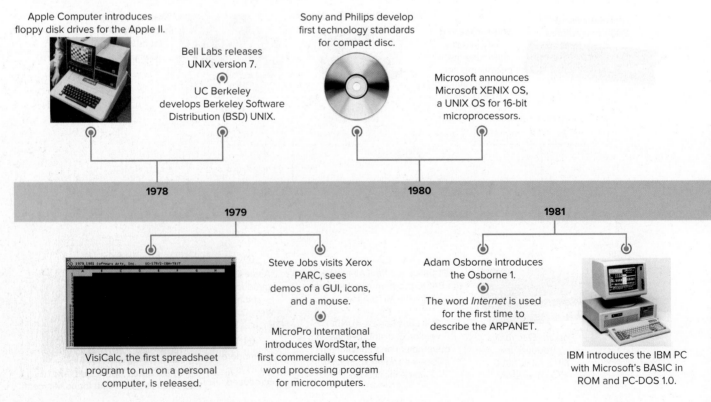

Apple Computer introduces floppy disk drives for the Apple II.

Bell Labs releases UNIX version 7.

UC Berkeley develops Berkeley Software Distribution (BSD) UNIX.

Sony and Philips develop first technology standards for compact disc.

Microsoft announces Microsoft XENIX OS, a UNIX OS for 16-bit microprocessors.

1978

1979

1980

1981

VisiCalc, the first spreadsheet program to run on a personal computer, is released.

Steve Jobs visits Xerox PARC, sees demos of a GUI, icons, and a mouse.

MicroPro International introduces WordStar, the first commercially successful word processing program for microcomputers.

Adam Osborne introduces the Osborne 1.

The word *Internet* is used for the first time to describe the ARPANET.

IBM introduces the IBM PC with Microsoft's BASIC in ROM and PC-DOS 1.0.

the world's Internet servers. Most versions of UNIX also offer several different user interfaces. Some use character mode, like the traditional shells, such as the Bourne shell and the C shell. Others use a graphical interface such as GNOME or KDE. As mentioned earlier, Apple's Mac OS X operating system is based on a version of UNIX, and it has a graphical user interface.

Even fierce UNIX advocates do not see UNIX taking over the desktop any time soon. However, it is very secure and stable. Versions of UNIX run on many of the world's Internet servers.

The Evolution of Desktop Operating Systems

The complex and powerful operating system like what you see on your desktop, laptop, or mobile devices didn't just magically pop into someone's head. An operating system as a separate entity didn't exist in the early years of digital computing (defined roughly as from World War II into the 1950s). Each computer was dedicated to a single purpose, such as performing trajectory calculations for weapons or mathematical analysis for a science lab, in addition to the system I/O functions. Loading a new program into a computer was a time-consuming process, and the software had to include system functions as well as the main purpose of the computer.

Small Steps

Operating systems evolved through many small steps over several decades, some in the form of technical advances and others in evolutionary changes in how people used computers, especially as they saw the need to use computers as multipurpose devices. The "user," at first a government agency, research institute, or large business, would define the computer's purpose at any given time by the program chosen to run. In the 1950s, some early "operating systems" managed data storage on tape for mainframe computers, but it was much more common for application programmers to write system I/O

TCP/IP becomes the network protocol standard for the Internet.

Apple introduces the Lisa, the first commercial computer with a purely graphical operating system and a mouse.

Mitch Kapor announces Lotus 1-2-3 spreadsheet application for the IBM-PC.

Apple Computer releases the Macintosh with the Mac OS 1.

Apple Computer releases the "Fat Mac" with 512K of memory.

Satellite Software International (SSI) introduces WordPerfect.

The 3½-inch floppy drives are introduced.

IBM introduces the PC-AT with PC-DOS 3.0.

1982

1983

1984

Microsoft introduces the Microsoft mouse for the IBM PC and compatibles.

Microsoft and IBM introduce PC DOS 2.0 to support the 20 MB hard drive of the IBM PC-XT.

Lotus 1-2-3 sells more than 200,000 copies the first year.

Bell Labs releases UNIX System V, release 2 through commercial licenses.

Motorola introduces the DynaTAC 800X mobile phone (the size and approximate weight of a brick).

routines (the stuff of today's OSs) right into their programs. By the mid-1960s, as disk systems became more common on large computers, we needed operating systems to manage these disks and to perform other common system-level routines.

The computer enthusiasts who bought the earliest microcomputers of the 1970s, such as the MITS Altair 8800, were infatuated with the technology. What we now consider slow CPU speeds, very limited memory, clumsy I/O devices, and lack of software was exciting and new technology at the time. They would network with like-minded people, have informal meetings and discussions, and then gather in self-help groups and form clubs such as the Home Brew Computer Club in California's Silicon Valley. They shared their techniques for creating hardware and programming language software for these computers. Almost every one of these early microcomputers exceeded the expectations of their makers and users, but before long, and for a variety of reasons, most of the early entrepreneurial companies and their products disappeared.

Software Versions

A software version is a unique level of an operating system. When a software publisher creates an entirely new OS, they give it a version number, usually 1.0. Software publishers constantly receive feedback from customers about problems and the need for additional features in each OS. In response, a publisher often introduces a modified version of the original product, in which case the number to the right of the decimal point will probably change (say, from version 1.0 to version 1.1—people often abbreviate *version* as simply "v"). An entirely new version number (2.0, 3.0, . . .) generally reflects an important change to an OS with major changes to the core components of the operating system as well as a distinctive and unifying look to the GUI.

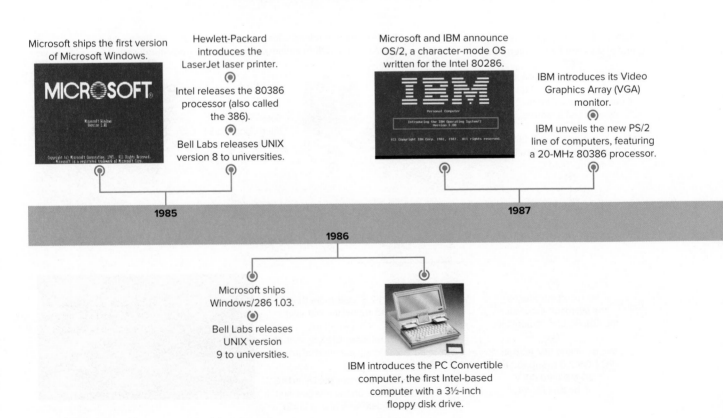

Microsoft ships the first version of Microsoft Windows.

Hewlett-Packard introduces the LaserJet laser printer.

Intel releases the 80386 processor (also called the 386).

Bell Labs releases UNIX version 8 to universities.

Microsoft and IBM announce OS/2, a character-mode OS written for the Intel 80286.

IBM introduces its Video Graphics Array (VGA) monitor.

IBM unveils the new PS/2 line of computers, featuring a 20-MHz 80386 processor.

1985

1987

1986

Microsoft ships Windows/286 1.03.

Bell Labs releases UNIX version 9 to universities.

IBM introduces the PC Convertible computer, the first Intel-based computer with a 3½-inch floppy disk drive.

The Killer App for the Apple II

For a microcomputer to truly become a successful, widely accepted product—used in businesses as well as by hobbyists—it had to be a tool that performed an important task; it had to have an application that many people needed enough to purchase a computer. We call that application a killer app.

One of these important tasks was spreadsheet calculations. Before microcomputers, people created spreadsheets manually, on large sheets of paper. They would enter a column of numbers—say, sales for one product in a drugstore—day-by-day for a month. Then they would add up the daily columns to get the total sales for that product for that month. The next column was for the next product, and so on. The process was tedious and error prone, but very valuable to the manager of the drugstore.

Thus, when VisiCalc, an electronic spreadsheet program, appeared it became a very successful application. It automated this thankless job, remembered the formulas for the calculations, and allowed people to recalculate a whole column of numbers after a single change was made. VisiCalc did more than this. It gave people a reason to want a personal computer. Many people were introduced to VisiCalc on the Apple II computer (running the Apple OS), and this contributed to the success of the Apple II in the late 1970s. However, as the 1980s arrived, Apple failed to come out with a successor to the Apple II in a timely fashion. So, when IBM introduced the IBM PC in 1981, the market was ready for a new microcomputer and VisiCalc was modified to run on the IBM PC, but VisiCalc wasn't the real killer app for this new type of microcomputer.

The IBM PC Operating System

Another fateful series of events revolved around the choice of an OS for the IBM PC. IBM representatives came to Microsoft, then a fledgling software company, for the Microsoft BASIC interpreter, which other machines were using at that time. The result of that visit was that IBM licensed Microsoft's

> *Note:* Want to learn more about the early history of PCs? Our favorite book on the subject is *Fire in the Valley: The Making of the Personal Computer* (ISBN 0-07-135892-7).

IBM and Microsoft release OS/2 1.1, adding a GUI to their first multitasking desktop operating system.

"Internet Worm" virus invades Internet, disables 10 percent of all Internet host computers.

NeXT, Inc. unveils the NeXT computer, featuring a 25-MHz Motorola 68030 processor.

Motorola announces its 32-bit microprocessor, the 68040.

Microsoft releases Windows 3.0.

1988

1989

1990

1991

Bell Labs releases UNIX version 10 to universities.

Intel releases the 80486 chip (also called the 486).

Tim Berners-Lee develops HTML, the foundation for the World Wide Web.

Microsoft releases MS-DOS 5.0.

Linus Torvalds creates Linux, a free UNIX-like operating system for the Intel platform.

Apple Computer launches the PowerBook series of portable computers.

Apple releases Macintosh System 7.0.

Internet opened to commercial use.

BASIC interpreter and installed it in the ROM of the IBM PC. The IBM folks also talked to Bill Gates about providing an OS; but he did not have one, and so he sent them to another company, Digital Research, the creators of the then-popular CP/M OS. Digital Research, however, refused to sign a contract with IBM, so the IBM guys went back to Bill Gates for the OS. Consequently, Microsoft bought an OS from another company, and this was the basis of the first versions of IBM PC DOS.

The IBM PC far exceeded IBM's sales forecast, which was for about a quarter of a million units during the predicted five-year lifetime of the product. According to one account, IBM took orders for half a million computers in the first few days after introducing the IBM PC. At first many enthusiasts bought it despite its roughly $5,000 price tag for a typical configuration. The IBM logo on the product also inspired many business users to buy it because this implied that it was a serious business computer.

The Killer App for PCs

Although many say that just having the letters *IBM* on the box was what sold that computer, the groundwork laid by VisiCalc was for what was arguably the second killer app, Lotus 1-2-3 by Lotus Corporation. Introduced in 1983, this spreadsheet application ran on the DOS operating system and used all of the 640KB of memory available to software (OS plus application)

Microsoft releases Windows 3.1, the first widely accepted version of Windows.

IBM releases OS/2 2.0, the first 32-bit OS for PCs.

Microsoft releases Windows for Workgroups 3.1, with integrated support for networking.

Yahoo! is born in a trailer on the Stanford University campus.

IBM releases OS/2 Warp (OS/2 version 3).

Microsoft releases MS-DOS 6.22 and Windows NT 3.5.

Netscape Communications releases Netscape Navigator.

1992

1994

1993

1995

Microsoft releases the first version of Windows NT (3.1).

Microsoft releases MS-DOS 6.0.

Apple introduces the Newton MessagePad, a handheld device with a stylus for use on the touch screen. It runs the Newton OS.

The National Center for Supercomputing Applications (NCSA) develops Mosaic, the first Web browser.

IBM introduces the Simon smartphone.

Microsoft ships Windows 95.

Intel releases the Pentium Pro microprocessor.

Motorola releases the PowerPC 604 chip.

Sun Microsystems creates the Java development language.

on the IBM PC. Both the Lotus 1-2-3 program and the spreadsheet were in memory while the user worked. It was very fast compared to VisiCalc, which was written to run under the CP/M OS and designed to use much less memory. Lotus 1-2-3 had additional features, including database functions and a program that could create and print graphs from the spreadsheet data. Lotus 1-2-3 was the real killer app, the software that made the IBM PC and PC DOS a must-have combination for people who worked all day crunching numbers and doing what-if calculations.

Apple OS

In 1976, Steve Jobs and Stephen Wozniak—two friends working out of a garage—founded Apple Computer, based on their first computer, the Apple I. Their real notoriety began in 1977 when they introduced the Apple II at the West Coast Computer Faire in San Francisco. This created interest in the brand, and the addition of disk drives in 1978 made it a sought-after product for the technically adventurous consumer. But the OS for the Apple computers at this point did not have a GUI interface—that showed up on the short-lived Apple Lisa computer.

In 1982 Apple introduced the Lisa, the first commercially available computer with a purely graphical operating system—and a mouse. However, this computer lacked something very important for consumers—applications. It was unsuccessful, and Apple's own Macintosh computer, released in 1984, overshadowed the Lisa and marked the beginning of consumer excitement and the near-cult following of the Apple computer products. The Macintosh came with Mac OS System 1, a GUI operating system that used a mouse. Apple improved the Mac OS over the years to include many easy-to-use features.

The final release of the classic Mac OS family was Mac OS 9, introduced in 1999. With its roots in the original 1984 OS, Apple revised and improved the operating system to support multiple users, but it was weak in memory management and full multitasking. In 2001 it was replaced by a completely new

> *Note:* Through the 1980s, PCs with DOS and a variety of DOS applications made great inroads into organizations of all sizes. In the decade after its introduction, thousands of applications were written for DOS, but Lotus 1-2-3, dBase (database management), and WordPerfect (word processing) were the de facto business standards at the end of that decade. All contributed to the mass adoption of PCs at work, at school, and at home.

IBM releases OS/2 Warp Server, an OS for network servers.

Apple Computer buys NeXT.

Microsoft releases Windows NT Workstation 4.0.

IBM releases OS/2 Warp 4, which can simultaneously connect to almost any network server.

U.S. Robotics releases the PalmPilot personal digital assistant running the Palm OS.

Intel releases Pentium II chip.

Apple Computer releases the iMac.

Microsoft releases Windows 98.

Sergey Brin and Larry Page found Google.

1996

1998

1997

Digital Video/Versatile Disc (DVD) technology is introduced.

Mac OS 8 ships.

operating system—Mac OS X, based on UNIX. There is a brief overview of OS X later in this chapter and more detail on this OS in Chapter 8.

MS-DOS

DOS, which stands for "disk operating system," provides support for interaction, or input and output (I/O), between the memory and disk drives. It is a single-tasking OS with very limited memory support, no support for virtual memory, no native GUI, and no built-in security function. *PC DOS* is the version for IBM computers. *MS-DOS* refers to the several versions of DOS developed by Microsoft and made available to non-IBM PC manufacturers. Each major version of DOS was released to support new disk capacities. PC DOS 1.0 supported single-sided 5¼-inch floppies; PC DOS 1.1 added support for double-sided 5¼-inch floppies; and PC DOS 2.0, released with the IBM PC-XT, included support for the XT's 10MB hard drives. PC DOS 3.0 was released with the IBM PC-AT and included support for the larger AT hard drives. Support for 3½-inch floppies and the larger hard drives of the IBM PS-2 computers were added in PC DOS 4.0. MS-DOS 6.22 was the last widely used version of MS-DOS. Some forms of DOS are now available from third-party sources, but these sources are dwindling.

DOS has a text-mode command-line interface that requires users to remember cryptic commands and their subcommands to perform file management functions and to launch DOS applications. Figure 1–5 shows a good example of how cryptic DOS can be to the uninitiated.

Although you will not find DOS as the preferred OS on desktop computers, you might find a variation of it as the OS on some handheld devices that do not require a GUI interface. In the past, computer professionals often found DOS handy as a very small OS that fit on a floppy disk, to which they added various utilities for troubleshooting computers. This practice has disappeared today, as have floppy disks and floppy disk drives. Those same techs are now more likely to carry either optical discs or a flash drive loaded with specialized software for their work.

> *Note:* Many of us still open a command line interface (CLI) in Windows to use certain advanced troubleshooting tools. There are two CLIs that come with Windows: the Command Prompt and the Windows Power Shell.

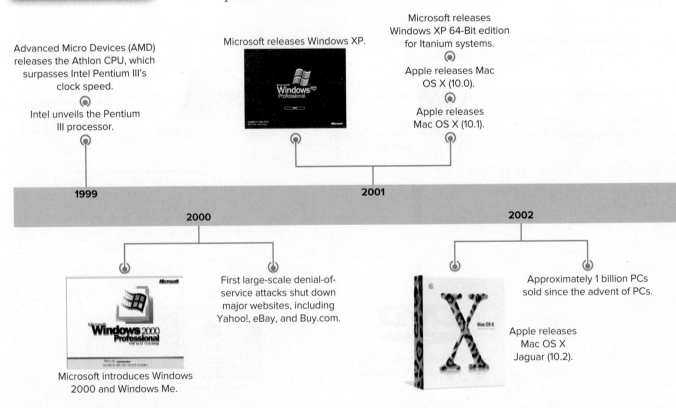

Advanced Micro Devices (AMD) releases the Athlon CPU, which surpasses Intel Pentium III's clock speed.

Intel unveils the Pentium III processor.

Microsoft releases Windows XP.

Microsoft releases Windows XP 64-Bit edition for Itanium systems.

Apple releases Mac OS X (10.0).

Apple releases Mac OS X (10.1).

1999

2001

2000

2002

Microsoft introduces Windows 2000 and Windows Me.

First large-scale denial-of-service attacks shut down major websites, including Yahoo!, eBay, and Buy.com.

Approximately 1 billion PCs sold since the advent of PCs.

Apple releases Mac OS X Jaguar (10.2).

```
A:\>format c: /s /u

WARNING: ALL DATA ON NON-REMOVABLE DISK
DRIVE C: WILL BE LOST!
Proceed with Format (Y/N)?y


Formatting   502M
Format complete.
System transferred

Volume label (11 characters, ENTER for none)?

  526,106,624 bytes total disk space
      212,992 bytes used by system
  525,893,632 bytes available on disk

        8,192 bytes in each allocation unit.
       64,196 allocation units available on disk.

Volume Serial Number is 3A4E-17DA


A:\>_
```

FIGURE 1–5 The MS-DOS prompt showing the Format command and the resulting output to the screen.

OS/2

In 1987, Microsoft and IBM introduced their jointly developed Operating System/2 (OS/2), intended to replace DOS. However, version 1.0 was written for the Intel 80286 processor, which had serious memory and operating limits. Despite the memory limits, OS/2 required much more memory and disk space (2MB of memory and 8MB of disk space) than either PC DOS or MS-DOS. This was at a time when 2MB of memory and a 40MB hard drive (considered large in the late 1980s) cost several thousand dollars. Although the first version of OS/2 could multitask applications in memory, it did not have a GUI, and only one application could be visible on the screen at a time. Also, people had to write applications specifically for OS/2, because it had very limited support for DOS applications.

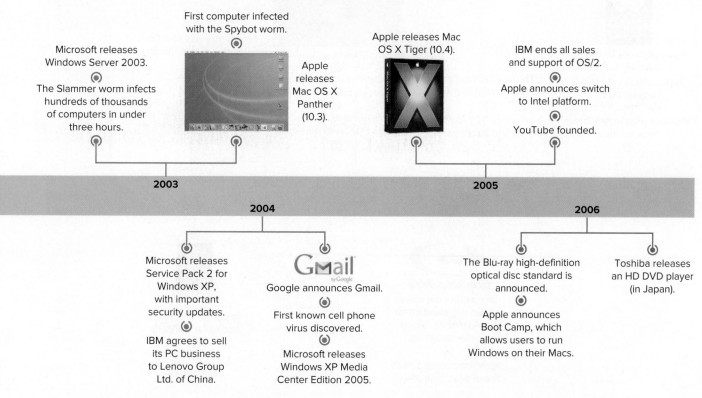

In the 1990s, IBM introduced OS/2 Warp, a greatly improved version of OS/2 with a very nice GUI. After about 18 months, however, IBM retreated from the battle for the desktop and targeted sales of OS/2 Warp to the high-end server market. It never rivaled Windows or UNIX in terms of sales. In 2003, IBM announced it would not develop any future versions of OS/2, and in December 2004 IBM sold its PC division to China-based Lenovo Group. In 2005 they discontinued support for OS/2.

Microsoft Windows

We'll begin our discussion of Windows by explaining Windows versions and editions, and then briefly go through the versions in chronological order.

Windows Versions and Editions. A Microsoft Windows version sometimes has a simple ordinal number, as in Windows 1 or Windows 2 (versions from the 1980s). Then some sub-versions appeared, such as Windows 3.1. In the mid-1990s, Microsoft moved away from the old convention and modified the names of several OSs to coincide with the calendar year of release, as in Windows 95, Windows 98, and Windows 2000. Then it created names such as Windows XP and Windows Vista, but underneath it all Microsoft still maintained a numeric version number.

Then there is the issue of editions. In recent years, each version of Microsoft Windows included separate products, each called an edition. Just a sampling of edition names includes Windows 7 Professional, Windows 7 Ultimate, Windows 8.1 Pro, and Windows 8.1 Enterprise. The differences among the editions for the same version are in the features. The more feature-rich editions cost more. But we are getting ahead of ourselves. We'll start our discussion of yesterday's Windows with the first version and make our way to Windows Vista. Then we will pick up the discussion of Today's Desktop OSs with Windows 7, Windows 8, and Windows 10.

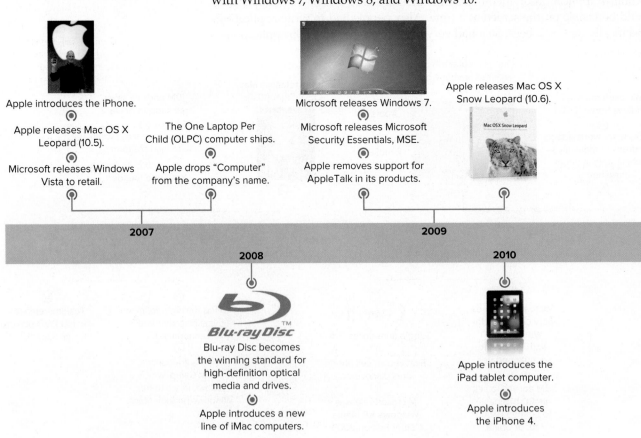

Apple introduces the iPhone.

Apple releases Mac OS X Leopard (10.5).

Microsoft releases Windows Vista to retail.

The One Laptop Per Child (OLPC) computer ships.

Apple drops "Computer" from the company's name.

Microsoft releases Windows 7.

Microsoft releases Microsoft Security Essentials, MSE.

Apple removes support for AppleTalk in its products.

Apple releases Mac OS X Snow Leopard (10.6).

2007

2009

2008

2010

Blu-ray Disc becomes the winning standard for high-definition optical media and drives.

Apple introduces a new line of iMac computers.

Apple introduces the iPad tablet computer.

Apple introduces the iPhone 4.

Windows 1 through 3. In 1985, when the first version of Windows appeared, it was more smoke than OS. It consisted of a not-very-good GUI by today's standards, balanced precariously on top of MS-DOS. The GUI code was separate from the OS code. It was slow and had a flat look—you couldn't lay one graphic on top of another. The ability to overlap graphical elements, such as windows and icons, did not show up until a later version.

From 1985 to 1990, Microsoft continued to work on both Windows and DOS, but Windows was not much more than a pretty face until 1990 and Windows 3.0, which supported the three Intel processor modes of operation available at that time. In Real mode, Windows 3.0 was just a GUI that ran on top of MS-DOS. In the other two modes, it added functionality to MS-DOS to take advantage of the Intel 286 (Standard mode) and the Intel 386 (386 Enhanced mode) processor modes.

The most important feature of Windows 3.0 was better support for legacy DOS applications within Windows. This was possible in the 386 Enhanced mode. This meant that both DOS apps and Windows apps could run simultaneously. This version still had its quirks, but for the first time, IT managers saw a potential GUI replacement for DOS as the desktop OS of choice.

In the spring of 1992, Microsoft brought out a minor upgrade, Windows 3.1, which many organizations adopted as the standard desktop OS. The fact that Microsoft's entire suite of productivity applications was also available in versions for Windows 3.*x* helped encourage adoption.

Figure 1–6 shows the Windows 3.1 desktop. Notice that there is no task bar at the bottom of the screen, just the Program Manager window (the main window) with other windows nested in it.

Windows for Workgroups. DOS and Windows OSs through Windows 3.*x* included only the operating system functions. If you wanted to connect to a network, you added a network operating system (NOS) on top of your installed OS. This separate network operating system might be from 3COM or Novell, or it might be Microsoft's LAN Manager NOS, developed in the late 1980s. You had to install the correct client software for the type of network and servers to which you connected.

Note: The success of a new version of an OS depends heavily on its ability to run old applications.

Note: Windows for Workgroups 3.1 was followed a year later by Windows for Workgroups 3.11, with the usual obligatory fixes and improvements including faster network and disk I/O operations. However, users were still working with a Windows OS that was running on top of MS-DOS; that is, first MS-DOS would start and then Windows. Windows depended on MS-DOS, which had to be installed on the computer.

Google Glass Explorer "smart glasses" prototype available for $1,500 to a limited number of "Glass Explorers."

◎

Microsoft releases Windows 8.1.

◎

Apple releases Mac OS X Mavericks (10.9).

Apple releases Mac OS X Lion (10.7).
◎
Amazon introduces the Kindle Fire.

Google introduces Chromebook computers running the Chrome OS.

Microsoft introduces the Microsoft Surface Pro tablet with pen.

2011

2013

2012

Apple releases Mac OS X Mountain Lion (10.8).
◉
Apple introduces the iPhone 5.
◉
Apple introduces the iPad mini.

Microsoft Windows 8 and the Microsoft Surface tablet are released.

FIGURE 1-6 The Windows 3.1 desktop.

Apple releases OS X Yosemite (10.10).

Apple introduces the iPhone 6 and iPhone 6 Plus.

2014

2015

Google Glass Explorer "smart glasses" prototype discontinued.

Apple releases the Apple Watch.

Microsoft releases Windows 10 with the Edge browser replacing Internet Explorer.

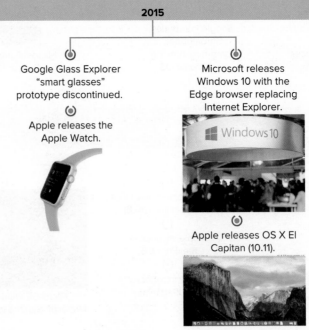

Apple releases OS X El Capitan (10.11).

Novell and LAN Manager were both network server operating systems that combined the operating system functions with the networking functions and also provided file and print sharing services to other computers. Additionally, to connect to a server, a client computer needed special client software so it could connect and request services from it.

Beginning in October 1992 with Windows for Workgroups 3.1, Microsoft included both the client and server software in all of its Windows OS products. This enabled peer-to-peer networking, meaning desktop computers could act as servers to their peers. This worked well in a small work group environment of 10 or fewer computers.

Windows NT. Because it had the same user interface as Windows 3.1, Windows NT was introduced in 1993 as Windows NT 3.1. That was where the similarity ended. To begin with, it was a server operating system, which included server protocols in its integrated network support. Furthermore, unlike Windows 3.x and Windows for Workgroups, the GUI did not sit on top of DOS, but was an entirely new operating system.

With Windows NT Microsoft introduced the New Technology File System (NTFS) with an entirely new logical structure for storing files. This file system is expandable and uses a transaction processing system to track changes to files, so that it can roll back incomplete transactions. It also includes several other features, including file compression, file encryption, file and folder security, and indexing. NTFS continues to be improved in each new version of Windows. It is the default file system in the current versions of Windows.

Windows NT was a stable and secure OS for its time. The next version, Windows NT 3.5, released in 1994, was the first Windows OS to have separate editions: Windows NT Workstation and Windows NT Server. Both of these used the same kernel and interface, but the Server version had enhancements and components that were needed only on a network server. The Workstation version was a robust desktop operating system targeted to corporate and advanced users. It had a higher price tag than Windows 95 (introduced in 1995), which was intended for consumers.

In 1996, Microsoft introduced Server and Workstation editions of Windows NT 4.0, which had a GUI similar to that of Windows 95 as well as other improvements and enhancements to the OS.

Note: The acronym *NTFS* is the preferred usage when talking about the file system first introduced in Windows NT. The longer name for it, the "New Technology File System," is rarely used.

Windows 95. Windows 95, released in 1995, predated Windows NT 4.0 Workstation. It was still a continuation of the Windows 3.x model with the graphical environment simply "sitting" on top of the DOS operating system. It did have some improvements in the operating system, including the GUI, which made it the most popular microcomputer operating system up to that time.

Windows 98. Windows 98 was an evolutionary development in the Windows desktop operating system, including improvements in both visible and under-the-hood components. It offered more stability than its immediate predecessor, Windows 95, meaning that it was less likely to stop in its tracks just when you were about to complete that book order on Amazon. Although improved, Windows 98 was not as stable as the newer Windows OSs. Figure 1–7 shows the Windows 98 desktop. Its biggest drawback was lack of security. It did not have a local security accounts database for local authentication, and it did not support the NTFS file system; therefore it did not have file and folder security.

Windows Me (Millennium Edition). Windows Me (Millennium edition), introduced in 2000, targeted the home market, especially the home game user. It was essentially Windows 98 with improved music, video, and home networking support. Windows Me was installed on many computers that were sold to individuals, but it was not an OS that organizations adopted.

FIGURE 1–7 The Windows 98 desktop with open windows.

Windows 2000. In 2000, Microsoft introduced the Windows 2000 family of OS products, which brought together the best of Windows 98 (the GUI) and Windows NT. Windows 2000 was available in several editions that all shared the same kernel and covered OS needs from the desktop (Windows 2000 Professional) to the enterprise server. The server editions included Windows 2000 Server, Advanced Server, and Datacenter Server. Figure 1–8 shows the Windows 2000 desktop.

FIGURE 1–8 The Windows 2000 desktop showing the Start menu and open windows.

FIGURE 1–9 The Windows XP desktop with open windows.

Windows XP. In 2001, Microsoft introduced Windows XP, intended only for the consumer desktop, not for the server environment. The new server products, introduced after Windows XP, began with Windows Server 2003.

There were several Windows XP editions, but the three most common were Windows XP Home edition, Windows XP Professional, and Windows XP Media Center. All were 32-bit OSs, had the same improved GUI, and shared many of the same features, but only Windows XP Professional included several important network- and security-related features. Additionally, Microsoft offered Windows XP 64-bit edition, which supported only 64-bit software and was limited to computers with the Intel Itanium processors.

The Windows XP desktop was very different from that of its main predecessor, Windows 98. Figure 1–9 shows the Windows XP desktop with several open windows. Microsoft redesigned and reorganized the Start menu, shown here.

The last service pack for the 32-bit version of Windows XP was SP 3. October 22, 2010, marked the last day you could buy a new PC with Windows XP preinstalled. This date was one year after the introduction of Windows 7. Support for Windows XP Service Pack 2 (SP2) ended July 13, 2010. Support for Windows XP Service Pack 3 (SP3) and for the 64-bit version with Service Pack 2 ended in April 2014, per Microsoft's published policy, the Microsoft Support Lifecycle.

Windows Vista. Microsoft released the first retail edition of Windows Vista early in 2007. Seen more as an upgrade of Windows XP, it included improvements in how Windows handles graphics, files, and communications. The GUI had a new look compared to previous versions of Windows (see Figure 1–10). It also had a feature called Aero, which included translucent windows, live thumbnails, live icons,

The Windows XP Start Menu.

try this!

Learn About the Microsoft Support Lifecycle

The Microsoft Lifecycle fact sheet describes the types of support Microsoft provides for its products and how long each support type will be available. Learn more about it. Try this:

1. Point your browser to support.microsoft.com/lifecycle.
2. On the Microsoft Support Lifecycle page there are links to general information on the Support Lifecycle Policy and to the life cycle of specific products.
3. Explore this Lifecycle information for Microsoft products described in this chapter.

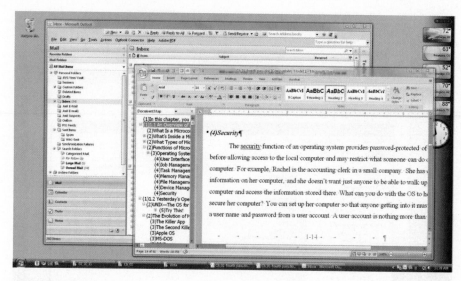

FIGURE 1–10 The Windows Vista desktop showing the transparent windows of the Aero feature.

and other enhancements to the GUI. Windows Vista was not widely adopted due to problems with speed on older hardware as well as high hardware requirements. Mainstream support for Windows Vista ended in April 2012.

LO 1.3 | Today's Desktop Operating Systems

Today's desktop microcomputer operating systems include Windows 7, Windows 8, Windows 10, OS X, and Linux. All of these OSs are multiuser/multitasking operating systems, with support for virtual memory and security. Each comes in versions that support either 32-bit or 64-bit processors.

Table 1–2 summarizes the current desktop OSs covered in later chapters of this book, listing the publisher, platform, and types of applications that you can run natively on each OS.

What follows is a brief description of these OSs, with more detail in the chapters devoted to each OS.

Today's Windows for the Desktop

Today's Windows for the desktop include Windows 7, Windows 8, and Windows 10.

Windows 7

Released in October 2009, Windows 7 includes several improvements correcting the shortcomings that kept Windows Vista from being widely accepted. Windows 7 is faster than Windows Vista in several ways, from starting up, to going

TABLE 1–2 Summary of Current Desktop/Laptop Operating Systems			
Desktop/Laptop OS	Company	Platform	Applications Supported
Windows 7	Microsoft	Intel/Microsoft	DOS, 16-bit Windows, 32-bit Windows, 64-bit Windows applications
Windows 8 and Windows 10	Microsoft	Intel/Microsoft	DOS, 16-bit Windows, 32-bit and 64-bit Windows applications for the Desktop and for the Windows 8 Modern GUI
OS X	Apple	Intel/Apple Mac	Mac applications
Linux	Various	Intel/Microsoft	UNIX/Linux applications

FIGURE 1–11 The Windows 7 desktop.

into and out of sleep mode, to recognizing new devices when you connect them. Windows 7 has many new features. The short list includes a redesigned desktop (see Figure 1–11) with a new taskbar that has many new features of its own, such as jump lists. Learn more about Windows 7 in Chapter 4.

Windows 8 and 8.1

Windows 8, released in October 2012, is faster than previous versions and includes better security and improved wireless connectivity as well as support for some newer hardware, such as USB 3.0 ports and improved touch screen support for simultaneous multiple touches and gestures.

The most controversial changes to Windows 8 are to the GUI, or rather GUIs. The default GUI, centered around the Start screen shown in Figure 1–12, is a departure from the Windows 7 desktop with its three-dimensional look.

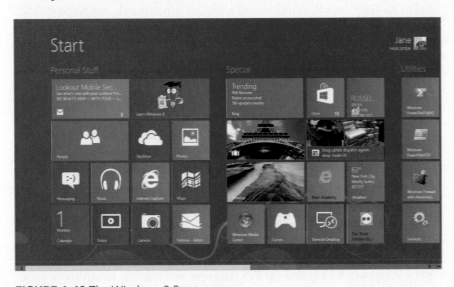

FIGURE 1–12 The Windows 8 Start screen.

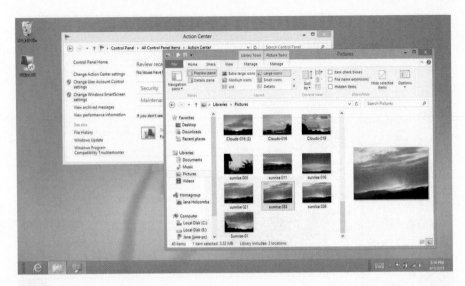

FIGURE 1–13 The Windows 8 desktop.

Note: In 2013, Windows 8 was followed by the important Windows 8.1 Update. Therefore, going forward in this book, we use the term Windows 8.x to refer to both releases.

Objects in this new GUI appear flat, without shading and borders so that they do not take up extra screen space. This is necessary because Windows 8 runs on a wide range of computing devices: PCs, laptops, and tablets. The new Windows 8 GUI inherited much of its look from the Metro user interface found in the Microsoft Windows Phone 7.5 OS. The Windows 8 Start screen contains tiles that represent apps. Each tile can show active content, such as newsfeeds, stock quotes, slideshows, and more, depending on the tile's app.

The second Windows 8 GUI, a modified version of the Windows 7 desktop (without the Start menu) has a very flat look to it in spite of having overlapping windows. Figure 1–13 shows the Windows 8 desktop. In 2013, Microsoft released an update to Windows 8—Windows 8.1—with changes to the Start screen and the desktop that they hoped would satisfy critics of the Windows 8 GUIs. Learn more about Windows 8.x on Desktops and Laptops in Chapter 5, and Windows 8.x on mobile devices in Chapter 11.

Windows 10

In 2015, Microsoft introduced Windows 10, skipping the logical naming progression to Windows 9. Windows 10 includes a modified, but recognizable, Start menu on the desktop (returned by popular demand). It also includes new or improved features. Figure 1–14 shows the Windows 10 desktop. The short list of new features are:

- A new Start menu.
- Windows Hello biometric authentication using facial features or fingerprint.
- The Cortana personal assistant.
- The Microsoft Edge browser (replacing the long-in-the-tooth Internet Explorer).
- Universal apps that run on all Windows 10 systems across all supported platforms.
- The Xbox app that brings game features to Windows 10.
- Support for multiple desktops.

Further, for a period of one year after its introduction, Windows 10 was available as a free upgrade to consumers running Windows 7 Service Pack 1 (SP1) or Windows 8.1 Update on PCs, laptops, and tablets. Learn more about Windows 10 in Chapter 6.

FIGURE 1–14 The Windows 10 desktop.

Apple OS X

Whereas the Linux and Microsoft OSs are available to install on hardware from many manufacturers, the Apple Inc. strategy has been to produce proprietary hardware and software for better integration of the OS and the hardware. They do not license OS X to run on other manufacturers' computers. This has historically resulted in a higher price for a Mac than for a comparable PC. For several years, beginning in the mid-1990s, Macintosh computers used the Motorola PowerPC chip with an architecture enhanced for graphics and multimedia. Since 2005 the Apple Mac line of computers have been Intel-based.

The Mac OSs in common use today are versions of OS X (X is the Roman numeral for 10). OS X is a revolutionary change from the previous Mac OS 9 because Apple based OS X on NextStep, an OS with a UNIX kernel. Until OS X, the Macintosh OSs were strictly GUI environments, with no command-line option. OS X, with its UNIX origins, gives you the option of a character-based interface, but most users will happily work solely in the GUI (see Figure 1–15). Apple has released several versions of OS X. Learn more about OS X and its features in Chapter 8.

FIGURE 1–15 The OS X GUI.

```
[cottrell@localhost ppp]$ ls -l
total 56
-rw-------   1 root     root         78 Feb 27 17:09 chap-secrets
-rw-r--r--   1 root     root        927 Apr 14 12:38 firewall-masq
-rw-r--r--   1 root     root        825 Apr 14 12:38 firewall-standalone
-rw-r--r--   1 root     root          0 Apr  8 09:08 ioptions
-rwxr-xr-x   1 root     root        310 Dec 26  2000 ip-down
-rwxr-xr-x   1 root     root       3564 Mar 20 22:17 ip-down.ipv6to4
-rwxr-xr-x   1 root     root        362 Dec 26  2000 ip-up
-rwxr-xr-x   1 root     root       5745 Mar 11 17:42 ip-up.ipv6to4
-rwxr-xr-x   1 root     root        918 Mar 11 17:43 ipv6-down
-rwxr-xr-x   1 root     root        918 Mar 11 17:43 ipv6-up
-rw-r--r--   1 root     root          5 Feb 27 17:09 options
-rw-------   1 root     root         77 Feb 27 17:09 pap-secrets
drwxr-xr-x   3 root     root       4096 Jul  5 15:02 peers
-rw-r--r--   1 root     root         93 Apr 14 12:38 pppoe-server-options
[cottrell@localhost ppp]$
```

FIGURE 1–16 A Red Hat Linux directory listing (the ls command).

Linux

Linux is an operating system modeled on UNIX and named in honor of its original developer, Linus Benedict Torvalds. He began it as a project in 1991 while a student at the University of Helsinki in his native Finland. He invited other programmers to work together to create an open-source operating system for modern computers. They created Linux using a powerful programming language called C, along with a free C compiler developed through the GNU project called GNU C Compiler (GCC). Linux has continued to evolve over the years, with programmers all over the globe testing and upgrading its code. Linus Torvalds could not have predicted in 1991 how well accepted the new operating system would be over 20 years later.

Linux is available in both 32-bit and 64-bit distributions, and it can be modified to run on nearly any computer. A distribution is a bundling of the Linux kernel and software—both enhancements to the OS and applications, such as word processors, spreadsheets, media players, and more. The person or organization providing the distribution may charge a fee for the enhancements and applications, but cannot charge a fee for the Linux code itself. Many distributions are free or very inexpensive.

Linux natively uses a command-line interface, and Figure 1–16 shows an example of a Linux directory list at the command line. Windows-like GUI environments, called shells, are available that make it as accessible to most users as Windows or OS X. We'll discuss selecting a Linux distribution in Chapter 9 along with other Linux-specific details.

> *Note:* A distribution is also called a "distro" or "flavor."

LO 1.4 | Today's Mobile Operating Systems

Mobile computing today has followed the trajectory of all computing, thanks to the miniaturization of components and new technologies. And like PCs, mobile devices became more desirable thanks to apps. However, don't look for a single "killer app" for mobile devices. Rather, the most popular mobile devices are those with a large number of compelling apps. Also, unlike the early PCs, which were seen more as office productivity tools, today's mobile devices are very personal devices used for communicating and entertainment as well as for work- and school-related tasks.

Of the three mobile OSs featured in this book, Apple licenses iOS only for use on Apple mobile devices; Microsoft charges manufacturers licensing fees for each device on which they install a Windows OS, adding to the cost of each device. Google does not charge manufacturers licensing fees for using

TABLE 1–3 Summary of Current Mobile OSs and Related Devices Featured in This Book

Mobile OS	Source of OS	Smartphones/Tablets	Sources for Apps
Apple iOS	Apple	Apple iPhone and iPad	Apple Apps Store
Android	Google	Smartphones and tablets from various manufacturers	Apps from Google Play and many other sources
Windows Phone 8 and Windows 10 Mobile	Microsoft	Smartphones from various manufacturers	Microsoft App Store
Windows 8 and Windows 10	Microsoft	Tablets from several sources	Apps from the Windows App store—and many other sources for Desktop apps

Android, but may require that certain Google apps and features be included. They license it for free under the Android Open Source Project. This helps hold down the cost of Android smartphones.

Mobile Devices

There are many manufacturers of mobile devices, but the ones we will focus on are those that use the Apple iOS, Android, or Windows operating systems. Two things they all have in common are support for a variety of wireless technologies and the ability to customize them with a variety of apps. Table 1–3 gives a summary of these OSs and the devices that use them. Following is a brief description of the hardware features of these devices:

Note: The iPod Touch runs iOS, but we are not covering this device. With its small screen and NO cell phone support, it is simply a digital music player with tablet features.

- Network adapters for various types of wireless networks.
- Great high-quality color touch screens that allow the OS to respond to several types of touch gestures.
- One or two (front and back) digital cameras.
- Built-in speakers and/or speaker ports for external speakers.
- Rechargeable batteries with battery life to get you through a normal day of use.
- An accelerometer that detects the physical tilt and acceleration of the device.
- Solid-state drives (SSDs).

Note: This book does not include coverage of the Watch OS, the operating system in the Apple Watch smartwatch.

Connectivity

The "smart" in smartphone comes from the computing ability that makes it a tool for work, home, and school. The "phone" in smartphone recognizes the ability to connect to a cellular network for voice communication. Typically you purchase a smartphone from a cellular provider, and connect the phone to the provider's network as your first ownership task.

Many tablets also have cellular network support for which you pay a premium—both for the cellular hardware in the tablet and for the cellular service. Most tablets with cellular support only offer data connections, not voice service.

To help control the cost of cellular data plans, we are fortunate to also have Wi-Fi connectivity in virtually all smartphones and tablets. If you enable Wi-Fi on your smartphone, you can save on your cellular data usage by connecting to an Internet-connected Wi-Fi network.

Another common wireless option is Bluetooth, a wireless networking technology for connecting over very short distances (a few yards or meters). Bluetooth is used to connect a mobile device to other computers and to wireless devices, such as keyboards and printers.

This is a test of the virtual keyboard on an iPad.

FIGURE 1–17 The virtual keyboard on an iPad.

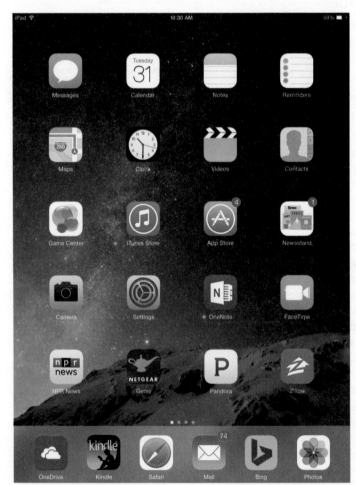

FIGURE 1–18 An iPad home screen in portrait orientation.

We will discuss how to enable and configure different types of network connections for mobile devices in Chapter 11.

Mobile Operating System Features

When discussing mobile operating systems it is difficult to separate the OS from the hardware, so the OS features we describe are closely tied to the previously listed hardware features of the mobile device.

Touch Screen and Virtual Keyboard Support

A mobile OS supports the touch screen by interpreting the various screen gestures we make. It also supports a feature called virtual keyboard. When you touch an area of screen that requires input from a keyboard, the OS will display the virtual keyboard, an on-screen image of a keyboard with labeled keys that you can tap. Figure 1–17 shows the virtual keyboard on an iPad. Many mobile devices will optionally connect to an external keyboard—usually via a Bluetooth wireless connection. Learn more about these features in Chapter 11.

Screen Rotation

Mobile operating systems take advantage of the hardware accelerometer by rotating the image on the screen to accommodate the position and allow you to read the screen. This feature is called screen rotation. Figure 1–18 shows the screen of an iPad

FIGURE 1–19 An iPad home screen in landscape orientation.

tablet in "portrait" orientation, and Figure 1–19 shows the screen of the same tablet in "landscape" orientation.

Updateable

As with desktop operating systems, the ability to update a mobile OS is important to the usability and security of the mobile device. While Microsoft's OSs are updateable during their clearly-defined life span, that is not quite as clear with mobile operating systems. In general, you can update an OS depending on the constraints of the hardware limits imposed by the cellular provider.

Availability of Apps

As we stated earlier, today's devices sell in part because of the number of useful apps, making the availability of a large selection of compelling apps more important than a single killer app that millions desire. All of the mobile OSs in this book have a large number of quality apps available to them, as well as many trivial and nonessential apps. Each mobile OS has one or more online sources, such as the Apple Store, shown in Figure 1–20.

Security

Mobile devices are targeted by the same security threats that target other computers. Being able to update the OS is only part of what you need to do to protect yourself and your data. Third-party solutions are available for some mobile OSs, and all of them come with some built-in security features. We will explore the security options for the various mobile operating systems in Chapter 11.

FIGURE 1–20 The Apple Store for iOS apps and other Apple products.

Data Synchronization

Data synchronization is an important feature supported by mobile OSs, especially for people who use multiple devices and wish to access the same data across all devices. For instance, you can access your contacts list and other data from anywhere with whatever device you are using. We will examine the synchronization options for mobile devices in Chapter 11.

Chapter 1 REVIEW

Chapter Summary

After reading this chapter and completing the exercises, you should know the following facts about operating systems.

An Overview of Microcomputer Operating Systems

- An operating system is a collection of programs that control all of the interactions among the various system components, freeing application programmers from needing to include such functions in their programs.

- A computer is a device that calculates. A central processing unit (CPU) is the component that performs the calculation for a computer.

- A microcomputer is a computer small enough and cheap enough for the use of one person. The integrated circuit (IC) is one of the inventions that made microcomputers possible.

- Interaction with a computer is called input/output (I/O).

- The CPU in a microcomputer is a microprocessor, which, along with several other important components (memory, firmware, and more), is installed onto a motherboard.

- System firmware contains the program code that informs the CPU of the devices present and how to communicate with them.

- Read only memory basic input output system (ROM BIOS) is a type of firmware used since the first IBM PC (circa 1981). It has been replaced by firmware that complies with a new standard, Unified Extensible Firmware Interface (UEFI).

- A device driver is a special program containing code for controlling a component.

- Common microcomputers in use today include desktops, laptops, tablets, and smartphones.
- Windows and Linux will run on a desktop PC or compatible laptop computer. OS X runs on the iMac desktop and MacBook laptop models.
- A server is a computer that provides one or more services to other computers.
- Smartphones and tablets are the two most popular mobile devices.
- Operating systems provide these functions:
  - User interface
  - Job management
  - Task management
  - File management
  - Device management
  - Memory management
  - Security

Yesterday's Operating Systems

- UNIX is the oldest operating system still in use. It comes in versions for large computers, as well as microcomputers.
- The complex and powerful OSs we now use evolved over many decades. How we use computers has changed along the way.
- Early microcomputers were introduced in the 1970s. The Apple computers came with the Apple OS.
- Software is created in versions, and some versions come in separate editions, products with bundled capabilities.
- Certain "killer apps," notably VisiCalc and Lotus 1-2-3, made microcomputers appeal to organizations and ordinary people.
- IBM introduced the IBM PC in 1981 with Microsoft BASIC in ROM. They offered PC DOS for computers with a floppy disk drive.
- In the 1980s, Microsoft made MS-DOS available to third-party PC manufacturers and no longer supports or sells MS-DOS. Other sources continued the development of non-Microsoft DOS.
- OS/2 was first developed in a joint effort between Microsoft and IBM. IBM soon continued development of it without Microsoft, bringing out OS/2 Warp, a GUI version. IBM discontinued support for OS/2 in 2005.
- Microsoft Windows evolved from the first version in 1985 to Windows 10, introduced in 2015. Each of the newer versions comes in multiple products, called editions.
- The Apple Mac computer, introduced in 1984, came with the MAC OS System. This OS line continued through Mac OS 9, introduced in 1999, and phased out after OS X was introduced in 2001.

Today's Desktop Operating Systems

- Today's desktop operating systems include Windows 7, Windows 8, Windows 10, OS X, and Linux.
- Windows 7, released in 2009, included many improvements over Windows Vista, convincing many businesses to migrate their desktops to this OS.
- Windows 8 was introduced in October 2012 with two GUIs. In 2013, Microsoft released the Windows 8.1 Update with changes to the Start screen and desktop.
- Windows 10 was introduced in 2015 with changes to the GUI and several new features.
- Apple's OS X, based on NextStep, an OS with a UNIX kernel, runs only on Apple Mac desktop and laptop computers.
- Linus Torvalds developed Linux as a collaborative effort beginning in 1991. It can run on nearly any computer. It natively uses a command-line interface, but GUI shells are available.

Today's Mobile OSs

- People use mobile devices for communicating and personal entertainment as well as for work- and school-related tasks.
- Apple's iOS runs on Apple's iPhone and iPad products (as well as on the iPod touch). Apps are only available from the Apple Apps Store.
- Google's Android OS runs on smartphones and tablets from many manufacturers. Apps are available from Google and from many other sources.
- Windows Phone 8.x and Windows Phone 10 run on smartphones from several manufacturers with apps available from the Microsoft App Store.
- Windows 8.x and Windows 10 run on tablets from many sources with apps available from the Microsoft App Store and many other sources.
- Features in mobile devices include:
  - Multiple types of wireless network adapters.
  - High-quality color touch screens.
  - One or two (front and back) digital cameras.
  - Built-in speakers and/or speaker ports.
  - Rechargeable batteries with battery life sufficient for a normal day of use.
  - An accelerometer that detects the physical tilt and acceleration.
  - Solid-state drives (SSDs).
- Smartphones and some tablets support cellular connections and are usually bought through a cellular provider.

- Smartphones and tablets also offer Wi-Fi connections, which give you a cheaper alternative to cellular for accessing the Internet with the device.
- Bluetooth is a wireless networking technology for connecting over very short distances.
- A mobile OS interprets screen gestures and displays a virtual keyboard when you touch an area of screen that requires text input.
- A mobile OS takes advantage of the hardware accelerometer in a device by rotating the image on the screen to accommodate the position of screen so that it is readable to the user.
- Most mobile operating systems can be updated to some degree.
- Popular mobile OSs have a large number of apps available to them.
- All mobile OSs have security features, and third-party solutions are available.
- It is important to have good options for synchronizing data across all devices used by an individual.

Key Terms List

accelerometer *(31)*

application *(2)*

central processing unit (CPU) *(2)*

client *(5)*

command-line interface (CLI) *(6)*

computer *(2)*

cursor *(6)*

device driver *(3)*

device management *(8)*

directory *(8)*

distribution *(30)*

edition *(20)*

embedded OS *(4)*

file management *(8)*

file system *(8)*

firmware *(3)*

folder *(8)*

formatting *(8)*

graphical user interface (GUI) *(6)*

input/output (I/O) *(3)*

integrated circuit (IC) *(2)*

Internet of Things (IoT) *(5)*

job management *(7)*

kernel *(6)*

Mac *(4)*

memory *(3)*

memory management *(8)*

microcomputer *(2)*

microprocessor or processor *(2)*

motherboard *(3)*

multitasking *(7)*

New Technology File System (NTFS), *(23)*

operating system (OS) *(2)*

partition *(8)*

personal computer (PC) *(4)*

portable operating system *(12)*

processes *(8)*

random-access memory (RAM) *(3)*

read only memory basic input output system (ROM BIOS) *(3)*

screen rotation *(32)*

security *(10)*

server *(5)*

smartphone *(4)*

solid-state drive (SSD) *(8)*

system-on-a-chip (SoC) *(4)*

tablet *(5)*

task management *(7)*

Unified Extensible Firmware Interface (UEFI) *(3)*

user interface (UI) *(6)*

version *(14)*

virtual keyboard *(32)*

virtual memory *(9)*

Key Terms Quiz

Use the Key Terms List to complete the sentences that follow. Not all terms will be used.

1. A/an _____ controls the interaction between a program and a computer's hardware, freeing application programmers from the task of including such functions in their programs.

2. The _____ is the main component of an OS that always remains in memory while the computer is running, managing low-level OS tasks.

3. The desktop operating systems described in this chapter all have an optional character mode _____.

4. An operating system that uses _____ will allow you to simultaneously run more programs than the physical memory of the computer will hold.

5. When you run several applications at once and switch between them, you are experiencing the _____ feature of an operating system.

6. Interaction with a computer involving getting data and commands into it and results out of it is called _____.

7. The role of a/an _____ is to provide services to other computers on a network.

8. Software that allows the operating system to control a hardware component is a/an _____

9. A/an _____ is a hardware component in a mobile device that an OS uses when it rotates the image on the screen so that it is readable in its current position.

10. The _____ function of an OS includes the visual components as well as the command processor that loads programs into memory.

Multiple-Choice Quiz

1. Which of the following operating systems cannot be licensed to run on a PC?
   a. Mac OS X
   b. Windows 10
   c. Windows 7
   d. Linux
   e. Windows 8

2. Which of the following is a small electronic component made up of transistors (tiny switches) and other miniaturized parts?
   a. Peripheral
   b. Integrated circuit (IC)
   c. Tablet
   d. Mouse
   e. Vacuum tube

3. Introduced in 1983, this application program became the "killer app" that made the IBM PC a must-have business tool.
   a. Microsoft Word
   b. VisiCalc
   c. BASIC
   d. PC DOS
   e. Lotus 1-2-3

4. Which of the following is not available as a desktop operating system?
   a. Windows 8
   b. OS X
   c. Windows 10
   d. Linux
   e. iOS

5. Which of the following is a computer input device? Select all correct answers.
   a. Mouse
   b. Printer
   c. Keyboard
   d. RAM
   e. ROM

6. On a network, the purpose of this type of computer is to allow users to connect over the network to save and access files stored on this computer, as well as to print to printers connected to this computer.
   a. Desktop computer
   b. File and print server

   c. Tablet
   d. Laptop
   e. Smartphone

7. Which acronym describes technology in which all or most of a device's electronic circuitry is on a single microchip?
   a. IoT
   b. ROM BIOS
   c. UEFI
   d. SSD
   e. SoC

8. OS X is built on NextStep, an OS based on what kernel?
   a. Linux
   b. UNIX
   c. DOS
   d. Windows
   e. BASIC

9. In the 1950s, a typical computer end user would have been a _____.
   a. computer gamer
   b. medical doctor
   c. politician
   d. government agency
   e. secretary

10. What acronym describes networked devices that contain microcomputers but are not thought of as computing devices, such as refrigerators, automobile components, light bulbs, and industrial control devices?
    a. IoT
    b. ROM BIOS
    c. UEFI
    d. SSD
    e. SoC

11. Which of the following accurately describes the overall trend in computing during the past 70-plus years?
    a. Toward physically larger, more powerful computers.
    b. Toward physically larger, less powerful computers.
    c. Toward physically smaller, less powerful computers.

d. Toward physically smaller, more powerful computers.
   e. Toward physically smaller, single-use computers.

12. When working with a mobile device, if you touch an area of screen that requires text input, the OS will display this for your use.
   a. Help screen
   b. Virtual keyboard
   c. A Bluetooth button so that you can connect a keyboard
   d. CLI
   e. Screen gestures

13. Using this type of wireless network connection when browsing the Internet with a smartphone or tablet can save you data fees.
   a. Bluetooth
   b. Wi-Fi
   c. USB
   d. Cellular
   e. Ethernet

14. What file system is the default for current Windows OSs?
   a. ROM BIOS
   b. IC
   c. RAM
   d. NTFS
   e. UEFI

15. What is the very first thing a user usually must do to gain access to a secure computer?
   a. Back up all data.
   b. Connect to the Internet.
   c. Log on with a user name and password.
   d. Double-click the Start menu.
   e. Reboot.

Essay Quiz

1. Describe the benefit to programmers of having an operating system when that programmer is creating a new application.

2. Based on your own observations, do you believe there are more differences or more commonalities among the different operating systems across devices: PCs, laptops, tablets, and smartphones?

3. Describe virtual memory and list an OS described in this chapter that does not use it.

4. Linux comes in distributions from many sources. Define the term *distribution* in this context.

5. In general terms, describe a mobile OS's use of a device's accelerometer.

Lab Projects

LAB PROJECT 1.1

Pick a typical day for you, and create a journal of all the interactions you have with computers from the time you wake up in the morning until you go to bed at night. *Hint:* Even a gas pump contains a computer.

LAB PROJECT 1.2

If you use both a desktop (or laptop) computer and a mobile device, describe the similarities and differences you notice in working with the GUI on each device. If you do not use both types of devices, find someone who does (classmate or other) and interview that person for this project. Create a report of these results to submit to your instructor or to use in a discussion of results with your classmates.

LAB PROJECT 1.3

Poll classmates or coworkers to determine how they use their mobile devices. Are they primarily entertainment devices? If so, describe why this is the case. How many people polled used a mobile device as a primary computer? In that case, what tasks did they perform on the mobile devices? Were there tasks they preferred to do on a desktop or laptop? Create a report describing the results and be prepared to discuss with other students who completed this project separately.

2 Computer Security Basics

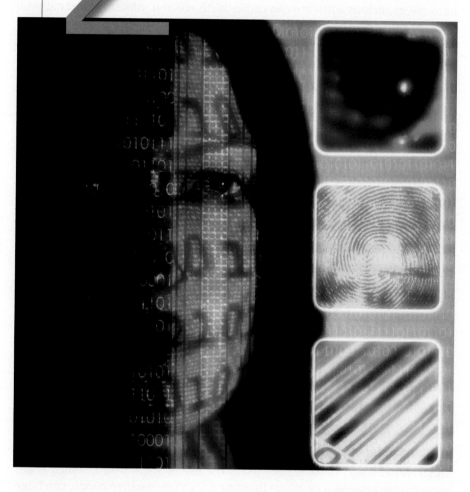

Learning Outcomes

In this chapter, you will learn how to:

LO **2.1** Describe security threats and vulnerabilities to computers and users.

LO **2.2** Identify methods for protecting against security threats.

LO **2.3** Troubleshoot common security problems.

Why do operating systems have a long list of security features? Why do we need to apply security patches to operating systems? Why has computer security become a multibillion-dollar business worldwide? Why? Because it's dangerous out there! And, as you will learn in this chapter, "out there" seems to be everywhere, because no place or technology is safe from threats. That includes the Internet, corporate extranets, desktop and laptop computers, and even your cell phone, tablet, or other mobile devices. Here you'll learn about the threats, and the methods, practices, and technologies for protecting your computer systems.

In this chapter we first attempt to instill a healthy dose of paranoia in your mind, and then we identify methods for securing a computer, such as authentication and authorization, encryption, firewalls, antispam, antivirus, anti-popup, privacy protection, and other types of protections. Then, in later chapters, you will learn how to implement OS-specific security. ✷

LO 2.1 | Threats to Computers and Users

What are you risking if your computer or mobile device is not secure? The short answer is that you risk your identity, the work you have created, your company's integrity, and your own job if you are responsible for loss of the company's equipment or data. Today, government regulations, such as the Sarbanes-Oxley Act or the Health Insurance Portability and Accountability Act (HIPAA) require that organizations protect certain personal information, such as health and personal financial data. The consequences to an organization that does not comply with these regulations, or that experiences a breach of security involving such data, can be very severe. In the extreme, malicious software can cause death when it infects critical national defense software or software in computers onboard an airplane or in a train switching system.

We'll begin the long answer with an overview of common threats and how they gain access to computers. Many of the threats described are severe enough to be considered cybercrimes. A cybercrime is illegal activity performed using computer technology.

Malicious Tools and Methods

We call software threats malware, a shortened form of "malicious software." This term covers a large and growing list of threats, including many that you no doubt know about, such as viruses, worms, Trojan horses, or spam. But have you heard of pop-up downloads, drive-by downloads, war driving, bluesnarfing, adware, spyware, back doors, spim, phishing, or hoaxes? Read on and learn about the various types of malware and their methods of infecting computers and networks.

Malware development has become a huge industry that targets all computing devices, with the greatest growth in malware targeting mobile devices. A large percentage of mobile malware targets Android devices. This is attributed by many to the less restrictive vetting process for Android applications compared to iOS applications.

Vectors

A vector is a method that malware uses to infect a computer. While some malware may use just a single vector, multivector malware uses an array of methods to infect computers and networks. Let's look at a few well-known vectors.

Social Networking. Social networking is the use of social media, which is any service (Internet-based or other) that provides a place where people can interact in online communities, sharing information in various forms. Community members generate social-media content. A social networking site is a website that provides space where members can communicate with one another and share details of their business or personal lives. Facebook is a very popular social networking site. Like all popular social media sources, Facebook has a membership requirement, and each member creates a password-protected account and provides personal information. LinkedIn is a social media site targeted to professionals who use it for business contacts. Twitter (Figure 2–1) allows users to send and receive short text messages (tweets) of up to 140 characters.

We see social media as a vector for malware and social engineering (defined later in this chapter) as well as a rich source of personal information on individuals. We are horrified to see the personal details that people reveal on their Facebook and Twitter sites.

Note: Malware continues to evolve with variations on the types of malware described in this chapter. A short list of such variations includes logic bombs, pharming, vishing, whaling, appender infection, and swiss cheese infection.

Note: Members of the Chinese People's Liberation Army hacked into Facebook and many other American companies and government agencies, stealing vast amounts of data. However, in what may be ironic justice, some of the hackers were later identified because they accessed Facebook (presumably with their personal accounts) from the same network from which they carried out the hacking attacks.

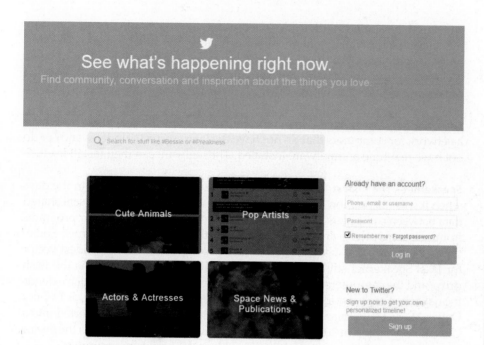

FIGURE 2–1 The Twitter home page.

try this!

Email. Some malware infects computers via email. You may have believed it was always safe to open email as long as you didn't open attachments, but the simple act of opening an email containing the Nimda virus can infect a computer, depending on the software you are using to read the message. This was true with Microsoft's Outlook Express email client included with Windows XP. Microsoft released a patch to close this vulnerability. This is just one argument for keeping your software updated with security patches.

Regardless of the email client you use, clicking on a link in an email message can launch malware from a website.

Malicious Code on Websites. Some malware infects computers by lurking in hidden code on websites. An unsuspecting user browses to a site and clicks on a link that launches and installs malware on her computer.

Trojan Horses. A Trojan horse, often simply called a Trojan, is both a type of malware and a vector. The modern-day Trojan horse program gains access to computers much like the ancient Greek warriors who, in Virgil's famous tale (the epic poem *The Aeneid*), gained access to the city of Troy by hiding in a large wooden horse presented as a gift to the city (a Trojan horse). A Trojan horse program installs and activates on a computer by appearing to be something harmless, which the user innocently installs. It may appear as just a useful free program that a user downloads and installs or a video with horrible or shocking content, but it is a common way for malware to infect your system.

Although it is hard to fit all threats into tidy categories, we consider threats similar to the "Complete a Quick Survey" exploit to be a Trojan because it

> **More About Social Media**
> Check out the latest in social media. Try this:
> 1. Open your favorite search engine, such as Google.com or Bing.com.
> 2. Enter the key words "social media."
> 3. Browse through the results and create a list of at least 10 social-media sites.
> 4. Return to the search engine and enter "social media security."
> 5. Browse through the results and look for recent articles on social media security concerns. Read some of the articles and discuss them with your classmates.

> **WARNING!**
> A worm can replicate itself via Bluetooth, infecting mobile devices when people are in crowded public places, such as sports bars. Turn Bluetooth off when not in use and when in close proximity to strangers.

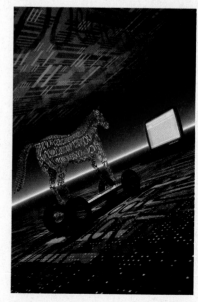

Trojan horse

appears to be something harmless, tempting you to comply. If you complete the survey it may take some action, such as pretending to scan your computer for problems, but the results will be bogus, offering to fix the problems it claims to find and asking for payment to support charities. A threat that causes you to take action out of fear is scareware.

Searching for Unprotected Computers. Still other malware searches throughout a network for computers that do not have the latest security updates and/or do not have real-time antimalware installed. The malware can then install itself.

Sneakernet—The Oldest Vector. Yet another vector is as old as PCs. In the days when it was uncommon for computers to connect to any network, users shared data between computers by carrying a floppy disk containing data or programs from one computer to another. The slang for this practice is sneakernet. Sometimes, the floppy disk contained malware, making sneakernet the oldest vector for PCs. Sneakernet still exists, but the storage device used today is the flash drive, and the computers are usually also connected to a network, which extends the risk when malware infects a single computer. In August 2010 the U.S. Deputy Defense Secretary declassified the information that a flash drive, inserted into a U.S. military laptop in 2008 on a military post in the Middle East, was the vector for malicious code that caused a significant breach of military computers.

Back Doors. In computing, a back door is a way in which someone can gain access to a computer, bypassing authentication security. Sometimes a program's author installs a back door into a single program so she can easily access it later for administering and/or for troubleshooting the program code. Or an attacker may create a back door by taking advantage of a discovered weakness in a program. Then any program using the back door can run in the security context of the invaded program and infect a computer with malware. The security context of the program encompasses the privileges granted to the logged-on user or to the program itself when it was installed. In one well-known situation, the Code Red worm took advantage of a specific vulnerability in Microsoft's Internet Information Server (IIS) Web server software to install a back door. The result was that the worm displayed a message on every Web page on the IIS server. The message included the phrase, "Hacked by Chinese." Then the Nimda worm took advantage of the back door left by the Code Red worm to infect computers.

Rootkits. A rootkit is malware that hides itself from detection by anti-malware programs by concealing itself within the OS code or any other program running on the computer. Someone who has administrator (root) access to the computer installs a rootkit, giving an attacker administrator privileges to the computer. Once installed, he can then run any type of malware to quietly carry out its mission. "Rootkit" also refers to the software components of a rootkit.

Pop-Up Downloads. A pop-up is a separate window that displays (pops up) uninvited from a Web page. The purpose of a pop-up may be as simple as an advertisement, but a pop-up can be a vector for malware. A pop-up download is a program downloaded to a user's computer through a pop-up page. It requires an action on the part of a user, such as clicking on a button that implies acceptance of something such as free information, although what that something may actually be is not clear. The program that downloads may be a virus or a worm.

Drive-By Downloads. A drive-by download is a program downloaded to a user's computer without consent. Often the simple act of browsing to a website, or opening an HTML email message, may result in such a surreptitious download. A drive-by download may also occur when installing another application. This is particularly true of certain file-sharing programs that users install to allow sharing of music, data, or photo files over the Internet. Some drive-by downloads may alter your Web browser home page and/or redirect all your browser searches to one site. A drive-by download may also install a virus, a worm, or even more likely, adware or spyware (which we describe later in this chapter).

War Driving. Secure all Wi-Fi networks with the latest standard of Wi-Fi security and require passwords to access the network. A Wi-Fi network that connects to the Internet through a router is a hotspot and should be protected from unauthorized access. Someone who detects an unprotected hotspot can access the Internet for free. Further, the reason we see this as a vector is that they also can capture keystrokes, email, passwords, and user names from the wireless traffic, giving them ways to send malware to connected users or use the information they gather to steal users' identities.

Some people actively seek out unsecured Wi-Fi networks, a practice called war driving. A war driver moves through a neighborhood in a vehicle or on foot, using a mobile device equipped with Wi-Fi wireless network capability and software that identifies Wi-Fi networks. The software detects the level of security (or lack of) on each detected Wi-Fi network.

Note: A less-dramatic term for "war driving" is "access point mapping."

Using an unsecured hotspot can expose you to threats. If you need to be inspired to secure your Wi-Fi network, check out the Internet, where numerous websites describe how to war drive, as well as how to protect your data from theft. There are even many war driving videos on YouTube, as shown in Figure 2–2.

Bluesnarfing. Similar to war driving, bluesnarfing is the act of covertly obtaining information broadcast from wireless devices using the Bluetooth standard, a short-range wireless standard used for data exchange between desktop computers and mobile devices. Bluetooth devices have a range of from 10 centimeters to 100 meters, depending on the power class of the device. Using a smartphone, a bluesnarfer can eavesdrop to acquire information, or even use the synchronizing feature of the device to pick up the user's information—all without the victim detecting it.

FIGURE 2–2 Online videos show examples of war driving.

Password Theft

A password is a string of characters that you enter, along with an identifier, such as a user name or email address, to authenticate yourself. If someone steals your passwords they can gain access to whatever you thought you were protecting with the password. We first considered calling this section "Discovering Passwords," but that phrase is far too innocent sounding—as if the perpetrator was innocently walking along and "discovered" your password lying on the sidewalk. What really happens is theft with intent to break into computers and networks. It is stealing, so let's call it that! People use many methods to steal passwords.

Stealing Passwords through Websites. There are numerous programs and techniques for stealing passwords. One commonly used technique is to invade an unsecured website to access information unwitting users provide to the site, such as user names and passwords, and such personal information as account numbers, Social Security numbers, birth dates, and much more.

Stealing Passwords with Password Crackers. Another technique used for stealing a password is a program called a password cracker. Some password crackers fall into the category of "brute-force" password crackers, which simply means the program tries a huge number of permutations of possible passwords. Often, because people tend to use simple passwords such as their initials, birth dates, addresses, etc., the brute-force method works. Other password crackers use more sophisticated statistical or mathematical methods to steal passwords.

Stealing Passwords with Keystroke Loggers. Another method for stealing passwords, as well as lots of other information, is the use of a keystroke logger, also called a keylogger. This is either a hardware device or a program that monitors and records every keystroke, usually without the user's knowledge. In the case of a hardware logger, the person desiring the keystroke log must physically install it before recording. The KeyCobra keystroke logger is a USB device the size of a flash drive that installs between the keyboard cable and a USB connector on the computer. There are also hardware keystroke loggers for PS/2 keyboard connectors. They are all very unobtrusive when connected to the back of a PC; one keystroke logger can hold a year's worth of keystroke data in flash memory and comes with software for reading the specially formatted data files. Some models are Wi-Fi enabled. When properly configured, a Wi-Fi keystroke logger can send reports on captured data via email, and the owner can also remotely access the keystroke logger. Without a network connection, a hardware keystroke logger must be physically retrieved to access the collected data.

A software keystroke logger program may not require physical access to the target computer but simply a method for downloading and installing it on the computer. This could occur through one of the vectors described earlier in this chapter. Once installed, such a program can send the logged information over the Internet via email, or using other methods, to the person desiring the log.

Some parents install keystroke loggers to monitor their children's Internet activity, but such programs have the potential for abuse by people with less benign motivations, such as stalkers and identity thieves. A simple Internet search of "keystroke logger" will yield many sources of both hardware and software keystroke loggers. The latter are now the more common.

Zero-Day Exploits

We also call a malware attack an exploit when it takes advantage of some vulnerability in our computers or networks. Experts are constantly discovering these vulnerabilities and attempting to stay ahead of the bad guys with appropriate defense techniques. However, sometimes someone finds a software vulnerability

Use unique and complex passwords.

Note: Advanced keystroke loggers may also capture screenshots of all activity on a computer.

in an operating system or application such as those we study in this book that is unknown to the publisher of the targeted software, and someone devises a way to exploit that vulnerability. We call this unknown exploit (often a virus) a zero-day exploit, and it is very difficult to protect against such a threat.

Viruses

While, in the broadest sense, "virus" is a term used for all malware, technically, a virus is one class of malware: a program installed and activated on a computer or mobile device without the knowledge or permission of the user. Viruses usually attach themselves to a file, such as a Microsoft Word document, and replicate and spread as you copy or share the infected file. Like a living virus that infects humans and animals, a computer virus can result in a wide range of symptoms and outcomes. Loss of data, damage to or complete failure of an operating system, or theft of personal and financial information are just a few of the potential results of computer virus infections. If you extend the range of a virus to a corporate or government network, the results can be far-reaching and even tragic. There are thousands of viruses "in the wild" today.

> *Note:* "In the wild" is a term frequently used to describe the overall computing environment, including private networks, and Internet and all other public networks. "In the zoo" refers to a controlled and isolated environment where viruses can be analyzed during the development of patches. This type of environment is also called a "sandbox."

Worms

Like a virus, a worm is a program installed and activated on a computer without the knowledge or permission of the user. But a worm replicates itself on the computer, or throughout a network. In other words, a worm is a network-aware virus that does not require action from the unwitting user to replicate, and it can have a similar range of outcomes. In recent years the Netsky and MyDoom worms caused chaos and loss of productivity just by the huge amount of network traffic they generated. The typical worm resides in a single file that it replicates onto multiple machines. However, the Nimda worm changed all that by inserting its code into other executable files on the local drive of each machine to which it replicated itself, making it difficult to locate and remove the worm.

Botnets and Zombies

A botnet is a group of networked computers that, usually unbeknown to their owners, are infected with programs that forward information to other computers over a network (usually the Internet). A bot, short for robot, is a program that acts as an agent for a user or master program, performing a variety of functions—for both good and evil. An individual computer in a botnet is a zombie because it mindlessly serves the person who originated the botnet code. A botherder is someone who initiates and controls a botnet. Most often affecting home computers, botnets have grown to be one of the biggest threats on the Internet.

Spyware

Spyware is a category of software that runs surreptitiously on a user's computer, gathers information without the user's permission, and then sends that information to the people or organizations that requested it. A virus may install Internet-based spyware, sometimes called tracking software or a spybot, on a computer. Spyware can be used by companies to trace users' surfing patterns to improve the company's marketing efforts; it can be used for industrial espionage; it is used by law enforcement to find sexual predators or criminals (with appropriate legal permissions); and it is used by governments to investigate terrorism.

Adware

Adware is a form of spyware that collects information about the user in order to display targeted advertisements to the user, either in the form of inline banners or pop-ups. Inline banners are advertisements that run within the context of the current page, just taking up screen real estate. Pop-ups are a greater annoyance, because they are ads that run in separate browser windows that you must close before you can continue with your present task. Clicking to accept an offer presented in an inline banner or a pop-up may trigger a pop-up download that can install a virus or worm.

Browser Hijacking

We received a call the other day from Dave, a finance officer at a large farm implement company. Every time he opened Internet Explorer, the home page pointed to a site advertising adware removal software. This is an example of browser hijacking, a practice that has been growing. Some unscrupulous people do this so that their website will register more visitors and then they can raise their rates to advertisers.

Dave was able to reverse this by changing the default page in Internet Options, but it was very annoying. He was lucky; hijackers can make it very difficult to defeat the hijack by modifying the registry (a database that stores configuration settings in the Windows OS) so that every time you restart Windows or your Web browser the hijack reinstates. Or you may even find that a registry change makes Internet Options unavailable.

Spam and Spim

Spam is unsolicited email, often called junk email. This includes email from a legitimate source selling a real service or product, but if you did not give the source permission to send such information to you, it is spam. Too often spam involves some form of scam—a bogus offer to sell a service or product that does not exist or tries to include you in a complicated moneymaking deal. If it sounds too good to be true, it is! We call spam perpetrators spammers, and spam is illegal. Spam accounts for a huge amount of traffic on the Internet and private networks, and a great loss in productivity as administrators work to protect their users from spam and individuals sort through and eliminate spam. Some corporate network administrators report that as much as 60 percent of the incoming email traffic is spam.

Spim is an acronym for spam over instant messaging, and the perpetrators are spimmers. A spimmer sends bots out over the Internet to collect instant-messaging screen names, and then a spimbot sends spim to the screen names. A typical spim message may contain a link to a website, where, like spam, the recipient will find products or services for sale, legitimate or otherwise.

try this!

Research Spam Statistics

Find out the latest bad news on the amount of Internet email identified as spam. Try this:

1. Open your Web browser and connect to your favorite search engine, such as Google, Bing, or Yahoo.
2. Search on the words "spam statistics." For a more targeted search include the current year in your search string.
3. In the results list, many of the links will be for antispam programs that provide individual statistics. Review the results and select a link that appears to give actual statistics on spam occurrences for Internet email users. Discuss the results with your classmates.

Social Engineering

Social engineering is the use of persuasion techniques to gain the confidence of individuals—for both good and bad purposes. People with malicious intent use social engineering to persuade targeted people to reveal confidential information or to obtain something else of value. Social engineering is as old as human interaction, so there are countless techniques. Following are just a few categories of computer security threats that employ social engineering.

Fraud Fraud is the use of deceit and trickery to persuade someone to hand over money or other valuables. Fraud is often associated with identify theft (discussed later), because the perpetrator will falsely claim to be the victim when using the victim's credit cards and other personal and financial information.

One form of fraud is ransomware, a type of scareware that threatens to do damage or lock a user out of a computer unless the user pays a "ransom." One type of ransomware encrypts the data on an infected computer and displays a message asking for payment, but there is no guarantee that your data will be unencrypted once the payment is made. A more frightening variation of ransomware claims that the victim has been observed in an illegal act, such as distributing child pornography, and threatens to report this to the authorities unless the victim pays a ransom. Ransomware may require payment through an online payment system, such as bitcoin.

Phishing Phishing is a fraudulent method of obtaining personal and financial information through Web page pop-ups, email, and even paper letters mailed via the postal service. Think of the metaphor of a fisherman preparing and casting his bait in an ocean full of fish. Even if only one in a hundred fish take the bait, he is statistically likely to have many successes. We'll concentrate our discussion on Web page pop-ups and email. A phishing message ("bait") purports to be from a legitimate organization, such as a bank, credit card company, retailer, and so on. In a typical phishing scenario, the email or pop-up may contain authentic-looking logos, and even links to the actual site, but the link specified for supplying personal financial information will take recipients (the "phish") to a "spoofed" Web page that asks them to enter their personal data. The Web page may look exactly like the company's legitimate Web page, but it's not. A common practice is for a phisher to use the credit information to make purchases over the Internet, choosing items that are easy to resell and having them delivered to a destination address to which the phisher has access, such as a vacant house.

While the typical phishing attack casts a wide net by sending out millions of messages, some phishing attacks are more targeted. We call these spear phishing, and the target of a spear-phishing attack is usually one that has a high probability of delivering a very valuable return. Such an attack may come in the form of a message with a greeting that includes your name and content that includes some of your personal information. If you work in a large organization, the attack may have language that seems to come from a coworker, detailing department information or referring to a recent (perhaps unnamed) meeting. The source of the message may actually be your coworker's valid address if the attacker managed to hijack the email account. Or it may appear to be your coworker's valid address, but in reality, it is a forged email address. Someone forges an email address by modifying the sender's address in the email message's header—the information that accompanies a message but does not appear in the message. We also call this type of forgery email spoofing.

Be very suspicious of email requesting personal or financial information. Legitimate businesses will never contact you by email and ask you for your access code, Social Security number, or password. Phishing (and spear phishing) are just old-fashioned scams in high-tech dress.

Hoaxes A hoax is a deception intended either for amusement or for some gain with malicious intent. Hoaxes take many forms. One example is an email message appearing to be from someone you know claiming she took an unplanned trip to London where she was mugged in the subway. The email

Take a Phishing IQ Test!

It is often difficult to discern which emails are legitimate and which are "phish." Test your ability to detect a phishing scam. To complete this test, you will need a computer or mobile device with an Internet connection.

Step 1

Use your Web browser to connect to the phishing test at www .sonicwall.com/phishing/. If this URL no longer works, use a search engine to find a phishing test.

Step 2

After reading the instructions and helpful hints, start the test.

Step 3

You will be presented with 10 messages and you must decide whether each is legitimate or phish.

Step 4

DELL SonicWALL

Protection at the Speed of Business

SonicWALL Phishing IQ Test

SonicWALL Phishing IQ Test
(Formerly the MailFrontier Phishing IQ Test)

Chances are that in the past week you've received an e-mail in your inbox that pretends to be from your bank, e-commerce vendor, or other on-line site. Hopefully you've realized that many times this e-mail is fake - a phishing e-mail. The sender (phisher) of these fake e-mails wants you to click on the link in the e-mail and go to a phishing Web site - which will look just like the Web site of the company being phished. Once on the phishers Web site they hope to obtain your account, financial, credit and even identity information. Of course not every e-mail you receive is a phish. In fact you should expect your bank or e-commerce vendor to send you legitimate e-mail. But how can you tell the difference? Well that's what the Phishing IQ test is all about - give it a try.

Instructions

To begin click the "Start the Test" button below. Each question will be displayed one at a time in a browser window and you decide if the e-mail is a "Phish" or "Legitimate." When you have completed the test you'll get a score along with a chance to see "why" a question was a phish or legitimate. Good Luck!

[Start The Test]

Helpful Hints

1. At the bottom of each "e-mail", on the status bar, there is the URL of the active link - the one being pointed to in the e-mail. You can decide if what is displayed is "real" or fake.
2. For this test, assume that you are "John Doe" or "Jane Doe" - in other words that you received the e-mail in your inbox addressed to you.

Phishing Facts

6.1 Billion - Number of phishing e-mails sent world-wide each month

$1,200 - Average loss to each person successfully phished (Federal Trade Commission)

22,273 - Number of unique phishing attacks in June 2011 (Anti-Phishing Working Group)

28,148 - Number of phishing Web sites found in June 2011 (Anti-Phishing Working Group)

US - The country hosting the most phishing sites (Anti-Phishing Working Group)

When you finish, the program will grade you on your choices and you will see the correct answers. Each message also has a detailed explanation as to why it is either legitimate or phish. Read these explanations carefully.

You got 9 out of 10 correct.

90%

address looks legitimate, but when you respond, you receive a message from someone else stating that your friend is now in jail and needs bail money. Sounds outlandish? We received such a message, but we were suspicious and called our friend who reported that she was safe at home and that several other of her friends had responded to the message and received the plea for money.

Enticements to Open Attachments Social engineering is also involved in the enticements to open attachments to emails. Called "gimmes," you find these enticements either in the subject line or in the body of the email message. Opening the attachment then executes and infects the local computer with some form of malware. A huge number of methods are used. Sadly, enticements often appeal to the less noble human characteristics such as greed (via an offer too good to be true), vanity (physical enhancement products), or simple curiosity (with a subject line that appears to be a response to an email from you). More tragic, these enticements may appeal to people's sympathy and compassion by way of a nonexistent charity or by fraudulently representing a legitimate charity.

Identity Theft

Identify theft occurs when someone collects personal information belonging to another person and uses that information to fraudulently make purchases, open new credit accounts, and even obtain new driver's licenses and other forms of identification in the victim's name. There are many ways not directly involved with computers for thieves to steal your identity. However, the use of computers and mobile devices for social networking and purchasing has greatly expanded the scope of this type of crime, turning it into a huge business involved in the theft of large numbers of persons' data from large databases. These criminals sell such identity information for pennies per record. Several websites maintained by the U.S. government offer valuable information for consumers who wish to protect themselves from identify theft. A starting place is the website www.idtheft.gov, by the President's Task Force on Identity Theft (see Figure 2–3); it includes steps to take if you have been a victim of identity theft. Connect to this website in the Try This.

try this!

Learn More About Identity Theft

Learn more about identity theft and what to do if you are a victim of identity theft. Try this:

1. Open your browser; enter www.idtheft.gov into the address box. The actual URL is www.identitytheft.gov, but the shorter version works and is easier to type.

2. This site, shown in Figure 2–3, gives clear step-by-step instructions for what to do if you are a victim of identity theft.

3. Notice that you can print out each checklist.

4. For prevention tips, direct your browser to ftc.gov/idtheft. This is also a link found on the bottom of the IdentityTheft.gov page accessed in the previous steps.

FIGURE 2–3 The FTC Identity Theft Web page.

Exposure to Inappropriate or Distasteful Content

The Internet, and especially the World Wide Web, is a treasure trove of information. It is hard to imagine a subject that cannot be found somewhere on the Internet. However, some of this content may be inappropriate or distasteful. To some extent, only an individual can judge what is inappropriate and distasteful; however, there are circumstances in which certain content harmful to some individuals—such as young children—is considered a threat and thus is inappropriate.

Invasion of Privacy

One can also view many of the threats discussed so far as invasions of privacy. Protecting against privacy invasion includes protecting your personal information at your bank, credit union, at online and brick-and-mortar retail stores, athletic clubs, and at any organization in which you are a customer, member, or employee. All steps you take to make your computer more secure also contribute to the protection of your privacy. Don't forget physical security and the ability of people to gather information by shoulder surfing, which entails reading information off your screen while you work on your computer in a busy office or public location.

Invasion of privacy by shoulder surfing.

Misuse of Cookies

One form of privacy invasion involves the misuse of something called cookies. Cookies are very small files a Web browser saves on the local hard drive at the request of a website. The next time you connect to that same website, it will request the cookies saved on previous visits—often giving you the convenience of automated log-ins to each site. Cookies are text files, so they cannot contain viruses, which are executable code, but they may contain the following:

- User preferences when visiting a specific site.
- Information you may have entered into a form at the website, including personal information.

- Browsing activity.
- Shopping selections on a website.

Users are not overtly aware of the saving and retrieving of cookies from their local hard disk, although most good websites clearly detail whether or not they use cookies and what they use them for. You can find this information in the privacy statement or policy of the site. Cookies are accessible by the website that created them, or through some subterfuge of the website creator. A cookie contains the name of the domain that originated that cookie. A first-party cookie is one that originates with the domain name of the URL to which you directly connect. A third-party cookie refers to a cookie that originates with a domain name beyond the one shown in your URL. An ad embedded in a Web page—often called banner ads—can use cookies to track your Web surfing habits, and third-party cookies play a part in this type of tracking, making third-party cookies less desirable than first-party cookies.

WARNING!

From now on, when you browse the Web, look for links to the privacy statement or site policy at each website you visit.

Computer Hardware Theft

Good security includes something as simple as locking doors, keeping hardware locked away from prying eyes and sticky fingers. That's obvious. What may not be obvious to you, especially if you use a laptop as your principal computer, is what happens if someone steals your computer. You would be astonished at how many computers, especially laptops and mobile devices, are stolen each year, and unless your computer has been properly secured, and all the data backed up, there goes your business information, your data files, your financial information, your address book, everything! Although a large percentage of computer thefts occur just so the thief can sell the hardware quickly and get some quick cash, an increasing number of thieves are technically sophisticated and will go through your hard drive looking for bank account, credit card, and other financial data so they can steal your identity.

Guard against computer theft.

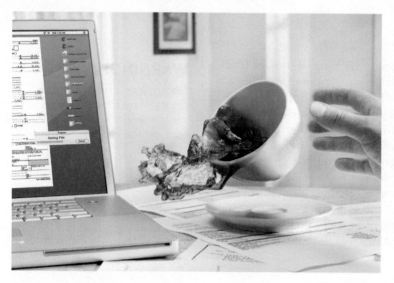

Computer accidents are common.

Accidents, Mistakes, and Disasters

Accidents and mistakes happen. We don't know of anyone who hasn't accidentally erased an important file, pressed the wrong button at the wrong instant, or created a file name he can't remember. Disasters also happen in many forms. Just a few are fires, earthquakes, and weather-induced disasters such as tornadoes, lightning strikes, and floods. Predicting such events is imperfect at best. The principal way to protect against accidents, mistakes, and disasters is to make frequent, comprehensive backups. You can make backups of an entire hard drive using programs that make an image of the drive, or you can use programs that back up your critical data files on a periodic basis. Organizations that have a lot of valuable data even make multiple backups and keep copies off-site. Then, in case of fire, flood, earthquake, or other natural disaster that destroys not only the on-site backups but also the computer, they can still recover.

Keeping Track of New Threats

We cannot begin to cover all the methods currently used to victimize computer users. However, various organizations work to keep track of these threats, counter them, and inform the public. The Federal Trade Commission (FTC) Bureau of Consumer Protection is one such organization. It maintains a website (www.ftc.gov/bcp/), shown in Figure 2–4, containing a list of documents about various consumer issues and threats. These documents are worth reviewing from time to time to learn about new threats. This site also posts the latest related news and hosts a blog.

FIGURE 2–4 The FTC Bureau of Consumer Protection website.

The People Behind the Threats

The people behind computer security threats are as varied as are their motivations. They come from all walks of life and are scattered all over the globe. The umbrella term for a person who breaks laws using computer technology is cybercriminal. Other terms further define the people behind these threats.

Organized Crime

Organized crime is a growing source of these threats. Organized crime cartels exist in every major country in the world, with certain areas notorious for their homegrown crime organizations. Online banking and online shopping are just two areas where billions of dollars exchange every day, and these cartels work to exploit weaknesses. Organized crime specialists work at stealing bank account login information and also are the source of many fraud attempts and money laundering via online shopping.

Cyberterrorists

Terrorists cause destruction without regard to its effect on humanity. Terrorists of all types have embraced cybercrime as a method by which individuals can wreak havoc on victims worldwide without putting themselves in physical danger. Such an attack is cyberterrorism, and a person who carries it out is a cyberterrorist.

Hackers

As any group of people engaged in similar endeavors grows and matures, it develops a set of terms and participant competency rankings. For years, the term "hacker" has been used, particularly by the press, to mean someone who uses sophisticated computer programming skills to invade private computers and networks to cause havoc, steal passwords, steal identities and money, and so on. But the people who work to invade computer systems actually fall into several classifications describing their action—classifications defined by the people within that community themselves. For instance, in some circles, a hacker is someone with a great deal of computing expertise, a white hat hacker. Like the classic good cowboy who wore a white hat in old westerns, a white hat hacker is not a cybercriminal and only explores computer system weaknesses for the purpose of making systems more secure, an activity considered to be ethical.

Note: The term "white hat" is so popular that a company that offers security software and services is named White Hat Security. They also offer online training in Web application security. They can be found at www.whitehatsec.com.

Hacker.

Crackers

A cracker is a member of a group of people who proudly call themselves hackers, but are regarded as black hat hackers. This again harks back to the old cowboy westerns in which the bad guys wore black hats. They may be after financial gain or simply get a kick out of causing damage after breaking into computers and making phone systems do things they aren't supposed to do (the latter is called phone phreaking). White hat hackers call these people "crackers" and want nothing to do with them because being able to break security doesn't make you a hacker any more than being able to hot-wire a car makes you an automotive engineer. The basic difference is this: Hackers build things and look for vulnerabilities in order to improve security; crackers break into systems illegally and do harm. The following also fall into the black hat category in spite of their lack of technical knowledge.

Script Kiddies

A script kiddie is someone who lacks the knowledge to personally develop a security threat, but uses scripted tools or programs created by others to break into computer systems to cause damage or mischief. The name implies enough knowledge to run computer scripts or programs.

Click Kiddies

A click kiddie is similar to a script kiddie, but with even less knowledge than a script kiddie, requiring a GUI to select and run a hacking tool. A click kiddie browses the Web, searching for sites that make it even easier by providing forms the click kiddie can fill out, enter a target IP address, and click to initiate an attack. Such sites provide the additional benefit of anonymity to the perpetrator.

Packet Monkeys

Packet monkeys are similar to script kiddies and click kiddies in that they need to use programs created by others to perform their attacks. They typically have little understanding of the harm they may cause, and their exploits are often random and without a purpose other than the thrill of trying to get away with something. Hackers call packet monkeys "bottom feeders."

Packet monkeys create denial-of-service attacks by inundating a site or a network with so much traffic (data packets) that the network is overwhelmed and denies service to additional traffic. Their attacks may be on a broad scale, which makes it more difficult to trace the identity of the packet monkey.

LO 2.2 | Defense Against Threats

No simple solutions exist to the damaging and mischievous threats that lurk on the Internet and on private networks, but doing nothing is not an option. We need to make our best efforts to thwart these threats, even if we cannot deter a determined and skilled invader. Most people do not have the necessary skills, motivation, or access to sophisticated tools, so implementing basic security will keep the majority out. Here are some basic defensive practices that you can apply in operating systems to avoid being a victim. Often you will need to install a third-party program (free or commercial) to add protection your operating system does not provide.

Education

This chapter may be just the beginning of your education about how threats, such as viruses, get access to computers and networks and how our own behavior can make us vulnerable to such threats as identity theft. Beyond understanding how these things can happen, also be actively alert to signs of a virus or that someone is using your credit cards or using your identity to obtain credit for themselves. Then you can take steps to defend against threats and recover from damage from threats.

Be suspicious of anything out of the ordinary on your computer. Any unusual computer event may indicate that a virus, some sort of browser hijack, or other form of spyware, adware, and so on has infected your computer. Signs to look for include:

- Strange screen messages.
- Sudden computer slowdown.
- Missing data.
- Inability to access the hard drive.

Similarly, unusual activity in any of your credit or savings accounts can indicate that you are a victim of identity theft, including:

- Charges on credit accounts that you are sure you or your family did not make.
- Calls from creditors about overdue payments on accounts you never opened.
- Being rejected when applying for new credit for reasons you know are not true.
- A credit bureau reports existing credit accounts you never opened.

Keep yourself informed by checking out reliable sources. ZDNet publishes articles on many technology topics. Just one of their regular security columns is the Zero Day Weekly, which gives an overview of the latest security-related news. Another good site for keeping up with security news is www.schneier.com.

Along with education about threats comes paranoia. However, if you use a computer at home, work, or school, and are on a network and/or the Internet, a touch of paranoia is healthy. Just don't let it distract you from your day-to-day tasks. Take proactive, responsible steps, as we outline here.

Security Policies

Every organization should have a set of established security policies describing how they protect and manage sensitive information. Security policies define data sensitivity and data security practices, including security classifications of data, and who (usually based on job function) may have access to the various classes of data. For instance, a security policy may state, "Only server administrators and advanced technicians may access the server room, and must not give access to any other individuals." Security policies should also describe the consequences of breaking policy rules.

Security policies should exist in both document form and software form. For instance, at work or school, if you are logging into a network with a central login, such as a Microsoft domain, administrators may configure the servers to enforce a password policy that accepts only strong passwords. How they define a strong password depends on the settings selected, such as minimum password length or complexity. Complexity requirements may say the characters must include a combination of lowercase alphabetical characters, uppercase alphabetical characters, numerals, punctuation characters, and math symbols. In addition, they may require that you create a new password every month, and that you cannot repeat any of the previous 10 passwords.

Windows has security policies implemented from the domain level on the computers as well as on the users that log on to the domain. Windows also

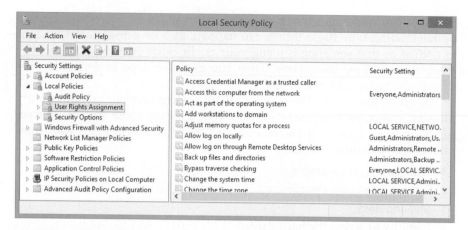

FIGURE 2–5 The Windows Local Security Policy console.

has a local security policy that affects the local computer and users, but can be overridden by domain policy when the computer and user are logged on to a Windows domain. The Local Security Policy console shown in Figure 2–5 allows an administrator to set local security policy. This is a very advanced task.

Firewalls

A firewall is either software or a physical device that examines network traffic. Based on predefined rules, a firewall rejects certain traffic coming into a computer or network. The two general types of firewalls are network-based hardware firewalls and personal firewalls that reside on individual computers. We recommend that you always have a reliable personal firewall installed, even if your computer is behind a hardware firewall. An attack can be from another computer behind the firewall, and that is when your personal firewall becomes your last line of defense between your computer and the world. Let's look at these two general types of firewalls.

Network-Based Firewalls

A network-based firewall is a hardware device designed to protect you against the dangers of having an unprotected connection to the Internet. It sits between a private network and the Internet (or other network) and examines all traffic in and out of the network it is protecting. It will block any traffic it recognizes as a potential threat, using a variety of techniques. Table 2–1 lists some of the most common technologies normally included in a firewall, although some of these are not strictly firewall technologies. Your ISP and most corporations employ hardware firewalls, expensive and specialized computers manufactured by companies such as Cisco, Palo Alto Networks, Fortinet, and others, and these sophisticated firewalls require highly trained people to manage them. Such a firewall probably protects the network at work or at school.

At home or in a small office, most people have a consumer-grade hardware firewall that comes in a small device that performs many of the same functions performed by a more professional-grade firewall. The most common name for these devices is broadband router or cable/DSL router. They combine the function of a firewall, a router (a device that "routes" traffic from one network to another), an Ethernet switch, and even a wireless access point all in one tiny box. These inexpensive devices can handle the traffic of just a few computers, while the more serious devices employed by ISPs and large organizations can handle thousands of simultaneous high-speed transmissions. These consumer-grade devices now come with the "one button" configuration that automatically configures a simple connection to the Internet, with the latest security turned

TABLE 2-1 Firewall Technologies

Technology	Description
IP packet filter	An IP packet filter inspects (or filters) each packet that enters or leaves the network, applying a set of security rules defined by a network administrator. Packets that fail inspection may not pass between the connected networks.
Proxy service	Sometimes referred to as an application-layer gateway, a proxy service watches for application-specific traffic. For example, a Web proxy only examines Web browser traffic. Acting as a stand-in (a proxy) for internal computers, it intercepts outbound connection requests to external servers and directs incoming traffic to the correct internal computer. You can configure a proxy service to block traffic from specific domains or addresses.
Encrypted authentication	Some firewalls require external users to provide a user name and password before they can open a connection through a firewall. Since the authentication information (user name and password) must pass over the Internet, it is important to encrypt it. This authentication involves the use of one of several encryption protocols. Encrypted authentication is a security service that is not limited to firewalls and is not always implemented on a firewall.
Virtual private network (VPN)	Not a true firewall technology, a virtual private network (VPN) is a virtual tunnel created between two endpoints over one or more physical networks, done by encapsulating the packets. Other security methods usually applied include encryption of the data and encrypted authentication. When set up in combination with properly configured firewalls, a VPN is the safest way to connect two private networks over the Internet.

on. You can also access the built-in Web page to make manual changes to the settings. Figure 2–6 shows the security page of a Cisco Wireless Router, which includes support for all the technologies listed in Table 2–1 and many more features, including support for the 802.11N standard for Wi-Fi communications and security. The setting labeled "Firewall" is just one option for securing your home network. Even with this device, you would need to research the impact of the various settings before changing from the default settings.

The firewall administrator configures a firewall to allow traffic into the private network or prohibit traffic from entering the private network based on the types of computers residing within the private network, and how they will interact with the Internet. If all the computers on a private network are desktop computers that connect to the Internet to browse Web pages and access FTP sites, the firewall protecting the network has a simple job. It simply blocks all in-bound traffic that is not the result of a request from a computer on the internal network; it matches incoming traffic with previous outgoing traffic that made requests that would result in incoming traffic. Then, when you connect to a website, outgoing traffic from your computer to the website requests to see a page. That page comes to you as incoming traffic and a firewall will allow it through based on your initial request.

But if the private network includes servers that offer services on the Internet, then the firewall must allow initiating traffic to come through, but it does not allow all incoming traffic through. In this case, an administrator configures a firewall to allow incoming traffic of the type that can only communicate with the internally based servers. The various types of traffic include email, Web, FTP, and others. Each type of traffic has a certain characteristic the firewall can recognize. Figure 2–7 shows a firewall protecting a network containing both servers and desktop computers (shown as clients).

A network professional would look at the simplified example of a firewall shown in Figure 2–7 and immediately talk about setting up a DMZ, named for a wartime demilitarized zone. In networking, a DMZ is a network between a private (inside) network and public (outside) network. An organization puts any servers that it wishes to have offer services to the Internet in the DMZ.

Note: A server created as a decoy to draw malware attacks and gather information about attackers is called a honey pot. A honey pot may be located outside a corporate firewall, within a DMZ, or inside the corporate network.

Personal Firewalls

Because many attacks come from within a private network, personal firewalls have become standard. The Windows Firewall is included in Windows. OS X

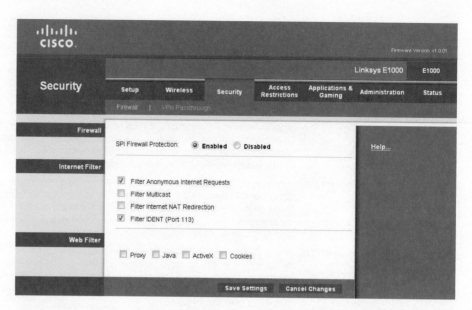

FIGURE 2–6 The Security page from a Cisco Wireless Router's configuration utility.

Note: Zone Labs (**www.zonelabs .com**) offers many excellent security products, including Zone Alarm, a personal firewall.

comes with a firewall, and there are many third-party firewalls for Windows, OS X, and Linux. There are two places where you can configure the Windows Firewall. One is the Windows Firewall Control Panel, shown in Figure 2–8. Using the links in the pane on the left, you can make changes to the Firewall. A more advanced configuration tool is Windows Firewall with Advanced Security, a Microsoft Management console shown in Figure 2–9.

If you have installed a third-party firewall—either separately or as part of a security suite—the Windows Firewall will be turned off. Opening the Windows Firewall applet in Control Panel will show you a message stating that your computer is unprotected and you need to turn on Windows Firewall. This informational message may simply mean that Windows Firewall is disabled because you are using a third-party firewall.

FIGURE 2–7 A private network protected by a firewall.

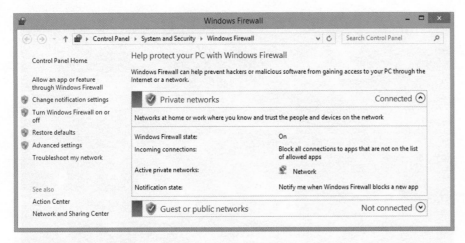

FIGURE 2–8 The Windows Firewall Control Panel.

Security Software

A logical progression through the appropriate defense against computer security threats would have us look at authentication and authorization at this point. However, because we include activities that require that you access the Internet, we will first talk about the comprehensive security software that should be in place before you connect to the Internet. This does not mean that security software is more important than authentication and authorization. They are all important pieces of every security defense strategy.

Comprehensive security software may come in one bundle of software from one source, or it can be separate software from many sources. The pieces should include (at minimum) a personal firewall, antivirus software, anti-spam software, and an email scanner. Figure 2–10 shows the console for Bitdefender with security components and various tools for managing the security package, such as the Update that automatically checks the Bitdefender site for updates and then downloads and installs them. The following sections will describe security components included with common security software.

FIGURE 2–9 Windows Firewall with Advanced Security console.

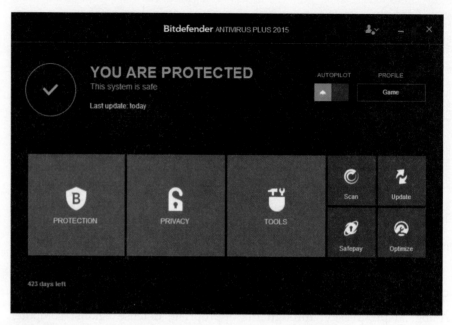

FIGURE 2–10 Security software with many bundled components.

Antispam Software

A spam filter is software designed to combat spam by examining incoming email messages and filtering out those that have characteristics of spam, including certain identified keywords. In an organization with centralized network and computer management, spam filter software installed on central mail servers can remove spam before it gets to a user's desktop. Other network administrators use Internet-based spam filtering services that block spam before it reaches the corporate network.

Individuals connected to the Internet from home or in small businesses are often on their own when it comes to eliminating spam. Luckily, many email clients, such as Microsoft Outlook, now offer spam filtering. Without a spam filter you must sort through your own email to find and delete the spam. Spam filters are not perfect—they often filter out legitimate messages, while allowing some spam messages through. For this reason, most spam filters require some configuration on the part of the user using rules or filters that will automate the process of removing spam from known sources. And the user will still often need to review a list of suspected spam messages. Figure 2–11 shows the Microsoft Outlook Junk Email Options dialog box with several tabbed pages of settings that allow you to configure the spam filter.

Junk E-mail Options - jane@

Options | Safe Senders | Safe Recipients | Blocked Senders | International

Outlook can move messages that appear to be junk e-mail into a special Junk E-mail folder.

Choose the level of junk e-mail protection you want:

○ No Automatic Filtering. Mail from blocked senders is still moved to the Junk E-mail folder.

○ Low: Move the most obvious junk e-mail to the Junk E-mail folder.

○ High: Most junk e-mail is caught, but some regular mail may be caught as well. Check your Junk E-mail folder often.

● Safe Lists Only: Only mail from people or domains on your Safe Senders List or Safe Recipients List will be delivered to your Inbox.

☐ Permanently delete suspected junk e-mail instead of moving it to the Junk E-mail folder

☑ Disable links and other functionality in phishing messages. (recommended)

☑ Warn me about suspicious domain names in e-mail addresses. (recommended)

OK | Cancel | Apply

FIGURE 2–11 The Outlook Junk Email Options page.

Antivirus Software

An antivirus program can examine the contents of a storage device or RAM looking for hidden viruses and files that may act as hosts for virus code. Effective antivirus products not only detect and remove viruses, but they also help you recover data that has been lost because of a virus. To remain current, they require frequent updating as to the virus threats to watch for. An antivirus program includes an antivirus engine (the main program) and a set of patterns of recognized viruses, usually contained in files called definition files. Retailers of antivirus software commonly charge an annual fee for updates to the antivirus engine and the definition files. There are excellent free services for home users. One example is AVG antivirus from GRIsoft. Software companies that offer free security software usually also offer a feature-rich commercial version to which you can upgrade for a fee. The free version gives you a chance to see if you like using it before you put out any money. Once installed, most antivirus programs will automatically connect to the manufacturer's website and check for these updates.

Pop-Up Blockers

Many free and commercial programs are available that effectively block various forms of adware, especially pop-ups, which are the easiest to block and the most annoying because a pop-up advertisement appears in its own window and must be closed or moved before you can see the content you were seeking. A program that works against pop-ups is a pop-up blocker, and all major Web browsers now have built-in pop-up blockers. You can configure a pop-up blocker so that it will block pop-ups quietly, but you can also configure one to make a sound and/or display a message allowing you to choose to make a decision on each pop-up or to automatically and quietly block all pop-ups. We have found a few websites where blocking all pop-ups has blocked much of the content we were seeking. In that case, we may configure the pop-up blocker to make an exception for that site. You can enable the pop-up blocker feature on the Privacy page of the Internet Options dialog box for Internet Explorer. Once enabled, click the Settings button to open the Pop-up Blocker Settings page.

To configure the pop-up blocker in Firefox, open Options and select the Content tab, where you will find the setting to turn the pop-up blocker off or on. You can also open the Exceptions dialog for Firefox, shown in Figure 2–12, and add any website where you wish to enable pop-ups.

Privacy Protection and Cookies

Web browsers and security programs offer privacy protection options. In Microsoft Internet Explorer, you can configure privacy settings, including the pop-up blocker, through the Internet Options dialog box, accessible from either the Control Panel or the Tools menu in Internet Explorer. This is also where you determine how Internet Explorer handles cookies. The settings range from "Block all cookies" to "Allow all cookies," with a variety of settings in between. Experiment with the settings by choosing one and then spending some time browsing the Internet. The balance here is between the convenience of cookies for automated login to frequently accessed sites and the risk of an invasion of privacy. The Sites button in Internet Explorer will block specific sites; you will see a list of known bad sites listed here. The Advanced button allows you to customize the handling of cookies, as shown in Figure 2–13. We recommend that you allow first-party cookies for the convenience (explained earlier) and block third-party cookies because the tracking methods often associated with third-party cookies are an invasion of privacy.

Parental Controls and Family Safety

The feature for protecting children from inappropriate content is known as Parental Controls in both OS X and Windows 7. Microsoft uses the name

FIGURE 2–12 The Firefox Pop-Up Blocker Exceptions page.

Family Safety beginning in Windows 8. In OS X look for Parental Controls in the System Preferences window or turn it on or off for a user in the Users and Groups dialog box. In Windows 7 enable this feature by first creating an account as a Standard user and then opening the Parental Controls control panel and selecting that user. In Windows 8 or later create a new account as a child account or change an existing account to a child's account. Once you create a child account you will receive weekly email updates on the child's activities. You can also go to Microsoft's Family Safety website, shown in Figure 2–14. Although Windows 8.1 allowed you to assign the child type to a local account, beginning with Windows 10, the child's account must be a Microsoft account, and the Family Safety settings will follow the child to other Windows 10 devices.

Content Filtering

You can use software that blocks content, called a content filter, to enable protection from inappropriate or distasteful content. A common type of content filter used on the Internet is a Web content filter, a software program designed to work with a Web browser to either block certain sites or to allow only certain sites. As with most types of software, you can find both free and commercial versions of Web content filters on the Internet. In fact, you may already have a Web content filter in your Web browser that you only need to enable and configure.

Many services are available on the Internet to evaluate website content and give each site ratings based on such parameters as language, nudity, sex, and violence. A content filter may use one or more of these rating services, and

Note: To learn more about content filters, use your favorite search engine to search on the key words "Web content filter."

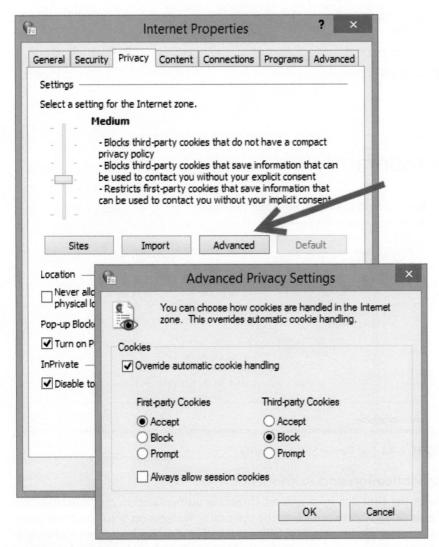

FIGURE 2–13 Use the Advanced Privacy Settings in Internet Options to control the use of cookies.

allow the administrator to choose the rating level to permit or exclude. Not all websites are rated, so if you enable a Web content filter, you will also have to decide what it should do in the event the user connects to an unrated site.

Software Updates

You should be sure to keep your operating system and applications up to date with security patches, especially if you are running Windows. Microsoft continues to update each version of Windows for several years (see the Microsoft Support Lifecycle at **www.microsoft.com**), and the versions discussed in this book automatically check for the updates that plug security holes that malware perpetrators exploit. Windows keeps a list of all the updates, as shown in Figure 2–15.

try this!

View the Windows Update History

You can see the update history on your Windows computer. Try this:

1. Open Control Panel. In Windows 7 open it from the Start menu. In Windows 8.*x* and 10 right-click on the start button and select *Control Panel*.
2. Tap or click on the Windows Update link in Control Panel to open it.
3. In the task pane (on the left) in Windows Update click or tap View Update History.
4. This opens the View Update History control panel, where you can scroll through the list of installed updates.

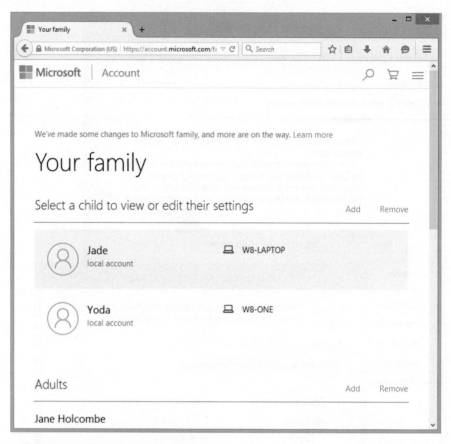

FIGURE 2–14 The Family Safety website.

Authentication and Authorization

One of the first defenses against threats is authentication and authorization by a security system built into the operating systems on your local computer and on network servers. The OSs surveyed in this book support authentication and authorization. In fact, Linux, Windows, and OS X require it.

After you, as the administrator, have set up an account for Rachel in accounting she must enter her username and password when she logs on to her computer. Before giving her access to the computer, security components of her operating system will verify that she used a valid user name and password. This validation of the user account and password is authentication.

FIGURE 2–15 Windows Update maintains a list of updates.

A recently hired part-time clerk, Kirsten, works at night entering accounts payable information into Rachel's computer. To allow Kirsten to also log on to Rachel's computer, you can create a new user account for Kirsten. Although only Rachel and Kirsten can log on to this computer, Rachel does not want Kirsten to be able to access the payroll information, also stored there, because this is private information. What might you do to help Rachel with this problem? One thing you could do (if her operating system supports it) is to set up Rachel's computer so that she can assign special permissions to the files and folders on her hard disk, giving each user account the level of permission it needs. For instance, one of Kirsten's tasks is to add accounting information to the accounts payable files, so you could give Kirsten's account the authorization that will allow her to write to the files in the accounts payable folder. You will not give Kirsten's account access to any of the other folders, and you will only give Rachel's account full control of the folders that she needs to use.

Right about now you're thinking that we're wrong about Windows and OS X requiring authentication. Your computer is running the latest version of Windows or OS X, but you don't have to enter a username or password to access your desktop and all your personal settings and data. So, obviously, you are not authenticated. Right? Wrong! Windows, OS X, and Linux always require authentication, but each has a feature called automatic login that the OS installation program system turns on under certain circumstances, such as when you bring home a PC or Mac that you just bought in a retail store. Automatic login authenticates anyone who powers up your computer using the same credentials, and they have access to everything that you normally do. You should never enable automatic login on a computer at school or at work.

Authentication

Authentication is the verification of who you are. Authentication may be one-factor, two-factor, or even three-factor. One-factor authentication is your use of a user name and password as you log on to your computer. In this case, you are authenticated based on something you know—your user name and password. One type of two-factor authentication involves the use of something you know plus something you have, referred to as a token. If you use a cash card at an ATM, you are familiar with two-factor authentication, because the something you know is your PIN (personal identification number) code, while the token is your cash card. Another type of two-factor authentication, common with many online services today, requires your authentication with a username and password followed by the service sending a one-time authentication code via a method you previously agreed to, such as a text message to your smartphone. For even more security, consider three-factor authentication, adding biometric data, such as a retinal scan, voice print, or fingerprint scan to the token and password.

Authorization

Authorization determines the level of access to a computer or a resource (files, folders, printers, and so on) to an authenticated user. Authorization includes authentication plus verification of your level of access to a computer or resource, including permissions and/or user rights. When you connect to a shared folder on your LAN, the security system of the computer hosting the folder will perform authorization, authenticating you and verifying that your account has some level of access to the folder. This level of access is called a permission. Permission describes an action that you may perform on an object. An example of a permission found on a file system is the read permission that allows reading of the contents of a file or folder, but by itself it does not allow any other action on that file, such as deleting or changing it. Another component that affects level of access is a user right. A **user right** defines a system-wide action that a user or group may perform such as logging on to a computer or installing device drivers.

Passwords

The most common method of authentication is the use of a password and identifier, such as a user name. A password is an important piece of the security puzzle. Don't take your password for granted. In fact, password should be plural, because you should not use the same password everywhere, and you should put a great deal of thought into creating passwords that truly help you protect yourself. This is important because, unless you deal strictly in cash and do all your transactions in person at the bank, secure authentication is your basic defense against an invasion of your privacy, and your password is central to having secure authentication. Passwords are a very important part of any security system. Most experts recommend using passwords that are at least eight characters long and that contain a mixture of numbers, letters (both uppercase and lowercase), and nonalphanumeric characters. It's easy to guess passwords that use common words—such as the name of a pet—and therefore they offer little in the way of real security.

Establish a method for creating strong passwords—whether it is some scheme that you think up or software that helps you create these passwords. Begin by thinking of a phrase that is easy to remember such as: "I love the Boston Red Sox." Then take the first letter of each word in that phrase and string the letters together. In our example, the result is: iltbrs. Now turn it into a more complex password by capitalizing some of the alpha characters and inserting numbers and other symbols between the letters: i-l,T.b+r-s. If this meets the minimum password requirements, you have a password. Now, the trick is to remember this password without the use of sticky notes!

A great alternative to "do-it-yourself" password creating is to use password management software. A **password manager** will create strong passwords, remember them for you, and even insert the correct password when you need it. Secure the password manager itself with a single strong password. Use a single password manager, such as Dashlane or LastPass, to manage the passwords across all your devices.

Security Account Basics

A **security account** is an account that can be assigned permission to take action on an object (such as a file, folder, or printer) or the right to take some action on an entire system, such as install device drivers into an operating system on a computer. A security account may identify a single entity (individual or computer) or a group of entities. Security accounts exist in security databases, such as those maintained by Novell servers, UNIX or Linux systems, OS X desktop and server OSs, and Windows server and desktop operating systems.

User Accounts

All operating systems discussed in this book have robust security that begins with using user and group accounts and the requirement to log in to the computer with a user account. The most common type of security account is an individual account, called a **user account**, assigned to a single person. In the security database, a user account contains, at minimum, a user name and password used to authenticate a user. Depending on the structure of the security accounts database, a user account may contain additional identifying information. Typically, a user account will include the user's full name, a description, and a variety of other fields including email address, department, phone numbers, and so on. User accounts exist in all Windows security accounts databases.

Built-In User Accounts

Each OS has a very special, very privileged built-in account—a super user—that can perform virtually all tasks on a computer, from installing a device driver to creating other security accounts. In Windows this privileged built-in user is Administrator, and it is disabled by default. In those operating systems with their ancestry in UNIX—OS X and Linux—root is the most powerful user account, as it is in UNIX. We'll discuss these accounts in the appropriate chapters.

At the other end of the privilege spectrum, we have a guest account, found in Windows, OS X, and Linux. This account is the least privileged and is disabled by default in Windows. If this account is enabled, a stranger can log in with the account (usually with no password), but cannot see anyone else's files and cannot make changes to the system.

Standard Versus Administrator Accounts

Linux and the versions of Windows and the OS featured in this book all have the notion of types of user accounts. In Windows Vista, Windows 7, and Windows 8 a standard user account is for an "ordinary" user without administrator status. A Windows child account is basically a standard account with the additional restrictions applied through Family Safety. A user logged on with a standard account can change her password and other personal settings, but cannot change computer settings, install or remove software and hardware, or perform other systemwide tasks. In contrast, a user logged on with an account that is an administrator account type can perform systemwide tasks that affect the overall operating system and other users. For example, an administrator can create new users, change user settings, install applications and operating system components, install hardware (and the drivers for that hardware), and access all files on a computer. Ignoring the built-in, but disabled, Administrator account, the first account created in any of these systems must be an administrator account type, and then you may use this account to create additional accounts. When an administrator creates a new account, the default type is Standard. Figure 2–16 shows the Windows 8.1 screen for selecting an account type.

In OS X, there is a check box in the Accounts dialog for a user: the "Allow user to administer this computer" check box. If this is checked, the user account is an administrator account; if it is unchecked the account is a standard account. As with the Windows administrator accounts, an OS X administrator account can install programs and do a range of systemwide tasks. An OS X standard user is limited much as a Windows standard user is.

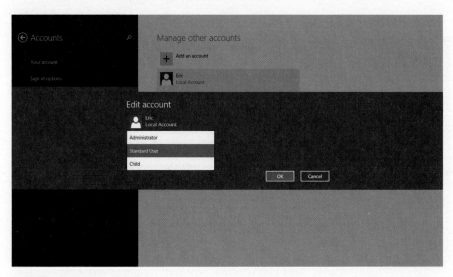

FIGURE 2–16 An administrator account can create accounts, assigning a type to each account.

The administrator type of account in Linux includes the all-powerful root, and some other accounts, but the standard account type is not as clear. For instance, "standard user" is the term used to describe the long list of accounts some distributions will create automatically if you choose a special installation. Since this includes the root account and others with a wide range of permissions, it is not the same as the standard type of account used in Windows and OS X.

Group Accounts

A group account is a security account that contains one or more individual accounts, and, in some security accounts databases, may contain other groups. Group accounts allow us to manage resources for multiple users and make administration of accounts much easier. Group accounts exist in the security accounts databases of all the OSs discussed here—some are built in and privileged users can create others. We will concern ourselves only with those groups that exist in the security accounts database on a desktop computer and not with the security accounts that exist on a network server, such as a Windows Domain Controller. We call the accounts on a desktop computer local user and group accounts. The built-in local groups in Windows include Administrators, Users, and Guests, but other groups are created for various services and applications as they install into Windows. Figure 2–17 shows the Local Users and Groups node of the Computer Management console, an advanced tool for managing users and groups in Windows.

Computer Accounts

Computers (and sometimes devices) may also have security accounts within a security accounts database maintained by a network server, such as in a Microsoft Windows Active Directory domain. This means your computer actually joins a domain before you, as a user, can log on to the network. When this occurs, new group accounts appear in the accounts database on your desktop Windows computer as it integrates into the domain. The details of this relationship are beyond the scope of this book, but be aware that this is the case if your computer is part of a Windows Active Directory Domain. How could this affect you? If you bring your personal laptop to the office, you will not be able to log on to the corporate network in the same way that you do from your desktop until an administrator makes your computer a member of the domain. If it's not desirable to join your personal laptop to the network, there are other methods to give you access to the corporate network.

Note: the Local Users and Groups manager is not available in the Home editions of Windows 7 or Windows 10, nor is it in the basic Windows 8.x edition. It is in the Pro and Enterprise editions.

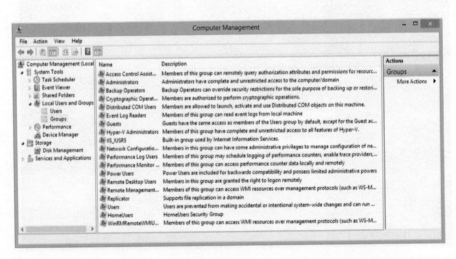

FIGURE 2–17 The Local Users and Groups node in Computer Management showing all groups on the local computer.

User Account Control

Before Windows Vista, if you wanted to make changes to your system such as installing a new device or program, you had to log on as an administrator. This meant, if you were already logged on with an account that did not have administrative access, you would have to log off and log on again with an administrator account before you could perform a major system task. To avoid this annoyance, many people stayed logged on all day every day using an account with administrator access. This meant that if malware infected your computer, it would have full control over your computer because it would have the same level of access as the logged-on user. To prevent this, Microsoft introduced User Account Control (UAC) in Windows Vista to prevent unauthorized changes to Windows. With UAC enabled, there are two scenarios.

In the first scenario, a user logged on with a privileged account with administrative rights only has the privileges of a standard account, until the user (or a malicious program) attempts to do something that requires higher privileges. At that point, UAC makes itself known, graying out (dimming) the desktop, and displaying the Consent Prompt, as shown here. You must click Yes to continue or No to cancel the operation.

In the second scenario, a user logs on with the privileges of a standard user and attempts to do something that requires administrative privileges. In this case, UAC displays the Credentials Prompt shown here, requiring the user name and password of an account with administrative privileges. If you provide these, the program or task will run with these elevated privileges, but you will return to the standard user privileges for all other activities. In either case, if you do not respond in a short time, UAC will time out, cancel the operation, and return the desktop to you.

By default, UAC is turned on in Windows 7 and Windows 8. Even with UAC turned off, Windows still may not allow you to perform all tasks and you will see a message such as "The requested operation requires elevation" when you attempt to perform certain functions.

OS X also has a function similar to Windows UAC, but it is more subtle. Certain dialog boxes have a lock symbol on the lower left. It will appear locked in some instances and unlocked in others. If you are in a dialog box, such as Accounts, you will find that when the lock symbol shows it is locked you can still make certain changes, such as changing your own picture, without a problem, but unlocking the lock reveals more settings that only an administrator may change. If you wish to access the advanced settings, you simply double-click on the lock and enter the user name (it will default to the currently logged-on user) and password of an administrator account, as shown in Figure 2–18. So, even if you have logged on with an account with administrator privileges, it acts like Windows UAC by requiring you to take an extra step before making systemwide changes.

The Windows 7 User Account Control Consent Prompt.

The Windows 7 User Account Control Credentials Prompt.

Best Practices When Assigning Permissions

The most important practice in assigning permissions to accounts in any operating system is to use the rule of least privilege. Give permissions to each user or group that allows each user the amount of access required to complete assigned tasks, but do not give users more access than required. Thus, the user has the least privileges necessary to function.

FIGURE 2–18 Unlock a dialog box in OS X to access advanced settings.

Best Practices with User Names and Passwords

You may actually have habits that make you vulnerable to identity theft or another type of attack on your computer, data, or personal information. Consider the following questions:

- Do you have too many passwords to remember?
- When you have an opportunity to create a new password, do you use your favorite password—the one that you use everywhere?
- At school or work, do you have your password written on sticky notes or your desk calendar?
- Have you used the same password for more than a few months?

If you can answer yes to any of these questions, you are at risk! And the risk is not only with your password. Because many websites allow you to provide a user name to use when you log in, you may also be reusing the same user name and password combination. Now a hacker doesn't even have to guess your account name.

Protect Your User Name and Password

If you use the same user name and password at your bank as you do at a website where you took what seemed like a harmless personality test, you may have put your bank account and your other financial assets at risk. Perhaps someone created the website to surreptitiously gather just such personal information, or it may have an innocent mission, but simply employ weak security practices. Either way, the outcome may be the same—someone now has information that could allow access to your bank account. "But," you say, "I didn't provide them with my bank account information." Are you sure? If you provided any personal information to the website, they may be able to use it to search online databases (some containing information illegally gathered), and to discover, or guess, which bank you use. Then, even though the bank has much better security practices than the website you went to, you have just given someone the key (so to speak) to your assets.

Create Strong Passwords

A strong password is one that meets certain criteria, and these criteria change over time as hackers create more techniques and tools for discovering passwords. An administrator should have a password that is a minimum of 15 characters long. Additionally, a strong password includes a combination of letters, numbers, and other symbols, as allowed by the security system accepting the password. Common sense requires that your personal password should be easy for you to remember, but difficult for others to guess.

> *Note:* Learn more about protecting your computer with passwords. Use an Internet search engine to search on "strong passwords." You will find great tips on how to create complex passwords that are easy to recall, but hard for others to crack.

Always use strong passwords for the following types of accounts:

- Banks, investments, credit cards, and online payment providers.
- Email.
- Work-related accounts.
- Online auction sites and retailers.
- Sites where you have provided personal information.

Avoid Creating Unnecessary Online Accounts

Many websites ask that you create an account and join, but what are the benefits of joining? Why do they need information about you?

Never Reuse Passwords

Every account should have a unique name (if possible) and a unique password (always). Many websites require your email address as the user name, so these will not be unique. When using your email address as a user name for an online account, be sure that you do not use the same password you use to access your email account, but a unique password, only to be used at that website.

Don't Provide More Information Than Necessary

Avoid creating accounts with websites that request your Social Security number and other personal and financial information. Avoid having your credit card numbers and bank account information stored on a website. Although it's not easy to do online, you can do this with a merchant in person: If asked for your Social Security number, ask these four questions:

1. Why do you need it?
2. How will you protect it?
3. How will you use it?
4. What happens if I don't give it to you?

You may have to make a decision as to whether to do business with that merchant if you don't receive satisfactory answers.

try this!

Get Help Creating Passwords

There are programs that will help you create passwords. While we strongly recommend that you come up with your own method to create and remember strong passwords, it is helpful to see some strong passwords. Try this:

1. Open your browser and connect to your favorite search engine. Search on "random password generator" (without the quotation marks).
2. Select a password generator from the results list and experiment.
3. For instance, the Secure Password Generator on the PC Tools website (**www.pctools.com/guides/password/**) allows you to define the password rules and then, after you click the Generate Password button, it will generate a password that complies with the rules.
4. Try creating a password, but do not use one you generated in this fashion. Rather, devise your own scheme for creating secure passwords. Then you are more likely to remember your password.

Encryption

Encryption is the transformation of data into an unreadable format (cipher text) that you can decrypt (decipher) only by using a secret key or password. A secret key is a special code used to decrypt encrypted data. You can encrypt data you are sending over a network. In addition, you can encrypt data files that are stored on a local computer or network server. Encryption protects sensitive or valuable data and only someone who knows the password or holds the secret key can decrypt the data back to its original state. The secret key may be held in a digital certificate (also called a security certificate, or simply a certificate), which is a file stored on a computer.

Encrypting Network Traffic

Without being aware, you participate in encrypting network traffic when you do online banking or shopping. Look at the address line and you will see the protocol prefix "http" replaced by "https." This means that you are now using Secure HTTP (HTTPS), which encrypts the communications between you and the bank or e-commerce server. HTTPS uses the Secure Sockets Layer (SSL) security protocol. For this encryption method, the user certificates contain identifying information used for verifying the holder of the certificate (your bank or the online retailer), including the holder's public key for use in encrypting a message for the user. Only the user holds the private key to decrypt the message. Your Web browser and its security protocols manage it all for you. If the browser detects a problem with a certificate as a page is loading, you will receive a warning that a website's security certificate is invalid. You should not continue loading the page and should block this website via your browser's security settings.

Windows Encrypting File System

Encryption is very useful for data stored on a laptop or in professional settings, where data theft is a concern. The Microsoft NTFS file system allows you to encrypt selected files and folders (not an entire drive) through a feature called Encrypting File System (EFS). Turn on encryption through the Advanced button of the Properties dialog box of a folder residing on an NTFS volume, and then all files created in that folder become encrypted. Figure 2–19 shows the Advanced Attributes dialog that opens from the Advanced button on the Properties of a folder named Data. Clicking the check box labeled Encrypt Contents To Secure Data will turn on encryption for this folder. Anyone who is logged on with your credentials has access to EFS encrypted data. If you copy or move an encrypted file to another NTFS-formatted volume, the encryption is maintained. If you copy or move an encrypted file to a volume that is not formatted with NTFS, the file is saved without encryption.

Whereas EFS is a useful tool, it is not without problems, including the risk that you will lock yourself out of your own files if you change your password. Only enable EFS if you have a knowledgeable administrator (such as at school or work) who will take certain precautions to ensure that someone can aid you in recovering your encrypted files should you be unable to access them yourself.

FIGURE 2–19 Turn NTFS encryption on or off using the Properties of a folder.

Encrypting with Windows BitLocker

BitLocker Drive Encryption is a feature of the Ultimate and Enterprise editions of Windows Vista and Windows 7 and Windows 8 Pro and Ultimate. It allows you to encrypt an entire drive. You or anyone else who is logged on with your credentials has access to the encrypted drive. When using BitLocker in Windows 7 Ultimate or Enterprise or in Windows 8 Pro or Enterprise, you can use a feature called BitLocker to Go to encrypt external hard drives and flash drives. When you create a BitLocker to Go volume, you select the method for unlocking. Because this is a portable drive, you can assign a password or a smart card to unlock the drive.

Older versions of Windows cannot create a BitLocker to Go volume, but they can read them, provided the user has the means to unlock the volume, owing to the program BITLOCKERTOGO.EXE, a BitLocker to Go Reader, that is installed on each BitLocker to Go volume. You will still need to unlock the drive, using a password or smart card.

WARNING!

Do not attempt this at home. You risk being locked out of your encrypted files if you change your password.

Encrypting with OS X FileVault

OS X has a feature called FileVault that began life as an encryption tool for all the files in your Home folder, and it has been improved in recent versions. Figure 2–20 shows the Security dialog box in which you can enable OS X FileVault. Someone logged on with your credentials can access the encrypted files.

Data Wiping

When you move computers from user to user or remove a computer from service within an organization and sell it or give it away, you should remove the data on the computer. This goes beyond a simple delete operation, because there are many methods for "undeleting" such files. To be sure that a

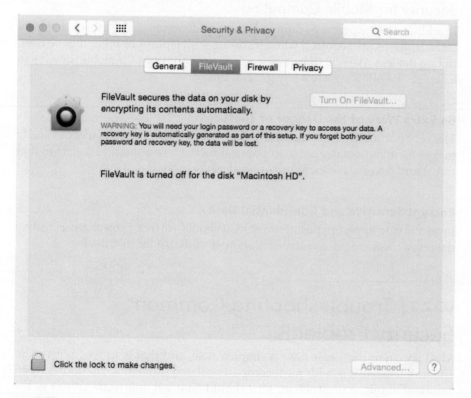

FIGURE 2–20 Configuring FileVault in OS X.

determined person will not access your old files, you must remove them completely. The permanent removal of data from a storage device is data wiping.

A reformat of the hard drive is one method, but it's not truly very secure, and it's a problem if you wanted to keep the operating system and programs on the disk. Another method is to use data wiping software that uses an algorithm for writing over an entire drive volume, or just those portions of a drive that contain data—whether it has been deleted or not. You can perform data wiping on any storage media that is rewritable, including hard drives, optical drives, and solid-state storage. Both free and commercial data wiping programs will do the trick for most purposes. Such programs are available for all storage types. Those written for hard drives can take advantage of a government-approved ability built in to newer hard drives—Secure Erase. You cannot recover data once you have used such a data-wiping program.

Physical Security

Physical security of computers and networks is yet another huge topic that we can only touch on here. Physical security for desktop computers and networks includes limiting who has access to the building or room in which the desktop computers or network servers reside. Physical security is part of a school or other organization's security policy, and that policy must define its implementation. Small organizations often simply rely on the trustworthiness of their employees—with mixed results—while larger organizations implement formal physical security protection. This can include a mode of identifying someone trying to get entry to a building or room. This mode can be a guarded entrance with confirmation of a person's credentials, key card access, or a variety of other methods depending on the security needs of the organization. Securing laptops and other mobile devices has its own challenges, addressed next.

Security for Mobile Computing

In addition to the practices outlined above as defenses against threats, special considerations are required when traveling with laptops or other mobile computing devices. We will discuss specific security options for mobile devices in Chapter 11. Following are a few general tips.

Be Extra Wary of the Danger of Theft

The very portability of laptops and other mobile computing devices obviously makes them more susceptible to physical theft, so you should be alert to that threat and never leave them unattended while traveling.

Encrypt Sensitive and Confidential Data

In addition to applying permissions, you should further protect any sensitive data on a mobile device with encryption, if available for that device.

LO 2.3 | Troubleshooting Common Security Problems

Most apparent problems have a simple cause, and that is as true with security problems as it is with most computer-related problems. Therefore, when troubleshooting any problem, you should first ask yourself, "What is the simplest (dumbest?) thing that could cause this problem?" This will keep you from going off in a panic looking for a high-tech solution before at least considering one or more simple solutions. In this section we discuss some common security problems we have encountered and our recommended solutions.

Troubleshooting Log-On Problems

There are certain nearly universal log-on problems. They include the following.

Caps Lock Key Turned On

Everyone does it! You're in a hurry, and when you type in your user name and password, you don't notice the placement of your hands and one or both of them are incorrect. You receive an error message indicating that the user name or password is incorrect, as in Figure 2–21. No problem; you type it in again, but don't notice that you have the caps lock on. Some operating systems, including Windows Vista and Windows 7, will warn you of this, but other operating systems will not. Therefore, be careful about the placement of your hands and ensure that Caps Lock is off before entering your user name and password.

Too Many Log-On Attempts

On a bad day, like your first day back at work after a vacation, you may try several times before you enter the password correctly. If you're logging on to a corporate network, it is counting all these tries and you may exceed a limit on the number of log-on attempts. This limit is part of account policies, which you learned about earlier in this chapter. Exceeding the number of log-on attempts (account lockout threshold) may result in your user account being locked out of the computer and the network for a period of time (account lockout duration), and you will see a message similar to that in Figure 2–22. There is usually a third parameter used for account policy: the period of time after which the counter for the number of log-on attempts resets to zero.

If a message like this appears when you are trying to log on to a network at school or work, you will have to call an administrator for help. An administrator may be able to override the lockout so that you can try again. Type carefully this time!

FIGURE 2–21 Log-on error message.

FIGURE 2–22 Log-on lockout message.

FIGURE 2–23 The Windows Account Lockout policy, where an administrator can set values for lockout duration, threshold, and a period of time after which the counter resets.

If no administrator is available, you will have to wait for the account lockout time to expire. An administrator configures these settings, usually to comply with a company's security standard (see Figure 2–23). So, it could be a matter of minutes, or it could even be days! Although at the time it can be a huge inconvenience, this is your protection against password crackers, who may need to make many tries before they guess the correct password.

In the unlikely event that you receive a lockout message when attempting to log on to a stand-alone or work group Windows computer, someone will have to log on with an account that is a member of the administrators' group and modify the account lockout policy, or you will have to wait out the lockout duration period.

Using the Administrator Account in Troubleshooting

Windows has an administrator account, cleverly named Administrator. It is disabled by default, as shown in Figure 2–24. The Administrator account is enabled if your computer starts in Safe Mode and if the computer is not a member of a Windows Active Directory domain. In this case, you can log on with this account and attempt to troubleshoot the reason for the computer going into Safe Mode.

Troubleshooting a Suspected Malware Attack

If you suspect a computer is infected by a virus and you have an antivirus program installed, first use it to run a scan of all drives and memory to see if you can discover and remove the virus. If this does not discover a virus but you are still suspicious, or if you do not have an up-to-date antivirus program installed, you can connect to one of many websites that offer free online scans. An online virus scanner does not fully install, so it should not conflict with your installed security software. Just one example of such a scanner is House-call, found at housecall.trendmicro.com. This scanner is by Trend Micro, which also offers a commercial security suite at www.trendmicro.com.

FIGURE 2–24 The Properties dialog box for the Administrator account shows it is disabled by default.

Step-by-Step 2.02

Perform an Online Virus Scan on a PC or Mac

Try one of the online virus scanners. All you need is a Windows computer or a Mac running OS X 10.7 and up, with a Web browser and a connection to the Internet. Use the online scanner at Trend Micro, or one recommended by your instructor.

Step 1

Open your browser and connect to http://housecall.trendmicro.com. Ensure that you are at this website, and were not redirected to one of the many download sites that entice you to download and install questionable software.

Step 2

On the Trend Micro HouseCall page, first select 32-bit or 64-bit. Then click or tap the Download button.

Step 3

Click the Save File button. The HouseCall launcher will download into your Downloads folder.

Step 4

Open your Downloads folder, locate the HouseCall Launcher, and double-click or tap it to run the program.

Step 5

Respond to any User Account Control prompt to enable the program to run. Then it will take a few minutes to load the program, checking for updates and doing other housekeeping. When prompted, accept the Trend Micro End User License Agreement and select Next.

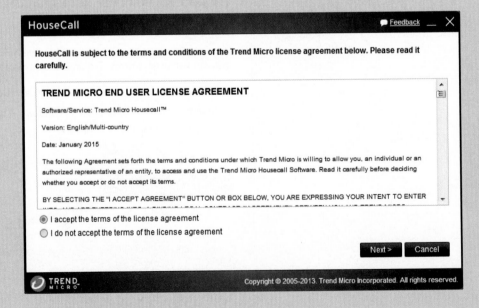

Step 6

Follow the on-screen instructions to run the scan. In the lab, open Settings and select Quick scan because a full system scan can take several hours, depending on the amount of programs and data on your computer. At home, you may want to perform a full system scan.

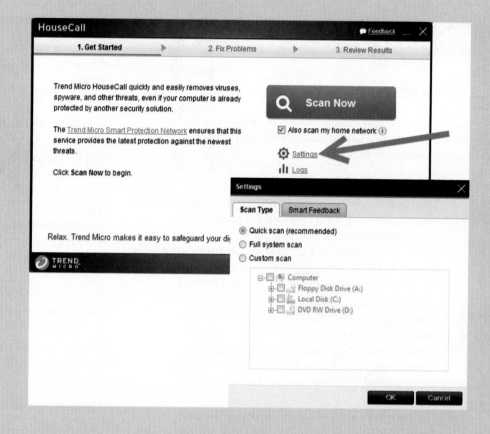

Step 7

When finished, the results dialog box displays.

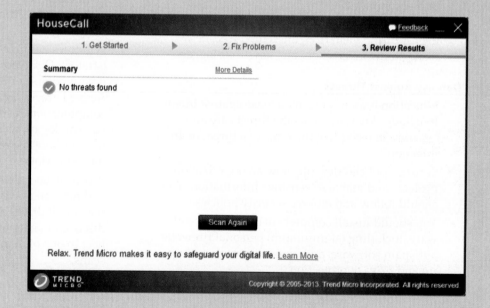

Chapter Summary

After reading this chapter and completing the exercises, you should understand the following facts about computer security.

Threats to Computers and Users

- Threats include malware, phishing, social engineering, identity theft and fraud, exposure to inappropriate or distasteful content, invasion of privacy, misuse of cookies, hoaxes, and computer hardware theft. Other threats include accidents, mistakes, and natural and unnatural disasters.

- A vector is the method that malware uses to infect a computer. Malware modes of infection include email, code on websites, Trojan horses, searching out unprotected computers, sneakernet, back doors, rootkits, pop-up downloads, drive-by downloads, war driving, and bluesnarfing.

- The people behind computer security threats come from all over the world, and increasingly they are part of terrorists groups and organized crime. Certain terms, describing their techniques, define the individuals. These terms include hackers, crackers, script kiddies, click kiddies, and packet monkeys.

- Many methods are used to steal passwords, including capturing them from unsecured websites, using password crackers, and keystroke loggers.

Defense Against Threats

- Education is an important defense against threats. It includes knowing what the threats are and learning to recognize the signs of a threat or an infection.

- Security policies describe how an organization protects and manages sensitive information. You should follow and enforce security policies.

- You should install comprehensive security software, including (at minimum) personal firewalls, antispam software, antivirus software, and pop-up and privacy protection.

- Keep your software up to date with security patches.

- You will improve your security if you understand authentication and authorization and its implementation on your computer and in your organization.

- You can combat threats by following the rule of least privilege when assigning permissions and using best practices with user names and passwords.

- Encryption technologies protect your data.

- Data wiping practices can remove even deleted data from computers.

- Physical security of computers and networks is also important, especially for mobile computing.

Troubleshooting Common Security Problems

- Log-on failure may be the result of something as simple as having the Caps Lock key turned on. The OS can lock you out from logging on to your computer if you exceed the number of failed log-on attempts configured in the Account Lockout policy for a network or an individual computer. An administrator may need to modify the policy.

- Windows has an administrator account, "Administrator." Disabled by default, it will be enabled if your computer is not a member of a Windows Active Directory domain (the norm for a home computer) *and* it starts in Safe Mode. In that case, you can log on with this account and attempt to troubleshoot the reason for the computer going into Safe Mode.

- If you suspect a computer is infected by a virus and have an antivirus program installed, run a scan of all drives and memory. If this does not discover a virus, and you are still suspicious, connect to one of many websites that offer free online scans.

Key Terms List

botnet *(45)*	hacker *(53)*	shoulder surfing *(50)*
browser hijacking *(46)*	header *(47)*	social engineering *(46)*
content filter *(62)*	honey pot, *(57)*	social media *(40)*
cookies *(50)*	hotspot *(43)*	social networking *(40)*
cybercriminal *(53)*	identity theft *(49)*	social networking site *(40)*
cybercrime *(40)*	keylogger *(44)*	spam *(46)*
cyberterrorist *(53)*	keystroke logger *(44)*	spam filter *(60)*
cyberterrorism *(53)*	malware *(40)*	spear phishing *(47)*
data wiping *(74)*	Parental Controls *(61)*	spim *(46)*
digital certificate *(72)*	password *(44)*	spyware *(45)*
DMZ *(57)*	password cracker *(44)*	standard user account *(67)*
drive-by download *(42)*	password manager *(66)*	third-party cookie *(51)*
email spoofing *(47)*	permission *(65)*	token *(65)*
Encrypting File System (EFS) *(72)*	phishing *(47)*	Trojan horse *(41)*
encryption *(72)*	pop-up *(42)*	user account *(66)*
exploit *(44)*	pop-up blocker *(61)*	User Account Control (UAC) *(69)*
Family Safety *(62)*	pop-up download *(42)*	user right *(66)*
FileVault *(73)*	ransomware *(47)*	vector *(40)*
firewall *(56)*	rootkit *(42)*	virus *(45)*
first-party cookie *(51)*	scareware *(42)*	war driving *(43)*
forged email address *(48)*	secret key *(72)*	white hat hacker *(53)*
fraud *(47)*	Secure HTTP (HTTPS) *(72)*	worm *(45)*
group account *(68)*	Secure Sockets Layer (SSL) *(72)*	zero-day exploit *(45)*
guest account *(67)*	security account *(66)*	zombie *(45)*

Key Terms Quiz

Use the Key Terms List to complete the sentences that follow. Not all terms will be used.

1. A/an _____ defines what a user or group can do to an object such as a file or folder.

2. Programs on a website may send very small text files called _____ to a Web browser, along with a request that the Web browser save the file on the user's computer.

3. Unsolicited email, usually sent to market a service or product (legitimate or otherwise), is called _____.

4. _____ occurs when someone collects personal information belonging to another person and uses that information fraudulently.

5. In Windows, a/an _____ defines a systemwide action a user or group may perform, such as logging on to a computer or installing device drivers.

6. _____ includes authentication, plus determination of a person's level of access to a computer or a resource.

7. The EFS feature in Windows NTFS and OS X FileVault feature are both examples of _____ at the file system level.

8. _____ is verification of who you are.

9. A parent wanting to protect a child from inappropriate Web content may use a/an _____.

10. A person or program with administrative access can install malicious code or a/an _____, which hides itself from detection within the operating system.

Multiple-Choice Quiz

1. What is the name for the defining rules and practices for protecting and managing an organization's sensitive information?
   a. Firewalls
   b. Security policies
   c. Security software
   d. Content filtering
   e. Antivirus

2. This type of annoyance appears uninvited in a separate window when you are browsing the Web and can provide a vector for malware infections.
   a. Inline banner
   b. Pop-up
   c. Spam
   d. Adware
   e. Back door

3. With this Windows feature turned on (as it is by default) a logged-on user only has the privileges of a standard account, even if that user is an administrator, and must provide credentials to perform most administrative tasks.
   a. Account lockout threshold
   b. EFS
   c. Lockout policy
   d. UAC
   e. Account lockout duration

4. This term describes unsolicited messages received via instant messaging.
   a. Spam
   b. Spyware
   c. Zombie
   d. Spim
   e. Bot

5. You open your browser and, rather than pointing to your home page, it opens to a Web page advertising adware removal or antivirus software. You reconfigure the browser to point to your home page, but when you restart the browser, it again points to the wrong Web page. This behavior is a symptom of what type of malware?
   a. Spyware
   b. Worm
   c. Browser hijacking
   d. Keystroke logger
   e. Trojan horse

6. What type of malware installs on a computer without the knowledge or permission of the user, and replicates itself on the computer or throughout a network?
   a. Virus
   b. Utility
   c. Worm
   d. Scam
   e. Spim

7. What term is used for a seemingly harmless program that has malicious code hidden inside?
   a. Worm

b. Trojan horse
c. Antivirus
d. Optimizer
e. Cookie

8. What utility or feature of a browser is used to inhibit the annoying windows that open when you are browsing the Web?
   a. Content filter
   b. Firewall
   c. Antivirus
   d. Spam filter
   e. Pop-up blocker

9. Strange screen messages, sudden computer slowdown, missing data, and inability to access the hard drive may be symptoms of what?
   a. War driving
   b. Spam
   c. Encryption
   d. Virus infection
   e. Fraud

10. This device sits between a private network and the Internet (or other network) and examines all traffic in and out of the network it is protecting, blocking any traffic it recognizes as a potential threat.
    a. Router
    b. Firewall
    c. Bridge
    d. Worm
    e. Keystroke logger

11. After several failed log-on attempts, a message appears stating that your account was locked out. This is the result of exceeding this setting in Account Lockout policy on a Windows computer.
    a. Password length
    b. Account lockout threshold
    c. Account lockout duration
    d. Maximum password age
    e. Password complexity requirements

12. This type of malware conceals itself within the OS code and gives someone administrative access to a computer.
    a. Rootkit
    b. Pop-up download
    c. Drive-by download
    d. Worm
    e. Hoax

13. What is the term used to describe the use of persuasion to gain the confidence of individuals?
    a. Hoax
    b. Fraud
    c. Phishing
    d. Social engineering
    e. Enticement
14. What term describes the action of a password cracker that simply tries a huge number of permutations of possible passwords?
    a. Keystroke logging
    b. Brute force

c. Statistical analysis
    d. Mathematical analysis
    e. Phishing
15. This firewall technology inspects each packet that enters or leaves the protected network, applying a set of security rules defined by a network administrator; packets that fail are not allowed to cross into the destination network.
    a. Proxy service
    b. VPN
    c. IP packet filter
    d. Encrypted authentication
    e. DMZ

Essay Quiz

1. Explain automatic log-in and why you should not allow it in a situation in which you require security.
2. Consider the following statement: User Account Control limits the damage that someone can do who accesses your computer when automatic log-in is enabled. Elaborate on this statement, describing why it is true, and why there is still a great risk.
3. Why should you disable the Guest account?
4. In your own words, describe why the use of Internet cookies can be an invasion of privacy.
5. Differentiate between permission and user right.

Lab Projects

These Lab Projects ask you to research various topics. In your answers, please provide links to websites you discovered that support your essay or project responses.

LAB PROJECT 2.1

Research identity theft/fraud to answer the following questions.

1 What is the estimated cost of identity theft/fraud in the United States in a recent year? What is the trend compared to previous years?

2 Identity theft can involve computers, but in many cases, computers play only a small part in identity theft. Find a recent article on an identity theft ring and describe how the thieves operated.

3 Share your findings with others in your class and compare the information you found.

LAB PROJECT 2.2

Research the latest malware threats. Many organizations, including antivirus vendors and security services, post information on the Internet about the latest malware threats. Use an Internet search engine to research the latest threats, which you may find at one of the top security software manufacturers, such as McAfee or Symantec. Using the information from one of these sites, make a list of five current threats and research each to learn more about it. Briefly describe each threat and how you will use security software or behavior to defend your computer from each one.

LAB PROJECT 2.3

Organizations require trained specialists to keep their computers and networks secure. One way prospective employers can determine how much someone knows about security is by requiring job applicants to hold certain appropriate security certifications that require study, experience, and passing exams. Find and research a security certification and give a brief description of this certification, including the organization that is behind this certification, who should seek it, what domains (topics) are included in the exam, and the job titles this certification would apply to.

chapter

3

Desktop Virtualization

Learning Outcomes

In this chapter, you will learn how to:

LO **3.1** Describe the various types of virtualization used in everyday computing and ways you might use desktop virtualization.

LO **3.2** Select and install a desktop virtualization option for a Windows desktop host computer.

LO **3.3** Select and install a desktop virtualization option for an OS X host computer.

When a software company such as Microsoft develops new software, they make it available to people outside of the company to test. One way to get to know a new OS is to take advantage of the opportunity to try it out, but not all of us have an extra computer to use for such testing. That is when desktop virtualization comes in handy, letting you run Windows or Linux in a special environment on your computer, while keeping your existing operating system intact. All you need in addition to specialized virtualization software is a computer with the processing power and enough RAM and hard drive space to support the number and types of OSs you wish to run. You also need appropriate licenses for all the software you run, including the OSs running in the virtual machines.

In this chapter we explore the exploding phenomenon of desktop virtualization, and prepare you to install the desktop OSs described in this book into virtual machines. This will save you the cost and physical desktop space of multiple physical computers. ✹

LO 3.1 | Virtualization Overview

In this section, we define virtualization and many of the terms associated with it, describe its background, and discuss how it has led to the virtualization of desktop operating systems.

Virtualization Is Everywhere

Virtualization is the creation of an environment that seems real, but isn't, and today it seems like virtualization is everywhere in the computing world. There are many types. You can spend time in a virtual world, such as Second Life (Figure 3–1). A virtual world often lets a user select an animated computer-generated human, an avatar, to represent him or her within it. People use virtual worlds in online training, marketing of products, and in games of many types. When this virtual world includes three-dimensional images and involves other senses, giving the participant a feeling of actually being present in that time and space, we call it virtual reality (VR).

Augmented reality (AR) is different from virtual reality, although the lines are sometimes blurred. Augmented reality involves viewing something in real time through a camera or other device while the image (or other input) is digitally modified. AR can involve any of the senses. AR technology is finding its way into gaming, retailing, job training, and education.

Many organizations use storage virtualization in which client computers can utilize many networked hard drives as though they are one. Network engineers work with network virtualization involving a network addressing space that exists within one or more physical networks, but which is logically independent of the physical network structure. Then there is server virtualization, in which a single machine hosts multiple servers, each of which performs tasks as independently from the others as separate physical machines would. Companies that provide low-cost web hosting services can create a separate virtual web server for each customer.

With only a small leap from these we come to desktop virtualization, the virtualization of a desktop computer into which you can install an operating system, its unique configuration, and all the applications and data normally used by a single person. This virtual desktop may reside on a server, allowing a user to access it from a computer with specialized client software, or it may exist on the local computer.

FIGURE 3–1 An avatar (at center bottom) walks on a London street in Second Life.

Each individual virtual environment in both server virtualization and desktop virtualization is a virtual machine (VM)—the software emulation of all hardware with which an operating system must interact. But wait, there's more! There is application virtualization, in which a user connects to a server and accesses one or more applications rather than an entire desktop environment. This chapter is devoted to today's desktop virtualization, but first we will look at the past.

Your (Great?) Grandparent's Virtual Machines

Today's virtual machines have a long pedigree: They can trace their roots back to the 1960s when mainframe computer manufacturers, such as IBM, routinely created multiple discrete environments on a single computer. A user connected using a dumb terminal that was little more than a keyboard and display with a connection to a host computer (mainframe or minicomputer) but it had little or no native processing power (hence the term *dumb*).

A dumb terminal connected to the host computer, sending keystrokes and displaying the keystrokes and responses on the display. During a single terminal session, a user connected to a discrete area on the host called a partition. The partition to which each user connected was not like today's virtual machines, but was an area where the user had access to programs and data. After the advent of the IBM PC in the 1980s, a PC configured to emulate a dumb terminal often replaced the dumb terminal.

For years, this model prevailed for those organizations that wished to have a centralized system where all the programs and data resided, with the individual users connecting from whatever served as a terminal. The 1990s implementation of this model included servers or minicomputers running terminal services to which users connected nearly

A 1970s-era computer terminal.

seamlessly to partitions from their desktop PCs using terminal client software. These were not, however, virtual machines because the entire hardware and operating system environment was not part of the partition to which users connected. They did not have a fully configurable desktop operating system, such as Windows, to work with beyond their application and data.

Today's Virtual Desktops

In the past decade or so, many large organizations have adopted the thin client for their desktop users. A thin client is a dedicated terminal or software installed on a PC. In either case, a thin client usually lacks such common peripherals as expansion slots and optical drives. The purpose of a thin client is to connect to a server, allowing the user to work in a server-hosted environment. When that environment provides the entire OS experience and the working applications it becomes a virtual machine. This virtual machine may reside on a server and be accessed by a client computer (thin or not), or it may reside on a desktop computer. This allows the interactive user (the one sitting in front of that computer) to switch between the host OS (the operating system installed directly on the computer) and one or more guest OSs (the operating system installed within a VM).

The term used today for hosting and managing multiple virtual desktops on network servers is virtual desktop infrastructure (VDI). The term is attributed

Note: Thin clients are the modern day dumb terminals.

to the VMware company. Today VDI applies to any server product that provides virtual desktop support.

Type I and Type II Hypervisors

A hypervisor, also called a virtual machine monitor (VMM), is the software layer that manages underlying hardware allocated to one or more virtual machines. The hardware virtualization allows multiple operating systems to run simultaneously on a single computer. Each hypervisor normally emulates a computer separate from the underlying computer, but it must use a virtual processor compatible with that of the underlying machine—mainly either an Intel processor or an AMD processor. There are two types of hypervisors, Type I and Type II. A Type I hypervisor—sometimes called a bare-metal hypervisor—can run directly on a computer without an underlying host operating system. A Type II hypervisor requires a host operating system.

Type I hypervisors first appeared on high-powered servers. At the time, desktop computers lacked the hardware support required for virtualization of some hardware. Of course, that was not a big hurdle, and Type I hypervisors are available from the major hypervisor manufacturers—notably Citrix, Microsoft, and VMware. These companies offer a selection of products that centrally manage desktop virtual machines, delivered to the desktop (laptop or PC) over a network.

Most of the hypervisors we use in our examples in this chapter are Type II hypervisors requiring an underlying operating system. Whatever hypervisor you use, you will find more and more organizations deploying server-based virtual machines that are the users' everyday work environment. The reason for this is easier central management of the operating systems and user environment.

You have several choices for Type II hypervisors for desktops, but today some of these run only on computers with hardware-assisted virtualization features, which means they require a computer with either the Intel Virtualization Technology for x86 (Intel VT-x) or AMD Virtualization (AMD-V) architecture extensions, which improve the performance of virtual machines on the host. Some hypervisors, such as the one that comes with Windows 8, requires even newer features. Figure 3–2 shows Windows 7 running in a virtual machine in OS X.

There are several choices of desktop Type II hypervisors, depending on both the hosting OS and the desired guest OSs. The ones we will discuss in this chapter all have several things in common; they are the tasks required to

> *Note:* Microsoft Hyper-V Server and VMware vSphere are examples of Type 1 hypervisors used on servers.

> *Note:* If your computer's documentation indicates that the processor supports virtualization but a hypervisor requiring this fails to install due to lack of support, look in the documentation for instructions on enabling this feature.

FIGURE 3–2 A Windows 7 client OS running in a virtual machine in OS X.

create a virtual machine, the order in which you do them, and how the host and guest OSs share the mouse and keyboard.

1. Prepare the host computer:
   - Select a computer that is not important for your everyday work.
   - Confirm that the computer's hardware and operating system meet the minimum requirements for hosting the hypervisor you intend to install.
   - Back up your hard drive.
   - Remove any conflicting software.
   - If you decide to install two or more different hypervisors on a single host system, do not try to run different hypervisors at the same time.
2. Install the hypervisor, such as Oracle's VirtualBox hypervisor (see Figure 3–3).
3. Create a virtual machine, selecting from a list of guest OSs that the hypervisor supports. Creating a virtual machine creates a number of files on the host. One is a virtual machine file containing all the settings; another is a virtual hard drive file containing all the operating system files, installed program files, and data created from within the virtual machine and appearing as a hard drive (drive C: on a Windows host) when the virtual machine is running. Other files, such as log files, may be created at this time.
4. Install the guest OS. This normally requires the full retail version of the OS. You may also use a compatible precreated virtual machine. You must have a legal license or a trial version for each guest OS. The guest OS can be installed directly from a physical disc (CD or DVD) or from a bootable ISO file, which is an image of the contents of a CD or DVD.
5. Install appropriate utilities for the guest OS. The hypervisor publisher provides these utilities, and they include special software for making a virtual machine work better for the guest OS.
6. Finally, once you have an OS installed into a virtual machine, you need to realize that the guest OS and host OS are sharing the same physical hardware, and certain things aren't easily shared. The keyboard and mouse are good examples of hardware that can serve only one master at a time. Normally, you give a VM control of a mouse by moving the pointer into the VM and clicking inside the guest window. The virtual machine captures the mouse and keyboard, giving the VM the focus. To release the mouse and keyboard, simply move the cursor outside the VM window and click or tap. At one time the only way to release the mouse and keyboard from VM control was with a host key, which varied by hypervisor. Clicking inside a VM window captured the mouse and keyboard, while you needed to use the host key (or key combination) to release the mouse and keyboard from the VM. If a hypervisor will not release the mouse and keyboard from a VM, look for an icon for the host key in the border of the window surrounding the virtual machine. Practice using it right away.

FIGURE 3–3 Installing a hypervisor.

Note: You must have a legal license for each guest OS.

Major Hypervisor Sources

The major hypervisor manufacturers are Citrix, VMware, Parallels, Microsoft, and Oracle. There are many other players in the field, described in articles and reviews in technical publications and websites.

FIGURE 3–4 The Windows 7 Start menu showing Windows Virtual PC and Windows XP Mode.

FIGURE 3–5 The Windows Features Control Panel showing Windows Virtual PC available, but not enabled.

LO 3.2 | Virtual Machines on Windows Desktops

You have several options—both paid for and free—for running Linux, DOS, or Windows on a Windows desktop computer. At this writing you cannot run any version of OS X in a VM on a PC, due to licensing issues. The hypervisors we describe here for Windows hosts are free. Two are from Microsoft (Windows Virtual PC, and Client Hyper-V) and one is from Oracle (VirtualBox).

Microsoft does not require that you register to acquire a free Microsoft Windows desktop hypervisor. However, the installation program will verify that your host OS is a legitimate version of Windows before the Microsoft virtualization products will install.

Windows XP Mode and Windows Virtual PC on Windows 7

Microsoft provides both Windows XP Mode and Windows Virtual PC as free, optional components of Windows 7. The main purpose of Windows XP Mode for Windows 7 is to run legacy Windows XP applications that will not run well in Windows 7. It uses a runtime version of Windows Virtual PC. You can install Windows XP Mode and/or Windows Virtual PC. Once installed, these features appear on the Start menu, as shown in Figure 3–4.

Microsoft recommends Windows XP Mode and Windows Virtual PC for small and midsize businesses with Windows 7 desktops. For larger organizations Microsoft recommends Microsoft Enterprise Desktop Virtualization (MED-V), which is server-based, centrally managed desktop virtualization.

With Windows Virtual PC you can also create VMs to run other guest systems, including older versions of Windows, and most versions of Linux. Once installed, it is so well-integrated into Windows 7 that you can start programs installed in the Windows Virtual PC VM from Start menu shortcuts of the host OS. Beyond that, if you have a certain data-file type that you prefer to run in a program that is in the VM, you can assign that file type to the program in the host. Then, double-clicking on such a data file will launch the VM and the program within it.

Only three editions of Windows 7 support Windows Virtual PC and Windows XP Mode. They are Windows 7 Professional, Enterprise, and Ultimate. You may only need to enable them in the Windows Features Control Panel, shown in Figure 3–5. The Try This! will show you how to locate this

try this!

Enable Windows Virtual PC or Windows XP Mode on your Windows 7 computer. Try this:

1. In the Start menu's Search box enter "windows features."
2. In the search results list select Turn Windows Features on or off. This opens the Windows Features dialog box.
3. In the Windows Features dialog box, the features list alphabetically. Scroll down to see if Windows Virtual PC is listed. If it is not, you will need to connect to the Microsoft site and install it. If it is listed but not checked, you will need to check it to enable it. Then follow the instructions.

dialog box and determine if Windows Virtual PC is listed and how to enable it if it is listed but not active.

Downloading and Installing Windows XP Mode in Windows 7

If you cannot start the installation of Windows XP Mode from the Windows Features dialog, you will need to connect to the Windows XP Mode Download page at Microsoft.com. Step-by-Step 3.01 describes how to do this.

Step-by-Step 3.01

Downloading and Installing Windows XP Mode

Complete this exercise using a computer running one of the supported versions of Windows 7: Professional, Enterprise, or Ultimate. Only do this exercise if you cannot start the Windows XP download and install from your Start menu or from the Windows Features Control Panel. Be prepared to install security software into the Windows XP Mode virtual machine when it starts up for the first time. Your instructor may provide this software for you.

Step 1

Open your browser and use a search engine, such as Google or Bing, to search on "windows xp mode download." Select the link to the correct download page at the Microsoft Download Center. Do not use any other download service. Double-check that the link is at microsoft.com before clicking on it.

Step 2

On the Windows XP Mode page of the Microsoft Download Center select a language and then click the Download button.

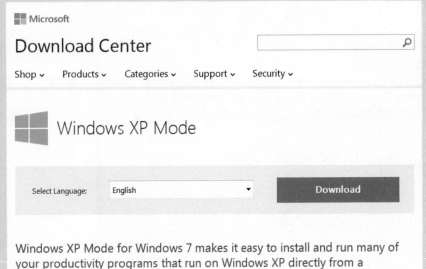

Step 3

Select the appropriate download. The N version came without Media Center, so it is smaller. Because you are not likely to need the Media Center features in a virtual machine, select the N version and click Next.

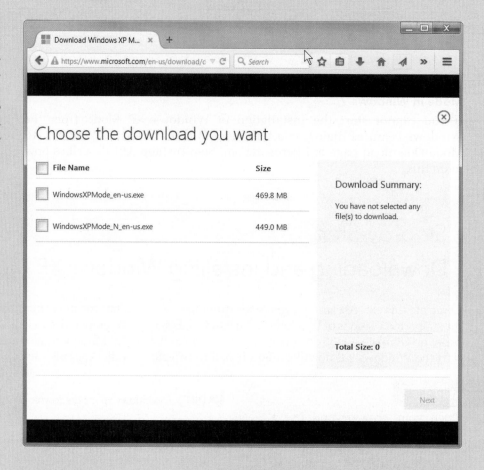

Step 4

After the download completes, open your Downloads folder and locate the Windows XP Mode executable file, shown here. Double-click to start the setup program.

Step 5

Follow the instructions on the screen, accepting defaults, as in the case of the location, and proceeding through the pages of the setup.

Step 6

Setup installs a virtual hard disk.

Step 7

Accept the license agreement and click the Next button.

Step 8

When this screen appears, select the first option and click Next.

Step 9

Setup will share the files on your computer with Windows XP Mode. This is normally what you would want to do. Click Start Setup unless instructed otherwise.

Step 10

The first time Windows XP Mode starts, install the antivirus software provided by your instructor.

Step 11

Windows XP Mode comes with Internet Explorer version 8, which is no longer supported. We strongly recommend that you not use a browser within Windows XP Mode, but only old apps that will no longer run in Windows 7.

Step 12

To exit from Windows XP Mode first select Log Off from the Windows XP Start menu. A Log Off Windows dialog box opens. Click Log Off in this box.

Step 13

You are not done yet! The Log On to Windows dialog box displays in the virtual machine. Select the Action menu and then select Sleep or Close. When you select Close, the virtual machine will hibernate, and the XP Mode window will close.

Removing Windows XP Mode

To remove Windows XP Mode open the Programs and Features Control Panel, locate Windows XP Mode in the list of programs and double-click on it. It will delete the XP Mode virtual hard disk and all data saved to the disk. It will not delete data you saved on the host drive.

If you also installed the full Windows Virtual PC, removing Windows XP Mode will not remove the hypervisor.

Installing Windows Virtual PC in Windows 7

If you have a version of Windrows 7 that supports Virtual PC, you should be able to enable it or initiate a download from the Windows Features dialog, shown back in Figure 3–5. If you cannot initiate Windows Virtual PC through the Windows Features dialog, connect to the Windows Virtual PC page in the Microsoft Download Center (shown in Figure 3–6). Click the Download button and follow the instructions to download your Windows Virtual PC software.

Once the download is complete, locate the correct file. If you are running 64-bit Windows 7, select the file with "x64" in its name. If you are running 32-bit Windows 7, select the file with "x86" in its name. Click to place a check in the box by the correct file name, and then click Next.

A dialog box will give you the choice of opening or saving the file. Select Save and click OK. After the download completes, open your Downloads folder and locate the file. Double-click it to start the setup program. Follow the prompts after that, including allowing the system to restart. After it restarts, go to the Start menu, and confirm that Windows Virtual PC is listed in All Programs. This is your starting point for Step-by-Step 3.02 in which you will create a virtual machine in Windows Virtual PC.

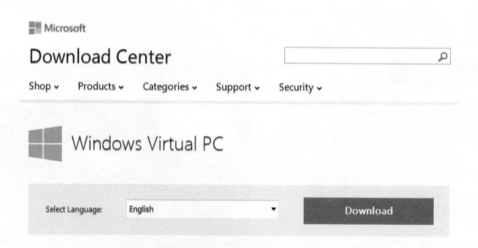

Windows Virtual PC is the latest Microsoft virtualization technology. You can use it to run more than one operating system at the same time on one computer, and to run many productivity applications on a virtual Windows environment, with a single click, directly from a computer running Windows 7.

FIGURE 3–6 The Windows Virtual PC Download page.

Step-by-Step 3.02

Creating a Virtual Machine in Windows Virtual PC

This exercise assumes you have a Windows 7 computer and that you have enabled Windows Virtual PC, as described in the previous text.

Step 1

Open the Start menu and locate and launch Windows Virtual PC.

Step 2

Click the Create Virtual Machine button to open the Create Virtual Machine Wizard.

Step 3

On the first page of the Wizard, enter the name for the new virtual machine. Leave the location as is and click the Next button.

Step 4

On the next page either accept the default Memory setting or enter the amount recommended by your instructor. Leave the check in the box by Networking unless told to remove it by your instructor. Click Next to continue.

Step 5

On the Add a Virtual Hard Disk page keep the default setting (the first option) unless instructed otherwise. Click Create to create the new virtual machine.

Step 6

Open Windows Virtual PC from the Start menu to see the new virtual machine listed.

Step 7

Now prepare the virtual machine to use the installation program of the OS you plan to install. Windows Virtual PC can install the new OS from a DVD drive or an ISO image file. With the new virtual machine selected in the Virtual Machines folder, click the Settings button. If you are using an ISO image make sure it is on a local hard drive.

In this step you enable the VM to boot from either a DVD or ISO image. In the Settings dialog box for the virtual machine select the source: DVD drive or ISO image. If you select ISO image you will need to browse to the location of the ISO image. Then click OK.

When you are ready to install the OS into the VM, open the Virtual Machine folder and either double-click the virtual machine or select it and click the Open button in the toolbar. This will start the installation, which should proceed like a normal OS installation, but it will all happen within the VM window.

Removing Windows Virtual PC

Windows Virtual PC is installed as an update to Windows 7, so to remove it, you must go into the Programs and Features Control Panel, select View Installed Updates, and then in the Installed Updates page scroll down to the Microsoft Windows category, as shown in Figure 3–7. Double-click Windows

FIGURE 3–7 To remove Virtual PC double-click Windows Virtual PC in Installed Updates page of Programs and Features.

Virtual PC. When the Uninstall an Update prompt appears, click the Yes button. When prompted to restart the computer, close all open Windows and then click the Restart Now button.

Client Hyper-V on Windows 8.x and Windows 10

The hypervisor introduced in Windows 8, Client Hyper-V, is a Type I (bare metal) hypervisor. This characteristic of Client Hyper-V is not apparent because you enable it from within Windows, but the host, or parent OS itself, runs in a virtual machine separate from the client VMs that you create. It does not include a Windows XP Mode virtual machine. It is based on the Hyper-V hypervisor found on Windows Servers. Client Hyper-V includes the Windows To Go Virtual Hard Disk (VHD) feature that allows you to create a virtual hard disk (VHD) on a USB drive, take it to another computer, and boot from it. This is an example of a Type 1 hypervisor at work.

Client Hyper-V is only available in the Pro and Enterprise editions of Windows 8.x and Windows 10. It requires at least 4 GB of RAM (more is better) and a CPU with the Second-Level Address Translation (SLAT) feature now found in many Intel and AMD CPUs.

Enabling Hyper-V

To enable Client Hyper-V, open the Windows Features dialog box (Figure 3–8). Locate the Hyper-V node and expand it so that you can see the two components of Client Hyper-V: Hyper-V Management Tools and Hyper-V Platform. Click to place a check in the Hyper-V box, which selects both components, as shown. Click OK; there will be a short wait while the files are found and installed. Then you will be prompted to Restart. Close any open windows, save any data files that are open, and click the Restart Now button.

> *Note:* At this writing the Intel Core i3, i5, and i7 CPUs support SLAT. AMD uses many different model names for their SLAT-compliant CPUs. Therefore, to see a list of AMD CPUs that support SLAT, enter the search string "amd hyper-v" in a search engine and select results at amd.com.

> *Note:* The Microsoft Windows Server versions of Hyper-V have more advanced capabilities for hosting server operating system clients.

FIGURE 3–8 Click to place a check in the Hyper-V box. This will select the two Hyper-V components.

Creating a Virtual Machine

After installing Hyper-V, two new tiles will display on the Start screen in Windows 8.*x* or in All Apps | Windows Accessories in Windows 10. Hyper-V Virtual Machine Connection and Hyper-V Manager. Click or tap the Hyper-V Manager to create and manage virtual machines. Figure 3–9 shows Hyper-V Manager with the New menu open. Selecting Virtual Machine from this menu will start the New Virtual Machine Wizard, which will walk you through creating a VM.

The Hyper-V tiles.

Connecting a Virtual Machine to a Network

In the Hyper-V Manager there are two procedures you must perform to connect a virtual machine to a network (virtual or real). The first step is to create a virtual switch (to which you can connect multiple VMs), and the second step is to configure each VM to connect to a virtual switch.

To create a virtual switch, open Hyper-V Manager and in the Actions list, shown on the right in Figure 3-9, click Virtual Switch Manager. The Virtual Switch Manager will open and offer the switch type options shown here. Choose the type of switch: an External switch type allows VMs on that switch to connect through the host to a physical network. The Internal switch type creates a switch that connects the VMs to each other and to their host computer, while a Private switch only allows network connections among the VMs on that host.

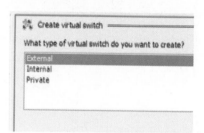

In Virtual Switch Manager select the type of switch.

FIGURE 3–9 Create and manage virtual machines using Hyper-V Manager.

FIGURE 3–10 Select the switch to which you will connect this VM.

The second procedure connects each VM to a switch. For instance, under the Actions list in Figure 3–9 you would locate the VM named W10-10130-June and click Settings (near the bottom of the Actions list). This opens the Settings dialog for that virtual machine. Click on the Network Adapter under the list of Hardware and then open the drop-down list of choices under the Virtual switch in the right pane, as shown in Figure 3–10. Select the switch from this list. Then click the Apply button at the bottom if you have more changes to make, or click the OK button if you are done making changes in this dialog box.

Removing Hyper-V

Because Hyper-V is enabled through the Windows Features Control Panel you need to remove it the same way. Locate the Hyper-V node shown in Figure 3–11 and click to clear the check box, and then click OK. The Windows Features dialog box will display progress information while it initiates the change, and then it will display a message stating that it needs to restart to complete the changes. Click the Restart Now button, and it will make changes as it shuts down and again when it restarts Windows.

Oracle VirtualBox

Oracle VirtualBox is a versatile free hypervisor that comes in versions for a variety of host operating systems, such as Windows, Linux, and OS X. It will run guest versions of Windows, Linux, and DOS. Oracle VirtualBox will run on hardware that does not support virtualization, so it is a good choice for older computers without hardware virtualization support. It is available for

Note: Possibly the biggest name in desktop virtualization is VMware with several products. The desktop products include two for Windows hosts (VMware Workstation 12 and VMware Workstation Player) and one for running Windows applications on Mac OS X (VMware Fusion 8). We did not use these excellent products in our examples because they are not available for free except as free trials that expire.

FIGURE 3-11 In Windows Features, clear the Hyper-V check box.

download at www.virtualbox.org. Because it also runs on an OS X host, we will use it in the next section when we discuss Virtual Machines on OS X.

LO 3.3 | Virtual Machines on OS X

You may want to use virtualization software on a Mac to test a distribution of Linux or a version of Windows or to run certain Windows apps that aren't available for OS X. There are several options for doing this, including Apple Boot Camp (not really a virtualization tool), VirtualBox, and Parallels. Apple Boot Camp is a multiboot solution, but VirtualBox and Parallels offer virtualization on the Apple desktop. Parallels Desktop by Parallels is a commercial product, and you can learn about it at www.parallels.com /products/desktop/.

Apple Boot Camp—A Dual-Boot Option

Apple Boot Camp is available with OS X. It is a dual-boot option, meaning it allows you to install Windows onto a separate disk partition, and then you can choose to boot into either OS. This is an either-or situation; you need to restart to change from one OS to the other. The advantage of a dual-boot solution is performance—each OS is running directly on the Mac with no performance loss from being in a virtual machine. However, today's hypervisors, when used on a recent Apple computer running OS X, perform well enough to discourage us from dedicating the disk space to a multiboot solution such as Apple Boot Camp.

Boot Camp comes with OS X 10.6 and later versions. Before running the Boot Camp Assistant to configure your computer and install Windows, back up your Mac because the first step requires that you create a new partition for

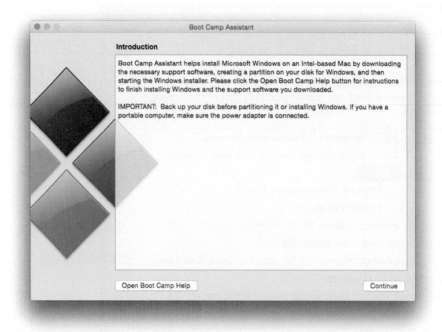

FIGURE 3–12 Open and read Boot Camp Help before proceeding.

the Windows OS. You will also need the installation disc or an ISO file for a full version of Windows (not an update).

Boot Camp installs only on an internal hard drive, so if you only have one drive with a single partition, Boot Camp Assistant will repartition that drive to create a new partition. Those of us with decades of experience working with hard drives cringe at partitioning an already fully partitioned drive containing data, but it works as long as there is room.

Run Boot Camp Assistant from the Applications Utilities folder. Notice that the first page, seen in Figure 3–12, gives you the option to open Boot Camp Help. This is an excellent idea. Click the button to open Help and read it before continuing. Then, if you still want to install and use Boot Camp, return to the Introduction screen, click Continue, and follow the instructions to prepare the disk and install Windows.

If you do continue, you should decide how big a partition you wish to have for your Windows OS. Remember that you will be installing applications into Windows, so you will need a bigger partition than the minimum recommended for the version of Windows you plan to install. For instance, when installing Windows 7 on an iMac with a 500 GB hard drive, we considered the minimum requirements for the OS itself (16 GB for 32-bit or 20 GB for 64-bit) and then we considered the requirements of the various applications we wish to install and the data we will generate (unless you are saving it to a server). Considering these needs, and the overall hard drive space, we decided to create a partition of 100 GB.

Oracle VirtualBox

The free version of Oracle VirtualBox will run on a variety of host operating systems including Windows, Linux, and OS X. It supports as guest OSs versions of Windows, Linux, and DOS. It will also run on hardware that does not support virtualization. Figure 3–13 shows Windows 10 running in VirtualBox in OS X.

FIGURE 3–13 Windows 10 running in VirtualBox on an OS X host.

Point your browser to the VirtualBox download page, shown in Figure 3–14. Click on the VirtualBox link for OS X hosts, shown under VirtualBox platform packages. This is the core software required for VirtualBox. You will also need to download the VirtualBox Extension Pack, also shown on this page.

Once you have downloaded the disk image file, when you are ready to install VirtualBox, simply open the Downloads folder and double-click on VirtualBox. Step-by-Step 3.03 describes how to install Oracle VirtualBox.

FIGURE 3–14 Download the OS X version from the VirtualBox Download page.

Step-by-Step 3.03

Installing Oracle VirtualBox

Using the file you downloaded or a file provided to you by your instructor, install Oracle VirtualBox. The instructions provided are for installing it into OS X using a disk image file (.dmg). To complete this exercise you will need the following:

- A computer running the version of OS X supported by the latest version of VirtualBox. You can find older versions on the VirtualBox website, if necessary.

- A computer that meets the hardware requirements for the version of VirtualBox you will install.

- The user name and password of an administrator account for this computer (even if you have logged on as an administrator, you will need these credentials to install new software).

- A broadband Internet connection.

Step 1	
Locate and double-click the VirtualBox disk image. It will be on the desktop or in the Downloads folder in Finder. This will open the VirtualBox drive. If you wish to read the documentation, open the UserManual.pdf file. Also, note that the VirtualBox Uninstall tool is located here, for when you decide you do not need this program.	

Step 2	
To start the VirtualBox installation, double-click on the VirtualBox.pkg icon. The VirtualBox installation wizard runs. At first it runs a test to verify that the computer can support VirtualBox. Follow the instructions and proceed through the pages, including providing the user name and password for an administrator account for the computer. Then you can either accept the defaults for a standard install or select a different destination and installation type.	

In a very short time the installation is complete, and you will find VirtualBox listed in Applications. Launch VirtualBox and then open the Machine menu at the top of the screen. Select New.

The New Virtual Machine app will guide you through the creation of a virtual machine. This process does not require the guest OS, but you do need to know which OS you will install into the virtual machine you are creating. You are simply configuring the machine to accept the guest OS. When prompted to name the virtual machine, use a meaningful name, such as the name and version of the OS you plan to install. Then select the OS you will install and continue.

On the Memory size page accept the default and click Continue.

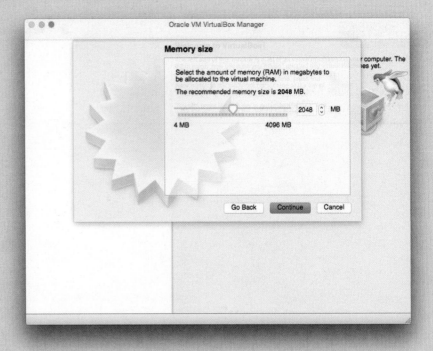

On the Hard Drive page select Create a Virtual Hard Drive Now and click Create. On the Hard Drive File Type page select the first type, which is VDI, the default for VirtualBox, and the one you should choose if you only plan to use this VM in VirtualBox. If you plan to use this VM in another hypervisor, select a type used by that hypervisor. Then click Continue.

Step 7

On the Storage on Physical Hard Drive page select Dynamically Allocated and click Continue.

Step 8

On the File Location and Size page the name will match the name you gave to the virtual machine. Accept the defaults for name, location, and size on this page and click Create. On the next page you will see a summary of the virtual disk settings. Confirm that these are correct and click the Done button to complete the creation of the virtual disk. Then you will see another summary page for all the settings for this virtual machine. Confirm the settings and click Done.

Step 9

When the console window opens check that your new virtual machine is listed. It is now ready for the installation of the OS.

Step 10

When you are ready to install an operating system, double-click on a virtual machine. This will launch the First Run Wizard, which will guide you through the process of beginning the installation of your OS.

Step 11

Secure the virtual machine. Assign a strong password to any user account you create within the guest OS, then update the OS with all security updates, and install antivirus and other security software.

Chapter Summary

After reading this chapter and completing the exercises, you should know the following facts about desktop virtualization.

Virtualization Overview

- There are many types of virtualization today, such as virtual worlds, virtual reality, storage virtualization, network virtualization, server virtualization, and desktop virtualization—the subject of this chapter.
- Virtualization had its roots in the dumb-terminal/ mainframe systems of the 1960s and the terminal service/terminal client systems of the 1990s.
- You can host today's virtual desktops on network servers or on PCs.
- A hypervisor, or virtual machine monitor (VMM), is the software that emulates the necessary hardware on which an operating system runs.
- A Type I hypervisor (a "bare-metal hypervisor") runs directly on a computer without an underlying host operating system.
- A Type II hypervisor requires a host operating system.
- The major sources of hypervisors are Citrix, VMware, Parallels, Microsoft, and Oracle.

Virtual Machines on Windows Desktops

- There are both commercial and free hypervisors for running Linux, DOS, or Windows on a Windows desktop computer.
- Windows XP Mode is a free hypervisor that installs on a Windows 7 host with a Windows XP guest OS preinstalled. It does not require hardware-assisted virtualization.
- Download Windows XP Mode from the Microsoft website and install it.

- Remove Windows XP Mode through Windows from the Programs and Features Control Panel.
- The free Windows Virtual PC requires both Windows 7 and hardware-assisted virtualization.
- Download and install Virtual PC from the Microsoft website. It installs as an update, so to remove it you will need to uninstall it from the Installed Updates Control Panel.
- Client Hyper-V is the Type I hypervisor that is included with Windows 8 Pro and Windows Enterprise editions.
- Client Hyper-V has more rigorous hardware requirements than other desktop hypervisors, requiring at least 4 GB of RAM and a CPU with the Second-Level Address Translation (SLAT) feature.
- Enable Client Hyper-V through the Windows Features Control Panel.
- Remove Hyper-V by deselecting it in the Windows Features Control Panel.
- Oracle VirtualBox is free and runs on several hosts including versions of Windows, Linux, and Max OS X, and it will run on hardware that does not support virtualization.

Virtual Machines on OS X

- You have several choices for hypervisors for OS X that will run versions of Windows and Linux.
- Apple Boot Camp is not actually a hypervisor but a dual-boot option that allows you to dual boot between OS X and Windows. This gives each OS full use of the hardware, but only one can be loaded at a time.
- Oracle VirtualBox is a free hypervisor and will run versions of Windows, Linux, and DOS. It does not require hardware virtualization.

Key Terms List

application virtualization *(86)*

augmented reality (AR) *(86)*

avatar *(86)*

desktop virtualization *(86)*

dumb terminal *(87)*

guest OS *(87)*

host key *(89)*

host OS *(87)*

hypervisor *(88)*

ISO file *(89)*

network virtualization *(86)*

Second-Level Address Translation (SLAT) *(100)*

server virtualization *(86)*

storage virtualization *(86)*

terminal client *(87)*

terminal services *(87)*

thin client *(87)*

Type I hypervisor *(88)*

Type II hypervisor *(88)*

virtual desktop infrastructure (VDI) *(87)*

virtual machine *(86)*

virtual machine monitor (VMM) *(88)*

virtual reality (VR) *(86)*

virtual world *(86)*

virtualization *(86)*

Windows XP Mode *(90)*

Key Terms Quiz

Use the Key Terms List to complete the sentences that follow. Not all terms will be used.

1. The software layer that emulates the necessary hardware on which an operating system runs in a virtual machine is a/an _____.

2. Viewing something in real time through a camera or other device while the image is digitally modified is an example of _____.

3. Many organization use _____ in which many networked hard drives are seen as one by the client computers.

4. _____ is the creation of an environment that seems real.

5. When you run a desktop OS within a hypervisor, it is called _____.

6. In the 1960s, a/an _____ was the very simple interface device to a mainframe computer.

7. In the 1990s, people often used _____ software on a PC to connect to a specialized server or minicomputer.

8. A/an _____ is a low-cost PC, usually without such common peripherals as expansion slots, and optical drives, and is used to allow a user to connect and work in a server-hosted environment.

9. In desktop or server virtualization, the software emulation of all hardware with which an operating system must interface is a/an _____.

10. Second Life is an example of a/an _____.

Multiple-Choice Quiz

1. In which type of virtualization does a user connect to a server and work within a program, without an entire virtualized desktop environment?
   a. Storage virtualization
   b. Application virtualization
   c. Terminal services
   d. Thin client
   e. Virtual world

2. What term describes the hosting and management of multiple virtual desktops on network servers?
   a. Thin client
   b. Terminal services
   c. Minicomputers
   d. Virtual desktop infrastructure (VDI)
   e. Partitioning

3. Which of the following does not require a host OS?
   a. Type II hypervisor
   b. Type I hypervisor
   c. Oracle VirtualBox
   d. Windows Virtual PC
   e. Windows XP Mode

4. What hypervisor, described in this chapter, is a "bare metal" hypervisor?
   a. Windows 10
   b. Windows Virtual PC
   c. Windows XP Mode
   d. Oracle VirtualBox
   e. Client Hyper-V

5. What type of hypervisor requires a host OS?
   a. Type II
   b. Type I
   c. Boot Camp
   d. A bare-metal hypervisor
   e. A dual-boot hypervisor

6. If you wanted to run Windows 7 on a Mac running OS X, which option would give you the best performance, but would not run Windows in a virtual machine?
   a. Windows XP Mode
   b. Hyper-V Client
   c. Oracle VirtualBox
   d. Parallels
   e. Apple Boot Camp

7. Which of these is a free hypervisor that runs on Windows, OS X, and Linux OSs?
   a. Client Hyper-V
   b. Windows Virtual PC
   c. Oracle VirtualBox
   d. Apple Boot Camp
   e. Windows XP Mode

8. Which acronym stands for a feature of many Intel and AMD CPUs required by Microsoft's Client Hyper-V?
   a. AR
   b. SLAT
   c. VMM
   d. VDI
   e. VR

9. Which of the following solutions should you select if you wish to run a Windows guest on OS X, but you need frequent access to both the host and guest OSs?
   a. Windows XP Mode
   b. Windows Virtual PC
   c. Oracle VirtualBox
   d. Boot Camp
   e. Client Hyper-V

10. Which of the following will release the mouse from the control of a virtual machine?
    a. Guest key
    b. Host key
    c. Host OS
    d. VDI
    e. Terminal service

11. Which of the following is synonymous with hypervisor?
    a. Terminal service
    b. Bare metal
    c. Virtual hard drive
    d. Virtual machine
    e. Virtual machine monitor (VMM)

12. Your Windows PC has an AMD processor installed that includes AMD-V technology and the motherboard fully supports this processor. Which is the most capable version of a Microsoft hypervisor you can install on this machine, provided the computer meets all the other requirements?
    a. VirtualBox
    b. Client Hyper-V
    c. Windows XP Mode
    d. Boot Camp
    e. Parallels Desktop

13. What legal issue must you consider when installing a guest OS into a hypervisor?
    a. Copyright of guest OS
    b. Antivirus
    c. Licensing of guest OS
    d. Guest key
    e. Supplying security credentials

14. After downloading VirtualBox to an iMac with OS X, which of the following is the name of the object you should double-click to install VirtualBox on your computer?
    a. VirtualBox.pkg
    b. VirtualBox.iso
    c. VirtualBox.exe
    d. VirtualBox.pdf
    e. VM.bat

15. Which of the following is a multiboot option for running Windows as a second OS on an OS X computer?
    a. VirtualBox
    b. Windows Virtual PC
    c. Windows XP Mode
    d. Boot Camp
    e. Parallels

Essay Quiz

1. What is the purpose of each of the two most important files created by a Type II hypervisor when preparing a new virtual machine?

2. Describe a feature of Client Hyper-V that allows you to take a virtual machine to another computer on a common small handheld device.

3. Explain why an IT person would want to use a hypervisor on a desktop computer.

4. Provide a reason why you would not run OS X in a virtual machine on a Windows computer.

5. You have Windows XP Mode installed on your Windows 7 computer, and you would like to do a side-by-side comparison of Windows XP Mode and Windows XP in a VirtualBox VM. What precautions should you take and how many computers are required for this comparison?

LAB PROJECT 3.1

Find out how virtualization is being used in an organization in your area. Arrange an interview with an IT manager, network engineer, or other knowledgeable IT staff person from an organization in your area. Consider approaching someone at a regional hospital or medical clinic because privacy laws require that they meet certain minimum standards in IT, and they often have the best IT staff in a community. Ask if they are using virtualization, and if so, what type. What are their future plans for virtualization? Report your findings to your classmates.

LAB PROJECT 3.2

If you installed a hypervisor on your computer, find another one that will run on your OS. Install the second hypervisor and attempt to open the virtual machines created for the first hypervisor. Compare the similarities and differences. Will the new hypervisor work with the virtual machines you created with the first one? Decide which one you prefer working with. If it is the second, then keep it; if you preferred the first one, uninstall the second.

LAB PROJECT 3.3

Find out the latest about Type I and Type II hypervisors. Browse the Internet using the keyword *virtualization* and watching for recent articles and news releases. Consider turning on Google alerts with the key term *virtualization*. Watch the number of alerts you receive over just a period of a few days.

4

Windows 7

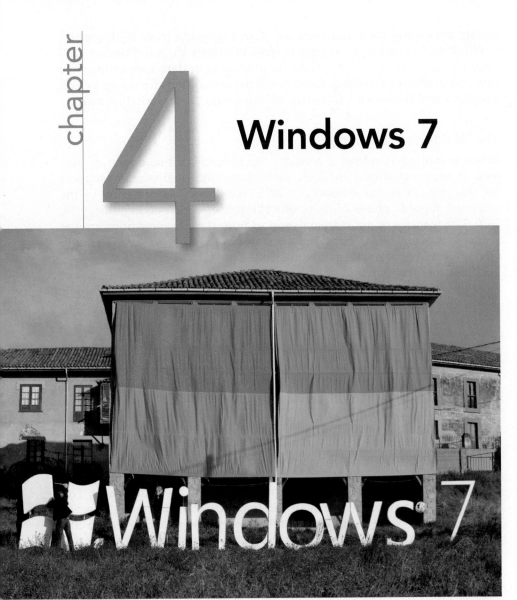

Learning Outcomes

In this chapter, you will learn how to:

LO **4.1** Install and configure Windows 7.

LO **4.2** Use the features of Windows 7.

LO **4.3** Manage Windows 7.

LO **4.4** Configure local security in Windows 7.

W indows Vista was released in 2007. The resistance to Windows Vista was so strong that Microsoft prolonged the life of Windows XP, allowing sales of new PCs with OEM (original equipment manufacturer) Windows XP installed until October 2010. This was one year after the release of Windows Vista's successor, Windows 7, and nine years since the introduction of Windows XP. History repeats itself. Although Windows 8 was introduced in 2012, many individuals and organizations decided not to upgrade, but to continue using Windows 7. In this chapter we consider the issues of installing and configuring Windows 7, followed by an overview of Windows 7 features and the basics of managing an installed OS. Finally, we'll explore issues for configuring local security in Windows 7. ✺

LO 4.1 | Installing Windows 7

In this section we will explore the options you have for installing Windows 7. We begin by identifying the upgrade paths available should you decide to install Windows 7 on an existing Windows desktop or laptop, answering such questions as, "Can I upgrade from Windows XP to Windows 7?" and "Can I upgrade from Windows Vista to Windows 7?" Then we will describe your options for moving your data and settings to a new installation of Windows 7 and detail the actual steps for doing a clean installation of Windows 7, following by important postinstallation tasks.

The Windows 7 Lifecycle

Before installing Windows 7 consider the lifecycle of this operating system. It was introduced in 2009, and Microsoft's mainstream support for this version ended January 13, 2015. Windows 7 is presently in the extended support phase of its product lifecycle, which ends January 14, 2020. The features of mainstream support important to most of us are the security updates, non-security updates, and some free support. The only one of these free services clearly available now during the extended support phase is security updating, but paid support is still available. Learn more about the Microsoft Product Lifecycle at **https://support.microsoft .com/en-us/lifecycle**.

Recommended System Requirements

Microsoft designed Windows 7 to provide better performance and to be more reliable on the same hardware required by its predecessor, Windows Vista. Table 4–1 shows the Windows 7 minimum requirements.

Windows 7 Editions

As with earlier versions of Windows, Microsoft offers Windows 7 as several separate products, called editions. Keep in mind that all editions of a single version of Windows have the same kernel and other core components. The differences among editions are mainly in the included components, targeted to specific types of users, and the more features the more expensive the edition. The three retail editions of Windows 7 are Home Premium, Professional, and Ultimate. Other Windows 7 editions are bundled with hardware as OEM Windows (with or without the accompanying DVD), while the Enterprise edition of any version of Windows is not available at retail, but sold only to customers of the Microsoft Software Assurance plan, a distribution channel for bulk licensing to organizations. The Enterprise editions have added features

WARNING!

If you plan to run Windows XP Mode, Microsoft recommends a PC with Intel-VT or AMD-V enabled in the CPU, plus you will need a minimum of 2 GB of memory and an additional 15 GB of free disk space.

TABLE 4–1 Windows 7 Minimum Requirements

	Windows 7 32-Bit Editions	Windows 7 64-Bit Editions
Processor	1 GHz 32-bit x86	1 GHz 64-bit x64 processor
System memory	1 GB	2 GB
Available hard drive space	16 GB	20 GB
Support for DirectX 9 graphics with WDDM 1.0 or higher driver (DirectX 10 required for certain games)	✓	✓
Graphics memory (to support Aero)	128 MB	128 MB
Audio output (if desired)	✓	✓
Internet access (for keeping the OS updated)	✓	✓

desirable to a large enterprise. These features include support for mass distribution, linking with enterprise security, compliance, collaborative productivity, and more.

Windows 7 also came in two scaled-down editions called Starter and Home Basic. The Starter edition was an OEM edition with many features removed or disabled, including the ability to change the desktop wallpaper or join a Windows domain. The Home Basic edition was available in emerging markets and was not available in the United States, most of Europe, the Middle East, Australia, New Zealand, and Japan.

Upgrade Paths

An upgrade of an operating system, also called an in-place installation, is an installation of a newer operating system directly over an existing installation. An upgrade preserves all your files and folders so that you do not have to restore you data. An upgrade also leaves existing programs in place, unless they are incompatible with either the installation program or the new OS.

The only in-place installation possible from an earlier version of Windows to Windows 7 is from Windows Vista.

> Note: The Windows 7 Upgrade product is different in two ways from the full Windows 7 retail product. The first is in how you install it, and the second is really a licensing issue. The upgrade product is cheaper than the full product because it is intended to replace the previously installed licensed Windows.

From Windows Vista to Windows 7

Table 4–2 lists the direct upgrade paths from Windows Vista to Windows 7. Blank fields indicate that you must do a clean install. You cannot directly upgrade from Windows XP or older versions to Windows 7.

An upgrade has its risks, since you end up with a new OS on an old computer with all the problems of the old installation as far as unnecessary installed programs, old hardware, and possible data loss or permission problems. With the Windows 7 Upgrade product you can still do a clean installation. Start the Windows 7 Setup from within the previous Windows version. At the screen that asks you to select the type of installation, Upgrade or Custom, simply select Custom and follow the prompts from there.

Windows 7 Anytime Upgrade Discontinued

Originally, Windows 7 Home Basic, Home Premium, or Starter editions came with the Anytime Upgrade option, listed under All Programs on the Start menu. When you ran this, you would follow the prompts to either enter an upgrade key you had previously purchased or you would connect to Microsoft online and purchase an upgrade key. Then Windows Anytime Upgrade would add the features of the upgraded edition to your installation of Windows 7. The Windows 7 Anytime Upgrade key is no longer available through the Microsoft Store.

TABLE 4–2 Upgrade Paths to Windows 7

Windows Vista Edition (with SP1 or SP2)	Windows 7 Home Basic	Windows 7 Home Premium	Windows 7 Professional	Windows 7 Enterprise	Windows 7 Ultimate
Business			✓	✓	✓
Enterprise					✓
Home Basic	✓	✓			✓
Home Premium		✓			✓
Ultimate					✓

Preparing to Install Windows 7

The preparation steps for installing Windows 7 vary based on whether you are doing an upgrade from Windows Vista, a side-by-side multiboot installation, or a clean installation. Here is a brief overview of each of the installation types:

Note: Use the Custom option when you want to do either a multiboot or clean installation.

- An upgrade, also called an in-place installation, installs directly into the folders in which the previous version of Windows installed. Windows 7 setup manages to preserve the old settings, while removing the old OS before installing the new OS. You can only upgrade from a Windows Vista edition that is upgradeable to the edition of Windows 7 you plan to install (see Table 4–2). However, if you simply aren't quite ready to break all ties with your old installation of Windows, then consider the next option.

- A multiboot installation leaves an old OS in place, installing a new OS in a separate partition or hard disk. This allows you to select the OS you wish to boot into every time you start the computer, and this is what we did on Jane's computer when Windows 7 was first available, because she still wanted an installation of Windows Vista for screen shots and comparison while writing about both Windows Vista and Windows 7. To install Windows 7 to multiboot, do a clean installation on a separate partition or hard disk, which means you will select the Custom installation choice. Windows 7 setup will preserve the earlier version of Windows and create a Windows Boot Manager menu, as Figure 4–1 shows, which will display for a short period at every restart. We often refer to a multiboot configuration with just two choices of operating system as a dual-boot configuration.

- A clean installation is an installation of an OS onto a completely empty hard disk or one from which all data is removed during the installation.

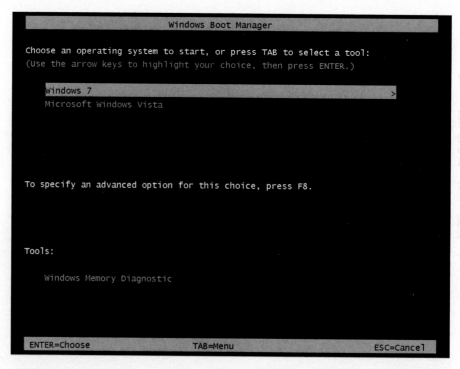

FIGURE 4–1 The Windows Boot Manager menu showing two choices: Windows 7 and Windows Vista.

It takes the least amount of disk space and is a new beginning for the new OS installation. You most often do a clean installation on a totally clean hard drive, although, in the case of a multiboot installation, you can direct Windows 7 setup to install as a clean installation on a different partition or drive from that of the existing OS. To start a clean installation select the Custom installation choice. To automate a clean installation onto many desktops, organizations use other, more advanced methods, such as hands-free, scripted install, or they use an image, which is an exact duplicate of the entire hard drive contents, including the OS and all installed software. The use of images is very popular in medium-to-large organizations that have dozens, hundreds, or thousands of desktop computers. Create a custom image for a large number of users by installing the OS and applications on a reference computer identical to those on which you will eventually place the images. Then use imaging software to copy the image of the hard drive. Products for enterprises centrally distribute images over a network out to the desktops.

Regardless of the type of installation you plan to do, you must ensure the hardware minimums are met, determine how to boot into the Windows setup program, and decide if you will activate immediately or later and if you wish to register the product with Microsoft. You can verify that your computer meets the recommended minimums by comparing the system configuration with Table 4–1.

Note: IT professionals use scripted installations or some type of imaged installations. These methods often take a great deal of preparation and knowledge and are best used when you must install an OS on many computers, using identical configurations as in a department, classroom, or computer lab.

Registration versus Activation

At some point, Windows setup will prompt you to register your product and to activate it. Many people confuse activation with registration. These are two separate operations for Microsoft software, although other popular software products combine these two functions, requiring that you give an email address and other personal information before the program is considered "legal" and activated.

Registration is when you inform Microsoft who the official owner or user of the product is and provide contact information, such as name, address, company, phone number, email address, and so on. Registration is generally optional with Microsoft products. Activation of Microsoft products is called Microsoft Product Activation (MPA), and is an antipiracy tool, meaning that Microsoft wishes to ensure that you are using your software per the software license, which normally limits its use to a single computer.

Microsoft Product Activation does not scan the contents of the hard disk, search for personal information, or gather information on the make, model, or manufacturer of the computer, and it sends no personal information about you as part of the activation process.

Activation is mandatory for retail versions of Windows 7 and you must do it within 30 days of installing the software. When prompted to activate during the installation, if you choose to activate at that time you enter a product key code from the Windows 7 packaging. The activation program communicates with Microsoft (you must have an Internet connection to do this online), and generates a product ID from the product key code and then combines it with a value that represents your hardware components to create an installation ID code. The activation program sends this code to Microsoft, which returns a 42-digit product activation code. Activating automatically online is the best way to do this.

Note: If you know that you will make major changes to the hardware in the first 30 days of using the new Windows 7 installation, then do not activate during installation, but wait until you have made the changes. This is because major hardware changes trigger the activation process again. Major hardware changes include: upgrading of the motherboard, CPU, hard drive, network interface card (NIC), graphics card, or RAM.

If you do not have an Internet connection when you try to activate, or if the activation program detects a problem, you will see a message telling you to call Microsoft. While sitting by the computer, dial the number provided. You will need to read the installation ID to a representative and enter the resulting 42-digit activation code in the Activate Windows By Phone dialog box.

Consider Windows Update Settings

Before you begin the Windows installation program you need to give some thought to how you want Windows to acquire the necessary updates that may improve its performance and make it more secure, because during Windows installation you will configure Windows Update, a Windows utility that can automatically connect to the Microsoft site and download and install updates. If you own the computer in question, then we recommend that you choose to have the updates downloaded and installed automatically. If the computer is part of a corporate or school network, then you need to ask your instructor or the IT staff how they want to handle updates.

Prepare to Transfer Settings and Data

Unless you are doing an in-place installation of Windows 7, you will want a way to transfer your data, email, and settings for Windows and your applications. Microsoft provides a utility that will do this for you, whether you plan to dual-boot between an older version of Windows and Windows 7 or do a clean installation. This utility, Windows Easy Transfer (WET), is available on the Windows 7 DVD. Before you run it, make sure you have an appropriate location where you want to transfer the files. This can be directly to a new computer, providing you have a special cable to use or a network connection between the two computers. However, you are most likely to do this using an external hard drive or USB flash drive. Just make sure that the location has plenty of free space for the files you will transfer. Make this location or drive available to the old computer, then insert the Windows 7 DVD into that computer and browse to the Support folder. Locate and double-click on the file MIG.WIZ to launch the Windows Easy Transfer wizard, shown in Figure 4–2. Carefully follow the instructions in the wizard for selecting the files and settings from the old computer to the location or drive.

Then, after Windows 7 is installed on the new computer, run the Windows Easy Transfer utility by entering "easy transfer" in Start | Search Programs

FIGURE 4–2 Windows Easy Transfer for Windows 7.

and Files. You will need to enter the location of the files into Windows Easy Transfer, and then identify your computer by selecting "This is my new computer." Then follow the instructions to transfer the files.

Prepare to Install into a Virtual Machine

If you have a hypervisor installed on a lab computer and plan to install Windows 7 into a virtual machine, you will need to first create a VM for the installation (as described in Chapter 3), and then ensure that the virtual machine will boot from the drive or ISO file containing the Windows 7 Setup files (also described in Chapter 3). By default, virtual machines in all the hypervisors discussed in Chapter 3 will connect and boot from an optical drive (CD or DVD) or an ISO file at startup, but you first need to configure the VM to use the drive or ISO file. Then, startup, the VM will boot into the Setup program.

The Installation

When you start the Windows 7 setup program the Windows Preinstallation Environment (Windows PE) starts. This is a scaled-down Windows operating system. Much like the old Windows setup program, it has limited drivers for basic hardware support for 32-bit and 64-bit programs. Windows PE supports the Windows setup GUI, collecting configuration information. The Windows 7 installation program requires very little user input. Step-by-Step 4.01 will walk you through the steps for performing a clean installation.

Step-by-Step 4.01

Installing Windows 7

In this step-by-step exercise, you will do a clean installation of Windows 7. To complete this exercise, you will need the following:

- A Microsoft/Intel standard personal computer (desktop or laptop) compatible with Windows 7, with at least the recommended minimum hardware and configured to boot from DVD, and an unpartitioned hard disk (disk 0, the first hard disk). Alternatively, use a virtual machine you have prepared before beginning the Windows 7 installation (see Chapter 3).

- The Windows 7 DVD or ISO file.
- The Product ID code. If you are using a retail version, look for this on the envelope or jewel case of your Windows 7 DVD. If you are not using a retail version, your instructor will provide a Product ID code or other instructions.
- A 15-character (or less) name, unique on your network, for your computer.
- A strong password for the user account created during setup.

Step 1

Using an ISO file or DVD, boot the computer or virtual machine. When using a DVD, watch the screen for instructions to boot from the optical drive. As the computer or VM boots, a plain black screen will briefly flash, followed by a black screen with the message: "Windows is loading files..." while Windows Preinstallation Environment is loaded and started. The Starting Windows screen signals that Windows PE is starting and will soon load the GUI for Windows 7 setup.

Step 2

On the first Install Windows page, select a language, time, currency format, and keyboard input methods. Then select Next.

Step 3

At the center of the next screen is the Install Now button, but you should notice two important links on the bottom left. One is labeled "What to know before installing Windows." Click on it to see if you have overlooked a preparation step. The second link, labeled "Repair your computer," is an important one to remember. If, after you install Windows 7 your system will not start, pull out your Windows 7 DVD, boot from it, and select this option.

Step 4

On the license page read the Microsoft Software License Terms, then click to place a check in the box labeled "I accept the license terms" and click the Next button.

Step 5

On the next page you are asked, "Which type of installation do you want?" Select Custom to perform a clean installation.

Step 6

On the next page, select the target drive for the installation and click Next. On most systems, this page will show a single disk with much more free space than shown here.

Step 7

Next, Windows 7 setup goes through the installation phases, restarting several times and returning to this page that displays progress with a green check by each completed phase.

Step 8

When it reaches the Completing Installation phase, the message "Setup will continue after restarting your computer" displays. After this, as Windows 7 restarts, the message "Setup is checking video performance" displays. Next enter a user name for the first user account (this will automatically be a Computer Administrator type, although that detail is not mentioned) and a name for the computer.

Step 9

Next create the password for the user account, entering it twice, and type a password hint that will help you to recall the password but not reveal it to others. The password hint will display anytime you enter an incorrect password when logging on.

Step 10

On the next page enter the 20-character Product Key. Notice the check box labeled "Automatically activate Windows when I'm online." Already checked by default, this means it will activate automatically if your computer connects to the Internet. If not activated within 30 days, Windows will stop functioning. Click Next to continue the final configuration steps.

Step 11

On the next page configure the Automatic Update Settings. Unless your instructor tells you otherwise, click the first option: "Use recommended settings." Windows setup will then continue. On the next page select your time and date settings, and click Next.

Step 12

Now select your computer's current location. If you are at home, select Home Network; if you are at school or work, select Work Network; if your computer has mobile broadband or you are using a public Wi-Fi network, select Public Network. There will be a short delay while Windows connects to the network and applies settings.

The Welcome page displays, followed by a message: "Preparing your desktop . . ." Soon the desktop displays and, depending on the setting you selected for updating and whether you have an Internet connection, you will see a message that Windows is downloading and installing updates. Some updates require restarting Windows to complete installing the update.

PostInstallation Tasks

After you install Windows 7, perform the necessary postinstallation tasks. They include verifying network access (assuming you connected to a network), installing security software, and installing at least the critical updates, including Service Packs. You should complete these tasks before moving on to customizing the desktop for yourself or another user and performing other desktop management tasks.

Verifying Network Access

Once you have completed the installation, look for the network status icon on the taskbar. If it does not show a red *x* then you have a network connection. If it shows a yellow exclamation mark, you have a local network connection, but do not have a connection to the Internet, although a router is present. Hover the mouse cursor over the icon. In the example shown here, the icon indicates a connection to a network named "ShortMoose" as well as to the Internet. If the network has no name, the top line would simply say "Network." In reality "ShortMoose" is the name of a wireless broadband router to which this computer connects via Ethernet. In Chapter 10 you will learn more about connecting to a private network as well as to the Internet.

The network status icon.

Installing Security Software

It's difficult to say which is more important: downloading and installing the all-important updates or installing a security package. We opt to install the security program before completing all the updates. If you do not have another program available to use, consider the free Microsoft Security Essentials, shown in Figure 4–3, available at www.microsoft.com/security_essentials. It includes general malware protection and free, automated updates. If you do not have another preferred security program, download and install this easy-to-use package as soon as possible.

Installing Updates

Now that you have verified that the computer has network access and installed security software, your next task is to install updates. Although some updates do install at the end of the Windows Vista and Windows 7 installation, you

FIGURE 4–3 Microsoft Security Essentials.

will need to ensure that additional updates install. How you actually obtain updates will depend on the organization (school or business) where you install Windows. In some organizations, the IT department may distribute updates for new installations on CD even before connecting a computer to a network. Other organizations may make them available on a shared folder on the private network. In most cases, if you have an Internet connection, you will configure Windows Update to automatically download and install updates. Figure 4–4 shows the options for configuring Windows Update.

If, during setup, you configured updates to download and install automatically, you can let nature take its course. In addition, we like to be more proactive,

FIGURE 4–4 Windows Update Settings.

because it can take Windows Update a few days before it downloads and installs all the updates for a new installation, especially as Microsoft continues to create more updates for a maturing Windows version. Therefore, even with automatic update configured, we recommend you use the Windows Update program to manually access the updates immediately after upgrading or installing Windows. This will still take several iterations, but you will bring it up-to-date sooner this way.

Configure Windows Update

If you are logged on as an administrator you can make changes to Windows Update. To configure Windows Update, try this:

1. Open the Start menu, in the Search Programs and Files box type "Windows Update," and select Windows Update from the results list.
2. In the task pane of Windows Update click Change Settings.
3. Using the drop-down lists and the check boxes, select the desired settings.
4. Click OK to close the Windows Update Change Settings box. Close Windows Update.

Virtual Machine Additions

If you installed Windows 7 into a virtual machine, be sure to install the virtual machine additions for Windows. Whatever hypervisor you are using will remind you to do this, usually when you start the newly installed OS in the virtual machine. Each hypervisor product has a different name for these additions, and you may simply need to respond to a pop-up window or you may need to look in one of the menus on the window surrounding your virtual machine to initiate the installation of the additions.

LO 4.2 | Windows 7 Features

This section offers an overview of Windows 7, including the separate Windows 7 products and some key features offered in Windows 7. Table 4–3 lists Windows 7 features and the editions in which each feature is included. We will examine just a few of these features in the following sections.

TABLE 4–3 Features in the Windows 7 Retail Editions

	Home Premium	Professional	Ultimate
Improved desktop navigation features such as Shake, Peek, and Snap	✓	✓	✓
Improved Instant Search organized into categories, searches external hard drives, networked PCs, and libraries	✓	✓	✓
Internet Explorer 8 (Upgrade this to Internet Explorer 10 for more improvements.)	✓	✓	✓
Windows Media Center (It requires a TV tuner and other hardware required for some functions.)	✓	✓	✓
HomeGroup for easy file-and-print sharing on a home network (HomeGroup requires a network and PCs running Windows 7.)	✓	✓	✓
Windows XP Mode for running Windows XP programs not compatible with Windows 7		✓	✓
Windows Touch (requires a touch-sensitive screen)	✓	✓	✓
Domain Join wizard for joining a Windows domain		✓	✓
Backup to a home or business network		✓	✓
BitLocker			✓
Switch among 35 languages			✓

A desktop shortcut.

The Windows 7 Desktop

The Windows 7 Desktop is only an evolutionary, not revolutionary change from that of its predecessors. For instance, the Windows 7 GUI can contain shortcuts in various locations, such as the desktop or the Start menu. A *shortcut* is an icon that represents a link to one of many types of objects. Double-clicking on a shortcut has the same results as taking the same action directly on the linked object. An object can be a folder, a data file, a program, or any other type of object an icon can represent in Windows. Shortcuts on the desktop are often, but not always, distinguished by a small bent arrow, as seen here on the shortcut for Mozilla Firefox. Shortcuts on the Start menu, such as those shown in Figure 4–5, typically do not have the bent arrow. The shortcuts highlighted in yellow in Figure 4–5 are pinned to the Start menu and will remain there until they are unpinned by the user. More on pinning later in this chapter. The shortcuts highlighted in mauve are shortcuts of recent programs that Windows dynamically adds to the Start menu. A horizontal line (barely visible) divides these two areas of the Start menu.

FIGURE 4–5 Shortcuts (at left) on the Start menu.

Aero

Windows Aero is Microsoft's name for a group of GUI desktop features and visual themes introduced in Windows Vista and improved somewhat in Windows 7. Windows 7 Aero includes transparent windows (referred to as "Glass"), Windows animations, Flip 3D, Aero Shake, Aero Snap, and Aero Peek.

Figure 4–6 is an example of the Windows 7 desktop with Aero enabled. *Flip 3D* lets you switch through your open windows as if they were a stack of cards or photos. Use the WINDOWS KEY+TAB combination to use Flip 3D, shown in Figure 4–7. It requires a video card that supports (at minimum) DirectX 9.0 and Shader Model 2.0. Figures 4–6 and 4–7 also show one of the desktop themes available with Windows 7.

FIGURE 4–6 Windows 7 with Aero enhancements, including transparent Glass.

FIGURE 4–7 Using Flip 3D in Windows 7.

Aero Snap lets you manipulate windows quickly. For instance, to maximize a window, drag it until its title bar touches the top edge of your display. Restore a maximized window by dragging it away from the top of the display. **Aero Shake** lets you quickly minimize all but one window by giving that window a quick shake. **Aero Peek** allows you to peek at the underlying desktop by hovering your mouse over the Show Desktop button, the small vertical bar at the far right edge of the taskbar. Aero Peek makes all open windows temporarily transparent.

> *Note:* If you click the Show Desktop button, all open windows will minimize. This button is also included in the Windows 8.*x* and Windows 10 desktops, as well as the peek at desktop feature.

Jump Lists and Pinning

Windows 7 improves the Start menu and taskbar with the Jump Lists and pinning features. The old pinned area of the Start menu is still available, and programs are often pinned there, but you can also pin items on the taskbar. When you right-click on a program shortcut on the Start menu or taskbar, a **Jump List** displays, as in Figure 4–8. This is a list of recently opened items such as files, folders, and websites. It automatically lists only the recently opened items, but you can select an item and "permanently" pin it to a Jump List. Practice pinning items in Step-by-Step 4.02.

Pinning allows you to place icons for applications and destinations on the taskbar and Start menu. Once pinned, an item's icon remains on the toolbar regardless of whether the program is open or closed. Simply click it to open the application or destination. When a program is running, its icon appears as a square button on the toolbar, as demonstrated by the Microsoft Outlook button on the toolbar in Figure 4–9, which shows a portion of a Windows 7 taskbar with the various icons labeled.

Figure 4–10 shows the Jump List for Microsoft Word that includes both Word documents and other types of files, such as recently embedded TIF files in Word documents.

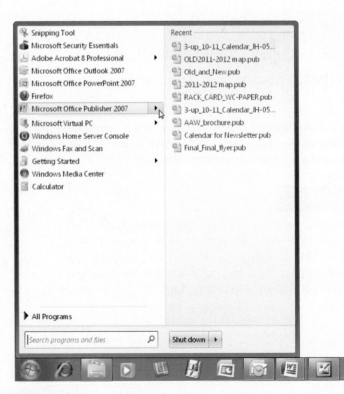

FIGURE 4–8 A Jump List (in the right column) for Microsoft Office Publisher.

Start button

Pinned items

Running program (Microsoft Outlook)

FIGURE 4–9 Pinned items on a taskbar, along with the button for a running program.

FIGURE 4–10 Right-click a pinned item to view its Jump List.

Note: We pin the apps we use the most to the taskbar, and now find we rarely launch apps from the Windows 7 Start menu.

Pin a program and then use that program's Jump List to pin several data files to the one program. When you pin a program to the taskbar, you use that one icon to open the program and switch to the program, and then you can select an item from the program's Jump List, which, like most pinned items, carries an automatically generated list of recently opened files for that item, but you can also add items to this list. There are several ways to pin programs. Learn more about pinning and Jump Lists in Step-by-Step 4.02.

Step-by-Step 4.02

Pinning Items

Practice pinning programs to the taskbar, and then pin files within a program's Jump List. In this step-by-step exercise, you will need the following:

- A computer with Windows 7 installed—either a conventional installation or an installation in a VM.

Step 1

Start a program, such as Microsoft Word. Then right-click the program's taskbar icon and select Pin This Program to Taskbar. The running icon will appear the same, but when you close the program, a pinned icon will remain.

You can also pin a program to the taskbar by dragging it. Open the Start menu and browse through the pinned items list or the All Programs menu until you locate the icon for a program you wish to pin. Then drag and drop the program icon onto the taskbar.

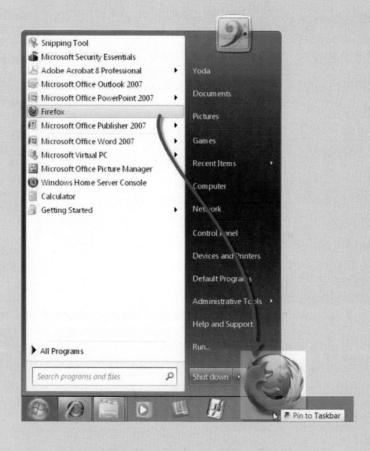

Windows 7 automatically generates Jump Lists, but you can ensure that an item stays on a Jump List by pinning it. To pin an item, right-click an icon on the Start menu to display the Jump List. Then hover the mouse cursor over an item in the list until the pushpin icon displays. Click the pushpin icon to pin the item.

Now you can see the distinction between the recent items Windows 7 automatically pins to the Jump List and those you choose to pin.

To unpin a program from the taskbar simply right-click on it and select Unpin This Program from Taskbar. To unpin an item from a Jump List, right-click on it and select Unpin from This List.

FIGURE 4–11 The hidden status icons revealed by clicking the Show hidden icons button shown here on the left side of the notification area.

Notification Area

The notification area, also called the system tray, is not new in Windows 7, but it is greatly improved over that of previous versions of Windows. The notification area holds status indicators and pop-up menus for a variety of devices and programs installed on your computer. It is so handy that many installation programs—both by Microsoft and by other software publishers—insert their own handy icons here. Before Windows 7, this practice resulted in clutter that detracted from the value of this feature. Windows 7 changed all that. To begin with, it does not display as many icons here itself, and best of all, it changed how icons appear and behave. Further, all those additional status icons are tucked away, but readily available with a click on the Show Hidden Icons button, as shown in Figure 4–11.

Figure 4–12 identifies the objects in the notification area. The Network icon shown indicates an Ethernet (wired) network, whereas an icon with five vertical bars in graduated sizes indicates a wireless network. If the network adapter is disconnected, a red X will appear on the icon. If there is another problem with the network, it will have a yellow triangle with a black

FIGURE 4–12 The Windows 7 notification area.

exclamation mark. Hover the mouse cursor over an icon to see a brief description; right-click to display a context menu, and click on the icon to open the related program.

Action Center

The Windows Action Center, represented in the taskbar notification area by the small flag icon, will briefly display a message balloon when there is a problem with your security programs or backup. Then it will quietly sit there with a white X against a red circle until you resolve the problem. A single click opens a message box, as shown in Figure 4–13. To open Action Center (see Figure 4–14) either click on the Open Action Center link in the message box or double-click the Action Center icon on the taskbar.

Libraries

Windows 7 introduced libraries. A library looks like a file system folder, but it is not, even though the four default libraries in Windows 7 carry the names of special folders: Documents, Music, Pictures, and Videos. While a folder is a container for files and other folders (called subfolders), a library only contains links to the locations of files and folders.

A library stores information about the locations of folders and files, displaying them as if they were all in one location, thus making it easier for you to find related information or types of files. For instance, in our example, the Documents library shows two default locations: My Documents (in this case D:\Yoda\Documents) and Public Documents (D:\Users\Public\Documents), as shown in Figure 4–15. Locations can be on the local computer or on shared locations on a network.

File System Support

Regardless of the file system used on a disk or disc, what you see in Windows Explorer remains the same: folders and files. Windows 7 supports the file systems described below.

FIGURE 4–13 The Action Center message box appears after a single click of the Action Center icon.

FIGURE 4–14 Open the Windows 7 Action Center by clicking on the Action Center link in the message box.

FIGURE 4–15 The two default locations for the Documents library.

FAT File Systems

The FAT file systems include FAT12, FAT16, FAT32, and exFAT. Each has a logical structure that includes a file allocation table (FAT)—hence the name of the file system—and a directory structure. The file allocation table enables the OS to allocate space for files, while a directory gives the OS a place for identifying information about each file. The FAT file system used many years ago on the diskettes and hard drives of the early PCs running IBM's PC-DOS and Microsoft's MS DOS is now called the FAT16 file system. The versions that are important to know about today are FAT32 and exFAT.

Recent versions of Apple OS X support FAT32, as well as exFAT (discussed next), so consider using one of these on a flash drive that you intend to use in both a Windows and Apple OS X computer.

The Extended File Allocation Table (exFAT) file system is intended for use with solid-state storage devices, such as flash drives. While exFAT theoretically supports volume sizes up to 64 zettabytes (ZBs), the recommended maximum is 512 terabytes (TBs).

Windows NTFS File System

The NTFS file system is available in all versions of Windows beginning with Windows NT, but excluding the Windows 95, Windows 98, and Windows Me versions. The main NTFS logical structure is a master file table (MFT) that is expandable, and therefore can be modified in future versions. Windows uses a transaction processing system to track changes to files, adding a measure of transaction-level recoverability to the file system, similar to what your bank uses to track transactions, and it will roll back incomplete transactions.

Over the years Microsoft improved NTFS. From the beginning, the NTFS file system provided file and folder security not available on FAT volumes. Today, in addition to file and folder security and transaction processing capability, NTFS supports many features. The short list includes file compression, file encryption, and an indexing service. NTFS is the preferred file system for hard drives in Windows and the default created when you install Windows.

File Systems for Optical Discs

Optical discs require special Windows file system drivers. The CD-ROM File System (CDFS) allows Windows OSs to read CD-ROMs and to read and write to writable CDs (CD-R) and rewritable CDs (CD-RW). The Universal Disk Format (UDF) is a file system driver required for Windows to read DVD ROMs and to read and write DVD-R and DVD-RW.

In addition to the traditional method for writing to optical drives (basically, a write once method), Microsoft introduced a new file system for optical drives in Windows Vista, which allows you to write to an optical disc, notably the DVD-RW and CD-R optical discs, adding files at any time, as long as the disc has room. Learn how to select between these two methods in the section titled "Managing Windows."

Security

In Windows 7, Microsoft improved existing security features such as User Account Control, BitLocker, and Windows Defender.

Improved User Account Control

As described in Chapter 2, User Account Control was introduced in Windows Vista. This security feature is designed to prevent malware from installing without the user's knowledge. It is less annoying in Windows 7, with fewer tasks requiring user intervention and use of an elevation prompt. Additionally, if you log on with an account with administrative privileges, you can adjust the User Account Control elevation prompt behavior.

Note: BitLocker and BitLocker To Go will encrypt an entire volume, regardless of the file system (NTFS, FAT, or exFAT).

BitLocker and BitLocker To Go

BitLocker, introduced in Windows Vista Enterprise and Ultimate editions, is also limited to the Enterprise and Ultimate editions in Windows 7. In Windows 7, as in Vista, you can encrypt the boot volume, but you can also encrypt any internal hard drive. Further, a feature called BitLocker To Go lets you encrypt external drives, such as flash drives. Later in this chapter you will learn how to use BitLocker in Windows 7.

AppLocker

AppLocker, a new feature in Windows 7, allows an administrator of a Windows Active Directory domain to control which applications each user can run, reducing the chance of malware running on the user's computer. This feature applies only to computers at work or school that are part of a Windows Active Directory domain.

Windows Defender

Introduced in Windows Vista, Windows Defender is a free built-in antispyware utility integrated into the Windows 7 Action Center where you can configure spyware scanning and updates.

Program Compatibility

If you need to run an old application that does not work well in Windows 7, open Help and Support from the Start menu, search on "compatibility," and check out the recommendations there. One recommendation is to run the Program Compatibility Troubleshooter. This will walk you through creating settings that may help your program to run better. Or you can do this manually by tweaking the compatibility settings for that application in the Properties for the application or its shortcut.

If the application still will not run, download and install Windows XP Mode, as described in Chapter 3. Install the application into the Windows XP VM. Windows 7 will even allow you to create a shortcut on the Start menu to an application installed in Windows XP Mode.

Recovery Tools

With each version of Windows, Microsoft has enhanced the recovery tools for repairing damage to the operating system. One of the most venerable of these tools is Task Manager, which has been in Windows through several versions and was extensively improved along the way. Task Manager allows you to see the state of individual processes and programs running on the computer, to view resource usage (CPU, memory, and disk), and to stop errant programs, when necessary.

You can access many of these tools while Windows is up and running, but in case a serious problem prevents Windows from starting, you can access an entire menu of tools by booting your system from the Windows 7 disc. Choose the language settings, click Next, and click the option Repair Your Computer. Select the OS you want to repair (if you installed more than one), click Next, and the System Recovery Options menu will display (see Figure 4–16). The following tools are available from this menu:

- Startup Repair scans for problems with missing or damaged system files and attempts to replace the problem files.
- System Restore allows you to create a restore point, which is a snapshot of Windows, its configuration, and all installed programs. Many restore points are created automatically when you make changes to your system. If your computer has problems after a change, use System Restore to roll it back to a selected restore point.
- System Image Recovery will let you restore a complete PC Image backup, providing you created one ahead of time.

FIGURE 4–16 The Windows 7 System Recovery Options.

> *Note:* Task Manager has abilities beyond managing tasks. If your Windows computer seems unusually slow, open Task Manager and select the Performance tab to determine if CPU or memory usage is high. Select the Networking tab to see state and speed of your network connections.

- **Windows Memory Diagnostic Tool** tests the system's RAM because RAM problems can prevent Windows from starting normally. If this tool detects a problem, replace the RAM before using any other recovery tool.

- **Command Prompt** provides a command-line interface in which you can use command-line tools to resolve a problem.

LO 4.3 | Customizing and Managing Windows 7

Once you have installed Windows 7, and completed the postinstallation tasks, it's time to customize Windows for the user. In this section, you will practice some of the common procedures for customizing and managing Windows 7, use Computer Management tools for a variety of tasks, install and remove applications, manage Windows components, and prepare the desktop for users, including modifications to display settings and adding a printer.

Computer Management

After you install Windows 7, if you add a new hard drive to your computer and need to partition it or do any other maintenance, open the Computer Management console and expand the Disk Management node. Figure 4–17 shows the disks on our Windows Vista/Windows 7 dual-boot computer. Windows Vista is installed on Disk 0 (drive C:) and Windows 7 is installed on Disk 1 (drive D:).

If you add a hard drive—internal or external—to a Windows computer, use Disk Management to partition and format the drive, if necessary. New external drives often come pre-formatted with FAT32, which does not provide security and cannot automatically repair damage to the disk. Therefore, if you wish to use the NTFS file system, open Computer Management and reformat your new drives. This will destroy all data on the target partition. There is also a method for converting a FAT partition to NTFS from the Command Prompt, which it will do without losing data. Although the danger of data loss is small, we recommend backing up your data before converting a FAT partition. To do this conversion, open a Command Prompt and enter **convert d: /fs:ntfs,** where *d:* is the letter of the target partition you wish to convert to

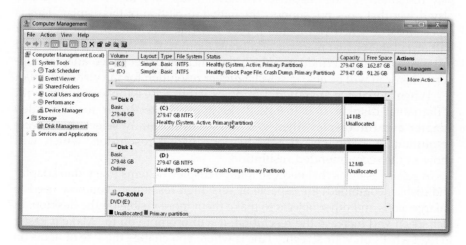

FIGURE 4–17 The Disk Management node in the Computer Management console.

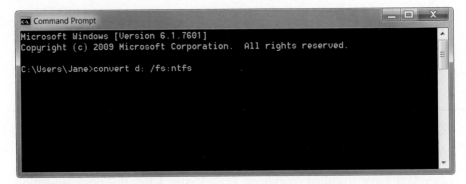

FIGURE 4–18 Convert a FAT partition to NTFS from the Windows Command Prompt.

NTFS. See Figure 4–18. You cannot use the convert command to go to any other format. If you want to convert from NTFS to another format, you must back up the drive, format it, and restore the data.

Preparing the Desktop for Users

In the many years we have worked with PCs running Windows OSs, we have noticed one phenomenon: A user who previously had to be shown the location of the on/off button will quickly figure out how to personalize the desktop. It seems like one day we help unpack the PC and a week later we come back to see dozens of shortcuts arrayed over desktop wallpaper of a child's crayon drawing. Whenever possible, we encourage such personalization because it means the person is making the computer his or her own and learning how to move around in Windows at the same time. Whether you are preparing a PC for yourself or another user, there are steps to take after you complete the immediate postinstallation tasks and before you install the necessary every-day applications. These include customizing the display settings—mainly the resolution—and adding a local printer.

Customizing Display Settings

After installing Windows 7 you may need to customize the display settings for resolution and (if you are lucky) for multiple displays.

Display Resolution. The Windows 7 installation program is very good at quickly installing Windows, but we still find that we need to tweak the display resolution settings because Windows setup may install a generic display driver that does not support the native resolution of the display. This is especially true when you install it into a virtual machine. In that case, you will install the virtual machine additions appropriate for the hypervisor and installed version of Windows, which will include better video adapter support. Then you will be able to select a higher resolution for the virtual display.

When you have installed Windows 7 on a desktop computer with a flat-panel display, if it installed the appropriate driver for the video adapter and the display, then Windows will normally select the correct resolution. A flat-panel display has one native resolution, which will show as the recommended resolution.

A related issue is that because today's display systems (the video adapter and display combined) are capable of very high resolution, you may need to enlarge icons and other objects to make them more visible on the desktop. In fact, when you increase the resolution, it will prompt you to "Make it easier to read what's on your screen." This is where you change the size of items on your screen. Practice adjusting screen resolution in Step-by-Step 4.03.

Note: A higher display resolution results in a smaller less readable screen font. To make it easier to read labels on icons and menus, change the size of text and objects on the screen, as shown in Step-by-Step 4.03.

Step-by-Step 4.03

Adjusting the Display Resolution

In this step-by-step exercise, you will familiarize yourself with the Windows 7 Appearance and Personalization settings and make a few changes to the desktop. You may see different settings than those shown in these steps, depending on the capabilities of your display. To complete this task, you will need the following:

- A PC or VM with Windows 7 installed.
- Administrative access.

Step 1

First change the screen resolution. A quick way to open the Screen Resolution page of the Appearance and Personalization applet is to right-click on an empty area of the desktop and select Screen Resolution from the context menu.

Step 2

Click on the down arrow in the drop-down list labeled Resolution, look for a recommended resolution, and select it. Click OK.

If you have increased your resolution, you will see this page, on which you can select the size of the text and other screen objects. This page is also available from the Screen Resolution page by clicking the link labeled "Make text and other items larger or smaller." Watch the Preview as you select a different size.

If you changed the text and object size, you will need to log off and then log on again for the change to take effect.

Multiple Displays. Although most PCs today only have a single display, more and more jobs require the increased screen real estate of multiple displays. Windows has supported multiple displays for several versions. All you need to add more display space to a typical desktop PC is a dual-headed video adapter and a second display. For most laptops the only cost is for a second display, because laptops usually come with a display connector for an external display that you can use simultaneously with the built-in display. We have worked with dual displays for over a decade on our computers and we have found that it can be a bit weird to work with displays of different sizes. Therefore, the ideal situation is to use identical displays.

When you have multiple displays, you can configure how Windows uses these displays on the Screen Resolution page. Our preferred mode is "Extend these displays," which leaves the taskbar on the main display (labeled 1 in Figure 4–19) and extends the desktop to the secondary display. It is great to have

FIGURE 4–19 Select how you want the desktop to appear on multiple displays.

FIGURE 4–20 When you click the Identify button a numeral will appear briefly on each display.

a document open on one display and an Internet browser open on the other, for instance. The setting "Duplicate these displays" shows the same desktop on both displays. You might use this if your laptop connects to a projector on which you wish to show the desktop. The remaining setting, "Show desktop only on 1" and "Show desktop only on 2" will leave the display you do not select blank.

Click the Identify button to have a number display on each physical display (see Figure 4–20) so that you can confirm that you have the displays oriented left to right as they are in the Screen Resolution page. If they are not, click and drag the display images on the Screen Resolution page to place them in the correct order.

If you want to change which display is the main display, go to the screen resolution page and, in the Change the Appearance of Your Displays box, click on the display labeled 2. Then a new option will show near the bottom of the settings below the box: Make This My Main Display. Click to place a check in this box, and that display will become the main display and will become number 1.

Desktop Gadgets

Windows Vista had a feature called the Sidebar in which you could configure one or more small programs called gadgets. The Sidebar is gone from Windows 7, but the gadgets remain; now you can position them anywhere you wish on the desktop. Each gadget performs some small function—usually involving keeping information handy in a small screen object. This information can be the date or time, stock quotes, weather in a certain city, and much more.

Note: Figure 4–20 is a screenshot captured on a dual-display with a window positioned to overlap both displays. It is one continuous image captured on two physically separate displays.

WARNING!

Do not use Windows 7 desktop gadgets because a gadget is a potential security hole.

Gadgets have proven to be a potential security hole. We no longer use them or recommend them.

Adding a Local Printer

Installing a new printer in Windows should be a nonevent because Windows is a plug-and-play OS, and new printers are plug-and-play. Therefore, you simply follow the setup guide for the new printer. In many cases, Windows will already have the printer driver and will install it without requiring a DVD from the manufacturer, but there can be another reason to run a setup program from the printer manufacturer. A new printer, especially one that includes other functions—primarily document scanning, copying, and faxing—will also include special software beyond the standard printer driver. Most common is software for scanning and organizing your documents.

Before connecting a printer, be sure to read the printer's setup guide—usually a hard-to-miss oversized sheet of paper with the basic instructions for setting up the printer. Often, a printer setup guide will instruct you to install the printer's software before connecting it, especially if it connects via USB. It will also guide you through making both the power connection and the connection to the computer. How will your printer connect to the computer? The most common wired printer interface is USB, but some printers also use IEEE 1394 (FireWire).

If a printer uses a cable (USB or IEEE 1394) you will first connect the printer, and then turn it on. If it connects via a wireless method, you will turn on the printer and establish the wireless connection. Once Windows detects a printer, it installs the driver and configures the printer for you. It will be added to the Devices and Printers applet, shown in Figure 4–21, and be available to all applications that can use a printer. The printer with the white check mark on a green circle is the default printer that Windows will use unless you select a different printer. Double-click on a printer icon to open the printer page with status information and links to the printer properties, print queue, and other pages for managing and controlling the printer and its features.

Connecting to a Network Printer

If you are installing a Bluetooth or Wi-Fi printer, or if a printer is available on your school or corporate network, and an administrator has configured it

Note: In the example in Figure 4–21, not all devices in the Printers and Faxes categories are physical printers or faxes. Some are software "printers" such as Adobe PDF and Snagit 9, which take a file from one format (a Word document or a graphic file) and "prints" it to a file in a new format, such as Adobe PDF, a file format commonly used for electronic document exchange that does not require users to have the same software that was used to create these documents, just software that can read them.

FIGURE 4–21 The Devices and Printers Control Panel.

with appropriate permissions so that you can connect and print to it, you can do just that. To do so, open Devices and Printers and click Add a printer. In the Add Printer wizard select "Add a network, wireless or Bluetooth printer." It will take time to search for all available network printers and then display them in the box. Select the Printer Name of the printer you wish to connect to, click Next, and follow the instructions. This will install the appropriate printer driver on your computer so that Windows can format each print job for that printer before sending it to the network printer.

Installing and Removing Applications

By now, you are ready to install applications into Windows to make your computer the tool you need for work, home, or school. If you purchased a computer with Windows preinstalled, you may also need to remove some of those preinstalled applications you have no desire or need to use.

Installing Applications

Today, each mainstream application comes with its own installation program that will walk you through the installation process. Some offer just a few options, installing with very little user input, while others will give you the option to do a custom install, in which you select the components to install and the location for the installed files. These programs copy the application files and make necessary changes to Windows, such as associating one or more file types with the application so that when you double-click on, say, a file with a DOCX extension, it knows to open Microsoft Word.

> **WARNING!**
>
> When installing new software, be careful that you do not install unwanted software or toolbars as part of the installation.

After completing an application installation, you should make sure to update the application. If you have an Internet connection, most applications will check for updates. This is very important today when malware targets our business productivity software. If your applications are from Microsoft, you can update them through Windows Update, which will list updates under Optional Updates, as shown in Figure 4–22.

FIGURE 4–22 Update Microsoft Applications through Windows Update.

FIGURE 4–23 Uninstall unwanted programs.

Removing Applications

When it comes time to remove an application, you should first look for an uninstall program for the application. If the application has a submenu off the Start menu, it may include the uninstall program, which is usually the best choice for uninstalling. You can also search the folder in which the application installed for an uninstall program. If you cannot find such a program for an application you wish to uninstall, open Control Panel, locate Programs, and click Uninstall A Program. It may take a few seconds for the list of installed programs to display in the Programs and Features page. Locate the program you wish to uninstall and double-click it. You will see a warning, as shown in Figure 4–23. Follow the instructions to complete the operation.

Managing Windows Components

Windows 7, like previous versions, includes many Windows components beyond the basic operating system files. You can view them by opening Windows features in Control Panel. Simply click a check box to turn individual features on or off, as shown in Figure 4–24.

Simple File Management

As with any operating system, file management in Windows 7 is mainly about organizing data files so that you can easily find the files you need when you need them. Windows provides a set of folders for just this purpose. Before you use them, get a basic understanding of the default file hierarchy in whatever version of Windows you are using. Then learn how to work with not just files and folders, but also the libraries that Windows 7 introduced. Finally, learn about the Windows file systems for optical discs and the ones that allow you to copy files to CD or DVD as easily as you copy them to a hard drive or flash drive.

Windows 7 Default File Hierarchy

All versions of Windows create one set of folders for the operating system, another set for application program files, and an additional set, personal folders, for each user account to hold user data files. The 32-bit and 64-bit distributions of Windows differ only in the location in which they store programs. The 32-bit distributions of Windows 7 stores all programs in the Program Files folder, while the 64-bit distributions store only 64-bit programs in this folder and store 32-bit programs in the folder named Program Files (x86). Figure 4–25 shows the folder hierarchy for a 64-bit installation of Windows 7. The default location for the majority of the Windows operating system files is in C:\Windows.

The default location for user data is C:\Users\<username> where <username> is the log-on user name. In Figure 4–26, note the folder for the user Jade. Within this folder are the personal folders created by Windows to hold various types of data or, as in the case of the Desktop folder, to hold files from a certain location. The Downloads folder holds files you download with your Internet browser.

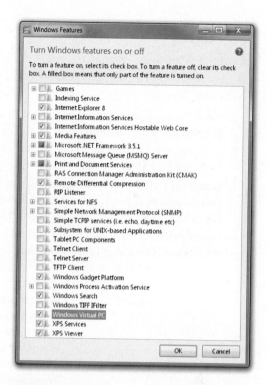

FIGURE 4–24 Use the check boxes to turn Windows features on or off.

FIGURE 4–25 The Windows 7 64-bit default folder hierarchy.

FIGURE 4–26 Windows 7 personal folders for the user Jade.

try this!

Explore Windows Folders

If you are sitting at a computer with Windows 7, explore the folder hierarchy. Try this:

1. Click Start | Computer or use the shortcut keys: Windows Key + E to open Windows Explorer.
2. In Windows Explorer double-click the icon for the Local Disk (C:). Note the folders in the root of drive C:.
3. Double-click the icon for Program Files and note the folders under Program Files. If you have a 64-bit installation of Windows, double-click the icon for Program Files (x86) and note the folders in this folder.
4. Now browse to the Users folder and open the folder for the account with which you logged on and explore the contents of this folder.

Navigating Windows Explorer

There are several ways to manage your files in Windows. The primary tool for saving files is the individual application you use to create and modify files of a certain type: for instance, a word processing program, spreadsheet program, photo editing program, or other application. When you issue the command within an application to save a file, you can navigate to the location of your choice and either save the file in an existing folder or create a new folder before saving. Similarly, when you decide to open an existing file from within an application, you can navigate to a location and open the desired file.

Although you can also do many file management tasks within an application, the primary tool for copying, moving, renaming, and deleting files is Windows Explorer. Microsoft introduced some features to the Windows Explorer folder windows, which we highlight here. Figure 4–27 shows the anatomy of a Windows Explorer folder window. By default, the Menu bar appears only when you press the ALT key, and you can use the Organize button and other buttons on the toolbar to modify the appearance and functionality of the Windows Explorer folder windows.

Navigate through Windows Explorer with mouse operations. When you hover the mouse over the navigation pane, small clear triangles appear next to each folder object that can be expanded. Click the triangle and it turns solid black and points down to the right in the navigation pane at the now-visible objects contained in the original folder. Click an object's icon in the navigation pane to open it in the contents pane. If you wish to open objects (folders, files, etc.) in the contents pane, you double-click on the object. You can move files and folders from one location to another by dragging and dropping the object you wish to move. Right-click on an object to access other possible operations.

Note: Open Windows Explorer quickly by pressing the Windows key and "e" key together.

Working with Libraries

Recall what you learned earlier in this chapter about libraries. A library points to one or more locations. Familiarize yourself with libraries by clicking the Windows Explorer pinned icon on the taskbar (it looks like a bunch of folders in a stand) and clicking on any library in the navigation pane. For instance, when you do this to the Documents pane, its contents appear in the contents pane and above that pane is the Library pane. The word *Includes* appears in the Library pane, and after that appears the number of locations. But this is also a link—click it to open the Documents Library Locations window.

You can add locations to a library and create libraries of your own. This is very handy if you want to organize all the files related to a project but those files are stored in folders in various locations on your local hard drive, external hard drives, or network servers. You can back up data in a library as if it were stored in one location. To add a location to the Documents library, simply click the Add button, which opens the Include Folder in Document window. Use this to browse to the folders you wish to add, select the folder, and click the Include Folder button. Windows then adds the new location to the library.

Note: By default, Windows Explorer hides extensions for known file types, an inconvenience for power users. To make file extensions visible, open Windows Explorer and press Alt-T to open the Tools menu, select Folder Options, then click the View tab. In Advanced Settings clear the check box labeled Hide extensions for known file types. Click OK to close Folder Options.

Control menu

Address bar

Minimize, Maximize, and Close buttons

Menu bar

Tool bar

Library pane

Navigation pane

Scroll bar

Contents pane

Details pane

Pictures library
Sample Pictures

Arrange by: Folder ▾

Blue hills (1).jpg   Blue hills(1).jpg   Chrysanthemum j...   Desert.jpg

Hydrangeas.jpg   Jellyfish.jpg   Koala.jpg   Lighthouse.jpg

Penguins.jpg   Tulips.jpg   WildCat.jpg

Blue hills (1).jpg   State: 🔗 Shared   Tags: Add a tag
JPEG image   Date taken: Specify date taken

FIGURE 4–27 A Windows Explorer folder window.

Notice the words *Default save location.* When you save files into this library, you are putting them in the default location for saving files. To change the default save location, first you need more than one save location in a library. Then all you need to do is right-click the desired location and select "Set as default save location."

To create a new library, first click on Libraries in the navigation pane, then notice the New Library tool that appears on the toolbar. Click New Library, which will create a new library folder, ready for a name and locations. If you missed entering the name when you created it, right-click on the New Library, select rename, enter the name, and press Enter. With the new library selected in the navigation pane, the contents pane will indicate that the library is empty. Click the "Include a folder" button to begin adding locations to this new library. You can continue to add locations. Figure 4–28 shows a new library named M-H with two locations—one on a network server named HTC-SERVER.

Working with Optical Discs

Even most inexpensive consumer-grade PCs come with optical drives capable of burning (writing data, music, or videos to disc), and optical discs are great for those files you wish to remove to make more room on the computer's hard drive. Whatever your need for burning CDs or DVDs, you should first understand the

FIGURE 4–28 A new library, M-H, with two locations: Manuscripts and Screenshots.

two formats Windows 7 uses when it burns discs: the ISO Mastered format and the Universal Disk Format (UDF) Live File System.

Use the Mastered format when you want to be able to use a CD or DVD in a conventional CD or DVD player or in any computer (older Apple Macs or PCs). The trouble with using this format is that each item you select to copy to the PC is stored temporarily in available hard disk space (in addition to the space used by the original file) until you finish selecting all you wish to copy, and then they are copied in one operation. This makes it difficult to copy files from a hard drive when you have very little free hard drive space on any hard drive in your computer.

Use the Live File System to burn a disc when you will only use the disc on newer Apple Macs and PCs running Windows XP or new OSs. Using Live File System you can directly copy items to the drive without requiring extra hard drive space. You can copy items individually, over time—either by leaving the disc in the drive or by reinserting the disc multiple times. If all the systems in which you plan to use a disc are newer PCs or Macs, then keep the default setting, which uses the Live File System. Step-by-Step 4.04 will walk you through copying files to an optical disc using the Live File System format.

Step-by-Step 4.04

Burning a CD or DVD

In this step-by-step exercise, you will burn a DVD using the Live File System, which allows you to copy files much as you would to any hard drive or flash drive. To complete this exercise, you will need the following:

- A computer with a DVD/CD drive and with Windows 7 installed—either a conventional-installation or an installation in a VM.
- A blank CD or DVD.

Step 1

Insert a blank disc into the optical drive. When the Autoplay dialog opens, select Burn Files to Disc.

Step 2

In the Burn a Disc dialog, provide a title for the disc (the default is the current date), enter a name, and then click Next.

Live File System format

Mastered format

Step 3

Windows formats the disc.

Step 4

After the disc is prepared, this message displays. You can now copy files to the disc from Windows Explorer—either click the button labeled "Open folder to view files" (just one way to open Windows Explorer), or close the box and continue working, copying files to the disc as you would normally copy files to a hard disk or USB drive.

Step 5

For instance, you can drag and drop folders and files to the disc, as we have done here with the folder titled "06-A+SG_7E." When you use the Live File System, you can continue to add files to the disc as long as it has available space. You can do that now, or add files to it later.

LO 4.4 | Managing Local Security in Windows 7

If your Windows computer is on a corporate network, the company will centrally manage it, including the security issues. A computer that is not part of a corporate network depends on the knowledge of the user for its security. Security implemented solely on a desktop or laptop computer is local security. Here we will look at administering local user accounts, local security for files and folders, Windows BitLocker drive encryption, Windows Defender antispam protection, and Windows Firewall.

Administering Local User Accounts

Local user accounts reside in the local accounts database on a Windows computer. You use a local account to give someone access to the Windows computer and local data. More than one person can log on to a Windows desktop computer as an interactive user (the one sitting at the keyboard), through a feature called Switch Users, but only one person at a time can physically use that Windows desktop computer's mouse, keyboard, and display. Typically, only one interactive user uses a desktop computer. Therefore, most users have little or no experience managing local accounts other than their own, and those same users rarely need to make any changes to their own account. This section gives you a chance to create and manage a local user account.

User Accounts Applet

The primary tool for administering local user accounts is User Accounts, a Control Panel applet shown in Figure 4–29. Either browse to it from Start | Control Panel or enter "user accounts" in the Start menu Search box and select User Accounts from the list of results. In the example shown here, the user Yoda is an Administrator and the account is password protected.

Working with User Accounts in Windows

You must log on with an account that is a member of the Administrators group to see all the local user accounts on your computer. Then open User Accounts

FIGURE 4–29 The User Accounts Control Panel.

and click Manage Another Account. The Manage Accounts window, shown in Figure 4–30, will show the existing accounts. In the example shown there are only two accounts: Yoda and Guest; the Guest account is off, which is the default for this account.

Windows 7 also has a local account built in named Administrator, disabled by default during a clean installation or an upgrade. The exception to this is when you upgrade a Windows Vista installation that only has the Administrator and has no other active local account that is a member of the local Administrators group, which would be a rare occurrence. In that case, the local Administrator account is enabled, so it would be visible in Local Users when an administrator selects Manage Another Account.

When you are performing an upgrade to Windows 7 on a Vista PC in a Microsoft Active Directory Domain, it will disable the local Administrator account regardless of the contents of the local accounts database. You can enable this account after installation, but we strongly recommend that you not do it because *this* account is all-powerful and immune to the User Account Control (UAC) security feature, whereas other accounts that are simply members of the local Administrators group are not immune to UAC.

Therefore, while the built-in Administrator account is logged on, the computer is more vulnerable to a malware attack. So it's good practice to not enable the Administrator account for everyday use, as you may never need this account.

FIGURE 4–30 The Manage Accounts window shows existing accounts.

Step-by-Step 4.05

Creating a New Account in Windows 7

In this step-by-step exercise, you will create a new Standard user account. To complete this exercise, you will need the following:

- A computer or virtual machine with Windows 7 installed.

- Be prepared to log on using an Administrator account (not necessarily *the* Administrator account).

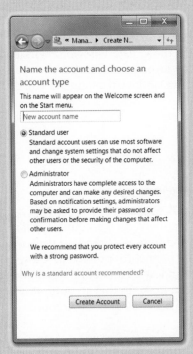

Step 1

Click Start | Control Panel | User Accounts and Family Safety | User Accounts. In the User Accounts window, click Manage Another Account. | Create a New Account. Enter a name for the account, read the descriptions of the Standard user and Administrator user account types, but leave Standard user selected and click Create Account.

Step 2

The Manage Accounts window opens with the new user added.

Step 3

The new account does not have a password. To password protect the account, you can either allow the user to log on and create a password, or you (as an Administrator) can create a password that the user will need to use when logging on. To create a password for this account, double-click on the account icon and click Create a Password.

Step 4

In the Create Password window, enter the new password twice in the New password and Confirm new password boxes. It is optional to enter a password hint, and we recommend you do that. Then click the Create Password button.

Step 5

The new user account appears in User Accounts as a Standard user account and is password protected. Close all open windows. Notice the other changes you can make to this account. When you are finished, close User Accounts.

User Account Control

Recall from Chapter 2 that User Account Control (UAC), introduced in Windows Vista and improved in Windows 7, is designed to protect the computer from having malware installed. In Vista or Windows 7, even if you log on as an Administrator, UAC will inform you that a program is trying to perform something for which it needs elevated permissions (administrator).

Windows 7 has eliminated many of the events that would have triggered a UAC prompt in Windows Vista. For instance, if you are logged on with an Administrator type account you will not see the Consent Prompt appear for certain advanced administrative tasks, such as opening the User Account Control Settings window. A Standard user will need to provide credentials.

Local Security for Files and Folders

Windows 7 supports the use of permissions to protect files and folders on local NTFS volumes. Additionally, it offers encryption on NTFS volumes, allowing you to turn on encryption for a folder, as described in Chapter 2. In this section, we will look at applying permissions on local NTFS volumes.

File and Folder Permissions

The NTFS file system allows you to control who has access to specified files and folders by assigning permissions. These permissions restrict access to local users and groups as well as to those who connect to these resources over the network. However, in the case of those connecting over a network, the share permissions (not related to NTFS permissions) take effect first and may block access to the underlying files and folders. Only NTFS volumes allow you to assign permissions to files and folders directly. In this section, we will focus on the security features of NTFS, including file and folder permissions.

On a volume formatted with the NTFS file system, each folder and file has a set of security permissions associated with it using the following mechanism. Each file and folder on an NTFS volume has an associated Access Control List (ACL), which is a table of users and/or groups and their permissions to access the file or folder. Each ACL has at least one Access Control Entry (ACE), which is like a record in this tiny ACL database that contains just one user or group account name and the permissions assigned to this account for that file or folder. An administrator, or someone with Full Control permission for the file or folder, creates the ACEs.

To view the ACEs in an ACL for a file or folder, open the Properties dialog box and select the Security tab. Figure 4–31 shows the Security page for a folder named Jade, which is the top-level personal folder automatically created by Windows the first time the user Jade logged on. Notice the list of permissions for the user Jade. This is an ACE. These are the default permissions set by Windows on the user's personal folders.

Change the permissions on a folder or file by opening its Security page and clicking the Edit button to reveal the page shown in Figure 4–32, where you can add a user or group, remove a user or group, and specify the permissions assigned to the file or folder for each user or group. Table 4–4 compares the standard permissions on folders versus those on files.

These permissions apply to files and folders on an NTFS volume and protect those resources from both locally logged-on users and those who may connect over a network. Windows only assigns network shares to folders, so

FIGURE 4–31 The list of permissions Windows creates on a user's personal folder.

FIGURE 4–32 Modify the permissions for the folder named Jade.

you must assign the permissions to the shared folder. This entirely different set of permissions is applied before a network user accesses the NTFS folder and file permissions. We will explore sharing files on a network and setting share permissions in Chapter 10.

NTFS Permission Inheritance

The folders and files on a volume are in a hierarchy, with the drive itself at the top, followed by the root folder and subfolders. Every subfolder and its contents inherits these permissions. If you wish one of the subfolders to have different permissions, you must first navigate to it and open its Properties dialog to explicitly set those permissions on the Security page. When you view permissions on a file or folder, the permissions inherited from the parent are visible but unavailable, as shown in Figure 4–33 by the gray checks and lack of boxes, and you will not be able to modify those permissions at that level. New permissions can be assigned, but inherited permissions cannot be altered. You can modify them in the folder in which they originated or you can choose to block inheritance on a folder or file to which you wish to assign different (usually more restrictive) permissions. To do this, you must

TABLE 4–4 Comparison of Folder and File Standard Permissions

Standard Folder Permissions	Standard File Permissions
Full control	Full control
Modify	Modify
Read and Execute	Read and Execute
Read	Read
Write	Write
List Folder Contents	

access the Advanced Security Settings, then click the Change Permissions button, and deselect the check box labeled Include inheritable permissions from this object's parent.

BitLocker Drive Encryption

If you have very high security needs and have either the Ultimate or Enterprise version of Windows Vista or Windows 7, consider enabling BitLocker Drive Encryption. Microsoft introduced it in Windows Vista as an optional feature for encrypting only the drive on which the Windows OS resides. It was enhanced in Windows 7 to include drives beyond the system drive, including internal hard drives and externally attached drives. This last feature is called BitLocker To Go.

BitLocker is off by default. When you enable it, BitLocker encrypts the entire contents of a drive, storing an encryption and decryption key in a hardware device that is separate from the encrypted hard disk. To do this, the computer must have either a chip with Trusted Platform Module (TPM) version 1.2 or higher or a removable USB memory device (a USB flash drive will do). When you use TPM, the drive and computer are married because the chip resides in the computer.

To encrypt the drive on which Windows is installed, BitLocker requires a hard drive with at least two partitions: one that contains Windows (the "system" partition), and a second partition (the "boot" partition) created by BitLocker and not directly usable by the user. When you perform a clean installation of Windows 7 it creates the hidden boot partition. This partition is critical to booting up your computer and without it, Windows cannot be started from the encrypted partition.

In Windows 7, when you wish to encrypt a drive—either internal or external—you simply open Windows Explorer, right-click a drive, and select BitLocker from the context menu, as shown in Figure 4–34. The existence of this choice on the menu indicates that the selected drive supports BitLocker.

BitLocker To Go may be the BitLocker feature most ordinary folks will use because many people carry flash drives, and when they have confidential information, such as medical records, it is important to protect that data. However, you will only be able to access the data on the drive on the computer on which you encrypted it or on a computer where you can make the keys available, which is limited to computers running Windows 7 or newer.

FIGURE 4–33 Inherited permissions are grayed out.

FIGURE 4–34 Right-click a drive and look for the option Turn on BitLocker.

try this!

View the BitLocker Status of All Drives at Once

Quickly view and manage the BitLocker status of your drives on a Windows 7 computer. Try this:

1. Enter "bitlocker" in the Start | Search box, and select BitLocker Drive Encryption from the results.
2. Click the link labeled TPM Administration to see if your computer supports TPM.
3. If you have a flash drive and have permission to do so, insert it into your computer and turn on BitLocker for that drive.

The tool for managing BitLocker for all your drives is the BitLocker Drive Encryption Control Panel shown in Figure 4–35. Notice the lock and key on the encrypted drive, named Cruzer. Once you encrypt a drive with BitLocker, Manage BitLocker becomes a choice on the context menu for that drive in Windows Explorer, so you can access the management options for the drive from either location. You can also open the BitLocker Drive Encryption Control Panel by

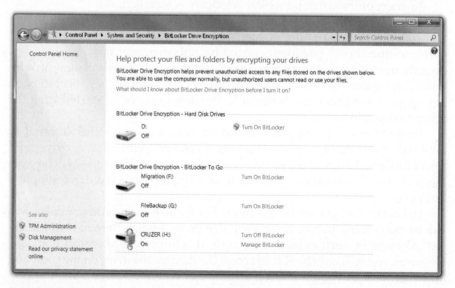

FIGURE 4–35 BitLocker is turned on for Drive H:.

entering "manage bitlocker" in the Start menu's Search box or from within the main Control Panel window.

Windows Defender

Windows Defender is free antispyware software included with Windows 7. This version protects only against spyware and does not protect against malware infecting your system. To see if Windows Defender is running on your computer click Start, type "defender," and select Windows Defender from the results list. If you see the message shown in Figure 4–36, Windows Defender is off, and if no other security software enabled, click the link "Click here to turn it on." However, if you have Microsoft Security Essentials (mentioned earlier in this chapter, and described next), or almost any full-featured third-party security software installed, it will include antispyware software.

FIGURE 4–36 Windows Defender is turned off.

Microsoft Security Essentials

Whereas Windows Defender in Windows 7 protects only against spyware, Microsoft Security Essentials (MSE) offers much broader real-time protection against malware as well as scheduled scans. MSE is available for Windows 7 and earlier versions as a free download from Microsoft. When you install MSE, Windows Defender is disabled because it is not necessary.

> *Note:* The Windows 7 version of Microsoft Security Essentials (MSE) will not run in Windows 8, but Windows 8 includes a replacement that is nearly identical to MSE and renamed Windows Defender! Learn more about this in Chapter 5.

Windows Firewall

We strongly recommend that you use a personal firewall on your PC if it connects to any network. Most security software suites come with a personal firewall. Windows Firewall has been a feature of Windows since Windows XP Service Pack 2. Each newer version of Windows has added its own enhancements to this personal firewall. So there is really no excuse for not using a personal firewall on your PC.

To open the Windows Firewall enter "windows firewall" into the Start Search box. The example shown in Figure 4–37 is on a computer connected to a private network. Notice that it shows we are not connected to a public network, which refers to an open Wi-Fi network like you would encounter if you used your laptop in an airport terminal or at your favorite coffee shop. The computer in question actually is connected to the biggest public network in the world—the Internet—but a firewall on a router guards our connection to the Internet.

FIGURE 4–37 On this page "Public networks" refers to public Wi-Fi networks and other untrusted public networks.

Chapter Summary

After reading this chapter and completing the Step-by-Step tutorials and Try This! exercises, you should understand the following facts about Windows 7.

Installing Windows 7

- The Windows 7 system requirements are nearly identical to the requirements for Windows Vista.

- As with earlier versions, Windows 7 is bundled as several products called editions—each with a set of features. Windows 7 has three retail editions: Home Premium, Professional, and Ultimate.

- You cannot directly upgrade Windows XP to Windows 7, and the ability to upgrade from Windows Vista to Windows 7 depends on the editions involved in the upgrade—both for Windows Vista and for Windows 7.

- You must decide on the type of installation: upgrade, multiboot, or clean installation. You achieve the latter two by using the Custom option in the Windows setup program.

- Retail editions of Windows must be activated, a process that confirms you are using a legal product, not a pirated copy.

- Decide how you want the Windows Update program to download and install updates because Windows 7 setup will query you about this.

- Unless you are doing an in-place installation to Windows 7, run a program, such as Windows Easy Transfer (WET) in the old installation to gather the settings and data you want to transfer to your new Windows installation. Then, after installing Windows 7, run the WET utility from the new installation to complete the transfer.

- The Windows 7 setup program runs a special scaled-down Windows OS, Windows PE.

- Immediately after installing Windows, verify network access, install security software, and finish updating Windows. If you installed Windows into a VM, do the same tasks, but also run the virtual machine additions for the hypervisor.

Windows 7 Features

- The Windows 7 desktop is enhanced with such features as Jump Lists and pinning.

- Windows 7 supports several file systems: FAT, exFAT, NTFS, and file systems for optical discs.

- Security features such as User Account Control, BitLocker, and Windows Defender are improved in Windows 7, and BitLocker To Go and App-Locker have been added.

- If an old app does not run in Windows 7, first use the Program Compatibility Troubleshooter. If it does not solve the problem, download and install Windows XP Mode and test the old app in that VM.

- Windows 7 has enhanced or added new recovery tools, including Startup Repair, System Restore, System Image Recovery, and Windows Memory Diagnostic Tool.

Customizing and Managing Windows 7

- Familiarize yourself with the tools in the Computer Management console, especially the Disk Management node, which will allow you to perform a variety of tasks on disks.

- If necessary, adjust the display resolution, and change the text and object size.

- If a computer has multiple displays, use the Display Resolution control panel to configure the displays for the way the user will use them.

- Install and uninstall a program using the program's own installation program. Some programs do not come with an uninstall option. In that case, use the Programs applet in the Control Panel to uninstall the program.

- Turn Windows features on and off in the Control Panel Programs applet.

- During installation, Windows creates a default folder hierarchy into which it installs operating system files and program files.

- The first time a user logs on, Windows creates the user's personal folders under the Users folder at the root of the drive on which Windows installed. If this is an NTFS volume, Windows will set permissions for the user's personal folders.

- Libraries appear to be folders when viewed in Windows Explorer, but a library is not a folder—it is an object that keeps track of one or more locations where certain folders and files are stored. There are four default libraries in Windows 7, and you can create custom libraries.

- If you burn an optical disc with the Mastered format you will be able to use it in a conventional CD or DVD player, or in any computer, including older Apple Macs or PCs, but the burn process for this format requires hard drive space to temporarily store the files before burning to disc.
- If you burn an optical disc with the Live File System you will only be able to use the disc on newer Apple Macs and newer PCs (Windows XP and newer support it, but older PCs may not). This format allows you to directly copy items to the drive without requiring extra hard drive space. You can also add files to a disc formatted with the Live File System.

Managing Local Security in Windows 7

- Local user accounts reside in the local accounts database on a Windows computer, and the User Account Control Panel applet is the primary tool for managing these accounts.
- You must log on as an Administrator to see all the local user accounts on your computer.

- User Account Control (UAC) has been improved in Windows 7 with fewer events that trigger UAC prompts.
- As with previous versions, Windows 7 supports the use of permissions on local NTFS volumes, as well as folder encryption.
- Each folder and file on an NTFS volume has a set of security permissions, Access Control Entries (ACEs), stored in an Access Control List (ACL). These permissions are inherited through the folder hierarchy.
- BitLocker Drive Encryption in Windows Vista can only encrypt the boot volume (the volume on which Windows resides). In Windows 7, it can encrypt other disk volumes, as well as external disks. This last feature is called BitLocker To Go.
- Windows Defender is a built-in antispam utility. Microsoft Security Essentials (MSE) is a broader antimalware program that is free from Microsoft. Windows Firewall is a personal firewall that comes with Windows.

Key Terms List

Access Control Entry (ACE) *(153)*

Access Control List (ACL) *(153)*

Action Center *(133)*

activation *(119)*

Add Printer wizard *(143)*

Aero Peek *(129)*

Aero Shake *(129)*

Aero Snap *(129)*

AppLocker *(135)*

BitLocker *(135)*

BitLocker To Go *(135)*

clean installation *(118)*

dual-boot *(118)*

FAT file systems *(134)*

Flip 3D *(128)*

gadget *(141)*

image *(119)*

Jump List *(129)*

library *(133)*

Live File System *(148)*

local security *(150)*

Mastered *(148)*

master file table (MFT) *(134)*

Microsoft Product Activation (MPA) *(119)*

Microsoft Security Essentials (MSE) *(125)*

multiboot *(118)*

personal folders *(145)*

pinning *(129)*

Program Compatibility Troubleshooter *(135)*

restore point *(136)*

shortcut *(128)*

Startup Repair *(136)*

System Image Recovery *(136)*

System Restore *(136)*

Task Manager *(136)*

upgrade *(118)*

Windows Aero *(128)*

Windows Defender *(135)*

Windows Easy Transfer (WET) *(120)*

Windows Explorer *(146)*

Windows Memory Diagnostic Tool *(137)*

Windows Preinstallation Environment (Windows PE) *(121)*

Windows Update *(120)*

Key Terms Quiz

Use the Key Terms List to complete the sentences that follow:

1. To preserve your installed programs and settings in place, install a new version of Windows as a/an _____.

2. Each file or folder on an NTFS volume has a/an _____ associated with it, containing security permissions.

3. _____ is a feature that lets you switch through your open windows as if they were a stack of cards or photos.

4. A/an _____ folder contains pointers to multiple locations on your computer and network, displaying the contents as if they were all stored in a single location.

5. _____ is a scaled-down Windows operating system that supports the Windows setup GUI.

6. The _____ feature allows you to temporarily make all open windows transparent when you hover your mouse over the Show Desktop button.

7. A/an _____ is a snapshot of Windows, its configuration, and all installed programs.

8. _____ is a Windows tool that has been greatly improved from version to version; it allows you to see the state of individual processes and programs running on a computer, and to stop programs, if needed.

9. _____ is a new feature in Windows 7 that allows you to encrypt a removable drive.

10. When you right-click on a program shortcut on the Windows 7 Start menu or taskbar, a _____ displays containing recently opened items and items you may have pinned there.

Multiple-Choice Quiz

1. What *retail* edition of Windows 7 includes BitLocker?
   a. Enterprise
   b. Home Basic
   c. Home Premium
   d. Professional
   e. Ultimate

2. What is the name for the desktop feature in Windows 7 that allows you to quickly minimize all but the current window with a simple mouse movement?
   a. Aero Snap
   b. Flip 3D
   c. Aero Shake
   d. AppLocker
   e. UAC

3. This Windows 7 feature requires a video card that supports (at minimum) DirectX 9.0 and Shader Model 2.0.
   a. BitLocker
   b. Windows Aero
   c. Instant Search
   d. Windows Defender
   e. Windows XP Mode

4. What alternative term correctly describes an upgrade of an operating system?
   a. Clean installation
   b. In-place installation
   c. Multiboot
   d. Optional installation
   e. Managed installation

5. After you complete a multiboot installation, you will see this special menu at every restart.
   a. Select OS
   b. F8
   c. System
   d. Windows Boot Manager
   e. Computer Management

6. You have Windows Vista Ultimate edition and want to upgrade to Windows 7. Which of the following editions would you select for an in-place installation of Windows 7?
   a. Ultimate
   b. Home Premium
   c. Home Basic
   d. Enterprise
   e. Business

7. What installation type should you choose in Windows setup if you want to do either a multiboot or clean installation?
   a. Upgrade
   b. Custom
   c. Dual-boot
   d. In-place
   e. Advanced

8. The Disk Management node exists in this console utility.
   a. Administrative Tools
   b. Control Panel
   c. Windows Explorer
   d. Computer Management
   e. System and Security

9. If you are setting up a multimonitor system, which Display option will let you put different windows and other objects on each multiple display, giving you more work space?
   a. Landscape
   b. Extend these displays
   c. Show desktop only on 1
   d. Duplicate these displays
   e. The recommended resolution

10. What feature of Windows is represented in the taskbar notification area by a small flag icon?
    a. AppLocker
    b. System Restore
    c. Action Center
    d. Task Manager
    e. BitLocker

11. What new feature of Windows 7 appears to be something it isn't, but allows you to organize and work with data from various locations as if they were together in one place?
    a. Windows Aero
    b. BitLocker To Go
    c. Library
    d. Notification Area
    e. Instant Search

12. What all-powerful user account built into Windows is disabled by default?
    a. Administrator
    b. Standard
    c. Local
    d. Guest
    e. Parental

13. During Windows setup one account is created for the user of that computer, and you provide a name and password for it. What type of account is this?
    a. Standard
    b. Administrator
    c. Parental
    d. Local
    e. Guest

14. What is the term used in the Windows Firewall Control Panel in Windows 7 to refer to Wi-Fi networks at coffee shops and other retail locations?
    a. Private networks
    b. Work networks
    c. Home networks
    d. Public networks
    e. Internetworks

15. What antispyware program comes bundled with Windows 7?
    a. Microsoft Security Essentials
    b. UAC
    c. BitLocker
    d. BitLocker To Go
    e. Windows Defender

Essay Quiz

1. Describe Flip 3D, including what it does and how to use it.

2. Your Windows XP computer is more than adequate for Windows 7. You would like to do a clean installation of Windows 7, discarding your old Windows XP installation, but you researched the hardware and software and you found that while all the hardware is compatible, one critical old application is incompatible and will not run in Windows 7. What is your best option for continuing to use this old application on a Windows 7 computer until you find a compatible replacement? Describe both the best solution and one other option, including the type of installation of Windows 7 required for each, and any other requirements beyond the minimums.

3. Windows setup now includes updating Windows. Does the inclusion of this step mean that you will not have to update immediately after installing Windows? Your answer must be more than a yes or no. Include why your answer is true.

4. A technician added a second display to your Windows 7 PC. After you log in the first time using the dual displays, you notice that the taskbar is on the right display. You prefer it on the left. Describe the steps you would take to place the taskbar on the left display.

5. Describe how UAC works to protect your computer from malware.

Lab Projects

LAB PROJECT 4.1

Using a computer with Windows 7 installed, open an app, pin the app to the taskbar, and repeat this for the three or four apps you use the most. Close all the apps, and then open each again from the pinned shortcut on the taskbar. Open two or more files in each app so that the file names appear on the Jump List for each app. Write a few sentences about how this did or didn't work for you compared to launching these apps from the Start menu.

LAB PROJECT 4.2

How successful is Windows 7? What is the latest information on the global operating system market share for Windows 7? Is Windows 7 more successful or less successful than Windows XP? How has Windows 10 affected the use of Windows 7? Research the answers to these questions and write about your findings.

LAB PROJECT 4.3

Use the Internet to research the conditions under which you read a flash drive on a Windows XP PC after the flash drive has been encrypted with Bit-Locker To Go on a Windows 7 computer, then test it: Prepare the flash drive as necessary. Copy data onto the flash drive. Then use BitLocker To Go to encrypt the drive, using the option to create a password (be sure to remember the password). Then take the flash drive to a Windows XP computer and insert the drive. Are you prompted to supply a password? Are you able to access the data on the drive? Describe how you prepared the flash drive and the results.

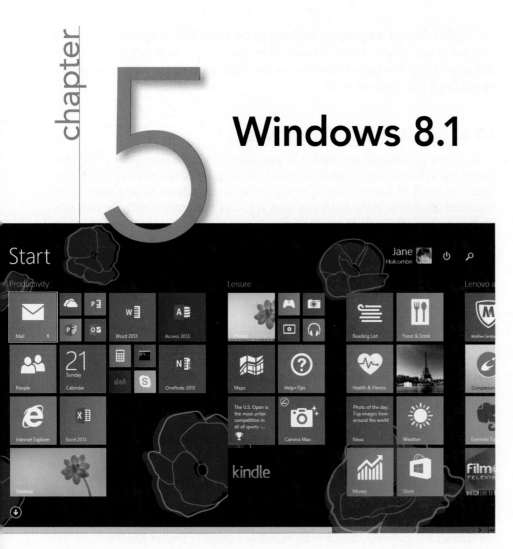

chapter

5 Windows 8.1

W ith Windows 8, Microsoft standardized the look of Windows across all types of devices from PCs to tablets. Introduced in 2012, Windows 8 came with a multitouch-enabled GUI modeled on the Metro interface of the Windows 7 Phone OS that preceded it. Windows Phone 8 is a separate operating system for smartphones with the Metro GUI. Windows 8 also included an updated desktop GUI that resembled Windows 7 without the Start menu. This is where the old-style Windows apps run.

Microsoft does not officially use the term "Metro" to describe the Windows 8 GUI. At first they used the term "Modern UI," or simply "Modern" to describe the GUI, and "Modern apps" to describe the applications designed to run in this GUI. Later, they called the apps that run in the new GUI "Windows Store Apps." For clarity, in this chapter we use the term "Modern" to refer to the new Windows 8 GUI, and "Desktop" to refer to the updated desktop GUI.

In 2013, Microsoft released Windows 8.1 in response to user dissatisfaction with the Modern GUI on traditional PCs. Then, in 2014, they released Windows 8.1 Update 1 with more improvements. This chapter uses the term "Windows 8.1" to describe Windows 8 as it is today with the most current updates at the time of writing. The majority of the screenshots were made using Windows 8.1 Update 1 on PCs, laptops, and tablets. When there was no change in a screen, we used images from the previous edition of this text.

In this chapter we practice working in the two GUIs of Windows 8.1. This chapter is not all you need to know to be productive in Windows 8.1, but it is a beginning. We hope to set you on the right path to learning more about Windows 8.1 on your own. ✺

LO 5.1 | Installing Windows 8.1

Before you can install any new OS you need to make sure your computer meets the system requirements. If you wish to upgrade from an older version, you will need to know what upgrade paths are available to you and determine ahead of time if the hardware and apps are compatible with the new OS. In this section, we will begin with the system requirements, followed by an explanation of the retail editions of Windows 8.1 and upgrade paths, then explore the tasks required to prepare for and install Windows 8.1. Finally, we do the common postinstallation tasks.

System Requirements

The minimum hardware requirements to install Windows 8.1 on an Intel/AMD architecture computer are nearly identical to those of Windows 7, with the exception of a minimum screen resolution. However, you will want much more RAM and more disk space than the minimum described if you plan to install many programs and store data locally. Today, even budget-level computers come with faster processors, much more RAM, very large hard drives, and great video adapters and displays, which seems to make the requirements irrelevant. But just for the record, the minimums are:

- 1 GHz or faster processor.
- 1 GB RAM (32-bit) or 2 GB RAM (64-bit).
- 16 GB available hard disk space (32-bit) or 20 GB (64-bit).
- DirectX 9 graphics device with Windows Display Driver Model (WDDM) driver.
- 1,024 × 768 minimum screen resolution (1,366 × 768 recommended).
- Broadband Internet connection for synchronizing settings and files from one Windows 8 PC to another.

Further, a multitouch-capable display, touchpad, or touch mouse is required if you wish to take advantage of Windows 8.1's multitouch support. A multitouch-capable screen or other device allows Windows 8.1 to interpret many simultaneous touch points. Multitouch hardware certified by Microsoft as Designed for Windows 8 must support a minimum of five simultaneous touches. Look for this on tablets, laptops, displays screens, touchpads, and devices similar to the Microsoft Touch Mouse.

Windows 8 and 8.1 Editions

In 2012, Microsoft introduced Windows 8 with three retail editions: Windows RT (which came preinstalled on ARM-based tablets), Windows 8, and Windows 8 Pro. They also offered the Windows 8 Starter edition, available only in emerging markets, and Windows 8 Enterprise, available to large corporate customers through Microsoft's Windows Software Assurance volume licensing program. The updated Windows RT 8.1 edition is only available preinstalled on tablets based on the ARM architecture or as an upgrade to an installation of Windows RT. The RT editions have had limited success, so we will not discuss these editions here, limiting our coverage to the

Windows 8.1 retail editions that run on traditional PCs and laptops as well as on tablets that conform to the Intel/AMD architecture. Those editions are Windows 8.1, Windows 8.1 Pro, and Windows 8.1 Pro for Students. The student edition sells for a discount and requires verification of student status prior to purchase.

The edition simply called Windows 8.1 is comparable to Windows 7 Home or Home Premium, containing the features that typical home users need on a PC, laptop, or tablet with a single CPU. This edition does not have certain advanced features, such as BitLocker and BitLocker to Go, Client Hyper-V, and Encrypting File System. This edition does include the Remote Desktop client, allowing the user to connect to a computer that has the Remote Desktop host turned on and work in the remote computer's desktop. Windows 8.1 cannot host this type of connection.

Windows 8.1 Pro has all the features included in Windows 8.1 as well as other features, such as the ability to host a Remote Desktop connection. It also includes features required to participate in a Windows Server network in an organization. We will look more closely at the features in Windows 8.1 Pro later in this chapter.

Upgrade Paths

The upgrade paths depend on the edition. For instance, Windows RT comes on certain tablets, and supports entirely different hardware architecture than was supported by previous versions of Windows. As such, you cannot upgrade to Windows RT from any previous version of Windows, so the upgrade paths are only available for the Intel/AMD computer architecture. If you have a PC or laptop with Windows 7, you may have a direct upgrade path. You can upgrade to Windows 8 and Windows 8 Pro from certain editions of Windows 7, as Table 5–1 shows.

Note: You can upgrade Windows 7 using either an upgrade version or a full version of Windows 8.

Preparing to Install Windows 8.1

With the advent of Windows 10, we do not expect a lot of interest in installing Windows 8.1, but we have been wrong before. We can think of scenarios in which we might find ourselves needing to do this, such as when a client needs their installed operating system reinstalled to remedy some problem, and the installed OS is Windows 8.1. We also continue to maintain a variety of OSs on our lab computers for testing and comparison. At any rate, in this section we present possible preparations for installing Windows 8.1 no matter your motivation to do so.

Activating a Retail Product

Before installing Windows 8.1, understand the new rule concerning activation of a retail edition. Activation is no longer something you can delay for 30 days. It occurs early in the installation process and requires the product

TABLE 5–1 Upgrade Paths to Windows 8.1 and Windows 8.1 Pro.

Upgrade from Windows 7 Edition	Upgrade to Windows 8.1	Upgrade to Windows 8.1 Pro
Starter	✓	✓
Home Basic	✓	✓
Home Premium	✓	✓
Professional		✓
Ultimate		✓

FIGURE 5–1 If you purchased the packaged Windows 8.1 discs, look for a card containing the product key.

key. If you purchase the Windows 8.1 retail package (either edition) with discs, the product key will be on a small card in the packaging, as shown in Figure 5–1. When you purchase Windows 8.1 as a download, you will also receive a product key, which you should save. You must manually enter this product key when you install the purchased software from disc or from the download file. The product key only works with one instance of the Windows 8.1 product. If you use the Windows 8.1 Web-based Installer, the product key will be entered automatically.

Purchasing Online from Microsoft

If you plan to purchase Windows 8 online from the Windows Store, you will need a Microsoft account, previously called a Windows Live ID. A Microsoft account (MSA) is simply an account with Microsoft that gives you access to Microsoft services, such as Hotmail, Messenger, OneDrive, Windows Phone, Xbox LIVE, and Outlook.com. A Microsoft account is free, as are many of the services. Fees apply when you upgrade services, such as increasing your maximum storage on OneDrive.

How Will You Sign In to Windows 8.1

You can sign in to Windows 8.1 with a local account that only exists on the Windows 8.1 computer, a Microsoft account, or a Windows Active Directory account if your computer is a member of a Windows Active Directory domain at work or school. Learn more about these accounts next.

Signing In with a Local Account. When you install Windows it creates a local account, but you can sign in using either that local account or a Microsoft account. If you use a local account, you will need to sign in separately to any Microsoft services. Figure 5–2 shows a Sign-in screen for a local account. This account has not yet been customized with a picture, which you can do after you install Windows 8.1.

Note: If you do not enter a password when you create a local account, sign in will not require a password, and the Sign-in screen will not show the password box. We strongly recommend that you create a password for your local account unless you are the only person with physical access to your computer.

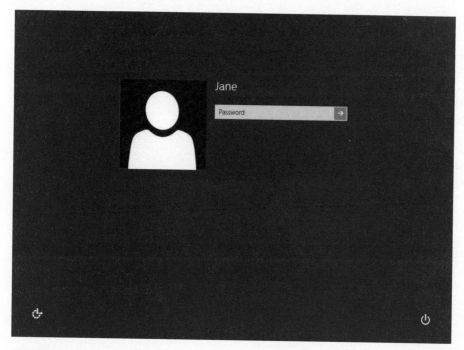

FIGURE 5–2 The initial Sign-in screen for a local account.

Signing In with a Microsoft Account. We prefer to use the Microsoft Account sign-in. If you use a Microsoft account, the Sign-in screen will display the name and the email address associated with your Microsoft account. The one sign-in gives you access to the local computer as well as to your Microsoft services. Then you can access all your data across other devices and services, and you can synchronize your settings on other Windows 8.1 computers that use the same sign-in.

Presently, you can acquire a Microsoft account by pointing your browser to live.com. You can also wait and create a Microsoft account during Windows 8.1 installation if you choose to configure Windows 8.1 with a Microsoft account sign-in. You will need an email address (any legitimate email address) and a password that you are not using for any other account. Select a password for use with the Microsoft account only. A Microsoft account is required for some Modern apps, such as Calendar, Mail, Messaging, and People, as well as Xbox Music, Xbox Video, and Xbox LIVE Games.

> *Note:* Microsoft now uses the term "sign in" rather than "log in" or "log on." These terms are interchangeable.

Signing In with a Domain Account. If your computer is running Windows 8.1 Pro or Windows 8.1 Enterprise, it includes the Domain Join feature that allows a Windows computer to join a Microsoft Active Directory Domain (based on Windows Server), and you will be required to sign in using a domain user account. In this case, you may not be involved in the installation or selection of the account at all but have a fully configured computer delivered to your desk. Alternatively (and there are several alternatives), the computer will show up on your desk, and the first time you turn it on you will go through the last portion of the installation (described later as the "Out of Box Experience"). You will then enter your domain credentials, as instructed by a domain administrator, and log in to both Windows 8.1 and the Active Directory Domain.

Running Upgrade Assistant before Purchasing Windows 8.1

Whether you plan to use the Web-based Installer or the more traditional Windows 8.1 setup from DVD, you can connect to the Microsoft website and run Upgrade Assistant, as described in Step-by-Step 5.01. This will prepare you for the changes you may need to make due to hardware or software incompatibility. You may need to find updated device drivers.

Step-by-Step 5.01

Check Out Compatibility before Upgrading

If you have access to a PC running Windows 7, connect to the Microsoft Windows website and run the Windows 8.1 Upgrade Assistant.

This exercise only works as shown from within Windows 7. The screens in Step 1 will differ depending on the browser you are using. To complete this exercise you will need the following:

- A computer running Windows 7.
- A Microsoft account.
- A broadband Internet connection.

Step 1

Open a browser. Using a search engine such as Bing or Google, search for "upgrade assistant Windows 7 to Windows 8.1." In the results, select the result that says "Upgrade Assistant FAQ" and points to Microsoft.com. This should open the Upgrade Assistant: FAQ page. Click Download Windows 8.1 Upgrade Assistant.

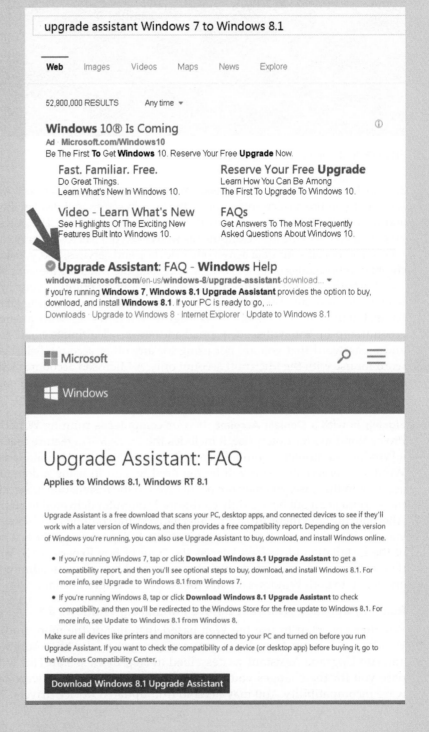

Click Save File. Then locate the file in the Downloads folder and launch it.

If the Open Executable File message appears, click OK. In the Open File box Click Run.

Step 4

The download will begin with a quick security scan. Respond to the User Account Control message; there may be a brief delay before the scan begins. The scan will take a few minutes, during which this page displays.

Step 5

When the scan is complete, you will see this screen with a statement summarizing the number of compatible devices and apps and a note concerning the items about which you will need to make a decision.

At this point, if you wish to see the details (recommended), select the link labeled "See compatibility details."

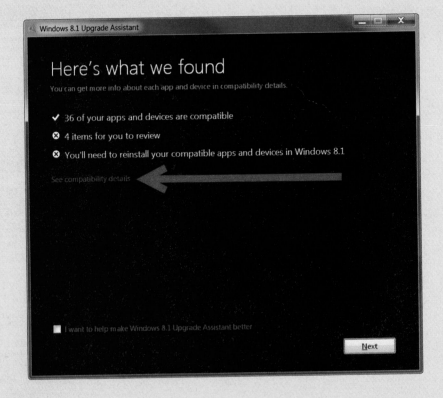

The compatibility report displays. You will have different results from those shown here. If you want a printed copy of this report select the Print button (at bottom), and if you wish to save the report in HTML format, click Save. You can do both. Also notice the link under each item. Click one of these to learn more about a compatibility issue. When done reviewing the compatibility details, click the Close button to return to the Upgrade Assistant.

Close the window to exit when you are finished.

If, after running the Upgrade advisor, you close the Compatibility Details window and click Next in the Windows 8 Upgrade Assistant, it opens a page that initiates a migration tool, shown in Figure 5–3. When we ran this on a Windows 7 Ultimate computer, we chose the first item, indicating that we wanted to keep Windows settings, personal files, and compatible apps. It then recommended an upgrade to Windows 8.1 Pro. If you chose the first item, but your apps are not compatible, the next message will state, "No compatible offers are available." When we chose just personal files or nothing, the Upgrade Assistant recommended either Windows 8.1 Pro or Windows 8.1.

The page shown in Figure 5–3 displayed when we chose "Just personal files" or "Nothing." If you select either "order" button, it will continue to the Review Your Order page, shown in Figure 5–4. On the page shown in Figure 5–5, you can choose just the download option or add an order for the DVD for an additional cost. If you proceed, you will go to the Checkout page. You can also change your mind at this point by clicking the Back button and then clicking the Close button on the previous page.

Acquiring Updated Drivers for Hardware

One of the incompatibilities you may discover using the Upgrade Assistant is that Windows 8.1 does not have drivers for some of your hardware, so you

Note: At this writing the Windows 8.1 Pro Student Edition is about one-third the cost of Windows 8.1 Pro.

FIGURE 5–3 Select what you want to keep when you upgrade.

FIGURE 5–4 You can order Windows 8.1 through the Upgrade Assistant.

may need to contact the manufacturer of your computer or of the specific incompatible component. You can usually do this on their website, and, if they have a new driver, download it ahead of time and have it available on a disc or USB drive. This is especially important if the Upgrade Assistant reported an

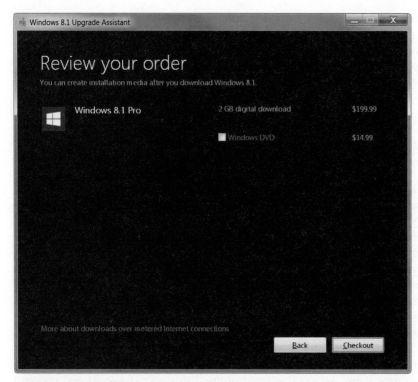

FIGURE 5–5 In addition to the download, you can order the Windows 8.1 Pro DVD.

incompatibility with the network interface card (NIC) because it is critical that you have the correct NIC driver installed.

If no updated driver is available for a component reported as incompatible, you may still want to wait until after installing Windows 8.1 to discover if a generic driver from Windows 8 takes care of the problem. Be prepared to replace any component that becomes unusable after the update.

The Installation

You can purchase Windows 8.1 as a download from the Windows Store, from other online retailers, or at a brick-and-mortar store. If purchasing online to upgrade from Windows 7, you can either do a Web-based install or a more conventional Windows setup install.

Web-Based Setup

If you purchase Windows 8.1 online, you have the option of doing a Web-based setup, using the Web-based Installer, which is quick and combines the more traditional Windows setup program with the features of the Windows Upgrade Advisor and the Windows 7 settings and data migration tools described in Chapter 4, which were separate from Windows 7 setup. Web-based setup requires very little interaction and is very fast. If downloading, follow the on-screen instructions to install it.

Although you will not need to enter the product key manually during a Web-based installation, you should still store the key in a safe place just in case you reinstall Windows 8.1 or need to reactivate your installation.

Traditional Windows Setup

Windows setup is the traditional program for installing and upgrading Windows. To install Windows 8.1 using this program, you must have the Windows 8.1 setup files on bootable media.

Note: If the computer fails to boot from either a USB or DVD drive, change the boot order setting in the computer's system settings. The actual steps for doing this vary by manufacturer. For instructions, do an online search using your computer model name and the key words "boot order."

WARNING!

Even if you do a Web-based install, be sure to record the product key and keep it in a safe place.

Acquiring Bootable Media. If you purchase the retail package you will have boot media in the form of DVDs. Use the appropriate disc (32-bit or 64-bit) for your computer.

If you purchase Windows 8.1 online and choose the option *Install later by creating Media,* you have the options to download to a USB drive or to an ISO file. If you install it to a USB drive, it creates a bootable USB setup drive.

If you choose ISO, it will download a bootable ISO image, a file containing a copy of the entire contents of a disc. After downloading it to a Windows 7 computer, simply double-click the file and the Windows Disc Image Burner dialog will display. Click Burn and it will create the disc.

Beginning Windows Setup. Once you have the media, you can either boot your computer from it (clean install) or if upgrading, simply insert the media into your Windows 7 computer after signing in. If it does not automatically run setup, browse to the disc in Windows Explorer and double-click the Setup file.

Windows 8.1 setup closely resembles the Windows 7 setup described in Step-by-Step 4.01 in Chapter 4. One important change is that you must enter the product key and activate Windows 8 during installation. You no longer have the 30-day grace period to activate that was possible with previous versions. The page for doing this, shown in Figure 5–6, appears very early, whereas in Windows 7 setup this page is near the end of Windows setup. Notice that you must enter the product key to continue.

After you enter the correct product key and click Next, you proceed to the License terms page. Accept the terms of the licensing agreement and proceed to the page where you select the type of installation, Upgrade or Custom, followed by other pages similar to those in Windows 7 setup. Setup will copy files and reboot. This type of restart, in which the operating system is restarted without a hardware power-down–power-up cycle, is called a warm boot.

We call the action of bringing a computer and operating system up from a no-power state by turning on the power switch, a cold boot. The restarts performed during setup are warm boots.

After a reboot, the Out of Box Experience begins, as described next.

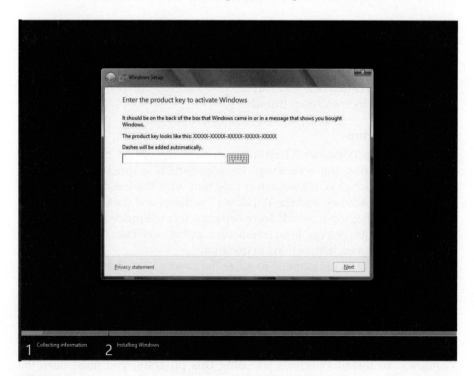

FIGURE 5–6 You must enter the product key before Windows setup will proceed.

The Out of Box Experience

Both the traditional Windows setup and the Web-based Installer end with the Out of Box Experience (OOBE) in which you customize your installation. The Out of Box Experience (OOBE) gets its name from the fact that when you buy a new computer with Windows 8.1 preinstalled, and you take it out of the box and turn it on, you will be greeted with this last phase of Windows installation where you personalize the GUI and configure how you will sign in.

Personalize Windows 8.1. The Personalize page (Figure 5–7) signals the beginning of the OOBE. This is where you can select the color for the screen and name the PC. The Settings page, shown in Figure 5–8, follows the Personalize page. We recommend reviewing the bulleted list of settings, and if these will work for you, click the "Use express settings" button. If you want different settings click Customize.

Selecting How to Sign In. Next, choose the type of account you will use to sign in. While you must make a decision during setup, you can change your choice any time after setup. The Sign-in screen, shown in Figure 5–9, offers a choice between a Microsoft account and a new account. If you have a Microsoft account and wish to use it, enter the email address and password and click Next. Windows setup will create a local administrator type of account and associate it with your Microsoft account. If you do not have a Microsoft account and want to create one, select the link shown in Figure 5–9 labeled *Create a new account,* indicated by an arrow. Enter the required information on the next page (Figure 5–10).

When you sign in with a Microsoft account you enter your Microsoft account credentials (email address and password). In a sense you have a dual identity, giving you access to your local computer and to your Microsoft

> *Note:* If your computer is offline (not connected to the Internet) during installation, OOBE will not display the option of using a Microsoft account. If that is the case, and you want to use the Microsoft account sign in, you can do it after-the-fact when you can connect the computer to the Internet. At that time, open the Users panel in the PC Settings screen (PC Settings is discussed later in this chapter) and select *Switch to a Microsoft account.*

> *Note:* If you have enabled two-step verification for signing in with your Microsoft account, you will need to first enter your email address and password, and then enter a one-time security code that is immediately sent to you by email, text, or phone call. Enable or disable two-step verification online in your Microsoft account settings.

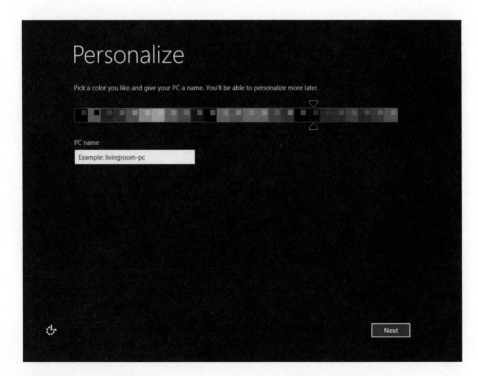

FIGURE 5–7 The Personalize page marks the beginning of the Out of Box Experience (OOBE).

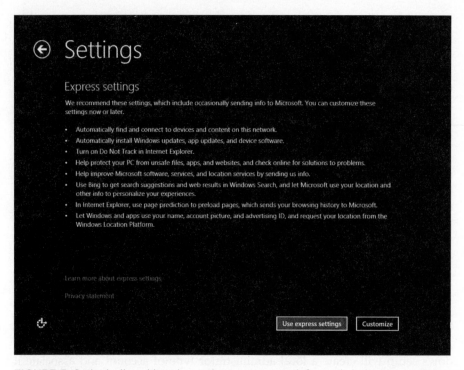

FIGURE 5–8 The bulleted list shows the settings used if you click the *Use express settings* button.

services. If you use this same account on multiple Windows 8 computers, you can choose to synchronize your data and settings.

If you do not want to use a Microsoft account for this installation, click the link labeled *Create a new account,* indicated by the arrow in Figure 5–9. When you choose that option, setup displays the page shown in

FIGURE 5–9 To create a new Microsoft account, choose the link labeled *Create a new account.*

FIGURE 5–10 Complete this page to create a new Microsoft account. If you want to create a local account, click *Sign in without a Microsoft account*.

Figure 5–10. Select the link labeled Sign in without a Microsoft account. This opens the page, shown in Figure 5–11, where you type in a user name and password (twice), as well as a password hint for the new account. If this is an upgrade from Windows 7, you will have a *Skip* button in addition to the *Finish* button. Selecting Skip tells setup to use your old local account.

Several more pages will display while Windows setup finishes configuring your installation and installs the default apps into Windows 8. Finally, the

Sign in to your PC

If you want a password, choose something that will be easy for you to remember but hard for others to guess.

User name	Yoda
Password	••••••
Reenter password	•••••••
Password hint	✕

Finish

FIGURE 5–11 Enter a user name and password (twice), as well as a password hint.

FIGURE 5–12 The Windows 8.1 Start screen.

Start screen displays, as Figure 5–12 shows. This is your home base and launching pad. Whenever you want to return to the Start screen, either swipe in from the right side of the screen to open the Charms bar and select the Start charm, press the ⊞ key on the bottom left on your keyboard, or touch or click the Start button at the bottom left of the Desktop screen. The Start button is also available from the Start screen: simply move your mouse cursor to the bottom left corner and the Start button displays.

Note: The ⊞ key returns you to the Start screen from anywhere in Windows 8.1. On a touch screen swipe in from the right edge and tap Start.

LO 5.2 | Postinstallation Tasks

You will need to do some tasks immediately after installing Windows 8.1. In previous versions of Windows we would have recommended you install security software at this point, but Windows 8.1 comes with a new and improved Windows Defender. It includes antivirus and antispyware. We will look at Windows Defender later in this chapter. Your postinstallation tasks should include installing drivers, if necessary, and running Windows Update.

Installing Drivers

If setup detected a device that would not work with one of the available drivers, you may have been prompted to provide the driver files. Setup may have simply installed a generic driver that works with a device but doesn't take advantage of all its features. Or you may have a noncritical device that simply does not work after Windows 8.1 is installed. Therefore, one postinstallation task is to install updated drivers. You have some choices for this which we will explore next.

Use Updated Drivers from Manufacturers

Note: Virtually all displays in use are flat panels as opposed to the old bulky CRT displays. A flat-panel display, which uses some variation of LCD or LED technologies, has just one physical resolution, and Microsoft shows that as the Recommended resolution in Screen Resolution.

If you were prepared to install new drivers during setup but did not have an opportunity to install them, then immediately after setup check for problems with the installed drivers in the form of error messages or a component not functioning properly. If you see such symptoms, install the drivers you prepared ahead of time. In most cases, when manufacturers supply a compatible driver, it comes as an executable. If you have the driver file on an external device, open File Explorer (the new name for the updated version of the Windows file management tool, Windows Explorer), locate the file, and double-click it to run the driver setup.

Check Display Driver

If the display does not seem to be functioning properly, check to see if the correct video driver was installed by looking at the Screen Resolution setting. To do that, from the Start screen click or tap the Desktop tile. This opens the Windows Desktop where you right-click to open the context menu, shown here. On a touch screen press on an empty area of the Desktop and hold until a small square appears, as shown in Figure 5–13, then immediately release. When the context menu (shown in Figure 5–14) displays select *Screen resolution*.

In the Screen Resolution dialog the resolution on a flat-panel display should be at the maximum resolution of the display. To confirm this, the resolution should have the word "Recommended" in parentheses, as shown in Figure 5–15 where the resolution is 1,366 × 768. If your setting is something other than the recommended, look for a compatible driver. Notice that Figure 5–15 has a check box for a setting: Allow the screen to auto-rotate. This is on a tablet with a detachable keyboard. When the keyboard is attached we don't want the screen to rotate.

One way to give Windows 8.1 a chance to automatically resolve any remaining driver problems is to run Windows Update, which we explain next.

Installing Updates

Although Windows installation includes some updating of the Windows code, and Windows 8.1 is configured for automatic updates by default, you should manually trigger updates soon after the installation because it can take several days for Windows Update to bring your installation completely up to date.

Windows Update will download and install updates it categorizes as "important." These are mostly security updates and updates to critical Windows components. However, you should also check out other updates available through Windows Update. Additionally, we recommend configuring Windows Update to update all your installed Microsoft software, not just Windows components.

Windows Update comes in a Modern version as well as a Desktop version nearly identical to that in Windows 7. Step-by-Step 5.02 walks through the steps for using Windows Update, showing how you may work in both versions. In the process, you will learn about the Windows 8.1 PC Settings panels, use Windows Update to download and install both important and optional updates, and learn how to configure Windows Update to update other Microsoft software.

FIGURE 5–13 On a touch screen, touch an empty area of the Desktop and hold until a small square appears, then release to display the context menu.

Note: Windows Update categorizes driver updates as "optional updates." Step-by-Step 5.02 gives an example of this.

FIGURE 5–14 Select Screen resolution from the Desktop context menu.

FIGURE 5–15 The resolution should be set at the Recommended resolution for the display.

Step-by-Step 5.02

Using and Configuring Windows Update

Windows Update in Windows 8.1 comes in both the Modern GUI and the traditional Control Panel GUI. Sometimes while working in the Modern GUI you will make a choice that opens the Desktop GUI. This exercise will help you to work with Windows Update in both GUIs.

- A computer running Windows 8.1 or Windows 8.1 Pro.
- You should sign in with an administrator account or have the user name and password of an administrator account for the computer.
- A broadbrand Internet connection.
- At least a 4 GB of free disk space.

Step 1

To run the Modern version of Windows Update you will need to first open the Windows 8.1 Settings bar. You can do this with a swipe from the right edge of the screen to open the Charms bar, shown here, which contains small graphic objects called charms. A charm acts as a shortcut to important systemwide tasks.

Step 2

Select the *Settings charm* to open the Settings bar. Or go directly to the Settings bar with the ⊞+I keyboard shortcut. The Settings bar slides out along the right side of the screen in both the Desktop and the Start screen. Click or tap *Change PC settings* at the bottom of the Settings bar.

The PC Settings screen contains several panels for configuring some Windows 8.1 settings. Scroll to the bottom of the list and select *Update & Recovery*. The Update and Recovery page displays. Assuming you do this immediately after installing Windows 8.1, the update information is current. However, click *Check now* to see what happens. Often additional updates are ready.

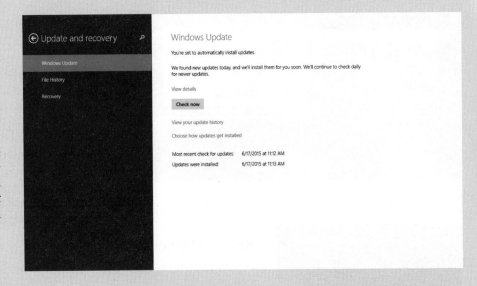

If Windows Update finds updates for your computer, it will display them in a list. If so, click the Install button and respond to any dialog boxes for User Account Control, license agreements, and to restart the computer. If your computer restarts, sign in and return to the Updates and Recovery page. Move on to the next step.

To configure Windows Update to include both Windows components and other Microsoft programs, select the *Choose how updates get installed* option on the Windows Update page. This opens a page where you can select how important updates, recommended updates, and updates for other Microsoft products (think Microsoft Office) are installed. For most users we recommend the settings shown here.

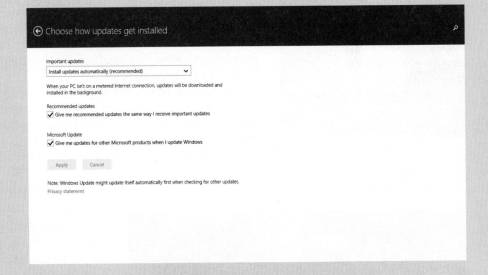

When you are finished, return to the Start screen using one of the following methods. Using a mouse, point the cursor in the lower left corner until the Start button displays, and then click; using a keyboard, press the Windows key; or on a touch screen swipe in from the right edge to open the Charms bar, and then tap the Start charm.

FIGURE 5–16 Installing Guest Additions in VirtualBox.

Virtual Machine Guest Additions

If you installed Windows 8.1 into a virtual machine, an important postinstallation task is to install the software into the virtual machine that will make it run better. The name for this software and how it installs vary by hypervisor. You may have already seen a message pop-up in Windows 8.1 in your virtual machine with instructions. Or look for an option in the hypervisor window surrounding the virtual machine, as we did when we installed Windows 8.1 into VirtualBox on an OS X Mac host, opening the VirtualBox Devices menu, shown in Figure 5–16. We selected the option *Install Guest Additions.*

Remove Unnecessary Software

If you purchase a computer with Windows 8.1 preinstalled, the first time you turn it on you will go through the personalization tasks in the Out of Box Experience, described earlier. When you finally arrive at the Start screen you may discover that the manufacturer installed a security package, along with lots of other software often called bloatware (one of the more civil terms for this software). We have found most of the bloatware to be more like "annoyware." We find it unnecessarily time-consuming to sort out what is useful and what was just installed to convince us to buy something else.

For instance, our touch-screen laptop from a major PC manufacturer came with a 30-day free trial of a security package. Every time we sign in, a reminder pops up asking us to connect and upgrade from the trial to the $60/year package. After a few days, we decided that the $5 savings for the 30 days was not worth being annoyed. We temporarily disabled our Internet connection (from the Start screen open Settings, select Change PC Settings) and removed the trial software. Then we opened Windows Defender (described later in this chapter). It soon became active, guarding against attacks, and when we enabled the Internet connection Windows Defender updated, and began a scan.

To remove bloatware applications, open the Apps screen from the Start screen by swiping up from the bottom or by moving your mouse to the bottom of the screen until a small arrow appears, as shown in Figure 5–17. Click on the arrow to open the Apps screen. Then, right-click on an app you wish to remove (Figure 5–18) and select Uninstall.

FIGURE 5–17 Click the down arrow at the bottom of the screen or swipe up from the bottom on a touch screen.

Create a Backup Image

Most new computers do not ship with installation or recovery discs, so you should look for some program from the manufacturer for creating an image of the factory-installed software in case you need to return the computer to its original state. Locate this software, create backup media, and put it in a safe place.

Alternatively, you can use a Windows 8.1 system image utility. Open the Control Panel and enter File History in the search box. From the File History applet, select the link at the bottom left labeled Create a system image. That will open the dialog box in Figure 5–19, where you can select a location for the image.

FIGURE 5–18 Right-click on an app and select Uninstall.

Turn on File History

Since the most important files on your computer are your data files, you should also plan for data backup. File History is a new and easy way to automatically back up files in your Documents, Music, Pictures, and Videos folders. File History is not turned on by default; if you have a spare external drive connected to your computer or a network location, turn on File History and point to the location. Turn on and configure File History using the File History page under Update and recovery in PC Settings as shown in Figure 5–20 On this page you can turn File History on or off, select a drive, and initiate a backup. File History works automatically, backing up files as you create or change them.

To make more changes, open File History in the Control Panel, shown in Figure 5–21. Here you can turn it on or off and select a location, as you can from the File History page. You can also add backup locations, exclude folders (from those within the default locations), and choose how often to save files and how long to keep saved versions (yes, File History saves versions of files).

FIGURE 5–19 The Windows 8.1 utility for creating a system image.

Shutting Down Windows 8.1

What do you do when you are done working at your computer? Do you press your computer's power button? Do you sign out or shut down from a menu in Windows?

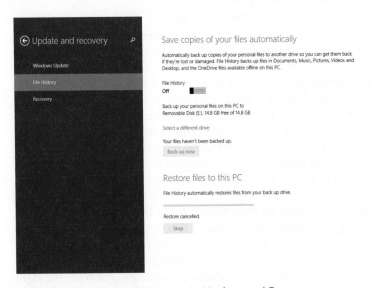

FIGURE 5–20 Open File History in Update and Recovery.

FIGURE 5–21 For more File History settings, open File History in the Control Panel.

Note: To open the Power User menu on a touch system, press and hold your finger on the Start button until a small shaded square appears around the Start button, then quickly release, to open the Power User menu.

If you press the power button, what happens depends on how the Power Options are configured in the Control Panel. On a laptop, pressing the power button will usually put the computer to sleep, saving the current state (all open programs and data files) so that the next time you press this button it will immediately wake up. Consider configuring the power button, through the Power Options, to power down the computer. Then, when you press your computer's power button, Windows will shut down programs, log out the current user, and power off the computer.

We prefer to close all our apps and data and open a menu that includes the option *Shut Down*. This signs out the currently signed in user and turns off the computer. There are several methods for accessing a menu to shut down Windows 8.1.

Using a Keyboard to Quickly Shut Down

A quick method for shutting down Windows 8.1 is to open the Power User menu (▣ + x), and then press u twice. Figure 5–22 shows the Power User menu with the Shutdown or Sign-out menu open. Notice the letter u is underlined in both menus.

Another not-so-quick method is to press CTRL-ALT-DELETE, which opens the CTRL-ALT-DELETE screen. This very plain screen displays four options in the middle: Lock, Switch user, Sign out, and Task Manager. It also has two buttons: the Accessibility button on the left and the Power button on the right. Select the Power button to open the Power menu from which you can select Sleep, Shut down, or Restart. Select Shut down from the Power menu to shut down Windows and power off the computer.

Using a Mouse or Touch to Shut Down from the Power Menu

The Power menu normally opens from a Power charm (or "button"), as shown in Figure 5–23. One way to access the Power menu is to open the Charms bar (shown in step 1 of Step-by-Step 5.02) by moving your mouse from the bottom-right corner of the screen or by swiping in from the right edge. Click the Settings charm to open the Settings Bar, shown earlier in

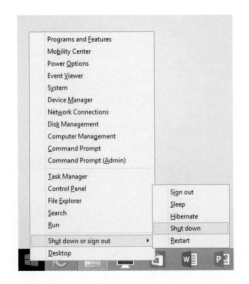

FIGURE 5–22 The Power User menu.

step 2 of Step-by-Step 5.02. Then click or tap the Power charm. This opens a small menu of power states, shown in Figure 5–23. The states available will depend on how your computer is configured. They may include *Sleep, Shut down, Restart* (or the option *Update and Restart* if updates are ready to install), and Hibernate. Hibernate is not a choice by default.

Update 1 for Windows 8.1 added both a Power charm and a Search charm on the upper right of the Start screen *for certain devices*. A PC or laptop will normally have both of these charms (or "buttons"), but the power charm does not appear on tablets. Some sources state that it doesn't appear on devices with touch screens, but one of the authors' laptops has a touch screen and a keyboard that folds under to act as a stand, so that the touch screen is the main input for the user. On this laptop both icons are visible on the Start screen.

FIGURE 5–23 The Power menu options depend on the configuration.

LO 5.3 | Navigating and Configuring Windows 8.1

Customizing and managing Windows 8.1 begins by understanding the two GUIs of Windows 8.1, and learning where you will find the tools for these tasks. If you followed along in the earlier sections of this chapter and did the Step-by-Step exercises, you worked with a few tools in both GUIs, including the PC Settings screen in the Modern GUI. We'll begin with a discussion of this operating system's optimization for working with touch devices, which leads us to the Lock screen and Start screen, features created especially for touch screens. You will learn basics of each of these as well as how to configure them, followed by an overview of the Desktop GUI and an introduction to File Explorer, the updated version of the Windows Explorer file management tool.

A GUI Optimized for Touch Devices

Whereas the mouse is the most common pointing device used on most PCs, the typical laptop has a touchpad integrated into the keyboard area. A touchpad is a pointing device that responds to finger touch gestures; newer touchpads respond to multitouch input. Touchpads also come as separate wireless or USB devices. Similarly, a touch mouse responds to touch gestures on its surface, in addition to the typical mouse gestures.

Whatever device you use, you can use touch gestures anywhere in Windows 8.1, even in the Desktop GUI, but the Windows 8.1 Modern GUI and its apps are optimized for touch devices (especially touch screens) that support multitouch. Multitouch is the ability of a multitouch-enabled screen, mouse, or touchpad to interpret multiple simultaneous touch gestures, such as the pinching gesture (sometimes called zoom out) in which fingers first touch the device at separate locations and then pinch together. The reverse of this gesture (zoom in) also has a special meaning in Windows 8.1, and there are many unique gestures with names, such as tapping, swiping, and panning. Multitouch support has been included with Windows since Windows Vista, but this support is now better integrated into the operating system and enhanced by a GUI designed for multitouch.

The Modern GUI is anchored by a home screen called the **Start screen**, which is shown in Figure 5–24. Notice the circles indicating 10 simultaneous finger touches. To capture this screenshot, we were careful not to touch the screen in a way that would be interpreted as a gesture by the OS. It took four hands: two to press on the screen and two to use the keyboard shortcut, ⊞+PRTSCN, to send a screenshot to the Pictures folder. This works on Windows 8 or Windows 8.1.

Overlapping windows and shortcuts are still available in the Desktop GUI. Missing from the Desktop is the Start menu, supposedly because it is not touch friendly. The first release of Windows 8 also came minus the Start button, but

FIGURE 5–24 The Start screen with circles indicating 10 simultaneous touches.

Microsoft added it back in with the first major update, Windows 8.1. Navigate both the Desktop and Modern GUIs using the more conventional keyboard and mouse.

Corners and Edges

While many touch gestures and mouse actions occur in the main area of the screen, some important mouse actions begin in the corners, while their touch counterparts originate at the edges. We will remind you of this difference as we introduce relevant touch and mouse actions.

Modern/Windows Store Apps

From the Start screen you can launch both Modern apps (also called Windows Store apps) and traditional windowed desktop apps (if they have a tile on the Start screen). When you tap or click the tile for a desktop app, the desktop opens. A Modern app normally runs full screen. In the first release of Windows 8, the exception to this was the use of a simple screen-sharing feature called Snap, which allows two Modern apps or one Modern app and the Desktop to share the screen, side-by-side with a vertical division, but no overlap. The updates to Windows 8 include the ability to do this with up to four areas.

The On-Screen Keyboard

An on-screen keyboard, much like those seen on smartphones, displays when you need to enter alphanumeric characters on a touch-screen device that lacks a hardware keyboard. On a touch-screen device that also has a keyboard, the on-screen keyboard displays when you touch a text box, rather than typing from the keyboard. Figure 5–25 shows the on-screen keyboard open for typing into the Search box, which is contained in the search bar that opens on the right of the screen whenever you start typing at the start screen.

Even though the on-screen keyboard is a necessary feature on devices without a keyboard, it is not entirely new to Windows. It was available in previous versions of Windows as an accessibility option, and you can still use it in that way. You can enable it from the Ease of Access button on the bottom left of

try this!

Open the On-Screen Keyboard from the Start Menu

If you have a physical keyboard but want to use the on-screen keyboard, you can use the method described in the text, or you can open it from the Start screen. Try this:

1. At the Start screen type "on" and the Search bar will open on the right side, along with results on the left.
2. Select the result that says *On-Screen Keyboard*.
3. The on-screen keyboard opens, and you can use it in either GUI.

FIGURE 5–25 On a device with a touch screen, the on-screen keyboard displays when you need to enter alphanumeric data.

FIGURE 5–26 Enable the on-screen keyboard from the Ease of Access menu.

the Sign-in screen. Simply click this button to open the Accessibility Menu, shown in Figure 5–26. When you open this menu, the Narrator will dictate the menu items to you. Select the on-screen keyboard to sign in.

Keyboard Shortcuts

It you are using a mouse and keyboard, you know that this OS is not just for touch devices. It supports most of the keyboard shortcuts included in previous versions, as well as a few new ones. A **keyboard shortcut** is a key and/or key-mouse combination that performs an assigned action, saving you several mouse, keyboard, or touch actions. Throughout this textbook we provide special notes, pointing out some of our favorite keyboard shortcuts. Many of them take advantage of the **Windows key** ⊞ located near the bottom left of most keyboards or as a special physical button on a tablet, the Microsoft Touch Mouse, or Windows Phone device. See Appendix A for a list of keyboard shortcuts.

The Lock Screen

By default, the Lock screen displays under certain conditions including: when you first start up your computer, after a period of inactivity, when you choose Lock from the User tile, or when you use the ⊞+L shortcut. The **Lock screen** is a screen that prevents you from accidentally triggering some action that you did not intend to happen. The classic example is "pocket dialing" someone on a smartphone while the phone is in your pocket. That is not the typical scenario on a touch-screen tablet where you are more likely to accidentally launch a program from the Start screen. To return to Windows from the Lock screen press any key or simply swipe on a touch screen and access the Sign-in screen.

To customize the Lock screen open PC Settings | PC and devices | Lock Screen, shown in Figure 5–27. Select a background (even one of your own photos) or a slide show, and decide what apps can run in background and display status and notifications and what apps can show alarms.

> *Note:* Press ⊞+L to lock your Windows computer before walking away from your desk at work or school. This will keep your current apps and data open, but requires unlocking the screen and signing in (if your computer is configured for a sign in).

The Start Screen

The **Start screen** features include live tiles, charms, Charms bar, Power charm, Settings bar, on-screen keyboard, and the Power User menu. Here we describe selected features of the Start screen.

FIGURE 5–27 The Lock screen settings page.

Start Screen Anatomy

Figure 5–28 shows the anatomy of the Start screen. Notice the various tiles. When Windows 8 was first introduced in Fall 2012 it had only two sizes of tiles on the Start screen—what we now know as Medium and Wide. The Windows 8.1 update added two more sizes: Small and Large. Figure 5–28 includes the four sizes of tiles. The smallest tiles on the screen are Small, the tiles that are approximately four times the size of the Small tiles are Medium, the tiles twice the size of Medium tiles are Wide, and the largest tile shown (Desktop) is an example of Large.

Live Tiles

The Start screen contains rectangular tiles with which you launch apps by the tap of a finger (on touch devices) or the click of a mouse. These tiles replace the old desktop shortcuts and are called live tiles. A live tile can display active content related to the app (if the app supports it) without

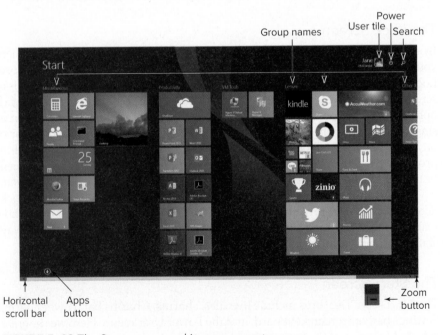

FIGURE 5–28 The Start screen and its components.

requiring you to launch the app. With live tiles, a glance at the Start screen can tell you the local weather, how many new emails you have received, current news headlines, and much more. A few of the tiles in Figure 5–28 show active content. You can choose to disable active content for a tile.

Navigating and Customizing the Start Screen

The horizontal scroll bar appears at the bottom of the Start screen when it contains more tiles than it can display at one time on the screen. Move the bar with your mouse or use a swiping touch motion to look at the additional tiles.

Drag a tile around with your mouse or finger to change its position on the Start screen. Arrange tiles in groups that work for you. Beginning in Windows 8.1 you can name these groups (or not), as shown in Figure 5–28, where we named three groups but did not name the fourth. Drag a tile to the empty space on the far right of the Start screen. Then pause, and a gray vertical bar appears. Release and Windows 8.1 creates a new group. At this point on a touch screen, a gray horizontal box opens above the new group labeled *Name Group*. Enter a name for the group and then tap outside the name box. When using a mouse to name a new group, right-click on the Start screen background and select Name Groups. The horizontal box will open above all groups, allowing you to name or rename any group. If you do not wish to name this group, tap or click anywhere on the background of the Start screen and the boxes will disappear and just the names you have created will appear above groups.

In order to move entire groups around, you must shrink the Start screen tiles on the screen as shown in Figure 5–29. In the bottom right of the Start screen is the Zoom button that you click to shrink the Start screen. On a touch screen use a pinching motion. When the Start screen is zoomed out (reduced in size), you can manipulate the groups of tiles (but not individual tiles). This zoom feature is called semantic zoom, and it also works within apps that support it.

try this!

Zoom the Start Screen

Use the mouse or touch actions to zoom the Start screen and rearrange the tile groups. Try this:

1. From the Start screen, use a pinching action or move the mouse to the bottom-right corner and click the Zoom button.

2. While the Start screen tiles are small, use your mouse or touch actions to rearrange the groups.

3. When you are ready to return the Start screen tiles to full size click or tap on the background.

FIGURE 5–29 Shrink the tiles (zoom out) and drag a group of tiles to rearrange the groups.

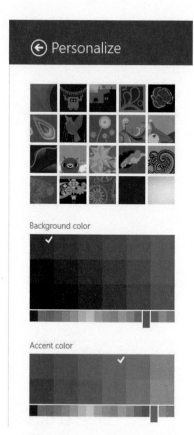

Background color

Accent color

FIGURE 5–31 The Personalize bar in Windows 8.1

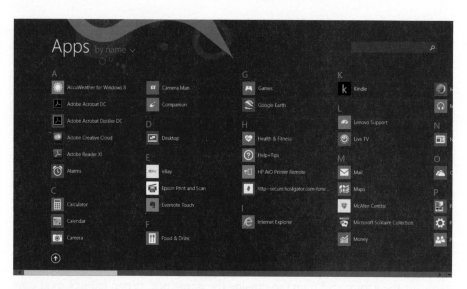

FIGURE 5–30 The Apps screen shows all installed apps.

FIGURE 5–32 The User menu.

Customizing Tiles from the Apps Screen. Beginning in Windows 8.1 an Apps button on the bottom left of the Start screen opens the Apps screen, Figure 5–30, where you can customize app tiles and uninstall apps from your computer.

Changing the Start Screen Background. Previous to Windows 8.1 you would do some Start screen customization from the Personalize page in PC Settings (open Charms bar, select Settings, Change PC Settings). In Windows 8.1 the Settings bar has a Personalize option that opens yet another bar on the right edge, the Personalize bar, shown in Figure 5–31, where you can change the patterns, background color, and accent colors.

Beginning in Windows 8.1 you can configure the same background on the Desktop and the Start screen. Make this change from the Desktop by right-clicking on the Taskbar, selecting Properties, and then in the Taskbar and Navigation properties dialog box, select the Navigation tab. Click to place a check in the box labeled *Show my desktop background on Start*.

Changing the User Tile Picture. On the top right of the Start screen is the User tile displaying your account name and an image. You can choose a custom picture. Click or tap the User tile to open the menu shown in Figure 5–32. From this menu you can Change your account picture, Lock the screen, or Sign Out. The Try This! describes how to change your account picture in Windows 8.1.

try this!

Change Your Account Picture

Would you like to personalize your account picture? You can easily use an existing photo or take a new picture with your computer's camera. Try this:

1. Click or tap the User tile and select *Change account picture*.
2. This opens the Accounts pane in PC Settings. From there you can browse to a location of an existing picture, select the Camera to take a picture, or open the People app to find a picture.
3. Once you select a picture, return to the Personalize pane with your new picture. This will display on the Start screen and on the Sign-in screen.

Moving between Apps

What you cannot see at first glance in both the Start screen and the Windows Desktop is also significant and discoverable, such as screen corners and edges, which make it easier to switch between apps. Mouse gestures activate the corner, and the edges respond to edge gestures, touch motions that begin close to the bezel of the screen.

After opening one or more apps, switch between running apps with a swiping gesture from the left bezel. Each swipe slides out one open app at a time. Repeat, and eventually you will cycle through all running apps. Or, if using a mouse, point it at the top-left corner to display the Back tip in that corner. A Back tip is a thumbnail (a small graphic image representing a larger object) that shows a tiny image, as shown in Figure 5–33. Click the Back tip to display the app on the screen. Repeat to bring previous apps to the screen, one at a time. A shortcoming of using either the swipe gesture or the Back tip to cycle through open apps is that Windows 8 treats the desktop as one app, no matter how many apps are open on the desktop.

But wait! There are even more ways to switch tasks. Press and hold the ALT KEY while tapping the TAB KEY. This opens Windows Flip, a visually flat version of Windows 7's Flip 3D (described in Chapter 4). Windows Flip displays a rectangle across the middle of the screen that shows all running apps, including individual Desktop apps. The app with the white outline in Figure 5–34 will open on the screen if you release the ALT KEY. If you continue holding the ALT KEY and tapping the TAB KEY, Windows Flip will cycle through the running apps.

Windows Flip is not a new feature in Windows 8, we just neglected to mention it in Chapter 4, choosing instead to talk about its fancier sibling, Flip 3D. Since Windows 8 has a flatter look, Flip 3D is not supported, and the keyboard shortcut for Flip 3D (WINDOWS KEY+TAB) now opens the Switcher, a black vertical bar with a thumbnail for each running app. To cycle through the running apps, continue to hold the Windows key while tapping the Tab key. Like Windows Snap, Switcher identifies the app it will open with an outline, as shown in Figure 5–35. However, like the Back tip and the swipe from the left edge, Switcher lumps all your running Desktop apps into one thumbnail.

To open the Switcher with a mouse, point the mouse at the bottom-left corner and move it up the left edge (do not drag it) until the Switcher appears. Open Switcher with an edge gesture, sliding a finger a short distance from the left edge of the screen and then quickly moving it back—a quick left-right gesture from the left bezel.

Search

Windows 8 improved the Search function for finding files, people, apps, and settings. In Windows 8.1 the Search function also searches the Internet using the Bing search engine. It centers on the Search bar shown back in Figure 5–25. Using a keyboard, open the Search bar from the Start screen by typing the first characters of the key word you want to use in a search. Open the Search bar from anywhere in Windows 8 with ⊞+Q, or by opening the Charms bar with a swipe from the right bezel and tapping the Search charm. In Windows 8.0, you had to select a search category. Search in Windows 8.1 is improved and, unless you are in a searchable Modern app such as People or Store, it will default to searching everywhere. Press Esc to close Search.

The Desktop

You will find yourself working on the desktop if you use any of the pre-Windows 8 versions of Microsoft productivity tools, such as Microsoft

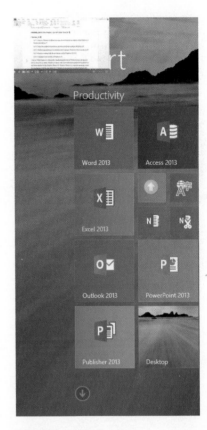

FIGURE 5–33 The Back tip displays in the upper-left corner.

FIGURE 5–35 The Switcher displays along the left side of the screen.

FIGURE 5–34 Windows Flip displays as a horizontal bar with a thumbnail of each running app.

Office. You will also gravitate here for many of the administrative tools, such as Control Panel and Computer Management until Microsoft improves on the new Windows 8 GUI tools.

Desktop Overview

From the Start screen tap or click the Desktop tile (or press ▦+D) to open the Desktop GUI. Open a Desktop app and then right-click on its Taskbar icon and select *Pin this program to taskbar*. After that, you can open the app from the Taskbar. Figure 5–36 shows the Windows 8.1 Desktop with two app windows open. It looks much like Windows 7. The Start screen replaces the Start menu. The Windows 8.1 Desktop includes the Start button that returns you to the Start screen. Notice that even the Desktop has lost the three-dimensional look of Windows 7. The Desktop windows and buttons have crisp corners and there is just the hint of shading around the current open window, the only nod to the third dimension.

Desktop-Centric Options

In Windows 8.1, in addition to adding the Start button, Microsoft also added options desired by people who work primarily with Desktop apps. These options are under *Start Screen* on the Taskbar and Navigation page of the Taskbar and Navigation Properties and dialog box, shown in Figure 5–37. One way to access this page is to first open Control Panel from the Power User Menu, enter "task" in the Search box, and select *Taskbar and Navigation* from the results. The one setting in this group not targeted at the Desktop crowd specifically is labeled *Always show Start on my main display when I press the Windows logo key.* This is for people with dual-displays, so that they can control where the Start screen displays. We explain the other Start screen settings next.

Open the Desktop at Startup. Select *When I sign in or close all apps on a screen, go to the desktop instead of Start* if you do not want to begin your day at the Start screen because you still use many Desktop apps. Then use the Start button when you want to open the Start screen.

Use the Same Background on the Desktop and the Start Screen. To do this, select *Show my desktop background on Start.* Then the background you configure in the Personalization Control Panel will show on both the Desktop and the Start screen.

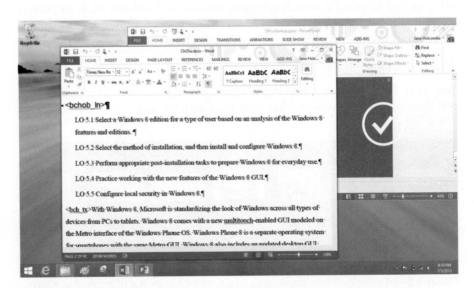

FIGURE 5–36 The Windows 8.1 Desktop with two application windows open.

Replace Start Screen with the Apps View. Select *Show the Apps view automatically when I go to Start.* This replaces the Start screen with the Apps view. In addition, selecting this also selects the normally unavailable option, *Search everywhere instead of just my apps when I search from the Apps view.* Because you have effectively disabled the Start screen, this second option gives you the default Search behavior (search everywhere) you would normally have from the Start screen.

Control Where Start Opens on a Multi-Display System. On a multi-display system when you press the Windows key, it is good to control which display reacts. To turn on this feature, select Show *Start on the display I'm using when I press the Windows logo key.*

List Desktop Apps First in Apps View. If you would like Desktop Apps to be listed first in Apps view, select this option.

File Explorer for File Management

Click or tap the folder icon on the Desktop Taskbar (or use the ◰+e shortcut) to open File Explorer, shown in Figure 5–38. This is an updated version of Windows Explorer, the Windows 7 file management tool, with some changes to the GUI. For one thing, the Quick Access toolbar at the left of the Title bar shows the return of the Control button that disappeared in Windows 7. Clicking the Control button opens a menu of options to control the File Explorer window itself: Restore, Move, Size, Minimize, Maximize, and Close. To the right of the Control button is the Properties button (ALT+ENTER) that opens the Properties dialog for the item selected in File Explorer. Next is the New Folder button (CTRL+SHIFT+N) that creates a new folder in the current location. The last default item on the Quick Access toolbar is a button that opens the Customize Quick Access Toolbar drop-down menu for adding or removing buttons on this toolbar.

On the far right of the File Explorer window are the Minimize, Maximize, and Close buttons, with some of the actions also found on the Control Button

FIGURE 5–37 The Taskbar and Navigation Properties dialog box.

Note: Figure 5–38 shows the ribbon that you can show or hide using the Minimize/Maximize Ribbon button on the right.

Note: In addition to file management, File Explorer also gives you a quick view of your devices and drives.

FIGURE 5–38 The Windows 8.1 File Explorer window.

FIGURE 5–39 Right-click on an empty area of the navigation pane to open this context menu.

menu. On the bottom left of the window is the Status bar that shows the status of the currently selected item. For instance, in the example, This PC is selected and it contains 11 items. On the far right are buttons for changing the display options for the Contents Pane.

When you first open File Explorer in Windows 8.1, you may notice that a feature introduced in Windows 7 and included in Windows 8 is missing: libraries. Libraries are still there, but hidden from the default view in File Explorer. To have libraries display, simply right-click in the navigation pane and select Show libraries from the context menu (Figure 5–39).

The more obvious difference between Windows Explorer in Windows 7 and File Explorer on the Windows 8.1 Desktop is the ribbon, a horizontal area below the title bar containing links to tools and options. The ribbon is similar to that found in recent versions of Microsoft Office. If the ribbon is not visible, click the Minimize/Maximize Ribbon button on the right of the menu bar below the Title bar.

The appearance of the ribbon changes based on the focus of the File Explorer window, bringing up tools and features you might need and sparing you the task of digging around in multilevel menus for those same features. While navigating File Explorer, take time to notice the buttons available on the ribbon as it changes with the file and folder location selected.

Further, File Explorer opens special contextual tabs that appear in the top bar. These tabs open based on the type of file or folder selected in File Explorer. Watch for these special tabs as you browse files. They include: Picture Tools, Music Tools, Disk Tools, and Application Tools. Figure 5–40 shows File Explorer focused on the Pictures folder, with the Picture Tools tab and its related ribbon.

Restoring Deleted Files

Most files on your hard drive are not permanently deleted when you use the Delete command or DEL key in File Explorer. Files deleted in this way are moved to the Recycle Bin, a special folder. To restore a file, open the Recycle Bin, select

FIGURE 5–40 File Explorer with the Picture Tools tab and its related ribbon.

FIGURE 5–41 Open File History for a folder and select a file to restore.

the file and then click or tap the button in the Recycle Bin Tools ribbon labeled *Restore the selected items.* The item is then restored to its original location.

If you delete a file permanently you cannot restore it from the Recycle Bin. That's when you need File History. If you turned on File History, as described earlier in this chapter, and if the file you deleted was in a location backed up by File History, you can open File History in File Explorer, locate your file (even a certain version of the file) and restore it. On the Home ribbon, click or tap the History button to open File History for that folder, as shown in Figure 5–41. Click the green button at the bottom of the window and your file is restored.

Managing Apps

The reason we have computers is to use apps for fun, school, or work. Therefore it is important to know how to acquire, install, update, and remove apps. Desktop apps will install and behave much as they did in Windows 7, only now you can launch a Desktop app from the Start screen, the Apps screen, or from a pinned icon on the Desktop taskbar.

Launch Modern apps from the Start screen, the taskbar, or the Apps screen. Windows 8.1 comes with some Modern productivity apps, such as People, Mail, Photos, and Maps. Internet Explorer comes in two GUIs—Modern and Desktop. Update and install Modern apps through the Windows Store.

In the first release of Windows 8, newly installed apps were automatically given tiles on the Start screen, but in Windows 8.1 you get to decide if you want an app on the Start screen. With the Apps screen so easy to access from the Start screen, you may not want to create Start screen tiles for an app you use infrequently. Launch those apps from the Apps screen.

Installing Apps from the Windows Store

The Windows Store is your only source of Modern apps, but you can still find Desktop apps from other sources. You will need a Microsoft account to use the Windows Store. Click or tap the Store tile (the shopping bag) on the Start screen to connect to the Windows Store and the Store page will open with a dynamically changing selection of apps and categories as shown in Figure 5–42.

Browse through the store by scrolling the screen horizontally, or use the Search box (on the upper right) to search for an app. Click or tap on a tile to

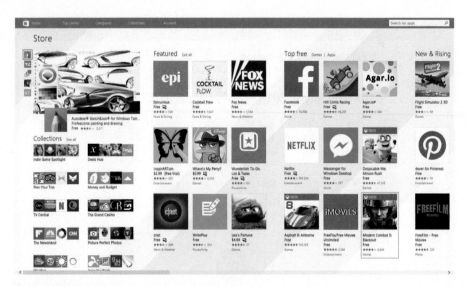

FIGURE 5–42 Find apps at the Windows Store.

learn more about an app, as shown in Figure 5–43, which opened when we tapped on the tile for PDF Touch. If you decide to buy an app, click the Buy button and follow the instructions to pay and then install the app. Return to the Start screen, open the Apps page (click or tap the down arrow button on the bottom left) and look for the new app. Right-click on the app tile to open the context menu for that app. Figure 5–44 shows the context menu for Adobe Acrobat DC, while Figure 5–45 depicts the context menu for another app. In the context menu, you can pin or unpin an app's tile, uninstall an app, and (in some cases) customize it.

Updating Apps from the Windows Store

Microsoft updates Modern apps from the Windows Store. The Store tile on the Start screen will let you

try this!

Install a Free App from the Windows Store

If you have an Internet connection, use the Store to browse for free apps at the Windows Store. Try this:

1. From the Start screen tap or click the Windows Store tile.
2. Enter a search string into the Search box or scroll through the selections and click those that interest you. Look for a free or free trial app.
3. Follow the on-screen instructions to download and install the app.

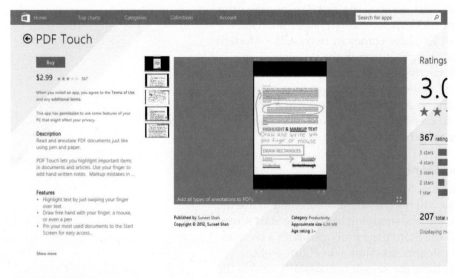

FIGURE 5–43 Read the details about an app before deciding to purchase and install it.

FIGURE 5–44 The context menu for an app contains actions that are appropriate for that app.

know when updates are available for your installed apps. The example shown in Figure 5–46 indicates that 16 apps have updates ready. Click on the tile to connect to the Windows Store and open the App updates page. On this page, select which apps to update and then click the *Install* button to install the updates.

The Taskbar and Title Bar in Modern Apps

In Windows 8.1 Update 1 Microsoft added a black title bar to Modern apps, shown in Figure 5–47. This appears on computers with a mouse briefly, as a modern app loads, and then whenever you move the mouse to the top of the screen. Additionally, when you move the mouse to the bottom of the screen in a Modern app, the Desktop taskbar appears. You can then access the usual title bar and taskbar functions.

Using Snap

To use the Snap screen-sharing feature, first open two Modern apps and/or one Modern app and the Desktop (with or without a Desktop app open). Then, if using touch, touch the left edge and drag your finger a short distance of about an inch until you see a thumbnail image for the second app and a vertical bar. If using a mouse, drag the pointer a short distance from the upper-left corner. Release the mouse button or lift your finger and the second app will appear in a vertical space next to the app that previously occupied the entire space. This takes practice. Previous to Windows 8.1, one app could only occupy a narrow vertical area on one side or the other, while the other app occupied the bulk of the screen. Beginning with 8.1, you can adjust the vertical divider to any position on the screen, and you can open more than two apps at a time, depending on your screen resolution. Figure 5–48 shows three apps sharing the screen on a display with a resolution of 1,920 x 1,080.

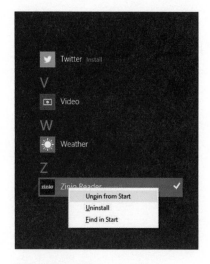

FIGURE 5–45 The options in a context menu vary by app.

FIGURE 5–46 The Store tile shows the number of updates available for installed apps.

FIGURE 5–47 The black title bar was added to Modern apps in Windows 8.1 Update 1.

FIGURE 5–48 Three apps sharing the screen using Snap.

LO 5.4 | Securing Windows 8.1

As with previous versions of Windows, securing Windows 8.1 involves using security software to protect against malware and spyware, using a personal firewall, enabling automatic updates, and using a secure sign-in. These security features are enabled by default during Windows installation.

Windows Firewall is turned on by default, and the Windows Firewall Control Panel looks and works like that in Windows 7. By default, Windows Update automatically downloads and installs important updates, which include security updates. You learned earlier how to configure Windows Update to update your other Microsoft software, which also helps to keep your system more secure. In this section, learn about Windows 8.1 security features and how you can use them. We begin with a discussion of the improved Windows Defender, and then describe what is new in administering user accounts.

Windows Defender

Securing your Windows 8.1 computer has become easier, because it comes with antispyware and antimalware protection in the form of Windows Defender. Now, rather than having to find and install a security package, Windows Defender comes installed and ready to go to work for you. Figure 5–49 shows Windows Defender's home page with minimal status information. It will automatically check for updates to virus and spyware definitions. Use the Update tab if you want to initiate a manual update. The History tab will describe suspected malware code that has been quarantined (isolated) so that it cannot become active and do harm. The History page also describes all detected items and any items allowed because you configured Windows Defender to allow them. This last you configure through options on the Settings tab: *Excluded files and locations* and *Excluded file types.*

Figure 5–50 shows the Advanced options on the Settings tab set to the defaults. For a higher level of security select *Scan removable drives.* If you select the option *Create a restore point,* then before Windows Defender quarantines a file it will create a restore point. If Windows or important software becomes unstable after files are quarantined, this allows you to restore your computer to

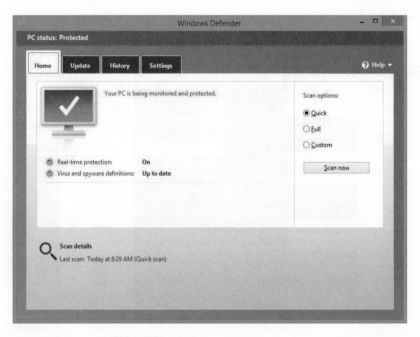

FIGURE 5–49 The Windows Defender home page.

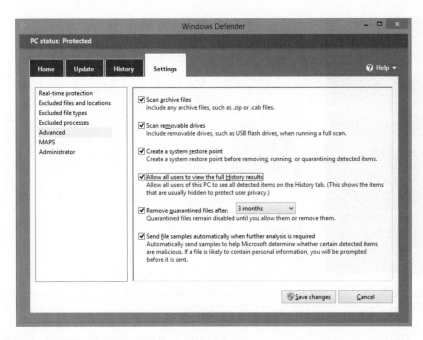

FIGURE 5-50 Windows Defender settings.

the prequarantined state. This is questionable, since you could be restoring your computer to an infected state if the files were, indeed, infected. It does make sense to select the option *Remove quarantined files after.* You configure the time period. A quarantined file is not allowed to run, so if some program requires a quarantined file, that program will not run at all or will issue error messages. Providing a time period before deleting the file gives you time to notice if the quarantined file was needed. The best action to take if quarantining a file disables an important program is to reinstall the program, provided it is first scanned for malware.

Administering Local User Accounts

As with Windows 7 (and many versions previous to it), local user accounts reside in the local accounts database on a Windows 8.1 computer, and use of a local account gives someone access to the computer and to local data. You can create multiple user accounts on a computer used by multiple people, with different permissions assigned to each user for accessing local files, folders, and printers.

Administer user accounts using the traditional Desktop tool, User Accounts Control Panel, which has not significantly changed since Windows 7. There is also a new Windows 8 GUI tool. In Windows 8, this tool was the Users panel in the PC Settings page. In Windows 8.1 it is the Accounts page in PC Settings, shown in Figure 5-51. In both releases, this tool allows you to do simple user management tasks. We will begin there.

Administering User Accounts

The Accounts page in PC Settings in Windows 8.1 has three panes: Your account, Sign-in options, and Other accounts. When the *Your account* pane is open it will resemble Figure 5-51 if you are signed on with a Microsoft account, and your email address will display under your name.

Options on Your Account Pane. If you are signed in with a local account, no email address will display, only the words *Local Account.* When signed in with a Microsoft account, the button labeled *Disconnect* lets you switch to signing in with a local account, at which point you will lose the benefits of the Microsoft account. If you are signed in with a local account, this button is replaced by one labeled *Connect to a Microsoft account.*

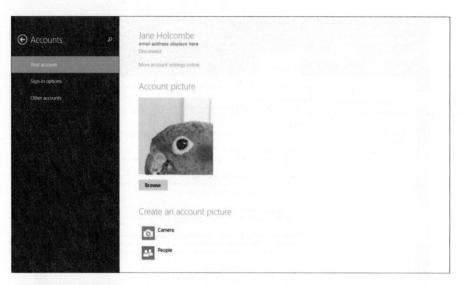

FIGURE 5–51 If you are signed in with a Microsoft account, the Your account pane will show these choices with your account picture.

The link *More account settings online,* only available for a Microsoft account, connects to your account settings online. You will need to enter your Microsoft account password before you can access your account settings. This is to protect you from someone using your unattended computer after you've signed in to connect and modify your settings. For both a Microsoft account or a local account, the only other options shown in the *Your account* pane in Windows 8.1 are for changing your account picture.

Sign-In Options Pane. The *Sign-in options* pane is where you change your password, and create or change a Picture password, create or change a PIN (a four-digit number) for signing in, or change the Password policy so that any user with a password doesn't need to enter it when waking the PC, or the opposite, requiring a password.

Adding Users. If you are signed in with an administrator account, you can add other users to your computer by selecting *Other accounts* on the Accounts page. In the *Other accounts* pane, click the + button labeled *Add an account.* The next page, shown in Figure 5–52, includes choices for signing in with

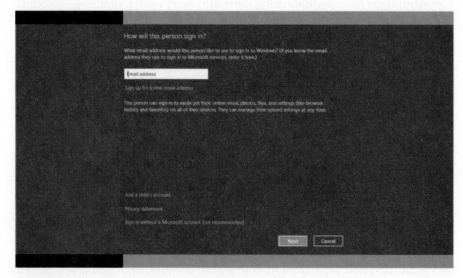

FIGURE 5–52 Select how a user will sign in.

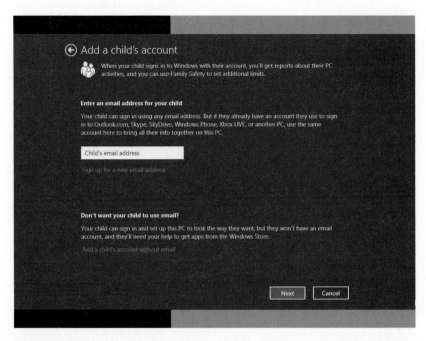

FIGURE 5–53 When you create a child's account in Windows 8.1, Family Safety will monitor that account's usage.

a Microsoft account, creating a new Microsoft account, or signing in with a local account. To have the new user sign in with a local account you choose the last option, *Sign in without a Microsoft account.*

Not so obvious is the fact that creating a new account using this tool creates a standard account (nonadministrator), and if you decide to change that you will need to take extra steps after the account is created, using the Users Account Control Panel.

Adding an Account for a Child and Enabling Family Safety. Monitor a child's use of a computer using a feature called Family Safety. In Windows 8.0 you would enable Family Safety after creating an account. In Windows 8.1, you can create an account with Family Safety turned on by selecting the link labeled *Add a child's account* near the bottom of the screen shown in Figure 5–52. This opens the screen shown in Figure 5–53, where you can choose to create a Microsoft account for the child or create a local account using the link at the bottom of the screen.

Now manage your Family Safety settings. In Control Panel, open Family Safety shown in Figure 5–54. Click the link to *Manage settings on the Family Safety website.* Sign in with your Microsoft account, and access the Activity Reporting page where you can turn on activity reporting, and view activity reports.

Windows SmartScreen

SmartScreen was introduced in Internet Explorer 9 to prevent downloading of suspicious programs during Web browsing. In Windows 8, Microsoft introduced a more powerful feature, Windows SmartScreen, that improves on the original. No longer just part of the Internet Explorer browser, Windows SmartScreen runs at the OS level so that it protects against malicious downloads from any source, such as browsers, email, and even your local network or locally attached drives. Windows SmartScreen uses special sensing features, as well as an online service to determine if software is malicious or from a known malware source.

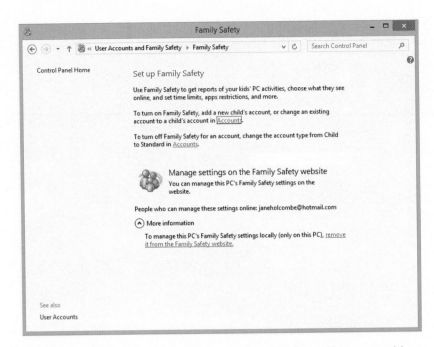

FIGURE 5–54 Select *Manage settings on the Family Safety website* to enable or disable activity reporting and view activity reports.

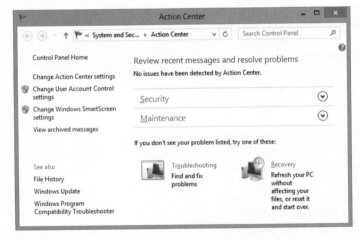

Open Action Center and select *Change Windows SmartScreen settings* (on left).

FIGURE 5–55 The default SmartScreen setting.

You can turn Windows SmartScreen off or on (it is on by default) for Windows Store apps. In Windows 8.1, open PC Settings and select Privacy. On the Privacy page select General, and the third choice is labeled *Turn on SmartScreen Filter to check web content (URLs) that Windows Store apps use.* You will find other settings for Windows SmartScreen in the Action Center Control Panel, shown here. Open it from the Desktop by clicking or tapping the Action Center icon (a small flag) on the Taskbar, then click or tap Open Action Center.

Select the link labeled *Change Windows SmartScreen settings.* This opens the Windows SmartScreen dialog box, shown in Figure 5–55, with just a few options. The default, as shown, is the most secure option.

A Windows 8.1 Computer in a Kiosk

Assigned Access is a feature added in Windows 8.1 that allows an administrator to assign a single user account to run just one app. This is done through the Other accounts pane of the PC Settings Accounts page. You can use this feature to turn a PC into a kiosk computer, meaning you could place the computer in a public place, configured to automatically sign in a user with limited permissions who can only run a single app. Imagine a physically secured touch-screen tablet in a mall kiosk running an app that helps visitors find the various businesses in the mall, but does not allow them to access any other files or programs on that computer.

Chapter 5 REVIEW

Chapter Summary

After reading this chapter and completing the exercises, you should know the following facts about Windows 8.1.

Installing Windows 8.1

- The current Windows 8.1 retail editions are Windows 8.1, Windows 8.1 Pro, and Windows 8.1 Pro for Students.

- Minimum requirements for the Intel/AMD computer architecture include a 1-GHz processor, 1-GB RAM (32 bit) or 2-GB RAM (64 bit), 16 GB available hard disk space (32 bit) or 20 GB (64 bit), a DirectX 9 graphics device with Windows Display Driver Model driver, and a minimum screen resolution of 1,024 × 768 (1,366 × 786 recommended), but most recently manufactured computers far exceed this minimum.

- Upgrade paths are limited to the Intel/AMD computer architecture and from certain editions of Windows 7 to certain editions of Windows 8.1.

- Activation is no longer something you can delay for 30 days, and it occurs early in the installation process.

- If you purchase Windows 8.1 from the Microsoft Store, you will need a Microsoft account. This account is free, as are many of the services. Fees apply when you upgrade services.

- Decide ahead of time how you will sign in to Windows 8.1. Your choices are local account, Microsoft account, and Microsoft Active Directory Domain account.

- The Windows 8.1 Web-based Installer is a new and improved installation method for a retail edition purchased through the Microsoft Store.

- If you plan an upgrade—whether you plan to use the more conventional Windows setup or the Web-based Installer, run the Upgrade Assistant ahead of time to be prepared for incompatibility issues.

- To run the traditional Windows setup you will need bootable media in the form of discs purchased at retail, a disc created from a downloaded ISO image file, or a bootable USB drive also created from a downloaded image.

- Both the traditional Windows setup and the Web-based Installer end with the Out of Box Experience (OOBE) in which you customize your installation.

Postinstallation Tasks

- If updated drivers did not all install during installation, take steps to install them afterward. Use driver update programs from manufacturers and/or Windows Update.

- Check that the correct display driver is installed by opening the Screen Resolution dialog in the Control Panel.

- Run Windows Update several times to bring all the Windows components up to date.

- Configure Windows Update to automatically update other Microsoft software in addition to Windows components.

- If you installed Windows 8.1 into a virtual machine, install the Guest Additions into the virtual machine so that Windows 8.1 will run better. How you do this, and the name for this software, varies by hypervisor.

- On a computer with factory-installed Windows 8 look for bloatware, the extra software the manufacturers often install. Remove software you do not want.

- Create a backup image.

- Turn on File History.

- There are several options for shutting down Windows 8.1. Just one is to open the Charms bar, select the Settings charm, and then from the Power charm, select Shut down.

Navigating and Configuring Windows 8.1

- Windows 8 has settings based in both GUIs: the new PC Settings page and the familiar Control Panel in the Desktop GUI.

- Windows 8.1 has traditional support for mouse and keyboard input, as well as multitouch support for a variety of touch devices. Touch-screen corners are sensitive to certain touch gestures, while screen edges are responsive to certain mouse gestures.

- The on-screen keyboard appears when alphanumeric characters need to be entered on a touch screen.

- The Lock screen is designed especially for touch-screen devices to prevent you from accidentally triggering some action.

- Start screen features include live tiles, charms, Charms bar, Power charm, User tile, scroll bar, and zoom button,
- Point the mouse at the bottom-left corner to display the Start button.
- When several apps are open, a swipe gesture from the left edge of the screen will switch among the open apps one at a time. A swipe gesture that begins at the left edge and almost immediately goes back to the edge reveals the Switcher, a bar containing thumbnails of all open apps.
- Use Search to find files, people, apps, and data. Open the Search bar when a Modern app is open and do a search related to the app.
- Change the User tile to a custom picture in the Personalize page in PC Settings.
- Zoom the Start screen out so that you can rearrange the groups of tiles.
- Open the Desktop from the Desktop tile on the Start screen.
- The Desktop resembles that of Windows 7, with a square Start button (added back in in Windows 8.1) the Start button. The Start menu was replaced by the Start screen.
- File Explorer (the new name for Windows Explorer) is the same file management tool that you used in Windows 7, with some changes to the GUI, including a menu ribbon similar to that in Microsoft Office.
- The Windows Store is your source of Modern apps as well as the updates to those apps.
- Several new GUI configuration options came in Windows 8.1, including (but not limited to) the option to open the Desktop at startup, use the same background on the Desktop and Start screen, and replace the Start screen with the Apps view.
- Use the Snap feature to display two or more Modern apps (as well as the Desktop) on the screen at once.

Securing Windows 8

- Security features are enabled and configured by default.
- Windows Defender provides antispyware and antimalware protection.
- Do simple administration of local user accounts in the Your account pane in the Accounts page of PC Settings. Any users you add here will be standard users. If an account will be used by a child, you can enable Family Settings to monitor the child's activities.
- SmartScreen was introduced in Internet Explorer 9 to prevent downloading of suspicious programs during Web browsing. An expanded version of this, Windows SmartScreen, in Windows 8 improves on the original feature by running at the OS level so that it protects against malicious downloads from any source, such as browsers, email, and even your local network or locally attached drives.
- If you need to run a Windows 8 computer in a public area, such as a kiosk, use the Assigned Access feature added in Windows 8.1 to create a user with limited access that is assigned to run just one program.

Key Terms List

Assigned Access *(202)*

Back tip *(191)*

bloatware *(182)*

charm *(180)*

Charms bar *(180)*

cold boot *(174)*

Domain Join *(167)*

edge gestures *(190)*

File Explorer *(178)*

keyboard shortcut *(185)*

live tile *(188)*

Lock screen *(187)*

Microsoft account (MSA) *(166)*

mouse *(185)*

multitouch *(164)*

on-screen keyboard *(186)*

Out of Box Experience (OOBE) *(175)*

PC Settings screen *(181)*

Power User menu *(184)*

Remote Desktop client *(165)*

Remote Desktop host *(165)*

Search bar *(191)*

semantic zoom *(189)*

Settings bar *(180)*

SmartScreen *(201)*

Snap *(186)*

Start button *(178)*

Start screen *(177)*

Switcher *(191)*

thumbnail *(191)*

touch mouse *(185)*

touchpad *(185)*

warm boot *(174)*

Web-based Installer *(173)*

Windows 8 *(164)*

Windows 8 Pro *(164)*

Windows 8.1 *(165)*

Windows 8.1 Pro *(165)*

Windows 8.1 Pro for Students *(165)*

Windows Flip *(191)*

Windows key (⊞) *(187)*

Windows RT *(164)*

Windows RT 8.1 *(164)*

Windows setup *(173)*

Windows SmartScreen *(201)*

Key Terms Quiz

Use the Key Terms List to complete the sentences that follow. Not all terms will be used.

1. Search, Share, Start, Devices, and Settings are all _____ on a bar that slides out from the right when you swipe in from the right edge of a touch screen.

2. A/an _____ is a rectangular object on the Start screen that acts as a shortcut to open an app, but can also display active content related to that app on the Start screen.

3. You can sign in to a Windows 8.1 computer using a Microsoft Active Directory Domain account, a local account, or a _____.

4. The _____ is the central screen of the new Modern GUI in Windows 8 and Windows 8.1.

5. The _____ edition only runs on devices with the ARM computer architecture.

6. If you need to configure a Windows 8.1 computer for a public space where it will run only a single app, use the _____ feature.

7. Both the Windows setup and Web-based Installer end in the _____, in which you customize your installation of Windows.

8. When you use _____ at the Start screen you can rearrange the groups of tiles by dragging them around.

9. The _____ opens when you right-click the Start button.

10. The _____ contains several panels for configuring Windows 8.1 settings.

Multiple-Choice Quiz

1. Which of the following represents the computer architecture supported by Windows RT?
   a. 64-bit
   b. Intel/AMD
   c. ARM
   d. Texas Instruments
   e. UEFI

2. A Windows 8.1 computer configured with default settings will start up to this screen.
   a. Sign-in
   b. Lock
   c. Settings
   d. Users
   e. Start

3. Your personal computer at home is running Windows 7 Professional and you want to do an in-place upgrade to Windows 8.1. Which edition should you purchase?
   a. Ultimate
   b. Windows 8.1
   c. Windows RT
   d. Windows 8.1 Pro
   e. Home Premium

4. A Modern app normally runs full screen. What Windows 8.1 feature allows multiple apps to share the screen?
   a. Charms
   b. Live tiles
   c. Start button
   d. Semantic zoom
   e. Snap

5. Swipe from the left side of the screen to cycle through open apps, or use a mouse to point at the top-left corner to open a _____ showing a thumbnail of the last open app.
   a. Charms
   b. Live tile
   c. Back tip
   d. Semantic zoom
   e. Snap

6. Previously only included in Internet Explorer 9, this improved and slightly renamed security feature works at the OS level beginning in Windows 8.1 to guard against malicious downloads from any source.
   a. Windows SmartScreen
   b. Charms bar
   c. Group Policy
   d. Lock screen
   e. Domain Join

7. In Windows 8.1 Update 1, what will appear at the top of a modern app when you move the pointer to the top of the screen?
   a. Back tip
   b. Title bar
   c. On-screen keyboard
   d. Lock screen
   e. SmartScreen

8. Use this key to return to the Start screen.
   a. ALT
   b. CTRL
   c. ESC
   d. RETURN
   e. WINDOWS

9. What is the updated file management tool that runs on the Desktop?
   a. File Manager
   b. File Explorer
   c. Windows Explorer
   d. SmartScreen
   e. Windows Manager

10. What is the name for the antivirus/antispyware software that is included in Windows 8.1?
    a. Windows Defender
    b. Microsoft Security Essentials
    c. OOBE
    d. Windows SmartScreen
    e. Assigned Access

11. You want to configure a Windows 8.1 computer to install in a kiosk in your school's lobby and run just one program that helps visitors find various offices. What feature will you use to limit visitor's access on that computer?
   a. Windows Defender
   b. Microsoft Security Essentials
   c. OOBE
   d. Windows SmartScreen
   e. Assigned Access

12. What do you "experience" the first time you power on a new computer with a factory installation of Windows 8.1?
   a. Windows Defender
   b. Microsoft Security Essentials
   c. OOBE
   d. Windows SmartScreen
   e. Assigned Access

13. Where will you find the Power charm?
   a. Scroll bar
   b. Switcher
   c. Settings bar
   d. Search bar
   e. Charms bar

14. This Windows 8.1 Feature, if enabled, automatically backs up certain folders, even tracking file versions, so that you can restore files after they are permanently deleted.
   a. Charms bar
   b. Recycle bin
   c. Settings bar
   d. Search bar
   e. File History

15. If you are using Windows 8.1 on a computer with a keyboard, use these keystrokes to quickly shut down Windows and the computer.
   a. CTRL-ALT-DELETE
   b. CTRL+SHIFT+N
   c. WINDOWS KEY + X
   d. WINDOWS KEY + X, U, U
   e. WINDOWS KEY+TAB

Essay Quiz

1. You plan to do a clean install of Windows 8.1 Pro onto a computer that currently is running Windows 7, and you plan to reinstall the Windows apps that are currently on that computer. Describe what steps you will take to see if your existing hardware and applications are compatible with Windows 8.1 and to prepare for any incompatibilities.

2. Describe how you would open the context menu on the Windows 8.1 Desktop on a touch-screen device without a keyboard.

3. Briefly explain the two computer architectures supported by Windows 8.1 and the edition or editions available for each architecture.

4. Describe a shortcoming of both the swipe and Back tip for use in cycling through open apps.

5. Describe how you are alerted that updates are available for your Windows 8.1 Modern apps.

Lab Projects

LAB PROJECT 5.1

The authors had to pick and choose what to present in a single chapter. One big topic that we could not cover is the specifics of working with the installed Modern apps and how well they share data. Pick two apps, such as Mail and People, and test them, even if you need to create a temporary Hotmail account with Microsoft and enter fictitious names and data into the People app. Or try the Music, Video, and Pictures apps and describe how they share data. Then describe what you did and how the two apps you selected share data.

LAB PROJECT 5.2

Another topic not included in this chapter is how this version of Windows handles digital media. Explore Windows Media Player (WMP), an app included with both editions, researching what it can and cannot do. Then provide a solution, available from Microsoft (or another source) including how you add this solution to each edition, Windows 8.1 and Windows 8.1 Pro.

LAB PROJECT 5.3

In addition to the three account types, you can also choose to sign in using a picture password or a PIN. Research these options and pick one and write a description of how you enable it and your opinion of the value and weakness of that option.

chapter

6 Windows 10

In this chapter, you will learn how to:

LO **6.1** Select a Windows 10 edition and the method of installation, and then install and configure Windows 10 on a laptop or PC.

LO **6.2** Perform appropriate postinstallation tasks to prepare Windows 10 for everyday use.

LO **6.3** Practice working with the new features of the Windows 10 GUI.

LO **6.4** Configure local security in Windows 10.

indows 10 was released in July 2015. It is a cross-platform OS, designed to give the user the same UI across all their devices—PCs, laptops, tablets, and smartphones. Windows 10 may be the last official Windows version, as Microsoft has stated that they will continually upgrade and add features to this OS rather than release separate versions at intervals that varied from two to five years as they have done over the past 30 years. Keep in mind as you progress through this chapter that what is true today may not be true by the time you read this book. We hope to get you started with the basics of the operating system so you can continue to learn and use new features as they appear in Windows on your devices.

LO 6.1 | Installing Windows 10

Perhaps you plan to purchase a new computer with Windows 10 preinstalled, or like many of us, you might decide to upgrade the operating system on your existing Windows PC or laptop.

In any event, you need to decide which edition of Windows 10 you will use and how to migrate data from your old computer or installation of Windows to Windows 10. Additionally, you may want all your old settings to apply in the new installation. Therefore, we begin by describing the Windows 10 editions, move on to reviewing the system requirements for this new OS, and then consider how you might upgrade from Windows 7 or Windows 8. In preparing to install Windows 10, decide how to sign in to the OS and take some necessary steps before installing it onto an older computer. After all this preparation, install Windows 10.

Windows 10 Editions

Windows 10 comes in several editions: one Education edition, one Enterprise edition, and three Retail editions. The Windows 10 Education edition is available only through Microsoft's Academic Volume Licensing program for the use of students, teachers, and other school employees. Windows 10 Enterprise and Mobile Enterprise are available only to large corporate customers through Microsoft's Windows Software Assurance volume licensing program.

In the following sections we briefly describe the three Retail Windows 10 editions: Windows 10 Home, Windows 10 Pro, and Windows 10 Mobile. The remainder of this chapter describes installing, configuring, and securing two of those editions: Windows 10 Home and Windows 10 Pro on PCs and laptops. These two editions also run on compatible tablets. Table 6–1 compares selected features of these two editions.

> *Note:* Another edition, Windows 10 IoT Core, comes preinstalled on small, inexpensive mobile devices that fall into the Internet of Things (IoT) category.

Windows 10 Home

Windows 10 Home Edition runs on PCs and tablets and is aimed at consumers who do not need some of the premium features of Windows 10 Pro. Owners of PCs or tablets with Windows 7 Home Basic, Windows 7 Home Premium, or the "basic" edition of Windows 8.x were able to upgrade to this edition for free for a year after the July 29, 2015, launch of Windows 10.

Windows 10 Pro

Windows 10 Pro also runs on PCs and tablets. It is equivalent to the Windows 8.x Pro, Windows 7 Professional, and Windows 7 Ultimate that offer features required for businesses, such as those described in Table 6–1. Users running

TABLE 6–1 Comparison of Selected Features in the Windows 10 Retail Editions for PCs and Laptops		
Features	**Windows 10 Home**	**Windows 10 Pro**
Maximum physical RAM memory	4 GB in 32-bit OS 128 GB in 64-bit OS	4 GB in 32-bit OS 512 GB in 64-bit OS
BitLocker		✓
BitLocker To Go		✓
Continuum	✓	✓
Cortana personal digital assistant	✓	✓
Domain Join support for joining a Windows domain		✓
Encrypting File System (EFS) on NTFS volumes		✓
Group Policy Management for Windows domain		✓
Hyper-V client	✓	✓
Hyper-V host (64-bit OS only)		✓
Microsoft Edge Web Browser	✓	✓
Universal Apps	✓	✓
Virtual Desktops	✓	✓
Windows Hello biometric login	✓	✓
Works on PCs, tablets, and two-in-ones	✓	✓

any of these systems, with appropriate updates, could upgrade for free for a year after the July 29, 2015, Windows 10 launch.

Windows 10 Mobile

Windows 10 Mobile is the replacement for Windows Phone 8 and 8.1. The distinction Microsoft makes by dropping "phone" from the name is that, not only is this intended for smartphones, they are also promoting it for small tablets with a screen size of eight inches or less. We describe mobile operating systems in Chapter 11.

System Requirements

The minimum hardware requirements to install Windows 10 on an Intel- or AMD-architecture computer are nearly identical to those of Windows 8. Keep in mind that the minimum RAM and disk space requirements are very minimal, and you will want much more RAM and disk space than the minimum described if you plan to install many programs and store data locally. Fortunately, even today's budget-level computers come with hardware that far exceeds the requirements for Windows 10, so we do not expect you to have a problem with the minimum requirements. What may be an issue is very old hardware that Windows 10 may not support because updated drivers are not available. Having said all that, here are the minimum system requirements:

- 1-GHz or faster processor or a 1-GHz system on a chip (SoC) (such as in a mobile device)
- Minimum 1-GB RAM for 32-bit Windows 10 or 2-GB RAM for 64-bit Windows 10
- 16 GB available hard disk space for 32-bit Windows 10; 20 GB for 64-bit Windows 10
- DirectX 9 graphics device with Windows Display Driver Model (WDDM) 1.0
- 1,024 × 600 minimum screen resolution (1,366 × 768 recommended)
- Internet access

Further, a multitouch-capable display, touchpad, or touch mouse is required if you wish to take advantage of Windows 10's multitouch support.

Upgrading to Windows 10

Upgrading to Windows 10 is an easy decision for many—both because it is (or was) free (see below) and because the system requirements are modest. The actual upgrade installation is also smoother and faster than for previous versions. In this section we discuss the free upgrade and what versions of Windows and which editions (free or not) you can upgrade to Windows 10.

Free Upgrade to Windows 10

Windows 10 was released July 29, 2015, and for a period of one year after that date it was a free upgrade for many existing installations of legally licensed and updated Windows 7 and Windows 8.1. A Windows 7 computer required Service Pack 1 (SP1) installed to qualify for the free update to Windows 10. A Windows 8 computer had to have Windows 8.1 Update 1 installed. A qualifying computer also had to have Windows Update configured to download and install updates automatically.

Beginning in late spring of 2015, users with qualifying Windows 7 and Windows 8.1 systems noticed a new Windows logo icon near the right side of their taskbars. Hovering the mouse over this icon showed that it was titled

Note: For a more complete list of Windows 10 features, check out the comparison table at www.microsoft.com/en-us /WindowsForBusiness/Compare. The table at that site compares core features found in most editions with business features found mainly in Enterprise and Education editions. Some, but not all, business features are included in Windows 10 Pro edition.

The Get Windows icon displayed on the Windows 8.1 taskbar.

FIGURE 6–1 The Get Windows 10 wizard as it appeared before the user reserved an upgrade.

Get Windows 10. Clicking on this icon opened a wizard, shown in Figure 6–1, which checked the system for compatibility and allowed you to reserve your free upgrade.

The Get Windows 10 wizard checked each PC and reported on the status. Figure 6–2 shows the report stating that the PC met the requirements, but that one app, Windows Media Center, would be removed during the installation. This caused us to delay upgrading that PC until later in the one-year window. Others received a report with the message, "This PC will have problems running Windows 10." They had to address each issue described before upgrading. In some cases, they had to manually uninstall an app.

FIGURE 6–2 The Get Windows 10 wizard displaying the results of a scan of the computer.

FIGURE 6–3 The Get Windows 10 wizard.

This reservation had to be made before July 29, 2015. Once you reserved an upgrade, Windows Update would then quietly download the upgrade to your system. Then, beginning on July 29, 2015, people who had made a reservation were notified that their free Windows 10 was available to install. This was done via a pop-up message over the Get Windows 10 icon. Figure 6–3 shows the wizard that opened when you clicked on that icon. People have also told us that they didn't make their reservation by the July 29, 2015, deadline, but did receive a free upgrade. This is anecdotal and we cannot confirm it, but we have no reason to doubt them.

Those who upgraded during this one-year period had the added benefit of free continued security updates as well as other feature and functionality updates to Windows 10 *for the supported lifetime of the device.*

If a computer and its installed operating system met the requirements, then the only other restriction we know of is that the installation had to be initiated from the qualifying Windows system. If you wanted to do a clean install of the free Windows 10 on your existing computer, you had to first upgrade, then after the upgrade was completed, you would enter the search string (without quote marks) "create recovery media" into the Cortana search box. This opened the Recovery Drive utility where you would select *Back up system files to the recovery drive.* It was necessary to provide blank discs or a USB drive with a capacity of 4 GB or larger for the utility to use. After the recovery drive was created, it could be used to do a clean installation on the same computer.

Also, computers that would otherwise qualify with the correct version of Windows and were not part of a volume license program, but were "Domain Joined" (members of a Windows domain), could not be upgraded while online. They had to upgrade using an ISO image file. The Get Windows 10 wizard and the setup program both check that a Windows installation is legally licensed, but you can also check for yourself. To do that in either Windows 7 or Windows 8.1, open the Control Panel System applet and look on the bottom of the page for the words "Windows is activated." It's as easy as that! Figure 6–4 shows the System applet in Windows 8.1 Pro.

Note: The authors interpret "supported lifetime of the device" to mean up to 10 years, because Windows 10 is subject to Microsoft's life-cycle policy, which is usually five years of mainstream support and five years of extended support. Microsoft stated that there would be no fees involved for those Windows 10 installations, and they would continue to receive updates for the life of the device.

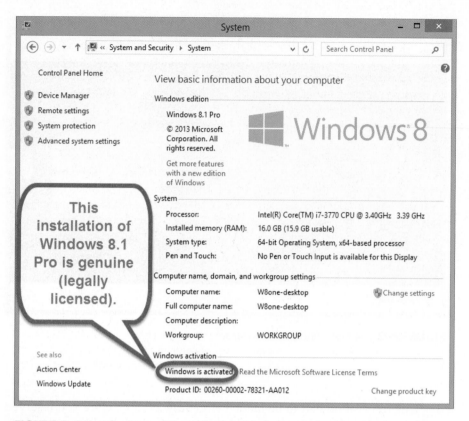

FIGURE 6–4 Use the Control Panel System applet to confirm that an installation of Windows is genuine.

Upgrading Editions

As described earlier, to upgrade an existing installation of Windows to Windows 10, the old version must be Windows 7 Service Pack 1 (SP1) or Windows 8.1 Update 1. However, it is important to understand which editions of each are directly upgradable, and to which Windows 10 editions. Table 6–2 shows the upgrade paths for Windows 7 SP1 to Windows 10, and Table 6–3 describes the upgrade paths from Windows 8.1 Update 1 to Windows 10.

TABLE 6–2	Upgrade Paths from Windows 7 (with Service Pack 1) to Windows 10 Retail Editions	
From	**To**
Windows 7 Starter	
Windows 7 Home Basic	Windows 10 Home
Windows 7 Home Premium	
Windows 7 Professional	Windows 10 Pro
Windows 7 Ultimate	

TABLE 6–3	Upgrade Paths from Windows 8.1 Update 1 to Windows 10 Retail Versions	
From	**To**
Windows 8.1	Windows 10 Home
Windows 8.1 with Bing	
Windows 8.1 Pro	Windows 10 Pro
Windows 8.1 Pro for Students	

Deciding When to Move to a New Version of Windows

There are countless factors that can influence the decision to move to a new version of Windows. The authors' needs are very different from most people's needs, as we must have at least one computer running each operating system we support. At the time that Windows 10 was released we had two PCs with Windows 7, one PC with Windows 8.1, two laptops with Windows 8.1, and a two-in-one laptop with Windows 8.1. After Windows 10 was released, we immediately upgraded the two-in-one and the other two laptops, but held off on upgrading one of the Windows 7 PCs until after the first major release. The second Windows 7 PC will stay as it is. The remaining Windows 8.1 PC will not be upgraded for the foreseeable future. That way, we have computers running all three versions (Windows 7, Windows 8.1, and Windows 10) for upcoming projects. We also have Apple products, a Linux computer, and an assortment of mobile devices here at the "Holcombe World Headquarters," just to be all-inclusive.

The Downside to Upgrading

As with any new version of an OS, not everyone should immediately upgrade their existing systems. It is always good to wait until the new OS proves its stability. Also, in the case of upgrading an existing system to Windows 10, some features will be removed. You should understand this ahead of time and consider if these are features you will miss. For instance, Windows Media Center was included in certain editions of Windows 7 but was a feature you would have paid for if you added it to Windows 8 or 8.1. Here is as complete a list as we can provide of those features that we know are removed, along with a few remarks:

- Windows Virtual PC with Windows XP Mode
- Windows Media Center
- Windows 7 Desktop gadgets
- The ability to disable automatic Windows Update for Windows 10 Home
- Solitaire, Minesweeper, and Hearts games (Setup installs a new version of Solitaire. Minesweeper is a free app at the Windows Store. Several non-Microsoft versions of Hearts are also free.)
- A USB floppy drive driver (if present) will be removed. (Install a new one with Windows Update or from the manufacturer of the floppy drive.)
- The Windows Live Essentials OneDrive app (Rather than being a separate app, in Windows 10 OneDrive is integrated into File Explorer as well as the inbox, allowing users to read emails and move them to OneDrive storage; they also can more easily attach files located on OneDrive to emails when using the Mail app. You will simply need to sign in to OneDrive.)

If you are planning an upgrade and will be adversely affected by one of these changes, you may want to stay with the previous Windows version until you find a solution to any problem that would be created by removing any of the above features. We advised clients to wait until at least one major upgrade before upgrading. In previous versions of Windows this would have been in the form of a service pack. Presently, however, we do not believe that there will be such a thing as a service pack for Windows 10 because Microsoft states that they will keep Windows 10 continually updated. This leads us to believe that they will no longer accumulate changes and release them bundled together in service packs.

Preparing to Install Windows 10

Before installing any operating system, there are preparation tasks—some requiring simple decisions, others requiring action beforehand. We will look at these in no special order, beginning with a few housekeeping issues for anyone who upgrades an existing system. Then we'll consider how Windows 10 activates itself as a legally licensed installation, and continue on to the decisions you need to make concerning how you will sign in to Windows 10.

Update Windows 7, Windows 8, or Windows 8.1

Before you upgraded a computer to Windows 7, you could connect to the Microsoft site and run the Windows 7 Upgrade Advisor to determine if your existing hardware, drivers, and software were compatible with the new OS. Similarly, when preparing to upgrade to Windows 8 or 8.1, you could connect and run the Windows 8 Upgrade Assistant for the same type of evaluation of your system. For Windows 10, Microsoft does a similar test, currently available through the Get Windows 10 app installed by Windows Update.

First ensure that you have one of the upgradable Windows versions and editions described in Table 6–2 or Table 6–3. Then open Windows Update and ensure that your Windows 7 or Windows 8.1 installation is up to date. Only then will you be able to run the Get Windows 10 app to determine if your hardware and installed drivers and software are compatible with Windows 10.

Back Up Your Data

If you are doing an in-place upgrade, your data and settings will be preserved, but you should still back up any important data stored on that computer before upgrading. Do this just in case something unexpected happens, like a power outage during the upgrade. If, like many people now, you save your data to the cloud using a file hosting service, such as Dropbox or Microsoft's OneDrive, then you may consider that file storage to be your backup. Or you may use a cloud-based backup service that is separate from the cloud-based file-storage service you use for saving your working files.

As an example, Jane had Windows 8.1 Pro on her primary work PC. She did and still does store data from recent and current projects—both personal and business—on Microsoft's OneDrive, and has archives of past projects stored offline. She keeps a secondary copy of some of the archive on the PC she uses the most so that she can dip into that archive more easily from time to time to recall what she previously wrote about a certain topic. Therefore, with a copy of the archive elsewhere, she could skip doing a local backup and restore the archive from the backup. However, just to be extra safe, she used Windows 8.1's image backup, found in the File History Control Panel applet.

Chuck was running Windows 7 Pro and stored all his data locally, backing up weekly to an external drive using the Windows 7 Backup and Restore utility. So he just had to do one final backup immediately before doing an upgrade. He opted to do a clean install of Windows 10, knowing that he could use the Windows 7 Backup and Restore utility that is included in Windows 10 to restore his data.

Update Firmware

If you are planning to use an existing computer with a functioning operating system installed, we suggest a rather advanced task for those who don't mind challenges: Update the system firmware while the previous OS is intact.

This is especially important on a computer that is more than a few years old because a firmware update may make the difference between using all the computer's features with the new version of Windows versus experiencing instability problems, such as the system hanging up when you try to shut down. Some manufacturers install update-manager software that checks for and downloads drivers and firmware, in which case, your system may be up to date. Otherwise, you may need to do a little searching for the computer model on the computer manufacturer's site to see if there are any firmware updates for that model. Then, follow the manufacturer's instructions for updating the firmware.

Acquire Updated Drivers

As with firmware updates, your existing computer may have a utility installed by the manufacturer that checks for updates to the system drivers for that model computer. Over time, these utilities have morphed into full-blown marketing apps for the manufacturer, but the updating function is useful because it may ensure that you have the latest drivers for the installed OS, and they may be acceptable to Windows 10. Windows 10 Setup will check your system to ensure that it has current device drivers. If Windows 10 does not have new drivers and the previously installed drivers are incompatible, Setup may install a generic driver, providing there is a reasonably compatible driver. If Setup issues an error message, you may need to acquire an updated Windows 10 driver. Alternatively, if Setup installed a generic driver, you may still need to install an updated driver from the manufacturer to take advantage of all of a device's features.

Microsoft Product Activation

As described in Chapter 4, activation, or Microsoft Product Activation (MPA), is an antipiracy tool that ensures you are using your software per the software license. One important change in the Windows 10 activation process is that you do not have to manually enter a product key during activation because Windows 10 comes "pre-keyed" and will automatically provide the key to Microsoft during the activation process. The product key only works with one instance of the Windows 10 product. If there is no Internet connection, it will try to activate the product key once the computer is connected. If it fails to activate after several tries, a message will display with instructions on how to manually activate the product—usually via telephone.

Choose How to Sign In to Windows 10

Decide ahead of time how you will sign in to Windows 10. As with Windows 8, you can sign in to Windows 10 with (1) a local account that exists only on the Windows 10 computer, (2) a Microsoft account, or (3) a Windows Active Directory account if your computer is a member of a Windows Active Directory domain (at work or school). One subtle difference between Windows 10 and Windows 8 or 8.1 is that the Windows 10 installation does not make it as difficult to create a local account during installation as it was in the Windows 8 or 8.1 Setup program.

Signing In with a Local Account. When you install Windows it creates a local account, but in Windows 8 or 8.1 and Windows 10 you can sign in using either that local account or a Microsoft account. As with Windows 8, if you use a local account, it only gives you access to local resources; you will need to sign in separately to any Microsoft services you use. Figure 6–5 shows a Sign-In screen for a local account. This account has not been customized with a picture, which you can do at any time after you install Windows 10.

Note: As with previous versions of Windows, if you do not enter a password when you create a local account, sign in will not require a password, and the sign-in screen will not show the password box. We strongly recommend that you create a password for your local account unless you are the only person with physical access to your computer.

FIGURE 6–5 The initial Sign-In screen for a local account.

Signing In with a Microsoft Account. If you use a Microsoft account (MSA), the Sign-In screen will display the name and the email address associated with your MSA. We prefer to use the MSA sign-in. This one sign-in gives you access to the local computer as well as to your Microsoft services, such as One-Drive, Skype, or Xbox. Then you can access all your data across other devices and services, and you can synchronize your settings on other Windows 8.1 and Windows 10 devices that use the same sign-in. Learn more about syncing your devices in the section titled *Postinstallation Tasks*.

You can use your existing MSA, create one ahead of time by going to the Microsoft site, or wait and create a new MSA during Windows 10 installation. Figure 6–6 shows the MSA sign-in page for Windows 10. Signing in with an MSA lets you use the same settings and Microsoft Store apps across your devices. An MSA is required for some apps as well as for Microsoft services, such as OneDrive and Xbox. An MSA is free, as are some basic Microsoft services, such as OneDrive and mail.

Note: In Windows 8 and 8.1, Microsoft required a Microsoft account to use certain Modern apps, such as Mail and Calendar. In Windows 10 they pulled back from this stand. For instance, if you wish, you can now use the Mail app without using an MSA—perhaps using a Gmail account (Microsoft calls it a "Google Account").

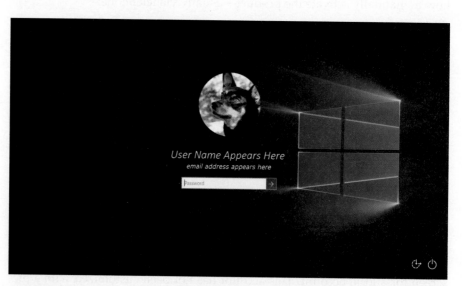

FIGURE 6–6 The Sign-In screen for a Microsoft account.

Signing In with a Domain Account. If your computer is running Windows 10 Pro, Windows 10 Enterprise, or Windows 10 Education it can join a Microsoft Active Directory Domain (based on Windows Server), and you will be required to sign in using a domain user account. In this case, you may not be involved in the installation of Windows or selection of the account at all but have a fully configured computer delivered to your desk. You will then enter your domain credentials, as instructed by a domain administrator.

Prepare to Install into a Virtual Machine

If you have a hypervisor installed on a lab computer and plan to install Windows 10 into a virtual machine, you will need to first create a VM for the installation (as described in Chapter 3), and then ensure that the virtual machine will boot from the drive containing the Windows 10 Setup files. By default, virtual machines in all the hypervisors discussed in Chapter 3 will connect to a computer's physical DVD drive as a virtual DVD drive and can boot from that drive at startup. Therefore, if you have a Windows 10 DVD, insert it into the host computer's DVD drive before starting the VM. At startup, the VM will boot into the Setup program. If the Windows 10 files are in an ISO image file, change the DVD settings for that virtual machine to point to the location of the ISO file before starting the VM, and then restart the VM and follow the prompts.

The Installation

If you wish to install Windows 10 on a computer that does not qualify for the free upgrade, or you are installing it after July 28, 2016, you must purchase it as a retail product. This is assuming you are not part of an Enterprise or Education program. If purchasing online to upgrade from Windows 7 or Windows 8.1, you can do either a Web-based install or a more conventional Windows Setup install.

Web-Based Setup

A Web-based setup is quick and combines the more traditional Windows Setup program with the features of the Windows Upgrade Advisor and the settings and data migration tools described in Chapter 4, which were separate from Windows Setup. Web-based setup requires very little interaction and is very fast. If you select this option, follow the on-screen instructions to install it.

Traditional Windows Setup

The traditional Windows Setup is available for Windows 10. To install Windows 10 using this program, you must have the Windows 10 Setup files on bootable media.

Bootable Media. If you purchase the physical retail package (see Figure 6–7), you will have bootable media. Use the appropriate media for the architecture (32-bit or 64-bit) supported by your computer.

Purchase Windows 10 online and choose the option "Install later by creating Media," and you will have the option to download to a USB drive or to an ISO file. If you install it to a USB drive, you will have a bootable USB Setup drive.

Choose ISO, and Microsoft will download an ISO image file containing a copy of the entire contents of a disc. After downloading it to a Windows computer, simply double-click the file and the Windows Disc Image Burner dialog will display. Insert a blank disc in your disc drive, click Burn, and it will create the disc.

Note: Exercise 6.01 requires a computer that can boot from either a USB or DVD drive. If your computer fails to do this, change the boot order setting in the computer's system settings. The actual steps for doing this vary by manufacturer. For instructions, do an online search using your computer model name and the key words "boot order."

FIGURE 6–7 The Windows 10 retail packaging.

Note: Windows PE was introduced in Chapter 4. It is a scaled-down Windows operating system with basic hardware support for 32-bit and 64-bit programs that is used during Setup and also during certain recovery scenarios.

Beginning Windows Setup. Once you have the media, you can either boot your computer from it (a clean install) or, if upgrading, first sign in to your Windows 7 or Windows 8.1 Update 1 computer and insert the disc. If it does not automatically run setup, open Windows Explorer or File Explorer (◻+E), browse to the disc, and double-click the Setup file.

Step-by-Step 6.01 will walk you through the steps for a clean install of Windows 10 from bootable media. An upgrade can also be done from bootable media. When you start the installation, the Windows Preinstallation Environment (Windows PE) starts as it did in Windows 7, Windows 8, and Windows 8.1.

Step-by-Step 6.01

Installing Windows 10

In this hands-on exercise, you will do a clean installation of Windows 10 from bootable media. To complete this exercise, you will need the following:

- A Microsoft/Intel standard personal computer (desktop or laptop) compatible with Windows 10, with at least the recommended minimum hardware and configured to boot from DVD or other media, and (ideally) an un-partitioned hard disk (disk 0, the first hard disk). Alternatively, you can install into a virtual machine you have prepared before beginning the Windows 10

installation (see Chapter 3 and the section in this chapter titled "Prepare to Install into a Virtual Machine").

- The Windows 10 DVD or other bootable media.
- If you plan on using a local account for sign in, you need to decide on a user name and password for that account.
- If you plan to use a Microsoft account, you need the email address and password for that account. If you do not have one you can create a Microsoft account during the Setup process.

Insert the bootable media containing the Windows 10 installation files and boot the computer. Watch the screen for instructions to boot from the optical (or other) drive. A plain black screen will briefly flash, followed by a black screen with the message: "Windows is loading files…" while the Windows Preinstallation Environment is loading and starting. The Starting Windows screen signals that Windows PE is starting and will soon load the GUI for Windows 10 setup.

On the first Setup screen, select a language, time, and currency format, and keyboard input methods and click Next.

On the next screen, take note of the link labeled "Repair your computer." This option is described in Chapter 7. To proceed with the installation, click Install now.

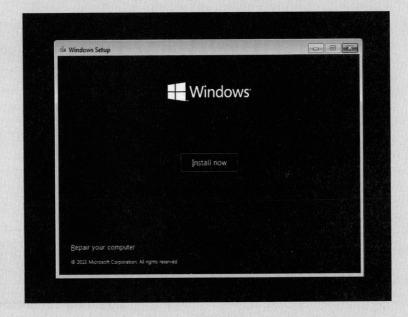

Step 4

When the license screen appears, read the Microsoft Software License Terms, then click to place a check in the box labeled "I accept the license terms" and click the Next button.

Step 5

On the screen after the license screen you are asked, "Which type of installation do you want?" Select Custom to perform a clean installation.

Step 6

On the next screen, you select the target drive for the installation. Anything currently stored on the drive you select will be deleted. If Windows 7 or Windows 8 was previously installed on the system on which you are doing a clean installation, this screen will show two partitions on the drive, as shown here. The smaller one is reserved by the operating system. In this case, select the larger of the two partitions and click Next.

If you are installing into a virtual machine or onto a clean hard drive without a previous installation of Windows, there will be only a single partition. Select it and click Next.

Step 7

Windows 10 Setup will now go through the installation phases. It may restart several times and return to this page that displays progress with a green check by each completed phase.

Step 8

A screen with the Windows logo in the center and a progress animation over the words "Getting ready" displays. Eventually a screen displays with an explanation of what will occur if you click the button at the bottom labeled "Use Express settings." Select this button unless your instructor or administrator gives you different instructions. Also note that this is the first time the Ease of Access icon displays (on the lower left). Select this to have audio and visual aids to make Setup more accessible. Ease of Access settings are also available after Windows is installed. Look for it on every sign-in screen and in the Control Panel.

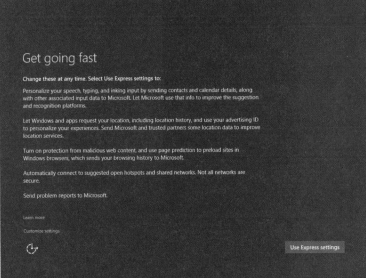

Step 9

After a short delay while Setup configures your system, this screen will display asking, "Who owns this PC?." Your response to this screen depends on your situation. In a classroom lab, you will probably select "My organization." At home, you will select "I do." Select one of the choices; then click Next.

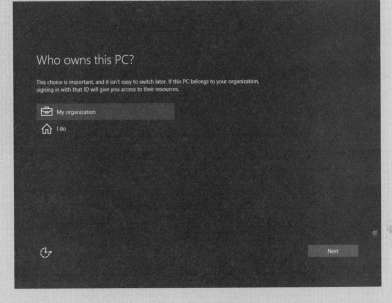

Step 10

After another short wait, during which a progress screen displays, a sign-in screen opens. The actual screen depends on your choice in step 9. If you selected "My Organization," then you will follow the screen prompts and enter your credentials for signing in to the organization's network.

If this is your own computer and you do not need to sign in to a Windows domain, sign in with a Microsoft account or create a local account. For this exercise we will sign in with a Microsoft account. If you wish to do that, enter the email address and password associated with your Microsoft account in this screen. Then click Sign In and skip to step 12.

If you wish to create and sign in with a local account, click on "Skip this step" and proceed to step 11.

Step 11

If you wish to sign in with a local account, create a user by entering a user name and password at this screen. Then click Next and skip to step 14.

Step 12

After signing in with your Microsoft account credentials, this screen will display if you have configured your Microsoft account with two-step verification for extra security and provided a telephone number where you can receive text messages. Just the last two digits of the phone number are shown in the first box. If this is correct, enter the last *four* digits in the second box, click Next, and a numeric code will be texted to your phone.

Step 13

On the following page enter the verification code that was sent to your phone and click Next.

Step 14

After a short wait you will see a screen suggesting that you create a PIN to use for signing in. You may choose "Skip this step" or "PIN me." If you choose to skip the step, proceed to step 15. If you choose "PIN me" you will see the "Set up a PIN" message. If you want to do this, we suggest that you clear the four-digit PIN checkbox and enter a PIN of at least six digits. Be sure to memorize it.

Step 15

The next page urges you to set up Cortana. For now select "Not now," and Setup will finish and sign you into the Desktop.

LO 6.2 | Postinstallation Tasks

You will need to do some tasks soon after installing Windows 10. In earlier versions of Windows we would normally have you install security software at this point, but, like Windows 8 and 8.1, Windows 10 comes with the Windows Defender security enabled during setup. We will look at Windows Defender later in this chapter. Your postinstallation tasks should include installing drivers, if necessary running Windows Update, and backing up Windows and your data files. But first, take a few minutes to familiarize yourself with the new GUI so that you can do these postinstallation tasks.

Get Acquainted with the New GUI

The Windows 10 GUI (and there is only one) is the Desktop; it opens up with the Recycle bin shortcut on the upper left and a taskbar with Start button along the bottom. This section is a brief introduction to some of the new features that you may need to work with when you do the postinstallation tasks. They include the new Start menu, the File Explorer file management tool, and the new Edge Web browser. Later, after taking care of any postinstallation tasks, we will look more closely at Windows 10 features.

The Windows 10 Start Menu

Click or tap the Start button (on the far left of the task bar) to open the Start menu, as shown in Figure 6–8, which shows the Start menu in Desktop mode, covering a portion, but not all, of the Desktop. This is how the Start menu appears on a computer with a keyboard attached. Notice the scroll bar on the right edge of the Start menu. If you had more tiles on the Windows 8.*x* Start screen, they were added off to the right side, and you scrolled horizontally to see them. In Windows 10, scroll vertically to see more tiles on the Start menu.

Click or tap Start again to close the Start menu. Microsoft calls the Start menu simply "Start," but in this book, we will continue to use the term "Start menu." After its absence in Windows 8 and 8.1, the Start menu has returned by popular demand, combining a selection of features from the Windows 7 Start menu and the Windows 8 Start screen along with new or improved features.

> *Note:* Later in this chapter learn about the special user interface mode for tablets: Tablet mode.

FIGURE 6–8 The Windows 10 Start menu open on the Desktop with a column of Quick links on the left and several Windows 8-style tiles on the right.

User Tile and Quick Links. At the very top of the left pane of the Start menu is the User tile for the currently signed-in user, with a picture if one is available. What we called a shortcut on the Start menu in Windows 7 is now called a Quick link. This is not exactly like the Windows 7 Start menu that so many are accustomed to using, but it does have a Quick link for Power, so that you can shut down, restart, or put Windows into Sleep mode. The Start menu covers only a portion of the screen when it is open on a PC or laptop. On a tablet, the Start menu is full screen so it is easier to see on a smaller screen. To make room for touch, the Quick links and tiles become larger, and menu choices are spaced farther apart. You can launch programs from Quick links, from tiles on the Start menu, from links pinned to the Taskbar, and from the All Apps list, which we look at next.

The Power menu options.

All Apps. Click the All Apps Quick link to see all the installed apps in a vertical, sorted list. Figure 6–9 shows the All Apps list in the left pane of the Start menu. Look closely to see the vertical scroll bar on the right side of the Apps list. Drag the scroll bar up or down to browse through the list. Folder items, such as the one labeled Articulate, have a drop-down button to the right that opens a list of the contents of that folder. To close the All Apps list, simply click or tap Back (at the bottom of the list).

Note: Later in this chapter we will use the new and improved features of the Start menu's search box (now occupied by Cortana) to get help, find apps and settings, and access the new features of Windows 10.

File Explorer

Another feature to check out before beginning your postinstallation tasks is File Explorer, the Windows 10 file management utility. This renamed

FIGURE 6–9 The All Apps list open on the left of the Start menu.

FIGURE 6–10 The File Explorer icon on the taskbar.

FIGURE 6–11 The Windows 10 File Explorer file management tool.

and updated replacement for Windows Explorer first appeared in Windows 8. Microsoft has made more changes in the File Explorer UI in Windows 10, but nothing that should keep you from finding your way around if you are experienced with either Windows Explorer or the Windows 8 or 8.1 File Explorer. Even the File Explorer icon on the taskbar (Figure 6–10), while updated somewhat, is recognizable from previous versions. In Figure 6–11 notice the ribbon containing menu buttons near the top of the window and the list of Quick links under Quick access on the left. When browsing your folders, select one you open frequently and click the Pin to Quick Access button on the left side of the ribbon. Briefly acquaint yourself with File Explorer by selecting it from the Start menu and browsing the folders.

Microsoft Edge

The last feature we will preview before discussing the postinstallation tasks is the Windows 10 Web browser, **Microsoft Edge**. This is an alternative to the decades-old Internet Explorer (IE), which is also included in Windows 10 for backward compatibility with some websites.

Why a new Web browser? Sure, IE was updated many times over the years and will continue to be updated for some time, but old apps have a way of keeping some of their old problems. One of IE's problems was its tight integration with the Windows operating system code, which caused security issues as well as legal issues for Microsoft with the European Union.

When browsing with Edge, if a website is incompatible with the new browser, Windows will automatically switch to IE. You can also choose to open IE manually. One way to do that is to type "Internet Explorer" in the Search box at the bottom of the Start menu. The top item in the results list should be Internet Explorer, with the description "Desktop app." Click it to open IE.

Launch Microsoft Edge from its taskbar icon, as shown in Figure 6–12. Notice the clean look of the Microsoft Edge window in Figure 6–13. Using Edge, you can run videos full screen. Edge has a reading mode that gives

Note: Windows 10 also supports Mozilla Firefox, Google Chrome, and Opera for applications that may be dependent on one of these browsers.

FIGURE 6–12 The Microsoft Edge icon is pinned to the taskbar by default.

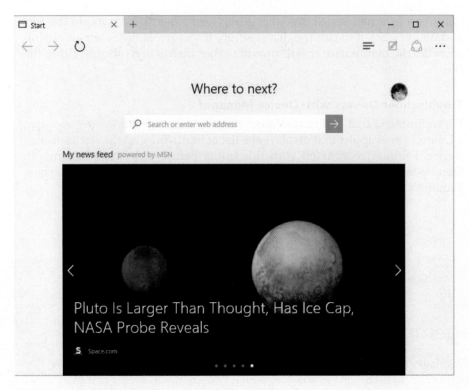

FIGURE 6-13 The Microsoft Edge browser window.

you choices for orientation and screen size, and you can pin settings, history, and reading list panes to the side of the Edge window. You can also mark up and save a Web page using a new feature called Web Note, which allows you to write or draw on a Web page, highlight items, erase your annotations, clip a portion of a page, and save the Web page with your annotations. You can then share it with other people. In Chapter 10 we will look more closely at configuration options and features in Microsoft Edge, as well as other Web browsers.

Install and Troubleshoot Drivers

Windows Setup detects your hardware devices and installs appropriate drivers. If Setup detects a noncritical device that does not work with one of the available drivers, you may be prompted to provide the driver files, or setup may quietly install a generic driver that works with a device, but doesn't take advantage of all its features. Or you may have a noncritical device that simply does not work after Windows 10 is installed. Therefore, one postinstallation task is to watch for error messages and devices that do not seem to function properly and install updated drivers. You have some choices for this that we will explore next.

Install Updated Drivers from Manufacturers

If you were prepared to install new drivers during setup, but did not have an opportunity to install them, then immediately after setup check for problems with the installed drivers in the form of error messages or a component not functioning properly. If you see such symptoms, install those drivers that you prepared ahead of time. In most cases, when manufacturers supply a compatible driver, it comes as an executable. If you downloaded the driver file, it will normally be in your Downloads folder, or you may have the driver file on an external device. In either case, open File Explorer, locate the file, and double-click it to run the driver setup. If the driver file is not an executable file, the manufacturer will provide other instructions for installing the file.

Troubleshoot Drivers with Device Manager

We recommend that you troubleshoot driver problems with Device Manager, a Control Panel applet that displays the list of hardware and the status of each device. Familiarize yourself with this utility before you have problems. In Step-by-Step 6.02, use Device Manager to look for problem drivers in the new Windows 10 installation and to correct problems, if necessary.

Step-by-Step 6.02

Using Device Manager in Windows 10

In this exercise you will open Device Manager to detect and resolve driver problems in Windows 10. To complete this exercise, you will need the following:

- A computer running Windows 10, preferably with a mouse and keyboard.

- You should be signed in with an administrator account, which you are if you are signed in as the user created during Windows 10 Setup.

- An Internet Connection will allow Device Manager to search online in Step 6.

Step 1

In the Start menu's Search box type "device manager." In the search results list notice that the results are shown in categories. Click on Device Manager, shown here at the top of the list.

Another way to open Device Manager is to use the ⊞+x shortcut to open the Power User Menu, and then select Device Manager.

Notice that the name of your computer displays at the top of the contents pane in Device Manager. Below that the devices are arranged in nodes. If Device Manager detects a problem with a device, the node will expand to show the device, along with a yellow error icon. In this example no errors were detected, but we clicked on the Monitors node to expand it and to learn more about the Monitor.

If Device Manager shows an error for a device, double-click that device. If there is no error, select a device, as we did, and double-click it to open the Properties. The box below Device Status shows that this device is working properly. If there is a problem an error message appears here. How you would troubleshoot a problem depends on the error. Device errors are often caused by the driver. Click the driver tab to see your options for managing the driver.

The Driver page has several buttons for managing drivers. Click on the Driver Details button.

The Driver File Details page shows the location and name of the driver file. There may be more than one file, but our example shows only one. Click OK to close Driver File Details and return to the Properties dialog box.

Step 6

Back on the Driver page of the Properties dialog box click the Update Driver button. On the Update Driver Software Page click the top option titled *Search automatically for updated driver software* and follow the instructions.

Step 7

A message and progress bar displays while Windows searches for a driver on your local computer and on the Internet.

Step 8

In our example, Windows determined that the best driver was already installed, displaying this message. If this is the case on your computer, click the Close button to return to the Properties dialog box where you can click the OK button to end the exercise, skipping the last step. If a message displays that a driver is being downloaded or installed, proceed to step 9.

Step 9

If Windows finds an appropriate updated driver on the local computer, it will proceed with the upgrade. If it finds one on the Internet, it will first download it, displaying a message with a progress bar. Then, after Windows 10 installs it, this message displays. Note, this screenshot is for a different device than the one shown in the earlier steps, which involved the monitor. This screenshot is the result of updating the driver for the display adapter, the device that controls the monitor.

Step 10

If you update a device driver, then the Properties for that device shows that the Roll Back button is live. Click the Close button to end the exercise.

If you upgrade a driver and then have problems with the device, or if Windows becomes unstable immediately after a driver upgrade, open the Properties dialog box for the device and use the Roll Back Driver button to remove the new driver and restore the old driver. The last two buttons on the Driver tab of the Properties dialog box for a device, Disable and Uninstall, trigger drastic measures that you would not normally take without advice from a very knowledgeable person.

Personalize Windows 10

After just a few minutes of using a new installation of Windows, you will feel the need to make it your own with your own preferences. Perhaps you want to change the size of icons on the desktop and taskbar or change pictures on the Lock screen, Desktop, or Sign-in screen. And we all have our own color preferences, which you can configure for the taskbar and windows. Begin by tweaking display settings, and then move on to the other ways to personalize Windows 10.

Tweak Display Settings

The Desktop context menu is one way to access Display settings. Open the context menu (Figure 6–14) by right-clicking an empty area of the Desktop. From the context menu select Display settings. In Windows 10 this opens the Display page of the Settings app where you change settings to suit how you work. Figure 6–15 shows the Display settings. The title at the top of the Display page (Customize Your Display) does not show because we scrolled down to show all the settings. Some settings take effect immediately, while others require that you click the Apply button. When this button remains grayed out, it is not usable or needed, but when it is required, it becomes brighter and you can click on it to keep changes. There may be other requirements before certain settings take effect, such as signing out and signing in again, as described below.

Identify, Detect, and Connect to Displays. Start with the row of items in blue text under the blue rectangle representing the display in Figure 6–15; if you

FIGURE 6–14 The Desktop context menu.

Note: To display the Desktop context menu on a touch screen press on an empty area of the Desktop and hold until a small square appears, then immediately release.

Note: If you are using Windows 10 in a virtual machine, you will be able to view the Display settings but not change them.

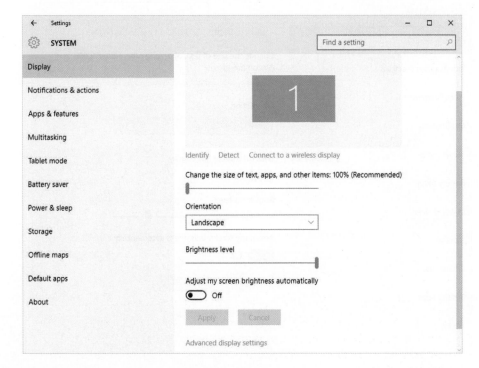

FIGURE 6–15 The Display settings on a laptop.

click on Identify, a number will appear on each display connected to your computer. This is very helpful when you have multiple displays, so that you can select which display is the main display, the one that will show the sign-in screen and will be the primary screen for the Desktop. Click Detect to detect all connected displays, and click Connect to a Wireless Display to initiate a connection with a wireless display.

Change the Size of Items on the Desktop. The next setting gives you some control over the size of displayed items; on our test systems this was limited to either 100% or 125%. The default is 100%, and if you change it, you will need to sign out and sign in again for it to take effect.

Orientation and Lock Rotation. The Orientation setting allows you to change the orientation from landscape (normal on desktops and laptops) to Portrait, as well as both of these orientations reversed, or "flipped." You normally will not change this setting. On a tablet, the Orientation setting will be grayed out, as shown in Figure 6–16, because sensors in a tablet will detect when you physically rotate the device and change the orientation without modifying these settings. Sometimes when using a tablet you want the tablet to stay in one orientation, even as you physically rotate it. For that reason tablets have the setting Lock rotation of this display, also shown in Figure 6–16.

Brightness Level. A Windows 10 laptop or tablet will automatically dim the screen when running on battery or, if the device has ambient light sensors, it will brighten the screen when it detects bright light. The laptop we used for the Figure 6–15 screenshot would dim the screen to an unacceptable

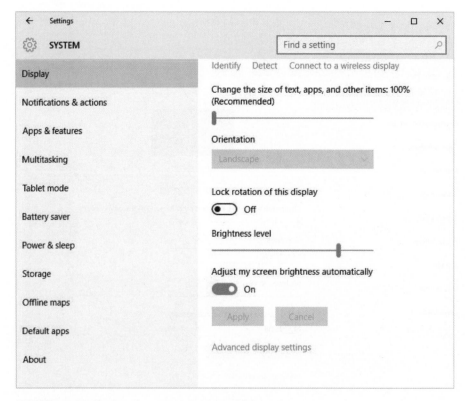

FIGURE 6–16 The Display settings on a tablet.

level, even when it was plugged into an outlet. To avoid this, we turned this setting off, and then manually set the brightness level to the highest setting. Experiment with this setting before following our example. In Figure 6–16 we have turned on the setting that allows Windows to automatically adjust screen brightness, and this works very well on the tablet. When you compare Figures 6–15 and 6–16, note that we scrolled down in Figure 6–16 to show the settings; otherwise the top of the page is identical to Figure 6–15.

Advanced Display Settings. Click the Advanced display settings link on the Display page to open the pane shown in Figure 6–17. Here is where you can check on the display resolution settings, which should be at the recommended setting on any modern flat screen display, as this is the native resolution determined by the display's design. The settings shown under Related Settings are settings that you will rarely need. For instance, use the Color Calibration utility if the colors on your screen appear wrong to you. This not a tool that artists or professionals would use to calibrate their screen.

The ClearType text setting allows you to enable or disable the ClearType technology that makes text more readable on your screen. This setting is turned on by default, and normally should not be turned off. Use the Advanced sizing of text and other items only if you are unhappy with the size of items and text on the desktop and the simpler setting on the first Display page did not make the improvement you needed. The last option under Related Settings opens the Properties dialog box for the display adapter, as shown back in step 10 of Step-by-Step 6.02.

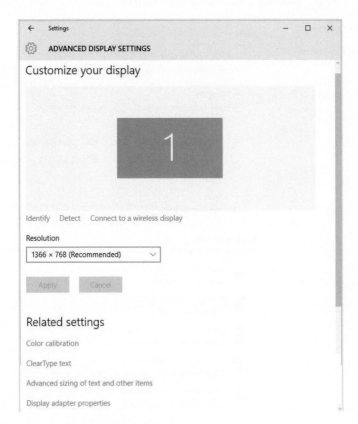

FIGURE 6–17 The Advanced Display Settings.

The Ease of Access button (left) and the Power button.

Ease of Access

Windows includes Ease of Access settings to make Windows more accessible for all types of needs. The Ease of Access and Power buttons, shown here, are on the bottom right of the Sign-in screen so that you can change some Ease of Access settings at sign-in. At this writing, the best place to find a complete list of Ease of Access settings or links to related settings is in Control Panel. In the Start menu Search box type "Ease of Access," and click or tap the result titled Ease of Access Center to open the Control Panel, as shown in Figure 6–18. There is a long list; some settings are out of view, and you can scroll down to see them.

Configure Windows Update

Windows Setup includes some updating of the Windows code, and Windows 10 is configured for automatic updates by default. In fact, in both retail editions, Windows 10 Home and Windows 10 Pro, updates are mandatory. In Windows 10 Pro you can defer upgrades that would add new features. Deferred upgrades will keep new Windows features from downloading and installing for several months.

However, you should manually trigger updates soon after the installation to ensure that your installation is completely up to date, and to help resolve any remaining driver issues. Additionally, we recommend configuring Windows Update to update all your installed Microsoft software, not just Windows components. Step-by-Step 6.03 walks through the steps for using Windows Update, available through the new Settings GUI.

Note: The keyboard shortcut ⊞+I opens Settings.

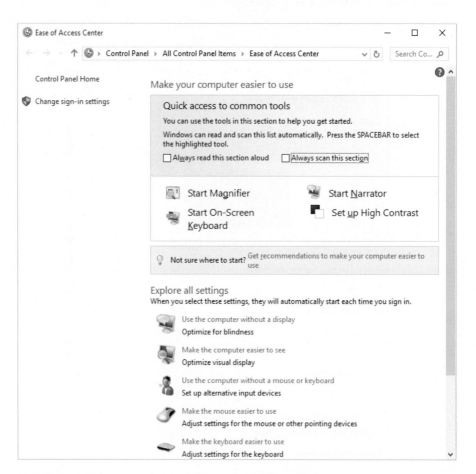

FIGURE 6–18 The Ease of Access Center in Control Panel.

Step-by-Step 6.03

Configuring and Using Windows Update

Open Windows Update from the new Windows Settings GUI, configure Update to update other Microsoft software, and check for more updates. To complete this exercise, you will need the following:

- A computer running Windows 10 Pro.
- You should be signed in with an administrator account or have the user name and password of an administrator account for the computer.

Step 1

Open Start and select Settings to open the Windows 10 Settings GUI. Alternatively, open Settings with the keyboard shortcut ⊞+I. Notice the grouping of settings into categories. Locate and select the Update & security category. You may need to scroll down in the Settings window to see this category.

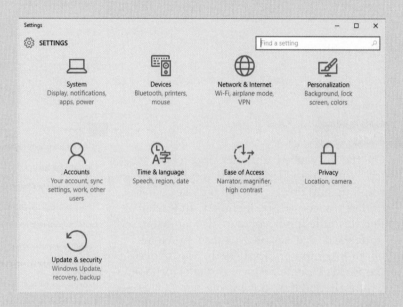

Step 2

This is the new Update & Security page. To see what choices you have for configuring Windows Update, click or tap Advanced Options.

Step 3

On the Advanced Options page ensure that installed Microsoft apps are kept up to date by clicking or tapping to place a check in the box labeled "Give me updates for other Microsoft products when I update Windows."

Step 4

On the Advanced Options page click or tap View Your Update History. If you scroll up and down, you not only see what updates successfully installed and what updates failed, but you can also uninstall updates if one seems to cause problems on your computer. Scroll to the top, above the words Update history, and click or tap Uninstall updates (not visible here). This opens a window in which you can select which update(s) to uninstall. Click it now, review the Uninstall an Update page, then close it to return to View Your Update History page.

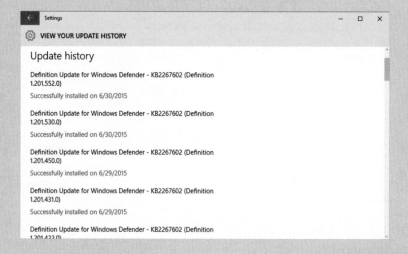

Step 5

Use the back arrow at the top of the View Your Update History page to return to the Advanced Options page. Repeat that action to return to the Windows Update page, shown in step 2. Then select Check for Updates to see just how up-to-date Windows is. In this example, Windows Update found a definition update for Windows Defender and proceeded to download and install it. When you are finished, close the Update & Security window to return to the Desktop.

Make Windows 10 Run Better in a Virtual Machine

If you installed Windows 10 into a virtual machine, an important postinstallation task is to install the software into the virtual machine that will make the OS run better. The name for this software and how it installs varies by hypervisor. In Microsoft's Hyper-V the software is labeled Integration Services, while Oracle VirtualBox uses the name Guest Additions. You may have already seen a message pop-up in Windows 10 in your virtual machine. If so, follow the instructions given. Otherwise, look for an option in the hypervisor window surrounding the virtual machine, as we did when we installed Windows 10 into a Hyper-V virtual machine on a PC running Windows 8.1 Pro. In that case, we opened the Action menu from the Virtual Machine Connection window and selected Insert Integration Services Setup Disk, as shown in Figure 6–19.

FIGURE 6–19 If you are using Hyper-V, open the Action menu on the Virtual Machine Connection window and select the last option (Integration Services).

If you installed Windows 10 into Oracle VirtualBox, open the Devices menu and select Install Guest Additions.

Remove Unwanted Software

If you purchase a computer with Windows 10 preinstalled, the first time you turn on your new computer you will go through the personalization tasks to configure your sign-in and to customize the Desktop. Then, when you arrive at the Desktop, you may find software installed by the manufacturer that you do not wish to use. Manufacturers received a lot of bad press a few years ago for some of the "junk" software that was preinstalled. Since then, new computers we have worked with have not had as much junk software, although we still find software that we simply do not use.

This preinstalled software falls roughly into two categories: trial software from various software publishers and free utilities provided by the manufacturer and labeled with the manufacturer's name.

Trial software is free to use for a period of time, usually 30 days. At the end of that time the trial software will cease to function unless you pay a fee to activate it. The two most common types of trial software are security, such as McAfee Antivirus, and productivity, such as Office 365. When you launch one of these, it clearly states that it is trial software and the length of the trial period. They also remind you before the trail period expires. What you choose to do about these trial apps depends on your own preferences and needs.

Apps installed by the manufacturer can usually be identified by the manufacturer's name in All Apps. Figure 6–20 shows the software installed by the manufacturer Lenovo. You may want to wait until you are more familiar with these apps before removing any.

When you decide to remove an app, open All Apps and scroll through the list to locate the app. You may need to open a folder, as in the case of Lenovo Reach, shown in Figure 6–21. Once you locate the app, right-click on it to bring up the context menu, also shown in Figure 6–21. Then select Uninstall.

FIGURE 6–20 The All Apps list showing software installed by the computer manufacturer Lenovo.

Migrate or Restore Data

If you did an in-place upgrade your data should be intact, but if you did a clean installation on an existing computer, you may have a data backup to restore. Your next task is to migrate or restore local data from a previous installation.

If you are migrating data from a Windows 7 computer and used the Windows 7 Backup and Restore utility before installing or upgrading, you

FIGURE 6–21 To remove an app, right-click on it, and select Uninstall.

are in luck because Windows 10 can do a restore from a Windows 7 backup. The Backup and Restore utility from Windows 7 is included in the Windows 10 Control Panel. Follow the steps in the Try This! to open this Backup and Restore utility.

Back Up Data and the System

In addition to the Windows 7 Backup and Restore utility, Windows 10, like Windows 8 and 8.1, comes with a File History tool for automatically backing up your local data. It also includes an image backup utility. You should configure these, or a third-party backup utility, soon after installing Windows 10.

Use Backup and Restore (Windows 7) to Back Up Files

Microsoft returned the Windows 7 Backup and Restore utility to Windows 10, and you can choose to use this to back up your data from any location on your local computer to the backup media of your choice.

Turn on File History

If you store your data files on the local hard drive, you will want to turn on File History. File History will automatically back up files in your Libraries, Desktop, Contacts, and Favorites. Therefore, you will need to save your files in those locations. It also backs up any OneDrive files that are available offline. File History is not turned on by default; if you have a spare external drive connected to your computer or to a network location, turn on and configure File History by opening Settings and selecting Update & Security. In Update & Security select Backup. On the Backup page, shown in Figure 6–22, click Add a drive. It should find the drive you attached or allow you to point to a network location. Once File History is turned on it works automatically, not only saving files as they change, but saving versions of each file, so that you can restore a file to a certain day and time.

FIGURE 6–22 Open File History in Update & Security.

FIGURE 6–23 Create a system image.

Create a System Image Backup

If you installed Windows 10 from bootable media, you already have the means to reinstall or repair the OS, if necessary. In the case of a new computer with Windows 10 preinstalled, look for some program from the manufacturer for creating an image of the factory-installed software in case you need to return the computer to its original state. Or you can create a System image using the Windows 10 utility. To do this follow the instructions for accessing File History in the previous section and select *More Options*. Then select *See Advanced Settings*. This will open the Advanced Settings for File History. On the bottom of this page select System Image Backup. This opens the page shown in Figure 6–23. Here you can create a System Image as well as a System Repair disc that will allow you to boot up the computer should the OS completely fail.

try this!

Use Backup and Restore (Windows 7)

Practice with the Windows 7 Backup and Restore utility in Windows 10. Try this:

1. In the Start Search box type "backup and."
2. From the search results list select Backup and Restore (Windows 7).
3. The Backup and Restore (Windows 7) Control Panel applet will open. If you have a Windows 7 backup, connect it to your computer; or you can click or tap **Select another backup to restore from** to point to a network location.
4. When you are finished, close the Backup and Restore window.

LO 6.3 | Working with Windows 10 Features

Microsoft has announced plans to release frequent updates to Windows 10, adding features along with bug fixes and security patches. Even though they used the update system to add features to Windows operating systems in the past, they continued to bring out new versions every three years or so, which meant that they held most features back until they could present them bundled in a new version. Now they are moving away from that practice, relying on incremental changes made through Windows Update, adding features when they have them ready to release. It looks like Windows 10 will continue to evolve as features are added through Windows Update. Therefore, we cannot promise to tell you everything about the Windows 10 you may have in front of you as you read this. After all, it is not the goal of this book to tell you about every single feature, but to present the selected features we believe are useful to experiment with and see which you will use every day.

Using the Start Menu

Earlier we introduced the Start menu, and now we will look at it more closely. When you start up Windows 10 on a PC or laptop, the Desktop strongly resembles the Windows 7 Desktop, clear of clutter, just showing the taskbar with the Start button and other features, and the Recycle bin shortcut near the top left. As you use your computer, you may add other objects to the Desktop or taskbar in addition to those placed there by default. Of course, Microsoft has changed the look of many of these objects, but not so much that you wouldn't recognize them. When you click on Start, the Start menu opens with features borrowed from the Start menu in Windows 7 and the Start screen in Windows 8 and 8.1.

As in Windows 7, the Start menu contains links and is customizable, letting you add or remove links to various folder locations such as Documents, Downloads, Pictures, Music, and Videos. The Start menu also highlights new apps right after they are installed, and contains the All Apps link that opens up a vertical alphabetical list of installed apps. After you have installed new software, All Apps will remind you with the word "New" positioned on its right in the Start menu. In Windows 10 the Start menu has two modes: Desktop and Tablet.

The Start Menu in Desktop Mode

On a PC or laptop the Start menu opens in Desktop mode, covering a large portion, but not all, of the Desktop as shown back in Figure 6–8. Desktop mode also displays apps windowed so they are easier to move around with a keyboard and mouse (or touchpad). You can use touch gestures in Desktop mode, but the GUI is not as convenient for touch use as it is in Tablet mode. In Desktop mode the Start menu contains a column along the left with your most used items at the top. Near the bottom are Quick links for File Explorer, Settings, Power, and All Apps, as well as a Cortana search box on the taskbar next to the Start button. In addition, out to the right on the Start menu are groups of Windows 8-style live tiles that can display active content.

The Start Menu in Tablet Mode

When Windows 10 wakes up on a tablet without an attached keyboard, the Start menu automatically opens in Tablet mode (full screen) to work better with a touch screen. In this mode, all your apps run full screen. In Tablet mode you do not have the option to switch to the Desktop unless you turn off Tablet mode. If you prefer the Windows 8 and 8.1 Start screen on your PC or laptop, simply click or tap the Action Center icon (or use the icon) in the keyboard shortcut Notification area of the taskbar (Figure 6–24), or use the keyboard shortcut ⊞+A. When the Action Center opens (Figure 6–25) tap or click Tablet mode. Figure 6–26 shows the Start menu in Tablet mode. Notice that the taskbar remains on the bottom of the screen. The column of Quick links on the left has disappeared to be replaced with a slender bar with a

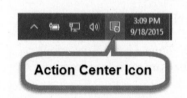

FIGURE 6–24 The Action Center icon is on the taskbar.

Note: The keyboard shortcut ⊞+A opens Action Center.

Note: The Action Center replaces the Windows 8 and 8.1 Charms bar. Action Center opens on touch devices with an edge gesture: a swipe from the right-side of the screen.

FIGURE 6–26 The Windows 10 Start menu in Tablet mode.

FIGURE 6–25 Open Action Center and select Tablet mode.

menu button at the top that opens up the Start menu list. At the bottom are the Power and All Apps Quick links. In Tablet mode, a Back icon, in the form of a left-facing arrow, appears on the taskbar. Click or tap this to go back to the last open app.

Selecting Tablet mode from the Action Center may only turn it on temporarily. Depending on the computer and other variables, the next time you restart a computer with keyboard attached it will go back to the default Desktop mode. So, if you are serious about working with the full Start screen on your computer with keyboard attached, then enable a setting under Start in the Personalization page of the Windows 10 Settings. As shown in Figure 6–27, the Use Start Full Screen setting is turned off by default. The Try This! exercise will show you how to enable this setting

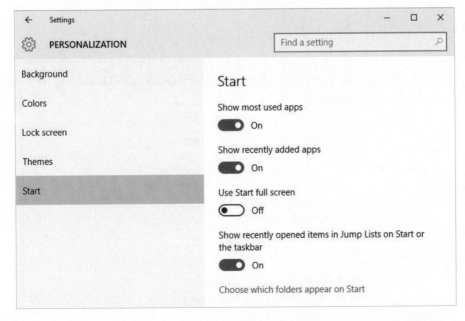

FIGURE 6–27 Enable Tablet mode at startup in Settings | Personalization | Start.

so that Tablet mode is the default. Learn more about personalizing Windows 10 in Step-by-Step 6.04.

Continuum

Continuum is a feature that is ideal for anyone working on a two-in-one device—a tablet with a detachable keyboard. With the keyboard attached, Windows 10 will display the PC-style Desktop mode. Detach the keyboard and the Continuum feature automatically changes to Tablet mode on the fly, converting the Start menu and open apps to full screen. Touch gestures let you move through the open apps. In addition, the Continuum feature enables a Windows 10 Mobile device to connect to monitors and keyboards.

Step-by-Step 6.04

Personalize the Windows 10 Desktop

The Windows 10 Desktop is more than just the Start menu, although that is an important feature. In this exercise, you will customize the Start menu and locate the Power User menu that gives you access to some of the utilities you used in previous versions of Windows. To complete this exercise, you will need:

- A PC or laptop running Windows 10.

Step 1

Open Settings | Personalization | Start.

Step 2

On the Start page click or tap "Choose what folders appear on Start."

Step 3

Scroll through the list and select a folder to appear on Start. We selected the Downloads folder.

Step 4

Close Settings and open Start to confirm that the folder you selected was added.

↓ Downloads

▥ File Explorer   ›

⚙ Settings

⏻ Power

≣ All apps

■ Ask me anything

Step 5

Customize the Desktop. Open Settings again and return to the Personalization page. Select Background. The background can be a picture, solid color, or a slideshow. As you choose different options, the Preview changes.

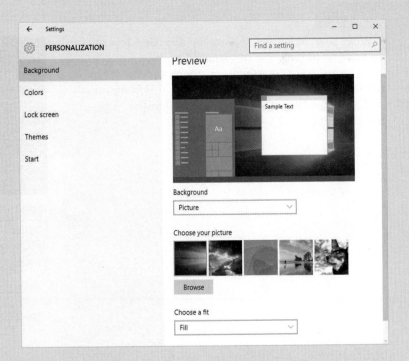

Click on the box labeled Picture in the step 5 example, and it will open to three choices: Picture, Solid color, and Slideshow. If it was not already selected, select Picture. You can select a different picture from the choices shown or browse to select a personal picture. The Preview reflects your changes, as shown here.

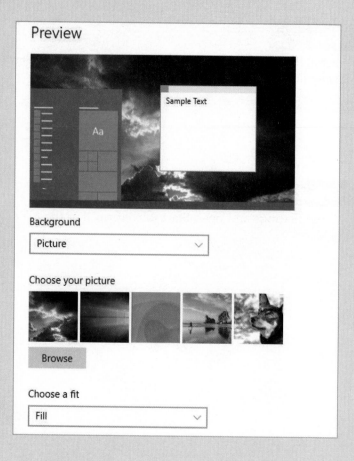

Change the fit of the picture on the Desktop by clicking or tapping the box under Choose a fit. This opens a list of fit treatments that temporarily cover up other settings. Experiment with different fits and see how they change the picture on the Desktop. Select one that you like.

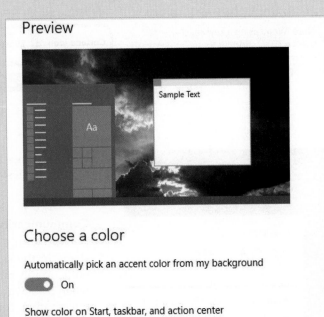

Step 8

Now select Colors in the left pane of the Personalization page. This opens the Colors pane. If the area below Choose a Color resembles the example shown here, change the first setting to Off so you can choose colors.

Step 9

Choose an accent color and add color to the Start menu, taskbar, and Action Center. You can also turn on or turn off the transparency of Start, taskbar, and Action Center. We prefer to have transparency turned off.

Step 10

Experiment with other Personalization options, such as choosing a picture for the Lock screen and selecting apps to appear on the Lock screen. When you have completed the changes you want, exit from Settings and return to the Desktop.

Note: When using a keyboard use the ⊞+C shortcut to open Cortana's Home panel.

FIGURE 6–28 The Cortana and Microphone icons.

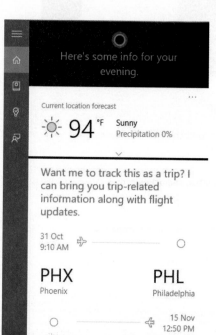

FIGURE 6–29 Cortana's Home pane.

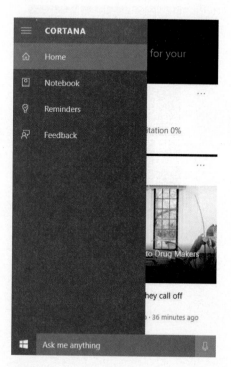

FIGURE 6–30 The Cortana Quick links.

Getting Started with Cortana

Cortana, a feature in Windows Phone 8.1, is now included in Windows 10. Cortana is an intelligent search system that searches the Web, your computer or device, and any cloud storage you use from that computer. It also learns about you, not by spying but by paying attention to things you give her permission to watch, using the Notebook feature. Let's start with the basics.

Communicating with Cortana

Interact with Cortana in several ways. You can simply enter a search string in the search box, as you did in previous versions of Windows, but Cortana can do much more for you. Click or tap the Cortana icon when you want to open her Home page where she keeps pertinent information for you. If you have a working microphone on your computer, click or tap the microphone icon, shown in Figure 6–28, on the right side of the search box, and start talking to Cortana. With either action, the area above the search box will open as she replies, as shown in Figure 6–29. This is the Home page where Cortana displays a configurable set of information for you as she learns more about you.

Control what Cortana displays in the Home page by changing settings, which we will discuss shortly. Click the menu icon at the top of the Cortana menu bar to expand it and see the label for each Quick link icon, as shown in Figure 6–30. They are, in order, Home, Notebook, Reminders, and Feedback (to Microsoft).

Select What Cortana Learns about You

Notebook, shown in Figure 6–31, is where you tell Cortana the things you want her to know about you and what she can use to learn more. This is where you change your name or its pronunciation, add favorite places, connect your online services (such as Office 365), and generally tell her your interests in the areas of dining, events, finance, transportation, movies, TV, music, news, sports, and travel. Notice the vertical scroll bar on the right, indicating that there are more items listed below.

Select Settings from Cortana's Notebook, and the Settings pane (Figure 6–32) opens. The options in blue text in this figure are links that will take you to additional settings. For instance, clicking "Manage what Cortana knows about me in the cloud," opens the Bing Settings Personalization page in the browser, shown in Figure 6–33.

Cortana can help you with many everyday tasks involving your installed apps, such as Music Player to select a play list, or creating an email using the Mail app. Cortana can go online to track a package based on information in an email. As Cortana learns, it will make appropriate suggestions and give reminders via posts on its Home page that opens up along the left of the screen. Providing a notice or other information in anticipation of a need is called a predictive notification, a feature long available in Google Now. This requires some history, but you can configure just how much of your life is revealed to Cortana. Need a little cheering up? Ask Cortana to tell you a joke.

Hey Cortana

The voice activation option, called Hey Cortana, was introduced in Windows Phone 8.1 and made available in Windows 10 for those devices that support voice input. This takes some training of the app by the user to ensure that Cortana responds to the voice query. You can either type your query or talk, and in both cases, you do not need to remember a syntax, but ask questions as you would if talking to or texting with a person.

Note: The autocorrect in apps for both PCs and mobile devices is another example of a predictive technology.

Using Apps in Windows 10

When working on the Desktop in Windows 10 you will find your apps behaving much like traditional Windows apps did in Windows 7. Launch an app from the Apps list and then pin it to the taskbar or create a shortcut on the Desktop. Windows 10 introduces Universal apps, which are an evolutionary change from the Modern apps of Windows 8. In this section, we introduce Universal apps, assure you that your old Windows apps will still run, try out the new Task view and Virtual Desktop features, and visit the Store.

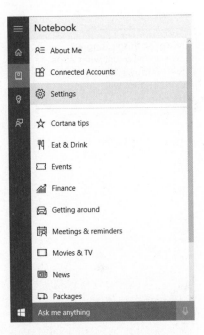

FIGURE 6–31 The Cortana Notebook.

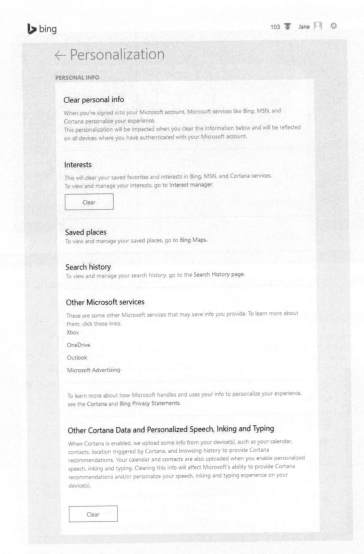

FIGURE 6–33 Use the Personalization page in Bing Settings to configure what Cortana knows about you through your online activities.

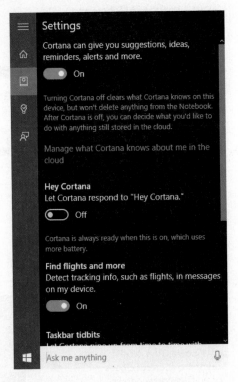

FIGURE 6–32 Configure Cortana through these settings and links.

Universal Apps

For Windows 10, Microsoft invested a large amount of effort into the notion that an application should be written once and run on many platforms—universally, so to speak. Therefore, while Windows 8 and 8.1 had Modern apps that covered the entire screen, and had a title bar added to them in Windows 8.1, Windows 10 introduced the Universal app that runs in Windows 10 on PCs and across all the devices this operating system supports, from the conventional PC to tablets and smartphones. A Universal app conforms to the different screen sizes and other features, such as input type (e.g., keyboard and mouse versus touch screen), making the switch automatically. Figure 6–34 shows Photos, a Universal app, running in a window. There are many other Universal apps, such as Photoshop Express, Dropbox, Netflix, and Twitter. On a tablet or smartphone, it will run full screen.

Support for Legacy Windows Apps

Windows 10 supports Windows Desktop apps. They run as they did in Windows 7 and on the Desktop in Windows 8 and 8.1. Figure 6–35 shows Microsoft Office 2013 apps open in Windows 10 in Desktop mode.

Note: At this writing we do not know just what apps the Windows 10 IoT Core edition will support.

Note: A Windows 8 Modern app also behaves like a Universal app, running in a window in Windows 10 on PCs and laptops, and switching to full screen on mobile devices.

FIGURE 6–34 A Universal app, Photos, runs in a window on a Windows 10 PC.

Note: As with previous versions of Windows, the Alt+F4 keyboard shortcut closes open Desktop windows and apps.

FIGURE 6–35 Traditional Desktop apps run in Windows 10.

FIGURE 6–37 Task view lets you quickly see your open apps.

Task View

Windows 10 **Task view** lets you quickly view all your open apps, improving on the Windows 7 Aero Flip 3D feature. Access Task view by clicking or tapping the Task view icon (Figure 6–36) on the taskbar. It opens with large tiles for each open app, as shown in Figure 6–37.

Virtual Desktops

Windows 10 includes a feature that has long been available in OS X and Linux: support for multiple Desktops—Microsoft calls it **Virtual Desktop**. This is a great way to group your projects. For instance, on your home PC you could create a new Desktop while working on personal finances with windows for Quicken, Excel, a calculator app, and your personal banking website open in one Desktop. Then you could also open a second Desktop where you work on an ancestry project. Task view, as shown in Figure 6–37, includes tiles at the bottom of the screen for two separate Desktops. From Task view simply click or tap to select a Desktop. When working in a Virtual Desktop, switch to other active Virtual Desktops by using the shortcut keys **Ctrl+⬛+left arrow** and **Ctrl+⬛+right arrow**.

Note: Two new keyboard shortcuts let you quickly move between virtual Desktops: Ctrl+⬛+ left arrow and Ctrl+⬛+right arrow.

Windows Store

The updated Windows Store is available from the Windows 10 Start menu. It requires an Internet connection and a Microsoft account. This one store provides Microsoft apps and services. It offers games, music, movies, and TV.

Be aware that many apps, especially games, have in-app purchases that can be quite expensive. They are very common in games, especially free games that often charge to turn off advertising for a period of time or charge for enhancements to the game. That is one reason the Store app in Windows 8.1 had a setting requiring an account password for every app purchase, but it could be turned off. This setting is not available in the Windows 10 Store app, but it is turned on. Our experience shows that it will ask for an account password with each purchase—even with in-app purchases.

Another important feature of the Store in both versions of Windows is the requirement that you add a payment method (credit card, cash card, or

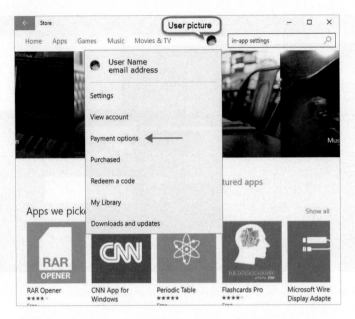

FIGURE 6–38 Add payment options for the Store.

PayPal) for app purchases through the Store. For instance, if you already have a payment method set up in your Microsoft account for a service, such as Office 365, that payment method will not be used for app purchases unless you add it. To do that, click on the User picture in the Menu bar to open the menu shown in Figure 6–38 and select Payment options. This will connect you to your Microsoft account settings where you can add a payment option for the Store. You do not need a payment option to download and install free apps.

The Store Settings page, shown in Figure 6–39, has an option for automatically updating apps. This is turned on by default, and we recommend keeping this setting. This is also where you can control whether or not the Live

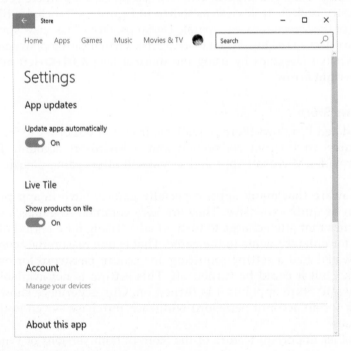

FIGURE 6–39 The Store Settings page.

Tile shows products. Under Account on this page is a link that will take you to the page in your Microsoft account settings where you can manage your devices on which you install apps.

The Try This! walks you through installing a free app from the Windows Store.

FIGURE 6–40 The Xbox Game bar.

Xbox Integration

If you have an Xbox One, use the Xbox app on your Windows 10 computer to access all your Xbox data, such as friends, activity, and game history. Additionally, you can record video game clips. With the Xbox app open, use keyboard shortcuts. ⊞+G opens the Xbox Game bar (Figure 6–40) containing buttons for working with Xbox recording games, taking screenshots of games, and configuring Xbox. Now either click or tap the record button or press ⊞+Alt+G to record the last 30 seconds of a game. Or use the ⊞+Alt+R shortcut to start a recording and repeat that shortcut to stop the recording. Take screenshots of a game with ⊞+Alt+Print Key.

If your Xbox One device can access live TV, you can stream it from your Xbox One to your Windows 10 PC using the Xbox app. The Xbox app also supports picture-in-picture (PIP) in which one show displays on the screen while another displays in a small box. This has been a feature in TVs for decades.

> **WARNING!**
>
> In-app purchases can quickly mount up. The Windows 10 Store app requires a password for each purchase. This is another reason to have a strong password.

try this!

Install a Free App from the Store

If you are signed in with a Microsoft account and have an Internet connection, browse for free apps at the Windows Store. Try this:

1. From the Start menu tap or click the Store tile.
2. Enter a search string into the Search box or scroll through the selections and click those that interest you. Look for a free or free trial app.
3. Follow the on-screen instructions to download and install the app.

> *Note:* Use ⊞+G to open the Xbox Game bar. Then use ⊞+Alt+G to record the last 30 seconds and ⊞+Alt+R to start recording a game. Repeat ⊞+Alt+R to end the recording of a game.

Changing the User Picture

On the top of the Start menu is the User tile displaying your account name and an image. You can choose a custom picture. Click or tap the User tile to open the menu shown in Figure 6–41. From this menu you can change your account settings, lock the screen, or sign out. The Try This! describes how to change your account picture in Windows 10.

FIGURE 6–41 The User menu.

try this!

Change Your Account Picture

Would you like to personalize your account picture? You can easily use an existing photo or take a new picture with your computer's camera. Try this:

1. Click or tap the User tile and select Change account settings.
2. This opens the Accounts pane in Settings. This page shows your present picture (or lack of one).
3. Click the Browse button and browse for a picture to use or select the Camera to take a picture.
4. Once you select a picture, return to the Accounts page where the new image will replace the previous one. Close the Settings window. The new picture will display on the Start menu and on the Sign-In screen.

LO 6.4 | Securing Windows 10

Windows 10 is the most secure version of Windows out-of-the-box because the default settings turn on the most critical security features. These include features from previous versions of Windows, such as Windows SmartScreen, Windows Defender, and Windows Firewall. Windows 10 security is also enhanced by new features: Windows Hello and Microsoft Passport. Although we include a description of Microsoft Passport here, it is one of several security features of Windows 10 designed for an Enterprise environment in which Windows 10 can be centrally managed to protect both the user and the enterprise. The other features we explore in this section are available to individual users who do not have the benefits of using Windows 10 in an enterprise. Further, in Chapter 10, Connecting Desktops and Laptops to Networks, you will learn security settings for popular Web browsers, including Microsoft Edge.

Privacy Settings

The Windows 10 Settings app's Privacy page contains many settings you should explore; carefully consider the trade-off between privacy and the convenience of allowing certain apps have access to your location and other personal information. One of the settings found in the General pane, if turned on, allows SmartScreen Filter to check URLs that Windows Store apps attempt to use. This is on by default, as shown in Figure 6–42.

Windows Hello

Windows Hello, a new biometric sign-in feature, lets you sign in to your Windows 10 device with a biometric sign-in: fingerprint, facial recognition,

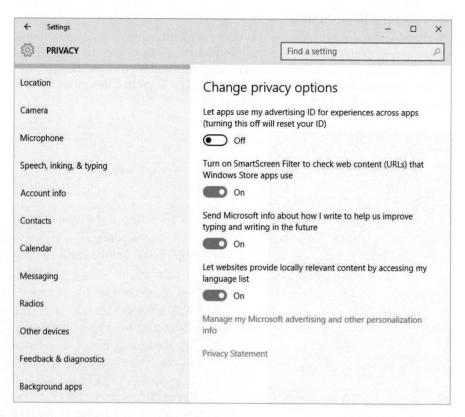

FIGURE 6–42 Windows 10 Privacy settings.

or iris scan. It requires the existence of special hardware in the Windows 10 computer. To sign in with a fingerprint, your computer must have a compatible fingerprint scanner. The facial and iris scanning requires a special depth camera that uses infrared light to see features under the less-than-ideal settings in the real world, such as poor light conditions and users wearing makeup or having facial hair.

Microsoft Passport

While Windows Hello allows you to log in to your Windows 10 device using biometrics, Microsoft Passport lets you securely sign in to network resources without sending a password or PIN over the network; the authentication is tied to the hardware. For greater security combine the secure local authentication of Windows Hello with Microsoft Passport authentication to network resources Microsoft Passport authentication to network resources. Presently Microsoft Passport gives you access to resources, such as Microsoft's Azure Active Directory services, and Web servers, but there is limited support beyond Microsoft's products. That may change, as Microsoft is among many companies representing such industries as banking, software, hardware, and more who joined the industry consortium FIDO Alliance (Fast Identity Online) to contribute their technology and work together to develop solutions that will allow users to securely access online services and conduct financial transactions without using password authentication and to reduce the risk of fraud.

Note: Learn more about the FIDO Alliance at **https://fidoalliance.org**.

Windows Defender

Windows Defender automatically provides antispyware and antimalware protection. Installing a third-party security app disables Windows Defender. Launch the Windows Defender app by entering "defender" into the Search box. Figure 6–43 shows the Home page of the Windows Defender app. From here you can initiate a scan outside of Windows Defender's normal schedule,

FIGURE 6–43 The Windows Defender app.

FIGURE 6–44 Windows Firewall Control Panel.

and choose the type of scan. Similarly, the Update tab lets you initiate an update of the Windows Defender virus and spyware definition files, while the History tab page lets you see what potential threats Defender has detected. So far, Windows Defender looks very much like Windows Defender in Windows 8 and 8.1, but the Settings tab is gone now, replaced by a Settings button that launches the Windows Defender page in Windows 10 Settings.

Windows Firewall

Windows 10 Firewall, like that in Windows 8.1, has a simple interface for basic settings, as shown in Figure 6–44. If you select the option on the left labeled "Allow an app or feature through Windows Firewall," a page opens with a list

FIGURE 6–45 Select apps to allow (or not allow) through the Windows Firewall on the private or public network.

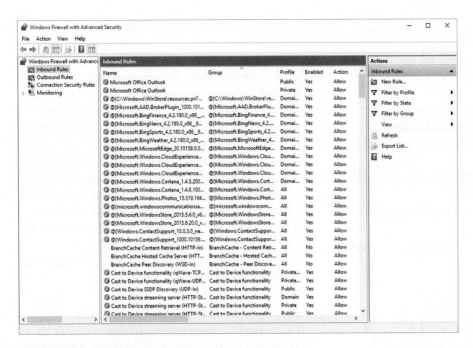

FIGURE 6–46 Windows Firewall with Advanced Security.

of allowed apps and features, shown in Figure 6–45. Here you can select those aps allowed (or not) through the firewall on the private network and/or on the public network.

Select Advanced settings from the Windows Firewall Control Panel to open the Windows Firewall with Advanced Security management console, shown in Figure 6–46. This is a very advanced tool for a knowledgeable administrator. Using this console, you can set inbound and outbound rules for the traffic identified by its source or app name, allowing or blocking certain types of traffic.

Chapter 6 REVIEW

Chapter Summary

After reading this chapter and completing the exercises, you should understand the following facts about Windows 10.

Installing Windows 10

- The three editions of Windows 10 are Windows 10 Home, Windows 10 Pro, and Windows 10 Mobile. The Home and Pro editions run on PCs and compatible tablets, while the Mobile edition is intended for both smartphones and tablets with a screen size of eight inches or smaller.
- Windows 10 has operating modes that work on PCs, tablets, two-in-ones, and phones.

- The minimum hardware requirements to install Windows 10 on a computer with Intel or AMD architecture are nearly identical to those of Windows 8. Fortunately, even budget-level computers today come with hardware that far exceeds Windows 10's requirements.
- Upgrades from certain retail editions of Windows 7 and Windows 8.1 were free for the first year after Windows 10's introduction date.
- Windows 10 includes Cortana, a personal virtual assistant integrated with the new Microsoft Edge Web browser.

- Cortana's voice activation option, Hey Cortana, was introduced in Windows Phone 8.1, and is available in Windows 10 for those devices that support voice input. Type a query or talk using natural language.
- To upgrade an installation of Windows to Windows 10, the old version must be either Windows 7 Service Pack 1 (SP1) or Windows 8.1 Update 1.
- Some features of Windows 7 and Windows 8.1 are not supported in Windows 10.
- Prior to upgrading there are several things you should do:
  - Update Windows 7, Windows 8, or 8.1 if they are not already updated.
  - Back up your data.
  - Update the firmware, if an update is available.
  - Acquire updated drivers if the manufacturer has not automatically updated them.
  - Choose whether you will sign in to Windows 10 with a local account, a Microsoft account, or a Windows Active Directory account.
- The Windows 10 comes "prekeyed" and will automatically provide the product key to Microsoft during the product activation process.
- If you purchase Windows 10 online you can do a Web-based setup that requires very little interaction and is very fast.
- To do a traditional Windows setup you must have the Windows 10 Setup files on bootable media. If you purchase a physical retail package you will have bootable media in either DVDs or a USB flash drive. If you purchase Windows 10 online and choose the option "Install later by creating Media," you will have the option to download to a USB drive or to an ISO file.

Postinstallation Tasks

- The Windows 10 Start menu: Apps are on the left and tiles on the right.
- Quick links replace the previous shortcuts.
- File Explorer is the Windows 10 file management utility. It is essentially the renamed and updated replacement for Windows Explorer.
- Microsoft Edge, a new Web browser, is an alternative to Internet Explorer (IE), which Microsoft also included in Windows 10 for backward compatibility with some websites.
- Install drivers. Windows Setup detects your hardware devices and installs appropriate drivers if it has them. If it doesn't, you will

have to find them, either online or from the manufacturer.
- Tweak the display settings from the Settings app, and make Windows more accessible with a long list of Ease of Access settings.
- Updates are mandatory in Windows 10 Home and Windows 10 Pro, but you can add updates for other Microsoft software.
- Make Windows 10 run better in a virtual machine. If you installed Windows 10 in a virtual machine, an important postinstallation task is to install the software in the virtual machine that will make it run better. The name of this software varies by hypervisor.
- Remove unwanted software from a computer that has Windows 10 preinstalled.
- Migrate or restore data.
- Back up both data and the system using either third-party utilities or the utilities available in Windows 10: Windows 7 Backup and Restore utility, File History, and image backup.

Working with Windows 10 Features

- Windows 10 default Desktop shows just the taskbar with the Start button, some other features, and the Recycle bin shortcut near the top left.
- On a computer with a keyboard, the Start menu opens in Desktop mode covering a large portion of the Desktop. Apps are windowed to make them easy to move around by keyboard, mouse, or touchpad.
- When Windows 10 wakes up on a tablet without an attached keyboard, the Start menu automatically opens in full-screen Tablet mode. In this mode, all your apps run full screen. You can manually switch between Screen mode and Tablet mode.
- The Continuum feature detects when the keyboard is attached so that Windows 10 will display the PC-style Desktop mode.
- Personalize the Start menu by adding Quick links to folders. Personalize the Desktop background and colors.
- Get started with Cortana, Windows 10's virtual assistant. Cortana learns as you use it and it will make appropriate suggestions and reminders. It includes a voice-activation option, Hey Cortana.
- When working in Desktop mode, all apps behave much as traditional Windows apps did in Windows 7. You can launch an app from the Apps list

and then pin it to the taskbar or create a shortcut on the Desktop.

- New Universal apps run on all the devices this operating system supports, from the conventional PC to tablets and smartphones. A Universal app conforms to the different screen sizes and other features, such as input type (e.g., keyboard and mouse versus touch screen), making the switch automatically.

- Windows 10 Task view lets you quickly view your open apps, improving on the Windows 7 Aero Flip 3D feature. Access Task view by clicking or tapping the Task view icon and it opens with large tiles for each open app.

- Windows 10 supports multiple virtual Desktops. This is a great way to group your projects.

- The Windows Store requires a Microsoft account and offers services, software, games, music, movies, and TV. The Store will not automatically use a payment method associated with your account for other services. To make purchases through the Store, add a payment method through the Store. The Store requires a password for each purchase.

- The Xbox app in Windows 10 accesses a user's Xbox One.

- Open the User menu from the User tile on the Start menu to change the user picture, lock the computer, or sign out.

Securing Windows 10

- Windows 10 is the most secure version of Windows with the most critical security features enabled. Explore the Privacy Settings to balance your privacy needs with the convenience offered by Windows features.

- Windows Hello, a new feature, lets you sign in to your Windows 10 device with a biometric sign-in type: fingerprint, facial recognition, or iris scan. It requires the existence of special hardware in the Windows 10 computer.

- Microsoft Passport lets you securely sign in to network resources without sending a password or PIN over the network. Once Passport authenticates you locally, it gives you access to resources, such as Microsoft's Azure Active Directory services, and some Web servers.

- Windows Defender automatically provides antispyware and antimalware protection. Installing a third-party security app disables Windows Defender. Launch the Windows Defender app by entering "defender" into the Search box.

- Windows 10 Firewall has a simple interface for basic settings. If you select the option labeled "Allow an app or feature through Windows Firewall," a page opens with a list of allowed apps and features.

Key Terms List

Continuum *(244)*	Microsoft Edge *(226)*	Task view *(251)*	Windows 10 Home Edition *(208)*
Cortana *(248)*	Microsoft Passport *(255)*	two-step verification *(223)*	Windows 10 Mobile *(209)*
Desktop mode *(224)*	picture-in-picture (PIP) *(253)*	Universal app *(250)*	Windows 10 Pro *(208)*
Device Manager *(228)*	predictive notification *(248)*	User tile *(225)*	Windows Hello *(254)*
Ease of Access icon *(221)*	Quick link *(225)*	Virtual Desktop *(251)*	Xbox Game bar *(253)*
FIDO Alliance *(255)*	Tablet mode *(242)*	Web Note *(227)*	
Hey Cortana *(249)*			

Key Terms Quiz

Use the Key Terms List to complete the sentences that follow. Not all terms will be used.

1. Although this sounds like you are greeting a female friend, _____ is a new feature of Windows that lets you activate your personal assistant with your voice.

2. In _____ the Start menu covers the entire screen, and universal apps are full screen.

3. The _____ feature of Windows 10 lets you quickly view all your open apps, improving on Aero Flip 3D, a feature of Windows 7.

4. The _____ feature is similar to ones long available in OS X and Linux, in which you can organize your open apps into individual groupings, with one grouping on your screen at a time.

5. The ⊞+G keyboard shortcut opens the _____ containing buttons for recording games, taking screenshots of games, and other tasks.

6. The _____ is an industry consortium working to develop technologies to allow users to securely access online services and conduct financial transactions without using password.

7. Windows 10 on a two-in-one device uses a new feature called _____, by which it detects when the keyboard is disconnected and automatically changes to Tablet mode.

8. An example of _____ is when Cortana provides a notice in anticipation of a need it discovered by learning about you and your interests.

9. A/an _____ automatically runs full screen on a Windows 10 tablet, and windowed on a computer with a keyboard.

10. _____ is the biometric sign-in feature in Windows 10, requiring special hardware.

Multiple-Choice Quiz

1. What previous versions of Windows could be upgraded to Windows 10 for free for one year from its release? Select all that apply.
   a. Windows Vista, Service Pack 2
   b. Windows 8.1 Update 1
   c. Windows 7 Service Pack 3
   d. Windows XP Service Pack 3
   e. Windows 7 Service Pack 1

2. Windows 10 introduced this new Web browser.
   a. Microsoft Edge
   b. Cortana
   c. Microsoft Passport
   d. Continuum
   e. Windows Defender

3. What are the words to look for in the Windows 7 and Windows 8 System app to determine if an installation is legally licensed?
   a. Hello Windows!
   b. Hey Cortana!
   c. License is legal.
   d. Windows is activated.
   e. Genuine Windows!

4. What is the name of the Windows 10 personal assistant that first appeared in Windows Phone 8.1?
   a. Microsoft Edge
   b. Cortana
   c. Microsoft Passport
   d. Continuum
   e. Windows Defender

5. This new method for authenticating to network resources does not send passwords or PINs across a network.
   a. Microsoft Edge
   b. Cortana

   c. Microsoft Passport
   d. Continuum
   e. Windows Defender

6. When working in Virtual Desktops in Windows 10, what feature will allow you to see a tile representing each Virtual Desktop, as well as all open apps?
   a. Quick link
   b. Predictive notification
   c. Task view
   d. Windows Hello
   e. Picture-in-picture (PIP)

7. This security antimalware and antispyware app comes with Windows 10 and is enabled during installation.
   a. Microsoft Edge
   b. Cortana
   c. Microsoft Passport
   d. Continuum
   e. Windows Defender

8. This feature, long available in TVs, allows someone with an Xbox One to use the Xbox app on Windows 10 to stream two shows at once and keep track of both of them on the screen.
   a. Quick link
   b. Predictive notification
   c. Task view
   d. Windows Hello
   e. Picture-in-picture (PIP)

9. Which one of these will be removed when upgrading a computer from Windows 7 to Windows 10? Select all correct answers.
   a. Windows Hello
   b. Windows Media Center

c. Desktop gadgets

d. Windows XP Mode

e. Minesweeper

10. Click or tap this to open the Windows 10 Start menu.

a. ⊞ KEY

b. Start button

c. Windows button

d. ⊞+I

e. ⊞+C

11. Which of the following is the acronym for Microsoft's antipiracy tool?

a. PIP

b. OS

c. MSA

d. ISO

e. MPA

12. What optional authentication feature for your Microsoft Account requires that you provide a method for Microsoft to contact you with a special code?

a. Hey Cortana

b. Windows Hello

c. Two-step verification

d. Windows Defender

e. Microsoft Passport

13. This feature of Windows Edge allows you to make annotations on a Web page, save the annotated page, and share it with others.

a. Cortana

b. Web Note

c. Microsoft Password

d. Windows Hello

e. Quick link

14. Which retail edition of Windows 10 will you buy for your home PC if you need to use BitLocker To Go?

a. Windows 10 Starter

b. Windows 10 Education

c. Windows 10 Enterprise

d. Windows 10 Home

e. Windows 10 Pro

15. Windows 8 introduced Modern apps and Windows 10 introduced this type of app.

a. Continuum

b. Windows Passport

c. Windows Firewall

d. Universal app

e. File Explorer

Essay Quiz

1. During the one-year period in which Windows 10 was a free upgrade for compatible systems running either Windows 7 Service Pack 1 or Windows 8.1 Update 1, describe the steps you would have had to go through to do a clean install on a qualifying computer.

2. You plan to do a clean install of Windows 10 Pro onto a computer that currently is running Windows 7, and you plan to reinstall the Windows apps that are currently on that computer. Describe what steps you will take to see if your existing hardware and applications are compatible with Windows 10 and to prepare for any incompatibilities.

3. I have Windows Live Essentials OneDrive app installed on my Windows 7 computer that I plan to upgrade to Windows 10. Describe what will happen during the upgrade and what I should do afterward.

4. Describe the differences between signing in with a local account and signing in with a Microsoft account.

5. Describe Windows Hello and Microsoft Passport and explain the relationship between these two features in making secure connections to network resources.

Lab Projects

LAB PROJECT 6.1

When Microsoft released Windows 10 as a free upgrade to many existing Windows computers, their hope was to replace old versions of Windows with one that would be continually upgraded as time went on. They also

hoped to gain market share of desktop and laptop computers. Research how successful this program was in terms of the percentage of qualifying computers that were upgraded and in terms of the resulting market share of Windows 10 on all PCs worldwide.

LAB PROJECT 6.2

Experiment with the Web Note feature. Find a website with content that interests you and use Windows 10 Web Note feature to add notes, highlight important facts, and circle items. Then share with a classmate by emailing a copy of the page. Is this a feature you will use? Discuss this with your classmates.

LAB PROJECT 6.3

Because of the limitation of introducing an entire new operating system in one chapter, the authors left out many interesting topics. One of those is HoloLens and holographic computing in general. At the time of this writing, HoloLens has only been presented as augmented reality technology, and demonstrations of it have mostly involved gaming. However, it has much broader applications. Microsoft is offering Microsoft HoloLens academic research grants. Research what is happening with this technology. Describe products using this technology and answer these questions: Is gaming the most important area? Provide examples of the use of HoloLens in research and education. Write up your findings and share them with your classmates.

7

Supporting and Troubleshooting Windows

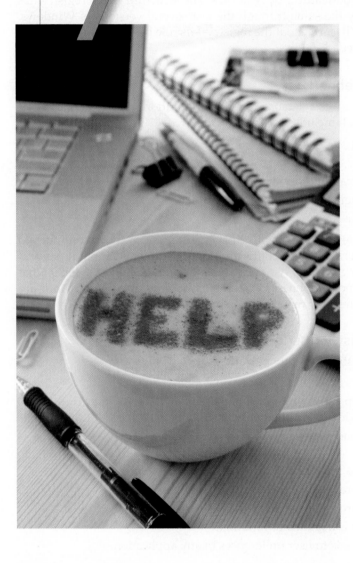

Learning Outcomes

In this chapter, you will learn how to:

LO **7.1** Define the role of the registry in Windows, and back up and modify the registry when needed.

LO **7.2** Describe the Windows user options and power options, and, given a scenario, select appropriate startup options.

LO **7.3** Install and manage device drivers.

LO **7.4** Troubleshoot common Windows problems.

T he world of computing has changed considerably during the decades since Windows was first introduced as a GUI operating system for PCs and laptops. The Windows PC or laptop, once required for students and people in innumerable jobs, has been losing ground to tablets and smartphones, as these devices offer more and more functionality. However, Windows still has a significant presence for millions worldwide, especially in the business world. If you are one of them you may occasionally find yourself needing to troubleshoot Windows. This chapter will guide you through a tour of some of the under-the-hood components and the tools for working with them.

Begin with the registry, a critical component of Windows. Then consider user options, power options, and various ways to start up Windows for resolving problems. Then move on to the topic of installing and managing device drivers, and lastly look at methods for troubleshooting common Windows problems. ☀

LO 7.1 | Understanding the Registry

The registry is one of several features that make Windows so adaptable that we can add the hardware and applications to turn a Windows computer into the computing tool we need. Ironically, it is also one of the most complicated and least understood features of Windows. The structure of the registry has remained virtually the same through the last several versions of Windows. In this section you'll learn about the registry—its role in Windows and how to modify it when needed.

The Registry Defined

The Windows registry is a database of all configuration settings in one installation of Windows. It includes settings for:

- Device drivers
- Services
- Installed application programs
- Operating system components
- User preferences

Windows creates the registry during its installation, and it continues to make modifications to it as you configure Windows and add applications and components. During startup, Windows depends on the registry to tell it what services, drivers, and components to load into memory, and how to configure each of them. The registry remains in memory while Windows is active.

Automatic Registry Changes

The Windows registry will automatically change when:

- Windows starts up or shuts down.
- Windows Setup runs (which occurs more often than you may think; e.g., each time Windows gets updated).
- Changes are made through a Control Panel applet or the newer Settings tool.
- A new device is installed.
- Any changes are made to the Windows configuration.
- Any changes are made to a user's desktop preferences.
- An application is installed or modified.
- Changes are made to user preferences in any application.

Registry Files

Although considered only a single entity when Windows is running, the registry is actually stored in a number of binary files on disk. A binary file contains program code. The Windows registry files include the following:

- BCD
- default
- ntuser.dat
- sam
- security
- software
- system

TABLE 7–1 Locations of the Hives within the Registry

Hive File	Registry Location
BCD	HKEY_LOCAL_MACHINE\BCD00000000
default	HKEY_USERS\.DEFAULT
ntuser.dat (of the currently logged-on user)	HKEY_CURRENT_USER and HKEY_USERS
sam	HKEY_LOCAL_MACHINE\SAM
security	HKEY_LOCAL_MACHINE\SECURITY
software	HKEY_LOCAL_MACHINE\SOFTWARE
system	HKEY_LOCAL_MACHINE\SYSTEM

The Windows developers named the portion of the registry represented in one of these registry files a hive. Table 7–1 shows where the data from each registry hive are located in the registry. Hive files are the permanent portions of the registry, with all the changes saved from use to use. With the exception of ntuser.dat and BCD, these registry files are in a disk folder named config, located below C:\Windows\ System32. Figure 7–1 shows the contents of the config folder in Windows 10. Look for the files that match the list above (except ntuser.dat and BCD). Notice that the registry files listed in the config folder have file names without file extensions. If you have Windows Explorer (Windows 7) or File Manager (Windows 8, 8.1, and Windows 10) configured to show hidden files, you will see other files in this location, including files with log extensions that have file names that match the registry files. The operating system uses LOG files for logging transactions to the registry files. Other hidden files with matching file names and SAV extensions are backup copies of registry files created at the end of the text mode stage of setup.

try this!

View Hidden Files and Extensions in Windows Explorer/File Explorer

By default Windows hides hidden files and extensions in the GUI. Make them visible in Windows Explorer/File Explorer. These steps work in Windows versions 7, 8.1, and Windows 10. Try this:

1. Open the **Start** menu (Windows 7) or **Power User** menu (Windows 8, 8.1, and Windows 10) and select **Control Panel**.
2. In **Control Panel** search on "folder options" and open **Folder Options** or **File Explorer Options** (Windows 10) from the results.
3. In Folder Options/File Explorer Options select **View**.
4. On the View tab enable the radio button labeled **Show hidden files, folders, and drives**.
5. Ensure that there is *no* check in the boxes labeled **Hide extensions for known file types** and **Hide protected operating system files**.
6. Click or tap the OK button.
7. Open Windows Explorer/File Explorer and browse to the **config** folder, usually found at C:\Windows\System32. Extensions and hidden files are now visible.

BCD

The BCD file resides in the Boot folder in the hidden system partition. As with other registry files, it is a binary file. It contains the Boot Configuration Database (BCD) store used by Windows during the bootloader phase of startup, providing the bootloader with information it needs to locate and load the operating system files.

Note: The Boot Configuration Database in the BCD file is used during the bootloader phase of startup.

DEFAULT

The default hive contains user desktop settings, called a user profile, used when there is no logged-on user. You do need desktop settings for the GUI even before you log on. You'll see evidence of this profile in the desktop settings used for the Logon screen shown in Figure 7–2.

FIGURE 7–1 This view of the Windows 10 config folder shows most of the registry files.

FIGURE 7–2 The default user profile is used until a user logs on.

NTUSER.DAT

The ntuser.dat hive file contains the user profile for a single user. These settings include application preferences, screen colors, network connections, and other personal choices. Each user who logs on to the computer has a separate ntuser.dat file. During startup, Window uses the other registry hives to load and configure the operating system. One of the last tasks of the operating system at startup is to request a user logon. When a user logs on, the settings from that user's ntuser.dat file apply and become part of the current registry. The first time a user logs on to a computer, Windows uses the ntuser.dat file from the C:\Users\Default folder to create the initial profile for the user. It saves the ntuser.dat file in the top-level personal folder for that user, and it is a hidden file so it is only visible if your Folder Options are set to Show hidden files, folders, and drives.

Note: We described personal folders in Chapter 4.

SAM

The sam hive contains the local security accounts database; sam is an acronym for Security Accounts Manager.

Note: the sam hive also stores user passwords, and it is used to authenticate users.

SECURITY

The security hive contains the local security policy settings for the computer, including rules for password complexity and for how the system will handle numerous failed attempts at entering a password.

SOFTWARE

The software hive contains configuration settings for software installed on the local computer, along with various items of miscellaneous configuration data.

SYSTEM

The system hive contains information used at startup, including device drivers to load as well as the order of their loading, and configuration settings, instructions for the starting and configuring of services, and various operating system settings.

The Temporary Portion of the Registry

The information stored in HKEY_LOCAL_MACHINE\HARDWARE is temporary information, gathered during the hardware detection process of the detect-and-configure-hardware phase of Windows startup. Windows does not save it to disk in a file, as it does other portions of the registry.

Viewing and Editing the Registry

You view and edit the hierarchical structure of the active registry using the Registry Editor utility, Regedit. Its executable file, regedit.exe, is located in the folder in which the operating system is installed (by default that is C:\Windows), but it does not have a shortcut on the Start menu or other handy locations in the Windows GUI. This is for a very good reason: It should not be too handy. When you need it, you can start it from the Run box. It will aid your understanding of the registry if you open the Regedit program now and refer to it as you read the following descriptions of the registry components. The Try This! will walk you through opening Regedit, viewing the registry locations shown in Table 7–1.

The first time Regedit runs on a computer, it looks like Figure 7–3. Each folder represents a **key**, an object that may contain one or more settings as well as other keys. Each of the top five folders is a **root key** (also called a subtree in Microsoft documentation). Each root key is at the top of a hierarchical structure containing more keys. Each key may contain one or more settings as well as other keys. A key that exists within another key is a **subkey**. Each setting within a key is a **value entry**. When you click on the folder for a key, it becomes

WARNING!

Do not directly edit the registry with a tool such as Regedit unless it is absolutely necessary; there are many safer ways to make a change to the registry. For example, when you change settings in a Control Panel applet, that applet in turn modifies the registry because that is where it maintains and uses the settings.

FIGURE 7–3 The registry root keys.

try this!

Start Registry Editor

Open Registry Editor and explore the contents of the registry. Try this:

1. Press ⊞+R. This opens the Run box. Type "regedit" and click OK.
2. Respond to any User Account Control dialog to continue.
3. Once Regedit is open be careful not to make any changes. Browse through the registry structure, much as you would navigate in Windows Explorer/File Explorer.
4. Notice the folders in the navigation pane and the various folders and settings in the contents pane. Keep Registry Editor open as you read this chapter section.

Note: Describing a registry location is similar to the way we describe file and folder locations on disk; we use a notation that shows the path from a root key down through the subkeys: HKEY_LOCAL_MACHINE\SYSTEM\CURRENTCONTROLSET\CONTROL.

the active key in Regedit, its folder icon "opens," and the contents of the key show in the right pane, as you see in Figure 7–4. Table 7–2 gives an overview of the information stored within each root key of the registry.

In Regedit, each value entry appears in three columns labeled: Name, Type, and Data. The Type column shows a label that describes the format of the data in that registry value, also called **data type**. There are many data types in the registry; take a few minutes to study Table 7–3, which shows just a few registry data types, to give you an idea of how diverse the data in the registry can be.

Backing Up the Registry

It is very important to remember that the last thing you should consider doing, even if your best friend or brother-in-law insists you do it, is to directly edit the registry using Regedit or a third-party registry editing tool. We are even more than a little squeamish about the registry cleaning tools promoted all over the Internet. But even though you should rarely if ever edit the registry, you should know how to back up the registry in case you decide that you have no choice but to use Regedit. Here are two methods for backing up the registry. The first, using System Restore, is a very broad approach that backs up the entire registry and more. The second method, backing up a portion of the registry with Regedit, is a more targeted approach.

FIGURE 7–4 Registry components.

TABLE 7–2 Contents of Registry Root Keys

Root Key	Description
HKEY_CLASSES_ROOT	Shows relationships (called associations) between applications and data file types defined by file extension. Thanks to the information in this key, you can double-click on a data file and the correct application will open and load the file. This root key is actually all the information located in HKEY_LOCAL_MACHINE\SOFTWARE\Classes.
HKEY_CURRENT_USER	Contains the user profile for the currently logged-on user, storing all the user settings that affect the desktop appearance and the default behavior of installed applications.
HKEY_LOCAL_MACHINE	Contains the system information, including detected hardware, application associations, and information for hardware configuration and device drivers.
HKEY_USERS	User profiles for all local user accounts, including the profile of the currently logged-on user (also shown under HKEY_CURRENT_USER), the default profile, and profiles for special user accounts used to run various services. Except for the default profile, each is labeled with a security ID (SID), a unique string of numbers preceded by S-1-5 that identifies a security principal (an entity that can be authenticated) in a Windows security accounts database, including users and groups.
HKEY_CURRENT_CONFIG	Contains configuration information for the current hardware profile, which is a set of changes (*only* changes) to the standard configuration in the Software and System subkeys under HKEY_LOCAL_MACHINE.

TABLE 7–3 Windows Registry Data Types (The Short List)

Data Type	Description
REG_BINARY	Raw binary data. It shows some hardware data in binary. Ironically, it shows binary data in hexadecimal and might look like this: ff 00 ff ff 02 05.
REG_DWORD	A 4-byte-long number (32 bits), stored in binary, hexadecimal, or decimal format. It may look something like this in hexadecimal: 0x00000002.
REG_EXPAND_SZ	A single string of text including a variable, which is a value that an application will replace when called. An example of a common variable is *%systemroot%*, which, when Windows uses it, is replaced by the path of the folder containing the Windows system files. Example: A registry entry containing *%systemroot%*\regedit.exe becomes c:\windows\regedit.exe.
REG_MULTI_SZ	Multiple strings of human-readable text separated by a special NULL character that it does not display. Example: wuauserv gpsvc trustedinstaller
REG_SZ	A sequence of characters representing human-readable text. It may use this data type when the data is quite simple, such as a string of alphanumeric characters—for example, ClosePerformanceData—or to represent an entire list: comm.drv commdlg.dll ctl3dv2.dll ddeml.dll.

Creating a Restore Point

Our favorite method is to simply create a restore point using System Restore. While Windows creates restore points on a regular basis, you can create one any time you want, knowing that you will have a snapshot of Windows at that point in time. Step-by-Step 7.01 will walk you through this process.

Step-by-Step 7.01

Creating a Restore Point

In this step-by-step exercise you will create a restore point. For this exercise you will need a computer running any of the three versions of Windows. The steps are written for all three versions, although the illustrations are from Windows 10. You will need to respond to a User Account Control (UAC) prompt. If you logged on as a standard account, you will need to enter an administrator password.

Step 1

In any of the three versions of Windows press ⊞+R. In the Run box type "sysdm.cpl." Do not type the quotation marks! Click OK.

Step 2

This brings up the System Properties dialog. Select the System Protection tab. Then click the Create button.

Step 3

Type a descriptive name for the restore point. Then press the Create button.

Step 4

It will take a minute or two, during which a progress message will display in the System Protection box. When Windows has created the restore point, this message will display. Click the Close button.

Step 5

The System Properties dialog box will remain open. To see the restore points, click the System Restore button. If a page displays with a recommended restore point, click Choose a different restore point. Then click the Next button. If a simpler page without the recommended restore point displays, as shown here, simply click Next.

Step 6

Caution: you want to view only the existing restore points—you do not want to actually roll back to a previous restore point. Simply view the list of restore points, noticing the descriptions. Press Cancel to exit from System Restore. Press Cancel again in the System Properties dialog.

Use Regedit to Back Up the Registry

Despite knowing the danger of directly editing the registry, you might find yourself in a position in which editing the registry is the only way to solve a problem. This may be the case when an administrator or help desk person has given you specific instructions for virus removal or some other necessary change. Do this only after attempting all other avenues, including using system restore to restore your computer to a previous state or doing a total restore of your computer from a complete backup set. But if all else fails, and you know the exact change that you must make to the registry, then before you attempt to edit the registry, use Regedit to back up the portion of the registry you plan to edit. To back up a registry key, right-click on the folder for the key in Registry Editor and select Export, as shown in Figure 7–5. Provide a location and name for the file, and Regedit will create a .reg file. If you need to restore the file, simply double-click on it.

LO 7.2 | Windows User and Power Options

Windows 7 combined both the user options and power options on one menu, while beginning in Windows 8, these options are separated. We will examine both types of options so that you understand how to use them. As part of the discussion on power options, we will also describe the shutdown and startup procedures for Windows 7 and the later versions. Understanding these can help you to troubleshoot problems that may occur as Windows starts up. It may seem a little backwards, but we will talk about power options, including Sleep, Hibernate, Shutdown, and Restart before describing how the different versions of Windows start up. This is because beginning with Windows 8, Fast Boot is the default startup mode, and it depends on a Hybrid Shutdown. It helps to understand Hybrid Shutdown before learning about Fast Boot.

The Windows 7 Shutdown button, if clicked, will shut down Windows and turn off the computer. The Shutdown button has a smaller button alongside it, and when you click it, the Shutdown options menu opens, shown in Figure 7–6. It includes *Switch user, Log off, Lock, Restart*, and *Sleep*. We call the first three options user options and the last two, *Restart* and *Sleep*, power options.

User Options

Beginning with Windows 8, Microsoft moved the user options to the User menu. Open this menu in Windows 8 or 8.1 by clicking or tapping the User tile on the Start screen. In Windows 10, open the Start menu and click or tap on the User tile at the top of the menu. Figure 7–7 shows the Windows 8.1 User menu. In Windows 7, selecting *Switch user* keeps the

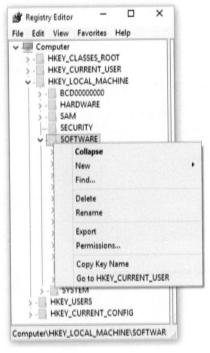

FIGURE 7–5 Back up a registry key and all its subkeys and values.

FIGURE 7–6 The Windows 7 Shutdown options menu includes Switch user, Log off, Lock, Restart, and Sleep.

current user's session in memory without closing any programs, and presents the logon screen. Another user can then log on and run in a separate user session with her own user profile, seeing her files, but not accessing the first user's open session.

In Windows 8, 8.1, and Windows 10, although the user options menu does not include *Switch user* it does allow you to switch users. If there is another user account on that computer, that user name and profile picture will display on the User menu, shown in Figure 7–7. In this example, the other user is Chrissy. Selecting Chrissy saves the current user's session in memory and shows the Sign-in screen ready (in this case) for Chrissy to provide her password.

Where Windows 7 provides *Log off* and *Lock* on the Shutdown options menu, Windows 8, 8.1, and Windows 10 display *Change Account Picture, Lock,* and *Sign out* on the User menu.

FIGURE 7–7 The Windows 8.1 User menu opens when you click or tap the User tile.

Power Options

While Windows 7 offers Restart, Sleep, and (in some cases) Hibernate from the Shutdown options menu, Windows 8, 8.1, and Windows 10 offer these choices from the Power menu, shown here. Access the Power menu In Windows 8 and 8.1 from the Settings bar or Sign-in screen. Windows 8.1 also added the Power button to the Start screen. In Windows 10 the Power button is located on the Start menu. In all versions of Windows since Windows 7, Hibernate is not a default option but you can enable it in Control Panel's Power Options. We will describe the difference between Sleep and Hibernate next.

Sleep

If you select the Sleep option, the computer stays on in a very-low-power mode; the system state and user session (applications and data) are saved in RAM, but the screen turns off. Wake up your computer (resume) by clicking a mouse button, tapping a touch screen, or pressing keys. On some computers, you may press the power button to bring Windows out of Sleep mode, but try these other actions first. When the computer resumes from Sleep, you may need to enter your password before you are back in Windows with all your apps open and data intact.

When should you use Sleep? A common scenario is when you must interrupt your work on a laptop or tablet, as when you board a plane. Select Sleep mode before boarding, and when you have settled in your seat, resume and continue working.

Do not use Sleep for a lengthy period of time because when the battery runs down, Sleep mode ends. Microsoft has safeguards built in, but we have never been comfortable using Sleep for an extended period of time because we have seen problems with network connections after bringing a computer back from Sleep mode.

Hibernate

If you select the Hibernate option, Windows saves to disk an image of the contents of RAM, including the OS, open apps, and all the associated data, in a file named hiberfil.sys, and then the OS sends the command to power down the computer. Hibernate does not require power.

When should you use Hibernate? If it is available, you may want to use it on a laptop or tablet when you would use Sleep. To resume, press the power button, and the Lock screen or the Sign-in screen will greet you. The apps that were open before you hibernated Windows will be open with the data intact.

Note: A small difference between the user options menu in these different versions of Windows is the naming of the option called *Change account picture*, shown in Figure 7–7, versus *Change account settings* in Windows 10. Either one will take you to the Your Account pane on the Accounts page of the Settings app.

The Power options menu.

Note: A computer recovers more quickly from Sleep than from Hibernate, but Sleep requires power, while Hibernate does not. As a user experience, Hibernate and Sleep are essentially the same: They return you to your open apps and data so that you continue working where you left off.

The Windows 7 Shutdown

When you select *Shutdown* from the Windows 7 Start menu, several events occur. Windows does the following:

1. Sends messages to all running apps to save data and settings.
2. Closes the session for each logged-on user.
3. Sends a shutdown message to all running services and then shuts them down.
4. Sends a shutdown message to all devices.
5. Closes the operating system's session.
6. Writes pending data to the system drive.
7. Sends a signal to power down the computer.

Windows 8, 8.1, and Windows 10 Hybrid Shutdown

When you select *Shutdown* from the Windows 8, 8.1, or Windows 10 Power menu it does a Hybrid Shutdown, during which Windows does the following:

1. Sends messages to all running apps to save data and settings, and then shuts down the apps.
2. Closes the session for each logged-on user.
3. Hibernates the Windows session and saves it in a file. It does not hibernate the User session.

Because the hibernate process saves an image of the system session to disk, the operating system does not have to reassemble all its parts every time it starts up.

Restart

Note: Restart is also a troubleshooting tool because a problem, such as system instability, that goes away after a restart may have been caused by a temporary problem. The problem is resolved by shutting down and restarting to let Windows reload all its components. It gives you a clean beginning, and you can then note if the problem reoccurs after you open an app or take some other action.

When you select the *Restart* option, all versions of Windows do a full shutdown and a full system startup. This is important to know because a Restart will seem slower on a Windows 8, 8.1, or Windows 10 computer than a cold boot because it will not do the Hybrid shutdown described above, nor the Windows Fast Boot, described later. A Restart is often required when updating Windows or installing an app to complete the installation.

Windows 7 Startup Phases

The Windows 7 startup has several phases on a typical desktop PC. These include:

1. Power-on self-test
2. Initial startup
3. Bootloader
4. Hardware detection and configuration
5. Kernel loading
6. Logon

In the first two phases, the hardware "wakes up" and system firmware searches for an operating system. Through the remaining phases, the operating system builds itself, much like a building, from the ground up, with more levels and complexity added at each phase.

Power-On Self-Test

When you power on your computer, the CPU loads firmware programs into memory. Firmware is software installed in nonvolatile memory chips. This memory may be read-only memory (ROM), erasable programmable read-only memory (EPROM), or a similar technology. All computing devices contain firmware. The common traditional name for the firmware in computers is ROM-BIOS, as defined in Chapter 1, but newer computers come with much more sophisticated firmware that complies with a specification called Unified Extensible Firmware Interface (UEFI), also described in Chapter 1.

Among the first firmware programs that run are those that perform the power-on self-test (POST)—a series of tests of the system hardware that determines the amount of memory present and verifies that devices required for OS startup are working. The POST most often only displays a brief black screen before Windows loads.

Initial Startup

During the initial startup the firmware bootstrap loader program uses hardware configuration settings stored in nonvolatile memory, commonly called CMOS, to determine what devices can start an OS and the order in which the system will search these devices while attempting to begin the OS startup process. The order may be optical drive or USB drive, then hard drive. On a computer with UEFI with Secure Boot turned on, this will normally be drive C only, unless you modify firmware settings, which is an advanced task. The bootstrap loader then looks in the location specified for Windows OS startup code, called the bootloader, and loads it into memory.

Bootloader

Bootmgr is the bootloader file that begins the loading of OS components for all current versions of Windows. Once bootmgr loads, the OS starts the file system, reads the Boot Configuration Database (BCD) file to learn the location and names of the remaining Windows OS files to load into memory at startup. Then it starts the winload.exe program, which is the OS loader boot program. Together, bootmgr and winload.exe manage the startup phases that follow.

> *Note:* Windows versions after Windows 7 have the same startup procedures and the files have the same names and roles as those used in Windows 7. But in the newer versions startup is made more secure by Trusted Boot and starts much faster when it uses Windows Fast Boot. We describe both later.

Detect and Configure Hardware

The Detect and Configure hardware phase includes a scan of the computer's hardware and creation of a hardware list for later inclusion in the registry.

Kernel Loading

During the kernel loading phase, the Windows kernel (ntoskrnl.exe) loads into memory from the location indicated in the BCD. Hardware information passes on to the kernel, and the hardware abstraction layer (HAL) file for the system loads into memory. The system hive of the registry loads, and components and drivers listed in the registry as required at startup are then loaded. All of this code is loaded into memory, but is not immediately initialized (made active).

Once all startup components are in memory, the kernel (ntoskrnl.exe) takes over the startup process and initializes the components (services and drivers) required for startup. Then the kernel scans the registry for other components that were not required during startup but are part of the configuration. It then loads and initializes them.

The kernel starts the session manager, which creates the system environment variables and loads the kernel-mode Windows subsystem code that switches Windows from text mode to graphics mode.

The Session manager then starts the user mode Windows subsystem code (csrss.exe). Just two of the session manager's other tasks include creating the virtual memory paging file (pagefile.sys) and starting the Windows logon service (winlogon.exe), which leads us to the next phase.

Logon

More things happen during the logon phase than simply authenticating the user, and they happen simultaneously. They include the following:

User Logon. The key player in this phase is the Windows Logon service, which supports logging on and logging off, and starts the service control manager (services.exe) and the local security authority (lsass.exe). At this point, depending on how your computer was configured, you may not be required to actually enter a user name and password. Figure 7–8 shows just one possible logon screen that you may see in Windows 7, in which you simply enter a password for the user name shown.

Program Startup. During program startup, logon scripts (if they exist) run, startup programs for various applications run, and noncritical services start. Windows finds instructions to run these programs and services in many locations in the registry.

Plug-and-Play Detection. Plug-and-play detection uses several methods to detect new plug-and-play devices, and when it detects a new device, it allocates system resources (memory and other OS resources) to the devices and installs appropriate device drivers.

Windows Secure Boot and Fast Boot

On a computer running Windows 8 or newer, all you see during startup may be the manufacturer's logo and, after a brief pause, the Lock screen. The system code in these newer versions of Windows is not much different from that of Windows 7, so it must go through a process similar to that of Windows 7 startup to assemble all the pieces of the OS along with settings, drivers, services, and apps. In view of what you learned earlier in this chapter about how Windows 7 starts up, you may wonder how these newer versions can get all of this done so quickly. We explain that mystery now.

FIGURE 7–8 Log on to Windows 7.

Firmware Startup

When you turn on your computer, the CPU loads firmware into memory and the power-on self-test occurs regardless of the OS installed, because it occurs before the OS is in control. If you have installed Windows 8, 8.1, or Windows 10 on an older computer with ROM-BIOS, the startup may be a bit longer than that same version of Windows on a UEFI-compliant computer, but it should be faster than Windows 7 on that same computer. Computers that come with Windows 8, 8.1, or Windows 10 preinstalled by the manufacturer must have UEFI firmware and must have security features of UEFI enabled by default to protect Windows during the startup process. Secure Boot is the UEFI firmware feature that loads only trusted operating system bootloaders. From there, as with the Windows 7 startup process described previously, the Windows components take over, with the addition of Windows Trusted Boot, described later.

While Windows proceeds with the phases of startup, up to the point when antimalware software loads, a UEFI firmware feature called Measured Boot logs the process, and antimalware software can analyze this log to determine if malware is on the computer or if the boot components were tampered with. In an enterprise environment with Windows Active Directory servers, Windows 8, 8.1, or Windows 10 can send this log to a trusted server that can assess the PC's startup and track the security and health of the PC.

Trusted Boot and Early Launch Anti-Malware

Trusted Boot is a feature, introduced in Windows 8, that examines each system file required for the boot process before it loads into memory. Another security component, called Early Launch Anti-Malware (ELAM) does the same for all device drivers before they load into memory, thus preventing drivers containing malware from loading.

> *Note:* During startup, as part of Trusted Boot, each operating system file is examined before it is loaded into memory. If one appears to have been altered, an unmodified version of the file is used.

Fast Boot

While the security features described above add complexity to the Windows startup, these newer versions of Windows actually start up very rapidly. The reason for this is the Fast Boot feature, which takes advantage of the hibernated kernel of the Hybrid Shutdown, described earlier in this chapter. Fast Boot simply brings the hibernated system session out of hibernation, saving all the work of the Kernel Loading phase. Additionally, on a computer with multiple CPU cores, the cores work in parallel when processing the hibernation file. Hybrid Shutdown is the default when you select the Shutdown option, and Fast Boot is the default when you power up your computer.

Modifying System Startup

You can modify the system startup on your Windows computer in many ways. First, determine if you can make the change you want through the GUI, such as using the Advanced System Settings page. As a last resort, you can directly edit these settings using the correct tool for the version of Windows in question. We'll look at modifying system startup for Windows 7, Windows 8/8.1, and Windows 10 including the settings for choosing the default OS started on a multiboot system and the length of time the selection menu displays.

> *Note:* Learn about special startup modes for troubleshooting later in this chapter.

In all versions of Windows discussed here, the Boot Configuration Database is actually a hidden part of the registry, stored in a registry file named BCD, located in a hidden partition. The basic information stored in BCD provides locale information, the location of the boot disk and the Windows files, and other information required for the startup process. View the contents of BCD using the BCDedit program, a utility that needs to run from a Command Prompt with elevated privileges, meaning that it runs with the privileges of a local administrator, as described in Step-by-Step 7.02.

The **Command Prompt** is a command-line interface (CLI) that you can launch from within Windows, from Safe Mode, or as a Recovery option. There are many commands that administrators use that run either in a Command Prompt or in another more advanced command-line interface, **PowerShell**. Both of these CLIs accept certain commands and can be used to run scripts that advanced technical people use to automate tasks, but Command Prompt is a much simpler and limited interface. Command Prompt, in all its forms, only accepts text input. PowerShell accepts text input, but it also accepts objects, as defined by object-oriented programming. A software object has fields that define its state, and each object has a set of behaviors. Modern operating systems use object-oriented programming.

To change Windows startup settings, one method is to use the Startup and Recovery page of System Properties. Step-by-Step 7.02 will walk you through making a change to BCD using the Startup and Recovery page, and then you will use BCDedit to view the changes made to the BCD file. Another method for configuring Windows System Startup is to use the MSCONFIG utility, described later in this chapter under *Using Windows Troubleshooting and Recovery Tools*.

Step-by-Step 7.02

Modifying Windows System Startup

In this step-by-step exercise you will modify the system startup for Windows using the Startup and Recovery page of System Properties. The steps work in Windows 7, Windows 8, 8.1, and Windows 10. The images are from Windows 8, but these are nearly identical to what you will see in the other versions.

Step 1

Use the keyboard shortcut ⊞+R to open the Run box. In the Run box, type "sysdm.cpl" (do not type the quotation marks). Click OK. In System Properties click the Advanced tab.

On the Advanced tab of System Properties, locate the Startup and Recovery section near the bottom and click the Settings button to open the Startup and Recovery page. If your computer is a multiboot computer you can choose the default operating system that it will select if you do not respond to the menu during the time that it displays the list of operating systems. Notice the time selected is 30 seconds.

Step 3

Change the selected time to 35 seconds and click OK to close the Startup and Recovery page. Click OK again to close System Properties. Windows will save the changes in a file named BCD, and they will take effect the next time Windows starts.

Step 4

To see the changes you made you will need to run BCDedit, an editor that will let you see the contents of BCD. If you are using Windows 7, go to step 5. If you are using a later version, skip to step 6.

In Windows 7, open Start Search and type **cmd**. Then right-click **cmd**, and select *Run as administrator* from the context menu, as shown here. Respond to the User Account Control (UAC) prompt (if required). The Command Prompt will then open. The Title bar of the window should say Administrator: Command Prompt. If it doesn't, carefully repeat this step. With the Command Prompt window open, skip to step 7.

In Windows 8, 8.1, or Windows 10 right-click on the Start button and select Command Prompt (Admin) from the Power User menu. This will first open the User Account Control (UAC) box. After you respond to the UAC message the Command Prompt window will open, and the Title bar of the window should say "Administrator: Command Prompt."

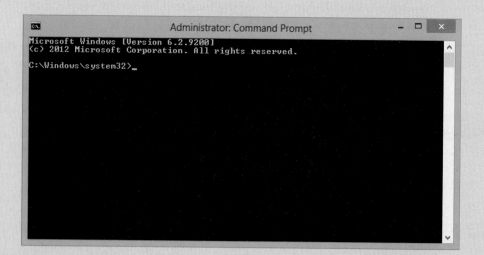

At the command prompt type "bcdedit" and press Enter. The result should look something like the example here. Notice the Timeout setting, which you changed in the earlier steps.

To close the Command Prompt windows type Exit and press Enter.

LO 7.3 | Installing and Managing Device Drivers

A huge number of devices work in Windows. There are the ones we take for granted, such as hard drives, flash drives, video adapters, network interface cards, displays, sound cards, and printers, as well as keyboards, mice, and other pointing devices. Then there are others, such as cameras, scanners, video capture cards, and game controllers. In this section we learn about installing device drivers and managing installed device drivers.

Installing Device Drivers

All devices need device drivers, and the latest versions of Windows come with huge caches of device drivers. Both Windows and virtually all devices for PCs are plug and play. Plug and play is the ability of a computer and OS to automatically detect and configure a hardware device. To work, the computer, the device, and the OS must all comply with the same plug-and-play standard. Therefore, when you connect a device, Windows recognizes it, and then finds and installs the appropriate driver.

But there are exceptions. For example, in some cases, even though the device is plug and play, you need to install the driver (and with it the companion software) before connecting the device. There is also the issue of when you should power on an external device. Some require that you power up the device before connecting it to the PC, while others require that you connect the device and then power it up. The supreme authority for each device is the manufacturer, so you really need to read the manufacturer's quick-start guide or user manual before connecting a new device.

Permissions

Regardless of how easily a device driver installs, you need administrator privileges to install or uninstall a device. In all current versions of Windows you can install a device driver while logged on as either a computer administrator or a standard user. When logged on as an administrator you will simply need to click Yes in the UAC Consent Prompt, whereas a standard user will need to provide computer administrator credentials in the Credentials Prompt.

Fortunately, unplugging a device does not uninstall the driver from your computer—it just gives the device a status of "not present." Therefore, once a device is installed, any local users may disconnect and reconnect the device without restriction and it will operate.

Working with Signed versus Unsigned Device Drivers

Because a device driver becomes a part of an operating system, a poorly written device driver can be a vector for malware and cause problems, including system crashes. For this reason bad device drivers have long been the top cause of operating system instability. Windows has features that help users avoid badly written program code.

One of the latest additions to protections against bad device drivers is Early Launch Anti-Malware (ELAM) during Windows 8, 8.1, or Windows 10 startup, described previously in this chapter. But one of the long-standing central features that protects against all types of bad program code is code signing, the use of a digital signature provided by Microsoft as its seal of approval on program code. A digital signature is encrypted data placed in the signed file. Windows decrypts the digital signature by a process called file signature verification. The digital signature includes information about the file so that the operating system can detect any alterations to the file. Driver signing is simply code signing of device drivers that indicates the integrity of the file or files and that the device driver has passed Microsoft's test for compatibility. This does not mean all nondigitally signed device drivers are bad. What it does mean is that Microsoft has provided a process that manufacturers can choose to use to have their device drivers tested and signed by Microsoft. This is part of the process of having a device added to Microsoft's compatibility list.

If you attempt to install a program that contains unsigned code, you may get a warning. It is then up to you if you want to continue using the unsigned code. If you trust the source, continue. By default, you cannot install unsigned drivers in 64-bit Windows; the installation will simply fail.

Managing Installed Devices

The Devices and Printers Control Panel applet, as well as the PC Settings Devices page in Windows 8, 8.1, and Windows 10 are simple tools for managing devices. The Device Manager Control Panel, available in all versions of Windows, is a more advanced tool. Learn about each of these.

Devices and Printers

You can manage many devices in all three versions of Windows through the user-friendly Devices and Printers Control Panel applet (see Figure 7–9). Open Devices and Printers in Windows 7 from the Start menu; open it in Windows 8, 8.1, and Windows 10 by searching on

try this!

Install a Plug-and-Play Device

Locate a plug-and-play USB device never before installed on your computer, such as a printer or wireless NIC. Try this:

1. Read the documentation for the device. If required, install the device driver before connecting the device.

2. Follow the instructions for the order in which you must power on and connect the USB device to a USB port. You may see a balloon by the notification area as Windows automatically recognizes it.

FIGURE 7–9 The Devices and Printers page.

"devices and printers." This gives you an overview of the most obvious devices attached to your computer. From here you can access the Properties dialog and other appropriate applications and actions by double-clicking on the device (for the default action) or right-clicking and selecting an action from the context menu. For instance, double-clicking on the Fax object will open Windows Fax and Scan. If you have installed special faxing and scanning software from the manufacturer, that software will open in place of Windows Fax and Scan.

In Figure 7–9, the Canon inkjet printer has a round green icon with a white check mark indicating it is the default printer that will be used unless you select a different printer when you select the Print command in an app. To change the default printer, right-click on a printer's icon and then select *Set as Default Printer* from the context menu, shown in Figure 7–10.

Expect newer devices to have a special "home page" that is part of the Device Stage feature. For instance, in Windows 7, double-clicking a printer's icon brought up the printer's print queue. That still happens if your installed printer does not have the Device Stage feature. If it has Device Stage, double-clicking on it will bring up a new page from which you can make many choices for managing the device, including a link to open your printer's print queue. Figure 7–11 shows the Device Stage page for a printer.

FIGURE 7–10 Set the default printer.

Windows 8 and Windows 8.1 PC Settings

In Windows 8 or 8.1 the Devices page of PC settings lists printers and other devices (see Figure 7–12). From this page you can add a plug-and-play device that Windows did not automatically detect and install by clicking the *Add a device* button.

At this writing, you can only add or remove devices in PC Settings in the Windows 8 or 8.1 Modern GUI. For more management tools, go to the Windows Desktop and use the same tools you used in Windows 7: Devices and Printers and Device Manager.

Windows 10 Settings

In Windows 10, launch Settings from the Start menu. In Settings, click or tap Devices and then select the type of device you want to add or remove. Windows 10 only has the one GUI, but it does have a limitation similar to that of Windows 8, described above, in that the new Settings dialog only lets you add or remove devices. It does include links within this utility to launch Device

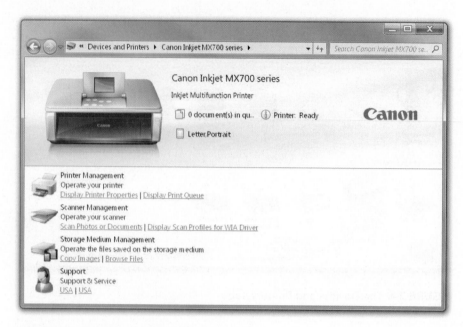

FIGURE 7–11 The Device Stage page for a printer.

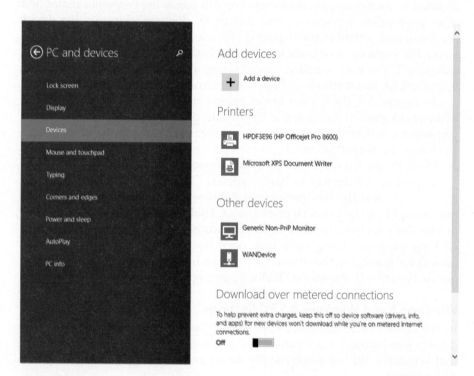

FIGURE 7–12 Add a new device in the Devices page of Windows 8.1 PC Settings.

Manager or Devices and Printers. This may change, as Microsoft continues to upgrade Windows 10.

Using Device Manager to Manage Device Drivers

Device Manager is a tool that allows an administrator to view and change device properties, update device drivers, configure device settings, uninstall devices, and roll back a driver update. Rollback is quite handy for those times when you find the new device driver causes problems. Device Manager has been in the last several versions of Windows and is still available in the current versions of Windows. Our favorite method for opening Device Manager is by entering "device manager" in the Windows 7 or Windows 10 Start Search box or in Windows 8, Search Settings. But if you find you need to work with Device Manager repeatedly on the same computer, consider making a desktop shortcut, as described in Step-by-Step 7.03.

Step-by-Step 7.03

Getting to Know Device Manager

In this step-by-step exercise you will create a shortcut to Device Manager on the desktop to make it more convenient to open. You'll then examine the information shown in Device Manager. This exercise can be completed on a computer running any of the versions of Windows discussed in this chapter. The screen shots are from Windows 8. You will need to either be logged on with an administrator account or be prepared with the credentials of an administrator on that computer.

Step 1

Right-click on an empty area of the Desktop; select New | Shortcut.

Step 2

In the Create Shortcut wizard, a text box prompts you to enter the location of the item. Simply enter the file name and extension for the Device Manager console: devmgmt.msc. Double-check your typing. Click the Next button.

On the following page of the Create Shortcut wizard, in the text box labeled "Type a name for this shortcut," type "Device Mgr," and click the Finish button.

Locate the new shortcut on the desktop.

Test your new shortcut by double-clicking on it to open Device Manager. Use the View menu to experiment with various ways of changing how it can display information—you have two options for viewing devices and two options for viewing resources that you can choose from the View menu. You will normally view devices by type because this approach is simpler and more understandable. Another option allows you to view hidden devices, which is handy when you want to remove a device driver for a device that is no longer connected or installed in the computer.

When viewing devices by type, there is a node for each device type, such as Audio inputs and outputs, Batteries, Bluetooth, Computer, Disk drives, and so on. Familiarize yourself with Device Manager by opening the nodes. Notice that the buttons on the button bar change as you click on the top node (the computer itself), then click on a type node (such as Display adapters), and then double-click on a device under a type node.

Double-clicking a device opens its Properties dialog box, where the Driver tab lets you manage a device (some of these actions are available from the button bar). Do not make any changes, and when you are finished, close all open windows. You will use other features of Device Manager in the troubleshooting section of this chapter.

LO 7.4 | Using Windows Troubleshooting and Recovery Tools

A short list of the handiest and most effective tools for troubleshooting Windows problems and recovering from virus infections includes the various Startup options, the System Configuration utility, and Device Manager. Explore these tools in this section.

For Startup Failures: The Windows Recovery Environment

In Chapter 4 we described the Windows Preinstallation Environment (Windows PE), the scaled-down Windows operating system that supports the Windows Setup GUI. This environment is available for Windows 7 and newer versions of Windows. It has limited drivers for basic hardware and support for the NTFS file system, networks, and programs. However, this

Note: When configuring a new installation or troubleshooting a problem, keep a journal of any changes you make. A record of the changes will help you return stability to your computer. This can be in the form of a note in a paper notebook or a word processing document. The advantage of the first method is that it will be available to you if Windows becomes unstable. The advantage of using a word processor, such as Microsoft Word, is that you can take screen shots and copy them into the document.

is still a very robust and specialized operating system, and when needed, it supports a powerful group of diagnostics and repair tools called the Windows Recovery Environment (Windows RE). Computer manufacturers who preinstall Windows have the option of adding their own repair tools to Windows RE.

If your Windows computer fails at startup, and if the damage is not too extensive, Windows RE will start and load the Windows Error Recovery page with the options: Launch Startup and Repair (Windows RE's built-in diagnostics and recovery tool) and Start Windows Normally. It is always worth trying the second option to see if the cause of the problem was something transient. Then, if it still doesn't start up normally, select the Launch Startup Repair and follow the instructions on the screen.

In situations where Windows starts up but you notice problems, you may want to use modified startups to troubleshoot and recover from the problem. We will look at them next.

Troubleshooting with Modified Startups

As you work with Windows computers, you may run into computers that fail to start normally or that behave oddly after startup. Windows offers a number of methods for starting with certain components disabled. Some of these are available through a special menu of startup options; others (including some of the same methods) are available through the System Configuration utility.

The Advanced Boot Options Menu in Windows 7

To access a list of startup options in Windows 7, restart the computer and press F8 before the graphical Windows start screen appears. This will bring up a special menu of startup options entitled "Advanced Boot Options Menu," shown in Figure 7–13. Following are brief descriptions of these options.

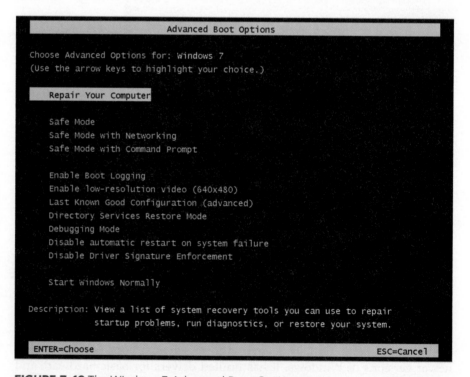

FIGURE 7–13 The Windows 7 Advanced Boot Options menu.

Repair Your Computer. If you select this option, Windows PE (the environment used by Windows setup) loads and first requires that you supply a keyboard input method, then requires that you log on, and finally displays the Windows RE System Recovery Options menu shown in Figure 4–16 in Chapter 4. From here you can select one of the following recovery tools, also described in Chapter 4:

- Startup Repair
- System Restore
- System Image Recovery
- Windows Memory Diagnostic
- Command Prompt

The System Recovery Command Prompt, is a command-line interface where you can enter commands to repair Windows. This is a very advanced task, but one command we have used in the past with some success is the command "chkdsk /r," a command that can repair certain logical damage to a disk.

Safe Mode. Safe Mode is a mode for starting Windows with certain drivers and components disabled. Access Safe Mode from the Advanced Options Menu in Windows 7, as shown in Step-by-Step 7.04. In Windows 8, 8.1, and Windows 10, access it from the Advanced Startup option on the General page of PC Settings, which we describe later. Safe Mode does not disable Windows security. You are required to log on in all variants of Safe Mode, and you can access only those resources for which you have permissions. If Windows will not start normally but starts just fine in Safe Mode, use Device Manager within Safe Mode to determine if the source of the problem is a faulty device. Run System Restore while in Safe Mode and roll back the entire system to a restore point from before the problem occurred.

Three Safe Mode variants are available:

- **Safe Mode** starts without using several drivers and components that it would normally start. It loads only very basic, non-vendor-specific drivers for mouse, video (loading Windows' very basic vga.sys driver), keyboard, mass storage, and system services. Because network components are not started, plain Safe Mode does not support networking.
- **Safe Mode with Networking** is identical to plain Safe Mode, except that it starts the networking components. Use the following debug sequence with Safe Mode with Networking:
  - If Windows will not start normally but starts OK in plain Safe Mode, restart and select Safe Mode with Networking.
  - If it fails to start in Safe Mode with Networking, the problem area is network drivers or components. Use Device Manager to disable the network adapter driver (the likely culprit), then boot up normally. If Windows now works, replace your network adapter driver.
  - If this problem appears immediately after upgrading a network driver, use Device Manager while in Safe Mode to roll back the updated driver. When an updated driver is available, install it.
- **Safe Mode with Command Prompt** is Safe Mode with only a command prompt as a user interface. In a normal startup, Windows loads your GUI desktop, but this depends on the program explorer.exe, the GUI shell to Windows. In place of this GUI shell, Safe Mode with Command Prompt loads a command prompt (cmd.exe) window. This is a handy option to remember if the desktop does not display at all. Once you have eliminated video drivers as the cause, corruption of the explorer.exe program may be the problem. From within the command prompt, you can delete the corrupted version of explorer.exe and copy an undamaged version. This requires knowledge of the command line commands for navigating the directory structure, as well as knowledge of the location of the file that you are replacing. You can launch programs, such as the Event Viewer

(eventvwr.msc), the Computer Management console (compmgmt.msc), or Device Manager (devmgmt.msc) from the command prompt.

Enable Boot Logging. While boot logging occurs automatically with each of the three Safe Modes, selecting Enable Boot Logging turns on boot logging and starts Windows normally. Boot logging causes Windows to write a log of the Windows startup in a file named ntbtlog.txt and save it in the system-root folder. This log file contains an entry for each component in the order in which it loaded into memory. It also lists drivers that were not loaded, which alerts an administrator to a possible source of a problem.

Enable Low-Resolution Video (640×480). This option starts Windows normally, except the video mode is changed to the lowest resolution (640×480), using the currently installed video driver. It does not switch to the basic Windows video driver. Select this option after making a video configuration change that the video adapter does not support and that prevents Windows from displaying properly.

Last Known Good Configuration. Last Known Good (LKG) Configuration is a startup option that will start Windows normally and select the configuration that existed at the last successful user logon (the "last known good configuration"), ignoring changes made after the last logon. This works if you made changes that caused obvious problems. On the very next restart, selecting this option will discard the changes. But if you have logged on since the changes occurred, those changes will be part of the last known good configuration, so this recovery option won't work. This rather crude system restore method only works if you did not restart and log on since making the change. Windows 7 is the last version to offer this option.

Directory Services Restore Mode. This option only works on Windows Servers acting as domain controllers.

Debugging Mode. This is a very advanced, (dare we say) obsolete, option in which Windows starts normally, and information about the Windows startup is sent over a serial cable to another computer that is running a special program called a debugger.

Disable Automatic Restart on System Failure. The default setting for Windows is for it to restart after a system crash. However, depending on the problem, restarting may simply lead to another restart—in fact you could find yourself faced with a continuous loop of restarts. If so, press F8 at the next restart and select the Disable automatic restart on system failure option. Windows will attempt to start normally (just once for each time you select this option) and may stay open long enough for you to troubleshoot. Do not attempt to work with any data file after restarting with this option because the system may be too unstable. If you are not able to solve the problem, then you will need to restart in Safe Mode to troubleshoot.

Disable Driver Signature Enforcement. If you are unable to install a driver due to Driver Signing, and you trust the manufacturer, select this option, which will start Windows normally, disabling driver signature enforcement just for that startup.

Start Windows Normally. Use this option to start Windows normally with no change in behavior. You would use this after using F8 to view the Advanced Options menu and deciding to continue with a normal startup. It does not restart the computer.

Return to OS Choices Menu (Multiboot Only). Selecting this option on a multi-boot computer will return to the OS Choices Menu (OS Loader menu).

Step-by-Step 7.04

Using Windows 7 in Safe Mode

In this step-by-step exercise you will start Windows in Safe Mode. The screen will not be identical, but you can experience Safe Mode in any of these OSs. Be prepared to provide credentials to access Safe Mode because security is still in place when you access Safe Mode. Once in Safe Mode you can run most Windows troubleshooting tools just as you would after a normal start.

Step 1

Restart the computer, pressing F8 as soon as the power down completes and before the splash screen appears. On the Advanced Boot Options menu use the up and down arrows to move the cursor around. Position the cursor on Safe Mode and press Enter.

Step 2

When prompted, provide credentials. Safe Mode loads with a black desktop background and the words *Safe Mode* in the corners of the screen. It also opens Windows Help and Support to the page on Safe Mode. Browse through the help information and click on the link labeled "Diagnostic tools to use in safe mode."

Step 3

On the resulting page, locate links to start several very handy tools in Safe Mode. In the following steps, practice opening some of these utilities.

Step 4

Click the link labeled *Click to open Recovery*. On the Recovery page notice the links to other tools. Click the button labeled *Open System Restore*. On the page labeled *Restore files and settings* click Next to see a list of the restore points on your computer. Click Cancel to leave System Restore and close the Recovery windows to return to Help and Support.

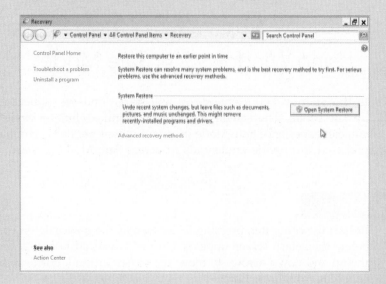

Step 5

Next, use the link that will open Control Panel. You can open most tools you would need from this page.

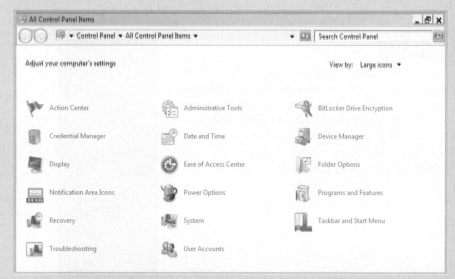

Step 6

When you are finished exploring Safe Mode, close all open windows, and either shut down or restart Windows, allowing it to start normally.

The Advanced Startup Options in Windows 8, 8.1, and Windows 10

Previously in this chapter you learned that if your Windows computer fails at startup and the damage is not too extensive, Windows RE will start and load the Windows Error Recovery page. Another option is to boot from the Windows installation DVD disc, but if Windows was preinstalled on your computer and UEFI boot is in effect, you may not be able to boot from disc unless you modify the UEFI settings, disabling Safe Boot security. How you do that differs from manufacturer to manufacturer.

The options you access from the Windows Error Recovery page are those that you can also access from the Advanced Startup options, available through the General page of Windows 8 PC Settings, the Update and Recovery page in Windows 8.1 PC Settings, and the Update and Security page in Settings in Windows 10. The quickest way to get to this page in any of these Windows versions is to search on "advanced startup" and select the result that says "Change advanced startup options." It is good to practice the Windows Advanced Startup options before you really need them for troubleshooting or recovery of the operating system. Step-by-Step 7.05 will walk you through a tour of the Windows 8 and 8.1 Advanced Startup options.

Note: Yet another way to access the Advanced Startup Options in Windows 8 is to open the Power menu from the Sign-in screen, the Start screen, or the Settings bar. Then hold down the Shift key while clicking or tapping Restart. After the restart the Choose an Option screen displays, as shown in step 2 of Step-by-Step 7.05, and you can continue from there as described in the remaining steps.

Step-by-Step 7.05

Exploring Windows 8 and 8.1 Advanced Options

If you have access to a computer running Windows 8 or Windows 8.1 and can sign in with an administrator account for that computer, you can do this exercise. The screen shots in this exercise were taken of a Windows 8 virtual machine installation, because we cannot create screen shots from within the Windows RE environment. Therefore, some of the screens do not have options that are available when installed directly onto a PC.

Step 1

Open the Charms bar, select Settings, and then from the Settings bar select *Change PC Settings*.

In Windows 8.0, from the PC Settings screen select *General*, and then scroll down to *Advanced startup*. Select *Restart now*. Skip the next paragraph and move to step 2.

In PC Settings in Windows 8.1 select *Update and Recovery*, and then select *Recovery*. Then select *Restart now*.

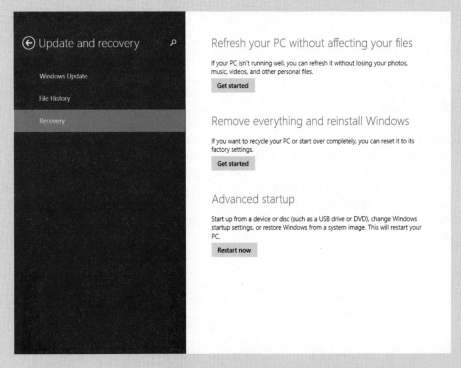

Windows Recovery Environment (Windows RE) launches. The resulting screen will resemble this, but will normally have more options showing. For instance, one of our Windows 10 systems had the option *Use a device* that would allow you to use a USB drive, network connection, or Windows recovery DVD. To restart in a troubleshooting mode, select Troubleshoot.

On the Troubleshoot screen, you will see these options, plus you may see one or more options added by the manufacturer of your computer. Our Windows 10 systems do not include the *Refresh your PC* option on this page. We will discuss the options labeled *Refresh your PC* and *Reset your PC* later. Do not select one of them at this time. From this screen select *Advanced options*.

Again, the Advanced Options screen shown here may look different on your computer. For instance, on a computer with UEFI rather than BIOS you will see a UEFI Firmware Settings option. This screen is from Windows 8.0. In Windows 8.1 and Windows 10 the Automatic Repair option is named Startup Repair. From this screen select *Startup Settings*.

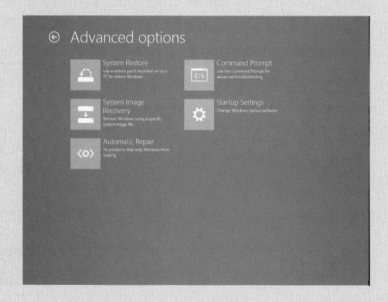

Step 5

This screen appears in all three versions of Windows, and it shows the options you will have from the next screen, so select Restart to move on.

Step 6

After a brief pause, the second Startup Settings screen displays with real choices. This is the replacement for the Windows 7 Advanced Boot Options menu. Press the 4 key to start in Safe Mode.

Step 7

At this point, you will see a normal sign-in screen. Enter your credentials to sign in and Windows will start in Safe Mode. Safe Mode starts in the Desktop view with one window open: Windows Help and Support.

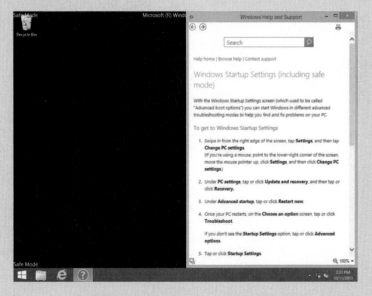

Spend a few minutes exploring the options available to you in Safe Mode. Open the Power User menu on the Safe Mode Desktop to access tools, such as Control Panel, Device Manager, Event Viewer, and System. When you have finished restart Windows.

Refresh. If you flip back to the illustration with step 3 in Step-by-Step 7.05, you will see an option labeled Refresh your PC. It refreshes the operating system without affecting your files. This is more involved than a system restore, but it is less drastic than some other measures you could take (such as the next option on the Troubleshoot page). Refresh is a very quick solution to a scenario that previously required advanced tasks and much time. For instance, in the past, if Windows had unexpected fatal errors in which a blue screen appeared, one solution was to reinstall Windows, but then you would have to restore your data and reinstall all your apps.

The Refresh option saves your user accounts, personal files, personal settings, all your installed apps that came with Windows, as well as any apps purchased through the Windows Store, and your important settings. Then it reinstalls Windows and reinstalls all the saved apps. However, it changes PC settings back to the defaults, removes apps installed from disc or sources other than the Windows Store, and saves a list of all removed apps on the desktop.

To begin Refresh from the Troubleshoot screen of Windows RE, click or tap the *Refresh your PC* option. After a short delay while Windows prepares your PC, a screen displays where you select an account to use for the sign-in. Enter your password and follow the prompts on the screen (see Figure 7–14). If asked, provide your Windows installation or recovery media on disc or flash

FIGURE 7–14 To complete a Refresh, follow the prompts on the screen.

drive. It will then take several minutes, showing progress messages. Finally, the Start screen displays after Refresh is complete.

Reset your PC. The Windows RE Troubleshoot screen (see step 3 in Step-by-Step 7.05) also includes the much more drastic Reset your PC option. It removes everything and reinstalls Windows, requiring that you enter a product key code. You would choose this option if you no longer plan to use this computer—maybe you are giving it away, because if you want to keep the computer, you will need to reinstall everything that does not come with Windows. As with Refresh, Reset may require the Windows installation or recovery media.

If Windows came preinstalled on your computer, you may want to use the manufacturer's restore option. This may be available from the same menu, but it may require that you previously created a set of backup discs.

Troubleshooting with MSCONFIG and Task Manager

System Configuration, more commonly known by its executable name MSCONFIG, is a GUI tool for temporarily modifying system startup. The easiest method for starting MSCONFIG is to open the Run box (■+R), type "msconfig," and press enter. MSCONFIG allows you to modify and test startup configuration settings without altering the settings directly. Use the options on the MSCONFIG General and Boot tabs to restart Windows in various troubleshooting modes, including Safe Mode, offered on the Boot menu.

MSCONFIG gives you access to settings buried within the registry through a moderately friendly user interface and it allows you to make temporary changes to try to pinpoint the source of a startup problem. For instance, open the Services tab page and stop a service from launching at startup, restart Windows, and see if that solves the problem. If it does not, then go back into MSCONFIG, enable that service, and disable another. Repeat until you locate the problem. If disabling services does not solve the problem, then move on to the programs.

MSCONFIG comes in all the versions of Windows discussed in this chapter. It works the same in all of these versions with one big exception. The Startup page in Windows 7, shown in Figure 7–15, contains a list of programs

WARNING!

The recovery options Refresh and Remove both require a lot of power while writing to storage and restarting the computer. Therefore, do not do a Refresh or Remove on a computer that is not plugged into a power source.

WARNING!

If you select the Safe option on the Boot page, it will also change settings on the General page. Therefore, any time you make changes, note the changes and be aware that before the system will restart normally, you will need to return to the General page and select Normal startup.

FIGURE 7–15 System Configuration (MSCONFIG) lets you test startup scenarios.

that Windows starts automatically, allowing you to disable programs one (or more) at a time at startup so that you can determine if a program is causing startup problems. In Windows 8, 8.1, and Windows 10 this tab contains a link only to the Task Manager utility where a new Startup page contains the list of programs, as shown in Figure 7–16.

Troubleshooting Device Problems

You will quickly learn if Windows detects a problem with a device when you open Device Manager. You will see an expanded device type, and the problem device will have an exclamation mark in a yellow triangle on the icon, as Figure 7–17 shows. The problem may be with the device itself, its device driver, or the ability of the operating system to automatically configure it. In Figure 7–17, Windows has placed the problem device under Other devices because it does not have enough information about it. This usually means that there is no installed device driver.

If you see the exclamation symbol on a device, double-click the device icon to open its Properties dialog box. You will see more information, as shown in the example in Figure 7–18. Follow the instructions in the Device Status box. In the example, it recommends running Update and provides the Update button (not normally shown on this page). Clicking update opened the Update Driver Software page with two choices: Search automatically for updated driver software and Browse my computer for

FIGURE 7–16 In Windows 8.1 and Windows 10 use the Startup tab to disable/enable individual programs.

FIGURE 7–17 Device Manager indicates a problem with a device.

FIGURE 7–18 On the General page of a device's Properties dialog, the *Device status* box describes the problem and recommends action to solve it.

driver software. Select the second one if you have the driver disc or have the driver on your local computer or on a network share. Select the first choice to have Windows search on the Internet. In the scenario shown, we selected the first choice and it found the driver, downloaded it, and installed it with no more interaction from us. In our example, the device was recognized and placed under the Network Infrastructure Devices category, as shown in Figure 7–19.

For other Device problems, open Device Manager and check out the Driver page of the Properties for the device. For instance, if you update a device driver and then find that the device fails or is not working as well as before the update, use the Roll Back Driver button on the Driver page to remove the updated driver and return to the previously installed driver. This button is active only after you have updated a driver, as shown in Figure 7–20. You can also use this page to update a driver, disable it, or uninstall it. You might disable a driver to see if it relates to another problem. Uninstall it if you do not need a device or if you believe there was a problem with the installation and plan to reinstall the driver.

WARNING!

If you are logged in as a standard user you will not be able to make changes to any settings in Device Manager, but it is still a good tool to use to see the status of devices. You can then report problems to a help desk if you are at school or work.

FIGURE 7–19 After installing the device driver, Windows places the device under the Network Infrastructure Devices category.

FIGURE 7–20 The *Roll Back Driver* button is active only after a driver update.

Chapter 7 REVIEW

Chapter Summary

After reading this chapter, and completing the Step-by-Step tutorials and Try This! exercises, you should understand the following facts about what is under the Windows desktop:

Understanding the Registry

- The registry is a database of all configuration settings in Windows. The Control Panel applets provide a safe way to edit the registry.
- Windows creates the registry during setup and modifies it any time a setup or installation program runs after that and during startup and shutdown. Windows also modifies it any time it installs a device driver and whenever it configures any application, Windows component, or device.
- Most of the registry is in several files, called hives. They include system, software, security, sam, default, and ntuser.dat. These are the permanent portions of the registry.
- View the registry in a hierarchical folder structure in Registry Editor.

- A key is a folder object that can contain one or more sets of settings as well as other keys.
- There are five top-level keys, or root keys.
- A key that exists within another key is a subkey.
- Settings within a key are value entries. Each value entry has a name, type, and data.

Windows User and Power Options

- Windows 7 combines user and power options on the Shutdown menu.
- Windows 7 user options are Switch user, Log off, and Lock. Power options are Restart, Sleep, and (sometimes) Hibernate.
- Windows 8 and later versions have power options on the Power menu and User options on the User tile.
- Windows 8, 8.1, and Windows 10 user options are Change account picture, Lock, and Sign out. Power options are the same as Windows 7.
- The phases of the Windows startup process are
  - Power-on self-test
  - Initial startup

- Bootloader
- Detect and configure hardware
- Kernel loading
- Logon

- If necessary, modify system startup using the Startup and Recovery page in System Properties. You can also modify the BCD file directly to modify startup, but only very advanced techs should do this.

Installing and Managing Device Drivers

- A device driver is program code, created by the device manufacturer, that allows an OS to control the use of a physical device.
- You need Administrator privileges to install any device driver in Windows.
- Once a device is installed, a standard user may disconnect and reconnect the device without restriction—the driver will not be uninstalled.
- Code signing exists to avoid problems caused by badly written code. It involves a digital signature, provided by Microsoft, as a seal of approval of program code.

- When an administrator installs or connects a plug-and-play device to a Windows computer, the computer will automatically detect the device and install and configure the driver.
- Plug-and-play devices connected to USB or IEEE 1394 (Firewire) can be disconnected without restarting.
- Device Manager is the Windows tool for managing and troubleshooting device problems.

Using Windows Troubleshooting and Recovery Tools

- Windows offers a variety of startup options, and some are well suited for troubleshooting. These include the Advanced Boot Options menu, the System Configuration utility (MSCONFIG), Task Manager, and the newer Advanced Startup Options in Windows 8 and newer versions.
- A yellow exclamation mark on a device in Device Manager indicates a problem. Open the properties dialog box to see an explanation.
- Use Device Manager to uninstall, update, and remove device drivers. You can also use it to disable a device without removing the driver.

Key Terms List

binary file *(264)*

bootloader *(275)*

bootstrap loader *(275)*

code signing *(282)*

Command Prompt *(278)*

Consent Prompt *(282)*

Credentials Prompt *(282)*

data type *(268)*

Device Stage *(283)*

digital signature *(282)*

driver signing *(282)*

Early Launch Anti-Malware (ELAM) *(277)*

Fast Boot *(277)*

file signature verification *(282)*

Hibernate *(273)*

hive *(265)*

Hybrid Shutdown *(274)*

key *(267)*

Last Known Good (LKG) Configuration *(290)*

logon phase *(276)*

Measured Boot *(277)*

MSCONFIG *(297)*

plug and play *(281)*

power-on self-test (POST) *(275)*

PowerShell *(278)*

registry *(264)*

root key *(267)*

Safe Mode *(289)*

Safe Mode with Command Prompt *(289)*

Secure Boot *(277)*

security ID (SID) *(269)*

Sleep *(273)*

subkey *(267)*

System Recovery Command Prompt *(289)*

Trusted Boot *(277)*

value entry *(267)*

Windows Recovery Environment (Windows RE) *(288)*

Key Terms Quiz

Use the Key Terms List to complete the sentences that follow.

1. A/an _____ is a portion of the Windows registry that is saved in a file.

2. _____ is a feature in Windows 7 that provides a special home page for a device containing options for managing the device.

3. When viewed with a registry editor, a/an _____ is a registry key located at the top level.

4. Many things occur during some of the startup phases. For instance, during the _____ programs start and plug-and-play devices are detected.

5. _____ is the use of a digital signature provided by Microsoft as its seal of approval on program code.

6. _____ is the ability of a computer and OS to automatically detect and configure a hardware device.

7. A/an _____ contains program code.

8. The _____ utility is very handy for troubleshooting startup problems, allowing you to temporarily disable programs you suspect are causing problems.

9. _____ is a startup mode for starting Windows with certain drivers and components disabled.

10. A/an _____ is a unique string of numbers preceded by S-1-5 that identifies a security principal (as in table 7-2) in a Windows security accounts database.

Multiple-Choice Quiz

1. Which of the following will you not find in the registry?
   a. Device driver settings
   b. Services settings
   c. User data files
   d. User preferences
   e. Application program settings

2. Any change to Windows or an installed application results in a change to this special database.
   a. Microsoft SQL Server
   b. Microsoft Excel
   c. ntuser.dat
   d. Registry
   e. Default

3. Most of the Windows registry files are stored in this location.
   a. *systemroot*\System32\config
   b. D:\Windows
   c. *systemroot*\System32\Registry
   d. *systemroot*\Windows
   e. *systemroot*\WINNT

4. If you select this option from the Power menu in Windows 8, 8.1, or Windows 10, both the system state and the user session are saved in memory, requiring a small amount of power.
   a. Fast Boot
   b. Hibernate
   c. Hybrid Shutdown
   d. Sleep
   e. Measured Boot

5. Beginning in Windows 8, the contents of the Startup tab page in MSCONFIG have been moved to this this utility.
   a. System Configuration
   b. Task Manager
   c. BCDedit
   d. Windows RE
   e. PowerShell

6. Which statement is true?
   a. Only the Administrator may disconnect or reconnect an installed device.
   b. Only members of the Administrators group may disconnect or reconnect an installed device.
   c. Only members of the Guests group may disconnect or reconnect an installed device.
   d. Any member of the local Users group may disconnect or reconnect an installed device.
   e. No one may disconnect or reconnect an installed device.

7. What UEFI security feature loads only trusted operating system bootloaders?
   a. Fast Boot
   b. Secure Boot
   c. Measured Boot
   d. Trusted Boot
   e. Early Launch Anti-Malware (ELAM)

8. Which of the following is a Device Manager feature only available after an installed driver updates?
   a. Uninstall
   b. Roll back driver
   c. Disable
   d. Update driver
   e. Remove driver

9. What registry hive does the bootloader use during startup to locate the operating system files it must load?
   a. BCD
   b. winload.exe
   c. bootmgr
   d. ntoskrnl.exe
   e. winlogon.exe

10. What page in System Properties would you open to modify the length of time the OS selection menu displays during Windows startup?
    a. Startup and Recovery
    b. Device Manager

    c. BCDedit

    d. Local Security Policy

    e. Computer Management

11. What choice on the Windows 7 Advanced Boot Options menu gives you a selection of tools that includes Startup Repair, System Restore, System Image Recovery, Windows Memory Diagnostic, and Command Prompt?

    a. Safe Mode with Command Prompt

    b. Debugging Mode

    c. Directory Services Restore Mode

    d. Last Known Good Configuration

    e. Repair Your Computer

12. Which of the following Windows 7 startup options will not do you any good if you have restarted and logged on after making a change that caused problems in Windows?

    a. System Restore

    b. Repair Your Computer

    c. Enable Boot Logging

    d. Safe Mode with Command Prompt

    e. Last Known Good Configuration

13. When Windows 8, 8.1, or Windows 10 does this, it hibernates the Windows session and saves it in a file but does not save the user session.

    a. Sleep

    b. Hybrid Shutdown

    c. Switch user

    d. Restart

    e. Hibernate

14. You upgraded a device driver, and Windows immediately failed and restarted. The problem is that it seems to be in a continuous restarting loop. What boot startup option will restart normally and give you an opportunity to try to troubleshoot the problem after a normal reboot?

    a. Debugging mode

    b. Enable boot logging

    c. Safe Mode with command prompt

    d. Disable automatic restart on system failure

    e. Safe Mode with networking

15. Which of the following is the executable name for the GUI utility that allows you to temporarily modify system startup?

    a. SYSCON

    b. MSCONFIG

    c. SYSEDIT

    d. regedit

    e. BCDedit

Essay Quiz

1. Describe at least five actions that will automatically change the Windows registry.

2. Your Windows 7 computer is having display problems when starting. You suspect that the cause is a video driver update that you installed. You managed to log on at the first restart after the update, despite being barely able to see the distorted logon dialog box. Then you found that, even though you had logged on, it was hopeless to try to work with the GUI. Describe how you would confirm that the problem is the video adapter and how you will correct the problem.

3. Describe a limit present in both Windows 8/8.1 and Windows 10 when it comes to using the PC Settings options for Devices.

4. A fellow student asked for your help in diagnosing a problem with a Windows computer. He believes there is a problem with the network adapter. He works in a small office and does not know the credentials for the Administrator account on that computer. The person who does know is out of town and is unwilling to give him the password until he can convince her that there truly is a problem. He wants to use Device Manager to see the status of the network adapter. What advice can you give him?

5. Describe what boot logging does and how you would use it as a troubleshooting tool.

Lab Projects

LAB PROJECT 7.1

Your Windows 7 computer will not start, and you believe the cause is a network card you recently installed.

1. Describe the steps you will take to isolate the problem.

2. Demonstrate the steps to your instructor.

LAB PROJECT 7.2

A fellow student asked for your help because his Windows 8.1 computer seems to be unstable. He is considering using either Refresh your PC or Reset your PC. Describe the differences, and if possible do a refresh of a Windows 8.1 or Windows 10 computer. Be sure you have permission to do this, and do not use a production computer. After the refresh, go into Windows and describe any changes you found.

LAB PROJECT 7.3

You are having a problem with your Windows computer that is isolated to a single graphics editing program that you use every day in your work. When you described the problem to the customer service support person for this product, she told you that the only fix for it is to edit a key under HKEY-LOCAL_MACHINE\SOFTWARE. She has assured you that this fix will work without causing any problems, but you are wary of doing this.

1 Describe the steps you will take before making the suggested registry changes.

2 Demonstrate only the steps you would take before modifying the registry. Do not actually modify the registry.

chapter

8 Apple OS X on the Desktop

Learning Outcomes

In this chapter, you will learn how to:

LO 8.1 Describe the important events in the history of Apple operating systems and the versions of OS X; determine what version of OS X is installed on an Apple computer.

LO 8.2 Prepare and implement an OS X upgrade or installation, and list the postinstallation tasks.

LO 8.3 Navigate and manage OS X on the desktop, including describing the Home folder, using Finder, performing file management tasks, and working with features and settings.

LO 8.4 Manage local security in OS X.

LO 8.5 Troubleshoot common OS X problems.

So far we have discussed operating systems in general, security for operating systems, virtualization of desktop operating systems, and the Windows operating systems. Now we change our focus to Apple OS X.

In this chapter, you will explore the OS X operating system beginning with an overview; then you'll learn how to install it, manage the desktop, and troubleshoot common OS X problems. You'll learn the basics of local security in OS X on the desktop. ✳

LO 8.1 | OS X History and Versions

In this overview, we explore the history of Apple's operating systems and the versions of the current line, OS X.

A Brief History of the Apple Operating Systems

Apple Computer (now officially Apple Inc.) was founded April 1, 1976, by Stephen Wozniak, Steven Jobs, and Ronald Wayne. They developed and manufactured their first product, the Apple I computer, in a garage

Personalize an OS X desktop to suit your tastes and needs.

in Los Altos, California. The following year, they introduced the Apple II computer at a local trade show. The Apple II was the first personal computer to have a plastic case and to include color graphics, although it didn't have a graphical user interface (GUI). In 1983, Apple launched the Lisa, the first production computer with a GUI operating system, and in 1984 the company launched the Macintosh 128k, the first *affordable* personal computer with a GUI. The Macintosh included a new operating system, and Apple shortened the name to Mac in later computer models.

These earliest incarnations of the Apple computers popularized the personal computer beyond the world of techies, leading to today's popular iMac, Mac Pro, MacBook, MacBook Pro, MacBook Air, and other models, not to mention the iPod, iPhone, iPad, and Apple Watch. Apple computers have had a profound impact on the computer industry and have inspired a strong community of proponents.

For many years the microprocessors and chipsets in Apple computers were different from those used in standard PCs that ran Windows, and therefore Apple computers could not run Windows. Apple abandoned this strategy around 2006 when they adopted Intel-compatible microprocessors and chipsets; since then you can configure a Mac to dual-boot between Windows and OS X using Apple Boot Camp, as described in Chapter 3.

As for the operating system, the Mac OS, or "System," was born along with the Macintosh in 1984 and went through many changes to the original code over the years until Apple left the old System behind when they introduced Mac OS X Server 1.0 in 1999 and the desktop version, OS X 10.0 in 2000. OS X is a very different OS from the earlier Mac OS. OS X has a UNIX core set of components, known as Darwin, that was originally a product of the open-source community.

OS X Versions

Apple has issued several major releases of OS X (referred to as "OS ten") beginning with the initial release for the desktop, 10.0, code-named Cheetah during its development. Although Apple did not publicly use the code names for releases 10.0 and 10.1, for each subsequent version they tied the

Note: Mac OS X Server came preinstalled on Apple's server computers, which Apple discontinued in 2011. Today it is not a standalone operating system. You must already have OS X installed before you can install OS X Server as an add-on. The good news is that it only costs $19.99. But in this chapter we discuss only the desktop versions of OS X.

Note: Most of the OS X screen shots in this book are from OS X version 10.11, El Capitan.

code name to the product and used it heavily in marketing and packaging. Apple continued to name OS X versions for species of big cats until 10.9, Mavericks.

Between the major releases Apple has made minor releases (10.8.1, 10.8.2, etc.). Each major release has added hundreds of improvements and new features—both minor and major. The last few versions include features first introduced by Apple in their iOS operating system for their popular portable devices, the iPod, iPhone, and iPad. With OS X 10.8 Mountain Lion, Apple dropped the "Mac" from the name of the OS, to make their desktop OS increasingly like the mobile OS, although OS X and iOS are still separate operating systems.

As you may notice while comparing the illustrations in this book to OS X on your lab computer, you always have the ability to customize the look so that no two installations need to be identical. The screenshots you see in this chapter all use either one of the backgrounds that comes with OS X or a white background for ease of viewing the captured windows and message boxes. Table 8–1 lists the major releases, their names, and release dates.

OS X has had many versions and minor releases since its introduction in 2001, and Apple has manufactured a variety of desktop and laptop computers running OS X. It is important to know both the version of OS X and the vintage of your computer before you make a decision to upgrade to a new version of OS X because the latest versions do not run on the older Macs, nor can you upgrade directly from some older versions of OS X to the latest version.

Whenever a new version is available, connect to the Apple website at **www.apple.com** and search on the product name of the new upgrade. Go to the Web page and select Tech Specs. This will list the requirements, including the OS X version, amount of memory and free disk space, the supported Apple computer models, and the requirements for special features of the new version.

To help you prepare for the next OS X upgrade, Step-by-Step 8.01 walks you through the process of checking out the OS X version and Mac computer vintage information.

TABLE 8–1   Release Dates of Major OS X Versions

Major OS X Release	Release Date
10.0 Cheetah	March 2001
10.1 Puma	September 2001
10.2 Jaguar	August 2002
10.3 Panther	October 2003
10.4 Tiger	April 2005
10.5 Leopard	October 2007
10.6 Snow Leopard	August 2009
10.7 Lion	July 2011
10.8 Mountain Lion	July 2012
10.9 Mavericks	October 2013
10.10 Yosemite	October 2014
10.11 El Capitan	October 2015

Step-by-Step 8.01

Checking Version and Hardware Information in OS X

It is simple to check the installed version of OS X, as well as the model information for a Mac. This exercise will walk you through the steps for checking out this information and more. You need:

- An Apple desktop or laptop computer running OS X.
- The user name and password of an administrator account for this computer.

Step 1

Log on to an Apple Mac computer running OS X. Click the Apple menu in the top-left corner of the screen and select *About this Mac*.

Step 2

The window that pops up displays the version of the installed OS X. It also lists the computer model and date of manufactur and other basic information about the computer: processor, memory, startup disk name, graphics adapter, and serial number. You may want to return to this window as you read the next section.

Step 3

Click the *System Report* button to see detailed technical information about the hardware, network, and software. Explore the three categories. When finished, close the open window.

LO 8.2 | Installing and Upgrading OS X

This section details the process of installing and configuring OS X, including the minimum hardware and software requirements, the installation process, and the postinstallation task of updating software. If you purchase a new Apple computer with OS X preinstalled, the OS will need to be personalized for you.

Setting Up a New Mac

The first time you turn on a brand-new Mac computer or a Mac with a fresh installation of OS X, the OS X Setup Assistant runs. Follow the instructions on the screen to create a local computer account that you will use to log in and to select user preferences, such as country, time zone, language, and keyboard layout. As with the Windows OSs, this first account has administrator privileges.

Preparing to Install OS X

A new Apple Mac computer has OS X preinstalled, but people with existing Macs will often upgrade to a new version of OS X, so we begin by discussing the minimum hardware requirements for upgrading to OS X.

Access a Fast Internet Connection

At this point, the latest OS X upgrade required downloading a file that was over 4 GB in size and may take a while to download. If your Internet connection is metered, meaning you pay for a certain amount of data usage per month, then you may want to take your computer to an Apple store and take advantage of their free fast Internet access to download the upgrade.

Back Up Your Computer

Before installing or upgrading OS X be sure to do a full backup. The best way to do this is to use an external hard drive and Time Machine, the backup software included with OS X since Snow Leopard (10.6). Time Machine requires a dedicated drive that is always available whenever the computer is on. This can be an external USB, FireWire, or Thunderbolt hard drive, an Apple Time Capsule (an Apple product that serves as a networked hard drive), an internal hard drive (in addition to the startup drive), or a separate partition on a drive. If you have one of these drives available and connected to your computer, open the Apple menu, a drop-down menu that appears when you click the Apple icon on the far left of the menu bar; select System Preferences. In System Preferences, select Time Machine. Turn on Time Machine and follow the instructions. The first backup will take hours. Figure 8–1 shows a first-time backup of a hard drive with 263.08 GB of programs and data. It took over four hours to complete, backing up to a USB hard drive.

Check the Computer Model and OS X Version before Upgrading

Before upgrading to the latest version of OS X, verify the version of the Mac OS already installed as well as the model (and vintage) of the computer, using the instructions in Step-by-Step 8.01. If your Mac computer is too old you may not be able to upgrade its OS. If the OS is too old you will not be able to directly upgrade. You may need to first upgrade to an interim version before upgrading to the latest version. Even if you have an upgradable version, run Software Update from the Apple menu, a drop-down menu

FIGURE 8–1 The first Time machine backup can take several hours.

that appears when you click the Apple icon on the far left of the menu bar. Running Software Update will bring your OS up to the latest incremental update before you upgrade.

Other Hardware Requirements

Ensure that you have adequate memory and disk space. Presently, you need 8 GB of free space and 2 GB of RAM to install the latest version. However, you will want much more of both for running programs and storing data. As we write this, OS X 10.11 El Capitan is the current release, and there may be an even newer version of OS X when you read this because, as Table 8–1 shows, Apple releases new versions at intervals of one to two years.

Check the Firmware Version before Upgrading

Finally, check to see if your computer requires a firmware update. Read the article "EFI and SMC firmware updates for Intel-based Macs" at **http://support.apple.com/kb/HT1237**, which explains that most firmware updates are automatically installed, but some need to be installed manually and describes how to find your firmware version and how to determine if a firmware update is available. Scroll down in that document to see the firmware list (Figure 8–2), which is regularly updated. Locate your computer model in the list, and then check to see if a firmware update is available. The Hardware report, shown in step 3 of Step-by-Step 8.01, displays the version

Note: Use Spotlight, the OS X search utility, to quickly locate the article on firmware updates. To do that, click on the magnifying glass icon on the right of the title bar then enter: "apple firmware updates." Look for **support.apple.com/kb/HT1237** in the search results and double-click it to launch Safari open to the article.

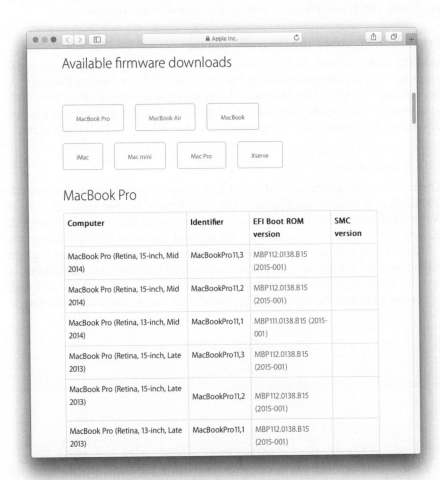

FIGURE 8–2 Locate your computer model in the list, and then check to see if a firmware update is available.

of firmware installed on your computer on the lines beginning with "Boot ROM Version" and "SMC Version." If the firmware version on your computer matches the one listed for that year and model, you do not need to do a manual update. If your firmware is not up-to-date, click the firmware version in the online article and follow the instructions to install the update.

Disable Disk Encryption

FileVault disk encryption has been included with OS X since Snow Leopard (10.6). If you have encrypted your files with either FileVault or a third-party program, temporarily disable it or turn it off. This is just a precaution to avoid any possible incompatibilities during the upgrade process or delays caused by the process of unencrypting. After a successful upgrade, enable encryption, unless you are using a third-party program that the new OS X version no longer supports.

Decide Where to Install OS X

Normally, you install OS X as an upgrade over a previous version. You can also install OS X onto a separate drive or separate partition on the same drive as your present version. This allows you to dual-boot between the two versions. The drive or partition must be empty when you begin the installation. The last OS installed will be the one that boots up by default, but you can change this on the fly by pressing the Option key as you turn on your computer. That is a good way to temporarily boot to the alternate OS. If you wish to change the default, then open the Startup Disk option in System Preferences and the drive you select will be the default startup drive.

Prepare to Purchase the Upgrade Online

Buy the latest version of OS X at the online App Store. Step-by-Step 8.02 includes instructions for accessing the App Store and purchasing the upgrade. Beginning with OS X 10.8 Mountain Lion, you can no longer order it on DVD; you must do an online upgrade or, if you want to do a clean installation, download the installation image and burn it to a DVD or USB flash drive.

The Installation

There are rarely surprises with an OS X installation—mainly because the installation is usually an upgrade; one can legally license this OS only on Apple Mac computers. If you do an upgrade, then at the end of the upgrade, you should only need to log in with the account you used before the upgrade.

Even when you buy a new Apple computer, which always has the OS preinstalled, you get to experience the final stages of the installation the first time you start the computer. That is when the Setup Assistant appears, and you will need to answer a few questions, including providing a user name and password.

Note: Before creating passwords, review the information on creating strong passwords in Chapter 2.

Note: In Step-by-Step 8.02 and other exercises we mention an OS X feature called the Dock. The Dock is a screen object resembling a floating tray usually located at the bottom of the desktop window. Like the Windows Taskbar, the Dock holds icons for commonly used programs, as well as for open applications. Click an icon to open a program. Learn how to configure the Dock later in this chapter.

Step-by-Step 8.02

Upgrading OS X

This exercise describes the steps for upgrading OS X. If you have an Apple Mac that meets the hardware requirements but is not using the latest version, you can perform an upgrade during this exercise.

- An Apple Mac that meets or exceeds the hardware requirements.
- An Apple ID.
- A broadband Internet connection.

Step 1

Begin an upgrade by first updating your current installation of OS X. Do this from the Apple Menu's Software Update option or by connecting directly to the App Store. To connect to the App Store, double-click on the App Store icon on the Dock.

Step 2

In the App Store, select Updates. When prompted, sign in to the Store and download the updates.

Step 3

While the update is downloading, an icon will display on the Dock with a progress bar.

Step 4

After downloading and installing all updates to the last version, select the new version from the Store. In our example, it is OS X 10.11 El Capitan. After it downloads the *Install OS X* window displays. Click *Continue*.

Step 5

Read the license agreement and click the *Agree* button to accept the terms of the license agreement.

Step 6

On the next screen, you will normally see only one location for installing the upgrade. If you decide to select another drive, click *Show all disks*. Otherwise, click *Install* to continue.

Step 7

This screen displays for a short time, and then the computer reboots and you see an Install OS X message box (against a plain background) with progress bar. After this, the message changes to *Install Succeeded* and it reboots again. What happens next depends on whether you did an upgrade over an older version of OS X or installed onto a clean hard drive.

Step 8

If you did an upgrade over an older version of OS X your apps will be intact, as will your settings, including your local user account. After the restart the logon screen displays, where you log in and meet the new version of OS X.

Step 9

If you did a clean install onto an empty hard drive you have more work to do. The Setup Assistant runs and you will need to answer screens of questions to complete the configuration of your computer, including a new user name and password.

Postinstallation Tasks

A benefit of Apple's requirement that you purchase OS X through the online App Store is that the installation image you download includes the latest updates to OS X. This requirement began with Mountain Lion, and eliminates the need to update OS X immediately after an upgrade or install. If you install OS X from an image you created days or weeks ago, you will need to check updates, as described earlier. Other postinstallation tasks include installing apps into a clean installation, updating apps, and enabling disabled components.

Installing Apps

If you did a clean install, you will need to install all your apps and personalize your computer to your own preferences.

Updating Apps

Apple does not include updates for your apps in the image, so you should check out available updates. An easy way to do this is by simply checking to see if a number appears on the top right of the App Store icon. When that happens, double-click the icon, the App Store window will open, and you can initiate the download and install the update from there.

Alternatively, when you do not see a message or indication of an update but want to see if any are available, open the Apple menu and select *Software Update*, which will also open the App Store window and check for updates.

In yet another scenario, you open an app and a message displays stating that an update is available. Unless you know of a reason to not update the software, simply respond to messages to start the download, including one allowing incoming network connections from the update program. Then you may see a message box giving choices to accept or reject individual updates and to start the install. A progress message will display while the update downloads. After the download completes, respond to more messages to continue, to accept the license terms, to select a destination drive, and finally to install the update.

try this!

Install Software Updates

It is simple to install updates. Try this:

1. Click the Apple menu in the top-left corner of your desktop and click Software Update in the window that displays.
2. In the Updates page of the App Store, see if any updates are available and respond to any messages to begin the Install.
3. Click Agree on any License Agreement page that displays (if you agree, of course). There may be several.
4. Click Restart, if requested.
5. It can take several minutes for the updates to install.

Enable Disabled Components or Apps

If you disabled any components, such as FileVault, before upgrading OS X, enable them after completing the upgrade. We describe FileVault later in this chapter.

LO 8.3 | Navigating and Managing the OS X Desktop

Navigating in OS X is much like it is in the Windows desktop. You move around by clicking graphical objects. Tasks include customizing the desktop, installing and removing applications, and adding a printer. You will learn how to set up system preferences, manage files, print, and create and manage user accounts. We also describe the features you use for your everyday work on a Mac, including launching programs and working with the newer OS X features.

The Desktop Menu Bar

One of the biggest differences between the OS X GUI and the Windows desktop is that Windows has a Taskbar at the bottom of the screen with general functions and notifications, and each app has its own menu bar at the top of its window. But OS X has a menu bar across the top of the screen with general functions and which also contains drop-down menus for the current app, and a notification area on the far right that serves some of the same functions as the right end of the Windows Taskbar. Depending on how OS X is configured, the notification area displays the day and time and contains icons for features such as the Spotlight search feature that searches local files and folders. Spotlight is also at the top of every Finder window. Figure 8–3 shows the OS X desktop with key features labeled. COMMAND+SPACE BAR opens the Spotlight search box. Spotlight presents results as soon as you start typing because Spotlight does a live search. Beginning in OS X 10.11 El Capitan, Spotlight searches everywhere,

> *Note:* The window for an app in OS X does not contain the menu bar, but it does contain buttons for accessing many of the same features available through the menu bar and the round window control buttons in the upper left corner for closing (red), minimizing (orange), and maximizing (green) the window.

FIGURE 8–3 Key features of the OS X desktop.

including the Web, and it is integrated into Safari. Another improvement in Spotlight is that you can ask natural language questions, as we have grown to expect to do with Apple's Siri and Microsoft's Cortana.

Click on the Apple icon on the left of the menu bar to open the Apple menu shown in Figure 8–4. This is where you find the version information (and details of the hardware and software), initiate a Software Update, connect to the App Store, open System Preferences to configure settings, put the computer into Sleep mode, restart the computer, shut down, and log out.

FIGURE 8–4 The Apple menu.

File Management in Finder

Like Windows, the OS X desktop has a file manager, Finder, as its foundation. When you launch OS X, Finder owns the desktop, as evidenced by the Finder menus at the top of the screen, but a Finder window is not open by default. Open the Finder windows from the smiling Finder shortcut on the Dock or with the shortcut keys: COMMAND+SHIFT+H. Apple is gradually replacing this focus on files in OS X by a focus on apps, which we discuss more in the sections on the Dock and Launchpad. However, Finder is your file management tool in OS X, and in the following sections we look at the Finder views, then practice creating folders, and learn other file management tasks.

Home Folder

Each person who logs on to an OS X computer has his or her own Home folder. When you open a Finder window, the Home folder for the currently logged-on user is identified in the Sidebar, the panel on the left of the Finder window, by an icon representing (what else?) a house. When you select your Home folder the house icon displays at the top of the window, as shown in Figure 8–5. Any time you want to open the Home folder, click on it in an open Finder window or simply press COMMAND+SHIFT+H. Several folders are created in the Home folder by OS X. They include Desktop, Documents, Downloads, Movies, Music, Pictures, and Public. You can also create custom folders to help you organize your files. The Documents folder is the default location that many apps use when saving your data files.

Note: Do you lose sight of your cursor when there is a lot of clutter on your desktop? Beginning in OS X 10.11 El Capitan, you just need to shake the mouse (or quickly swipe back and forth on a touchpad) and the mouse moves and temporarily enlarges on the screen.

Note: COMMAND+SHIFT+H opens the Home folder. COMMAND+SHIFT+D opens the Desktop folder that contains files and folders that appear on your OS X Desktop.

FIGURE 8–5 The Home folder has a house icon and displays the user's name.

FIGURE 8–6 The Finder menu.

The Finder menus—Finder, File, Edit, View, Go, Window, and Help—offer a variety of file management and configuration tools. The Finder menu, shown in Figure 8–6, lets you manage Finder itself, as does the menu in this position for any open app. The About Finder option gives its version number. Since Finder is part of the OS, it has the same version number as the OS, but when you open the About menu for an app that is not part of the OS you will see a different version number, and often, much more information about the app. The Window menu arranges window views, and the Go menu offers shortcuts to folders used for storage both on the computer and out on a network.

Select Preferences from the Finder menu and personalize Finder's default behavior. For instance, use the Sidebar options (see Figure 8–7) to add or remove items from Finder's Sidebar.

Finder Views

Note: Beginning in OS X 10.9 (Mavericks), Finder includes Finder Tabs, which act much like the tabs in Safari and other browsers. This reduces clutter by allowing you to have multiple tab pages in one window.

Finder has four views or ways of displaying objects: Icon, List, Column, and Cover Flow. Finder saves the preferred view of the first folder or disk opened in a new Finder window. The unifying factor in all four viewing modes in OS X is the ability to navigate the file and folder structure of your disks and to open files and folders by double-clicking them. If you are sitting at a Mac, follow the instructions in the Try This exercise, and then, while reading the following paragraphs describing the four views, experiment with the different views. You can set view options from the View menu, or from the View buttons, which we labeled in Figure 8–8.

Icon View. In Icon view, shown in Figure 8–9, you simply see the icon for each object in the selected location. This example shows the Applications folder open in Icon view. OS X stores application executables in this folder; double-click an icon to launch its app. We describe other methods for launching apps later in this chapter.

List View. List view, shown in Figure 8–10, displays content in an indented outline format that allows you to see the contents of enclosed folders. This is a powerful means of viewing and organizing your folders and files without having to open new windows for each subfolder, a process that can make your virtual desktop as messy as a real one!

To expand a folder, click the triangular icon to the left of the folder icon. To close the folder, simply click the icon again to hide the contents of that folder. The List view offers a wealth of

try this!

Explore Finder Views

Open Finder and browse through it while reading about the different types of views. Try this:

1. Open a Finder folder by clicking the Finder icon on the Dock.
2. Click each object in the left pane and then settle on one object that displays many files and folders in the right pane.
3. Locate the View buttons on the Finder window toolbar.
4. As you read through the description of Finder views here in the chapter, select the appropriate View button to select a view.

try this!

Sorting Files in List View

In List view, four columns offer information about your files: Name, Date Modified, Size, and Kind. The default view is an alphabetical sort by name. You can change that order. Try this:

1. Open a Finder folder by clicking the Finder icon on the Dock.
2. Double-click a folder or hard disk.
3. Click the title of any of these columns, and you will see your files sorted by that attribute. Sorting based on the size and data columns is useful when you want to recover hard disk space. Look for big, obsolete files this way.
4. Click the same title again to see the files sorted by that attribute in reverse order. Used most often with the Date column, this technique is effective when you want to search for recently changed or out-of-date files.

information about folders and files such as date last opened, date added, size, and kind (for example, application or file). If you double-click a folder, that folder opens either in the same folder window or in a new window, as in the other two view options.

Column View. In Column view, shown in Figure 8–11, when you select a file by clicking it once, the file's icon or a preview of its contents, either text or graphics, displays in a column to the right. If you click on a folder, the contents display in the column to the right, and if you click on a subfolder, yet another column opens with that folder's contents. When a window is in Column view, you can change the size of columns by dragging the bottom of the column divider.

Cover Flow View. Cover Flow view, shown in Figure 8–12, opens a pane containing small images of each object in the currently selected folder. Below this pane is a list pane. Select a file or folder in this list and it will appear in the center of the Cover Flow.

Creating Folders in the Finder

Organize your documents and applications in the contents pane. Create a new folder to contain copied or moved files or folders by choosing New Folder from the File menu in the Finder or by right-clicking an area of the contents pane and selecting New Folder. Practice creating a new folder in Step-by-Step 8.03.

FIGURE 8–7 Use Finder Preferences to add or remove items from the Sidebar.

FIGURE 8–8 Change the view from the Finder View menu or by clicking one of the View buttons on the toolbar.

Note: COMMAND+SHIFT+A opens the Applications folder.

FIGURE 8–9 The Finder window with the Applications folder open in Icon view.

FIGURE 8–10 The Finder window in List view.

FIGURE 8–11 The Finder window in Column view.

Copying, Pasting, and Deleting Files and Folders

Copy and paste files and folders into local or network locations.

- To copy, select the item and choose Copy from the Edit menu (or press Command+c).
- To cut, select the item and choose Cut from the Edit menu (or press Command+x).
- To paste, first either copy or cut a file or folder. Then open the destination location and select Paste from the Edit menu (or press Command+v).
- To delete, choose Delete from the Edit menu (or press Command-Delete). This moves the file or folder into the Trash. To empty the Trash, select Empty Trash from the Finder menu (or press Command+Shift+Delete).

FIGURE 8–12 The Finder window in Cover Flow view.

- If you drag a file or folder and drop it onto a different drive, that operation is a copy, meaning that you have copied the file or folder to the new location and the original remains in the old location. To copy a file or folder onto the same drive with a drag operation, hold down the Option key as you let go of the file or folder. Otherwise, it will be a move (discussed next).

The Finder Edit menu.

Moving and Renaming Files and Folders in Finder

If you drag a file or folder and drop it in a different folder on the same drive, that operation is a move, meaning that it is first copied to the new location and then automatically deleted from the old location. When you cut and paste a file or folder, it results in a move regardless of the locations. In Step-by-Step 8.03 you create a folder, and then drag files into the new folder.

Renaming Files and Folders in Finder

Open Finder and locate the file or folder you want to rename; click on it once to select it, and then after a short pause click again. This will highlight the name of the item and you will be able to edit the file name without changing the extension. (You should almost never change a file's extension.) When you are ready to save the item with the new name, either click away from the item or press RETURN.

WARNING!

When you rename files, be careful not to change the file extension. This can keep the operating system from recognizing a file type and the OS would not know which program to use to open the file.

Step-by-Step 8.03

Creating a New Folder and Organizing Files

In this exercise, you will create a folder within an existing folder, rename it, and move files into it. To complete this exercise, you will need the following:

- A Mac computer with OS X installed.

- A user name and password that will allow you to log on to your computer.
- Files in at least one of the folders of your home directory.

Step 1

Open Finder by clicking its icon (the rectangular, blue and white icon with a face image) on the Dock. If the Home folder is not visible in the Sidebar, first check Finder Preferences, as described earlier, and make sure there is a check by your Home folder. If it is still not visible, it may be hidden. Hover your mouse over the word "Favorites" at the top of the Sidebar. If the word on the right is "Show," click it to make the Home folder visible. Click on your Home folder in the left pane to see its contents on the right. Switch to Column view.

Step 2

Create a new folder. Press COMMAND+ SHIFT+N or select New Folder from the Finder's File menu. A new folder, called "untitled folder," will appear in the list of files and folders.

Step 3

Type a new name for the folder and press ENTER to save it. Or click the folder once, pause, and then click it a second time to highlight its name, and then type a new name and press ENTER to save the file with the new name.

Step 4

If a column is not already open to the right of the new folder, double-click on the folder.

Step 5

On the menu bar, select File, New Finder Window. Position the new window next to the window for the new folder. In the newly opened window, navigate to a folder containing files or folders you wish to move to the new folder. In this example, the window on the left shows the new folder "Dog-Pics." The window on the right shows that we selected a file named "Jazzy_3-08-08.jpg."

Step 6

Select a file or folder that you want to place into this folder by clicking it once and then dragging it to the window containing the new folder. If you want to select multiple files or folders, hold down the COMMAND key while clicking each file until you have selected all the files.

When you are finished selecting items, press COMMAND key+C to copy them. Then click in the empty folder area in the other Finder window. Press COMMAND key+V to paste into the new folder. When you have completed the task, close all open windows.

Changing Settings in OS X

The System Preferences icon on the Dock.

Open System Preferences from the Apple menu or from the Dock where its icon is a gray box containing a gear. This is the OS X equivalent of the Windows Control Panel. Figure 8–13 shows the main System Preferences window. Notice the *Show All* button in the title bar; this will always return you to the main System Preferences window. The icons are in rows by category. The actual icons in each row depend on the installed features and devices. While any logged-on user can change some settings, others can only be changed by an administrator, and some can be configured to be changed by either type of user. We describe the System Preferences categories by row below, using category names that are no longer visible in System Preferences.

- **Personal**—Desktop, security, and privacy settings for the currently logged-on user.

FIGURE 8–13 System Preferences organized by category.

- **Hardware**—Settings for hardware devices. Some of these are obviously associated with a single device, but Energy Saver controls the conditions under which different components are put into a low-power sleep mode and/or awakened.
- **Internet and Wireless**—Settings that apply to any form of network available to the computer and to certain services that rely on networking.
- **System**—Software settings that apply to all users of the computer.
- **Other**—Settings that apply to miscellaneous services and devices that do not quite fit into the other categories. This row does not exist in Figure 8–13.

If you have trouble with the default organization of the System Preferences icons, you can sort them in alphabetical order by clicking the View menu (in the Menu bar at the top of the screen) and selecting *Organize Alphabetically*. When you do that, the settings in the System Preferences window are sorted, and the shading that previously separated the categories disappears. However, you don't really need to change the View; simply select the setting name from the View menu, as shown in Figure 8–14. This is helpful when you know the name of a Preference pane but do not recall its category.

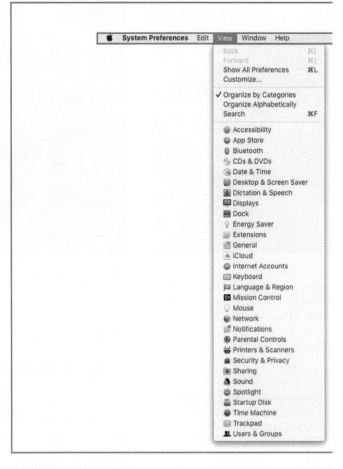

FIGURE 8–14 The View menu lets you change the appearance of the System Preferences folder.

Launching and Switching between Apps with the Dock

While early versions of Mac OS used the Finder as a task switcher, OS X delegates the task of launching frequently used apps and switching between open apps to the Dock, shown in Figure 8–2. A subtle line "engraved" in the Dock separates program icons from icons representing disks, folders, and documents. A single click on an icon on the Dock launches the program.

When you launch a program, a small dot appears under the app's icon on the Dock; simply click on one of these icons to quickly switch between tasks. The Trash icon sits on the Dock, waiting for you to drag unwanted files, folders, and apps into it. Add a file, folder, application, or Internet bookmark to the Dock by simply dragging it there. If you want to remove something from the Dock, just drag it off and onto the desktop until the word "Remove" appears over it, as shown in Figure 8–15; release the mouse button. The icon disappears. An icon on the Dock

Note: Press COMMAND+OPTION+D to hide the Dock. Press it again to unhide the Dock.

try this!

Add an Icon to the Dock

Add a shortcut icon to the Dock. Try this:

1. Open the Application folder in Finder and select something you would like to call up quickly from the Dock.
2. Click the item's icon and drag it onto the Dock. Before letting go of the mouse button, move the icon over the Dock to position it between existing Dock icons. Depending on the type of icon, you will be able to position it to the right or left of the divider.
3. Release the mouse button when you are satisfied with the position of the icon.
4. To reposition the Dock on the screen, click the Apple menu and select Dock. From the Dock menu click to select one of the position options. Notice the change in the appearance of the Dock as well as the orientation of the icons.
5. To remove the icon, drag it to the Trash icon.

FIGURE 8–15 To remove an icon simply drag it off the Dock until the word "Remove" appears, then release the mouse button.

FIGURE 8–16 The Launchpad contains app icons.

Note: Press and hold COMMAND while tapping TAB to open the heads-up switcher. Repeat until you have selected the desired app.

The Heads-Up Program Switcher.

Note: Launchpad, like the Windows 8 Apps screen and Windows 10 All Apps list, displays all installed apps.

behaves like a Windows shortcut, pointing to a file, program, or location. Therefore, removing it from the Dock only removes the icon.

Using the Heads-Up Program Switcher

There are several ways to switch among open apps, but we find using the Dock, as described above, and using the Heads-Up Program Switcher to be the methods we use the most. Simply press and hold the COMMAND key and tap the TAB key. The heads-up display of open app icons appears in the middle of the screen. Keep the COMMAND key down while you repeatedly tap the TAB key to cycle through the app icons. When the app you want is selected, release the COMMAND key.

View and Manage All Programs in Launchpad

Launchpad, a feature introduced in OS X Mountain Lion, resembles the home screen on Apple iOS devices (shown in Chapter 11). Click the Launchpad "rocket" icon on the Dock to open Launchpad. With Launchpad open, the menu bar at the top of the screen and objects on the desktop disappear, but the Dock remains visible. Now you can view all the existing apps on your computer and launch one with a single click. If you have more program icons than will fit on a page, scroll to see additional pages, just as in iOS.

Figure 8–16 shows Launchpad open with one page of app icons. The computer represented in Figure 8–16 does not have more apps than would fit on one page of the Launchpad. When two or more pages of apps are installed, the number of pages is indicated by dots positioned just above the Dock. Click a dot or swipe to move to another page. Customize Launchpad by clicking on an icon and holding the mouse button until all the icons in Launchpad start jiggling. Then drag the selected icon to different positions on the page or pages. If you drag an icon on top of another program icon (without releasing it), a horizontal band opens in the middle of the screen. Drop the icon into this band to group it into a folder with the other icon. When we dragged the iTunes icon on top of the Game Center icon the band opened with the suggested folder name of "Games." When we dropped the iTunes icon, Launchpad created the folder and showed the name above the band, as shown in Figure 8–17.

FIGURE 8–17 Group apps that you use together in a folder in Launchpad.

Declutter the Desktop with Mission Control

Mission Control is a window-management program that combines the functions of the Exposé, Dashboard, and **Spaces** features. "Exposé" was the term Apple previously used to refer to the feature that let you view all open windows on the screen at once. Dashboard is a screen containing small applets that act somewhat like Windows widgets. A Space is a virtual screen; OS X supports up to 16 Spaces. Use Spaces for separating work, play, and school projects into virtual desktops. Or open an app full screen and place it in its own Space. OS X Mountain Lion introduced full-screen apps that hide the menu bar and give you the maximum space in which to work.

Open the **Mission Control** screen to manage these features. While you can open Mission Control from the Launchpad, check out the keystroke or key combination to open Mission Control in the Mission Control preferences pane, shown here. The Mission Control shortcut is usually Ctrl+Up Arrow. The shortcut is a toggle: Use it once to open Mission Control. Use it again to close Mission Control.

> *Note:* A more generic term for Apple's Spaces feature is desktop, easily confused with the virtual desktops discussed in Chapter 2, but altogether different. Linux and Windows 10 each have features similar to Spaces.

Change Mission Control settings in this preferences pane.

> *Note:* To see a list of all keyboard shortcuts for OS X, open the Shortcuts tab of the Keyboard pane in System Preferences.

FIGURE 8–18 Mission Control.

When you open Mission Control, each window displays as a tile with no overlaps and a thin bar is across the top with the current space or spaces identified as "Desktop 1," "Desktop 2," and so on. Move your cursor to the top of the screen and the bar will broaden, showing thumbnails for the current spaces, as shown in Figure 8–18. To add a space, simply click on the plus (+) at the top right and a desktop will be added showing a thumbnail of the desktop. You can drag an open window from below to another desktop up on the bar. Switch between spaces by selecting a space within Mission Control or by simply using the CTRL+RIGHT ARROW key or CTRL+LEFT ARROW key.

OS X 10.11 El Capitan added the ability to make two full-screen apps share the screen, a feature called Split View. This will work only with apps that are capable of this feature, so it may take a bit of experimentation at first. To begin, open the two apps you wish to have share the screen side by side. In one of the apps click-hold the green Open Window button on the top left of the app window. The screen should split behind the app, and if the second app is capable, it will also open in the other half of the screen. This is great when you need information from one app while working in another app. Figure 8–19 shows an example of Split View. Split View is automatically assigned its own desktop space.

Note: Press CTRL+RIGHT ARROW key or CTRL+LEFT ARROW key to switch between Spaces.

FIGURE 8–19 Split View in OS X 10.11 El Capitan.

Notification Center

The Notification Center displays important status messages, notifying you of events, such as a new email or text message or the availability of a new update. These messages pop down on the top right of the Desktop. To open the Notification Center itself, click on its icon to the right of the Spotlight (magnifying glass) icon that opens OS X's search feature. In Notification Center, shown in Figure 8–20, you can see all your messages at once. Click the tiny icon in the bottom-right corner of the open Notification Center to open the Notifications preferences window (the open windows in Figure 8–20), where you can configure settings for notifications. Alternatively, open Notifications preferences from System Preferences.

Menu Extras

The OS X Menu bar has a variety of icons on the right side—some open up menus, while others, like the speaker icon, open controls as shown in Figure 8–21. These icons that give you quick access to some System Preferences settings are called Menu Extras. Add Menu Extras to the Menu bar through the individual preferences panes in System Preferences. For instance, the day and time are visible on the Menu bar because of a setting enabled on the Clock page of the Date & Time preferences pane. This setting is *Show date and time in menu bar*. Similarly, the Volume Control is on the menu bar because of a setting titled *Show volume in menu bar*.

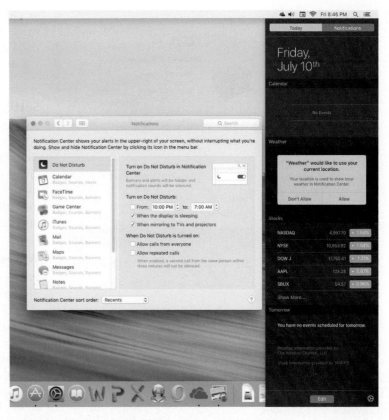

FIGURE 8–20 Open Notification Center to see all current notifications.

FIGURE 8–21 Some Menu Extras have menus; others have controls.

Printing in OS X

No matter what type of printer you have, almost every OS X application manages the printing process in the same way, including giving you the ability to create an Adobe PDF document from any Print menu.

Installing a Printer

Installing a printer in OS X is a nonevent. You simply connect the printer, power up, and it installs without any fuss or obvious activity. OS X quietly goes searching for the driver, downloading it from the Internet if the computer has an Internet connection.

To verify that the printer did install, open Printers and Scanners in System Preferences. With the Print tab selected, installed printers are listed on the left. If your new printer is not listed, click the plus (+) button under the list (shown in Figure 8–22) to initiate the printer detection process. This is often necessary before OS X recognizes a printer over a Wi-Fi connection. If this doesn't work, use the disc that was packed with the printer or, if you do not have a disc, contact the manufacturer for help finding a driver.

Note: While Menu Extras is the official term for these little menus and controls, some users call them *menulets*.

Note: Previous to OS X Snow Leopard (10.6), OS X kept a large cache of printer drivers on the local hard drive, taking up a good deal of space. Snow Leopard and newer versions no longer do that.

FIGURE 8-22 Click the plus (+) at the bottom of the list to add a new printer.

Most of your printer interaction takes place in the Print dialog box within applications. During printing, the Print Center icon appears in the Dock, allowing you to view, hold, or delete jobs.

Setting Printing Options

A printer has a variety of configurable options, which you may modify from the Print menu in any application's File menu (or the Print and Scan preferences pane). These options are specific to the printer model. You should explore these options for your own printer so that you are aware of its capabilities and can plan to take advantage of them.

Where to Find the Print Queue

When you are ready to send a job to the printer, simply open the Print menu in the application, select the printer, and if you need to change paper size, orientation, or scale, click the Page Setup button and make those changes. When you are ready to print, click the Print button. While a job is printing, an icon displays on the Dock, and if you're fast, you can open it in time to see the print queue, which closes when the print job is finished. Otherwise, you can find the print queue for an individual printer by calling up the Print and Scan preferences pane. Select a printer from the list on the left and double-click on any printer or click the *Open Print Queue* button to view its print queue, check the ink or toner level, print a test page, or open a printer utility that will let you do certain printer maintenance and testing.

AirPlay

Apple added AirPlay, a feature that was first introduced in iOS, to OS X in Mountain Lion. Use AirPlay to connect to an Apple TV, which acts as an intermediary device for sending your iTunes songs, video, pictures, and other data from your computer to a high definition (HD) TV via Wi-Fi.

LO 8.4 | Managing Local Security in OS X

Although most malware attacking desktop computers target Microsoft Windows, OS X is not impregnable, and anyone who connects to a network, plugs in a flash drive, or inserts an optical disc in their computer is vulnerable—not to mention the threats you can encounter browsing the Web and even in the messages you receive.

Apple is aware of the threats and has built in many security features that are on by default. Make sure you have updated your software, as described earlier in this chapter. It also doesn't hurt to add an antivirus program to your Mac. However, the greatest threats may be from scams and frauds, and your best defense against them is self-education and skepticism (even paranoia) when faced with messages that ask for information or require that you click on a link. In this section we examine the OS X security features that do a pretty good job of protecting you from everything but social engineering.

So where do you begin? Start your relationship with your Mac by exploring the security features of OS X and ensuring that you are using every security option available to you.

Note: We use a third-party antivirus, Sophos. Do your own research and make your own decision about this. Enter "antivirus for Mac" into a search engine and see what others think about this issue.

Check Out the OS X Firewall

How does your Mac connect to the Internet? Is it through a broadband router at home, or through a Wi-Fi hotspot at the school cafeteria or the local coffee shop? However your computer connects—whether it is a network you trust (at home or school) or an untrusted network, such as many of the public Wi-Fi hotspots, you need to ensure that you have the OS X Firewall turned on. While the most recent versions of OS X turn it on by default, you should check it out and familiarize yourself with it.

To view and modify Firewall settings, open the Security and Privacy pane in System Preferences and click on Firewall. Ensure that the firewall is on. If it is not, turn it on. You may need to click on the lock icon on the lower left of the window to unlock the settings, in which case you will need to provide a password. Then click the button labeled **Turn on Firewall**. Figure 8–23 shows the Firewall turned on.

After ensuring that the firewall is on, click the Firewall Options button to view the settings. Figure 8–24 shows this page. This requires some explanation. You could block all incoming connections if all you are doing is simple Web browsing and sending and receiving email. During these operations you initiate the connection to a Web server or mail server. The traffic that comes to your computer because of these actions is not seeking to initiate a connection to your computer; it is simply responding to your request for Web pages or email messages. Therefore, you could block all incoming connections, but still browse the Internet and send and receive email.

Our example in Figure 8–24 is more complicated because we have enabled sharing services on the Mac. If you install or enable services on your Mac that require incoming traffic (not initiated from within), it will configure the Firewall to allow this type of traffic. However, if you do not plan to do any type of sharing and have not enabled any service requiring incoming traffic, Firewall will block all incoming connections and it will turn on stealth mode, which it will gray out so that you cannot disable it. If you later wish to use a sharing service, the installation will change the setting to allow incoming connections for that service.

FIGURE 8–23 Firewall is on.

FIGURE 8–24 Incoming connections are allowed for sharing and for certain apps.

Gatekeeper

Gatekeeper, a feature introduced in OS X Mountain Lion, limits the online sources from which you can download programs. You will not find an icon labeled Gatekeeper, but you can configure Gatekeeper settings by selecting one of the options labeled *Allow applications downloaded from* on the General page of the Security & Privacy preferences pane. Here is a description of each of those settings (shown in Figure 8–25):

1. **Mac App Store**: Only install apps from the App Store. The most restrictive setting.

2. **Mac App Store and identified developers**: Download and install apps that include a Developer ID signature as well as apps from the Apps Store. Less restrictive.

3. **Anywhere**: Download and install apps from any location, as long as other security features of OS X allow this action. The only restrictions will be from other security components. This turns Gatekeeper off.

> **WARNING!**
> Anytime you unlock a settings pane, be sure to lock it again when you finish.

FIGURE 8–25 View and change the Gatekeeper settings by selecting one of the options under *Allow applications downloaded from:*

WARNING!

Do not turn on FileVault if you cannot allow the computer to run until encryption is completed. It can take several hours for FileVault to encrypt your disk, which it does after a restart. Once you turn on FileVault and the computer is restarted you are committed to this course of action.

WARNING!

If you forget your password or recovery key, you will not be able to access your startup drive and any data stored on it.

Kernel ASLR

Using a security feature called address space layout randomization (ASLR), OS X Mountain Lion and newer OSs load the core operating system code, the kernel, into random locations in memory, rather than loading into the same memory addresses every time. This prevents malware from accessing operating system functions based on their known location in memory.

Digitally Signed and Sandboxed Apps

All apps available through the App Store are digitally signed. A digitally signed app will issue a warning if its code is modified. In addition, each app available through the App Store is sandboxed, meaning that it cannot access any code or device it is not authorized to access. It is in a virtual sandbox where it can only play with those "toys" it is permitted to access.

FileVault

FileVault is OS X's file and disk encryption feature. Earlier versions only encrypted the Home folder, but in recent versions of OS X, FileVault encrypts everything on your startup drive every time you log out. With FileVault disk encryption turned on, your files are accessible only while you are logged on. Unless someone has access to your password, or you walk away from your computer without logging out, no one can open the encrypted files. An administrator must turn on FileVault using the FileVault page of the Security pane, as shown in Figure 8–26. On the next screen (Figure 8–27) choose how you wish to unlock your disk: with your iCloud account or with a recovery key. If you choose to use a recovery key, it will be created and displayed on the screen. Be sure to copy down the recovery key and store it in a safe place. You only need one recovery key on each computer. The encryption of your disk will begin after a restart, and it may take hours to complete. During this time you cannot turn off FileVault.

Secure Virtual Memory

OS X uses a swap file, much as Windows does. The swap file is disk space the OS uses as if it is memory, so they call it virtual memory. All multitasking

FIGURE 8–26 Click the *Turn On FileVault* button in the FileVault page of the Security preferences pane.

FIGURE 8–27 Choose how you want to unlock the disk.

operating systems use virtual memory to allow you to have several applications open. While you are actively using your word processor, most other open applications are just waiting for you to switch back to them. Therefore, it temporarily saves at least part of the code and data for these other apps to the swap file. Clever hackers can access the swap file, so Apple includes a feature in OS X called Secure Virtual Memory, which encrypts the swap file. Before OS X Mountain Lion, when you turned on FileVault it turned on Secure Virtual Memory, but beginning with Mountain Lion, this feature is on by default, without a way to turn it off in System Preferences.

Keychain

The keychain is part of a credentials management system using the name "keychain" as a metaphor for a physical keychain. The password to the keychain gives the user access to all the passwords or "keys" on that keychain. Each keychain is a secure database of a user's passwords, collected the first time it asks you to supply a user name and password to something, such as shared folders on your school or work network, at websites, FTP sites, and more.

Two default keychains, System and System Roots, belong to the OS. The first time you log in, OS X creates your first keychain, called login, using your account password as a master password for the keychain. Then as you go about your business, logging in to various servers to access email and other resources, as well as various websites, the credentials you supply are saved in your keychain, provided you respond to a prompt asking if you want to save the password. Although some websites have login programs that will not allow this, many do, and if you save the password for a website in your key chain, it will complete the login boxes (a process called AutoFill in Safari) each time you reconnect to one of these sites.

Safari turns AutoFill on by default, and you can turn it off if you do not want keychain to remember your credentials. Look for a setting similar to AutoFill, or one that mentions remembering passwords in any Internet browser to enable keychain with that browser.

For most of us, the login keychain is sufficient for all our needs, but you can create multiple keychains, each with a separate purpose, such as for your online shopping or as a place to save your personal credit information. Create additional keychains if you need varying security levels. For instance, you can configure one keychain so that the keychain locks if there is idle time over a certain threshold. This is where you keep your keys for accessing online banking accounts. Then create another keychain that will not have such a restriction because it is for low-security activity, such as a website you access purely for entertainment, such as Pandora, or for your instant messaging account. To create multiple keychains for various purposes, use Keychain Access, a utility found in Finder | Applications | Utilities, shown in Figure 8–28.

There's more to this topic. Now that many if not most of us work on multiple devices, we need a keychain that will work across those devices as we access the same networks and websites. The last few versions of OS X iOS include support for iCloud Keychain. This is a keychain stored in iCloud and is accessible to all your devices that support it and that you have enabled. Turn on iCloud Keychain in iOS 7.0.3 or later in Settings | iCloud. Do the same in OS X 10.9 Mavericks or later in the iCloud page of System Preferences.

FIGURE 8–28 The Keychain Access utility.

Managing Local User Accounts

OS X supports multiple local user accounts. At home, school, or work, you can set up a single computer with multiple accounts so that each person is restricted to his or her own home folder, preserving preferences from one session to another. As in Microsoft Windows, two users can log in to the same computer at the same time, but only one can have control of the "console," the keyboard, screen, and mouse, at any given time. OS X preserves each account's session in memory and users can switch back and forth using fast user switching. Alternatively, users can log in and log out when they finish working or step away.

Parental Controls

Note: You cannot apply Parental Controls to an administrator-type account.

Access Parental Controls in System Preferences through the Parental Controls pane or through the settings for individual users in the Users & Groups pane. Parental Controls have four categories of restrictions you can apply to a Standard or Guest account. They are:

- **Apps**—The desktop (Finder) for ease of use and/or to restrict which apps the user can open. Allow or deny the ability to modify the Dock.
- **Web**—Restrict access to adult websites or allow access only to certain websites.
- **People**—Control access to multiplayer games through Game Center, or limit mail and/or messages to a list of allowed contacts.
- **Time Limits**—Assign time limits during weekday and/or weekend and prevent access during defined times.

When you turn on Parental Controls for an account, it becomes a managed account.

Types of Users and Privileges

There are several types of user accounts; two of them, Administrator and Standard, are like the Windows account types of the same name. The others are Sharing Only, Guest account, and Root account. We describe the main functionality of the account types here.

Administrator Account. The Administrator account type, also simply called "admin," is for advanced users or for the person who will administer this computer. The first account created during installation is an Administrator. Open the Accounts preferences pane from System Preferences and view the local accounts on a Mac. Notice the description "Admin" on the left under the first account name in Figure 8–29. An Administrator account can do the following:

- Change all system preference settings and install software in the main application and library folders.
- Create, modify, and delete user accounts.

Standard Account. This account type is for ordinary users in an organization with tech support to take care of configuring and supporting computers. A Standard account type gets into far less trouble because of these restrictions:

- File access is limited to only the user's Home folder and the Shared folder (/Users/Shared/) that is accessible to other users without restriction.
- Access is denied to higher-level system preferences, such as network settings, sharing, software update settings, user setup, and date and time settings.

FIGURE 8–29 The Users & Groups preferences pane.

Sharing Only Account. You can create a Sharing Only account for someone who only needs to access shared folders on your Mac over a network. With a Sharing Only account type someone can connect remotely and log in with the local account, but will not have her own set of Home folders on the local computer. A person with a Sharing Only account cannot log on locally at the computer where the Sharing Only account resides.

Guest User. Guest is an account type with very limited access, but OS X no longer allows you to assign this account type to a new user. Instead, it creates a single Guest account, called Guest User. This account does not require a password, has access only to the Guest Home folder, and when a guest logs out, all files and folders created during that session in the Guest's Home folder are deleted. Enable the Guest Account in the Users & Groups preferences pane. To further restrict the Guest account, turn on Parental Controls, described previously.

Root Account. The Root account, often called a super-user account, exists mainly for the use of the OS. It is not enabled for interactive users in the standard installation of OS X. Root is only for people familiar with the inner workings of UNIX, and changing things on your computer using this account can result in serious system dysfunction and lost data. We will not describe how to enable it. Root gives you complete control over all folders and files on the Mac.

You rarely will require the amount of control over OS X system files that the Root account allows. Apple specifically organized OS X to limit the need to change the system files and folders.

Automatic Login

Automatic Login bypasses the login page and logs into the selected user account when the computer powers on. With Automatic Login turned off (the recommended setting), OS X prompts a user to enter passwords to log in. In recent versions of OS X an administrator configures automatic login by selecting the Login Options at the bottom of the Users & Groups preferences pane. This opens a page where you can enable or disable Automatic Login for individual local users, as well as modify the appearance of the login window (if Automatic Login is disabled).

Creating and Deleting User Accounts

The first user account is set up when you install OS X. This account is automatically an administrator-type account and it is automatically associated with the user's Apple account. After the installation process is complete, you can create additional user accounts, as described in Step-by-Step 8.04. We recommend that you take an additional step and enable an option on the user account page for the first user labeled *Allow user to reset password using Apple ID*. This setting will make life easier for you if you should forget your password for this account, which we discuss later.

> **WARNING!**
> Only use Automatic Login in a very safe environment, such as your home, where the convenience outweighs any threat to your data.

Step-by-Step 8.04

Creating a New User/Deleting a User Account

In this exercise, you will add a new user to your computer. To complete this exercise, you will need the following:

- A Mac computer with OS X installed.

- You must be logged on to the computer as an administrator.
- If Automatic Login is turned on, turn it off before beginning this exercise.

Step 1

Begin the process of creating a new user by opening the Users & Groups preferences pane. In the Users & Groups pane click on the lock on the bottom left. In the box that opens enter your password and click *Unlock*. Back in Users & Groups click the button with the plus sign at the bottom left. Enter a Full Name and press the TAB key. This will create the account name based on the full name. You can change the full name and password later, but the account name is permanent. Next, if you choose the iCloud option, enter the user's iCloud ID. Internet access is mandatory for the first login to a device using an iCloud ID. If you created a user using an iCloud password, click the Create User button. Step 2 describes creating a user account that will use a local password.

Step 2

If you are creating a local password, enter it in both the Password and Verify boxes. Enter a password hint, and then click Create User.

Step 3

The new user appears in the sidebar of Users & Groups, and the settings for that user display on the right. The new user in this example is a Standard User. If you want to change this account to an administrator-type account, click to place a check in the box labeled *Allow user to administer this computer* on this page. If the new user is a child, you may want to enable Parental Controls.

To delete a user account you will need to ensure that Users & Groups is unlocked for changes. If the lock on the bottom left is locked, click it and enter your password. Then select the user account in the sidebar of Users & Groups and click the minus button (–) at the bottom of the sidebar. When prompted, select an option for saving or deleting the user's Home folder, and then click *Delete User*.

LO 8.5 | Troubleshooting Common Mac OS Problems

In this section you learn where to find basic help and a guide to the system utilities and keyboard shortcuts that can help you get out of trouble. You'll also learn how to handle the larger files that you'll encounter in today's computing environment.

Note: COMMAND+SPACEBAR opens the Spotlight bar on the desktop.

Where to Find Help

When problems arise, where do you go to find general help in OS X or from within an application?

Help with the OS

With the improvements in Spotlight search, we rely more and more on simply asking a question in natural language and selecting a likely source for help among the results it produces. Quickly open the Spotlight bar on the desktop with the COMMAND key+SPACEBAR shortcut. Or go directly to Apple's Support Center at www.apple.com/support, select the product being used, and search there.

Alternatively, members of the network of Apple user groups around the world can get support from other users and learn more about their computers. Apple user groups are a useful and affordable way to increase your knowledge of your system and the software you choose and use. For more information, see www.apple.com/usergroups/.

If self-help fails and your computer is still under warranty, contact Apple directly, using the information that came with your computer. Technical support is expensive if your computer is outside its warranty period. Novice users who use their computers enough to increase the likelihood of multiple requests for support should consider signing up for an AppleCare service and support package to keep technical support costs down. Find more information at www.apple.com/support/products/.

Note: COMMAND+Q quits the open app. OPTION+COMMAND+ESC opens the Force Quit Applications box.

Help within Applications

If a problem with an open application persists, click the Help menu from the menu bar. In many cases, there will be a local help utility and an option to find online help for the application. Search through the help utility to find an answer to your problem or search the software publisher's website or the Web at large using a brief description of the problem or a part of the error message in the search string. Figure 8–30 shows the PowerPoint help utility.

FIGURE 8–30 The PowerPoint Help utility.

FIGURE 8–32 Select the application from the Force Quit Applications box.

FIGURE 8–33 An application failed.

Note: If you *change* a password, OS X lets you keep your login keychain and assigns the new password to the keychain. When you *reset* a password, OS X creates a new login keychain for that user, and you will need to manually enter passwords and allow them to be saved in the new keychain.

FIGURE 8–31 An application's Quit option.

When to Quit

When you finish working with an app, you can quickly quit the app by pressing COMMAND-Q or by opening the app's menu (shown in Figure 8–31), and selecting Quit. If an open application is behaving strangely—maybe it freezes, displaying the "busy" icon for no apparent reason—quit the application and restart it. This will resolve many transient problems.

Sometimes an application will not politely quit; that's when you must use Force Quit—either from the Apple menu or with the key combination of COMMAND+OPTION+ESC. This will bring up the Force Quit Applications box, shown in Figure 8–32. It shows you all the running applications, so you can select the correct one. A force quit allows you to safely remove an application from memory without requiring a restart of your computer and without adversely affecting the rest of the programs running in memory.

OS X Failure to Quit

Sometimes, when you attempt to shut down, log off, or restart, you see a message similar to Figure 8–33, stating that you haven't been logged out because an application has failed to quit, like the one shown here. Return to the app and close it out properly. If that does not work, use the Force Quit tool. If the application still refuses to quit, do a hard power-down by pressing and holding the power button for several seconds.

Forgotten Password

The majority of calls to help desks are for forgotten passwords. Here we describe your options for recovering from this minor disaster.

Resetting a Password in OS X Snow Leopard or Older

The first-created user account on your computer is automatically designated an administrator. If you happen to forget or lose the administrator password, and if you have OS X Snow Leopard (10.6) or older, reset the password with the help of the installation disc. To do this insert the DVD and from the Install screen choose Utilities | Reset Password. Select the hard drive that contains the System folder, and use the first pop-up menu to select the name of your account. Enter your new password twice. You should keep the DVD in a safe place, because anyone with the OS X DVD can gain complete access to your system.

Resetting a Password in OS X Lion or Newer

With OS X Lion (10.7) or newer how you reset a password depends on the scenario. We will look at each scenario next.

You are logged in with an administrator account. If OS X is running and you are logged in with an administrator account and wish to reset the password for another account, open System Preferences | Users & Groups. If the lock is in the locked position, click it and enter your password. Select the user in the Users and Groups sidebar, and then select *Reset Password*. Enter a password, verify it by entering it a second time, provide a password hint, and then click *Reset Password*.

You have forgotten your password and cannot log in and FileVault is off. If you cannot get into OS X because you have forgotten your password, and if you don't have FileVault turned on, then at the login screen when you enter a wrong password, the Password Hint box will pop up. If the hint doesn't help, or if there is no hint, click Reset password with Apple ID. The Reset Password box will display, and you can enter your Apple ID and password, and then click Reset Password. Follow the instructions from there.

You have forgotten your password and cannot log in and FileVault is turned on. If FileVault is enabled on your computer, you may be able to use the FileVault recovery key to reset your login password. For detailed instructions, you will need to go to another computer and search support.apple.com for the article titled "If you forget your login password and FileVault is on."

The article cited walks you through the necessary steps. In short, you will first have the opportunity to attempt to login again. If that fails, and you cannot reset the password using your Apple ID, select the option to "reset it using your Recovery Key." Then enter your recovery key and reset the password. Be sure to save the new password in a safe location. Or memorize it.

try this!

Help to the Rescue!

If you're in OS X and can't remember the keyboard shortcuts for escaping a program freeze or some other action, jog your memory with OS X Help Center. Try this:

1. Click the desktop or the Finder icon on the Dock to make sure you're in the Finder.
2. Select the Help menu.
3. Type "Freeze" in the Help Search box and press ENTER.
4. Choose Shortcuts for Freezes.

Note: There is a difference between the Change Password and Reset Password features in Users & Groups. The *Change Password* button appears on the account page for the currently logged-on user, and that user must provide his or her current password before entering a new password. When you choose *Reset Password*, which an administrator can do for another user, you need to provide only the new password.

Disappearing Sidebar Items

Our mantra is "Disaster is only a mouse-click away." We could write an entire book on the foibles of blithely moving objects around in any GUI. One minor but annoying problem we have had in OS X is the disappearance of Applications in the Finder Sidebar. Here is a simple solution to standard items disappearing from the Sidebar: Simply open the Finder menu, select *Preferences*, and then click *Sidebar* in the button bar. In the list of items, ensure that all the items you wish displayed have a check mark, and then if items are still missing from the Sidebar, hover your mouse over the word "Favorites." If the word "Show" appears on the right, select it to unhide items.

Useful System Utilities

The utilities described here for OS X are useful for basic troubleshooting. As with any situation, if you find yourself in deep water, seek expert advice. Here is a quick guide to OS X's hard disk and network software utilities.

Note: If your system is crashing a lot, one of the reasons may be damage to the hard disk. Running a diagnostic test with Disk Utility will reveal if there is damage.

Disk Utility

Found in the OS X Utilities folder (Applications | Utilities), Disk Utility, shown in Figure 8–34, offers summary and usage statistics for all volumes attached to the computer. The utility also includes Disk First Aid, accessed from the button on the upper left, which enables you to verify or repair OS Standard, OS Extended, and UFS formatted disks, including hard disks and CD-ROMs. The software also works as a one-stop shop for erasing and partitioning volumes.

FIGURE 8–34 The Disk Utility.

FIGURE 8–35 Advanced page of the Network preferences pane.

Network Preferences

Have you ever had a problem with your home Internet connection and found yourself talking to a help desk person from your Internet service provider (ISP)? The help desk often wants you to provide information about your network connection, such as the IP address and other configuration settings. To do that in OS X, open the Network pane in System Preferences, select the network connection in the sidebar, click the Advanced button, and then click the appropriate tab. For instance, the TCP/IP tab shows the IP configuration, while the Wi-Fi tab shows the network or networks to which your computer connects as preferred networks and the type of security used. Figure 8–35 shows the TCP/IP settings.

Using Terminal in OS X

OS X includes another source of utilities for troubleshooting the many programs an advanced user can run from its Command-line interface (CLI) Terminal, a window where you can get in touch with OS X's UNIX roots. OS X security applies to your activities while working in Terminal. In this section we give an overview of Terminal features and opportunities for you to practice using the commands in Terminal. Terminal includes many of the same CLI commands as Linux, the topic of Chapter 9.

try this!

Open a Terminal Window in OS X

Open a Terminal window in OS X. Try this:

1. Open a Finder window by clicking on the Finder icon on the Dock and browsing to **Applications | Utilities | Terminal**.
2. Double-click **Terminal** to launch it.
3. With Terminal open, right-click on its icon in the Dock and select **Options | Keep in Dock**.
4. Leave it open as you read through the chapter.

Launch Terminal

Launch Terminal from the Utilities folder located in the Applications folder. The first thing you will see is the character mode user interface, or shell. Terminal uses the BASH shell, which we will discuss further in Chapter 9. Launch Terminal and add it to the Dock so that it is easy to quickly launch. See how in the Try This!

FIGURE 8–36 The Terminal Shell menu.

The default Terminal $ prompt, as shown in Figure 8–36, begins with the computer name followed by a colon (:) with a tilde (~) representing your home directory. These are followed by the user name of the currently logged-on user and the $ sign. After opening Terminal, notice that just like all other windows in OS X, it has its own menu at the top of the screen, as shown in Figure 8–36. Use the Shell menu to launch a new Terminal window so that you can have multiple windows open at once. The Terminal window also supports multiple tabs. Select New Tab to open a new tab in the current Terminal window.

Add the Terminal to the Dock.

Shell Commands in Terminal

A shell command is a command entered through a CLI shell. There are well over a thousand commands available in Terminal, and one way to quickly see a list is to use the command completion feature. Simply type the first letter and Terminal will try to guess what you are typing, completing the command for you. If you press the Tab key twice at an empty Terminal Command Prompt, it will first pause and prompt you by asking if you want it to display all the possibilities. Press **y** to proceed or **n** to cancel. If you let it proceed, it will display all commands, as shown in Figure 8–37. Notice the word "More" at the bottom of the window. When you see this, press the spacebar to see another window full of the results. Move the scroll bar up to see the commands that scrolled out of the window area. This is not a very satisfying way to see the commands, but it gives you a sense of the quantity of commands.

Note: For a short list of frequently used commands see the *UNIX Command Summary* at www.bsd.org/unixcmds .html.

FIGURE 8–37 Press the Tab key twice; then type y to see the complete command list.

Note: UNIX-based OS X Terminal provides for the temporary use of the Root account security context when you precede a command with the sudo command and provide your password. This works only if you have logged in as an Administrator. Because of this feature, Terminal does not need the option to "Run as administrator" that the Windows Command Prompt uses.

Before you start typing commands at the $ prompt you should understand that OS X Terminal is case sensitive and case aware, as are both Linux and UNIX. Commands are (mostly) in lower case, but options may vary, and whenever you type a directory or file name in Terminal, pay attention to case.

Working with Manual Pages

Once you know the name of a command that you want to use, tap into the power of the **man** command to learn how to use that command. This command lets you view the manual page for a Terminal command, called a manpage, usually many "pages." Simply type the **man** command followed by the name of the command.

Note: Whenever the screen gets too cluttered, simply use the **clear** command.

For instance, to see the manual page for the **ls** command type **man ls**. The documentation for the command will display one screen at a time. A colon (:) and a blinking cursor display on the last line of the window, indicating that there is more of the manpage to display. When you are ready to move to the next screenful of the manpage press the spacebar (or press RETURN to advance one line at a time). To go back up, press the up arrow. When it gets to the end of the manpage "(END)" replaces the colon. You can quit a manpage at any time by pressing the **q** key. Practice in Step-by-Step 8.05.

Step-by-Step 8.05

Using the Man Command

Open two Terminal windows in OS X and practice using the **man** command in one window as a guide for working in a command in the second window.

Step 1

At the $ prompt type **man ls** and press ENTER.

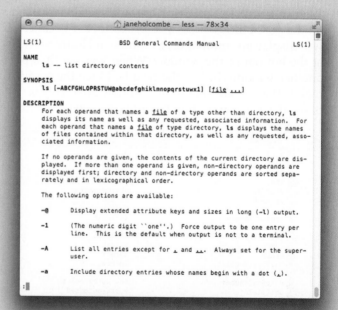

Step 2

Notice what the manpage says will occur if no operands (options) are entered at the command line. Test this by opening a second Terminal window while leaving the one with the manpage open. To do this, click the **Shell** menu and then select **New Window**.

Step 3

Use the **ls** command without any options. In the new window type **ls** and press ENTER. This displays a list of the nonhidden files and directories in the current directory.

Step 4

Back in the first Terminal window, the first page of the **ls** manpage describes the **-a** option. In the second Terminal window add the **-a** option to the **ls** command to see a list that includes both hidden and nonhidden files and directories. Type **ls -a** and press ENTER. All the normally hidden entries appear. They are the files and directories that begin with a period (.).

Step 5

You know which entries are hidden and which are not, but so far, it is not clear which is a file and which is a directory. The second page of the **ls** manpage describes the **-F** option. To see all entries (as in step 4), and to also see directories identified with an ending slash (/), type **ls -aF** and press ENTER. Be sure to type the correct case.

Step 6

The output of the **ls** command with the **-aF** identifies all the directories with the forward slash (/). Notice the . and .. entries. The single period (.) represents the current directory and the double period (..) represents the parent directory—the directory above the current directory.

Step 7

In the window where you have been experimenting with the **ls** command, use the **cd** (change directory) command to move up to the parent directory. Type **cd ..** and press ENTER. This changes the current directory to the parent directory.

Return to the Home directory: Type **cd ~** and press ENTER.

Change to the Documents directory: Type **cd Documents** and press ENTER.

Step 8

When you are finished with the **ls** manpage in the first window press **q** to quit.

Chapter Summary

After reading this chapter and completing the Step-by-Step tutorials and Try This! exercises you should understand the following facts about Mac OS:

OS X History and Versions

- Stephen Wozniak, Steven Jobs, and Ronald Wayne started Apple Computer, now Apple Inc., in April 1976.
- Apple introduced the Macintosh in 1984, the first affordable personal computer with a GUI.
- Apple introduced Mac OS X Server 1.0 in 1999 and the desktop version Mac OS X 10.0 in 2000. OS X has a UNIX core, known as Darwin.
- Apple has introduced several major versions of OS X—some within a year of the last version. It also has released many interim minor versions.
- Find the version information on the Apple menu's *About This Mac* option.

Installing and Upgrading OS X

- OS X installs only on proprietary Apple hardware, which normally comes with the OS preinstalled.
- Before upgrading, check the version of the installed OS; you may need to upgrade to another version before upgrading to the latest version.
- Hardware requirements have not increased since OS X Leopard (10.5). You cannot upgrade some older Mac computers to the latest version. If the model is upgradable, check the firmware and make sure it has enough RAM and disk space.
- Disable disk encryption before upgrading.
- OS X is no longer available on DVD; you must do an online upgrade or download the installation image and burn it to DVD or USB flash drive.
- If you buy a new Mac, you complete the personalization of the installation with the OS X Setup Assistant.
- After the installation, if you disabled disk compression or any other component or app, enable it. If you did a clean installation, you will need to install and update apps and personalize the computer to your own preferences.
- The online installation of OS X includes all the latest updates, so you no longer need to immediately update the OS.

Navigating and Managing the OS X Desktop

- The OS X desktop has a menu bar across the top containing general functions as well as the drop-down menus for the current app.
- The Apple menu opens when you click the Apple icon in the upper left of the OS X window. Use this menu to shut down, restart, or log out, and a few other tasks.
- The Finder in OS X is the GUI face of OS X with a variety of file management tools.
- Each person who logs on to an OS X computer has a Home folder identified in the Finder windows with a house icon and the user's name. The Documents folder in Home is the default location used by many apps for each user's data files.
- System Preferences is the OS X equivalent of the Windows Control Panel.
- Switch between apps using the Dock or the Heads-Up Program Switcher.
- Drag icons on and off the Dock and configure the Dock to be on the left side, right side, or bottom of the screen.
- See icons for all your installed programs using Launchpad. Group program icons together in folders.
- Declutter the desktop with Mission Control, which lets you create and manage desktop Spaces.
- Notification Center displays messages at the top right of the screen. Open Notification Center to see all messages.
- Menu Extras are icons you can install at the top right of the menu bar; they open menus or controls.
- Most printers install automatically, appearing in the application's Print menu.
- If a printer does not automatically install, use the Print box, click Add Printer to detect the printer.
- Use AirPlay to send local media files through an Apple TV device to a high-definition (HD) TV via Wi-Fi.

Managing Local Security in OS X

- The OS X Firewall is enabled by default. If you install or enable services on your Mac that require incoming traffic, it will configure the Firewall to allow this type of traffic.
- Gatekeeper limits sources from which you can download apps. The most restrictive setting

limits program downloads to the App Store. The Anywhere setting turns off Gatekeeper altogether.

- Using ASLR, OS X loads the kernel into random locations in memory.
- OS X apps are digitally signed and sandboxed, meaning that an app cannot access any code or devices it is not authorized to access.
- If you have important and sensitive information on your Mac, ensure that you securely encrypt your startup drive with FileVault.
- The keychain is a secure database of a user's passwords. By default, OS X creates a keychain for you the first time you log in, using your account password as a master password for the keychain.
- Create an iCloud Keychain to save your passwords across all your devices.
- OS X supports multiple local user accounts.
- The first user account in OS X is automatically designated an administrator.
- The types of user accounts in OS X are Administrator, Standard account, Sharing Only account, Guest account, and Root account.
- The Administrator account type can create new accounts, change all system preference settings, and install software in the main application and library folders.
- The Standard user account type can only access files in the user's home folder and the Shared folder (/Users/Shared/).
- The Sharing Only account type gives a remote user access to shared folders on the local computer, but this account cannot log on locally and does not have a local home folder.
- You cannot assign the Guest account type to any user other than the Guest User account created by OS X by default. It does not require a password, only has access to the Guest Home folder, and when the Guest logs off, the folder's contents are deleted.
- The Root account has complete control over all folders and files on the Mac. Only the OS uses this account and it is disabled for interactive users by default.

- Automatic Login bypasses the login page and logs into the designated user account when the computer powers on.

Troubleshooting Common OS X Problems

- When you need help with OS X, do a natural language search in Spotlight. If you have narrowed the problem to one application, use that application's Help utility.
- If an application freezes, press COMMAND-OPTION-Esc to force it to quit.
- A user can change his own password using Users & Groups. If a user forgets a password an administrator can reset the password, but the user will have a new, empty keychain associated with the new password. An administrator should configure her account so that she can reset her password using an Apple account.
- Use the Finder preferences pane to make folders display in the Finder sidebar.
- Erase and partition volumes and repair a damaged disk with Disk First Aid in the Disk Utility.
- The OS X CLI is the Terminal window where you can run OS X's UNIX commands at the $ prompt.
- Open a Terminal window from the Utilities directory.
- You can open multiple Terminal windows, and each window can have multiple tabs open.
- The default Terminal $ prompt begins with the computer name followed by a colon and a tilde (~) to represent the home directory. These are followed by the user name of the currently logged-on user and the $ sign.
- The Terminal window has a menu at the top of the OS X screen. Use the Shell menu to open new windows and/or new tabs within an open Terminal window.
- At the $ prompt press the Tab key twice and respond to the resulting message with a **y** to see a list of all command names (without descriptions).
- OS X Terminal is case-sensitive. Commands are usually in lower case, but options can vary, as do directory and file names.

Key Terms List

Menu Extras *(329)*

Mission Control *(327)*

Notification Center *(329)*

OS X *(306)*

OS X Setup Assistant *(309)*

recovery key *(332)*

sandboxed *(332)*

Secure Virtual Memory *(333)*

Shared folder *(334)*

Sharing Only account *(335)*

shell *(340)*

shell command *(341)*

Spaces *(327)*

Split View *(328)*

Spotlight *(316)*

Standard account *(334)*

System Preferences *(324)*

Terminal *(340)*

Time Machine *(310)*

Key Terms Quiz

Use the Key Terms List to complete the sentences that follow:

1. In a safe environment, such as your home, you can avoid entering your password at login by enabling _____.

2. To search for files use _____, a feature found in the desktop menu bar and at the top of every Finder window.

3. A user's passwords for logging on to various servers and websites from a single computer are saved in a secure database called a/an _____.

4. At the core of OS X is a powerful UNIX system called _____.

5. The _____ screen displays icons for all installed apps.

6. The _____ account does not require a password, and any file or folder it creates is deleted when this user logs out.

7. _____, introduced in OS X 10.11 El Capitan, allows two full-screen apps to share the desktop.

8. The _____ is a GUI object on the OS X desktop that holds program icons for fast launching, as well as icons for open applications you can use for task switching.

9. The _____ limits the online sources from which you can download programs.

10. The _____, accessed through a small icon at the extreme top left of the OS X screen, sounds like something the hostess hands you in a vegetarian restaurant.

Multiple-Choice Quiz

1. When did the first Mac OS appear?
   a. 1976
   b. 1983
   c. 1999
   d. 1984
   e. 2000

2. What major revision of OS X was released in the fall of 2015?
   a. Leopard
   b. Cheetah
   c. Snow Leopard
   d. El Capitan
   e. Lion

3. When you first power up a new Mac, what program starts automatically and prompts you for information?
   a. Dock
   b. Safari

   c. OS X Setup Assistant
   d. iChat
   e. System Preferences

4. Complete this sentence: In OS X, forced quits of applications . . .
   a. often cause other applications to fail.
   b. always require a restart of the OS.
   c. is not an option.
   d. usually cause system crashes.
   e. rarely affect the performance of the rest of the computer's functions.

5. Where will you quickly find version information about your OS X installation?
   a. Recent items
   b. Window menu
   c. Help menu
   d. Apple menu
   e. Finder

6. Which of the following is one of the four views available in Finder windows?
   a. Date
   b. Cover Flow
   c. Reverse
   d. Finder
   e. Jukebox

7. The Applications folder has disappeared from the Finder Sidebar. Where in the GUI can you go to put the Applications folder back into the Sidebar?
   a. System Preferences | General
   b. Utilities
   c. Sidebar | Preferences
   d. Finder | Preferences
   e. Windows | Restore

8. In addition to having an upgradable version of OS X running on one of the compatible models of Apple computer, you should also check to see if this (another system requirement) is up-to-date before upgrading to a new version of OS X.
   a. Apple ID
   b. Video drivers
   c. Firmware
   d. FileVault
   e. Gatekeeper

9. Which all-powerful account is used by the operating system, but is disabled for interactive users?
   a. Standard
   b. Group
   c. Administrator
   d. Root
   e. Global

10. You have an external hard drive from another Mac, and you would like to remove all the data on it and use it as backup for your new Mac. What will you use to prepare this disk for use?
    a. Finder
    b. Boot Camp Assistant
    c. System Preferences
    d. Tools
    e. Disk Utility

11. What type of service should you disable as a precaution before beginning an upgrade OS X?
    a. Networking
    b. Launchpad
    c. Mission Control
    d. Sharing
    e. Disk encryption

12. What keyboard shortcut can you use to force an application to quit?
    a. COMMAND-POWER key
    b. SHIFT-ESC
    c. SHIFT-RETURN
    d. COMMAND-OPTION-ESC
    e. Press C during startup

13. A Sharing Only type of account is not allowed to do which of the following?
    a. Connect over a network.
    b. Access shared folders.
    c. Log in locally.
    d. Enter a password.
    e. Enter a user name.

14. This account is automatically created by OS X; it does not require a password associated with it, has limited local access, and when this user logs out, the contents of its Home folder are deleted.
    a. Sharing Only
    b. Administrator
    c. Root
    d. Guest User
    e. Standard Account

15. Which of the following preference panes allows you to configure settings for Spaces, Dashboard, and shortcuts?
    a. Finder
    b. Mission Control
    c. Desktop & Screen Saver
    d. Dock
    e. Notifications

Essay Quiz

1. Research the significance of the UNIX core of OS X and write a few sentences describing your findings.

2. Your Mac laptop has both personal financial information and files for all your in-process school projects, including data from research for a major project in one of your classes. This laptop has two equal-sized partitions on the hard drive, and is always with you at home, at school, and at work. Describe how you will ensure the security of your valuable data.

3. Your copy of Microsoft Word suddenly freezes in midsentence. Describe the best way to regain control of your Mac.

4. When you brought your new iMac home and completed the information in the Mac OS Setup Assistant, you did not have Internet access. You have signed up for Internet access and the setup instructions from your ISP request the hardware address (MAC address) of your Wireless network card. First research and then explain where you will find this information within the OS X GUI and describe how it represents this value.

5. Describe the purpose of the Dock.

Lab Projects

LAB PROJECT 8.1

One of the users on your network, Helen Bandora, married Jon Moz, and changed her name to Helen Moz.

While it is simple enough to log into OS X as an administrator and alter her long user name to reflect her name change, changing her short name is not possible in OS X because it was used to create the Home directory *hbandora*. Her Home directory is not particularly full, with some Microsoft Word files in the Documents folder and some MP3s in her Music folder.

You decide that it would be polite to change both login names. What do you do to give her a correctly named account?

You will need a computer with OS X installed on which you have administrator rights.

You will need to do the following:

1 Research the solution for setting up Mrs. Moz with a correctly named account.

2 Find Helen's Home directory on the hard drive.

3 Implement your solution on the lab computer.

LAB PROJECT 8.2

OS X has a feature called Smart Folders that was not described in the chapter. Research Smart Folders and create at least one Smart Folder for yourself. Then, in your own words, write a short definition of Smart Folders, and describe a practical application of Smart Folders giving specifics.

LAB PROJECT 8.3

If you ever find yourself the administrator of a large network, you would want to minimize your network's electricity consumption by instituting good energy practices.

You will need a computer with OS X installed and do the following:

1 Go into the Energy Saver preferences pane and assess the various options you have for controlling the display and hard disk sleep features. Your goal is to reduce the display and hard disk sleep times to the minimum possible without causing the display to dim or the hard disk to spin down intrusively for users.

2 This is a chance to be creative and aware of the types of users of your network, and how they interact with the lab environment. Are computers used constantly, requiring a generous display or hard disk sleep time? Is the amount of RAM sufficient for working with files in memory or does the hard disk need to be accessed constantly? What kinds of software do your users use: processor and hard drive-intensive programs such as image manipulation and multimedia programs, or email and word processing software?

9

Linux on the Desktop

Learning Outcomes

In this chapter, you will learn how to:

LO 9.1 Describe Linux and its origins, and list benefits and drawbacks.

LO 9.2 Select, acquire, and install a distribution of Linux for the desktop.

LO 9.3 Identify certain features and utilities in a Linux GUI for customizing it and performing common tasks.

LO 9.4 Demonstrate the use of shell commands to accomplish common tasks.

LO 9.5 Secure a Linux desktop by creating user accounts, assigning passwords, and applying file and folder permissions.

Linux, a free operating system with many of the same qualities as UNIX, has the potential to save corporations millions of dollars. To grasp how important a free operating system is, think of an operating system as the software engine of your computer. Then consider the engine in your car. An engine costs thousands of dollars, but if a company started making and distributing free engines, the cost of your new car would drop dramatically, requiring just the cost of the body and chassis, electrical system, radiator, passenger heater and air conditioner, radio, and many other components. Of course, the Linux community offers many of the additional software components for the OS free.

In this chapter, learn the basics of Linux on the desktop with one of the many GUIs available. Linux is far too broad a topic to give a detailed exploration here, but you will learn why Linux is growing in popularity. You will learn where to obtain Linux to test on your computer and basic configuration and navigation tasks in a Linux environment. If you have never worked with Linux before, this chapter will serve as an introduction to this OS and perhaps inspire you to study it further. ✸

LO 9.1 | Linux Overview

Linux is an open-source operating system based on UNIX. In this section discover why you should learn Linux, the features and benefits of Linux, and how and why Linux is used today.

Why Learn Linux?

Learning Linux can be very beneficial to your future career because of its growing importance on all types of computers. Like Windows and OS X, you will find Linux on both desktops and servers.

Qualifying for a Job

If you are interested in a job in Information Technology (IT) or a related field, you should familiarize yourself with Linux. Because it is similar to UNIX, learning Linux prepares you for working with UNIX. Both Linux and UNIX are recognized as stable and used on servers worldwide. By learning Linux you are advertising your intelligence, initiative, and computer ability. A potential employer reviewing your résumé would see Linux knowledge as a big plus for an employee in many technology-related areas. Their reasoning is simple—if you can learn Linux, then you should quickly learn the idiosyncrasies of an organization's internal computer systems.

Improving Your Skills

Another reason to learn Linux is to improve your computer skills for working in a non-GUI environment, thus forcing you to be precise. Any OS is unforgiving when given the wrong instructions, but it doesn't take precision to browse a GUI and select the correct graphical object, which is how a GUI buffers users from the precision the operating system requires. The command-line interface (CLI) does not offer that buffer. In the IT networking environment the typical router or switch is managed using shell commands in a CLI.

The Evolution of Linux

In the early 1970s, Ken Thompson, a developer working at Bell Labs, was criticized for playing a computer game on company equipment. He then found an unused computer and wrote an operating system that would run his game. This operating system became the foundation of UNIX, which has gone on to power the computers of many universities, corporations, and governments of the world. It is a powerful, stable, and fast system. While UNIX is not Linux, the latter does owe its existence to individuals who looked at what Thompson had done with UNIX and decided to create something similar. Below are just some of the important milestones in the evolution of Linux.

Note: Learn more about GNU at www.gnu.org.

1984

In 1984, interested persons created the GNU organization to develop a free version of a UNIX-like operating system (GNU is a recursive acronym for GNU's Not Unix). Since its founding, GNU members have developed versions of Linux, as well as thousands of applications that run on

UNIX and Linux platforms. Some of these apps are bundled with distributions of Linux.

1988

In 1988, a group of UNIX licensees formed the Open Systems Foundation (OSF) to lobby for an "open" UNIX after AT&T formed a partnership with Sun Microsystems to develop a single proprietary UNIX. In response, AT&T and other licensees formed UNIX International to oppose the OSF. The trade press called the maneuverings of these two groups the "UNIX wars."

1991

In 1991, Linus Torvalds wanted to write a better, open-source version of MINIX, a UNIX-like operating system. Open-source software is distributed with all of its source code, which is the uncompiled program statements that can be viewed and edited with a text editor or special programming software. Linux is written in the C language as one or more text files, and then compiled, using a program called a C compiler, into binary object code. Object code is, essentially, an executable program in yet another language (machine language) that can be interpreted by a computer's CPU and loaded into memory as a running program. Object code cannot be edited.

Torvalds and a team of programmers succeeded in his original goal, but he receives no direct financial gain because he does not own Linux—just the name—and the open-source community could easily decide to rename it. But we don't believe that will happen because of Torvalds' fame and the very nature of the Linux community.

1994

Because the software was open source, many individuals and several companies modified the kernel. Two of the versions available in 1994 were the Slackware and Red Hat kernels, both written in the C++ language; both with TCP/IP functionality for communicating on the Internet as well as primitive Web servers. To obtain a copy, one simply went to an Internet site and selected the distribution to download. This is true today, with many more sources for the code.

Linux Today

The open-source movement has gained credibility in part because vendors such as Novell and IBM integrated open-source software into their product mix. The notion of free and open software, with no one entity owning the source code, thrives today and has the support of many organizations that previously opposed it. Several vendors offer inexpensive Linux servers running the open-source Apache HTTP Server, often simply called "Apache." This Web server software was originally written for UNIX but also runs on Linux. Separate versions have been available for other operating systems, including Windows. Apache is one of the most widely used Web servers due to its stability, security, and cost (free).

Note: The kernel is the core of the operating system. It contains all of the program code needed to allow the user to interact with the computer. The Linux kernel's code is freely available to any who wish to download it. Along with a great deal of other information, you can find the latest version of the Linux kernel at www.kernel.org. However, that alone is not what we download and install on our computers in this chapter; we download the kernel, plus drivers, services, and apps, all bundled together in a single ISO image.

Note: The World Wide Web (WWW) (also called the Web) is the graphical Internet consisting of a vast array of documents located on millions of specialized servers worldwide. Hypertext Transfer Protocol (HTTP) is the protocol for transferring the files that make up the rich graphical Web pages we view on the Web. Using HTTP commands, a Web browser requests Web pages from a Web server to display on the screen of a local computer.

try this!

Research the Open-Source Debate

View the current arguments in the open-source debate. Try this:

1. Use your favorite Internet search engine to find recent articles on "open-source debate."
2. Look at the arguments on the pro-open-source side and the proprietary side.
3. Who appear to be the major players on each side?

Linux Distributions

try this!

Research Linux Distributions

You can learn a lot about the various Linux distributions at the DistroWatch website. Try this:

1. Point your web browser to distrowatch.com.

2. Notice the organization of this site. The large center column of the Home page contains announcements of new releases, with the latest first.

3. The middle column also contains a brief description with links to the *DistroWatch Weekly,* an online newsletter containing reviews, news, tips, and other articles of interest to the Linux community. Click on links to read the articles. Read a few articles that interest you.

4. Return to the DistroWatch Home page at any time; clicking the Home page link at the top of each page will return you to the DistroWatch Home page.

5. On the Home page, look for the list of distributions ranked by page hits.

6. Close your browser when you have finished.

As mentioned in Chapter 1, when you buy or download a version of Linux you get a distribution, sometimes called a "distro," that includes the Linux kernel and a whole set of programs that work together to make a functional version of Linux. Most distributions include a number of applications. A distribution targeting desktop users will include an office suite and other productivity apps, while a server distribution will include server-related tools. A good source of the latest information about Linux distributions is DistroWatch. First published in May 2001, this website has grown from a simple comparison of a handful of distributions to the go-to source for the latest information on Linux distributions. Learn more about Linux distributions in the Try This!

Note: Terminology for Linux is a little different from other OSs. When you buy or download a version of Linux you get a distribution, sometimes called a "distro," that includes the Linux kernel and a whole set of programs that work together to make a functioning version of Linux. Most distributions include a number of Linux applications. There are many distributions of Linux!

Benefits of Linux

There are several benefits to using Linux on your desktop computer.

Linux Is Free

The first benefit of Linux is cost. You may freely download many versions of Linux from the Web. Many sites offer Linux distributions in convenient ISO images. If you don't want to download these distributions, you may purchase prepackaged versions of Linux online or in computer stores for modest cost.

Canonical is the company behind the open-source Ubuntu Linux distributions, updating the OS frequently. In addition, they are involved in other open-source projects and offer consulting services, which is how they pay their employees and keep the lights on and the servers running.

The Fedora Project is the organization founded in 2003 by Red Hat and other contributors. The resulting Fedora Linux distributions are open source, and also the basis for Red Hat's commercially available Red Hat Enterprise Linux (RHEL).

Linux Can Run on Old Equipment

In addition to being free or inexpensive, Linux can run on old equipment. A nonprofit organization can provide computers for its employees with donated or very inexpensive equipment. There are countless situations in which computers too underpowered to run even an outdated version of Windows continue to run reliably for years—as Web servers! The requirements for the latest version of the Ubuntu Linux Desktop Edition are:

- 700 MHz processor.
- 512 MB RAM.
- 5 GB of free space on a hard drive, USB thumb drive, or external hard drive.
- VGA-compatible video adapter capable of 1,024 × 768 screen resolution.
- A CD or DVD drive or a USB port if using USB-attached installation media.

Linux Is Fast

While Linux runs respectably well on old computers, it is even faster on newer computers. This is because Linux programs are very lean and efficient. They

FIGURE 9–1 The KDE GUI in a Fedora installation.

use as few resources as possible, graphics use in Linux is optional, and many Linux applications use few, if any, graphics. Graphics can slow a system's response time, making it seem slower than it truly is.

Linux Can Have a GUI

Unlike Windows, Linux was not intended to have a GUI, but rather just a text-only shell. A shell is the user interface to an OS; it accepts commands and displays error messages and other screen output. The traditional Linux shell is a command-line interface (CLI), such as the BASH shell. The term "shell command" is most often applied to text commands entered through a CLI shell.

Many distributions of Linux, especially those for desktop computers, come with a GUI shell created to a standard for Linux, X Window System. This standard was developed in 1984 at MIT for use with UNIX. The X Consortium then continued development of the X Window System (commonly called X Window or simply "X"). Today the Open Group continues the work.

Many Linux GUIs are available today, including but not limited to GNOME (usually pronounced "nome") and KDE. These competing Linux GUIs have improved over the years and various groups have developed their own GUIs, targeting different types of users. We find them as easy to work with as the Microsoft Windows or OS X GUIs, after some practice. Figure 9–1 shows the KDE GUI bundled with a Fedora distribution. It has a bar across the bottom, much like the Windows taskbar, as well as a Fedora button (with a script "f" on it) on the far left of the bar. This button opens Kickoff Application Launcher. Figure 9–1 shows the result of clicking this button.

> *Note:* BASH is an acronym for Bourne-Again SHell. The BASH shell in use today (the default in most Linux systems) is an enhanced version of the original shell program written by Steve Bourne.

Linux Is Stable

Linux code is well written, which increases the speed at which Linux runs and improves the stability of the operating system. Linux is next to impossible to crash. If an application crashes, you can simply remove the program from memory and restart it (the program). This is why people use Linux on Web servers where stability is crucial.

Linux Is Secure

Linux is a secure operating system with all the appropriate security options, as well as the benefit of not being as much of a hacker target as Windows operating systems are. As open-source software, Linux has the advantage of having legions of programmers working to make it a better and more secure OS.

Linux Is Open Source

Finally, Linux is open-source software; users can read the source code and modify it as needed. This probably means little to the average user of the final version of a Linux kernel. However, during development, "beta" releases of the kernel are available to developers who download the code and test it thoroughly, searching for problems and correcting the code. This process helps to ensure an as-well-written-as-possible final release of the kernel.

Once they release a final version, developers can adjust the kernel as needed. We know a developer who modified his kernel to be more usable for vision-impaired users. He added better support for large-print output and a command-line narrator that reads the information on the command line out loud. Being Open source lets the developer modify his code to suit his needs.

Drawbacks of Linux

Even though Linux is widely used on corporate servers, websites, and large-scale networking environments, you still won't find many people using it on their home desktop computers. There are several reasons for this.

Lack of Centralized Support

No system is 100 percent secure; however, Microsoft products do have extensive documentation and support. Microsoft releases service packs and frequent updates to fix discovered vulnerabilities. Linux does not have this centralized support. When you purchase Linux from vendors it is often supported by vendor-provided documentation and user groups, but support and documentation for free Linux can be spotty. A user who downloads Linux from the Internet may receive only a downloadable manual and access to online help pages. It is true that the Linux community is growing, and there are many active user groups, but one must search them out and expend considerable time and effort to get questions answered.

Choice of GUIs Is Confusing

The fact that you can choose from various GUIs is confusing. Users want what they know, and the Linux GUIs, while responding to most of the same mouse and keyboard shortcuts as Windows and OS X, are still different from both Windows and each other, requiring some exploration and self-training. For instance, the desktop shown in the Ubuntu example in Figure 9–2 shows the Unity desktop with a menu bar across the top, similar to OS X, and a Launcher bar along the side, unlike the GUIs for either OS X or Windows. However, the GUI shown in a Fedora distribution with a KDE GUI in Figure 9–1 has an entirely different look that is closer to the Windows Desktop with a bar across the bottom and a menu that opens from a button on the far left similar to the Windows Start Menu. Need we say more?

Limited Software Selection

People purchase computers to run applications—whether for business or for pleasure. There are important titles for Windows that are not available for Linux, so you need to check the software selection before moving to Linux on the desktop. But more titles are becoming available for Linux every year—even some very well-known titles. For example, consider Internet browsers. The most popular browsers, Mozilla Firefox, Google Chrome, and Microsoft Internet Explorer, are available for Linux, as are other browsers.

Note: If you have a recent distribution of Linux with the Linux GNOME desktop, look for accessibility options listed under Universal Access in the System category of System Settings.

Note: To add to the GUI confusion, several years ago Ubuntu moved to the Unity GUI, a departure from the previous GNOME GUI. At first glance, the main difference is the Launcher bar, but the Unity GUI actually has more stringent video requirements and is designed to work on a wider range of computers, from desktop to touch-screen tablets.

FIGURE 9–2 The Unity GUI desktop in an Ubuntu installation.

You are also limited in your choice of word processors. The most popular word processor is Microsoft Word. Chances are good that every desktop computer in your school uses Word. But Word is not available for Linux, although there are open-source programs that allow Word to work under Linux in certain circumstances. Various distributions of Linux have bundled excellent substitutions, including LibreOffice and Apache OpenOffice. Each of these is an applications suite that contains a word processor and other office productivity tools. However, although both are very nice products, a proficient Microsoft Office user would have to learn how to use one with the same level of proficiency.

Figure 9–3 shows the Ubuntu Software Center, where you can search for software for an Ubuntu installation. This is similar to what Apple and Microsoft offer for their OS platforms.

Limited Hardware Support

Not all hardware products work with Linux, but we see this situation improving. Linux vendors work very hard to support the more common devices by providing drivers for them. Having the correct driver is crucial. If you have a new or unusual device, you may need to search the Internet for a driver. Maybe the vendor has not created a Linux driver for your new device, but there is great support among Linux users who create drivers and make them available on the Internet.

Complexity

The last block in the wall between Linux and greater success as a desktop OS is Linux's

Notification Center icon

Menu bar

Notifications and Menu Extras

Dock

Trash

FIGURE 9–3 The Ubuntu Software Center.

difficulty of use at the command shell, which continues to be where advanced tasks must be done. Only a limited subset of users care to invest the time and effort to learn its intricacies. Linux, like UNIX, assumes that you know what you are doing, and it assumes that you know the consequences of every command you type.

Even with the new, improved GUI shells for Linux, it is not as easy to use as the more common operating systems. So if you implement Linux as a desktop OS, be prepared to spend time configuring Linux and providing training for other users who might need to use your computer.

Don't let this discourage you, however. By now, you have spent sufficient time working with operating systems so that you know the basic theory. You'll do fine in Linux. In this chapter we will explore how to work in Linux in a GUI as well as the basics of working in the Linux terminal window.

LO 9.2 | Linux on Your Desktop

So now that you know some of the history of Linux and its benefits and drawbacks, how will you experience it? Do you have a computer to dedicate to Linux so that you can install it? Do you plan to install it in a dual-boot configuration and continue to boot into another OS? Do you have a computer with a hypervisor in which you can create a virtual machine for testing Linux? In this section, we will describe the sources of Linux distributions for desktop computers and test an option you may not have considered for experiencing Linux: a live image.

Acquiring Linux for the Desktop

There are many distributions of Linux, and many sources for them. The most important criterion to keep in mind before selecting one is the role you wish the Linux computer to play—will it be a server or a desktop? When selecting a source, select one that meets your support needs. Are you a developer who wants to participate in the further development of Linux and Linux apps? If so, you can join a community of like-minded people at one of many websites where they gather. Since this is a survey class, we will assume that most students reading this are only interested in getting acquainted with Linux to understand its place in the world.

Our criteria for a distribution to feature in this chapter was for a desktop version of Linux that we can download and use quickly and easily. We selected two: Ubuntu and Fedora. Learn more about each of these distributions at the following websites:

- Ubuntu (www.ubuntu.com)
- Fedora (getfedora.org)

While we have downloaded and installed Linux from both sources, we chose Ubuntu Desktop Edition for most of our examples in this chapter mainly because we had worked with it with some success in the past. Both sources provide an ISO file that allows you to create a bootable disc. When you boot from the disc, you choose to install Linux onto the local computer or to boot into a live image of Linux. A live image is a bootable image of the operating system that will run from disc or other bootable media without requiring that the OS be installed on the local computer. This feature is sometimes called a Live CD, but that term is becoming outdated by the fact that you can now create a bootable CD, DVD, or solid-state drive (USB flash drive). Many system administrators create custom live images that include both an OS and handy utilities. When an OS fails, an administrator can boot up with the live image and use the utilities for diagnostics, troubleshooting, and data recovery. After downloading an ISO file, burn it to a disc or install it on a flash drive and you can then boot up the OS.

The Ubuntu distribution we selected includes a complete software bundle: the Unity GUI desktop and a number of GUI applications including

LibreOffice, Firefox, and software selections for many other functions, such as email, chat, social networking, music streaming, photo management and editing, and more. The download for this edition is 1 GB.

The various versions of Linux have many things in common, so what you learn about one version will carry over to another version.

Step-by-Step 9.01

Downloading Linux and Creating a Bootable USB Flash Drive

This step-by-step exercise takes you through downloading a distribution of Linux and burning the image to a disc, which you can then use in the remainder of the class. The instructions and illustrations are for using a Windows computer to download an Ubuntu Linux ISO file and to create a bootable DVD. You can complete this exercise using a different distribution of Linux, and the steps will be similar. To complete this exercise you will need:

- A Windows computer (if using another OS, the steps and screens will differ from those shown here).
- An optical drive capable of burning a disc.
- A blank DVD disc.
- Broadband Internet access.

Step 1

Use your browser to connect to www.ubuntu.com. Click the *Download* link at the top of the Ubuntu home page. On the resulting page click to select Ubuntu desktop. On the next page, shown here, select the version with Long Term Support (LTS). Then select either 64-bit (shown in the white box) or click on 64-bit to open the drop-down menu and select 32-bit. The latter is necessary if the computer or VM where you will install Linux has 2 GB or less memory. When ready to proceed, click Download.

Step 2

On the next page you are asked to contribute. At the time that we downloaded Ubuntu, this page showed an itemized list of areas to which we could contribute, but this is not required for a download. Scroll to the bottom of the page and select either *Not now, take me to the download,* or *Pay with PayPal.* For this exercise, we selected the first choice, which started the download.

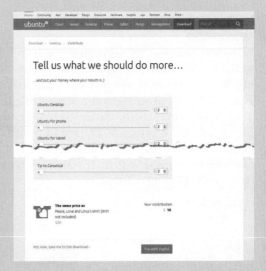

Step 3

Your browser will now open a dialog box asking you to open or save the file. This example is from Firefox. Other browsers will offer the same choices. Select Save File to have it saved in the Downloads folder on your computer. Then click OK.

Step 4

The Ubuntu *Thank you* page will display, and you can check on the progress in the menu bar of the Web browser.

Step 5

Create the bootable disc by using the ISO image you downloaded. To do that in Windows browse to the Downloads folder, right-click on the Ubuntu file, and select *Burn disc image*.

Step 6

Now test the disc by rebooting the computer with the disc inserted. After a brief delay during which you will see text on a black background, the Ubuntu Welcome screen displays. You have successfully downloaded Ubuntu Linux, created a bootable DVD, and are ready either to boot into Linux and explore it as a Guest or to proceed with an installation. Stay at this screen as you continue.

Installing Linux or Using a Live Image

If you completed Step-by-Step 9.01, you should be at the Welcome screen. If so, select a language, and then click *Try Ubuntu* if you just want to try out Ubuntu without installing it, using the live image. If you run the live image, you will not need to log in, as you will be automatically logged in with the Guest account.

Only select the second option, *Install Ubuntu*, if you are ready to install it on the same computer. If you plan to install it to another location, click the System (gear) icon on the title bar in the upper right (see the illustration in step 6), select *Shut Down* from the System menu and remove the disc before selecting *Shut Down* again in the confirmation box.

There are several possible scenarios for installing Linux. Just a few include a clean installation on a spare computer, a clean installation onto a second drive on a computer running another OS to create a dual-boot configuration, or an installation into a virtual machine. We installed both distributions of Linux into virtual machines on Windows 7 and Windows 8 computers. We also did clean installs onto a spare computer. We used VirtualBox as our hypervisor on both Windows 7 and Windows 8 and found Ubuntu simply worked better without tweaking it in the virtual machine, while Fedora, which was quirky in the virtual machine, ran and installed beautifully on the spare computer. Your experience may be different, as may the distribution you select.

If you did the exercises in Chapter 3 and installed a hypervisor, you only need to create a virtual machine for Linux, insert the disc you created, and start the virtual machine. If the virtual machine does not see the disc, you may need to modify the settings for the virtual machine to include the disc. If it recognizes the disc, the VM should start up and boot into the Ubuntu Welcome screen.

For the remainder of this chapter, leave Linux open—using the live image or an installation of Linux. If you choose to install it, you will find the installation is very similar to a clean installation of OS X or Windows, and shortly after you install Linux, you will see a notice that updates are ready to install.

If you are installing Linux in a school lab and have limited time, do not install the updates at this point; wait until you have the time for them to install. Plan on restarting after installing the updates.

> *Note:* We recommend that you create a virtual machine for Linux, even if you plan only to boot into the live image because when you use a live image in a virtual machine you will still have access to your computer and can take notes, browse the Web, or take screen shots of the contents of the virtual machine.

LO 9.3 | Exploring a Linux GUI

In this section you will practice certain tasks in Linux using a GUI, beginning with logging in, exploring the GUI Desktop, locating tools for changing settings, modifying the desktop, and ending a Linux session.

Logging In to Ubuntu Linux

If you are running a live image of Linux, you are logged in as a Guest; but if you installed Linux, you will log in with the username and password you provided during installation. Normally, a login box will display, as shown in Figure 9–4. If you configured the Automatic Login, which is an option during the Ubuntu installation, you will not need to enter a password and will go directly to the desktop when you turn on your computer.

In our example, the login page displays the full username we provided, which was simply uppercase initials, although full username implies both first and last names. The login username in this case is "jane" in all lowercase letters, but it is not displayed in the GUI. Whether it has a GUI or not, Linux is

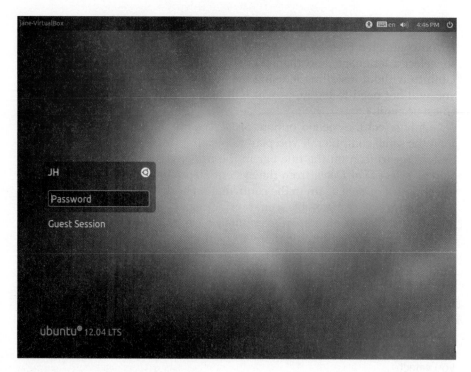

FIGURE 9–4 Log in to the Linux GUI.

pervasively case-sensitive, so while the full username can include a mixture of upper and lower case, the installation program will only accept all lower case for the login username.

Notice in Figure 9–4 that you can also select *Guest Session* and log in as a Guest with no password. In that case, you will have more limited access than other users, but you will still be able to experience Linux.

The Ubuntu Unity Desktop

The Ubuntu Unity desktop has a bar across the top, which behaves much like the menu bar at the top of an OS X desktop. When no program is open on the desktop, the bar is titled *Ubuntu Desktop* on the far left and has a notification area containing various menu icons on the far right. If you simply move the cursor to the bar, a menu will display on the left with the desktop drop-down menus named *File*, *Edit*, *View*, *Go*, and *Help*.

Note: If the menu does not display when you move the cursor to the bar, click on the Home Folder.

The Ubuntu Desktop bar displays at the top of the screen in the Unity GUI.

Move the cursor to the Desktop bar to show the menus.

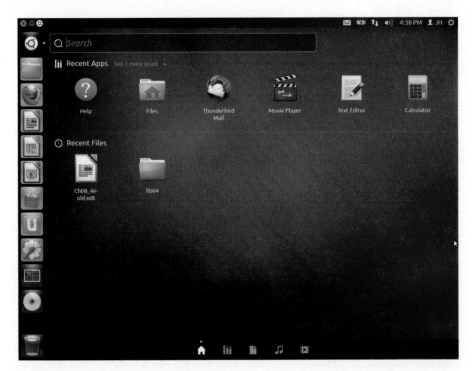

FIGURE 9–6 The Dash search utility displays recently used apps and files when it opens.

FIGURE 9–5 The Launcher with icons labeled.

The Ubuntu Unity desktop includes the Launcher, a bar on the left side of the screen that serves the same purpose as the OS X Dock or the pinned items feature on the taskbar on the Windows Desktop. Simply pause the mouse cursor over one of the icons on the Launcher and a title will pop out. Figure 9–5 is a screenshot we modified with a photo editor to show all the titles for the standard set of Launcher icons.

Searching in the Ubuntu Unity Desktop

The Dash is your search tool for finding apps and all types of files. To open it, click the Dash button on the Launcher or simply press the Windows key. Notice that the Dash also displays recently used apps and files or folders, as shown in Figure 9–6. Clicking on the file named Ch08-4e-old.odt launches the LibreOffice Writer with that file open in it. Dash anticipates that a user may often need to search for a recently used app or file and therefore presents that information without requiring a search.

To search for a file or app, enter a search string into the Search box, shown in Figure 9–6. Dash shows matching app results in one row and file results in another row. The Try This! exercise will walk you through a search. Control where Dash searches using the icons across the bottom of the screen. When you select the house-shaped icon Dash searches your Home directory; if you select the next icon Dash searches Applications—both those that are installed and those available for download in the Ubuntu Software Center. The middle icon (resembling a document) tells Dash

Note: Use the Windows key to quickly toggle the Dash open or close.

try this!

Use a Linux GUI Search Tool

Whether you are using the Ubuntu Unity desktop or another GUI, it will have a search utility. If it is not apparent to you how to open the Search utility, use the Help utility for your distribution of Linux, which should be readily available from a menu. Try this:

1. Locate and open the Search utility.
2. In the Search box enter a search string and press the Enter key.
3. What were the results? Did it find both apps and files that matched the search string?
4. Compare your results to others in your class.

to search files and folders; selecting the musical note icon selects a search of music files; and the last icon, resembling the play button, searches for videos or movies.

Browse Directories in the GUI

Before browsing directories in either the GUI or the CLI take time to learn about the Linux directory hierarchy. It contains two types of directories. The first type consists of directories in which an ordinary user can make changes. We call these home directories. Every user has a home directory, the one place in Linux where a user has full control over files and directories without requiring elevated privileges. The second category consists of directories that the user cannot change: system directories, such as /etc and /bin, or home directories for other users.

To work with Linux directories you should understand how to use paths. A path is a description that an operating system uses to identify the location of a file or directory. In Windows, a full path to a file or directory begins with the drive designator (letter plus colon) and you build it using the backslash (\) character as separators between the drive and root directory (first backslash) and then between each of the subsequent directories in the path. Thus, a valid Windows path is C:\Winnt\System32. In Linux, you do not use a drive letter, but you use a forward slash (/) at the beginning of a path to represent the root and a forward slash (/) to separate directories in a path. A valid path is **/etc/gtk**. In Linux everything is a file identified within the file system. Files represent drives and other devices, as well as directories and files.

When you log in to Linux, your home directory becomes your current (working) directory. If you installed Linux with the defaults, your home directory path is **/home/**username, where username is the user name for the account you used to log in. The default installation includes several other directories. The **/bin** directory within your home directory contains many of the Linux commands. The **/usr/bin** directory is an example of a symbolic link that points to another directory, in this case, **/bin**. Table 9–1 shows some of the default directories with brief descriptions.

Now that you know something about the directory structure on your Linux computer, find a tool in the Linux GUI for browsing the Linux

TABLE 9–1 Linux Default Directories

Directory	Purpose or Contents
/	The top, or root directory of a storage volume
/bin	Linux commands
/boot	Files to be loaded during Linux boot up
/dev	Files that represent physical devices
/etc	Linux system configuration files
/home	Home directories for each user
/lib	Shared libraries for programs and commands to use
/mnt	Mount points for removable devices
/opt	Optional (add-on) software packages
/proc	Current status of OS processes
/root	Root account home directory
/sbin	System commands and binary files
/tmp	Temporary files
/usr	Secondary hierarchy
/var	Several directories containing variable data

directories and explore the directories on your computer. A big advantage of working in a GUI is that you do not need to carefully type the names of files and directories—a fact made more important, since Linux is case-sensitive, meaning that it preserves the case used in the characters of a file name when created, and requires that you enter the correct case to open or manage the file. Step-by-Step 9.02 will guide you through the process of browsing the Linux directory structure. Notice that some directories have upper and lower case. You will want to remember that later when you explore Linux directories from the CLI.

> Note: While Linux is case-sensitive, Windows is case-aware, meaning that it will preserve the case used for the characters in a file name when you create it, but it does not require the correct case when retrieving or managing the file.

Step-by-Step 9.02

Browsing the Linux File System in a GUI

In this exercise, use a GUI to browse the Linux directory structure. You will need the following:

- A computer running Linux with a GUI.
- The username and password for a user account.

Step 1

Log in to a Linux installation with a GUI. In our case, we logged in to Ubuntu Linux with the Unity GUI.

Step 2

The Unity GUI has an icon on the Launcher titled Home Folder (shown previously in Figure 9–5). Click it and a window opens focused on the currently logged-on user's home directory. This home directory contains directories created during the installation of this distribution of Linux, as well as directories created by the user.

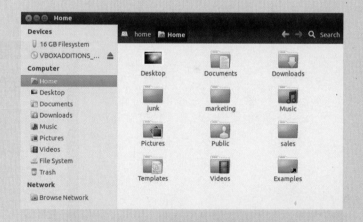

Step 3

Browse through the directories in the home directory, then return to the home directory, and click the item on the left labeled File System. This opens focused on the root (the top level of the file system).

In File System double-click on the home folder to open the top-level home directory. A home directory should display for each user.

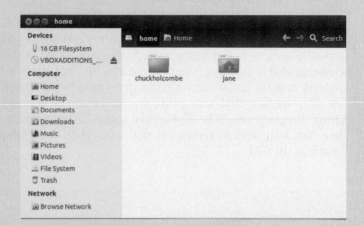

When you are finished browsing the directories, close the window.

Updating Ubuntu from the Unity Desktop

When updates to Ubuntu are available, the Update Manager icon appears in the Launcher displaying the number of updates, as shown at the left where the icon indicates that there are 10 updates available. Click it to open the Update Manager and install the updates.

The Update Manager icon appears on the Launcher.

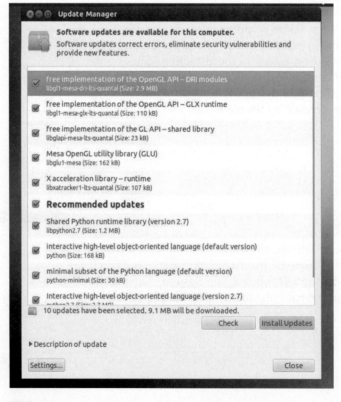

Open the Update Manager and install the updates.

System Settings

Launch System Settings from the System (gear) icon on the Launcher. Like the Control Panel in Windows and System Preferences in OS X, System Settings includes icons representing a number of settings, organized here by category. And, like the other OSs, you can call up the various control panels by other actions. Like OS X System Preferences, once you open a panel, such as Appearance, you can return to the main System Settings page by selecting *All Settings* from the bar at the top of the window.

Modify the Desktop

Modify the desktop to suit your personal tastes. As with Windows you can access desktop background settings by locating these settings through something like Control Panel, called System Settings (shown here) or right-click on the desktop and select *Change Desktop Background* to open the Appearance page, to make changes as described in Step-by-Step 9.03.

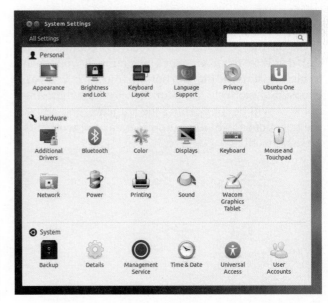

Unity's System Settings window serves the same purpose as Windows' Control Panel and OS X's System Preferences.

Step-by-Step 9.03

Modifying the Desktop

You will need the following:

- A computer with Ubuntu installed. The steps are written for Ubuntu with the Unity GUI.

- The username and password of an administrator account for this computer.

Step 1

Right-click on an empty space on the desktop to open a context menu. Select *Change Desktop Background*.

Step 2

In the Appearance control panel select a wallpaper. As you click on a wallpaper selection on the right, the small screen on the left shows the wallpaper, and it also displays behind the window.

Click on the Behavior tab to see the changes you can make to the Launcher's behavior. If you wish to change it, click the Off button, and then you can choose to auto-hide the Launcher, decide where the hot spot will be for opening the launcher, and adjust the hot spot sensitivity. Auto-hide may not work in a virtual machine.

No need to click an OK button; changes are made as soon as you select them. In our case, we selected a new wallpaper but did not change the behavior of the Launcher.

Return to System Settings and open Brightness and Lock. Here you can select the amount of time your computer can be inactive before the screen turns off. If Lock is off, then a simple key press or mouse motion will wake up the screen. You can also turn on Lock and require a password to wake the computer from suspend. Return to All Settings when you finish with this window.

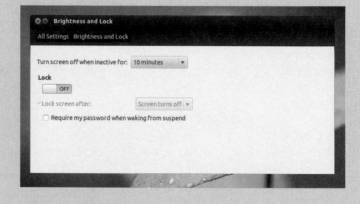

Step 6

In All Settings, select *Displays*. This is where you can modify display settings. This example shows the display in a virtual machine. Return to All Settings.

Step 7

Select *Universal Access*. This is where you can customize the Unity desktop to make it more accessible to someone who needs adjustments made for viewing the screen, listening, typing, or using a pointing device. When you are finished close the window.

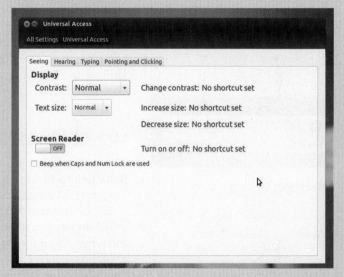

Ending a Linux Session from the GUI

As with Windows and OS X, you have choices for ending your session in Windows. You can simply log out, which is a reasonable choice if you are sharing a computer with someone else. You can shut down, which will both log you out and shut down your computer. You can restart Linux.

Logging Out of a Linux GUI Session

When you log out of Linux it ends your session, giving you an opportunity to save files before closing down all apps (and your desktop if in a GUI), but does not turn off the computer. After logging out, another user can log in, as Guest or using another account on that computer. How you log on or off a Linux GUI session depends on which GUI you are using.

If you are using the Ubuntu Unity desktop click on the System (gear) icon in the upper-right corner to open the drop-down menu shown in Figure 9–7. Then select *Log Out*. You will need to respond to the "Are you sure" to continue with Log Out. Then the session will end and after a delay a login page similar to the one shown back in Figure 9–4 will display.

FIGURE 9–7 The Ubuntu Unity System menu.

The Switch User Accounts menu.

Note: The switch users feature is also available in Windows and OS X.

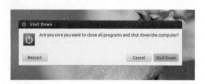

Select Shut Down.

Note: If Ubuntu Linux with the Unity GUI is installed on a computer that supports Suspend, it will be an option from the System menu.

Note: Type the **exit** command to leave (log off) the Linux CLI. If you are using a terminal window, this closes the window—only ending that session, it does not shut down the Linux GUI in which the terminal window resides. The command **sudo shutdown now** shuts down the computer.

Switching Users

If you have multiple accounts on a Linux computer you can take advantage of switch users, a feature that allows the currently logged-on user to leave their apps and data open in memory, switching away so that another user can log in to a separate session. Each user's session is protected, requiring a password to access again.

To switch users in Unity GUI in Ubuntu, open the Switch User Accounts menu by clicking the user icon on the right of the Desktop bar. Then either select another user to log on or click on **Switch User Account** at the top of the menu. This opens a login screen where you can select a local account and enter a password to switch to another account.

Shutting Down, Restarting, or Suspending a Linux GUI

When you shut down a Linux computer, you are logged out and the operating system closes all files and powers off the computer. When you select restart on a Linux computer, you are logged out and the operating system closes all files and then issues a restart command to the computer, without turning the power off. The operating system is then restarted and the login screen displays.

The option to Shut Down a computer from a Linux GUI is usually on the same menu as the Log Out option. When you select this choice in Ubuntu Unity, the Shut Down dialog box, shown here, displays. From here you can choose to *Restart*, *Cancel*, *Suspend*, or *Shut Down*.

LO 9.4 | Linux Command-Line Interface

The native Linux user interface is the command-line interface (CLI). Many installations of Linux, especially on servers, have only a CLI. Although there are great GUI options for working in Linux, system administrators still do much of the real work of supporting and managing Linux from the CLI, which forces you to be precise when entering commands. Any OS is unforgiving when given the wrong instructions, but it doesn't take precision to browse a GUI and select the correct graphical object, which is how a GUI buffers users from the precision required from a command prompt. Acquiring the habit of being precise now will help you succeed in future computer work.

To learn the commands, you must enter them at a Linux prompt. Sit at a Linux computer while reading the following sections because, as we examine various commands, you will have frequent opportunities to try them. Feel free also to experiment on your own. Note that your screen may not look exactly like the examples shown.

The Terminal Window in Linux

If you installed Linux with a GUI or are running it from a live image booted into a GUI, you can open a terminal window, equivalent to a Windows Command Prompt window, where you can experience the Linux CLI. How you do this depends on the GUI. For instance, in the Ubuntu Unity GUI, click on the Dash search tool and enter "terminal." Then select *Terminal* from the results list. That will open a terminal window, similar to the one shown in Figure 9–8.

When you open a terminal window you will see the $ prompt, which consists of the name of the currently logged-on user and the computer name. These are separated by the @ sign, which in turn is followed by a tilde (~) representing the path to your home directory. When you start a session at the $ prompt the current directory is your logged-on user's Home directory. The prompt ends with the dollar sign ($).

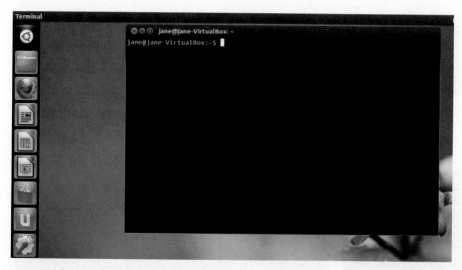

FIGURE 9–8 A terminal window in the Ubuntu Unity GUI.

Later in this chapter you will learn how to use the **cd** command to change the current directory. If you make another directory current, the name of that directory will be included in the $ prompt. The appearance of the $ prompt may vary somewhat among Linux versions. The blinking cursor that follows the $ prompt, seen in Figure 9–8 as a white rectangle, indicates that it is awaiting your command.

Using Linux Shell Commands

The most important thing to learn and remember about working in the Linux shell (in a terminal window or in Linux without a GUI) is that it is case-sensitive. Commands are entered in lowercase, and so are most options.

Linux Shell Command Syntax

When working at the CLI, the Linux shell command syntax follows these rules:

- All lines start with a Linux command (the first string of characters).
- A space must follow the command.
- Next come options, specific to the command, that modify its behavior. Most options are short options using a single character, while more recent options may be long (more than one character).
- Order of options is usually of little importance.
- Use a space between each option.
- Short options are preceded by a hyphen (-d); long options are preceded by two hyphens (--help).
- If you want to use multiple short options for a command you can combine them into one long option with a single hyphen at the beginning.
- Some commands are followed by a parameter, which is a file name, directory, or device name. A parameter is the object that the command action targets.

try this!

Test Case Sensitivity in Linux

Test Linux case sensitivity while using the **man** command that, when entered correctly, opens the user manual page for the command you provide, such as the **list directory contents** command, **ls**. Try this:

1. At the Linux $ prompt enter the following command in all caps:

   MAN LS

2. Notice the resulting error message.
3. Now reenter the command in all lower case. The result is that the Linux user manual will open to the page on the command **ls**.
4. Use the SPACEBAR and UP and DOWN arrow keys to move through the manual page.
5. To quit a manual page, press **q**.

FIGURE 9–9 The **ls** command showing a simple listing of the current directory.

FIGURE 9–10 The **ls -a** command showing a listing of all items in the current directory.

FIGURE 9–11 The **ls** command using two options (**-a** and **-l**) showing a listing of all items in the current directory and the "long" information on each item.

In general, the command syntax in Linux follows this format:

command -option parameter

Combining Options

Now let's practice combining options. Consider the **ls** command, which lists contents of a directory, as shown in Figure 9–9, in which the command is run without any options or parameters.

It has several options, two of which are **a** (all files including hidden files) and **l** (lowercase "L") for long format listing that will include permissions, owner, size, modification time, and more. Figures 9–10 and 9–11 show the use of each of these commands alone. To use **ls** with the **a** option enter **ls –a**, which will simply list the files, as shown in Figure 9–10, but give no information about them, other than the color coding for the type of file, explained later. To use both options at once, enter **ls –al** or **ls –la**, as shown in Figure 9–11. Either will work. When too much text displays for the size of the terminal window, a scroll bar appears on the side, and you can use it to scroll through the results.

try this!

Using Multiple Options

Practice using **ls**. Run the command with a single option and then with multiple options. Try this:

1. Enter the command **ls**.
2. Notice that **ls** defaults to a column output (four across).
3. To get a long listing of this directory, enter **ls -l**. This runs the -l option on the current directory.
4. Now use multiple options. Enter **ls -la**. This provides a long listing for all files, including hidden files, in the current directory.

Note: The screen (or terminal window) gets pretty cluttered. To clear the screen and return the $ prompt to the top of an empty screen enter the **clear** command. If the screen has unusual characters on it that do not disappear with the **clear** command, use the **reset** command for a more thorough reset of the terminal window.

The Help Manual

Help is always at hand in the form of the online user manual, accessed with the **man** command. Type **man** *command*, where *command* is the shell command you wish to learn more about. Figure 9–12 shows the result of entering **man ls**. This is the first page of the explanation for the **ls** command. Notice the instructions in white at the bottom of the screen. Press *h* to see an explanation of how to move through the manual. Press *q* to quit the **man** command. You can even see the documentation for the **man** command itself by entering **man man** at the $ prompt.

Command-Line History

Linux saves the shell commands you enter for the duration of the session (called command-line history), and you can scroll through these commands while at the $ prompt. Simply use the up and down arrow keys to move through the history. When you find the command you would like to reuse, you can edit the command by moving back and forth through it with the left and right arrow keys. When you are ready to use the command, simply press ENTER. Linux saves these commands in a file called .bash_history, but you do not need to know anything about this file to take advantage of this feature.

Command Completion

As you enter a command at the $ prompt, experiment with the command completion feature. Enter the command name and a few more characters of the options, then press the TAB key. Linux tries to automatically fill in partially typed commands, and is especially clever at doing this when it looks like you are entering a directory name, indicated by the forward slash (/), but you need to give it more information than just the forward slash. For instance, when using the cd (change directory) command, if you enter cd /e and then press the TAB key, it will guess that you intended to type "etc/" and will complete it that way so that it reads cd /etc/. A more general term for this feature, when used in applications and search engines, is *autocompletion*.

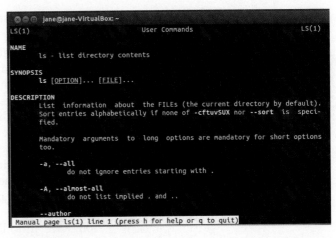

FIGURE 9–12 Enter the **man ls** command to see the manual page for the **ls** command.

try this!

What Time Is It?

Practice entering the date and calendar commands. Try this:

1. Type the command **date** and press ENTER. This will display the current date, along with the day of the week and time.

2. Now type the command **cal** and press ENTER. This will display the calendar for the current month with the day highlighted.

Linux Feedback

When it comes to feedback, Linux commands are actually similar to Windows Command Prompt commands, in that they all provide cryptic feedback, communicating with you only if there is a problem. A Linux BASH command does not report when it is successful, though you'll get an error message if the command is incorrect. In this example, we first tried to change to the documents directory using the command **cd documents**. The second line shows an error. We then ran the **ls** command (third line) to see the contents (fourth and fifth lines) that showed the directory was actually named "Documents." We entered it again (sixth line), using the correct case: **cd Documents**. No message resulted from this command, although it is clear that we changed directories because the dollar prompt on the seventh line now shows Documents as the current location.

Like Windows, Linux relies heavily on a directory structure that has several predefined directories created by default during installation. Some hold important system files, and others hold user data. Linux is very similar. It has several directories for system files and a home directory for each user. You have already been introduced to a few of the file and directory management tools: **ls** and **cd** while learning the basics of working with shell commands. In this section you will use these and other commands to explore the default directories and learn more about working with Linux at the CLI.

The **date** and **cal** commands.

A message appears only if a command causes an error.

Using Shell Commands for the Linux File System

A shorthand for the path, or location, of the Home directory both at the $ prompt and in a shell command is the tilde (~). Use the **ls** command to see other directories. Some have rather strange names.

In Linux everything is a file, even physical objects like a hard drive or other storage devices. Therefore, Linux shows each drive and other device simply as a part of the file system and gives it a path that begins at the root of the file system (/). Drives and other devices have assigned names, such as **/dev/sda0**, the first hard drive on a SCSI interface (indicated by **sda**); or **/dev/hda1**, the first hard drive on an IDE interface (**hda**).

Practice using shell commands to work with files and directories on your computer. Table 9–2 provides a list of basic file management commands for your reference.

You were introduced to the **ls** command earlier in this chapter, and Figure 9–12 showed the use of the **man ls** command to display the manual page for this command. Table 9–3 lists and explains the commonly used options for **ls**. Recall that Linux is case-sensitive, so pay attention to the case of each option. By itself, **ls** provides only the names of visible files in the current directory, and the **–a** option that you learned about earlier lists all files and directories, even hidden files. Hidden files have names that begin with a period (.).

Listing the Contents of a Specified Directory. If you do not specify the directory you want **ls** to work on, it uses the current directory. To point ls to another directory, use the directory name and the appropriate path as a parameter in the command. Figure 9–13 shows the result of typing **ls /etc**. The colors of the names tell you more about that file or directory.

- Blue = directory
- Green = program or binary data file such as jpeg
- Light blue or aqua = link to files in a different directory
- Pink = image file

TABLE 9–2 Basic Shell Commands for File Management

Command	Description
cd	Changes to another directory
chmod	Changes the mode or file permissions
cp	Copies a file
ls	Lists contents of a directory
mkdir	Makes a directory
more	Displays a text file, one screenful at a time
pwd	Prints the working directory
rm	Deletes a file

TABLE 9–3 Commonly Used Options for the ls Command

ls Option	Description
-a	Lists all files in the directory, including the hidden files. Files are hidden in Linux by making the first character a period, like this: **.bash_profile**
-l	Displays a long listing of the directory contents with all file attributes and permissions listed
-F	Classifies the listed objects. In particular, directory names have a / character after the name
-S	Sorts the output by size
-t	Sorts the output by time

FIGURE 9–13 A listing of the **/etc** directory.

FIGURE 9–14 A listing of the **/etc** directory with more details.

- Red = compressed archive file
- White = text file
- Yellow = device

To view more details of the files in the **/etc** directory enter the command **ls -l /etc**; the output will be similar to that shown in Figure 9–14. This listing does not include hidden files because we did not use the **–a** option to see hidden files, as we did back in Figure 9–12.

In the results from using the **-l** option the first column is 10 characters wide and lists the attributes on the file or folder, which you will examine a little later in this chapter. The next column indicates the number of links to a file. The next two columns list the owner (normally the user who created the file) and last modifier of the file, respectively. The next number indicates the size of the file. The next columns indicate the file creation date and time. Lastly, it shows the name of the file. If a file is a link, it next lists the link location; the file after the arrow is the original file.

Changing the Current Directory. The command to change the current directory in Linux is **cd**. The **cd** command was used in previous examples in this chapter to illustrate the command completion feature and the need to pay attention to letter case. Let's focus on this command for itself now.

The **cd** command requires one parameter: the directory to change to. If the directory is a child of the current directory, then you only need the name to change to this directory. For example, suppose that in your home directory you have a child directory called private. To change to this directory, you enter **cd private**. If the directory is not a child of the current directory, you will need to enter the path to the directory. An absolute path will start with / (the root directory). Each directory in the path is listed after the / and separated from the next by another /. For example, to change to the **sbin** directory under the **/usr** directory, you would enter **cd /usr/sbin**. It is called an absolute path because you clearly provide its location beginning with the top level, which in Linux is the root directory.

> **WARNING!**
>
> To avoid seeing error messages in place of results, whenever you need to use a shell command to perform an operation on a hidden file or directory, be sure to include the (.) at the beginning of the name.

FIGURE 9–15 Changing to the /usr/sbin directory.

FIGURE 9–16 Changing to the Home directory using the tilde (~).

Use the **pwd** command to display the path to the current directory.

When you correctly use **cd** to change to a different directory, it rewards you with a change in your prompt. In Figure 9–15 the user started in the Home directory of the user jane, as indicated by the tilde (~) in the $ prompt, and changed to the /usr/sbin directory. The prompt changed to reflect the new directory. You can quickly change back to your personal home directory from any directory by entering **cd** ~. Figure 9–16 shows the result of entering this command.

Where Am I? Unfortunately, the Linux prompt does not (by default) show the entire path to the current directory. If you are unsure of where you are, use the command **pwd**, which stands for print working directory. It does not send anything to your printer; rather it displays (prints) the path to the working (current) directory on your screen, as shown here where the **pwd** command shows the path to the current directory (/home/jane) on the second line and then returns to the $ prompt on the third line.

try this!

Display the Contents of a File

Use the **more** command to display the contents of a file on the screen. Try this:

1. If a terminal window is not open, open it now.
2. If the prompt does not include a tilde (~), enter **cd** ~ to ensure that you are in the Home directory.
3. Enter the command: **more .bash_history**. This will display the contents of the hidden file .bash_history, pausing after the screen is full.
4. Press the ENTER key (repeatedly) to scroll one line at a time or press the SPACEBAR to scroll one screenful at a time. Continue to the end of the output.

Relative Path. Linux allows you to use commands to navigate directories, using special symbols as shorthand for moving to directories that are relative to your current directory. For instance, the command **cd ..** will change the current directory to the next directory up in the hierarchy. If you are in your personal home directory, this command will move you to the home directory, one level up. In Figure 9–17 the first two lines show the **pwd** command and its result, showing that the /home/jane directory is current. The third line shows the command **cd ..** followed by the resulting $ prompt on the fourth line in which the /home directory is current. The /home directory is the parent directory of all the home directories on a Linux computer.

Place the .. characters between forward slashes (/) to move up additional levels. In addition, throw in a specific directory that exists at that level. For example, the command **cd ../../etc** moves up two levels and then to the etc directory. Be sure you know where you want to go, and remember, using one of these characters is supposed to save you typing. Rather than use the command string **cd ../../etc**, it is shorter to type **cd /etc**. Another special symbol is the single dot (.), which refers to the current directory.

FIGURE 9–17 Use the command **cd ..** to move to the parent directory of the current directory.

try this!

Using Relative Path Statements

A little practice with relative paths is helpful. Try this:

1. Type the command: **cd ..**
2. Return to your home directory by typing: **cd** ~
3. Now move to the /etc directory using a relative path: **cd ../../etc**
4. Return to your home directory by typing: **cd** ~

Wildcards. Linux supports the use of wildcards. A wildcard is a symbol that replaces any character or string of characters in a command parameter. It is also supported in other CLIs for other OSs. The use of the asterisk (*) as a wildcard in a file name or directory name replaces all the characters from the point at which you place the asterisk to the end of the name. For instance **ls bi*** would list all files or directories that begin with "bi."

Linux wildcard support is flexible. You can enter a range of characters as a wildcard. For instance, if you enter **ls [c-d]*** the **ls** command will display all files in the current directory that begin with the letters *c* through *d*. The bracket symbols ([]) are part of a Linux feature called regular expressions. Linux also allows you to use the dollar sign (**$**) to represent a single character within a file name, a feature also supported by DOS and the Windows Command Prompt. We considered ourselves very experienced DOS users (back in its heyday), and we found that using the dollar sign was rarely worth the bother.

When a parameter for the **ls** command is the name of a directory the result will include the contents of that directory. Therefore, if you try the command in the example given in the previous paragraph from within the **/etc** directory the **ls [c-d]*** command will result in a long listing because each of the items that begins with either a "c" or "d" that is also a directory will cause **ls** to list the contents of that directory. Figure 9–18 shows just a portion of the output from running this command with the /etc directory current. Each line that ends with a colon is for a directory and the following line or lines display the contents of that directory.

FIGURE 9–18 A portion of the results of the command **ls [c-d]*** when run from the **/etc** directory.

try this!

Using Wildcards

1. Change to the /etc directory (enter **cd /etc**).
2. Enter the command **ls e***. You'll see all files that begin with the letter *e*.
3. Now enter the command **ls [c-d]* /etc**.

Creating Directories

Create a directory in Linux with the **mkdir** command, which requires at least one parameter: the name of the directory to create. For example, to create a directory called junk within the current directory, enter the command **mkdir junk**. Because Linux gives you no feedback after you create a directory, use **ls** to verify that it built the directory.

If you list more than one parameter, then it will create a directory for each. Therefore, to create two directories named "sales" and "marketing" with one command, enter the command **mkdir sales marketing** (see Figure 9–19).

FIGURE 9–19 Use **mkdir** to create directories and **ls** to confirm that they were created.

try this!

Create Directories

Create directories in your home folder. Try this:

1. Enter the command **mkdir data**.
2. Use the **ls** command to confirm that it created the data directory.
3. Make several directories by entering the **mkdir** command followed by two or more names for new directories.
4. Use the **ls** command to confirm that it created the new directories.

Copying Files in Linux

The command to copy files is **cp**. We recommend you make a copy of a file before you change it. This allows you to recover from any changes you make.

The **cp** command requires two parameters. The first is the source file, which can be a file in the current directory or a file in another

FIGURE 9–20 Copying the hosts file from the **/etc** directory to the user's home directory.

directory, as long as you provide the correct path. The second parameter is the target, which can be a target location to copy to and/or a name for the file. This makes more sense after you practice using the command.

As you can see in Figure 9–20, the file named hosts was copied from the /etc directory to the current directory. (The period at the end of the command represents the current directory.) This is just a copy, leaving the original hosts file in the /etc directory. Notice that Linux does not report that it copied a file. The figure also shows that we used the **ls** command to verify a successful copy of the file.

LO 9.5 | Securing a Linux Desktop

Linux is a very secure OS—whether you are using a GUI or a CLI. It is important to know how to configure a computer for the needs of its users. This includes managing user accounts and applying security to directories.

Managing Users

Linux allows several users to use one computer, but each user should have a unique account. When you create a user account, Linux also creates a home directory within the **/home** directory, using the user's name for the directory name. This is the place in the Linux file system where an ordinary user account has full control over directories and files. The user can both save files and create new subdirectories. Users can further protect files from other users by changing the permissions on files and folders in their home directories.

The Linux Root Account

Each installation of Linux has a root account, an all-powerful account that is only used when absolutely necessary to do advanced tasks. Ubuntu Linux comes with this account disabled in such a way that no one can log in directly with the account, but there is a way to temporarily use it whenever you need it for tasks, such as creating or deleting users. However, you must be logged on with an administrator-type account to do this. You can do this from within a GUI or at a CLI in Linux. You will practice this when you create a user account in the next section.

Creating a User Account in a GUI

Step-by-Step 9.04 describes how to temporarily take on the power of the root account and add a new user in the Ubuntu Unity GUI. If you are using a different GUI, you will need to locate the GUI tool for administering user accounts. In Unity for Ubuntu, this is User Accounts.

Step-by-Step 9.04

Add a New User for User Accounts in Unity for Ubuntu

If you are adding no more than a few users to a desktop installation of Ubuntu, a GUI tool is the easiest to use. In this example we use the User Accounts tool in Unity for Ubuntu.

To complete this exercise you will need:

• A computer running Ubuntu with the Unity GUI.
• The username and password of an administrator-type account for this computer.

Step 1

Open *System Settings* in the Ubuntu Unity GUI and select *User Accounts* (on the bottom right) to open the User Accounts window. In this example there are two users. The first user created in Ubuntu, in this case JH, is automatically an administrator-type account. This user can perform administrative functions by temporarily borrowing the use of a root account. Standard users cannot do this.

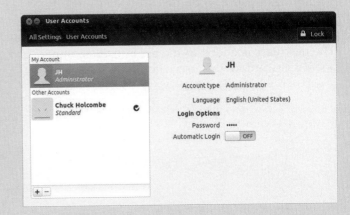

Step 2

Before you can add a user you need to unlock the advanced settings in User Accounts. Do that by clicking on the Unlock icon on the top right of the User Accounts window. This opens the Authenticate dialog box. Enter your password and click the Authenticate button. This elevates your effective permissions to root, but only temporarily.

Step 3

After entering your password, you are returned to the User Accounts window. Notice that the icon on the top right has changed to a closed lock. Pause the cursor over it until the tool tip pops up with an explanation.

Step 4

To create a new user click the plus (+) button under the list of users to open the Create new account dialog box. Enter the Full name, and Linux will automatically create a Username, using the full name in all lower case with all illegal characters removed, such as the space. You can shorten the Username, if you want, as we did here.

The new user is added to the list of user accounts. To add a password for this user, click in the Password box.

Enter a password twice and click Change.

In the User Accounts dialog box click the close button in the upper left. The next time you open User Accounts, it will automatically be locked again.

Managing User Accounts with Shell Commands

When adding many users to either a Linux desktop or server, an advanced Linux administrator will add users by creating a special script that will create a list of users much faster than using a GUI. We believe that if you need to create only a few users on a few computers, it is easier to work through the GUI. However, if you need to manage users on a Linux computer without a GUI, you will need to know how to work with shell commands. Table 9–4 lists useful commands for managing users with shell commands.

When working from a Linux CLI, temporarily assign root account (also called Superuser) privileges to the currently logged-on user (who must be an

Note: When you enter a password in a Linux CLI the characters you enter do not show on the line as you enter them. In fact nothing shows. The cursor does not move. Don't forget to press ENTER at the end of the password.

TABLE 9–4	Shell Commands for User Management
Command	**Description**
useradd	Adds a user to the system
userdel	Removes a user from the system
passwd	Changes a user's password
finger	Finds a username

administrator-type account) by preceding the command you wish to run with the **sudo** (Superuser Do) command. When you use **sudo** it will prompt you to enter your password (not the root password). Then, for the next five minutes (by default) you will be able to run **sudo** without requiring a password. After this time has passed, if you run **sudo** again, you will need to enter your password. The following includes examples of using the **sudo** command to run administrative commands, beginning with the installation of software to add a command to Linux.

The **finger** command allows you to look up user information, but some installations of Linux (including Ubuntu) do not automatically install it. Therefore, if you want to experiment with the **finger** command, you must install the finger daemon. A daemon is a program that runs in background until it is activated by a command. Once installed, the **finger** daemon is activated by running the **finger** command. Install the **finger** daemon with this command: **sudo apt-get install finger**. This should result in the output shown here.

From the command shell, use the **useradd** command preceded by **sudo** to create a user. This command requires at least one parameter, the username you want to add. If you want to create a password for this user in the same operation, use the **useradd** option **–p** followed by the password. For instance, to create an account for Ashley Phoenix using the username of aphoenix with the password pa22w0rD, enter the command **sudo useradd –p pa22w0rD aphoenix**. To verify that it created the user account, use **finger aphoenix** (see Figure 9–21).

Installing the **finger** daemon.

Changing User Passwords

Changing a user's password involves the command **passwd**. Entering **passwd** without any additional parameters will let you change your own password. Any user can change his or her own password, but only a user with root privileges can change the password on other user accounts. For example, enter **sudo passwd aphoenix** to change the password for the aphoenix account. The administrator doing this does not need to know the current password for the account before changing it to the new one, but can simply enter the new password twice. Note that, as always, Linux doesn't display passwords, but it does provide the useful feedback that the password was updated successfully.

FIGURE 9–21 Create a user with the **useradd** command. Confirm its creation with the **finger** command.

Deleting Users

In any organization, employees leave. For security reasons, you should remove these accounts from the system shortly after the employee leaves. The command **userdel** allows you to remove a user from a Linux account, but you must run this command using **sudo**.

The syntax for userdel is similar to that for **passwd** and **useradd**. For example, you can remove the aphoenix account with the command **sudo userdel aphoenix**.

try this!

Creating New Users

Practice creating user accounts for Ashley Phoenix (aphoenix), Jose Martinez (jmartinez), Kiesha Olson (kolson), and Beverly Chung (bchung). Try this:

1. Precede each command with **sudo**. Start by creating one user, Ashley Phoenix.
2. Enter the command **sudo useradd –p** *password* **aphoenix**. Provide a password in place of *password*.
3. Confirm that Linux added the account by entering the command **finger aphoenix**.
4. Now add accounts for the other three people.

Recall that every user has a home directory in which to store his or her files. When you delete a user you do not remove this directory—you must remove these files manually. The long explanation for doing this is to delete the files contained in the user's home directory first; then delete the user's home directory itself. It will have the user's name. However, if a directory has subdirectories, you first need to switch into each subdirectory and delete all files in those as well. Once you have deleted the files, you change the directory to one level above and use the **rmdir** command. The syntax for **rmdir** is as follows: **rmdir** *directoryname.*

Now, for the quicker method for deleting a directory and its contents. The **rmdir** command can only remove empty directories, but the **rm** command removes a file or a directory and its contents. Use the **rm** command with the -r (remove) and -f (force) type **rm -rf** *directory-or-file-name* to remove a directory and everything below it.

File and Folder Permissions

To implement security for a file or folder, you must first understand Linux file and folder attributes. When you use the **-l** option with the **ls** command you will see the attributes listed in a column of 10 characters on the far left. Each character is significant in both its placement (first, second, etc.) and in what each single character represents. The first character at the far left indicates whether the entry is a file (**-**), directory (**d**), or link (**l**). The next nine characters show the permissions on the file or folder for three different entities. Figure 9–22 shows a listing of a directory using the -l option to show all the attributes of nonhidden entries. To decode the permissions, use the following list:

r = read

w = write

x = execute

- = disabled

FIGURE 9–22 A sample listing showing attributes.

Notice the set of permissions for the link named **initrd.img**. The attributes r (read), w (write), and x (execute) repeat three times. Linux is not repeating itself; it is listing permissions for three different individuals or groups. The first set of three permissions applies to the user who owns the files. Normally, if you create a file, then you are the owner.

The second set of three permissions applies to the group the user belongs to. We use groups to organize users, joining those with similar needs and access privileges. For example, a school may group all faculty members into a single group. This will allow instructors to create files that other instructors can read, but that students cannot read.

The third set of three permissions applies to all others. So the read, write, and execute permissions on initrd.img apply to the owner (root, in this case), the owner's group, and all others. Look at the permissions for the first entry, **bin**. The permissions on this directory are set so that the owner has read, write, and execute permissions, but the owner's group and all others have only read and execute permissions, meaning only the owner can change or delete the file.

The command to change a file's or a directory's permissions is **chmod** (called change mode). The **chmod** command requires two options. The first option is the access mode number. The second option is the file to change.

Note:
To remember the order of the groups, think of the name UGO. UGO stands for User, Group, Other.

TABLE 9-5   Access Mode Numbers

Permission	Value
Read	4
Write	2
Execute	1

There is a small calculation to perform to determine the access mode number. In Figure 9–22, the link named **initrd.img** has access mode number 777, and the directory **bin** has access mode number 755. You can calculate this number by using the values in Table 9–5. Determine the permission for each user or group by adding the values together. Thus, if the owner needs to read, write, and execute a file, the first number is $4 + 2 + 1 = 7$. If the group is also to read, write, and execute the file, the second number is also 7. If a user has permission only to read and execute a file, the value is $4 + 1 = 5$.

WARNING!

Always be sure the file owner has at least an access mode number of 6 for a file, which allows for read and write permissions. If the mode for the owner drops below 6, on some Linux installations any future access to this file is blocked. You should rarely have a file with permissions of 777 because it means that anyone can change the file.

Step-by-Step 9.05

Working with Directories

Imagine that a marketing firm that uses Linux as its primary OS hired you. You will work with a group of users. You need to create a series of directories that the group can see as well as a private directory that no one else but you can see. The following steps will allow you to create directories and set permissions on the directories. You will create these directories in your own home directory.

You will need the following:

- An account on a Linux computer with or without a GUI. If you log in to a GUI, open the terminal.
- Read access to the /etc directory.

Step 1

First create the directories needed to work. Use **mkdir** to create two directories, called wineProject and private, entering this command: **mkdir wineProject private.**

Step 2

Use the command **ls -l** to verify that Linux created the directories and to view the permissions assigned to the directories by default.

```
[jh@classlab01 wineProject]$ ls -l
total 8
-rw-rw-r--    1 jh       jh          70 Dec  3 10:11 busplan2006
-rw-rw-r--    1 jh       jh         178 Dec  3 10:10 instructor_letter
[jh@classlab01 wineProject]$ cd ~
[jh@classlab01 jh]$ ls -l
total 216
-rw-rw-r--    1 jh       jh          70 Dec  3 08:14 busplan2006
-rw-rw-r--    1 jh       jh         178 Dec  2 19:51 instructor_letter
-rw-r--r--    1 jh       jh        9283 Dec  2 22:03 mailcap
-rw-r--r--    1 jh       jh         112 Dec  2 22:03 mail.rc
-rw-r--r--    1 jh       jh        4426 Dec  2 22:03 man.config
-rw-r--r--    1 jh       jh       36823 Dec  3 06:49 mime-magic
-rw-r--r--    1 jh       jh       99960 Dec  2 22:03 mime-magic.dat
-rw-r--r--    1 jh       jh       12786 Dec  2 22:03 mime.types
-rw-r--r--    1 jh       jh        1110 Dec  2 22:03 minicom.users
-rw-r--r--    1 jh       jh         311 Dec  2 22:03 modules.conf
-rw-r--r--    1 jh       jh         281 Dec  2 22:03 modules.conf~
-rw-r--r--    1 jh       jh           0 Dec  2 22:03 motd
-rw-r--r--    1 jh       jh         242 Dec  2 22:03 mtab
-rw-r--r--    1 jh       jh        1913 Dec  2 22:04 mtools.conf
drwxrwxr-x    2 jh       jh        4096 Dec  3 10:10 private
drwxrwxr-x    2 jh       jh        4096 Dec  3 10:11 wineProject
[jh@classlab01 jh]$
```

Step 3

You are now the owner of these directories. Set the permissions on the private directory so that only you can access it, and on the wineProject directory give yourself read, write, and execute permissions, only read and write permissions to users in your group, and no permissions for others. To set the permissions appropriately enter these two commands: **chmod 700 private** and **chmod 760 wineProject.**

```
[jh@classlab01 jh1$ chmod 700 private
[jh@classlab01 jh1$ chmod 760 wineProject
[jh@classlab01 jh1$ ls -l
total 216
-rw-rw-r--   1 jh       jh             70 Dec  3 08:14 busplan2006
-rw-rw-r--   1 jh       jh            178 Dec  2 19:51 instructor_letter
-rw-r--r--   1 jh       jh           9203 Dec  2 22:03 mailcap
-rw-r--r--   1 jh       jh            112 Dec  2 22:03 mail.rc
-rw-r--r--   1 jh       jh           4426 Dec  2 22:03 man.config
-rw-r--r--   1 jh       jh          36823 Dec  3 06:49 mime-magic
-rw-r--r--   1 jh       jh          99960 Dec  2 22:03 mime-magic.dat
-rw-r--r--   1 jh       jh          12786 Dec  2 22:03 mime.types
-rw-r--r--   1 jh       jh           1110 Dec  2 22:03 minicom.users
-rw-r--r--   1 jh       jh            311 Dec  2 22:03 modules.conf
-rw-r--r--   1 jh       jh            281 Dec  2 22:03 modules.conf~
-rw-r--r--   1 jh       jh              0 Dec  2 22:03 motd
-rw-r--r--   1 jh       jh            242 Dec  2 22:03 mtab
-rw-r--r--   1 jh       jh           1913 Dec  2 22:04 mtools.conf
drwx------   2 jh       jh           4096 Dec  3 10:10 private
drwxrw----   2 jh       jh           4096 Dec  3 10:11 wineProject
[jh@classlab01 jh1$ _
```

Step 4

Confirm the new permissions using **ls -l**.

Step 5

Populate the wineProject directory by copying two files into it from your home directory, using the **cp** command. For instance, to copy the file named "letter" type **cp letter wineProject.**

Step 6

Change to the wineProject directory by entering the command **cd wineProject.** Confirm that the files are there and view the permissions on the files. They do not inherit the permissions of the directory. You will need to modify the permissions on the files if you wish permissions more restrictive than those assigned to the directory. However, any restrictive directory permissions will keep users from accessing the contents of the directory.

```
[jh@classlab01 jh1$ cp instructor_letter wineProject
[jh@classlab01 jh1$ cp busplan2006 wineProject
[jh@classlab01 jh1$ cd wineProject
[jh@classlab01 wineProject]$ ls
busplan2006  instructor_letter
[jh@classlab01 wineProject]$ ls -l
total 8
-rw-rw-r--   1 jh       jh             70 Dec  3 10:11 busplan2006
-rw-rw-r--   1 jh       jh            178 Dec  3 10:10 instructor_letter
[jh@classlab01 wineProject]$ _
```

Chapter 9 REVIEW

Chapter Summary

After reading this chapter and completing the Step-by-Step tutorials and Try This! exercises, you should understand the following facts about Linux:

Linux Overview

- Linux, originally created by Linus Torvalds, is free, open-source software that is like UNIX in stability and function.
- Many versions of Linux exist for all types of computers, and it is used on many Web servers.
- Linux benefits include cost (it is free or inexpensively bundled), the ability to run on old hardware, speed, and stability.

- Drawbacks of Linux include lack of centralized support, choice of GUIs is confusing, limited software selection, limited hardware support, and complexity.

Linux on Your Desktop

- There are many sources of Linux distributions: just two are Ubuntu (www.ubuntu.com) and Fedora (getfedora.org).
- Software distributions are available with GUIs and a complete software bundle of apps.

- Download a distribution as an ISO file and create a bootable DVD or USB flash drive for installing. Popular distributions include a live image from which you can boot and run Linux without having to install it.
- Install Linux as a clean installation on a spare computer, in a dual boot configuration, or into a virtual machine.
- After installing Linux, initiate updates, as you would with Windows.

Exploring a Linux GUI

- If you boot into a live image of Ubuntu Linux, you are logged in as a Guest, but if you install Ubuntu Linux, you will log in with the username and password you provided during the installation.
- In a GUI, or at the CLI, Linux is case-sensitive.
- A Linux distribution with a GUI will have graphical objects similar, but not identical, to those in Windows and OS X.
- The Ubuntu Desktop bar displays at the top of the screen in the Unity GUI.
- The Ubuntu Unity desktop includes the Launcher, a bar on the left side of the screen.
- The Ubuntu Unity desktop has a search tool named Dash that lets you search for files and applications.
- Every user on a Linux computer has a home directory, the one place in Linux where a user has full control over files and directories without requiring elevated privileges. Users cannot normally change system directories, such as /etc and /bin or the directories of other users.
- A path is a description that an operating system uses to identify the location of a file or directory. In Linux you do not use a drive letter; you use a forward slash (/) character at the beginning of a path to represent the top level (root) of the file system.
- The path to a user's home directory is **/home/*username*.**
- The **bin** directory within each user's home directory contains many of the Linux commands.
- The **/etc** directory resides in the root of the file system and contains settings and configuration data for a Linux installation.
- It is far easier to browse the Linux directory structure in a GUI than in a Linux CLI.
- The Unity GUI on Ubuntu includes an Update Manager utility for downloading and installing updates.

- Unity's System Settings window serves the same purpose as Windows' Control Panel and OS X's System Preferences.
- Modify the Unity Desktop using GUI tools similar to those in Windows and OS X.
- End a Unity Ubuntu Linux session with the Shutdown command, which will log out the currently logged-on user and turn off the computer. You can also choose to restart or suspend.

Linux Command-Line Interface

- The Linux native user interface is the CLI, and many installations, especially on servers, only have a CLI.
- If you installed Linux with a GUI or are running it from a live image booted into a GUI, you can open a terminal window, where you can try the Linux CLI.
- You can combine short options and precede them with a single hyphen (-).
- Some options are followed by a parameter, such as a file name, directory, or device name that the command action targets.
- The command syntax in Linux follows this format:
  command –option parameter
- The **reset** command clears the screen and returns the $ prompt to the top:
- The **man** command gives you access to the Linux manual.
- Linux saves the shell commands you enter for the duration of the session, and you can scroll through these commands while at the $ prompt.
- Linux has a command completion feature in which it tries to guess what you want to type next.
- The **date** command displays the day, date, and time. The **cal** command displays the calendar for the month with the current day highlighted.
- Linux gives very little feedback at the CLI, but it does issue error messages when you enter something wrong.
- Certain shell commands are useful when managing the file system. They are **cd**, **chmod**, **cp**, **ls**, **mkdir**, **more**, **pwd**, and **rm**.
- When you list the contents of a directory, the items are color coded to identify different types of entries.
- Linux allows you to use commands to navigate directories, using special symbols as shorthand for moving to directories that are relative to your current directory.

- The wildcard asterisk (*) is a symbol that replaces any character or string of characters, in a command parameter.
- Create a directory in Linux with the **mkdir** command, which requires at least one parameter: the name of the directory to create. Use multiple parameters to create multiple directories with one command.
- Use the **cp** command to copy files. It requires a parameter for the source file, and one for the target location and/or name of a file.

Securing a Linux Desktop

- If multiple people need to use one computer, each should have a unique account.
- When you create a Linux account, it also creates a home directory for the account using the user's name for the directory name.
- The **root account** is an all-powerful account that is only used when absolutely necessary to do advanced tasks. Ubuntu Linux comes with this account disabled in such a way that no one can log in directly with the account, but there is a way to temporarily use it.
- Create an account using a GUI tool or by using the **useradd** command at the CLI. The **userdel** command will delete specified users, **passwd** is used to change a user's password, and the **finger** daemon will confirm that a user has been created.

- Temporarily assign root account privileges to the currently logged-on user by preceding the command you intend to run with the **sudo** command. **Sudo** will prompt you to enter your password (not the root password). Then, for the next five minutes (by default), you will be able to run **sudo** without requiring a password.
- The **rmdir** command can only delete empty directories, while the **rm** command will delete a directory and its contents. This is a very dangerous command.
- When you use the **ls** command with the **-l** option it lists files and directory details. The first 10 characters are attributes. The first character is the type of entry: file (**-**), directory (**d**), or link (**l**). The next nine characters show the permission on the file or folder for three different entities (owner, group, and others).
- The characters that represent permissions are **r** for read, **w** for write, **x** for execute, and **-** for disabled.
- The command to change a file's or a directory's permissions is **chmod**.
- Access mode values are 4 for read, 2 for write, and 1 for execute. These are added together to create the access mode number. If the owner, group, or other has read (4), write (2), and execute (1) permission to a file, the access mode number for that entity on that file is 7.

Key Terms List

absolute path *(373)*

access mode number *(380)*

Apache HTTP Server *(351)*

BASH *(353)*

burn *(356)*

case-aware *(363)*

case-sensitive *(363)*

command completion *(371)*

command-line history *(371)*

daemon *(379)*

GNOME *(353)*

GNU *(350)*

home directory *(362)*

Hypertext Transfer Protocol (HTTP) *(351)*

Kickoff Application Launcher *(353)*

Launcher *(361)*

Linux *(350)*

live image *(356)*

object code *(351)*

open-source software *(351)*

owner *(380)*

path *(362)*

Red Hat Enterprise Linux (RHEL) *(352)*

root account *(376)*

source code *(351)*

switch users *(368)*

symbolic link *(362)*

terminal window *(368)*

Ubuntu *(352)*

Web *(351)*

wildcard *(374)*

World Wide Web (WWW) *(351)*

X Window *(353)*

X Window System *(353)*

Key Terms Quiz

Use the Key Terms List to complete the sentences that follow. Not all terms will be used.

1. To access the CLI in the GNOME GUI, you open a _____.

2. GNOME is an example of a/an _____ GUI.

3. A/an _____ is a bootable image of the operating system that will run from bootable

media without requiring that the OS be installed on the local computer.

4. When you create a user in Linux, the OS creates a _____ on disk for that user.

5. When you write digital data to an optical disc, you are said to _____ it.

6. A/an _____ is a program that runs in background until it is activated by a command.

7. The _____ organization was created in 1984 to develop a free UNIX-like operating system.

8. A/an _____ is a special symbol, such as an asterisk (*), that replaces a character or string of characters in a command parameter.

9. _____ is the uncompiled program statements that can be viewed and edited.

10. The most powerful account in Linux is the _____.

Multiple-Choice Quiz

1. Linux is modeled on which operating system?
   a. Windows
   b. UNIX
   c. NT
   d. VMS
   e. CP/M

2. If the access mode number for the owner of a file or directory drops below this on some Linux installations, any future access to this file is blocked.
   a. 5
   b. 8
   c. 1
   d. 7
   e. 6

3. Who was the initial developer responsible for Linux?
   a. Ken Thompson
   b. Linus Torvalds
   c. Steve Jobs
   d. Dennis Ritchie
   e. Fred Linux

4. Which user has the most power and privileges in Linux?
   a. Administrator
   b. Admin
   c. Absolute
   d. Root
   e. Linus

5. What is the command a user invokes to log off when working at the Linux shell?
   a. exit
   b. shutdown
   c. bye
   d. log off
   e. quit

6. What is the Linux shell command to copy a file?
   a. cpy
   b. rm
   c. mv
   d. copy
   e. cp

7. What option for the **ls** command lists all files in a directory, including the hidden files?
   a. -S
   b. -F
   c. -l
   d. -a
   e. -t

8. What is the shell command (and option) to turn off a Linux computer immediately?
   a. sudo down
   b. sudo shutdown now
   c. exit stat
   d. off now
   e. power off

9. What feature preserves your open apps and data, but allows another user to log in to his or her own session on the same computer?
   a. daemon
   b. lock screen
   c. live image
   d. switch users
   e. Guest

10. What organization formed in 1988 to lobby for an "open" UNIX after AT&T formed a partnership with Sun Microsystems to develop a single proprietary UNIX?
    a. GNU
    b. Apache
    c. Ubuntu
    d. BASH
    e. OSF

11. Which command displays a text file one page (screenful) at a time?
   a. mkdir
   b. more
   c. pwd
   d. cd
   e. rm

12. What command can you use at the CLI to temporarily borrow the privileges of the most powerful account in a Linux system?
   a. sudo
   b. root
   c. rm
   d. switch users
   e. chmod

13. Which Linux command can you use to change file permissions?
   a. cd
   b. ls

   c. more
   d. chmod
   e. rm

14. Why would an advanced Linux administrator use shell commands rather than a Linux GUI when creating many users at once?
   a. The shell commands are more intuitive.
   b. Linux GUIs are too cryptic.
   c. Shell commands are faster.
   d. The Linux CLI is more secure.
   e. You cannot create users from a Linux GUI.

15. When in the terminal window, which command would return you to your Home directory, no matter what directory is current?
   a. cd ..
   b. cd ~
   c. cd /
   d. chmod ~
   e. cd.

Essay Quiz

1. List and explain the reasons that Linux has not yet taken over the desktop OS market.
2. Discuss how your school or work could use Linux.
3. Discuss how open-source software can benefit an organization.
4. The Helping Hand, a charitable organization, has asked you to set up its computer systems. The

organization has a very limited budget. Describe how Linux can allow users to be productive while costing very little.

5. Explain the merits of sudo, as implemented in Ubuntu Linux.

Lab Projects

LAB PROJECT 9.1

The Unity GUI includes workspaces, a feature not described in this chapter, although a button for using it was shown on the Launcher in Figure 9–5. Research the workspaces and write a few sentences describing the notion of workspaces in Linux.

LAB PROJECT 9.2

When installing Ubuntu Linux the **Who are you?** page has an option entitled **Require my password to log in**, and below that is another option entitled **Encrypt my** home folder. Research this last option and describe another option you should not enable after you have selected this option, along with the reason not to. Hint: locate the Getting Started with Ubuntu manual.

LAB PROJECT 9.3

Research and describe the Suspend and Hibernate options sometimes available from the Unity Shutdown menu (accessed from the icon on the far right of the menu bar).

10 Connecting Desktops and Laptops to Networks

Learning Outcomes

In this chapter, you will learn how to:

LO **10.1** Configure a computer for a TCP/IP network.

LO **10.2** Connect to the Internet.

LO **10.3** Work with basic Internet clients.

LO **10.4** Configure File and Printer clients.

LO **10.5** Troubleshoot common network client problems.

A stand-alone PC—one with no connection whatsoever to a network—is a rare thing today. Most of us can find some reason or need to connect to a network, whether it is a small home network, a corporate intranet, or the Internet. Without a network connection, a PC is like a remote island where the inhabitants have resolved to be isolated from civilization. And it does take resolve today to be so isolated because there are means by which a computer in the most remote location can connect to the Internet or another network. The heart and soul of all networks are the servers that provide the services we, as clients, seek on a network. These services are as simple as those that give us access to files and printers, Web pages, applications, and much more. Each of these services provides an important role on a network.

At work, at school, and at home, computer users depend on client software components that connect to services—whether for online research, playing games, engaging in a community through social media, using email, or downloading and uploading files.

In this chapter you will study the client side of networking. Because a client computer cannot interact with network servers unless you properly configure it to communicate on a network, begin with how to configure network connection settings on a client computer. Then move on to the Internet, first examining methods for connecting to the Internet, and then look at the most common Internet clients for browsing and email. Finally, practice methods for troubleshooting common connection problems. ✳

LO 10.1 | Configuring a Network Connection

In this section we will briefly describe the TCP/IP protocol suite, the basics of the addressing scheme of the IP protocol, and how to view and configure the important IP settings on your devices.

Understanding the TCP/IP Protocol Suite

TCP/IP is a group of protocols that evolved from the work of the Defense Advanced Research Projects Agency (DARPA); the Internet Engineering Task Force (IETF) now oversees TCP/IP development. TCP/IP is the underlying protocol suite of the Internet and nearly all private networks, regardless of the network medium (wired or wireless). It is supported by all operating systems on desktops, servers, and common mobile devices.

Each software implementation of a component of TCP/IP is a protocol, regardless of whether it is a driver, a service, or an application. So, in computer networking, a protocol is both the set of rules for doing some task as well as the software that accomplishes it. In this section we will work at understanding the TCP/IP protocol suite, software bundled together in what we call a protocol stack.

The TCP/IP protocols work together to allow both similar and dissimilar computers to communicate. You need this protocol suite to access the Internet, and it is the most common protocol suite used on private intranets. It gets its name from two of its many protocols: Transmission Control Protocol (TCP) and Internet Protocol (IP)—the core protocols of TCP/IP. If, during Windows installation, Windows detects a wired or wireless network adapter it will install a driver for that adapter card and the TCP/IP protocol will automatically install.

TCP/IP is a subject of epic proportions! We offer only an introduction to TCP/IP, in which we attempt to arm you with useful information, but not overwhelm you with detail. Our goal is to give you an overview of TCP/IP, and familiarize you with the settings that you may need to enter or modify for your desktop or laptop computer. Of course, this knowledge should also help you with your mobile devices, the subject of Chapter 11. Most computers and mobile devices need little or no help in acquiring the address they need to connect to a network, but knowing more about how this works is very helpful when things don't work as they should.

Transmission Control Protocol

Transmission Control Protocol (TCP) is the protocol responsible for the accurate delivery of messages, verifying and resending any pieces that fail to make the trip from source to destination. Several other protocols act as subprotocols, helping TCP accomplish this.

Internet Protocol

Internet Protocol (IP) is the protocol that delivers each IP packet (a small "package" containing chunks of data) from a source to a destination over a network on an Internetwork (a network of networks connected through routers). Special routing protocols use a destination IP address to choose the

Note: TCP/IP was developed for connecting networks to networks. For this reason it is routable, meaning that messages can be sent from one TCP/IP network to another through routers, the devices that connect networks. The Internet consists of millions of such connected networks.

Note: For an entertaining overview of TCP/IP and the workings of network devices (routers, switches, and firewalls), check out YouTube video *TCP/IP the Movie* (Parts 1 and 2).

The logo of the World IPv6 Launch organization.

best route for a packet to take through a very complex internetwork. IP has subprotocols that help it accomplish its work, but we will not discuss the subprotocols.

Note: What progress has the Internet community made in moving toward an IPv4-free world? Check out the website **www.worldipv6launch.org** to see where things stand in the IP protocol world.

Presently there are two versions of Internet Protocol: IPv4 and IPv6, each with its own addressing scheme. Both protocols are present on the Internet, as it slowly transitions away from the older IPv4 (the standard since 1983) to IPv6. A lot of attention is focused on the differences in addresses used by these two protocols, but there are many reasons for the Internet's move to IPv6.

The short list of reasons IPv6 is better than IPv4 includes:

- IPv4 has run out of addresses.
- IPv6 has many more addresses: 340 trillion trillion trillion unique identifiers.
- IPv6 works better with mobile devices using a subprotocol, Mobile IP.
- IPv6 automatically assigns addresses to devices in a very reliable and no-fuss way.
- IPv6 manages addresses better.
- IPv6 has subprotocols that support better security.

It is important for you to learn about IP addresses because you cannot participate on a TCP/IP network without a valid IP address.

IP Addressing Fundamentals

Let's explore the basics of IP addressing. First, an IP address is not assigned to a computer but to each network interface card (NIC) on a TCP/IP network, whether wired (Ethernet) or wireless (Wi-Fi). A modem (whether it is a cable modem, DSL modem, or an old analog "dial-up" modem) also has an address when you use it to connect to the Internet. If your computer or mobile device has multiple network connection devices connected to different networks, such as an Ethernet network adapter connected to a LAN and a Wi-Fi or cellular connection, each must have an address when it connects to a network.

That is why you see the Internet Protocol as a component of a connection in Windows (see Figure 10–1). The Connect Using box near the top of the Ethernet Properties dialog box identifies the connecting device to which these settings apply. Figure 10–1 shows that Windows supports both IPv4 and IPv6.

An IP address, along with a subnet mask (explained later) identifies your network card (a "host" in Internet terms), and the network on which it resides. An IP address, when added to a message packet as the destination address, allows the message to move from one network to another until it reaches its destination. At the connecting point between networks, a special network device called a router uses its routing protocols to determine the route to the destination IP address, before sending each packet along to the next router closer to the destination network. Each computer that directly attaches to the Internet must have a globally unique IP address. Both versions of IP have this much, and more, in common. Following are short explanations of IPv4 and IPv6 addresses.

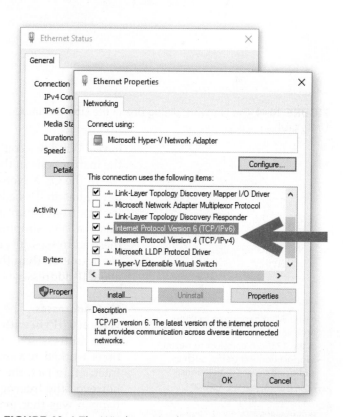

FIGURE 10–1 The Windows 10 Ethernet Properties dialog box.

FIGURE 10–2 The Windows 10 Network Connection Details box.

FIGURE 10–3 The OS X Network preferences pane.

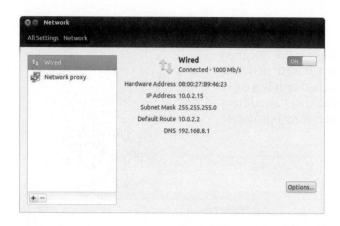

FIGURE 10–4 The Network dialog box in the Ubuntu Linux Unity GUI.

IPv4 Addresses. IPv4 has been used on the Internet and other internetworks for over three decades. With 32-bit addressing, calculated by raising 2 to the 32nd power (2^{32}), IPv4 offers almost 4.3 billion possible IP addresses, but the way in which they were initially allocated to organizations greatly reduced the number of usable addresses, and we have now run out of IPv4 addresses.

An IPv4 address is 32 bits long in binary notation, but it usually appears as four decimal numbers, each in the range of 0–255, separated by a period. See examples of IPv4 addresses in Figures 10–2, 10–3, and 10–4. Figure 10–2 shows the Windows 10 Network Connection Details with the address of the local connection set as 192.168.1.10. The other IP addresses shown are to other network devices. If you have a Windows computer you can open the Details dialog box by following the instructions in the Try This!

In the OS X Network preferences pane, shown in Figure 10–3, the Wi-Fi device has an IPv4 address of 192.168.1.16. Figure 10–4 shows the Network dialog box from Ubuntu's Unity GUI with an IPv4 address of 10.0.2.15. Because this is a very simplified explanation, we will not go into the exact rules for these addresses, just an overview. And, as you can see, there is more to an IP configuration than the address of the device itself, but we will tell you more about IP addresses before we discuss these other settings.

IPv6 Addresses. The Internet is currently transitioning to Internet Protocol version 6 (IPv6) with a new addressing scheme that provides astronomically more addresses. For many years, manufacturers and standards organizations worked toward the day when they could fully support IPv6 on the Internet. In fact, the World IPv6 Launch Day was June 6, 2012. On that day, however, the Internet world did not become an IPv6-only world. What did happen was that many important Internet service providers and websites became available to computers using either IPv4 or IPv6. They included

Note: What happened to IPv5? An IPv5 standard was developed in the 1980s in an effort to better support nontext traffic, such as audio, video, and simulations. However, it did not replace IPv4, which was then still a recent standard.

An IPv6 Address in hexadecimal notation:

2002:0470:b8f9:0000:020c:29ff:fe53:45ca

The same address in hexadecimal notation with leading zeros removed:

2002:470:b8f9::20c:29ff:fe53:45ca

The same address in binary notation:

```
0010000000000010  0000010001110000  1011100011111001  0000000000000000
0000001000001100  0010100111111111  1111111001010011  0100010111001010
```

FIGURE 10–5 An IPv6 address expressed in both hexadecimal and binary notation.

Bing, Facebook, Google, and Yahoo!, and many more continue to join them. For the near future (perhaps decades), IPv4 and IPv6 will coexist on the Internet and on private and governmental internetworks of the world. Recent versions of operating systems and all new networking equipment come with support for IPv6 built in.

IPv6 has 128-bit addressing, calculated by raising 2 to the 128th power (2^{128}), which supports a huge number of unique addresses—340,282,366,920, 938,463,463,374,607,431,768,211,456 to be exact. An IPv6 address appears as eight groups of four hexadecimal digits separated by colons. You will often see an IPv6 address shortened by eliminating leading zeros in a group, and if there are all zeros between a set of colons, the zeros won't show and you will see just two colons together. If two or more groups of all zeros are adjacent there will still only be two colons. In Figure 10–5 an IPv6 address is first shown in full hexadecimal notation, then with leading zeros removed, and finally as eight groups of binary numbers.

Which Addresses Can You Use?

While we described both IPv4 and IPv6 addresses above, our discussion here centers around IPv4 because it will be around for a while, and you are more likely to need help resolving a problem with an IPv4 address than with an IPv6 address. We doubt anyone other than a network administrator will be concerned about IPv6 addresses.

There are billions of addresses, so how do you pick an address to use? Of course, the answer is—it all depends. Will you be using the address on a public network (the Internet) or on a private network? A central organization decides how to allocate all these addresses for use on the public Internet. They also understand that organizations need to use IP addresses within their private networks, and schemes were developed to slow down the depletion of addresses. One of those schemes involved dividing the possible IP addresses into two broad categories: public addresses and private addresses.

Public Addresses. Public IP addresses are designated for hosts on the Internet. In IP terminology, a host is any computer or device that has an IP address. To communicate over the Internet, you must send your message from an IP address that is unique on the entire Internet, and your message must go to a unique IP address. The centrally responsible organization for allocation of

TABLE 10–1 IPv4 Private IP Address Ranges
Private IPv4 Address Ranges
10.0.0.0 through 10.255.255.255
172.16.0.0 through 172.31.255.255
192.168.0.0 through 192.168.255.255

public IP addresses is the Internet Assigned Numbers Authority (IANA). This organization allocates numbers to various Regional Internet Registries (RIRs), which have the task of allocating IP addresses to Internet service providers. The largest ISPs, in turn, allocate addresses to other ISPs. You or your school or employer receive addresses for each Internet connection from your ISP. The addresses provided are from selected portions of those many billions of possible addresses specifically used on the Internet.

Private Addresses. A private IP address is an address from one of three ranges of IPv4 addresses designated for use only on private networks, so they are unusable on the Internet. All the IPv4 addresses in Figures 10–2, 10–3, and 10–4 are private addresses. In fact, many organizations use these addresses on their private IP networks, and you do not need to get permission to do so.

If a computer with a private address connects to the Internet, it will not be able to communicate because Internet routers will not forward packets with private addresses. Therefore, the same private address can be in use on millions of private networks, thus relieving some of the pressure on the limited supply of IPv4 addresses. Table 10–1 (above) shows the three ranges used as private IPv4 addresses. All other IPv4 addresses either have specialized uses or are public addresses valid for computers and devices that are on the Internet.

If a user on a private network using private IP addresses wishes to connect to the Internet, a device between the local network and the Internet must intercept, repackage, and give a public IP address as its source address to each data packet before it goes onto the Internet. Then, if there is a response, each returning packet will go through the same in reverse process before returning to the private address.

If you connect to the Internet from home, or through your school or work, there is a device between your computer and the ISP that substitutes (or translates) your actual IP address to a unique Internet IP address. There are a couple of methods for doing this. One involves a special network service called a proxy server, and another involves a special service called network address translation (NAT), which a NAT router provides. These are services that your ISP or network administrator manages for your school or organization. Such services also exist in the devices called Internet routers, which allow home or small-office computers to connect to the Internet, usually through a cable or DSL connection. A cable provider or telephone company will normally supply this equipment along with the Internet service.

How Does a NIC Get an IP Address?

A NIC gets an IP address in one of two ways: static address assignment or automatic address assignment. Automatic address assignment is the most common method used today and automatic IP address assignment itself has two methods.

Note: Most home routers use the IPv4 address 192.168.1.1 or 192.168.0.1. The examples given in Figures 10–2 and 10–3 are from computers connected to a home router. In Figure 10–2 the address of the router to which a Windows computer connects is labeled "Default Gateway." In Figure 10–3 OS X uses "Router" for the label to this address. Figure 10–4 shows the Network Settings dialog box on Linux running in a virtual machine. It labels a router address as "Default Route." The address the virtual router uses is not used by most home routers.

Static Address Assignment. A static IP address is manually configured by an administrator for a host and can, therefore, be considered semipermanent—that is, it stays with the device until someone takes action to change it. Manually configuring an IP address involves manually entering the IP address and other necessary IP settings. Most organizations do static IP addressing only on servers, network printers, and network devices such as routers that are required to have static addresses.

Where will you find this information on your desktop or laptop computer? Actually, unless you are setting up your own TCP/IP network (a very advanced task!), you will be given the IP addressing information by a network administrator, if you are connecting to a LAN at school or work, or by your Internet service provider. But most ISPs automate all the configuration of home Internet connections.

If you need to manually configure an address, be sure to carefully enter the numbers given to you, and double-check them! In Windows, you will enter these in the TCP/IP properties found in the properties dialog box for the network connection. See Figure 10–6.

Automatic Address Assignment. One nearly universal method is used for assigning IP addresses to computers: automatic IP addressing. Another method is used as a sort of fail-safe: Automatic Private IP Addressing (APIPA).

- Most organizations use automatic IP addressing for their desktop computers. It requires a special server or service on the network, called a Dynamic Host Configuration Protocol (DHCP) server, which issues IP addresses and settings to computers configured to obtain an IP address automatically, thus making them DHCP clients. The news gets even better since the default configuration of TCP/IP on a Windows, Mac, or Linux computer is to obtain an IP address automatically. Look for the line in Figure 10–2 that shows that DHCP is enabled for Windows 10, and Figure 10–3 shows that it is using DHCP to configure IPv4. However, in the Ubuntu Linux Network dialog box in Figure 10–4, you would need to click the Options button and bring up the Editing Wired connection 1 dialog box (not shown) to learn how the network card receives an IP address.

- Do not confuse *automatic* with *automatic private*. Most operating systems will enable a feature of DHCP—Automatic Private IP Addressing (APIPA), whereby a DHCP client computer that fails to receive an address from a DHCP server will automatically give itself an address from a special range that has 169.254 in the first two octets of the IPv4 address. This is also called a link-local address, and IPv6 uses link-local addresses that begin with fe80. If a computer uses a link-local address, it will only be able to communicate on the local network segment, and then only with other devices and computers that use the same network ID. *When a computer is using an APIPA address, it continues to look for a DHCP server. Windows will check every 5 minutes.*

    APIPA allows a novice to set up a small TCP/IP network without needing to learn about IP addressing. Each computer would use APIPA to assign itself an address, first testing that no other computer on the LAN is also using that same host ID.

IP Configuration Settings

If you must manually configure IPv4, you will need to understand the other settings to enter in addition to the IP address. Refer to the Windows 10 Internet

WARNING!

Incorrect IP configuration settings can make your network connection useless. Modify IP configuration settings only if a network administrator or your ISP provides you with settings and tells you to. Then take great care to be accurate!

Note: Flip back to Figure 10–2 showing the Network Connection Details. The third line from the bottom contains the link-local IPv6 address fe80:fd8b:1940:be8:f6ff%6. In this case, the NIC assigned this address to itself because it did not receive an IPv6 address. This NIC communicates on the network using the IPv4 address.

WARNING!

An APIPA address can indicate that a router is turned off or faulty.

FIGURE 10–6 Manually configure TCP/IP in Windows 10 using the Internet Protocol Version 4 (TCP/IPv4) Properties dialog box.

Protocol Version 4 Properties dialog box in Figure 10–6 while reading the following descriptions of the various IP settings.

Subnet Mask. When a network device gets an IP address, it must also get a subnet mask. The subnet mask for an IPv4 address is as critical as the address itself because it takes what looks like a single address and divides it into two addresses by masking off part of the address. It is a little like your house address. The house number gives the address on the street, but you also need the street name. If you look at the Properties dialog box in Figure 10–6, the IPv4 address 192.168.1.132 has a mask of 255.255.255.0. The IP protocol now knows that this network device has the host address of 132 (its house number) on network 192.168.1 (its street name). The host address is the host ID, and the network address is the net ID.

Let's take a brief look at how masking works. Technically, it is done using binary math (base-2 math that uses only 0s and 1s), but you do not have to be a binary math whiz to understand the concept of masking; just look at the IP address and the mask in its binary form. You can use the scientific setting of the Calculator program that comes with Windows to convert each octet (a group of eight binary digits) of an IP address from binary to decimal or vice versa. As an example, if you convert an address of 192.168.100.2 to binary it looks like this:

11000000.10101000.01100100.00000010.

If you convert the mask of 255.255.255.0 to binary, it looks like this:

11111111.11111111.11111111.00000000.

If you lay the mask on top of the IP address, the ones cover (mask) the first 24 bits (short for binary digits). What falls under the ones of the mask is the network address, and what falls under the zeros of the mask is the host address. Figure 10–7 should make this concept clearer.

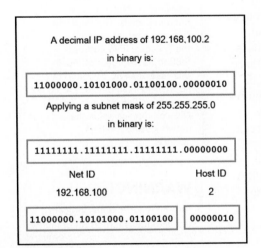

FIGURE 10–7 A subnet mask covers a portion of an IP address.

Default Gateway. The next entry shown back in Figure 10–6 is the default gateway. This is the IP address of the router connected to your network. The router is the network device that directs traffic to destinations beyond the local network. The net ID of the gateway address should be identical to the net ID of your NIC. Without a properly configured router, as well as the correct address (Default Gateway) for reaching this router, you cannot communicate with computers beyond your network. In our example in Figure 10–6, the router connects network 192.168.1 to other networks. Anytime your computer has a packet destined for a network with a network address other than 192.168.1, IP will send the packet to the gateway address to be forwarded to a host on another network.

DNS Servers. The last two settings are addresses of Domain Name System (DNS) servers. DNS is a distributed hierarchical online database containing registered domain names mapped to IP addresses. Thousands of name servers on the Internet maintain this distributed database. When you attempt to connect to a website, such as www.mhhe.com, your computer's DNS client queries a DNS server to determine the IP address for that website.

You may enter two addresses in the Microsoft Properties dialog shown in Figure 10–6—a primary DNS server and a secondary DNS server. The primary DNS server is the server the DNS client on your computer contacts any time you make a request to connect to a server using a domain name rather than an IP address. The DNS server will attempt to resolve the name to an IP address. The DNS client contacts the second DNS server only if there is no response from the first DNS server, but it does not use the second DNS server when the first DNS server responds that it cannot resolve the name. This is when you see an error similar to: "DNS query for www.somedomainname.com failed: host not found."

The Internet Corporation for Assigned Names and Numbers (ICANN), a California nonprofit corporation, currently oversees the Domain Name System, after having replaced an organization called InterNIC. The U.S. government sanctions ICANN, which reports to the U.S. Department of Commerce. Anyone wishing to acquire a domain name contacts one of the roughly 200 domain name registrars of top-level domains (.com, .org, .pro, .info, .biz, and so on) accredited by ICANN. Once registered with ICANN, each domain name and its IP address go on the Internet Domain Name Servers so that users can access Internet services offered under those domain names.

Step-by-Step 10.01

Examine a Connection's IP Configuration in a GUI

In this step-by-step exercise, you will examine a connection's IP configuration in the Windows GUI. The illustrations are from Windows 7, but this also works in the newer versions of Windows. You will need:

- A computer running Windows.
- An administrator account and password for the computer.

Step 1

In Control Panel open the Network and Sharing Center.

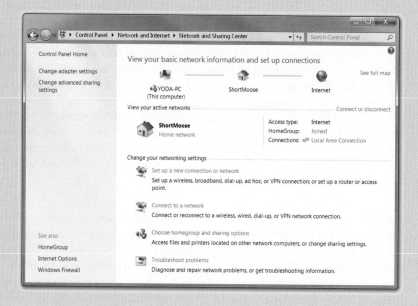

Step 2

In the Network and Sharing Center click **Change adapter settings** in the task list on the left. This opens the Network Connection window. Our example has only one network connection device, but you may have more than one listed.

Step 3

Double-click on the network connection you wish to examine. This opens the Status dialog box for the connection.

Step 4

Click the Details button. This will open the Network Connection Details box. The Windows 10 version of this dialog box is shown back in Figure 10–2. This is a good place to see the IP address of your NIC in the GUI.

Step 5

If you wish to make changes to the configuration, click the Close button to return to the Status dialog box. Then click the Properties button on the Status page to open the properties for this connection.

Step 6

Keep in mind that only an advanced user should make changes to the network configuration. To look at the Properties dialog box for IPv4 for this connection double-click Internet Protocol Version 4 (TCP/IPv4).

Step 7

When you have examined the configuration, click Cancel to close each open box without making changes. Then click Close to close the connection you examined, and then close the Network Connections window.

```
D:\Windows\system32\cmd.exe                                    _ □ X

D:\Users\Yoda>ipconfig /all

Windows IP Configuration

   Host Name . . . . . . . . . . . . : Yoda-PC
   Primary Dns Suffix  . . . . . . . :
   Node Type . . . . . . . . . . . . : Hybrid
   IP Routing Enabled. . . . . . . . : No
   WINS Proxy Enabled. . . . . . . . : No

Ethernet adapter Local Area Connection:

   Connection-specific DNS Suffix  . :
   Description . . . . . . . . . . . : Realtek PCI GBE Family Controller
   Physical Address. . . . . . . . . : 00-27-19-CD-2F-C2
   DHCP Enabled. . . . . . . . . . . : Yes
   Autoconfiguration Enabled . . . . : Yes
   Link-local IPv6 Address . . . . . : fe80::607f:c2b:3650:edcb%11(Preferred)
   IPv4 Address. . . . . . . . . . . : 192.168.1.134(Preferred)
   Subnet Mask . . . . . . . . . . . : 255.255.255.0
   Lease Obtained. . . . . . . . . . : Sunday, November 21, 2010 7:05:43 AM
   Lease Expires . . . . . . . . . . : Monday, November 22, 2010 7:05:51 AM
   Default Gateway . . . . . . . . . : 192.168.1.1
   DHCP Server . . . . . . . . . . . : 192.168.1.1
   DHCPv6 IAID . . . . . . . . . . . : 234891033
   DHCPv6 Client DUID. . . . . . . . : 00-01-00-01-14-2D-C9-A0-00-27-19-CD-2F-C2

   DNS Servers . . . . . . . . . . . : 192.168.8.1
   NetBIOS over Tcpip. . . . . . . . : Enabled
```

FIGURE 10–8 The output from running the command ipconfig /all.

Viewing an IP Configuration from a Command Prompt

You can view the IP configuration of a Windows, Linux, or OS X computer from a Command Prompt using either **ipconfig** (Windows) or **ifconfig** (Linux and OS X).

In the Windows Command Prompt use the **ipconfig** command without any command-line switches to have it display only the IP address (both IPv4 and IPv6, when present), subnet mask, and default gateway for each NIC that is connected to a network. Using the command with the **/all** switch will display much more information for each NIC. For instance, without this switch no detail is listed under Windows IP Configuration, but with the **/all** switch, as shown in Figure 10–8, several lines display, beginning with the Host Name. Then, for each adapter, in addition to the basic IP address, subnet mask, and default gateway, all the IP configuration information for each NIC displays. This includes the physical address, several lines of information pertaining to DHCP, and one or more DNS server addresses, if available, as well as the status of NetBIOS over TCP/IP, a protocol used for downward compatibility in networks with older Windows versions.

The equivalent of the Windows **ipconfig** command in the OS X Terminal window or at a $ prompt in Linux is the **ifconfig** command. Open a Terminal window in OS X or access the $ prompt in Linux and enter the **ifconfig** command with the **-a** switch to see all information about all network interfaces in that computer. The results for a OS X Terminal window are shown in Figure 10–9 and from the $ prompt in Linux in

try this!

View Your IP Configuration from a Windows Command Prompt

Check out your current IP configuration using the **ipconfig** command. Try this:

1. Open a Command Prompt.
2. At the prompt type **ipconfig**.
3. After viewing the results of the command, type the command again with the **/all** switch: **ipconfig /all**.
4. Notice the additional information the **/all** switch provides.
5. Learn about other options for **ipconfig** using the **/?** switch.

Figure 10–10. Notice that the information in OS X and in Linux is more difficult to decipher than it is in Windows. For instance, in both Figures 10–9 and 10–10 the lines labeled "inet6" refer to IPv6, while those beginning with "inet" refer to IPv4. You'll find the physical addresses of installed NICs in Figure 10–9 on lines beginning with "ether." In Figure 10–10 the line containing the physical address of the Ethernet NIC is in the first line of the section labeled eth0.

```
Last login: Sun Nov 21 15:46:24 on ttys000
Janes-iMac:~ janeholcombe$ ifconfig -a
lo0: flags=8049<UP,LOOPBACK,RUNNING,MULTICAST> mtu 16384
        inet6 ::1 prefixlen 128
        inet6 fe80::1%lo0 prefixlen 64 scopeid 0x1
        inet 127.0.0.1 netmask 0xff000000
gif0: flags=8010<POINTOPOINT,MULTICAST> mtu 1280
stf0: flags=0<> mtu 1280
en0: flags=8863<UP,BROADCAST,SMART,RUNNING,SIMPLEX,MULTICAST> mtu 1500
        ether c4:2c:03:11:f5:1b
        media: autoselect
        status: inactive
fw0: flags=8863<UP,BROADCAST,SMART,RUNNING,SIMPLEX,MULTICAST> mtu 4078
        lladdr e8:06:88:ff:fe:fb:26:62
        media: autoselect <full-duplex>
        status: inactive
en1: flags=8863<UP,BROADCAST,SMART,RUNNING,SIMPLEX,MULTICAST> mtu 1500
        ether d8:30:62:57:17:fc
        inet6 fe80::da30:62ff:fe57:17fc%en1 prefixlen 64 scopeid 0x6
        inet 192.168.1.135 netmask 0xffffff00 broadcast 192.168.1.255
        media: autoselect
        status: active
vboxnet0: flags=8842<BROADCAST,RUNNING,SIMPLEX,MULTICAST> mtu 1500
        ether 0a:00:27:00:00:00
vnic0: flags=8843<UP,BROADCAST,RUNNING,SIMPLEX,MULTICAST> mtu 1500
        ether 00:1c:42:00:00:08
        inet 10.211.55.2 netmask 0xffffff00 broadcast 10.211.55.255
        media: autoselect
        status: active
vnic1: flags=8843<UP,BROADCAST,RUNNING,SIMPLEX,MULTICAST> mtu 1500
        ether 00:1c:42:00:00:09
        inet 10.37.129.2 netmask 0xffffff00 broadcast 10.37.129.255
        media: autoselect
        status: active
Janes-iMac:~ janeholcombe$
```

FIGURE 10–9 The result of running the **ifconfig -a** command in a Terminal window in OS X.

```
chuck@chuck-linux:~$ ifconfig -a
eth0      Link encap:Ethernet  HWaddr 08:00:27:17:fe:b0
          inet addr:10.0.2.15  Bcast:10.0.2.255  Mask:255.255.255.0
          inet6 addr: fe80::a00:27ff:fe17:feb0/64 Scope:Link
          UP BROADCAST RUNNING MULTICAST  MTU:1500  Metric:1
          RX packets:2286 errors:0 dropped:0 overruns:0 frame:0
          TX packets:1853 errors:0 dropped:0 overruns:0 carrier:0
          collisions:0 txqueuelen:1000
          RX bytes:1718199 (1.7 MB)  TX bytes:247442 (247.4 KB)

lo        Link encap:Local Loopback
          inet addr:127.0.0.1  Mask:255.0.0.0
          inet6 addr: ::1/128 Scope:Host
          UP LOOPBACK RUNNING  MTU:16436  Metric:1
          RX packets:9 errors:0 dropped:0 overruns:0 frame:0
          TX packets:9 errors:0 dropped:0 overruns:0 carrier:0
          collisions:0 txqueuelen:0
          RX bytes:1056 (1.0 KB)  TX bytes:1056 (1.0 KB)

chuck@chuck-linux:~$
```

FIGURE 10–10 The result of running the **ifconfig -a** command at the $ prompt in Linux.

LO 10.2 | Connecting to the Internet

A connection to the Internet is a wide area network (WAN) connection. A wide area network (WAN) is a network that covers a very large geographic area (miles). There are several WAN technologies to choose from. Some of these are wired technologies, and some are wireless. Most connection methods described here remain available 24/7, in which case, Internet access is as simple as opening your browser or sending an email. The connections include a wide range of speeds. In this section, we will compare the various means of connecting a network or computer to the Internet and discuss the most common methods for doing so from home or a small business so that you can make a decision for yourself. This will also help you to understand something about how you are connecting to the Internet from school or work, although we will not discuss the very expensive high-speed WAN services for connecting a large enterprise (commercial, government, or educational) to the Internet.

The choice of physical means of connecting to the Internet closely relates to your choice of an organization that will give you access to the Internet. This section includes an overview of these organizations first. Then you will learn about the technologies used at the connection point to the Internet, regardless of whether it is a single computer or a LAN connection.

Internet Service Providers

An Internet service provider (ISP) is an organization that provides access to the Internet for individuals and organizations. For a fee, an ISP provides you with this connection service and may offer other Internet-related services, such as Web-server hosting and email. Some ISPs specialize in certain connection types. For instance, HughesNet and Dish are both ISPs that specialize in satellite Internet services. T-Mobile (www.tmobile.com), Verizon, and AT&T all provide ISP services for their cellular customers; and your local telephone company may provide ISP services for dial-up, DSL, and cable customers. Virtually all cable TV providers also provide Internet service.

try this!

Find Internet Service Providers

You can use the Internet to find ISPs you might want to use. Try this:

1. Use your Web browser to connect to your favorite search engine, search on "Internet Service Provider," and brace yourself for a *long* list of ISPs and sites related to ISPs.

2. To find ISPs that specialize in satellite connections, for example, search on "Internet Satellite Data Service Provider."

3. Then, further refine your search to just one country by entering a country name in the search by results box.

Computer-to-Internet versus LAN-to-Internet

A local area network (LAN) is a network that covers a building, home, office, or campus. It can be wired or wireless. The traditional wired network uses Ethernet connectors and cables; Ethernet connectors are still standard on many desktops and some laptops. A Wi-Fi network is a wireless LAN (WLAN) that complies with IEEE 802.11 standards. The maximum distance covered by WLAN signals or LAN cabling is measured in hundreds of feet. Almost any computer will first connect to a LAN or WLAN, which in turn connects to a router connected (directly or indirectly) to the Internet. There is usually at least one router between your computing device and the Internet. More likely, there are many routers.

At the point of connection at home, you will have some sort of modem (cable, DSL, or analog). One port of the modem connects to a WAN connection and through that to an ISP. The other port may connect directly to a computer or, most often, to a router that in many cases is also a wireless access point

FIGURE 10–11 Connecting to the Internet from a single computer or from a LAN.

(WAP) and an Ethernet switch. Therefore, you are connecting via a WLAN (Wi-Fi) or LAN (Ethernet) to the Internet. This is also the case at school or work, only on a larger scale, because the LAN or WLAN ultimately connects through a router to a high-speed Internet connection. Figure 10–11 shows these two scenarios.

Wired Connectivity Technologies

Many wired WAN technologies for connecting to the Internet utilize the telecommunications infrastructure of the telephone system—either in its traditional state or with upgrades and equipment added to that infrastructure. Another private network often used for wired Internet connections belongs to the cable TV companies, which provide Internet access for their customers.

Dial-Up Connections Using Analog Modems

A technology that clearly takes advantage of the traditional phone system is dial-up, an inexpensive choice available to anyone with a standard phone line and an analog modem. At one time every laptop came with an internal analog modem.

Analog modems as standard equipment in laptops have gone the way of the buggy whip. Never heard of buggy whips? That's our point. However, dial-up is the only low-cost means of connecting to the Internet in remote areas of the world, including some within the United States, and millions still use dial-up, so we will devote some space to this topic.

The longtime speed standard for dial-up is 56 kilobits per second (Kbps). The dial-up connection at 56 Kbps is very slow compared to a LAN running at 100 megabits per second (Mbps) or 1 gigabit per second (Gbps). In addition to a standard phone line (what we often call a "land line") you also need to subscribe to an Internet connection service from an ISP. The cost of the ISP subscription should be your only cost in addition to your phone service. When using an analog modem you may not use the phone line simultaneously for voice or fax.

In a dial-up connection to the Internet, your computer uses its modem to dial a telephone number provided by the ISP (hence the term *dial-up connection*). One of many modems maintained by the ISP at its facility answers your computer's call; a server maintained by the ISP for authenticating customers authenticates you, and then the ISP routes traffic between your computer and the Internet for that session. Like a voice phone conversation, the connection is only temporary and ends when either your PC or the ISP's server ends the call. Most ISP servers disconnect a dial-up connection automatically after a certain period of inactivity.

High-Speed Wired Access

If multiple users need to share an Internet connection, the connection between the network and the ISP must be adequate to simultaneously carry the traffic created by all the users at peak usage times. The authors presently have a Wi-Fi router connected to a DSL modem. Through that wireless router we connect five desktop computers (three Windows PCs, one Linux computer, one iMac), two Windows laptops, two Kindles, two smartphones, an iPad, an Android tablet, an ASUS 2-in-1, a TiVO DVR, and a ROKU device. That's 15 devices for just two people. Many families exceed that number. For this you need high-speed WAN connections, such as the three wired options we describe here, or one of the wireless options detailed later.

Integrated Services Digital Network. Integrated services digital network (ISDN) is a digital telephone service that simultaneously transmits voice, data, and control signaling over a single telephone line. ISDN service operates on standard telephone lines but requires a special modem and phone service, which adds to the cost. An ISDN data connection can transfer data at up to 128,000 bits per second (128 Kbps). This seems extremely slow to most of us with faster options. While rarely used in homes in the United States, ISDN may be all that is available for a wired WAN connection in some areas, especially outside of the United States.

The benefits of ISDN (beyond the faster speed compared to a dial-up connection) include being able to connect a PC, telephone, and fax machine to a single ISDN line and use them simultaneously.

ISDN has fallen out of favor in many areas where there are higher performance options, such as cable and DSL. In remote parts of the world, another optional broadband service, satellite communications, may be a more viable option than ISDN because it does not require the wired infrastructure needed by ISDN.

Digital Subscriber Line. Digital subscriber line (DSL) service is similar to ISDN in its use of the telephone network, but it uses more advanced digital signal processing to compress more signals through the telephone lines. DSL requires component changes in the telephone network before they can offer it. DSL service can provide simultaneous data, voice, and fax transmissions on the same line. It gives you a dedicated circuit from your home or office to the central office and the service can usually guarantee consistent upload and download speeds.

Several versions of DSL services are available for home and business use. Each version provides a different level of service, speed, and distance, and each normally provides full-time connections. The two most common are asynchronous DSL (ADSL) and synchronous DSL (SDSL). ADSL is the type of service normally available to home users. Other versions include high-data-rate DSL (HDSL) and very high-data-rate DSL (VDSL). The abbreviation often used to refer to DSL service in general begins with an *x* (*x*DSL), reflecting the varied first character in the DSL implementations.

Across the DSL services offered by various ISPs, data transmission speeds range from 128 Kbps for basic DSL service through 24 Mbps for high-end service. When describing DSL speeds, they usually refer to the speed of traffic flowing "downstream"—that is, from the ISP to your computer. For instance, the authors subscribe to a rural phone company's ADSL service, which provides a downstream speed of 10 Mbps, but an upstream speed of 1 Mbps. While SDSL provides the same speed in each direction, it is much more expensive and not widely available. Most home users only require the higher speeds for downloads (browsing the Internet, downloading streaming video, and so on), so SDSL service is only practical for customers who must upload a great deal of data.

Because servers must upload a great deal of data in response to user requests, commercial Internet servers are normally hosted on much faster links than those discussed here.

Cable. Many cable television companies now use a portion of their network's bandwidth to offer Internet access through existing cable television connections. They call this Internet connection option cable modem service because of the need to use a special cable modem to connect.

Cable networks use coaxial cable, which can transmit data as much as 100 times faster than common telephone lines. Coaxial cable allows transmission over several channels simultaneously. Internet data can be on one channel while transmitting audio, video, and control signals separately. A user can access the Internet from his or her computer and watch cable television at the same time, over the same cable connection, without the two data streams interfering with one another.

The biggest drawback to cable modem service is the fact that the subscribers in a defined area share the signal. As the number of users in an area increases, less bandwidth is available to each user. Therefore, while cable providers advertise higher speeds than DSL, they cannot guarantee consistent speeds.

Wireless Connectivity Technologies

Like wired communications, wireless has moved from analog to digital over the years. Today, you can connect to the Internet through cellular networks, wireless wide area networks (WWANs), wireless LAN (WLAN) connections (if the WLAN ultimately connects to the Internet), and by satellite.

Smartphones support both voice and high-speed cellular data service, allowing users to surf the Internet from any location offering the required signal. Cellular Internet companies usually meter their connections, meaning that your plan allows only a predetermined amount of downstream data per month. Extra charges apply if you exceed the permitted amount.

In addition, modern smartphones also come with Wi-Fi. This allows users to configure their phones to use a Wi-Fi connection, when available, for connecting to a router that, in turn, is connected to the Internet, thus saving on connection and data charges from their cellular provider.

Tablets optionally have cellular communications features as well as Wi-Fi, allowing Web browsing and communicating by email and other features.

Wireless WAN Connections

A wireless wide area network (WWAN) is a digital network that extends over a large geographical area. A WWAN receives and transmits data using radio signals over cellular sites and satellites, which makes the network accessible to mobile computer systems. At the switching center, the WWAN splits off into segments and then connects to a public or private network via telephone or other high-speed communication links. The data then links to

Wireless wide area network (WWAN) structure

Laptop connected through a cellular hotspot

Company
LAN/WAN

FIGURE 10–12 A WWAN includes devices that retransmit the wireless signal.

an organization's existing LAN/WAN infrastructure (see Figure 10–12). The coverage area for a WWAN, normally measured in miles or kilometers, makes it therefore more susceptible than wired networks to environmental factors such as weather and terrain.

A WWAN is a fully bidirectional wireless network capable of data transfer at speeds in excess of 100 Mbps. Usually, basic WWAN services offer connection speeds between 1 and 10 Mbps. With dedicated equipment, the downllink speeds can reach 100 Mbps. The uplink speeds are less. A WWAN system requires an antenna tuned to receive the proper radio frequency (RF).

A cellular Internet connection is an example of a WWAN. Many cellular services offer Internet data service. In addition to using your smartphone or tablet on a cellular network, providers offer cellular hotspot plans, in which your smartphone or a separate hotspot device acts as a Wi-Fi router for your other computers and devices to access the Internet.

Satellite

Satellite connections are as suitable for large businesses as for small offices, cybercafés, individuals, homes, and the armed forces. Satellite is the WAN of choice when it is not possible or practical to use a wired connection and when cellular WAN services are not available or are too slow or costly. Satellite Internet providers offer several levels of service based on speed and they offer either stationary installations or mobile installations. The hardware cost for a mobile satellite installation is considerably higher than that for a stationary installation, and the ongoing service fees are higher, too.

Satellite Internet Connection Speeds. Like ADSL, satellite data communication is usually faster downstream than upstream. The discrepancy can be huge, as we found when we had our own mobile satellite system installed on our motor home in 2003. During our three years of living and working on the road, we often achieved download speeds of 400 Kbps to 800 Kbps (and occasionally more), but upload speeds were only in the range of 25 to 45 Kbps. While these speeds seem minimal compared to the mobile satellite options available today, the system worked well for us because, like most Internet users, our greatest need was for fast downloads as we browsed the Internet or downloaded files. At the time, cellular service was slow or simply did not exist in most locations, and so we found a mobile satellite connection was the best solution as long as we were careful not to park under trees or other obstacles to the satellite signal.

Satellite Internet Connection Costs. Today, the price of consumer-grade mobile satellite equipment and the basic monthly service fees are generally more expensive than they were in 2003. But the base plan speeds are much faster, at 3 or more Mbps down. If you are willing to spend the money on the appropriate equipment and service, you can have mobile satellite speeds of up to 5 Mbps down and 2 Mbps up.

Satellite Internet Connection Latency. Satellite communications tend to have a higher latency, or lag. Think of watching a news broadcast that includes a foreign correspondent reporting over a satellite link. The news anchor in the studio asks a question, and you see the correspondent on the screen with a frozen smile while he or she waits to hear the question in its entirety. While it is barely noticeable when someone is reporting the news, such latency is very undesirable for real-time Internet applications, such as online games. Many IT professionals consider satellite connections unreliable, but it can be the best solution for Internet communications in remote areas.

When individuals or organizations contract with an ISP for stationary satellite service, they install an Earth-based communications station. It usually includes three parts: a transceiver (a combined transmitter and receiver), a device that for simplicity we call a modem, and the satellite dish on its mount. You place the satellite dish outdoors in direct line-of-sight of one of several data satellites in geostationary orbit around the Earth. The modem connects the other components to the computer or LAN. A mobile installation (on a land- or water-based vehicle) is generally much more expensive than a stationary installation because the mount must allow for moving the dish to align on the satellite, and therefore requires controlling circuitry and a costly motor-driven mount to achieve this with precision. The monthly service plans for mobile satellite communications are also more expensive than those for stationary installations.

Because a satellite traveling in a geostationary orbit moves at the same speed as the Earth's rotation, it hovers over the same location on the Earth— therefore you can align a satellite dish antenna precisely on the satellite. The satellite links the user's satellite dish to a land-based satellite operations center, through which the signal goes to the Internet (see Figure 10–13).

WLAN Connections

A is a local area network, usually using one of the standards referred to as Wi-Fi (for wireless fidelity). The Wi-Fi standards of the Institute of Electrical and Electronics Engineers include 802.11a, 802.11b, 802.11g, 802.11n, and 802.11ac listed from oldest to newest. The maximum distance covered by a WLAN is a few hundred feet rather than miles. Therefore, this is not a technology that connects directly to an ISP (as a WWAN or satellite connection will) but can be used to connect to another LAN or device with a WAN connection. This is the technology of Internet cafés, wireless laptops, tablets, and smartphones. With enough wireless hubs, called wireless access points (WAPs), an entire community can offer wireless access to a shared Internet connection.

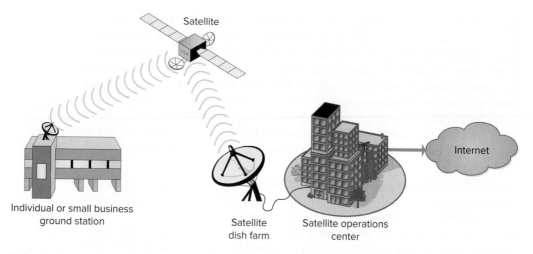

Satellite

Individual or small business
ground station

Satellite
dish farm

Satellite operations
center

Internet

FIGURE 10–13 Accessing the Internet through a satellite WAN connection.

Many of us have one of the high-speed WAN technologies described above and connect multiple devices to them through a device that is both a wireless access point (WAP) and an Internet router. The authors presently have a Wi-Fi router connected to an ADSL connection. Through that wireless router we connect all our computing devices to the Internet.

The latest IEEE 802.11 standards are both faster and more secure owing to encryption technology. Therefore, we regularly replace our Wi-Fi devices with newer ones that are up to the new standards.

Using a Virtual Private Network

Mobile users and remote offices often need to connect to a corporate intranet through the Internet using any of the connection technologies discussed earlier. You can make such a connection more secure by connecting through a virtual private network (VPN), over an existing WAN connection. Think of a VPN as a simulated private network that runs inside a "tunnel" from end point to end point. When an individual connects from a computer or mobile device we call this connection a remote access VPN (see Figure 10–14). One end is a computer connected to the Internet, while the other end is a VPN server in the private network. When two networks connect by VPN, we call it a site-to-site VPN.

VPN
client

VPN
tunnel

Internet

ISP

Corporate
VPN server

Corporate
network
servers

FIGURE 10–14 A remote access VPN.

The tunnel effect is the result of encapsulating each data packet sent at one end of the tunnel and removing it from the encapsulation at the receiving end. Because the encapsulation itself provides only a very small amount of protection VPN providers apply other measures to protect the data, such as encrypting the data, and requiring authentication at both ends of the tunnel.

Anyone who connects to the Internet while away from home, school, or work should consider using a VPN for secure access. Organizations often provide this service to their employees. Individuals can subscribe to VPN services targeted to consumers, such as Private Internet Access (PIA) or TunnelBear. This is not an endorsement of either of these services. If you are interested in protecting yourself while connected to public hotspots, research VPN services to find one that meets your needs and budget.

LO 10.3 | Using Internet Clients

The growth in the number and type of Internet services has increased the number of client types required to access those services. We will limit our discussion of Internet clients to Web browsers and email clients. Many services are accessible through Web browsers. Email may be the most important service on the Internet—many people, who have no other use for the Internet, use email.

Web Browsers

While the World Wide Web (the Web) is just one of many services that exist on the Internet, it alone is responsible for most of the huge growth in Internet use that began after the Web's introduction in the early 1990s. Web technologies changed the look of Internet content from all text to rich and colorful graphics, and made it simple to navigate the Web by using a special type of client called a Web browser. In this section, learn about common browser features and the most common browsers used on desktop and laptop computers.

Common Browser Features

The Web browser's ease of use hides the complexity of the Internet, as protocols help to transfer the content of a Web page to the user's computer. There the Web browser translates the plain-text language into a rich, colorful document that may contain links to other pages—often at disparate locations on the Internet. Today, the popular free Web browsers come in versions for OS X, Microsoft Windows, and Linux. Beyond the desktop, you'll find versions of these and other Web browsers with scaled-down screens for smartphones and tablets. In short, just about any electronic device that can connect to the Internet and has a display has some kind of browser.

Popular browsers share many of the same features for both general browsing and security. General browser features found in most browsers include:

- Active search
- Add-ons
- Autofill
- Automatic updates
- Bookmarks
- Integrated search engine
- Password manager

- Reading mode
- Personalization
- RSS feeds
- Search within page
- Synchronization
- Tabbed browsing
- Zoom

> **WARNING!**
>
> Many innocent-looking download sites are like mine fields with multiple links to malware displayed more prominently than the legitimate software you seek. Therefore, be careful when downloading and installing even the most popular software, such as the Chrome and Safari browsers. Navigate directly to the website of the publisher (Microsoft, Google, Mozilla, and Apple) and search for the download page.

Google Chrome

Google Chrome is software from the Chromium open-source project and other sources. It is in its 44th major version at this writing and has

FIGURE 10–15 Google Chrome with three tabs open across the top and the Chrome menu open on the right.

a clean look with no menu bar, but a small button on the right called the Chrome button that opens the Customize and Control menu (shown in Figure 10–15). From this menu you can access any feature you would find in a menu bar. The Settings option opens your personal settings page (saved with your Google account). The Help option connects to Chrome's online help.

Mozilla Firefox

Mozilla Firefox, a product of the Mozilla Foundation, is currently at version 41, In the latest versions of Firefox, a menu button has been added to the right side of the button bar containing the most-used functions. If you don't find what you need there, check out the menu bar. If it is not visible, press the ALT key to open it whenever you need it. If you wish to keep the menu bar visible, press ALT, select the View menu and select Toolbars. Then click to place a check by Menu Bar and any other toolbar you want to stay visible. We believe that Firefox will eventually do away with the menu bar, but until they do, it is there for those who expect it to be. Figure 10–16 shows Firefox with the menu open on the right and the menu bar visible across the top.

Internet Explorer

Microsoft introduced the Internet Explorer (IE) Web browser with the Windows 95 operating system, and IE is still bundled with Windows and available for free for Windows and OS X at the Microsoft website. Figure 10–17 shows the open Tools menu for IE version 11 running in Windows 10. As with Firefox, the IE menu bar is hidden until you press the ALT key. And, like Firefox, you can use the View options to select what toolbars you want to stay visible in IE. Microsoft's replacement for IE, Microsoft Edge, comes with Windows 10. Internet Explorer is also included with Windows 10, for use with websites that require features of IE.

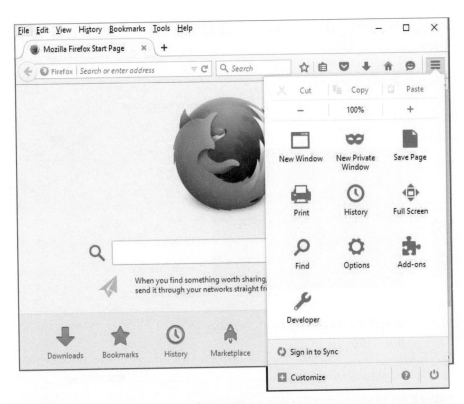

FIGURE 10–16 Mozilla Firefox with the menu open on the right and the menu bar visible across the top of the window.

FIGURE 10–17 Microsoft Internet Explorer 11 with the Tools menu open on the right.

Microsoft Edge

Microsoft Edge was introduced with Windows 10 as a replacement for IE. It is a Universal app, capable of adapting itself to all devices and screen sizes supported by Windows 10. Like Chrome, Edge has a very clean look. It will be kept up-to-date with Windows Update. Figure 10–18 shows Microsoft Edge with the menu open on the right.

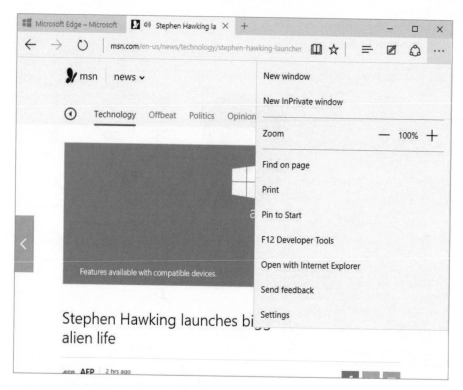

FIGURE 10–18 Microsoft Edge with its menu open.

Other Browsers

Other browsers include Opera (www.opera.com) and Apple Safari (www.apple.com/safari) for OS X and Windows PCs.

The Opera Web browser logo.

The Apple Safari browser logo.

Security and Web Browsers

Rather than dive into the details of every security setting in your Web browser, we'll define certain security threats and describe how to manage them through modern Web browsers.

Cookies. As you learned in Chapter 2, cookies are good—mostly. Under some circumstances people can use them for the wrong purposes, but for the most part, their benefits outweigh the negatives. Normally, only the website that creates the cookies can access them. However, some advertisers on websites have the browser create so-called third-party cookies, which other sites that include this advertiser can use. Look for options to manage cookies when configuring a Web browser. Figure 10–19 shows the Content settings where you can change how Chrome handles cookies.

To check out the cookies settings for Firefox click the menu button, select Options, and click the Privacy button from the sidebar (a mask).

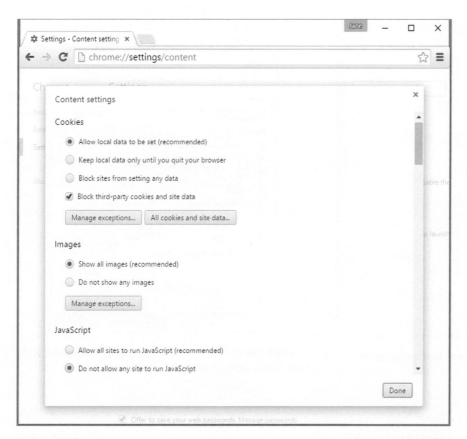

FIGURE 10–19 The Chrome Content Settings page includes settings for cookies.

Figure 10–20 shows the Firefox Privacy page with the settings for History. When you click on the down arrow in the box labeled *Firefox will*, and select *Use custom settings for history*, Firefox displays the options for controlling how it treats history and the use of Cookies. Notice that we configured it to never accept third-party cookies.

In IE, you need to dig a little deeper to find the settings for cookies. Open the Privacy page in Internet Options and click the Advanced button. On the Advanced Privacy Settings dialog box you can manage first-party and second-party cookies, with options to accept, block, or prompt you for first-party and third-party cookies, as shown in Figure 10–21.

To change the Cookies settings in Microsoft Edge click or tap the menu button on the far right of the button bar, select *Settings, Advanced Settings*. Scroll down to Cookies and select a setting. Figure 10–22 shows the advanced settings.

Browsing History. Your browsing history is useful information to marketers and others who want to learn more about you. At the same time, this information also makes life a bit easier for you when you return to favorite sites. While your browser does not divulge this information, a system compromised by spyware or malware could reveal this information to the wrong persons. Additionally, if you leave your computer unattended but logged on with your account, anyone with access to your computer could look at your browsing history; system administrators or others who have administrative access to your computer can do the same. Once again, your security needs may be at odds with your need for convenience on the Web. Therefore, Web browsers allow you to manage your browsing history.

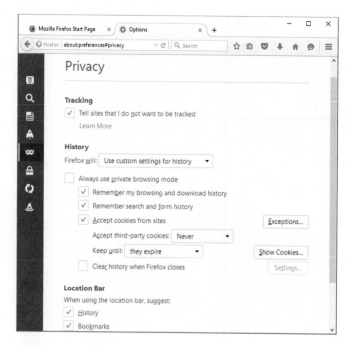

FIGURE 10–20 The Firefox privacy page with settings to protect you while browsing.

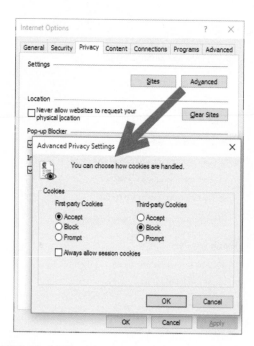

FIGURE 10–21 The Internet Explorer privacy page with settings to protect you while browsing.

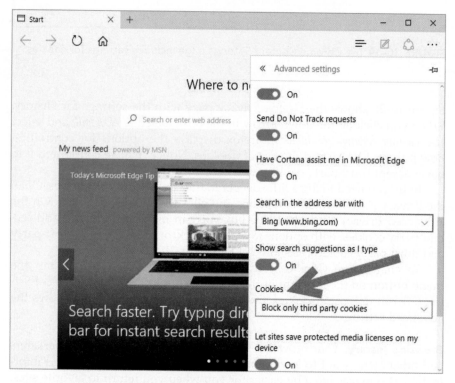

FIGURE 10–22 The Microsoft Edge Advanced Settings box.

Access the Chrome browser History page by selecting History from the Chrome menu. Figure 10–23 shows the History page. From this page you can search through the history (see button at top), clear all browsing history, and select items using the check boxes to the left of each one. Or you can click the Actions button to the right of each item, which allows you to see more items from that site (searching) or remove the item from history.

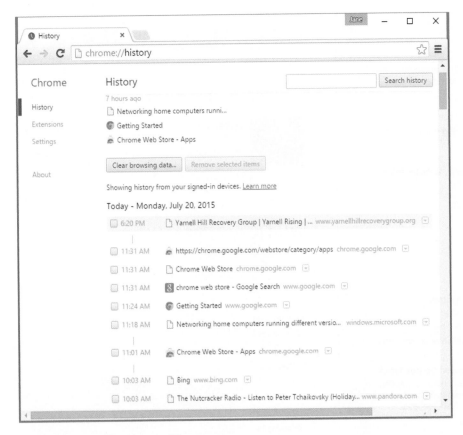

FIGURE 10–23 The Chrome History page.

In Firefox, manage browsing history settings on the Privacy page in the Options dialog box, shown previously.

In IE if you want to quickly delete all browsing history, press CTRL-SHIFT-DELETE. When the Delete Browsing History box opens (Figure 10–24) select or deselect items and then click the Delete button.

In Microsoft Edge the Hub is a bar that opens on the right of the window when you click or press the Hub button on the button bar, shown in Figure 10–25. In the Hub click on the button with the clock icon to open History. Here you can clear all history, clear history in a certain time frame, or expand a time frame and select items to clear.

Private Browsing. Private browsing is a browser security feature that allows you to browse the Web without saving any history on the local computer. All of the browsers discussed here offer private browsing. When you turn on private browsing you open a new window, and your protection exists as long as you remain in that window, even as you open new tabs within the window. Always use private browsing when you use a shared computer, as in a library or school lab.

Chrome's name for private browsing is incognito. To start a private browsing session in Chrome select **new incognito window** from the Chrome menu or use the shortcut CTRL-SHIFT-N. Then notice the icon in the upper-left corner, shown here, resembling a man with dark glasses and hat peering down on your folders. As long as this is present you are browsing incognito in Chrome.

Firefox simply calls the feature Private Browsing, and to use it click on the menu button on the right side of the button bar and select **New Private**

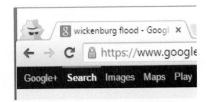

While a Chrome incognito window is open, this character at the upper left watches over the window.

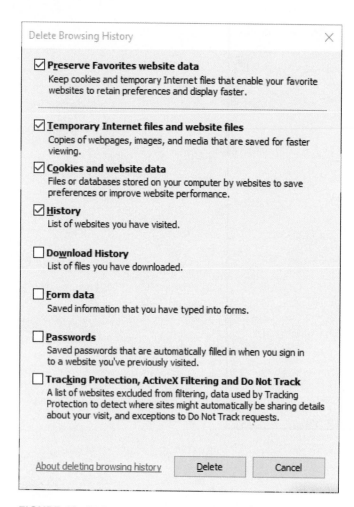

FIGURE 10–24 Press CTRL-SHIFT-DELETE to open the Internet Explorer Delete Browsing History page.

FIGURE 10–25 In Microsoft Edge open History in the Hub to manage browsing history.

A purple mask appears at the top of a Firefox Private Browsing window.

Internet Explorer InPrivate Browsing window.

Window or use the shortcut CTRL-SHIFT-P. The Firefox Private Browsing window is clearly marked, with a purple mask on the top of the window, as shown here.

Both Microsoft Edge and Internet Explorer call private browsing InPrivate Browsing. In Internet Explorer open the Tools menu and select InPrivate Browsing. In Microsoft Edge click the menu button on the far right of the button bar and select *New InPrivate window*. When you open an InPrivate window in either browser, the address box is clearly labeled, as shown here. It opens a page that alerts you that InPrivate is turned on and provides a link to online information about this feature, which opens in a new InPrivate browsing window. When you are ready to continue browsing, simply enter a universal resource locator (URL) or a search string in the address box.

Passwords. Do you like to have your browser remember your password to websites, or would you rather enter your user name and password every time you access a site? While it is convenient to have the browser remember passwords, this practice is a security risk if your computer is not protected with a strong password, or if you leave your computer unattended while you are logged in. Configure the browser password settings that work best for you.

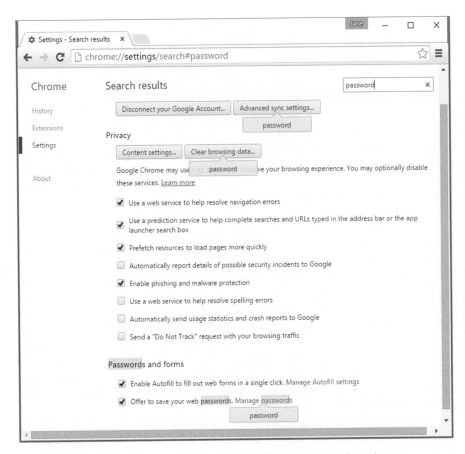

FIGURE 10–26 The Search results from searching on **password** in Chrome Settings.

In Chrome open the Chrome menu and select Settings. In Settings enter **password** in the search box. The search results will resemble Figure 10–26, showing all the settings having to do with passwords in Chrome. The first one is for synchronizing your settings across your devices, a handy feature if you sign in to Chrome with a Google account and want all your Google preferences synchronized across your devices. If you click on the **Clear browsing data** button, a dialog box opens that allows you to select what browsing data to clear. The last section in the Search results for password is the section Passwords and forms. The first setting allows you to enable Autofill with information such as your mailing address, so if you start typing this into a form in the Chrome browser, it will complete it. Finally, the last item includes the link **Manage saved passwords**. Click on this to see what passwords are saved and to delete those you no longer want to save.

Manage passwords in Firefox on the Options Security page where you can add a master password to your password list by clicking to place a "√" by **Use a master password**. That opens the dialog box shown in Figure 10–27. If you decide to set a password, it will prompt you to enter it once per Firefox session in which Firefox retrieves a password for a website.

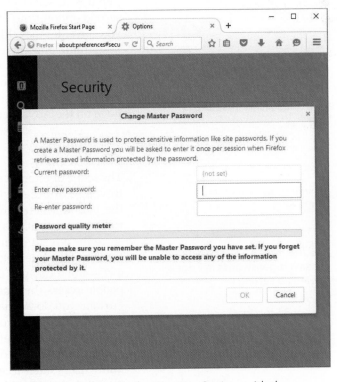

FIGURE 10–27 The Firefox Security Options with the Change Master Password dialog box open.

FIGURE 10–28 The Internet Explorer AutoComplete Settings dialog box.

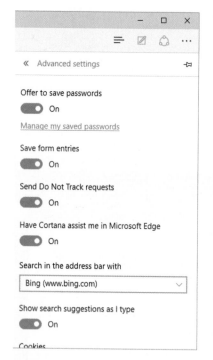

FIGURE 10–29 Select **Manage my saved passwords** in Edge's Advanced settings.

Back in the Security dialog box click on the Saved Passwords button to see and manage the saved passwords.

Internet Explorer also saves passwords and other information you enter at websites. To turn this on select Internet Options from the tools menu. In Internet Options open the **Content** tab and then select **Settings** under AutoComplete. Figure 10–28 shows the AutoComplete Settings dialog box in Windows 10. Select the types of entries you want AutoComplete to save.

In Microsoft Edge open Advanced settings and select **Manage my saved passwords** (Figure 10–29). This will open a list of websites with your user name for each site. Click on a website to make changes to your username or password.

Pop-Ups. We've all seen them. Those windows that pop up on top of your browser from a website advertising products, wanting to show you videos, or any number of excuses to get your attention and interrupt your stream of thought. We call them pop-ups, and not all pop-ups are bad. Some of our favorite websites use pop-up windows to open something we requested, such as a downloaded page or a login page, but the latest standard for creating Web pages discourages pop-ups because they do not work on all platforms and they interfere with assistive browsing technologies. Therefore, the use of pop-ups should wane in coming years. For the foreseeable future software that blocks pop-ups is necessary, but it also needs to be configurable so you can block pop-ups from all but the sites you trust.

To access the Pop-up settings for Chrome click on the menu button on the far right of the button bar, then click **Settings**. In the Settings page, scroll down to the bottom and click **Show advanced settings**. This expands the settings. Under **Privacy** click the **Content settings** button and then scroll down through the Content settings list to **Pop-ups**. Here you can either allow all sites to show pop-ups or select **Do not allow any site to show pop-ups**. If you select the second option, you can click the Manage exceptions button to open a box where you can enter the URLs of sites that you will allow to show pop-ups.

Firefox and Internet Explorer also allow you to enable/disable pop-ups and have exceptions when you enable it. Configure Firefox's pop-up blocker on the **Content** page of the **Options** dialog box and configure IE's on the **Privacy** page of Internet Options. Turn on the pop-up blocker in Microsoft Edge on the Advanced Settings page.

Email Clients

The scope of Internet email has made several major jumps in the past decades. It evolved from a service used by academics and government workers, through the period when early PC users accessed services such as CompuServ, to today's casual PC users, numbered in the billions, who joined the Internet since the advent of the World Wide Web in 1991. Because of the explosion in the use of the Internet, email has long been the most compelling reason to own a PC—but today you do not need to use a PC to send and receive email. Many people access their personal and business email from their mobile devices. Further, you do not need to own the device you use for Internet access.

An email client used in a school or corporate network may be specific to the private mail servers the user connects to, such as Microsoft Exchange, or the client may be one that you can use for different types of mail servers. Many users have access to email client software such as Microsoft Outlook, Apple Mail, or Mozilla Thunderbird. Users who subscribe to Web mail or free email services such as Gmail, MSN, or Yahoo! can use a Web browser rather than special email client software. Regardless of the type of client software, they all accomplish the task of sending and receiving in the same way.

The client software will show a list of all of the messages in the mailbox by displaying information it reads from the message headers. The message header is information added to the beginning of the message that contains details such as who sent it and the subject, and also may show the time and date of the message along with the message's size. Then the user may click on a message to open it and read the body of the email. Users can then respond to the message, save the message, create a new message, add attachments, and/or send it to the intended recipient.

Email clients have become much easier to use, even to the point of automatically detecting and configuring the underlying settings for connecting to an email server, given your personal account information. They also will import your email and contact information from other accounts.

Email Protocols

There are three types of email accounts: POP, IMAP, and Web mail. The first two are protocols, while the third describes email that you access via the Web, and therefore, the protocol is some form of HTTP. When you configure an email client, you need to know the address and type of server, defined by the account type.

POP. Post Office Protocol (POP) is a protocol that enables email client computers to pick up email from mail servers, so that you can open it and read it in your email client. When it picks up a message, it deletes it from the POP server. The current version is POP3. This has been very popular with ISPs because it minimizes the amount of disk space required on the email server for each account. The user is responsible for maintaining and backing up messages. When the client computer does not connect to the email server, the user can still access all the locally stored messages.

IMAP. Internet Message Access Protocol (IMAP) is a protocol that will allow users to maintain the messages stored on an email server (usually on the Internet) without removing them from the server. This type of account allows you to log in and access your message store from any computer. Of course, the message store is not available to you when you are offline, and you may run out of allotted disk space on the mail server, at which point it rejects new messages.

Web Mail. Web mail is a generic term for using a Web browser (and therefore, either HTTPS or HTTP) to retrieve email, often replacing the traditional email client, such as Microsoft Outlook. In fact, this may be the method the tech support at school or work instructs you to use, allowing you to access your email from any browser on any device. With the increase in Internet hosting services offering a wide range of services, many individuals as well as both small and large organizations have their own Internet domains. The hosting services typically include hosting and management of both websites and email accounts for each domain. To do that, consult the Help utility at the provider.

Configuring and Using an Email Client

Whether you use Outlook, Apple Mail, or one of many third-party email clients, you should be prepared with the information to configure your email client. This includes:

- The protocol used by the mail server you are accessing (POP3, IMAP, HTTPS, or HTTP).
- Your account name and password.

Note: A variation on a pop-up is a pop-under, a window that opens behind your browser window. Anytime you close a browser window and are puzzled to see a browser window (usually with an advertisement) lurking behind it, you have encountered a pop-under. These are also controlled through the pop-up settings for each browser.

Note: Don't confuse Microsoft Outlook, the email client, with Microsoft Outlook .com, the Web mail service.

- The DNS name of the incoming mail server.
- If you are preparing to connect to a POP3 or IMAP server you will also need to know the name of an outgoing mail server.

If you do not have this information, ask your ISP, in the case of a private account, or ask a network administrator if your mail server is a school or corporate mail server. ISPs often provide email configuration information on their websites. Check this out before configuring your email client because it will help you avoid certain pitfalls. For instance, when configuring a client using a cell data connection you may have to configure it to authenticate to a certain mail server in the home service area.

In Step-by-Step 10.02 we use Microsoft Outlook 2016 to demonstrate how to configure an email account. Although we stated that you need the information listed above, you might be lucky because email clients, such as Apple Mail and Outlook, can automatically configure some types of email accounts given just the user name and password. This is where you should start. Then, if that doesn't work, use the other information you gathered.

Step-by-Step 10.02

Connecting a Client to an Email Account

To complete this step-by-step exercise you will need a PC with an Internet connection and an email client. In this exercise we use Microsoft Outlook 2016 running on a Mac. The basic steps are similar in other email clients. We assume you are adding an account and that the email client already has one account configured. If this is the first account for this email client, you may have introductory screens that will walk you through the process. To complete the exercise you will need the first two items listed here for all accounts, and the last four only if the client fails to automatically connect to your account with the basic login information.

- The type of account.
- Your password, account name, and email address. The last two are often just the email address.
- The DNS names of the outgoing and incoming mail server.
- The DNS name or IP address of an incoming mail server for POP3, IMAP, or HTTP.
- The DNS name or IP address of an outgoing mail server (SMTP).
- If using a provider, such as Gmail, you may need to change the settings for your Gmail account to allow IMAP access.

Step 1

Locate the option for adding an account. In Outlook first select the Tools ribbon, and then select Accounts on the far left of the ribbon.

Step 2

In the Accounts dialog box locate the list of accounts and click the plus (+) button at the bottom to open the **Add New Account** page.

Step 3

Select the account type.

Step 4

If you select Exchange or Office 365, enter the account information on the following page. Click the scroll button on the right of the **Method** box to select an authentication method.

Step 5

If you select **Other Email**, try using just your email address and password. If that fails, enter the information you obtained from your provider. For instance, we have an account with our hosted domain, so we had to enter the names of the incoming and outgoing mail servers. *Note:* Identifying information is obscured in this image.

Step 6

If you connect to this email account from multiple devices, you should configure the email clients on each device to leave messages on the server. To do that in Outlook, select the Advanced button in the Account page, shown in step 5, and choose if and when you want messages deleted on the server. Outlook 2016 also allows you to delete messages individually from Inbox.

Step 7

Select **Security** to enable digital signing and encryption if supported by your email provider.

FTP Clients

We use **File Transfer Protocol (FTP)** to transfer files between a computer running the FTP server service and an FTP client. It is a simple and fast method for transferring files over a TCP/IP network, such as the Internet. Before the advent of the World Wide Web and the use of GUI tools for working on the Internet, people used character-mode FTP clients because that was all there was. Because of the tremendous growth in the number of Internet and Web users, we now have a variety of GUI FTP client programs. You can even use some of the popular Web browsers as FTP clients, although programs designed specifically as FTP clients are usually easier to use and allow you to save the connection settings, including (but not limited to) the URL for the site, user name, and password.

Note: FTP services have not completely disappeared, but they have diminished in importance since the advent of such cloud-based file storage services as Dropbox, OneDrive, and Google Drive. These services offer many more features, appealing to both organizations and individuals.

Anonymous FTP

An **anonymous FTP site** does not require a user name and password, and all users connecting are using the Anonymous account, which may mean they can only read and copy the files from the FTP site but cannot copy files to the site. It is simple to connect to such a site using your browser by entering the URL, including the protocol suffix, **ftp**. You can download by selecting and copying files from the site, but we don't recommend that you do this from an unfamiliar FTP site.

try this!

Find FTP Sites

Look for lists of FTP sites on the Internet. Try this:

1. Use your Web browser to connect to your favorite search engine and search on "FTP sites."
2. Browse through the results. Notice that many of the results are links to compiled lists of sites, often organized by topic.

Configuring an FTP Client

When connecting to an FTP site that requires a user name and password, you can use a Web browser and the site will prompt you to log in. A Web browser is fine for connecting to an FTP site you will visit only once, but when you wish to save the site settings, or manage settings for many FTP sites, you should find a free or commercial FTP client that suits your needs. A quick search of "FTP client" using an Internet search engine will yield a long list of clients. The free Mozilla FireFTP, an add-on to Mozilla Firefox, is a favorite of ours. To configure an FTP client you will need:

- The host name of the FTP server.
- A user ID and password.

You may also need to know if the FTP server allows passive mode connections and/or secure (SSL) connections. Figure 10–30 shows FireFTP. The left pane is open to the local hard drive, while the right pane shows the contents of a folder on the FTP site.

LO 10.4 | Sharing Files and Printers

File and printer sharing allows users to share and access files and printers over a network. All the OSs discussed in this book have methods for allowing file and printer sharing. There are two sides to file and printer sharing: the server side and the client side, and before you implement either side of this equation, take a few minutes to understand how they interact. Both sides must use complementary file and printer services that can talk to each other. Then you can implement sharing on the server side (even on a desktop computer) and users can access it from the client side. For our examples we'll use Microsoft Windows 7.

FIGURE 10–30 The user interface of FireFTP.

The Server Side of File and Printer Sharing

A file and printer server (often simply called a file server), is a computer that gives client computers access to files and printers over a network. The actual folder or printer being shared acts as a connecting point on the server and is called a share. A share is visible as a folder over the network, but it is a separate entity from the disk folder or printer to which it points. Like other file-sharing services, the one installed with Windows allows you to share both files and printers. This service is installed and enabled by default, although it is up to you to decide how to use it. On a Windows desktop computer, look for File and Printer Sharing for Microsoft Networks in the Properties dialog box for a network connection, as shown in Figure 10–31.

The Client Side of File and Printer Sharing

A file and printer client includes both the user interface and the underlying file-sharing protocols to access its matching file-sharing server service on a network server. The client for Microsoft file and printer sharing is installed and enabled by default. With the client installed, you can use the Windows GUI to see those Microsoft computers on the network that have file and printer sharing turned on. You can see both dedicated Windows network servers and Windows desktops that have this service turned on. Your ability to connect to any shares on those computers depends on the permissions applied to each share. Figure 10–32 shows four computers and a printer (EPSON0E0C4E) that are visible because they have the file and printer service turned on.

With appropriate permissions, you will be able to browse to the shared folders on a server and perform file operations, such as copying, moving, deleting, and opening files in your locally installed applications.

Sharing Files and Printers with Windows HomeGroups

To illustrate how to share files and printers from your Windows desktop we will use the HomeGroup feature introduced in Windows 7.

Note: As a rule, a desktop computer should not have File and Printer Sharing turned on, especially if the computer is a member of a domain and connects to dedicated servers for file and printer services. The exception to this is when a desktop computer is participating in a HomeGroup or work group and must share local files and printers with other computers. This is common in the small office/home office (SOHO) situation.

FIGURE 10–31 File and Printer Sharing for Microsoft Networks is listed for a network connection.

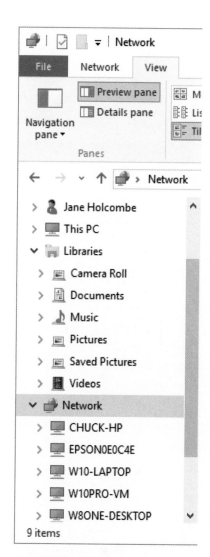

FIGURE 10–32 The computers and printer listed at the bottom under Network have File and Printer Sharing turned on.

Sharing with HomeGroups

HomeGroup is an easy-to-configure implementation of Microsoft's file and printer sharing, with only a single password protecting the HomeGroup shares on all Windows computers that join a HomeGroup. You only have to enter the password once on every client computer in the HomeGroup when it first joins the HomeGroup. All editions of Windows 8, 8.1, and 10 can create a HomeGroup, but only certain editions of Windows 7 can create a HomeGroup. They are Windows 7 Home Premium, Professional, Ultimate, and Enterprise editions. Beyond this, there are several requirements and restrictions:

- Versions of Windows prior to Windows 7 cannot participate in HomeGroups.
- A Windows computer can belong to only one HomeGroup at a time, and only one HomeGroup can exist on one LAN or WLAN.
- Windows computers that are part of a Windows Active Directory Domain cannot create a HomeGroup but they can join one.

try this!

Find Microsoft File and Printer Servers

You can use Windows Explorer in Windows 7 or open File Explorer on newer versions of Windows to look for the file and printer servers on your network. Try this:

1. Open Windows Explorer/File Explorer.
2. Browse to the Network folder in the left pane.
3. View the icons in the contents pane. The icons resembling a computer with a blue screen are file and printer servers.
4. If any file and printer servers are visible, double-click one to access it and browse. If you do not have permissions, you will see a Network Error message. If you have permissions to a server, you will be able to browse the folders to which you have permissions.

FIGURE 10–33 Open Network and Sharing and ensure that your computer is a member of a Home network (Windows 7) or a Private network (Windows 8 and newer).

- To create or join a HomeGroup a Windows 7 computer must connect to a Home network location (see Figure 10–33). Windows 8 or newer must connect to a Private network (the new name for the same location).
- IPv6 must be enabled on participating computers, and all firewalls between HomeGroup computers must support IPv6 and allow file and printer sharing. IPv6 is enabled by default in Windows, as well in the Windows Firewall.
- When you join a HomeGroup you decide what, if any, local libraries and printers you will share with the HomeGroup.

Step-by-Step 10.03

Creating and Joining a HomeGroup

Create a HomeGroup to share your local files and printers with others on your home or small business network. The screenshots are from a Windows 7 computer, but the steps will work on newer versions of Windows. The exercise will not work if a HomeGroup already exists on the network. To complete this exercise you will need the following:

- Windows 7 Home Premium, Professional, Ultimate, or Enterprise edition or a newer version of Windows. The computer must not be joined to a Windows Active Directory Domain.
- The computer must connect to a Home network (Open Network and Sharing Center to confirm).

Step 1

From the Start menu or Start screen enter HomeGroup in the Search box and select HomeGroup from the results list. On the HomeGroup page click Create a HomeGroup.

Step 2

The first page of the Create a HomeGroup wizard lists your personal folders and any local printer with checks for those that are shared and empty check boxes for those that are not shared. By default, Windows does not share your Documents folder. Select what you would like to share, and click Next.

Step 3

Windows will generate a password for your HomeGroup. Write it down or use the link to print the password and instructions. You will need to enter the password on the other computers on your network as you join them to the HomeGroup. After writing down or printing out the password, click the Finish button. *Note:* If you lose the password you can open Home-Group on any computer that has successfully joined and view it.

Step 4

Go to another Windows computer on your network, and from the Start menu or Start screen enter "homegroup" in the Search box. Then click Join now and follow the instructions to enter the HomeGroup password.

LO 10.5 | Troubleshooting Common Network Client Problems

If you are unable to access another computer on the network, several command-line utilities will help in pinpointing the source of a problem and arriving at a solution. In this section you will learn to troubleshoot common client connection problems using each of these utilities, as indicated by the symptoms. Each utility provides different information and is most valuable when used appropriately. For instance, you should first view the IP configuration using the **ipconfig** or **ifconfig** utility and verify that it is correct for the network to which you are connected. If you discover any obvious problems when you view the IP configuration, correct them before proceeding. Then test the ability to communicate using the **ping** command. Here you will practice this procedure and a few others.

Built-In Network Diagnostics

Each of the operating systems surveyed in this book has a variety of utilities for diagnosing network problems. From the command-line utilities discussed later in this section to GUI tools that combine the functions of several tools into one broad-stroke diagnostics tool, each generation of OS brings improvements in these tools. In Windows 7 and Windows 8, the Windows Network Diagnostics, the Windows 7 version of which is shown in Figure 10–34, will diagnose the problem area (the broadband modem in this example) and instruct you on how to solve the problem. Similarly, if your Internet connection fails, the Network Diagnostics window will display and attempt to diagnose the problem.

The Network Utility in OS X, shown in Figure 10–35, requires more knowledge of the individual tools, but it does spare you from entering the commands from the OS X Terminal window.

Testing IP Configurations and Connectivity

When the TCP/IP suite is installed on a computer, it includes many protocols and many handy little programs that network professionals quickly learn to use. You should learn two right away, for those times when you find yourself sitting at your computer and talking to a network professional while trying to resolve a network problem. These are commands you enter at a command line. In Windows these commands are **ipconfig** and **ping**. In OS X and Linux they are **ifconfig** and **ping**. Learn about these commands below, and then do Step-by-Step 10.04, in which you will use both of these commands to test a network connection.

Verifying IP Configuration with ipconfig

The **ipconfig** command will display the IP configuration of all network interface cards, including those that receive their addresses and configuration through DHCP. Using this command shows whether the IP settings have been successfully bound to your network adapter. *Bound* means that

FIGURE 10–34 The Windows 7 Network Diagnostics tool.

there is a linking relationship, called a binding, between network components—in this case, between the network protocol and the adapter. A binding establishes the order in which each network component handles network communications. When troubleshooting network connectivity problems on an IP network, always use the **ipconfig** command to verify the IP configuration.

If the **ipconfig** command reveals an address beginning with 169.254, it is an APIPA address and a symptom of a failure of a Windows DHCP client to receive an IP address from a DHCP server (for whatever reason). Troubleshoot the DHCP server on your network (such as the DHCP service in a broadband router).

Troubleshooting Connection Errors with the ping Command

The **ping** command is useful for testing the communications between two computers. The name of this command is actually an acronym for packet Internet groper, but we prefer to think (as many do) that it was named after the sound of underwater sonar. Instead of bouncing sound waves off surfaces, the **ping** command uses data packets, and it sends them to specific IP addresses, requesting a response (hence the idea of pinging). This is a great test to see if you can access a certain computer.

To use the **ping** command, give it an address and it sends packets to the specified address, "listens" for a reply, and then displays the results.

1. Pinging the IP address of the computer's own NIC and receiving a successful response indicates that the IP protocol and the local address is working. Using the example in Figure 10–36, from Host_1-1 you would type: **ping 192.168.1.101** to ping the local NIC.

2. Then ping another computer on the same network to test the ability to communicate between the two computers. Again, from Host_1-1 you would type **ping 192.168.1.102** to ping Host_1-2, a computer on the same network.

FIGURE 10–35 The OS X Network Utility at work (notice the various network diagnostic tools listed across the top).

FIGURE 10–36 Two networks connected by a router.

3. Next, ping the gateway address to ensure that your computer can communicate with the router. Again, working from Host_1-1 in Figure 10–36, type **ping 192.168.1.1** to ping the gateway address for Network 1, which is the address of the router interface (NIC) connected to Network 1.

4. Finally, ping an address beyond your network, to test the router and the ability to communicate with a computer via the router. Using Figure 10–36, from Host_1-1 type **ping 192.168.2.101** to ping the address of Host_2-1 on Network 2.

Now the bad news about the **ping** command. First, a firewall can block specific types of traffic or configure an individual computer not to respond to a ping. Hence, you may not be able to ping a computer, even if you can communicate with that same computer in other ways such as by Web browsing or downloading email.

The reason firewalls or individual computers block or ignore the requests from a **ping** command is because people can use this command in malicious ways—most notoriously in a denial of service (DoS) attack, in which someone sends a large number of ping requests to an address, overwhelming the server so that it is unavailable to accept other traffic.

Step-by-Step 10.04
Testing an IP Configuration

In this step-by-step exercise, you will look at the IP configuration settings to determine whether they are automatic or static; then you will test the current configuration. The first test will let you confirm that you can communicate with a computer on your network, and the second test will confirm that you can communicate with a router on your network. The last test will confirm that you can communicate with a computer beyond your network. To complete this exercise, you will need the following:

● A computer with Windows.

● A working connection to the Internet.

● The IP address of another computer on your local network (use this when a step asks for *NearbyIPaddress*). Enter this in the appropriate line in step 3.

● The IP address of a computer beyond your local network (use this when a step asks for *RemoteIPaddress*). Enter this in the appropriate line in step 3.

● The user name and password of an account that is a member of your computer's Administrators group.

Step 1

Check out your current IP configuration using the **ipconfig** command. To do that, first open a Command Prompt by selecting Start | Run, and in the Open dialog box, type "**cmd**" and press ENTER. Type **ipconfig /all** at the Command Prompt.

```
C:\Documents and Settings\Jane>ipconfig /all

Windows IP Configuration

        Host Name . . . . . . . . . . . . : Wickenburg
        Primary Dns Suffix  . . . . . . . :
        Node Type . . . . . . . . . . . . : Hybrid
        IP Routing Enabled. . . . . . . . : No
        WINS Proxy Enabled. . . . . . . . : No

Ethernet adapter Local Area Connection:

        Connection-specific DNS Suffix  . :
        Description . . . . . . . . . . . : Realtek RTL8139/810x Family Fast Eth
ernet NIC
        Physical Address. . . . . . . . . : 08-00-46-A7-29-3B
        Dhcp Enabled. . . . . . . . . . . : No
        IP Address. . . . . . . . . . . . : 192.168.100.48
        Subnet Mask . . . . . . . . . . . : 255.255.255.0
        Default Gateway . . . . . . . . . : 192.168.100.1
        DNS Servers . . . . . . . . . . . : 192.168.100.1

C:\Documents and Settings\Jane>
```

Step 2

If the current settings show an IP address other than 0.0.0.0, IP has successfully bound an IP address to the network adapter. If the current settings include DHCP enabled = **Yes**, and shows an IP address for a DHCP server, then your network adapter is configured to receive an address automatically and has received its address from the DHCP server whose address is listed. If your DHCP Enabled setting = **No** and your computer has a set of values for the IP address and subnet mask, then it has a static IP configuration that is successfully bound to the network adapter.

Step 3

Gather the information from the **ipconfig /all** command and fill in the first three lines provided below. Your instructor will give you the last two items, *NearbyIPaddress* and *RemoteIPaddress*. You will need these addresses in the following steps.

    IPaddress: _____

    Default GatewayIPaddress: _____

    DNSServerIPaddress: _____

    NearbyIPaddress: _____

    RemoteIPaddress: _____

Step 4

At the Command Prompt, enter **ping** *IPaddress*, where *"IPaddress"* is the address of your computer from step 3. You should receive four replies if your computer is properly configured. If you receive an error message or fewer than four replies, report this to your instructor.

Step 5

At the Command Prompt, enter **ping** *NearbyIPaddress*, where *"NearbyIPaddress"* is the address of another computer on your same network. You should receive four replies if your computer is properly configured and if the other computer is also powered up and properly configured. If you receive an error message or fewer than four replies, report this to your instructor.

```
C:\Documents and Settings\Jane>ping 192.168.100.48

Pinging 192.168.100.48 with 32 bytes of data:

Reply from 192.168.100.48: bytes=32 time<1ms TTL=128
Reply from 192.168.100.48: bytes=32 time<1ms TTL=128
Reply from 192.168.100.48: bytes=32 time<1ms TTL=128
Reply from 192.168.100.48: bytes=32 time<1ms TTL=128

Ping statistics for 192.168.100.48:
    Packets: Sent = 4, Received = 4, Lost = 0 (0% loss),
Approximate round trip times in milli-seconds:
    Minimum = 0ms, Maximum = 0ms, Average = 0ms

C:\Documents and Settings\Jane>_
```

Step 6

If the last test was successful, and if your computer has a gateway address, test this address now. Return to the Command Prompt and enter **ping** *Default gatewayIPaddress*, where *"Default gatewayIPaddress"* equals the Default Gateway address recorded in step 3. You should receive four replies if your computer is properly configured and if the default gateway is active on your network.

```
C:\Documents and Settings\Jane>ping 192.168.100.1

Pinging 192.168.100.1 with 32 bytes of data:

Reply from 192.168.100.1: bytes=32 time<1ms TTL=128
Reply from 192.168.100.1: bytes=32 time=1ms TTL=128
Reply from 192.168.100.1: bytes=32 time<1ms TTL=128
Reply from 192.168.100.1: bytes=32 time<1ms TTL=128

Ping statistics for 192.168.100.1:
    Packets: Sent = 4, Received = 4, Lost = 0 (0% loss),
Approximate round trip times in milli-seconds:
    Minimum = 0ms, Maximum = 1ms, Average = 0ms

C:\Documents and Settings\Jane>
```

If your IP configuration includes the address of a DNS server, you should test connectivity to the DNS server now. Return to the Command Prompt and enter **ping** *DNSServerIPaddress*, where "*DNSServerIPaddress*" equals the DNSServer address recorded in step 3. You should receive four replies if your computer is properly configured and if the default gateway is active on your network.

Step 8

If you were given the address of a computer beyond your local network, test this address now by returning to the Command Prompt and entering **ping** *RemoteIPaddress*, where "*RemoteIPaddress*" is the address of the remote computer.

Note: The equivalent command in Linux or OS X Terminal is **traceroute**.

Troubleshooting Connection Problems with tracert

You may have situations in which you can connect to a website or other remote resource, but the connection is very slow. If this connection is critical to business, you will want to gather information so that a network administrator or ISP can troubleshoot the source of the bottleneck. You can use the **tracert** command to gather this information. **tracert** is a command-line utility that traces the route taken by packets to a destination. When you use this command with the name or IP address of the target host, it will **ping** each of the intervening routers, from the nearest to the farthest, as shown in Figure 10–37. You see the length of the delay at each router, and you will be able to determine the location of the bottleneck. You can then provide this information to the people who will troubleshoot it for you. Consider a scenario in which your connection to the Google search engine (www .google.com) is extremely slow. You can use this command to run **tracert** and save the results to a file: **tracert www.google.com tracegoogle.txt**.

try this!

Use tracert

You can use **tracert** to determine where a problem is occurring. Try this:

1. Open a Command Prompt.
2. Type **tracert www.google.com.**
3. If the command runs successfully, you will see output similar to Figure 10–37, but with different intervening routers.

Troubleshooting DNS Errors Using ping, netstat, and nslookup

Have you ever attempted to browse to a Web page, only to have your browser display an error message such as "Cannot find server or DNS Error"? This

Note: If you want to save a copy of the information displayed by a command-line command (such as **tracert**), you can send the screen output of this command to a text file, using the command-line redirection symbol (>). You can use any file name and any path to which you have write access. For instance, type **tracert www.google .com >tracegoogle.txt**. No output will appear on the screen.

```
C:\>tracert www.google.com

Tracing route to www.google.akadns.net [216.239.41.99]
over a maximum of 30 hops:

  1    <1 ms    <1 ms    <1 ms  192.168.100.1
  2   858 ms   810 ms   812 ms  hh1095067.direcpc.com [205.177.62.67]
  3   875 ms   819 ms   807 ms  dpc6682016181.direcpc.com [66.82.16.181]
  4   803 ms   746 ms   872 ms  dpc6682016073.direcpc.com [66.82.16.73]
  5   749 ms   820 ms   747 ms  so-5-1.hsa1.Washington1.Level3.net [63.215.128.129]
  6   806 ms   867 ms   879 ms  ge-9-2.ipcolo2.Washington1.Level3.net [4.68.121.172]

  7   815 ms   806 ms   760 ms  unknown.Level3.net [166.90.148.174]
  8   749 ms   812 ms   811 ms  216.239.47.69
  9   821 ms   805 ms   812 ms  216.239.47.154
 10   871 ms   747 ms   811 ms  216.239.48.77
 11   755 ms   867 ms   880 ms  216.239.41.99

Trace complete.

C:\>_
```

FIGURE 10–37 The tracert results.

may be a name resolution problem because the fully qualified domain name (FQDN) portion of a URL, such as www.google.com, must be resolved to an IP address before a single packet goes to the website.

Using the ping Command to Troubleshoot DNS

One way to test if the problem is a connectivity problem or a DNS error is to first test for connectivity by either pinging the IP address of the website or using the IP address in place of the FQDN in the URL. If you cannot reach the website by using its IP address, then it is a connectivity problem and you should resolve it by contacting your network administrator or ISP and telling them the symptoms and the results of the **ping** test.

If you can reach the website by pinging the IP address but cannot access it through your browser, then it is a name resolution problem. A simple test to see if DNS name resolution is working is to ping the FQDN. Figure 10–38 shows the result of pinging the FQDN www.google.com. Notice that this displays the IP address of the website, confirming the DNS name-to-IP address resolution is working.

Troubleshooting with the netstat Command

When you are troubleshooting networking problems, it is very helpful to have a second computer that does not display the same problems. Then you can use the second computer to discover the IP address of a website by using your browser to connect. Once connected, you can use the **netstat** command to discover the IP address of the website. **netstat** displays network statistics, protocol statistics, and information about current TCP/IP connections. Figure 10–39 shows the result of running the **netstat** command after connecting to a website with a browser. The IP address for this website, www.google.com, is shown under Foreign Address, and the protocol used to connect to the website, http, is shown after the colon.

```
C:\>ping www.google.com

Pinging www.google.akadns.net [216.239.41.104] with 32 bytes of data:

Reply from 216.239.41.104: bytes=32 time=923ms TTL=245
Reply from 216.239.41.104: bytes=32 time=856ms TTL=245
Reply from 216.239.41.104: bytes=32 time=855ms TTL=245
Reply from 216.239.41.104: bytes=32 time=858ms TTL=245

Ping statistics for 216.239.41.104:
    Packets: Sent = 4, Received = 4, Lost = 0 (0% loss),
Approximate round trip times in milli-seconds:
    Minimum = 855ms, Maximum = 923ms, Average = 873ms

C:\>
```

FIGURE 10–38 Pinging the FQDN www.google.com reveals the IP address.

```
C:\>netstat

Active Connections

  Proto  Local Address          Foreign Address        State
  TCP    Wickenburg:1175        216.239.41.104:http    ESTABLISHED

C:\>
```

FIGURE 10–39 The netstat command displays the IP address and protocol information of current connections.

```
C:\>nslookup
*** Can't find server name for address 192.168.100.1: Non-existent domain
*** Default servers are not available
Default Server:  UnKnown
Address:  192.168.100.1

>  _
```

FIGURE 10–40 The **nslookup** command reveals a DNS problem.

Using the nslookup Command to Troubleshoot DNS

Finally, the classic command for troubleshooting DNS, used for many years on the Internet and other TCP/IP networks, is **nslookup**. The NS in this command name stands for "name server." This command allows you to send queries to a DNS name server directly and see the results. It is a very powerful command, but you can use it to test your DNS setting without learning all of its subcommands. Running **nslookup** in a Command Prompt without any additional command-line parameters will cause it to attempt to connect to the name server address in your IP configuration. Then it displays the **nslookup** prompt, a greater-than sign (>). You may enter subcommands at this prompt. If it cannot connect to the DNS server, it will display an error, as shown in Figure 10–40. If you see this error, contact your network administrator or ISP. Type **exit** at the **nslookup** prompt to exit from the command. Then type **exit** again to exit from the Command Prompt.

Note: To learn more about the **nslookup** command, search on **nslookup** in the Windows Help program.

Chapter 10 REVIEW

Chapter Summary

After reading this chapter and completing the Step-by-Step tutorials and Try This! exercises, you should understand the following facts about networking:

Configuring a Network Connection

- A protocol is a set of rules, usually formalized in a standard published by one of many standards organizations. A software implementation of a protocol is also called a protocol.
- TCP/IP is the protocol suite needed to access the Internet.
- Transmission Control Protocol (TCP) and Internet Protocol (IP) are the core protocols of TCP/IP.
- An IP address assigned to a network adapter or modem connects it to a network.
- IPv4, an old version of the protocol, is slowly being replaced by IPv6.
- Public IP addresses are for hosts on the Internet, and each address must be unique on the entire Internet.
- A private IP address is one of three ranges of IP addresses designated for use only on private networks. They are not for use on the Internet, and you do not need to obtain permission to use these addresses on a private network.

- Computers on a private network using private IP addresses get access to the Internet through a specialized device, usually a router.
- Each host on a TCP/IP network must have an IP address. A host receives an address by two general methods: automatically as a DHCP client via a network DHCP server (or a self-assigned APIPA address), or as a static address.
- In addition to the IP address there are several IP configuration settings including subnet mask, default gateway, DNS server, advanced DNS settings, and WINS settings.

Connecting to the Internet

- A connection to the Internet is a wide area network (WAN) connection.
- An Internet service provider (ISP) is an organization that provides individuals or entire companies access to the Internet.
- Common wired WAN technologies include dial-up, ISDN, DSL, and cable.
- ISDN is a digital telephone service that simultaneously transmits voice, data, and control signaling over a single telephone line and can

transfer data at up to 128,000 bits per second (128 Kbps).

- Digital subscriber line (DSL) service is similar to ISDN in its use of the telephone network, but it uses more advanced digital signal processing to compress more signals through the telephone lines and so is much faster than ISDN.
- Many cable television companies now offer Internet access through existing cable television connections using special cable modems.
- Wireless options for connecting to the Internet include cellular networks, wireless wide area networks (WWANs), wireless LAN (WLAN) connections (if the WLAN ultimately connects to the Internet), and satellite.
- Mobile users and remote offices often need to connect to the corporate intranet through the Internet using any of the connection technologies discussed previously, with the addition of a virtual private network (VPN) for security.

Using Internet Clients

- Web technologies changed the look of Internet content from all text to rich and colorful graphics, and made it simple to navigate the Web by using a special type of client called a Web browser.
- The top Web browsers are Google Chrome, Mozilla Firefox, and Internet Explorer.
- Both Firefox and IE have a large number of configuration settings that range from GUI preferences to settings critical to protecting your privacy and maintaining security for your computer and personal data.
- An email service and client are defined by the protocols they use, which are POP3, IMAP, and Web mail (HTML protocol).
- While some email services require dedicated clients, some email clients can interact with a variety of email server types.
- To configure any email client you need a specific set of information. This includes:
  - The type of mail server you are accessing (POP3, IMAP, or HTTP).
  - Your account name and password.
  - The DNS name of the incoming mail server.
  - If you are preparing to connect to a POP3 or IMAP server, you will also need to know the name of an outgoing mail server.
- File Transfer Protocol (FTP) is a protocol used to transfer files between a computer running the FTP server service and an FTP client. It is simple and fast.

- An FTP site that allows anonymous connections is an anonymous FTP site.
- If a site requires a user name and password, it will prompt you, whether you are using a Web browser to connect or an FTP client.
- A Web browser is fine for occasionally connecting to FTP sites, but use an FTP client to save settings for FTP sites you visit repeatedly.
- To configure an FTP client you will need the following, including:
  - The host name of the FTP server.
  - User ID and password (if applicable).
  - Account (if applicable).

Sharing Files and Printers

- A file and printer sharing protocol allows a computer to share files and printers with compatible clients.
- A file and printer client includes both the user interface and the underlying file-sharing protocols to access a file-sharing system on a network file and printer server.
- Windows installs with both the server and client components for file and printer sharing.
- Windows 7 and newer version have the Home-Group feature that allows sharing with other Windows 7 and newer installations. It only requires a password the first time the computer connects to the HomeGroup.
- To join or create a HomeGroup a Windows 7 computer must be connected to a Home network location; Windows 8 or newer must be connected to a Private network location. Same location; different names.
- To join or create a HomeGroup, a Windows computer must have IPv6 enabled; all firewalls between HomeGroup computers must also support IPv6 and must allow file and printer sharing.

Troubleshooting Common Network Client Connection Problems

- All the OSs surveyed in this book have GUI-based Network Diagnostics that combine many functions.
- Several command-line commands help in diagnosing and solving network client connection problems. These utilities include:
  - **ipconfig**
  - **ifconfig**
  - **ping**
  - **tracert**
  - **netstat**
  - **nslookup**

Key Terms List

anonymous FTP site *(421)*

automatic IP addressing *(393)*

Automatic Private IP Addressing
(APIPA) *(393)*

cellular hotspot *(404)*

default gateway *(395)*

dial-up *(401)*

digital subscriber line (DSL) *(402)*

Domain Name System (DNS) *(395)*

Dynamic Host Configuration
Protocol (DHCP) server *(393)*

file and printer server *(422)*

File Transfer Protocol (FTP) *(421)*

fully qualified domain name
(FQDN) *(431)*

host ID *(394)*

integrated services digital network
(ISDN) *(402)*

Internet Protocol (IP) *(388)*

Internet service provider (ISP) *(400)*

internetwork *(388)*

IP address *(389)*

IPv4 *(389)*

IPv6 *(389)*

local area network (LAN) *(400)*

net ID *(394)*

octet *(394)*

packet *(388)*

private browsing *(413)*

private IP address *(392)*

protocol *(388)*

protocol stack *(388)*

public IP addresses *(391)*

remote access VPN *(406)*

router *(395)*

share *(422)*

site-to-site VPN *(406)*

static IP address *(393)*

subnet mask *(394)*

TCP/IP *(388)*

Transmission Control Protocol
(TCP) *(388)*

virtual private network (VPN) *(406)*

Web browser *(407)*

Web mail *(417)*

Wi-Fi network *(400)*

wide area network (WAN) *(400)*

wireless LAN (WLAN) *(400)*

wireless wide area network
(WWAN) *(403)*

Key Terms Quiz

Use the Key Terms List to complete the sentences that follow:

1. The IP addresses designated for hosts connected directly to the Internet are _____.

2. _____ is the version of the Internet Protocol that is slowly replacing the version that has been in use since 1983.

3. A/an _____ uses encapsulation to protect data sent over a public network. Encryption makes the data more secure.

4. An IPv4 address beginning with 169.254 is a/an _____ address.

5. A/an _____ is not used for hosts on the Internet.

6. A/an _____ is an organization that provides individuals or entire companies with access to the Internet.

7. In an IPv4 address, each grouping of decimal numbers is called a/an _____ because it represent eight bits.

8. Among IP configuration settings, the _____ is the IP address of the router used to send packets beyond the local network.

9. _____ is a term for a group of wired high-speed technologies offered through the phone company, and capable of much greater speeds than ISDN.

10. Most organizations use a _____ to assign IP addresses to desktop computers.

Multiple-Choice Quiz

1. The IPv4 address 192.168.30.24 is an example of one of these.
   a. DNS server address
   b. Public IP address
   c. Private IP address
   d. Automatic private IP address
   e. WINS server address

2. This protocol has 340 trillion, trillion, trillion unique identifiers.
   a. DNS
   b. IPv6
   c. DSL
   d. DHCP
   e. IMAP

3. In the chapter, which form of DSL is described as having the same speed upstream as downstream?
   a. ADSL
   b. *x*DSL
   c. VDSL
   d. HDSL
   e. SDSL

4. Your neighbor tells you that he has to initiate a connection to the Internet and complains that the connection is much slower than the connection he enjoys at work—and he is disconnected if there is a period of inactivity. From his description, which type of connection would you assume he has?
   a. ISDN
   b. Dial-up
   c. ADSL
   d. SDSL
   e. Cable

5. What appears in the Windows Connect Using box in the connection properties dialog box?
   a. A connection device
   b. An ISP name
   c. A user name
   d. A password
   e. A phone number

6. Which of the following is obviously *not* a valid IPv4 address?
   a. 192.168.100.48
   b. 10.0.33.50
   c. 172.300.256.100
   d. 30.88.29.1
   e. 200.100.99.99

7. You connect to Wi-Fi from your smartphone or laptop in public places, such as airports and coffee shops. What type of service should you use to protect your communications?
   a. VPN
   b. Firewall
   c. Private browsing
   d. IPv6
   e. Private IP address

8. What command can you use to view the status of current connections, including the IP address and protocol used for each connection?
   a. ipconfig
   b. cmd
   c. ping
   d. netstat
   e. tracert

9. Which of the following is an example of an IPv6 address with the leading zeros removed?
   a. 2002:0470:b8f9:0000:020c:29ff:fe53:45ca
   b. 192.168.1.1
   c. 10.0.0.1
   d. 2002:470:b8f9::20c:29ff:fe53:45ca
   e. 0.0.0.0

10. Which command would you use as a test to see if a DNS server will respond to a request to resolve a name?
    a. ping
    b. nslookup
    c. ipconfig
    d. netstat
    e. tracert

11. This IPv4 configuration setting defines the two parts of an IP address: the Host ID and the Net ID.
    a. Gateway
    b. Subnet mask
    c. DNS
    d. DHCP
    e. Host name

12. Where in Internet Options can you configure how IE manages cookies?
    a. General page
    b. Security page
    c. Tabs page
    d. Advanced Privacy Settings dialog box
    e. Exceptions button

13. Your neighbor, a retiree on a modest fixed income, has asked your help in acquiring an Internet connection for his computer, a desktop computer running Windows 7. His only interest in Internet access is to use email to keep in touch with his children, who live in other states. He has a reliable phone connection. Based on this information, which service will you recommend?
    a. Cable
    b. ISDN
    c. Dial-up
    d. DSL
    e. Satellite

14. If you wanted to see the IP configuration from the $ prompt on a MAC, Linux, or UNIX system, which command would you use?
    a. ipconfig
    b. netstat
    c. nslookup
    d. ping
    e. ifconfig

15. What protocol is responsible for the accurate delivery of messages, verifying and resending

pieces that fail to make the trip from source to destination?

a. Internet Protocol

b. Transmit Control Protocol (TCP)

c. Secure Sockets Layer (SSL)

d. File Transfer Protocol (FTP)

e. Transmission Control Protocol (TCP)

Essay Quiz

1. Your computer was recently connected via a network adapter to a LAN that includes a router through which traffic passes to the Internet. You know the adapter was configured to use TCP/IP, and you need to test its ability to communicate with computers on the LAN and on the Internet. In your own words describe the steps you will take.

2. After reviewing Web browsers in this chapter, do you see a commonality in the user interface and in the less obvious features of these different apps? Describe your observations.

3. In a large western state an agency that dispatches mobile units to disaster areas to monitor the disaster sites for hazardous chemical and biological contamination requires reliable Internet access for these units from any location in the state. They need to keep up-to-date with technical information via postings on federal websites and to upload their data to state and federal sites. Which Internet connection option is the best fit for their needs? Explain your answer.

4. In Step-by-Step 10.02, step 6, you are instructed to configure when messages should be deleted from a mail server. This is a setting in most email clients. Consider how you would configure your email clients on several devices connecting to the same email service, including an explanation of why you would (or would not) configure all your clients to delete messages as soon as they are picked up.

5. Explain subnet masking in simple terms, including why a subnet mask is required when an adapter is configured with an IP address.

Lab Projects

LAB PROJECT 10.1

Research VPN services for individuals and answer these questions.

1. How do the various VPN services differ?

2. What is the advantage of the feature called geo-shifting?

3. What does it mean when a provider says that they do not keep logs?

4. Why is it important to know where the VPN servers are located when selecting a VPN service?

5. Why would someone want the feature that makes it appear that they are connected from a different country?

6. What are the advantages to hiding the type of content you are downloading?

LAB PROJECT 10.2

This project requires the use of a Windows, Linux, or Mac computer that has Internet access. Using methods you learned in this chapter, find the answers to the following questions:

1. How is an IP address assigned to the lab computer?

2. Record the IP configuration settings for the lab computer below:
   a. IP address
   b. Subnet mask
   c. Default gateway
   d. DNS server

LAB PROJECT 10.3

Interview the IT staff at your school, place of work, or another organization and determine what Internet services they offer to students (Web pages, email, etc.).

The list will usually go beyond the basic services studied in this chapter. Create a list of these services and the clients they require.

11

Mobile Operating Systems

Mobile computing in the 21st century has evolved from two branches of the technology tree: the telephony branch and the personal computing branch. Today's mobile devices only remotely resemble their awkward ancestors because today's devices are remarkably tiny and powerful, more like fictional *Star Trek* communicators than any 20th-century phones or computers. The versatility and widespread consumer appeal of today's mobile devices exceeds the extraordinary imagination and vision of *Star Trek* creator Gene Roddenberry, at least in their use by consumers. Perhaps no one could have predicted three decades ago how tiny and powerful computing and communicating devices would become, and that they would be so common that individuals would insist on using them at work.

Chapter 1 introduced mobile devices and mobile operating systems. Before reading this chapter, we urge you to review the Chapter 1 section titled "Today's Mobile OSs." The coverage includes a description of the hardware features of popular smartphones and tablets. They include cameras, speakers, speaker jacks, adapters for a growing number of wireless technologies, and several types of sensors. Sensors include the accelerometer (described in the overview of mobile devices in Chapter 1), GPS, magnetometer, proximity sensor, compass, and ambient light sensors. We will also look at a few mobile accessories.

In this chapter, we first explore the issues surrounding employees using their personal mobile devices at work and then we describe common configuration tasks for your mobile device and finally we look at security for mobile devices. ☀

LO 11.1 | From Luggable to BYOD

Mobile computing was once something only certain business travelers did using computers that were just luggable versions of the PCs they left at the office. Mobile computing has evolved, and in just the last few years the mobile computing market has been flooded with tiny and powerful mobile devices. Now consumers in every walk of life practice mobile computing, children carry smartphones to preschool, and teachers uncrate boxes of iPads preloaded with student coursework. The "mobile" aspect seems to mean we are not tethered to power and data lines, even as we practice mobile computing at home and everyplace else we go day or night.

In this section, you'll peek at the past of mobile computing, which wasn't very mobile, rarely connected, and involved little computing power. Then you'll examine the issue of using personal mobile devices in the workplace.

Mobile Computing Then and Now

In a span of 30 years mobile computing devices went from a few heavy underpowered devices to today's large number of mobile devices that fit nicely in the hand and whose weight is measured in ounces rather than in tens of pounds. Hence, personal mobile devices are rarely out of reach of their owners, who have come to depend on them at home, school, work, and play. Some of us have lived through this history.

Sometime in the mid-1980s our friend Amber was waiting in the baggage area of an airport as a gray plastic bin rose into view at the center of the baggage carousel and made a precarious slide down to the moving stainless-steel track. She recognized its clattering contents as the components of a Compaq portable computer, its cracked case the size of a 21st-century gaming tower.

Obviously some road warrior had wearied of lugging 28 pounds of technology and checked it as baggage. Amber smugly snatched up her own suitcase and placed it on top of her luggage cart that already contained her carry-on: a 16-pound Zenith Data Systems Z-180 Portable PC. She had spent the flight with her feet resting uneasily on the portion of the laptop that did not fit under the passenger seat in front of her, while the luggage cart rode in the overhead compartment. There was no way she could actually put the laptop on her lap and get real work done. Computer professionals like Amber, rather than the typical consumer of the time, were the target market for portable computers. To quote the Welcome page of the Zenith Data Systems Z-180 Owner's Manual:

This Owner's Manual is for you, the new computer user. In the first part of this manual, you will learn how to set up and operate your new computer for the first time. In the second part, you will learn about the firmware of the computer and how to program it. In the third part, you will learn about the hardware and how to use the programmable registers in the computer.

Programmable registers? Times have changed. Three decades later we no longer expect or need a manual for a new tablet or smartphone. Another big change is that modern mobile devices are almost always connected to one or more networks, whereas the old devices did not connect to any network while in transit. Amber had to wait until she arrived in a classroom with a connection to a local area network (LAN) or hotel room that included a "modem line" for a slow dial-up connection. The more expensive the hotel, the more they charged for this service. Today's travelers demand that hotels provide free high-speed Internet access, and many of them have cellular data plans so that their mobile devices can wirelessly connect to the Internet 24/7.

And consider what they do with those connections! Mobile device users collectively upload and share hundreds of millions of photos every day. They upload an estimated three hundred hours of video to YouTube per minute. And this type of traffic is increasing as more and more mobile users stay in touch, sharing their thoughts and opinions via social media, and keeping up with work and personal email. This pervasiveness of mobile devices has led to a phenomenon in the workplace that we explore next.

The home screen on an Android smartphone.

Note: Mobile devices have evolved into entertainment devices. In addition to uploading videos to YouTube, mobile users stream videos and movies from services such as YouTube and Netflix and listen to music from Pandora and Spotify.

Mobile Devices and BYOD

Smartphones and tablets present a challenge for schools and employers because many individuals come to school or work armed with a pocket or a backpack full of technology. And they don't care to spend any time separated from these devices. Many demand to be able to use these devices for accessing work email, text messages, and data. This practice is called bring your own device (BYOD), and it occurs in many organizations, whether or not they officially condone it.

There are variations of policies (or lack of them) governing BYOD in the workplace. Here are just a few examples:

- Companies may reimburse an employee who uses their own device for cellular voice and data usage. This is important, because cellular voice charges are usually by the minute, and cellular data services are metered, with the cost going up with the amount of data downloaded. Charges can quickly mount up for someone using their personal device for work.

- In a form of shared ownership, an employer subsidizes the purchase of an employee's personal mobile device, giving the employee the option of buying a more expensive device than budgeted.

- An employer may allow or require use of personal mobile devices but not compensate the employee or have any clear policies regarding how to protect work data.

An Apple iOS home screen.

Advantages of BYOD to Employers

There are many advantages to employers of BYOD; a short list includes:

- Quicker response by the employee to communications.
- It saves the employer the cost of the device.
- Some jobs either require, or at least benefit from, the use of mobile devices.
- Acceptance of employees' use of mobile devices attracts tech-savvy people.
- Employees are inclined to work outside of normal work hours.
- You can deliver important job training to mobile devices that employees can use when needed.

Disadvantages of BYOD to Employers

There are risks to allowing employees to access email and corporate data using their personal mobile devices. A few of the issues with BYOD include:

- Personal mobile devices can significantly increase the load on the employer's network infrastructure.
- It may conflict with corporate security policy.
- It may violate government regulations for employees to have certain data on their mobile devices.
- If a device is lost or stolen, it puts the employer at risk.
- Employees may leave a job and still have sensitive work-related data on their personal devices.
- Normally intellectual property created as part of a job belongs to the employer. It is unclear who owns the intellectual property if it is created on the employee's device.

Risks of BYOD to Employees

There are risks and concerns for the employee. Consider these issues:

- Who will pay for the cost of the device?
- Who will pay for added voice and data usage due to business use?
- What protects the employees if the employer's policy mandates monitoring BYOD devices?
- Can an employer or law enforcement agency confiscate an employee's device for any work-related reason?

Basic BYOD Policies

Basic BYOD policies should address these areas:

- Who owns intellectual property created on an employee's device—the employee or the employer?
- What security requirements should there be and how should they be enforced, including but not limited to passwords, encryption, and remote wipe (remotely deleting data from a lost or stolen device)?

- How and when does the employee back up the employer's data?
- Will video- and audio-recording features in BYOD devices be allowed in the workplace?
- Will the employer take advantage of location services on devices to monitor an employee's location during working hours? A location service is one that allows an app to track your location, using one or more methods, often with the help of the Internet.

Managing BYOD

Managing BYOD begins with company policies covering work behavior, security, and employee reimbursement. Existing policies may cover the use of personal devices in very broad terms and need updating. Employers have many options for managing BYOD to protect themselves and their employees. They also want to make the mobile devices more useful to the employees.

Employers' awareness of BYOD and the need to manage it varies. Therefore some experts on security and BYOD promote a bottom-up approach, seeking to educate the employees so that they will be aware of the risks to themselves and request more clarity in BYOD policies from their employers.

In addition to modifying policies for BYOD, employers can enforce those policies and manage mobile devices using a category of software called mobile device management (MDM). Companies such as Citrix, VMware, Sophos, MobileIron, Acronis, and Microsoft offer such products—sometimes integrated into existing suites of products. Mobile device management is a broad term for the variety of features offered and the different approaches by the vendors of this type of software.

Some employers use products that include some form of virtualization. That may be in the form of a virtual machine running on the remote device or some variation of application virtualization—with processing occurring either on the mobile device or on remote servers.

Others prefer to create a Web-based portal to work apps and data, making this available to a wider range of devices, since the only required client software is a browser.

LO 11.2 | Configuring Accounts and Wireless Connections on Mobile Devices

Chapter 1 described some of the wireless options for mobile devices and Chapter 10 described and compared networking technologies. In this section we first describe the accounts required for each of the mobile operating systems discussed in this chapter. Then we detail how to configure your mobile operating system to connect your device to four types of wireless networks: cellular data networks, Wi-Fi WLAN networks, Bluetooth connections for connecting to nearby devices, and another type of wireless connection over very short distances, called Near Field Communication (NFC).

Note: In spite of its small market share in the smartphone market, Microsoft does have an important presence on tablets, so we have included Windows in this chapter. However, we have not included details about Windows Mobile.

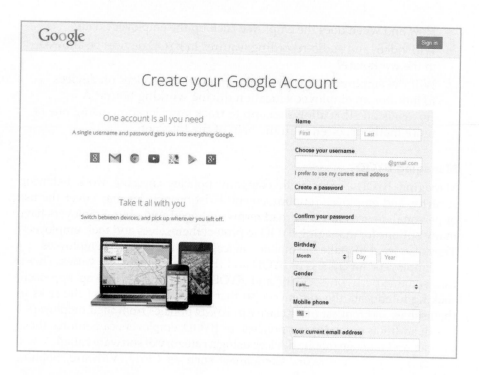

The Create your Google Account page.

Your Mobile Device Account

All popular smartphones and tablets require a user account. That includes Apple's iPhone and iPad, Android devices, and mobile devices running Microsoft Windows.

Google Account

A Google account is an account that gives you access to Google services and is normally required on Android devices. A Google account is free and you can have more than one. To create a Google account, connect to accounts.google.com, shown above. You can use/create a Google Gmail account or use any existing email account. If you wish to use an email address other than a Gmail account, simply click on the blue link titled **I prefer to use my current email address** located under the **Choose your username** box.

Apple ID

An Apple ID is your account as a customer of Apple for Apple services and products. Like a Google account, an Apple ID is a free account, although some of the services may be fee-based. The credentials include an email address (any working email address) and a password for the Apple ID—*not* the password for using the email account.

If this is your first Apple product, you will create a new account at the time of purchase. To create or manage an Apple ID point your browser to appleid.apple.com. This account is associated with your iTunes account and the credit card used for purchasing music for the iPod. Therefore, many think of it as an iTunes account, but you can use this one account for all your Apple devices and services, such as iCloud and Apple Online Support. For security reasons consider creating a second Apple ID without an associated credit card that you use for downloading free apps from the Apple store and for synchronizing data across devices. Connect to the My Apple ID page, shown on the next page, where you can log in with an existing account and manage it, or create a new Apple ID account.

Another reason for having multiple accounts is for more iCloud data storage because each account has a limit on free data storage. A family with

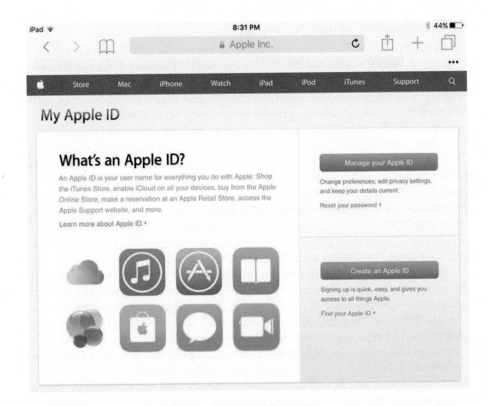

Manage an existing account or create a new Apple ID at appleid.apple.com.

multiple devices may want a separate account for each member. Or an individual with multiple devices may want one account for a device used mostly for work and another account just for personal use.

Microsoft Account

A Microsoft account is a free account that gives the subscriber access to Microsoft services, such as Hotmail, Messenger, OneDrive, Office 365, Skype, Xbox Live, and Outlook.com. Although the account is free, some of the services may be fee-based. To sign up for a Microsoft account, connect to signup.live.com, shown here, and provide the required information.

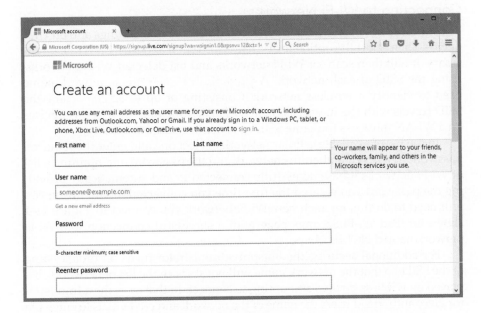

Create a new Account at the **Microsoft account** page.

Connecting to Cellular Networks

When preparing to buy a smartphone, first shop for the cellular provider, such as Verizon, AT&T, Sprint, T-Mobile, Cricket, or U.S. Cellular. Look for the best service and options in your area. Having only one or two providers with coverage in your area narrows down the choices, but if you live in an area with coverage from several cellular providers, you may want to visit several stores or websites to compare plans and costs before making your final choice.

After selecting the carrier and the plan you would like, select the device. Once you have selected the device that fits your needs and budget, you normally sign a contract for a certain level of service before you gain possession of the device. While there are many plans, they generally charge you a flat rate for up to a certain number of voice minutes, and a separate flat rate for a certain amount of cellular data usage. Research this and read customer reviews of cellular data plans before you buy because reviews will tell you a lot about other customers' experiences with the provider.

Before you receive the phone the cellular service provider will program it for your cellular account. This process often includes inserting a card called a Subscriber Identity Module (SIM) into the device. If you purchase the device over the Internet, the SIM card may come with the device, with instructions on installing it and activating the phone. If you purchase a smartphone in a brick-and-mortar store, you will usually configure the cellular connection while still in the store, or the salesperson may do it for you.

The first time you power up a new smartphone that has not been prepared or one that has the basic configuration but still needs your personal settings, a setup screen will display and lead you through the process. This will include accepting a language and terms of use. You will also have an opportunity to read a privacy statement and then go through steps for setting up your phone.

Cellular data communications is optional in a tablet, adding a premium to the cost of the device because of the required internal cellular modem as well as the ongoing cost for the cellular data plan. As with a smartphone, the cellular provider will either configure the device or give you special instructions. The device may come preconfigured for connecting to the cellular network, and the first time you start it up, you personalize it by moving through screens where you answer questions.

Connecting to Wi-Fi Networks

To connect to a Wi-Fi network for the first time, open the Settings app on your device. Then select the option for Wireless (or Wi-Fi) and turn on Wi-Fi, if necessary. It will then scan for Wi-Fi networks and list detected Wi-Fi networks, using the SSID of each network. A Service Set ID (SSID) is a network name used to identify a wireless network. Consisting of up to 32 characters, the SSID travels with the messages on a Wi-Fi network, and all wireless devices on a WLAN must use the same SSID in order to communicate.

In the list of available cellular networks, select one and enter the required password. It will remember this network and the password, maintaining a list of Wi-Fi networks it has successfully connected to and automatically providing the password you entered the first time you connected. If you travel, you will need to do this for each new Wi-Fi network you connect to. Figure 11–1 shows an iPad Wi-Fi Settings page with a successful connection to a Wi-Fi network named HOME-24.

For additional security, the hotspot administrator turns off broadcasting of the SSID, so that the network name will not show in the list of networks displayed on wireless devices attempting to connect. In that case, the administrator gives authorized users the name of the network and credentials to enter. On an iOS device, select Other to open the drop-down box shown in Figure 11–2.

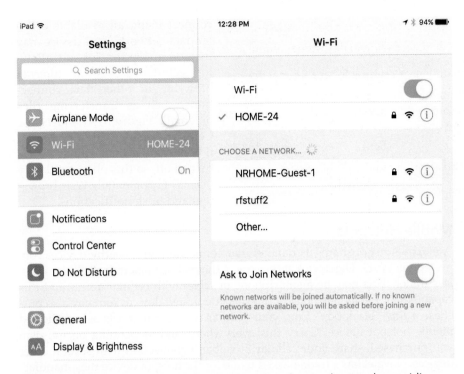

FIGURE 11–1 Turn on Wi-Fi and then connect to a detected network, providing a password, if necessary.

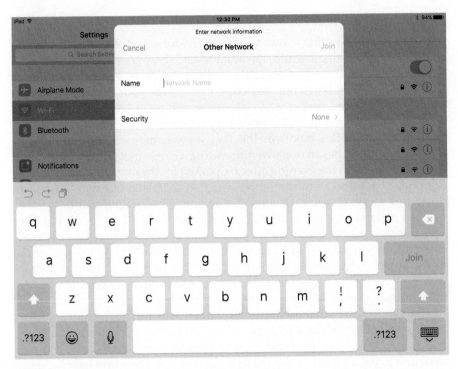

FIGURE 11–2 If the network name (SSID) is not visible because it is hidden, enter the network name and required credentials.

There is an important money-saving feature that is enabled by default in some mobile devices with both cellular and Wi-Fi connections. If the device connects to a Wi-Fi network, it will use that rather than the cellular network for data. So, when you open your browser, the device will automatically use the Wi-Fi network. If a Wi-Fi network is not available, when you open your browser or other app requiring Internet access the device will connect using an available cellular data network. Your device may include an option for not allowing cellular access for Internet browsing or other data connections, such as transferring files or email. Figure 11–3 shows the Cellular settings in iOS on an iPhone. Notice that cellular data is turned off, so this phone will only use Wi-Fi for email, Web browsing, and push notifications.

Mobile Hotspots

A mobile hotspot shares its data cellular connection with nearby devices connected via Wi-Fi. The device at the core of the mobile hotspot is a cellular wireless router. This may be a smartphone or tablet with cellular access and this capability, or the mobile hotspot may be a dedicated device. You may also purchase a tiny "black box" from your cellular provider that acts as a dedicated mobile hotspot device. Carry this everywhere, and, depending on the plan you purchased, share your cellular broadband connection with several other devices. Novatel has a trademarked name for the hotspot device they manufacturer: MiFi, which stands for "my Wi-Fi." Contact your provider to ask for the terms and cost, and to have them enable the service you select for your account.

Tethering

Tethering is a feature that allows you to share your smartphone's cellular data connection with a single computer—one-to-one sharing of your Internet connection. The actual connection to the computer, laptop, or tablet can be via USB cable, Wi-Fi, or Bluetooth. Tethering mode turns your phone into a cellular modem. During a period of three years beginning in 2003 the authors lived and worked full-time in an RV while they traveled around the United States. Fortunately, in our first month on the road, we were between writing and editing projects, so we began our adventure using a single mobile cell phone as an Internet modem. In the evening after we parked for the day we would pass the cell phone back and forth across the aisle that separated our two "offices" to take turns connecting to each computer, mainly for accessing email.

Our cellular modem in 2003 operated at about 56 Kbps, so we did very little Internet browsing and within a month we parked for two days in a business park in San Jose to have a data satellite dish installed on the roof of the motor home. A few weeks later we picked up a new book contract and we were ready with the high-speed Internet access required for research and for uploading chapters and figure files to our publisher.

Back in 2003, we purchased that cell phone just to use it as a cellular modem; it had a data plan without a voice plan. We each already carried a conventional cell phone. Today, when you have a data plan for your smartphone you may also need to pay an extra fee for the tethering service. The world has changed a great deal since 2003. Today's cellular devices offer much faster speeds, and are competitive in both speeds and pricing with mobile satellite service. However, tethering may not be your best option, and it may not even be an option from your carrier. It may be included with a mobile hotspot service.

Connecting to Bluetooth Devices

Bluetooth is a wireless standard used for communicating over very short distances. The most common implementation of Bluetooth connects devices

---

●●○○○ Verizon 🗺	8:16 PM	🗺 97% ▬
‹ Settings	**Cellular**	

Cellular Data	⚪

Turn off cellular data to restrict all data to Wi-Fi, including email, web browsing, and push notifications.

| **Roaming** | Off › |

CALL TIME

| **Current Period** | 13 Minutes |
| **Lifetime** | 13 Minutes |

CELLULAR DATA USAGE

| **Current Period** | 16.4 MB |
| **Current Period Roaming** | 0 bytes |

FIGURE 11–3 The Cellular settings page on an iPhone.

Note: Tethering is also used to describe a connection between your mobile device and another mobile device or computer for the sake of synchronizing or backing up data.

FIGURE 11–4 When pairing an iMac and iPad, the codes must match on both devices.

Bluetooth Pairing Request

"Jane's iMac" would like to pair with your iPad. Confirm that the code "536655" is shown on "Jane's iMac".

Cancel   Pair

FIGURE 11–5 Verify that the code is the same on each device, and then tap **Pair** on the iPad.

at a distance of up to one meter. You might want to use Bluetooth to connect a Bluetooth headset or keyboard to your mobile device, to connect your smartphone to your car stereo, or to connect a mobile device to a PC or Mac to synchronize data. Bluetooth consumes battery power, so it is disabled by default. To connect devices via Bluetooth, first open the Settings app on your mobile device and enable Bluetooth. Then enable it on the computer or Bluetooth device you wish to connect to so that they can discover (find) each other, which they will attempt to do as soon as you enable Bluetooth. We call a connection between two Bluetooth devices a pairing.

When connecting two computing devices, such as an iMac and an iPhone or iPad tablet, go to the Settings screen on each one and select the other device for pairing. After a short pause a message will display with a pairing code (also called a PIN code), as shown in Figure 11–4 showing the message on an iMac when pairing with an iPad. Then simply confirm that the same pairing code shows on the screen for both devices and tap the Pair button on the iPad, as shown in Figure 11–5.

When connecting a Bluetooth device without a screen (such as a headset or keyboard) to a computer or mobile device, turn on the device and allow the smartphone, tablet, or PC to discover it. A message will display on the computer or mobile device. Enter the code at the keyboard to complete the pairing. After this, you will not need to enter the code each time they pair, but you will need to turn on Bluetooth if you turn it off after using it.

Finally, test connectivity between the devices. We have found that just entering the pairing code on a keyboard is not enough confirmation that the connection is working. So in the case of a keyboard, open an app, such as an Internet browser, tap on a box requiring text (such as an address box), and then start typing on the keyboard. If it does not work you may not have confirmed the pairing on both sides (not always necessary). We have also found that a failure to connect is often a case of impatience, so a short wait is in order. However, if you have a problem with the pairing, disable Bluetooth on both devices and start over again.

WARNING!

Disable Bluetooth when you do not absolutely need it. The Bluetooth pairing process is a security vulnerability, allowing someone with a Bluetooth-enabled device to connect and install malware, listen to your conversations, make phone calls, and more. Turn it off manually, or install a battery management app that will turn it off when you disconnect a Bluetooth device.

Note: On devices that we have tested, the order for setting up a Bluetooth connection is: (1) enable Bluetooth, (2) find a device for pairing, (3) enable pairing, (4) confirm or enter the code, and (5) test connectivity.

try this!

Pair Two Devices with Bluetooth

Connect your mobile device to a computer or peripheral using Bluetooth. Try this:

1. Open the Settings utility in your mobile device.
2. Locate the Bluetooth setting and turn it on.
3. Turn on your Bluetooth device.
4. The mobile device should show that it is searching, connecting, and pairing.
5. It if is a keyboard, enter the code that appears on the mobile device.
6. Test the connection: for instance, play music to test a Bluetooth headset.
7. Disable Bluetooth when you are finished.

Connecting with Near Field Communications

Some newer mobile devices include a special chipset that supports Near Field Communication (NFC). With this enabled and configured, you can position your phone very close to another that also has NFC enabled and share data and even pay for purchases at locations using this type of device. The Windows 8.1 implementation of NFC, as described in Chapter 5, is Tap to Send.

Apple uses NFC technology for the Apple Pay automatic system for Apple Watch and iPhones. The app for this service was first called Passbook and later renamed Wallet. Credit and debit card data is stored in Wallet. Add this data from your iTunes account, enter card information manually, or use the iSight camera on your iPhone to capture this information for the app. It requires at least an iPhone 6 with the Touch ID feature, as well as the built-in NFC in that and newer devices. Hold your iPhone 6 (or newer) or Apple Watch near a contactless reader while holding your finger on Touch ID. An Apple Watch requires a double-click of the side button.

try this!

Enable or Disable Airplane Mode

If you have a mobile device, it should have a setting for enabling or disabling Airplane mode. Try this:

1. Open the Settings utility in your mobile device.
2. Locate the Airplane mode setting.
3. Turn Airplane mode on (this turns off wireless communications).
4. Test Airplane mode by opening a browser and attempting to connect to a website.
5. When you have tested it, turn Airplane mode off.

Airplane Mode

When traveling on a commercial airliner you are required to turn off radio frequency (RF) signals from all personal devices for at least part of the flight. At one time this required powering down cell phones, but modern mobile devices are actually useful to their owners, even when they are not connected. Therefore, these devices have a feature called Airplane mode.

When you turn on Airplane mode all radios in your device are turned off, including cellular, Wi-Fi, Bluetooth, and NFC, but you can continue calculating your expense account or playing Angry Birds, as long as you don't require a wireless connection. Use Airplane mode when traveling to save battery power and money. Airplane mode prevents your device from repeatedly attempting to connect to Wi-Fi while you are out of range, saving on battery power. This mode also saves money for the traveler who wants to avoid expensive roaming charges while outside your cellular provider's network. Although you may be careful not to initiate phone calls and messages while roaming charges apply, you may be charged for incoming voice calls and text messages unless you turn on Airplane mode. Look for Airplane mode in the Settings app. Figure 11–6 shows the settings screen on an Android smartphone containing the switch for enabling or disabling Airplane mode.

LO 11.3 | Email, Apps, and Synchronization

Once you know how to work with your mobile device's connection settings, you will want to configure email, acquire new apps, and enable synchronization.

Configuring Email

In order to use your mobile device to access your email, begin by adding the account. Mobile devices support several types of accounts for email, social networking, data backup, and more. And you can configure a single

FIGURE 11–6 The Wi-Fi page on an Android smartphone.

device to use several accounts. Mobile operating systems know the basic connection information for many types of accounts. Therefore, for many accounts, you only need to provide your personal login information to the account, which is usually an email address and password. Figure 11–7 shows a list of account types supported on an iPad. Chapter 10 described email account types as well as the settings required to connect to an email account.

Web mail Accounts

For Web mail accounts, such as Hotmail or Gmail, you do not have to specify a sending and receiving server. All you need to enter is your user name and password. All the mobile OSs described here work with Web mail accounts.

Accounts Requiring IMAP, POP, or SMTP Settings

If you want to use an account type other than a Web mail service, you will need server names for the incoming and outgoing mail servers. Obtain these from your mail server administrator. To receive mail you will need a name for a Post Office Protocol 3 (POP3) or an Internet Message Access Protocol 4 (IMAP4) server that receives your incoming mail and forwards it to you. An email client uses one or the other of these. To send mail you usually need the name of your Simple Mail Transfer Protocol (SMTP) server that accepts your outgoing mail and forwards it to the recipient's mail server.

A POP3 name will simply be the name of a mail server in an Internet domain, and may resemble this: pop.domainname.com; while the name for an IMAP4 server might look something like this: imap.domainname.com. Then, we probably don't need to say this, but the SMTP name might look like this: smtp.domainname.com. These are just examples, and you need to get the names for these servers from your email administrator.

> Note: Enable and disable several features in iOS by swiping up from the bottom of the screen to open the **control center**. Features you can turn on or off from here include **Airplane Mode**, **Wi-Fi**, **Bluetooth**, **Do Not Disturb**, and **Mute**. **Control center** also has screen controls for video, sound, and brightness, and you can also launch **Camera** and the **Clock** (World Clock, Alarm, Stopwatch, and Timer) from this handy tool.

FIGURE 11–7 Mobile OSs allow you to use many types of accounts for email and social networking.

> Note: The name of the server for sending and/or receiving email will not always match the domain name seen after the @ in the email address. The name of the server is irrelevant, as long as it points to the correct mail server.

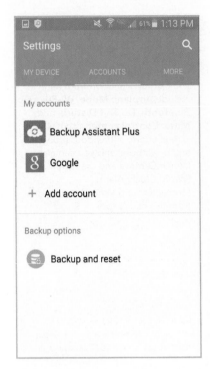

Select **Add account** on the Android **Accounts** screen.

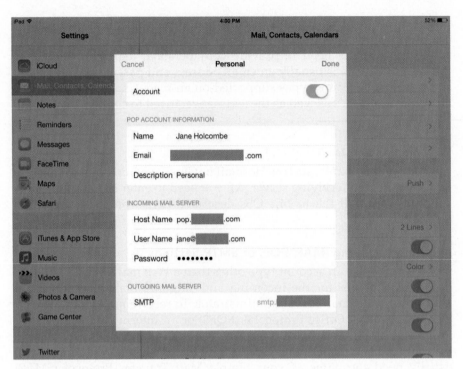

FIGURE 11–8 The settings for a POP email account.

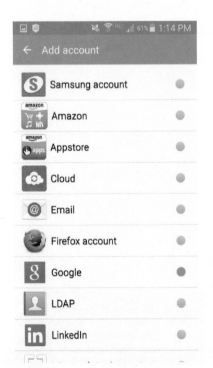

FIGURE 11–9 Select the account type from the long list in the Android **Add account** page.

Armed with the needed information, locate the email settings on your mobile device and carefully enter the information. On an iPad, open the Settings app and tap **Mail, Contacts, Calendars**. Then, in the **Accounts** category in the right pane tap **Add Account**. Does the list include the type of email account you need to use? If it does, tap it and continue. If not, tap **Other** at the bottom of the list and then tap **Add Mail Account**. The **New Account** dialog box will display, along with the virtual keyboard (unless you have an external keyboard connected). Enter your name (not a user account name), email address, password for that email account, and a description for the email account that will identify it for you in the list of accounts. Tap **Next**, and follow the instructions, using the addresses you obtained from your mail server administrator. Figure 11–8 shows the settings for a POP account named "Personal" by the user. If you slide the green button to the right of "Account" you can disable the account without deleting it. If you scroll down in this list of settings, you will find the Delete Account option that allows you to delete the account.

On an Android device you will have a Google account for accessing Google services and Gmail. To add another type of account in Android, open **Settings**. Then under the **Accounts** category select **Add Account**. This opens the **Add an Account** screen that lists a variety of account types, not just email accounts but social networking sites, photo sharing sites, data backup sites, and other accounts added as you install certain apps.

From the **Add an Account** screen scroll through the list of account types and select the type of account you wish to add, shown in Figure 11–9. Then enter the appropriate information for that account type.

In Windows Phone and Windows Mobile, your Microsoft account is your first email account as well as your account for accessing Microsoft services. You can add other accounts as well. As with Android and iOS, these other accounts include email accounts and social networking accounts. The Mail app for Windows Phone only works with cloud-based email accounts, relying on an Internet-based email service to store email data, rather than save all your saved messages on your smartphone.

To add accounts to Windows Phone, open **Settings** | **System** | **email+ account** (Figure 11–10). You may see a different list of accounts, depending on what accounts you have added to your phone. To add a new account of any type click **add an account**. Then on the **Add an Account** screen select from the accounts listed. Select one of these options and enter your email address and the password for using that email account. Then tap **sign in** and Mail will attempt to detect other settings required for the connection; you may be prompted to enter more information.

Select **other account** on the **Add an Account** page to configure an email service using IMAP or POP. Again, enter your email address and password for the account and attempt to sign in. Then use the **advanced setup** option only if Mail fails to detect the correct settings and you need to enter mail server settings manually.

Configuring an Exchange Client

Many organizations use internally maintained Microsoft Exchange mail servers for employee email accounts and for email within the organization as well as over the Internet. Also, many hosting services for Internet domain names offer Exchange email hosting services to their clients. Exchange gives the organization full administrative control, while providing users with a central location for their email history, contacts, tasks, and many collaborative tools.

If you need to connect your device to an Exchange server, first open Accounts from Settings. All the mobile OSs described in this chapter list Microsoft Exchange as an account type. Select it and enter the email address, user name, password, and a description for the list of accounts.

Mobile Apps

Apps are what make your mobile device the high-tech version of a Swiss Army knife. All mobile devices come with some built-in apps, but everyone installs more apps. Whatever mobile OS you select, you can choose from among hundreds of thousands of mobile apps. Apps are OS specific, so you must find apps that work with your OS and device. The major mobile operating systems differ in how the apps are available and what apps are available. The home screens on these mobile devices will normally have an icon for connecting to an online retail site for buying apps for that mobile OS and (sometimes) device type.

When you find an app that sounds like what you need, read through the description, paying close attention to the requirements. An app may require certain services in order to work as advertised. For instance, you may need to give the app full control of your device or turn on the location service and/or global positioning system (GPS) service.

Apps for Android

Play Store is an Android app that connects you to the Google Play online app store, the official source for Android apps, but since this is an open OS, there are other sources in the open-source market, such as AndroidPIT at www.androidpit.com. Pay very close attention to the specs for an app, as there are many versions of Android, with features that are only supported on some devices. Figure 11–11 shows a small sampling of the Android apps at the Google Play store.

FIGURE 11–10 Click **add an account** to add a new account to Windows Phone.

Note: The organization owning the Exchange server and domain, such as a company or university, centrally manages and owns all Exchange accounts stored in one Exchange accounts database. Google and Microsoft centrally maintain and administer the individual accounts stored in Gmail and Hotmail, respectively. Due to the complexity and cost of managing large numbers of email accounts, organizations are increasingly outsourcing email services to companies like Google and Microsoft.

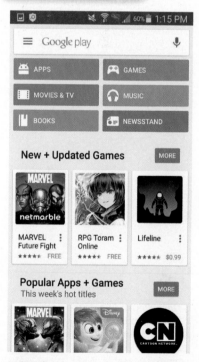

FIGURE 11–11 A small sampling of apps at the Google Play online app store.

The number on this App Store icon indicates that one update is available.

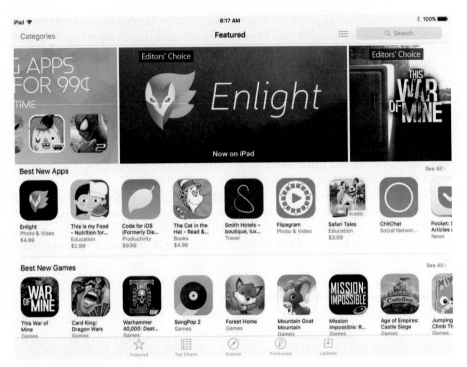

FIGURE 11–12 The Apple online App Store.

Apps for Apple iOS

Apple's online App Store or the brick-and-mortar Apple stores are the only app sources for Apple devices of any type. They sell only Apple-sanctioned software from many publishers. Because of the screen size differences some apps display best on the device for which they were written. Tap the App Store on the home page of your iOS device to connect to the App Store; the first time you connect from a device you will need to provide your Apple ID and password. Figure 11–12 shows the App Store. You update apps through the App Store, and when one or more updates are ready, the number of updates will appear on the App Store icon, as shown above. When you open the App Store, the updates will display, and if you decide to update or download an app, you will need to enter your Apple ID and password before continuing.

Apps for Microsoft Windows

The Windows Store is the main source of apps for Windows smartphones and tablets. With Windows 10 Microsoft broadened the scope of products in the Windows Store, and you can buy apps as well as music and video for all the current Windows operating systems. However, the number of apps for Windows mobile devices does not compare with the huge selection for Apple's iOS devices in the Apple App Store or Android's selection in Google Play.

Synchronization

Some of us have multiple computing devices. The authors each have a desktop PC, a laptop, and a smartphone. In addition, Jane has an iMac and iPad and Chuck has an Android tablet. With so many devices (and we know people with more), it is a challenge to keep track of our data. Therefore, we **synchronize** certain data between devices. When data is synchronized between two locations, the files are examined and newer

Note: Depending on the device and the options available to you, you can synchronize data using four connection types: USB cable, Wi-Fi, Bluetooth, or cellular data network.

files replace the older files—sometimes, but not always, in both directions so that the contents match. Synchronizing can be to another computer or mobile device or to a cloud-based service to ensure against data loss if the device is lost or stolen.

We don't do this between the two users, but each of us synchronizes our own data between mobile devices and PCs and between mobile devices and a cloud service.

Connecting Mobile Devices for Syncing

You can synchronize your smartphone or tablet with your computer, using a USB cable, Wi-Fi, Bluetooth, or over the Internet using a cloud-based service. If you choose a cable, use the USB cable that came with the smartphone; it is usually attached to an alternating current (AC) adapter for charging. Disconnect it from the AC adapter and connect the end previously connected to the power supply (usually a standard USB connector) to the computer and connect the other end to the device. On smartphones, this will usually be a micro USB connector; on iPad and some other tablets, it is a proprietary 30-pin connector. On some devices, this connection will cause two programs to run on the PC—one from your cellular provider (if the device has cellular service) for configuring your online account (if you already have one, you simply log in). The second program will be device-specific to aid in transferring files.

Syncing Android Devices

When you connect an Android device to your computer it is treated like an external drive, and you can copy files back and forth once you figure out the directory structure and locate the files you want to copy or back up. Strictly speaking, this isn't syncing. There are individual solutions for various types of data. For instance, when you create a contact in Android it asks you to pick an account to store (or back up) the contact information. The choices are Google or one provided by your cellular carrier. Select Google and they will be automatically backed up and synced to Google over the Internet, either through a cellular connection or via Wi-Fi. Who do you expect to have the longest relationship with, Google or your cellular provider? We use Google to back up our contacts because it will be available to use if we cancel the contract with the cellular provider.

Syncing an iOS Device with a Mac or PC

Use Apple iTunes for syncing an iOS device with a Mac or PC. It comes with all Apple computers and is a free download for Windows PCs. You can synchronize apps, several types of audio content, books, contacts, calendars, movies, TV shows, photos, notes, documents, and ringtones.

If you have a Mac, you may still need to update to the latest version of iTunes. Whether you are using a PC or Apple Mac computer, download and install the latest version of iTunes. To do that connect to the iTunes page at the Apple website (currently at www.apple.com/itunes/download/).

There are other requirements for playing music and video through iTunes on a PC, but we are only concerned with the requirements to synchronize your contacts, email, pictures, music, and videos from the device to the Mac or PC. You cannot copy files from the Mac or PC to the mobile device, but you can back up (not sync) your apps using iTunes.

Another option that is more of a backup than a synchronizing option is iCloud, an Apple Internet-based service for backing up your data from any Apple device to the iCloud service. This data is available to all devices from any location with Internet access.

Step-by-Step 11.01

Configuring Synchronization in iOS using iTunes

This step-by-step exercise goes through the steps for synchronizing your iPad or iPhone data using iTunes. To complete this exercise, you will need the following:

- The latest version of iTunes on your Mac or Windows PC.
- An iPhone or iPad as well as the USB cable that came with the device.

Step 1

Open iTunes on your Mac or Windows PC. Connect the USB cable to the iPad and the computer. The first time you do this on a Windows PC there will be a slight delay while it installs the driver. When the iPad is recognized, the iPad button will appear in the button bar. Select the iPad button.

Step 2

Under Backups select This computer. If you want to encrypt your account passwords and data, select that box, and then select **Back Up Now**.

Step 3

You may see a message similar to this. It is a little confusing, but if you want your apps on the iPad synchronized with your computer, you will go through the steps to authorize that computer, providing your Apple ID and password.

When the backup is complete, the date and time shown under Latest Backup will change.

Backups

Automatically Back Up

○ iCloud
Back up the most important data on your iPad to iCloud.

● This computer
A full backup of your iPad will be stored on this computer.

☐ Encrypt local backup
This will allow account passwords and Health data to be backed up.

Change Password...

Manually Back Up and Restore

Manually back up your iPad to this computer or restore a backup stored on this computer.

Back Up Now   Restore Backup...

Latest Backup:
Today 7:03 PM to this computer

Exit iTunes and disconnect your iPad.

Syncing Windows Phone

In Windows Phone you have several ways to synchronize different types of data. You can sync email accounts, podcasts from iTunes, and you can synchronize your Windows Phone data with the cloud and with your PC.

If you sign in to your Windows Phone device with a Microsoft account you can back up your settings, text messages, photos, and videos to OneDrive. You can Enable Backup during the initial Windows Phone setup or later by opening Settings | Backup. On the Backup page (Figure 11–13) select what you want backed up. You need to turn Backup on for each type of data.

LO 11.4 | Securing Mobile Devices

How do you protect a mobile device from malware? How do you keep the wrong people from logging on to a device they stole or found? How do you keep mobile operating systems up to date? How can you find lost devices?

Security Software for Mobile Devices

Many security programs are available for each of the mobile operating systems. They include such features as antivirus, antispam, browsing protection, and privacy features that will alert you if an app attempts to access your private information (for example, location, contacts, and messages). These free or inexpensive security suites may also include backup and missing device features. If a device is missing, you can use this software to locate it over the Internet (if you previously enabled location services), initiate a loud alarm on the device, and/or do a remote wipe (deleting all contents), making it effectively unusable by anyone who steals or finds it. We describe remote wipe later in the chapter.

Mobile OSs also have built-in security features. We will describe the steps you can take to make your mobile device more secure with built-in settings.

Patching and OS Updates

As with any computer, you need to keep your device updated with operating system patches and security updates. All the mobile OSs described here are automatically updated. You can check on the status for each OS.

FIGURE 11–13 On the **Backup** page select each type of data and enable backup.

This Windows Store tile shows three updates ready to download and install.

Presently, Android has updates turned on by default. You can see the status of updates on your Android device by opening **Settings**. Then scroll down and tap **About device** (or **About phone**). This opens a list of information about your device. Locate and tap **Software update** (or System updates) included in this list. This will give you the status of updates, and on some devices you can disable or enable this setting. We recommend that you leave it turned on.

To check the status of updates on an Apple iOS device, open Settings, then tap General, and on that page locate and tap Software Update to see the current state. Figure 11–14 shows the General page from the iPad's Settings app. Tap on Software Update and it will give the status. Later we will discuss several security settings on the General page.

Windows 8, Windows RT, Windows Phone 8, and Windows 10 all update automatically, as do their apps, through the Windows Store. The Store tile will display the number of app updates waiting to download and install. Simply tap the tile and the first screen will be the update screen. You can select apps individually or choose to update all of them.

Securing Lock Screens on Mobile Devices

A mobile device has a lock screen that keeps you from accidental touch actions, such as inadvertently "pocket dialing" your boss when you are at lunch. Mobile devices usually have a setting for a passcode lock that keeps the lock screen in place until you perform some action, such as entering a code or password. Without a passcode lock a simple swipe closes the lock screen and gives anyone access to the device. Android, iOS, Windows, and Windows Phone include this feature, although they use different terms to describe it as well as different options.

Android Screen Lock

The Android tablet and phones used for research for this chapter are all up to date, but the settings, screens, and options vary slightly between the tablet and the phones. The Lock screen settings on the tablet include None, Swipe, Face unlock, Pattern, PIN, and Password. The Lock screen options on our Android phones use the term "Slide" in place of "Swipe." These settings vary by manufacturer of the device.

Passcode Lock for iOS

The iPad has **Passcode** as an option on the Settings page. Tap it to open the **Passcode Lock** page, shown in Figure 11–15. Notice the two messages below the Erase Data setting. One begins with "Erase all data on this iPad." All data will *only* be erased after 10 failed passcode attempts, *if* you turn on **Erase Data.** However, the second statement, "Data protection is enabled," is true because the iOS data protection feature is enabled when you turn Passcode on. In iOS data protection encrypts mail messages and attachments on the device, using the passcode as the encryption key.

In iOS a simple passcode is only four digits long. When you enable Passcode, the **Set Passcode** box opens with just four spaces for the passcode. Select **Passcode Options** and then select options to make your passcode harder to break (see Figure 11–16).

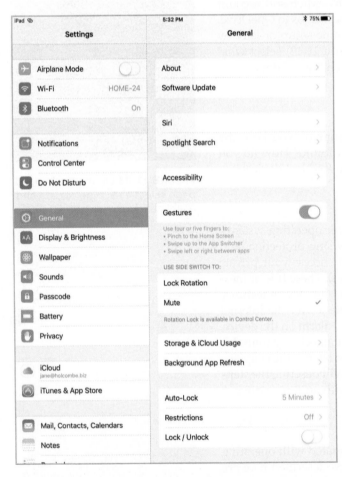

FIGURE 11–14 The **General** page of the iPad's Settings app.

Figure 11–17 shows the passcode keypad that displays when you turn the Passcode Lock on and choose to have a six-digit numeric code.

If you do not require a passcode, you simply use a swipe to close the lock screen and access the device.

Windows Phone Lock Screen Password

When you use a Lock screen password in Windows Phone, a password entry screen displays after you swipe on the Lock screen. Configure a Lock screen password by opening Settings | Lock Screen. Then locate the Password option at the bottom of the Lock Screen page (Figure 11–18) and move the slider to **On**. Then in the **Create a password** page enter a code of four digits or more and tap Done.

After you create a password, the Lock Screen settings include two new options: **Change password** and **Require a password after**. The first allows you to change the password. You will be required to enter the old password before you can change it. The second option controls how often you need to enter a password. The default is **Each time**. You can change this to a screen time set in minutes (1, 3, 5, 15, or 30). Securing your Windows Phone device with a password will still allow you to make an emergency call (911 in the United States) without entering a password.

Location Settings

Locator applications have a variety of uses, such as allowing you to find your lost or stolen mobile device from another device or computer, plotting driving directions from your current location, and much more. For these apps to work

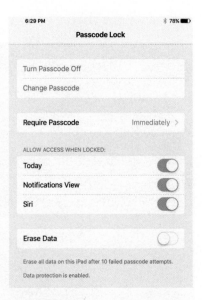

FIGURE 11–15 The iOS **Passcode Lock** settings.

Note: If your iPhone or iPad supports Touch ID, you can configure Passcode Lock to unlock using your fingerprint.

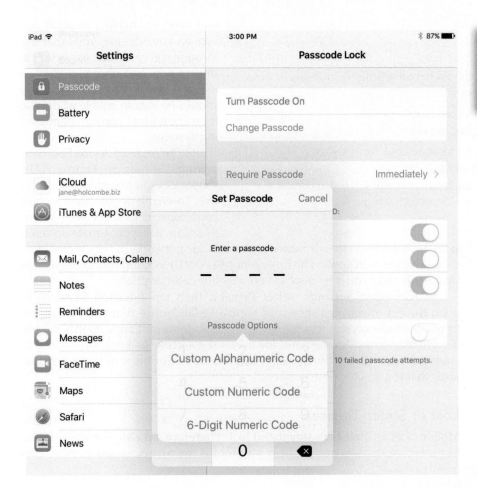

FIGURE 11–16 Use Passcode Options to enable a more complex passcode.

FIGURE 11–17 The **Passcode keypad** displays on the iPad **Lock** screen.

FIGURE 11–18 Enable Windows Phone Lock Screen password by moving the **Password** slider to the **On** position.

FIGURE 11–19 Location services on an Android device using the Verizon cellular network.

try this!

Enable or Disable Location Services

If you have a mobile device, it should have a setting for enabling or disabling location services. Try this:

1. Open the Settings utility in your mobile device.
2. Look for a setting for location and tap it.
3. If you do not see a setting for location, look for "privacy."
4. Once you find it, disable it and test it by opening a mapping program and trying to find your location. It will fail if you turned the location service off, and it will succeed if you turned it on.

you need to enable a location service on your device. Apps that use location services are expected to inform you, and once you turn on location services for a device, you should be able to enable or disable it for individual apps in all operating systems.

On an Android device, Locations settings, shown in Figure 11–19, shows Google Location Service in use. To enable it you need to give your consent to allow your phone to share its approximate location with apps and services. It may use the cellular network, in which case data usage charges will apply. The Emergency 911 (E911) location service is enabled by default and cannot be disabled on a mobile cellular phone.

In iOS, open **Settings**, select **Privacy**, then tap **Location Services** to open the list of settings shown in Figure 11–20. Notice that you can enable or disable location services for various components and apps on this device.

On Windows devices look for a Privacy setting or Location setting to enable the service for the device. Then enable or disable it in the individual apps that request location services.

Lost or Stolen Devices

Mobile devices are easily stolen and lost. Therefore, take steps ahead of time to protect your data and to help you locate the lost or stolen device. This will usually involve enabling a locator service on the device that tracks its location.

Android Device Manager and Samsung Find My Mobile

Beginning in August 2013 Google quietly enabled a service, previously available only to business accounts, to all Google accounts with Android devices. This service is called Device Manager and it will help you locate your device, change the lock screen settings, and even remotely wipe all the data if necessary.

Enable this service or one tied to the manufacturer of your device by searching in Settings.

If you enabled Android Device Manager you can manage your Android smartphone from any computer by connecting to **https://www.google.com/android/devicemanager**. Sign in with the Google account associated with your device, and the **Android Device Manager** page will display. After a short delay the map will show the location of your device. If you have simply misplaced the device at home, select **Ring** and the device will ring until you turn it off and on again. If it is stolen, but appears to be physically near you, selecting **Ring** will alert you to who has the phone. You can also remotely erase all the data from the device by selecting Erase Device.

If you have a Samsung device and if it has the Find My Mobile option in Security settings, you can use the Samsung Find My Mobile service. Register your Samsung account on the device in the Add account page, shown back in Figure 11–9. Then enable the service. If your phone is lost or stolen (or misplaced), use another computer and browse to findmymobile.samsung.com and sign in.

Apple iCloud Find My iPhone

On an Apple OS X or iOS device you can enable a free feature that uses iCloud to locate a lost or stolen iMac, iPad, iPhone, or iPod and then select from several actions, including a remote wipe if your device is lost or stolen. On an iOS device open Settings and select iCloud. Then enable **Find My iPhone** (or iPad or iPod) and **Send Last Location**, as shown in Figure 11–21. Tap **Allow** in the confirmation message that displays.

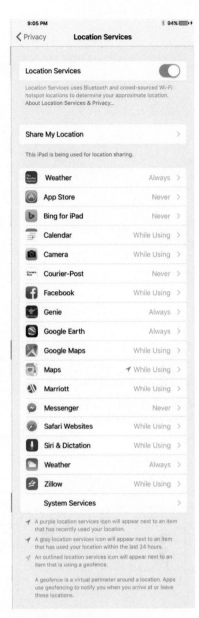

FIGURE 11–20 The iOS **Location Services** settings.

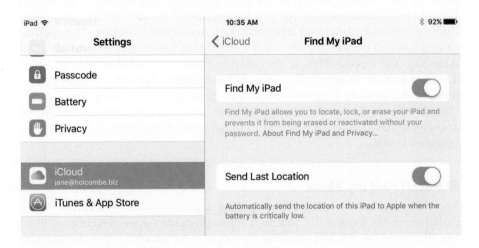

FIGURE 11–21 Open **iCloud** settings and enable **Find My iPad** and **Send Last Location**.

FIGURE 11–22 After you log in to the iCloud home page from another computer, select Find My iPhone.

FIGURE 11–23 Select the actions for a lost device.

Microsoft's **Find My Phone** settings.

Once enabled, you can connect to **www.icloud.com** from another computer and log in with your Apple ID. You will be prompted to verify your access to all of iCloud.com from that device (if you haven't already authorized it), but you can still use Find My iPhone without this verification. Notice the iCloud home screen in Figure 11–22. The one feature that is available to you without verification is Find My iPhone. On the iCloud home screen select **Find My iPhone** (that is the name of this service, whether you have an iPhone or not). Then on the next screen a map will display with the location of your devices.

Select All Devices at the top left of this page to open a menu of your devices. Select the lost or stolen device, and **All Devices** changes to the name of the selected device and a box opens for that device, as shown in Figure 11–23. This box tells you the battery life of the device (see the upper-right corner of the box) and lets you take some action. Clicking **Play Sound** causes a sound on the device, and it will display the message "Find My iPad Alert" on the device. This is very handy when your iPad is hiding under a pile of papers in your office. Select **Lost Mode** and enter a passcode to lock the device (this appears if the device does not already have a passcode). Once the passcode is entered on the device itself, it is no longer in Lost Mode and can be used. The last option is **Erase iPad**. Select this if you are convinced it is stolen.

Microsoft Find My Phone

Microsoft has a free service for locating a lost or stolen Windows Phone called Find My Phone. To enable it on your device open **Settings | Find My Phone**, shown at left. Tap the first option to remotely ring, lock, erase data, or send apps to the phone from Microsoft's Windows Phone website, **WindowsPhone.com**. Tap to place a check in the second box and Windows Phone will save its location to OneDrive until the battery runs out.

Chapter 11 REVIEW

Chapter Summary

After reading this chapter and completing the Step-by-Step tutorial and Try This! exercises, you should understand the following facts about mobile operating systems.

From Luggable to BYOD

- Just 30 years ago mobile computing involved lugging heavy computers that could not connect to a network when in transit. They were not meant for the typical consumer, but for technically savvy persons.
- Today's mobile devices are popular consumer devices that are tiny, powerful, and connected 24/7.
- People bring their personal mobile devices to school and work, a practice called bring your own device (BYOD).
- Most employers do not have an adequate policy for BYOD to address the many issues of security, ownership, and cost.
- Mobile device management (MDM) is a category of software for managing mobile devices.

Configuring Accounts and Wireless Connections on Mobile Devices

- All popular smartphones and tablets require a user account.
- An Android device has a Google account associated with it for accessing Google services. The Google account can be your Gmail account or you can associate it with another existing email account.
- An Apple ID is a customer account for accessing Apple services and products. Any working email address will do as the account name, and then create a password for the Apple ID.
- You only need one Apple ID, but since the free iCloud storage has a set limit per account, a person with many devices and/or many family members sharing the account may want to have multiple accounts in order not to run out of free storage space.
- A Microsoft account is a free account that gives the subscriber access to Microsoft services.
- A smartphone requires a cellular connection from a cellular provider.

- A cellular data connection is an extra option for a tablet, adding a premium to the cost of the device, plus requiring a cellular data plan.
- All popular mobile devices offer Wi-Fi connections, which you can enable and connect to hotspots using appropriate credentials. Using Wi-Fi for data when it is available saves on cellular data costs.
- A mobile device with a cellular connection may be able to share that connection, turning the device into a mobile hotspot. Cellular providers charge a service fee for allowing you to do this.
- You can purchase a separate device to use as a dedicated mobile hotspot. Novatel calls their mobile hotspot device MiFi.
- Tethering is a feature that allows you to share your smartphone's cellular data connection with a single computer.
- Near Field Communication (NFC) is a special chipset in some mobile devices that allows you to position your device close to another that also has NFC enabled and share data, pair with a Bluetooth device, or pay for purchases.
- Airplane mode is a feature of mobile devices that, when enabled, turns off all radio frequency (RF) signals. It complies with commercial airline requirements.

Email, Apps, and Synchronization

- Any popular mobile device can support multiple accounts of different types at once.
- Mobile operating systems understand the basic connection information required for many types of accounts, so you may only need to enter the personal login information for the account and it will attempt to connect.
- Sometimes when configuring an email account you may have to provide more information, such as the name of POP, IMAP, or SMTP servers.
- Each mobile OS has some service for synchronizing data between the mobile device and other devices or to the cloud.

Securing Mobile Devices

- There are security apps available for mobile devices that are free or inexpensive.

- Mobile OSs also have some security features built in.
- By default, mobile operating systems have updates enabled, so that security patches and updates of the OS are downloaded and installed automatically.
- A mobile device has a lock screen to prevent accidental touch actions. You can protect a lock screen with various security measures so that a simple swiping gesture does not give the wrong person access to the device.
- There are many locator applications, such as mapping programs or an app or service for finding your lost or stolen mobile device. They require a location service. Your device may have multiple location services available.
- Android Device Manager is a free service from Google that will help you locate and manage a lost or stolen device, remotely wipe the device, and cause it to ring. Samsung offers the Find My Mobile service to users of their Android devices.
- Apple iCloud has the free Find My iPhone service. Enable it through iCloud settings on your device.
- Enable Microsoft's Find My Phone on a Windows Phone device and it will save your phone's location to OneDrive until the battery runs out. Then, before the battery runs out and using another computer, connect and sign in to Microsoft's Windows Phone website and you can cause the lost or stolen phone to ring, lock, erase data, and show you its location.

Key Terms List

Airplane mode *(448)*

Apple ID *(442)*

Apple Pay *(448)*

Bluetooth *(446)*

bring your own device (BYOD) *(439)*

data protection *(457)*

Google account *(442)*

location service *(441)*

MiFi *(446)*

mobile device management (MDM) *(441)*

mobile hotspot *(446)*

Near Field Communication (NFC) *(448)*

pairing *(447)*

passcode lock *(456)*

remote wipe *(456)*

Service Set ID (SSID) *(444)*

Subscriber Identity Module *(SIM) (444)*

synchronize *(452)*

tethering *(446)*

Touch ID *(448)*

Wallet *(448)*

Key Terms Quiz

Use the Key Terms List to complete the sentences that follow:

1. If you turn on the _____ feature of a cell-enabled mobile device the device serves as a cellular modem for an attached computer.

2. Turn on _____ to turn off all radios in your mobile device.

3. The list of available Wi-Fi networks that display on your device or computer are each identified by a/an _____.

4. The practice of people using their own mobile devices at work is called _____.

5. One company uses the trademarked name of _____ to identify their line of small devices that act as dedicated mobile hotspots.

6. A connection between two Bluetooth devices is called a _____.

7. Some organizations use a type of software called _____ to manage mobile devices used by their employees.

8. If your device is stolen, be prepared to protect it by learning what you need to do to cause a/an _____, which will delete all your data on the device.

9. A/an _____ secures the lock screen on a mobile device.

10. _____ is a service offered by Apple on their newer devices that have both Touch ID and NFC, allowing the user to pay for purchases wirelessly.

Multiple-Choice Quiz

1. Which of the following is *not* true concerning BYOD?
   a. Employees may personally incur higher voice and data costs when they bring their own devices to work.
   b. A lost or stolen device can put the employer at risk.
   c. It is unclear who owns intellectual property created.
   d. An employee's private data on their personally owned device may be at risk.
   e. Most organizations have adequate policies in place for BYOD.

2. Which of the following is not a type of wireless communications?
   a. NFC
   b. USB
   c. Wi-Fi
   d. Cellular
   e. Bluetooth

3. Which of the following is an account required for using an Android smartphone?
   a. Apple ID
   b. Microsoft account
   c. Yahoo!
   d. Google account
   e. Hotmail

4. Which type of connection is the primary connection type for a smartphone?
   a. NFC
   b. USB
   c. Wi-Fi
   d. Cellular
   e. Bluetooth

5. Which type of connection is an option for a tablet that adds cost to the hardware as well as a fee for data usage?
   a. NFC
   b. USB
   c. Wi-Fi
   d. Cellular
   e. Bluetooth

6. Which feature, if available, allows you to share your smartphone's cellular data connection with just a single computer?
   a. Mobile hotspot
   b. Tethering
   c. MiFi
   d. SSID
   e. BYOD

7. Which mode turns off all radio frequency (RF) signals on a device?
   a. Tethering
   b. Mobile hotspot
   c. Airplane mode
   d. Synchronization
   e. Data protection

8. What wireless connection feature, if available in your phone, would allow you to pay for purchases by simply positioning the device very close to another device with this feature?
   a. NFC
   b. USB
   c. Wi-Fi
   d. Cellular
   e. Bluetooth

9. Without this type of feature on a mobile device, a simple swipe gives anyone access to the device. What is the term for this feature?
   a. Location service
   b. Passcode lock
   c. Updates
   d. Screen saver
   e. Device manager

10. This very short-range wireless connection option is often used to connect keyboard and headsets to mobile devices.
    a. NFC
    b. USB
    c. Wi-Fi
    d. Cellular
    e. Bluetooth

11. What free Google service is available to all Google accounts, allowing them to locate their lost or stolen Android mobile devices?
    a. iCloud
    b. Find My Phone
    c. Android Device Manager
    d. Find My iPhone
    e. Google Play

12. Use this Apple service to synchronize your iOS device with a Mac or PC.
    a. iCloud
    b. Apple ID
    c. Find My iPhone
    d. iTunes
    e. iMac

13. What Apple service allows you to back up your data from any Apple device so that it is available to all your devices?
    a. iCloud
    b. Apple ID
    c. Find My iPhone
    d. iTunes
    e. iMac

14. What type of card inserted into a mobile device programs it for a user's cellular account information?
    a. NFC

b. SSID
c. MDM
d. SIM
e. MiFi

15. This name identifies a Wi-Fi network.
    a. NFC
    b. SSID
    c. MDM
    d. SIM
    e. MiFi

Essay Quiz

1. Describe your ideal mobile device, whether it exists or not.

2. What options do you have for cellular service in your area? Write a paragraph listing the cellular providers who service your area and which one you would choose if you were shopping for a mobile device today. Explain your choice.

3. Take a poll of your fellow students or coworkers. What mobile operating systems are on their mobile devices? Record the results of your poll and compute the percentage using Android, iOS, and Windows.

4. What is the U.S. Federal Aviation Administration policy for the use of electronic devices on an airliner? If you live in another country, research the policy of the equivalent agency in your country. Does this policy allow for Airplane mode?

5. Has this chapter influenced your attitude toward mobile devices? Explain your answer and discuss with your instructor and fellow students.

Lab Projects

LAB PROJECT 11.1

Research mobile device management (MDM) software products by searching for recent product reviews and answer the following questions.

1. What mobile operating systems did the majority of the MDM products you found support?

2. How many of the reviewed products included support for desktop OSs in addition to mobile OSs? List the OSs and the number of MDM products you found that supported them.

3. How many of the MDM products reviewed included a feature that would block devices from accessing email if MDM policies were violated?

LAB PROJECT 11.2

An organization that hosts email services for clients does not need to view the content of the messages in order to provide this service. They can deliver messages by simply examining the header information of the packets that comprise each message. Storing email messages on servers also does not require scanning the content.

Two popular email service providers, Microsoft (hotmail.com and outlook.com) and Google (Gmail), both include advertising next to your messages in their Web-based email GUIs. Research this practice by these two providers and see if you discern any difference in their use of advertising. Write up your findings and share them with your instructor or class.

LAB PROJECT 11.3

This book describes mobile devices at a point in time: summer of 2015. What do you see as the most significant change in mobile devices since then? Is it a new type of mobile device or a revolutionary new app? Is this change a law concerning mobile devices? Discuss this change with your classmates, and tell why you believe it is the most significant change.

Windows Mouse and Keyboard Shortcuts

Mouse Action or Mouse+Key Combination	Result in Windows 7 and Earlier	Result in Windows 8 and Newer
ALT + PRTSCR	Captures the current window and saves it in the Clipboard.	
CTRL + −	Zoom out (where supported in the GUI).	
CTRL + +	Zoom in (after a zoom out and where supported in the GUI).	
CTRL + A	Select all.	
CTRL + F1	Expand or minimize the ribbon in an app with the ribbon. (Includes File Explorer in Windows 8 and newer versions).	
CTRL + Roll middle scroll wheel	Semantic zoom (in and out).	
CTRL + SHIFT + ESC	Opens Task Manager.	
CTRL-ALT-DELETE	Opens the CTRL-ALT-DELETE menu.	
Double left-click	Selects or activates the object, performing the default command. If the pointer is in a document, this action selects the word at the insertion point, and a third click selects the sentence or paragraph (depending on the application and the version of the application). The third click for selecting an entire paragraph disappeared from Microsoft Word several versions ago.	
Drag and drop	After pointing at a graphic object, hold the primary pointing device button down while moving the pointing device to visually drag the object. At the destination, release the button to drop the object.	
F1	Opens context-sensitive Help where supported.	Opens context-sensitive Help where supported on the Desktop. It does not work in Modern apps or the Start screen.
Hover	The object the mouse pointer hovers over will display a tooltip, infotip, or similar information, if enabled for the object.	
PAGE DOWN	Depending on context, moves cursor/current screen to next screen.	
PAGE UP	Depending on context, moves cursor/current screen to previous screen.	
PRTSCR	Captures the screen and saves it in the Clipboard.	
SHIFT key + single left-click	For selectable objects, this action contiguously extends the selection.	
Single left-click	Selects or activates an object, depending on the current context and location of the pointer. For instance, if the pointer is in a document, this action sets the insertion point.	
Single right-click	Selects the object and displays its context menu.	
WINDOWS KEY + F1	Opens Windows Help and Support window.	Opens Windows Help and Support window on the Desktop.
WINDOWS KEY ALONE	Opens the Start menu.	Returns to Start screen or returns to previous app from Start screen.

Mouse Action or Mouse+Key Combination	Result in Windows 7 and Earlier	Result in Windows 8 and Newer
WINDOWS KEY + PrtScr	Captures the screen and saves it in the Clipboard.	Captures the screen and saves it in a folder named *Screenshots* in the Pictures folder.
WINDOWS KEY + TAB KEY (repeat)	N/A	Cycles through Modern app history in the task switcher bar on the left of the screen. Desktop apps appear as one app (Windows 8.x).
WINDOWS KEY + TAB KEY (release)	N/A	Opens Task view for current virtual desktop (Windows 10).
WINDOWS KEY + SHIFT + LEFT ARROW KEY	On dual display system, switches contents of windows.	On dual display system moves desktop window to left display.
WINDOWS KEY + SHIFT + RIGHT ARROW KEY	On dual display system, switches contents of windows.	On dual display system moves desktop window to right display.
WINDOWS KEY + +	Opens Magnifier to magnify all or part of the screen.	
WINDOWS KEY + ESC	Closes Magnifier.	
WINDOWS KEY + , (COMMA)	N/A	Peek at the Desktop. Release to return to previous screen or Desktop window.
WINDOWS KEY + HOME	Minimize nonactive desktop windows.	
WINDOWS KEY + LEFT ARROW KEY	Snaps current desktop window to left.	
WINDOWS KEY + RIGHT ARROW KEY	Snaps current desktop window to right.	
WINDOWS KEY + UP ARROW KEY	Maximizes current desktop window.	
WINDOWS KEY + DOWN ARROW KEY	Restores/minimizes current desktop window.	
WINDOWS KEY + PGUP KEY	Same as PGUP KEY alone.	Moves Start screen to left monitor.
WINDOWS KEY + PGDN KEY	Same as PGDN KEY alone.	Moves Start screen to right monitor.
WINDOWS KEY + 1–9	Opens desktop app at the given position on the task bar.	
WINDOWS KEY + C	N/A	Opens Charms bar (Windows 8.x). Opens Cortana (Windows 10).
WINDOWS KEY + D	Minimizes all open windows and displays the desktop.	Same as Windows 7 (Windows 8.x). From Start screen or Modern app, opens the Desktop or returns to Desktop (Windows 8.x).
WINDOWS KEY + E	Opens a Windows Explorer window.	Opens a File Explorer window on the Desktop.
WINDOWS KEY + F	Opens a Search window.	Opens Search focused on files (Windows 8.x).
WINDOWS KEY + H	N/A	Opens the Share bar.
WINDOWS KEY + I	N/A	Opens the Settings bar (Windows 8.x). Opens Settings (Windows 10).
WINDOWS KEY + J	N/A	When using Snap, switches focus between apps (Windows 8.x).
WINDOWS KEY + K	N/A	Opens the Devices bar (Windows 8.x). Opens Connect bar (Windows 10).

Mouse Action or Mouse+Key Combination	Result in Windows 7 and Earlier	Result in Windows 8 and Newer
WINDOWS KEY + L	Locks the PC displaying the Sign-In screen.	Locks the PC displaying either the Lock screen (if enabled) or the Sign-In screen.
WINDOWS KEY + M	Minimizes all windows.	Minimizes all Desktop windows.
WINDOWS KEY + O	N/A	Toggles the device orientation of mobile devices on and off in portrait or landscape.
WINDOWS KEY + P	Opens projection/second monitor options.	
WINDOWS KEY + Q	N/A	Opens the Apps Search bar (Windows 8.x). Opens Cortana Home (Windows 10).
WINDOWS KEY + R	Opens the Desktop Run box.	
WINDOWS KEY + T	Cycles through open Desktop apps.	
WINDOWS KEY + U	Opens Ease of Access Center.	
WINDOWS KEY + W	N/A	Opens Settings Search (Windows 8.x).
WINDOWS KEY + X	N/A	Opens Power User menu.
WINDOWS KEY + Z	N/A	When in Start screen or a Modern app, opens Apps bar on bottom of screen (Windows 8.x).
WINDOWS KEY + CTRL + D	N/A	Opens New virtual desktop (Windows 10).
WINDOWS KEY + CTRL + F4	N/A	Closes current virtual desktop (Windows 10).
WINDOWS KEY + CTRL + RIGHT ARROW KEY	N/A	Switches to next virtual desktop (Windows 10).
WINDOWS KEY + CTRL + LEFT ARROW KEY	N/A	Switches to previous virtual desktop (Windows 10).

Glossary

The number at the end of the entry refers to the chapter where the term is introduced.

$ prompt (Pronounced "dollar prompt.") The command prompt displayed in a Terminal window in OS X. The $ prompt is also used in the Linux CLI. (8)

absolute path A directory path that begins with the top level. in Linux, an absolute path begins with a forward slash (/) to indicate the root directory. (9)

accelerometer A component of a mobile device that detects the physical tilt and acceleration of the device, allowing the device to change the screen orientation for readability. (1)

Access Control Entry (ACE) An entry in an Access Control List, containing just one user or group account name and the permissions assigned to this account for that file or folder. (4)

Access Control List (ACL) A table of users and/or groups and their permissions to access the file or folder associated with the ACL. (4)

access mode number A value assigned to a file permission in Linux. The user (owner), group, and others each have a different access mode number calculated using the following values: read = 4, write = 2, and execute = 1. (9)

Action Center A Windows feature, represented by the small flag icon on the right of the toolbar; it will briefly display a message balloon when there is a problem with security programs or backup. (4)

activation A method of combating software piracy, intended to ensure that each software license used solely on a single computer. (4)

Add Printer wizard A series of onscreen instructions that guide you through the installation of a printer's driver and utilities. (4)

address space layout randomization (ASLR) A security feature of OS X Mountain Lion and newer that loads the core operating system code, the kernel, into random locations in memory, rather than loading into the same memory addresses every time. This prevents malware from accessing operating system functions based on where they are known to be in memory. (8)

administrator account type An account type in the OSs surveyed in this book. A user logged on with an administrator account type can perform systemwide tasks such as changing computer settings and installing or removing software and hardware. (2)

adware A form of spyware software downloaded to a computer without permission. It collects information about the user in order to display targeted advertisements, either in the form of inline banners or pop-ups. (2)

Aero Peek A Windows 7 feature that allows the user to peek at the underlying desktop by hovering the mouse over the Show Desktop button on the taskbar. (4)

Aero Shake A Windows Aero feature that lets you quickly minimize all but one window by giving that window a quick shake. (4)

Aero Snap A Windows Aero feature that lets you manipulate windows quickly. To maximize a window drag it until its title bar touches the top edge of your display. Restore a maximized window by dragging it away from the top of the display. (4)

Airplane mode A feature of mobile devices that turns off all wireless communications (cellular, Wi-Fi, Bluetooth, and NFC) without powering off the device. (11)

AirPlay A feature that was first introduced in iOS, and later added to OS X in Mountain Lion for connecting to an Apple TV, which acts as an intermediary device for sending iTunes songs, video, pictures, and other data from the computer to a high definition (HD) TV via Wi-Fi. (8)

anonymous FTP site An FTP site that does not require a user name and password, but allows anonymous connection, which means that all users connecting are using the Anonymous account. (10)

Apache HTTP Server Open source Web server software, originally written for UNIX, runs on Linux. (9)

Apple ID A free account that identifies the holder as a customer of Apple for all Apple services and products. (11)

Apple menu A pop-up menu opened by clicking on the Apple icon in the upper left of the OS X desktop. (8)

Apple Pay An automatic payment system for Apple Watch and iPhones that uses NFC wireless technology. (11)

application Software that allows a computer user to perform useful functions such as writing a report or calculating a budget. (1)

application virtualization Virtualization of an application whereby a user connects to a server and accesses one or more applications rather than an entire desktop environment. (3)

AppLocker A feature introduced in Windows 7 for controlling which applications each user can run, reducing the chance of malware running on the user's computer. Administer AppLocker with Group Policy, centrally managed through a Windows Active Directory domain. (4)

Assigned Access A feature added in Windows 8.1 that allows an administrator to assign a single user account to run just one app. (5)

augmented reality (AR) Similar to virtual reality, but AR involves viewing something in real time through a camera or other device while the image (or other input) is digitally modified. (3)

authentication Validation of a user account and password that occurs before the security components of an OS give a user access to the computer or network. (2)

authorization The process of both authenticating a user and determining the permissions that the user has for a resource. (2)

automatic IP addressing A method by which a host can be assigned an IP address and all the additional configuration settings automatically. (10)

Automatic login In OS X (and other operating systems), a setting that bypasses the login when the computer powers on, page and logs into the selected user account with requiring a user to enter a password or passcode. (8)

Automatic Private IP Addressing (APIPA) A method by which a DHCP client computer that fails to receive an address from a DHCP server will automatically give itself an address from a special range that has the value 169 (base-10) in the first octet (eight binary digits) of the IP address. (10)

avatar An animated computer-generated human used in a virtual world to represent an individual. (3)

back door A way to use software to bypass security and gain access to a computer. (2)

Back tip In Windows 8, a thumbnail image of the previous active app that appears when the user points a mouse in the upper left corner. (5)

BASH An acronym for Bourne Again Shell; the Linux component (shell) that provides the character-mode user interface for entering and processing commands, issuing error messages, and other limited feedback. (9)

binary file A file that contains program code, as opposed to a file containing data. (7)

bitcoin An online payment system. (2)

BitLocker A feature introduced in the Enterprise and Ultimate editions of Windows Vista and Windows 7 for encrypting the drive on which the Windows OS resides and other drives beyond the system drive. (4)

BitLocker To Go An enhanced feature of BitLocker that includes encryption of removable devices. (4)

black hat hacker Someone who breaks into computers (hacks) to do harm. (2)

bloatware Slang for the software added to a computer when it is purchased with Windows preinstalled. Some of these programs are useful, but most of it is annoying or may be free trial software that you can try, but must purchase to use after the trial period (often 30 days) expires. (5)

bluesnarfing The act of covertly obtaining information broadcast from wireless devices using the Bluetooth standard. (2)

Bluetooth A wireless standard for using radio waves to communicate over very short distances between devices. The most common implementation of Bluetooth wirelessly connects devices at a distance of up to one meter. (11)

bootloader OS startup code that must be loaded into early in the startup process. The Windows bootloader is a file named BOOTMGR. (7)

bootstrap loader A firmware program that uses hardware configuration settings stored in nonvolatile memory, commonly called CMOS, to determine what devices can start an OS and the order in which the system will search these devices while attempting to begin the OS startup process. It then loads the bootloader program. (7)

botherder Someone who initiates and controls a botnet. (2)

botnet A group of networked computers that, usually unbeknown to their owners, have been infected with programs that forward information to other computers over the network (usually the Internet). (2)

Bring Your Own Device (BYOD) The practice of using personal mobile devices at work. (11)

browser hijacking Malware installed on a computer that causes the Internet Explorer home page to always point to a specific site, often advertising something. Hijackers make it very difficult to defeat the hijack by modifying the registry so that every time you restart Windows or Internet Explorer the hijack reinstates. (2)

burn To write digital data just once to a disc. Traditionally this term refers to the writing of data to a disc (CD-R, DVD-R, or BD-R) that can only be written to once in any given area of the disc. Once full, you cannot add data to the disc. It is "write-once." The source files can be individual files or an ISO file. (9)

case-aware In an operating system, a feature that allows the OS to preserve the case used for the characters in a file name when creating it, but does not require the correct case when opening or managing the file. (9)

case-sensitive In an operating system, a feature that allows the OS to preserve the case used for the characters in a file name when creating it, and requires the correct case to open or manage the file. (9)

cellular hotspot A service offered by cell providers in which a customer's smartphone or a separate device acts as a Wi-Fi router to allow other computers and devices to access the Internet. (10)

central processing unit (CPU) An integrated circuit (chip) that performs the calculations, or processing, for a computer. See also *microprocessor*. (1)

charm Shortcut-like object that appears on the Charms bar in Windows 8. This bar slides out from the right side of the screen. (5)

Charms bar A bar that displays on the right side of a Windows 8 screen and contains charms. (5)

clean installation An installation of an OS onto a completely empty hard disk or one from which all data is removed during the installation. (4)

client A software component on a computer that accesses services from a network server. (1)

code signing A Windows feature in which all of the operating system code is digitally signed to show that it has not been tampered with. See also *driver signing*. (7)

cold boot A method of starting up a computer and operating system by turning on the power switch. (5)

command completion A feature of Linux (and OS X Terminal UNIX) that completes what is entered at the command line with a command name or file or directory name. (9)

command-line history The Linux and UNIX (and OS X Terminal) feature that saves command-line history in a file named bash_history. (9)

command-line interface (CLI) A user interface that includes a character-based command line that requires text input. (1)

Command Prompt In Windows, the command-line interface that is launched from within Windows or in Safe Mode or as a Recovery option. (7)

computer. A device that calculates. (1)

Consent Prompt Part of the User Account Control security feature since Windows Vista, this prompt appears when a user is logged on as an administrator and a program attempts to perform a task requiring administrative permissions. The task is allowed to complete only if the user selects the Yes button. (7)

content filter In an Internet browser, software that blocks content. (2)

Continuum A feature of Windows 10 that senses when a keyboard is attached versus when a keyboard is removed and presents the appropriate desktop for each configuration. (6)

cookies Very small text files an Internet browser saves on the local hard drive at the request of a website. Cookies may contain user preferences for a specific site, information entered into a form at a website (including personal information), browsing activity, and shopping selections made at a website. (2)

Cortana An intelligent search system introduced in Windows Phone 8.1, and improved on as a personal assistant in Windows 10. (6)

Credentials Prompt Part of the User Account Control security feature since Windows Vista, this prompt appears when a user is logged on as a standard user and a program attempts to perform a task requiring administrative permission. The prompt will ask the user for an administrator password to continue. (7)

cursor In a command-line interface (CLI), the cursor is a marker for the current position where what you type on the keyboard will go. In a GUI the cursor is replaced by a graphical pointer that can have a variety of shapes you can move around by manipulating a pointing device. (1)

cybercriminal A person who breaks laws using computer technology. (2)

cybercrime Illegal activity performed using computer technology. (2)

cyberterrorism A computer-based attack that wreaks havoc on victims. (2)

cyberterrorist A person who commits a computer-based attack that wreaks havoc on victims. (2)

daemon In Linux, software that runs in background until it is activated. (9)

Darwin The name of the core operating system on which OS X is based. A product of the open-source community. (8)

data protection In iOS a feature that is turned on when you enable the Passcode Lock that encrypts mail messages and attachments on the device, using the passcode as the encryption key. (11)

data type In the Windows registry, a special data format. There are several registry data types, such as REG_BINARY, REG_DWORD, and so forth. (7)

data wiping The permanent removal of data from a storage device. (2)

default gateway The IP address of the router connected to your network. The net ID of the default gateway address should be identical to that of your NIC. The router is a network device that sits between networks and directs traffic to destinations beyond the local network. (10)

Desktop mode A feature of Windows 10 that displays the desktop and apps appropriately for a computer with a keyboard attached. (6)

desktop virtualization The virtualization of a desktop computer into which you can install an operating system, its unique configuration, and applications and user data. (3)

device driver Software that is added to an OS to control a physical component (device). A component-specific device driver is needed for each unique hardware device connected to a computer. (1)

device management An OS function that controls hardware devices through the use of device drivers. (1)

Device Manager A Windows recovery tool that aids in troubleshooting device problems. This Windows Control Panel applet displays the list of hardware and the status and properties of each device. Use this to disable a device or to update or roll back a device driver. (6)

Device Stage A feature introduced in Windows 7 that, if the device supports it, will bring up a page from which you can make many choices for managing the device; it often includes an accurate image of the device. (7)

dial-up An inexpensive WAN option available to anyone with a phone line and a standard analog modem (the long-time standard runs at 56 Kbps). (10)

digital certificate A special file stored on a computer that may hold a secret key for decrypting data. (2)

digital signature In Windows, encrypted data that can be unencrypted by Windows in a process called file signature verification. (7)

digital subscriber line (DSL) A WAN service similar to ISDN in its use of the telephone network, but using more advanced digital signal processing to compress more signals through the telephone lines. (10)

directory A special file that can contain files as well as other directories. This term is most often used with non-GUI operating systems, while *folder* is most often used when describing a directory in a GUI. (1)

distribution A bundling of the Linux kernel and software—both enhancements to the OS and applications—such as word processors, spreadsheets, media players, and more. (1)

DMZ A network between the internal network and the Internet with a firewall on both sides. (2)

Dock A floating bar on the OS X desktop that holds icons for commonly used programs, as well as icons for open applications. A single click on an icon launches the program. (8)

Domain Join A feature that allows a Windows computer to join a Microsoft Active Directory Domain. (5)

Domain Name System (DNS) A distributed online database containing registered domain names mapped to IP addresses. Thousands of name servers on the Internet maintain this distributed database. When you attempt to connect to a website, your computer's DNS client queries a DNS server to determine the IP address of the website. (10)

drive-by download A program downloaded to a user's computer without consent. Often the simple act of browsing to a website or opening an HTML email message may result in such a surreptitious download. A drive-by download may also occur when installing another application. (2)

driver signing Code signing of device drivers that indicates two things: the integrity of the file or files, and that the device driver has passed Microsoft's tests for compatibility. (7)

dual-boot A multiboot configuration with just two choices of operating systems. (4)

dumb terminal A device consisting of little more than a keyboard and display with a connection to a host computer (mainframe or minicomputer) and having no native processing power of its own. (3)

Dynamic Host Configuration Protocol (DHCP) server A server that issues IP addresses and settings to computers that are configured to obtain an IP address automatically, thus making them DHCP clients. (10)

Early Launch Anti-Malware (ELAM) A security feature, introduced in Windows 8, that examines all device drivers before they are loaded into memory, preventing suspicious drivers from loading. (7)

Ease of Access icon An icon that appears in the Windows Setup screen and other screens. Click this icon to access Windows settings for audio and visual aids. (6)

edge gestures Touch gestures that begin close to the bezel of the screen on a Windows 8 computer. (5)

edition A packaging of a Windows version. (1)

email spoofing Forging of the sender's address in the email message's header (the information that accompanies a message but does not appear in the message) so that an incorrect address appears in the "from" field of an email message. (2)

embedded OS An operating system stored in firmware, as in a mobile device (1)

Encrypting File System (EFS) An NTFS file encryption feature for encrypting selected files and folders (not entire drives). (2)

encryption The transformation of data into a code that can be decrypted only through the use of a secret key or password. (2)

exploit A malware attack. (2)

Family Safety The Windows 7 term for features for protecting children from inappropriate content. (2)

Fast Boot A feature of Windows 8 and newer in which startup takes advantage of the hibernated kernel (if the last shutdown was a Hybrid Shutdown), bringing the hibernated system session out of hibernation, saving all the work of the Kernel Loading phase. (7)

FAT file systems Several related file systems based on the original FAT file system. They include FAT12, FAT16, FAT32, and exFAT. Each has a logical structure that includes a file allocation table (FAT) and a directory structure. (4)

FIDO Alliance An industry consortium that works together on solutions that will allow users to securely access online services and conduct financial transactions without using password authentication and to reduce the rick of fraud. (6)

file and printer server A network server that gives client computers access to files and printers. Also simply called a file server. (10)

File Explorer Previously named Windows Explorer, the name of the Windows file management tool beginning with Windows 8. (5)

file management An operating system function that allows the operating system to read, write, and modify data and programs organized into files. (1)

file signature verification The process by which Windows unencrypts a digital signature and verifies that the file has not been tampered with. (7)

file system The logical structure used on a storage device for the purpose of storing files, as well as the code within an operating system that allows the OS to store and manage files on a storage device. (1)

File Transfer Protocol (FTP) A protocol used to transfer files between a computer running the FTP server service and an FTP client. It is a simple and fast method for transferring files over a TCP/IP network. (10)

FileVault A feature in Mac Os X that, in earlier versions of OS X, encrypted the Home folder. In recent versions, it encrypts the entire startup disk. (2)

Finder The foundation of the OS X GUI and the equivalent to Windows Explorer, the Windows file management tool. (8)

firewall A firewall is either software or a physical device that examines network traffic. Based on predefined rules, a firewall rejects certain traffic coming into a computer or network. The two general types of firewalls are network-based firewalls and personal firewalls that reside on individual computers. (2)

firmware Software resident in integrated circuits. (1)

first-party cookie A cookie that originates with the domain name of the URL to which you directly connect. (2)

Flip 3D A Windows Aero feature that lets you switch through your open windows as if they were in a stack of cards or photos. (4)

folder A special file that can contain files as well as other directories. This term is most often used with GUI operating systems, while *directory* is most often used when describing a directory in a non-GUI. (1)

forged email address An address that appears in the "from" field of an email address because the sender address was modified in the email message's header (the information that accompanies a message but does not appear in the message). This type of forgery is also called *email spoofing*. (2)

formatting The action of an operating system when it maps the logical organization of the file system to physical locations on the storage device (most often a conventional hard disk drive or solid-state drive) so that it can store and retrieve the data. (1)

fraud The use of deceit and trickery to persuade someone to hand over money or other valuables. (2)

fully qualified domain name (FQDN) The human-readable TCP/IP name corresponding to the TCP/IP address of a host, as found on a computer, router, or other networked device. It includes both its host name and its domain name. (10)

gadget In Windows 7 a small program represented by an icon on the desktop. Gadgets are no longer recommended because they were found to be potential security holes. (4)

Gatekeeper A security feature of OS X that limits sources from which you can download apps. (8)

GNOME An acronym for GNU network object model environment, a Linux GUI that uses the Linux X Windows system. (9)

GNU An organization created in 1984 to develop a free version of a UNIX-like operating system. GNU, a recursive acronym for GNU's Not UNIX, has developed thousands of applications that run on UNIX and Linux platforms. Many are distributed with versions of Linux. (9)

Google account A free account that gives the account holder access to Google services. (11)

graphical user interface (GUI) A user interface that takes advantage of a computer's graphics capabilities to make it easier to use with graphical elements that a user can manipulate to perform tasks such as system and file management and running applications. (1)

group account A security account that may contain one or more individual accounts. In some security accounts databases, it may contain other groups. (2)

guest account A special account used when someone connects to a computer over a network but is not a member of a security account recognized on that computer. That person connects as a guest (if the guest account is enabled) and will only have the permissions assigned to the guest account. (2)

guest OS An operating system running within a virtual machine. (3)

Guest User An account created by OS X that does not require a password, has access only to the Guest Home folder, and when this account logs out, all files and folders created during that session are deleted. (8)

hacker Someone with a great deal of computing expertise. One who does no harm is a white hat hacker. One who does harm is a black hat hacker. (2)

header The information that accompanies a message but does not appear in the message. (2)

Hey Cortana The voice activation options for the Cortana feature of Windows Phone 8.1 and Windows 10. (6)

hibernate A Windows power or shutdown option that, if enabled, saves both the system state and the user session in a file named hiberfil.sys. (7)

hive The portion of the Windows registry represented in one registry file. (7)

home directory In Linux, a directory created for a user, using the user's login name, and located under the /home directory. This is the one place in Linux where an ordinary user account has full control over files without logging in as the root account. (9)

Home folder A folder created by OS X for a user that displays in the Finder when that user is logged on, identified in the sidebar by a house icon and the user's name. (8)

honey pot A server created as a decoy to draw malware attacks and gather information about attackers. (2)

host ID The portion of an IP address that identifies the host on a network, as determined using the subnet mask. (10)

host key A key or key combination that releases the mouse and keyboard from a virtual machine to the host OS. (3)

Host OS The operating system installed directly on the computer. A Type II hypervisor runs on this OS. (3)

hotspot A Wi-Fi network that connects to the Internet through a router. (2)

Hybrid Shutdown The default when you select Shutdown from the Windows 8 (or newer version) Power menu: Windows closes the session for each logged-on user, and hibernates the Windows session and saves it in a file. (7)

Hypertext Transfer Protocol (HTTP) The protocol for transferring the files that make up the rich graphical Web pages we view on the World Wide Web (WWW). It includes the commands a Web browser uses to request Web pages from a Web server to display on the screen of a local computer. (9)

hypervisor The software layer that emulates the necessary hardware for an operating system to run in. It is the hardware virtualization that lets multiple operating systems run simultaneously on a single computer, such as a network server. (3)

iCloud keychain A database of user names passwords to various locations stored in iCloud and accessible to all devices that support it and that have been enabled by the user. (8)

identity theft This occurs when someone collects personal information belonging to another person and uses that information to fraudulently make purchases, open new credit accounts, or even obtain new driver's licenses and other forms of identification in the victim's name. (2)

image An exact duplicate of the entire hard drive contents, including the OS and all installed software, that is used to install copies of an OS and associated applications on multiple computers. (4)

input/output (I/O) Anything sent into a computer (input); anything coming out of a computer (output). (1)

integrated circuit (IC) A small electronic component made up of transistors (tiny switches) and other miniaturized parts. (1)

integrated services digital network (ISDN) A digital telephone service that simultaneously transmits voice, data, and control signaling over a single telephone line. ISDN service operates on standard telephone lines, but requires a special modem and phone service, which adds to the cost. An ISDN data connection can transfer data at up to 128,000 bits per second (128 Kbps). (10)

Internet of Things (IoT) Not really a separate Internet, but a term that describes the trend to have devices such as appliances connected to networks—even to the Internet. (1)

Internet Protocol (IP) The core TCP/IP protocol that delivers communications in chunks, called packets. This protocol allows your computer to be identified on an internetwork by a logical address called an IP address. Special routing protocols can use a destination IP address to choose the best route for a packet to take through a very complex internetwork. IP also has subprotocols that help it accomplish its work. (10)

Internet service provider (ISP) An organization that provides individuals or entire organizations access to the Internet. For a fee, an ISP provides you with this connection service and may offer other Internet-related services such as Web server hosting and email. (10)

internetwork A network of interconnected networks. (10)

IP address The logical address used on a TCP/IP network to identify a network interface card (NIC). (10)

IPv4 The version of the Internet Protocol in use since 1983 (with updates). (10)

IPv6 The latest version of the Internet Protocol that is gradually replacing IPv4. (10)

ISO file A copy of the entire contents of a CD or DVD that can be easily transferred to a writable CD or DVD with ISO image copy software. (3)

job management An operating system function that controls the order and time in which programs are run. (1)

Jump List In Windows, a list of recently opened items such as files, folders, and websites that appear when you right-click on a program on the Start menu or taskbar. (4)

kernel The main component of an operating system that always remains in memory while a computer is running. (1)

key In the Windows registry, a folder object that may contain one or more sets of settings as well as other keys. (7)

keyboard shortcut A key combination that performs an assigned action, saving you several mouse or keyboard actions. (5)

keychain A database in which OS X saves encrypted passwords for a single computer. The first keychain, login, is created for each user and associated with the user's login password. (8)

Keychain Access The OS X utility for managing the keychain. (8)

keylogger See *keystroke logger*. (2)

keystroke logger A hardware device or a program that monitors and records a user's every keystroke, usually without the user's knowledge. Also called a keylogger. (2)

Kickoff Application Launcher A GUI object on the KDE GUI bundled with Fedora that, when clicked, opens a menu (similar to the Windows Start menu) for launching programs. (9)

Last Known Good (LKG) Configuration A Windows start-up option for start-up failures due to a configuration change. It lets you restore the system to a single restore point (not called that). You must use LKG on the first reboot after making a configuration change, and *before* logging on. (7)

Launcher A GUI object (a bar) on the left side of the Ubuntu Unity desktop that serves the same purpose as the OS X Dock and the pinned items feature on the taskbar on the Windows Desktop. (9)

Launchpad A feature in OS X that resembles the home screen on Apple iOS devices. It consists of one or more screens holding icons for all installed apps. Apps can be grouped together and/or launched from the Launchpad. (8)

library A feature introduced in Windows 7, in which a library is a special folder with pointers to disk folders that can be in many locations, but will all appear to be in the same library. (4)

Linux An open source operating system based on UNIX that was developed by Linus Torvalds and others beginning in 1991. (9)

Live File System A file format used by Windows to burn discs that will only be used on newer Apple Macs and newer PCs. Using Live File System you can directly copy items to a CD or DVD without requiring extra hard drive space. You can copy items individually, multiple times. (4)

live image A bootable image of the operating system that will run from disc or other bootable media without requiring that the OS be installed on the local compute. (9)

live tile A rectangle on the Windows 8 Start screen that when tapped with a finger or clicked with a mouse launches an app. The "live" part of the name is due to each tile's ability to display active content related to the app without requiring that you launch the app. (5)

local area network (LAN) A network that covers a building, home, office, or campus. It can be wireless or wired. A Wi-Fi network is a wireless LAN (WLAN). The typical maximum distance covered by WLAN signals or LAN cabling is measured in hundreds of feet. (10)

local security The security options available and limited to a local computer. In Windows, this includes local security accounts and local security for files and folders, Windows BitLocker drive encryption, Windows Defender antispam protection, and Windows Firewall. (4)

location service A service on a computer or mobile device that allows an app to track your location, using one or more methods, often with the help of the Internet. (11)

Lock screen A screen that displays at startup of a Windows 8 computer, when Windows is locked, or when a period of inactivity triggers the screen saver. You must use a swiping motion (with finger or mouse) to close the Lock screen and access either the Sign-in screen or the Start screen. (5)

logon phase A phase of Windows startup during which a user is authenticated, the service control manager starts, logon scripts run, startup programs run, and noncritical services start. Plug-and-play detection occurs during this startup phase. (7)

Mac The product name for Apple's computers. (1)

Mac OS X Server The first of the Mac OS X line designed for Mac Server computers. It was introduced in 1999, shipping preinstalled on Mac Server. Today you can only buy it as an add-on to OS X. (8)

malware A shortened form of "malicious software" that covers a large and growing list of threats such as viruses, worms, Trojan horses, or spam. (2)

manpage In Linux, UNIX, and the OS X Terminal window, a manual page is the documentation for a command, accessed with the **man** command. (8)

Mastered When burning a disc in Windows this option allows you to use the burned CD or DVD in a conventional CD or DVD player or in any computer (older Apple Macs or PCs). (4)

master file table (MFT) The main logical structure of the NTFS file system that is expandable and uses transaction processing to track changes to files. (4)

Measured Boot A UEFI firmware feature that logs the startup process. Antimalware software can analyze this log to determine if malware is on the computer or if the boot components were tampered with. (7)

memory The physical chips that store programs and data. There are two basic types: random-access memory (RAM) and read-only memory (ROM). (1)

memory management An operating system function that manages and tracks the placement of programs and data in memory. (1)

Menu Extras Icons on the right side of the OS X menu bar that give quick access to some System Preferences settings. (8)

microcomputer A computer built around a microprocessor. (1)

microprocessor An integrated circuit (chip) that performs the calculations, or processing, for a computer. Also called a processor or central processing unit (CPU). (1)

Microsoft account (MSA) A free account with Microsoft that gives the subscriber access to Microsoft services, such

as Hotmail, Messenger, SkyDrive, Windows Phone, Xbox LIVE, and Outlook.com. (5)

Microsoft Edge The Internet browser introduced with Windows 10. (6)

Microsoft Passport A feature that securely signs in to network resources without sending a password or PIN over the network. (6)

Microsoft Product Activation (MPA) Microsoft's method of combating software piracy, intended to ensure that each software license is used solely on a single computer. After installing Microsoft software, MPA will attempt to contact Microsoft's site to confirm the product is authentic. Normally, during activation the user is prompted to enter a product code, found on the packaging. Many other software vendors require activation. See *activation*. (4)

Microsoft Security Essentials (MSE) A free security app from Microsoft includes general malware protection and free, automated updates. Available for Windows Vista and Windows 7 at www.microsoft.com/security_essentials. MSE was replaced in Windows 8 by Windows Defender. (4)

Microsoft Store The name for brick-and-mortar stores and an online site that sell hardware and software compatible and approved by Microsoft. (5)

MiFi Novatel's trademarked name for the hotspot device they manufactured. It stands for "my Wi-Fi." (11)

Mission Control A screen in OS X where you can create and organize Spaces. (8)

mobile device management (MDM) A category of software for enforcing policies and managing mobile devices. (11)

mobile hotspot A mobile device that shares its data cellular connection with nearby devices connected via Wi-Fi. (11)

motherboard The central circuit board of a computer to which all other devices connect. (1)

mouse A pointing device that you move with your hand on a level surface to manipulate objects on the computer screen. (5)

MSCONFIG The System Configuration Utility, a Windows tool for modifying system startup, allows you to modify and test start-up configuration settings without having to alter the settings directly. (7)

multiboot An installation that leaves an old OS in place, installing a new OS in a separate location. This allows you to select the OS you want to boot into every time you start the computer. (4)

multitasking Two or more programs (tasks) running simultaneously on a computer. (1)

multitouch The ability to interpret multiple simultaneous touch gestures, such as the pinching gesture in which fingers first touch the device (screen, touch mouse, or touch pad) at separate locations and then pinch them together. (5)

Near Field Communication (NFC) A chipset that supports a short-distance wireless standard that requires two devices to touch before communicating. (11)

net ID The network portion of an IP address, as determined through the subnet mask. (10)

network virtualization A network addressing space that exists within one or more physical networks, but which is logically independent of the physical network structure. (3)

New Technology File System (NTFS) The preferred Windows file system that is expandable and uses a transaction processing system to track changes to files, so that it can roll back incomplete transactions. It also includes several other features: file compression, file encryption, file and folder security, and indexing. (1)

Notification Center An OS X feature that displays important status messages, notifying the user of important events, such as a new email or text message or that an update is available. (8)

object code An executable program, the result of compiling programming statements, that can be interpreted by a computer's CPU or operating system and loaded into memory as a running program. (9)

octet A group of eight binary digits. (10)

on-screen keyboard A virtual keyboard that is available as an accessibility option. It also displays in Windows 8 on devices without a keyboard when you need to enter alphanumeric characters on a device that lacks a keyboard. (5)

open source software Software distributed with all its source code, allowing developers to customize it as necessary. (9)

operating system (OS) A collection of programs that provides a computer with critical functionality, such as a user interface, management of hardware and software, and ways of creating, managing, and using files. (1)

OS X The Apple desktop operating system. (8)

OS X Setup Assistant In a new computer with Mac OS X preinstalled, the OS is not configured, so the first time it is powered up, this program prompts you for the user preferences information. (8)

Out of Box Experience (OOBE) A feature on a new computer with Windows 8 preinstalled. When you take it out of the box and turn it on, you will be greeted with this last phase of Windows installation where you personalize the GUI and configure how you will sign in. (5)

owner In Linux, the user account that creates a file or directory. This term is also used in Windows. (9)

packet A piece of a message packaged by the Internet Protocol. In addition to the portion of a message, each packet is given a header that contains information including the source address (local host address) and the destination address. (10)

pairing A connection between two devices using the Bluetooth wireless standard. (11)

Parental Controls A feature in Internet Explorer that allows parents using a password-protected administrator account to protect their children from harm by setting specific Parental Controls for a child's user account. Apple OS X uses the same name for this type of feature. (2)

partition An area of a physical hard disk that defines space used for a logical drive. (1)

passcode lock A string of characters (or gestures) that a user enters to close the lock screen and access a device. (11)

password A confidential string of characters that a user enters (along with a user name) in order to be authenticated. (2)

password cracker A program used to discover a password. (2)

password manager Software that creates and remembers passwords, and can manage your use of passwords across all your devices. (2)

path A description that an operating system uses to identify the location of a file or directory. (9)

PC Settings screen A Windows 8 screen containing several panels for configuring Windows 8 settings. (5)

permission A level of access to an object, such as a file or folder, that is granted to a user account or group account. (2)

personal computer (PC) A microcomputer that complies with the Microsoft/Intel standards. (1)

personal folders A set of folders created by Windows for each user account to hold user data files. (4)

phishing A fraudulent method of obtaining personal financial information through Web page pop-ups, email, and even paper letters mailed via the postal service. Often purports to be from a legitimate organization, such as a bank, credit card company, or retailer. Phishing is a form of social engineering. (2)

picture-in-picture (PIP) A TV display feature supported by the Xbox app in which one show displays on the screen while another displays in a small box. (6)

pinning A feature introduced in Windows 7 that allows you to place icons for applications and destinations on the taskbar and Start menu. Once pinned, an item's icon remains on the toolbar regardless of whether the program is open or closed. The user clicks it to open the application or destination. (4)

plug and play The ability of a computer to detect and configure a hardware device automatically. To work, the computer, the device, and the OS must all comply with the same plug-and-play standard. (7)

pop-up An ad that runs in a separate browser window you must close before you can continue with your present task. (2)

pop-up blocker A program that works against pop-ups. (2)

pop-up download A program that is downloaded to a user's computer through the use of a pop-up page that appears while surfing the Web. (2)

portable operating system An operating system that you can use on a variety of computer system platforms, with only minor alterations required to be compatible with the underlying architecture. (1)

power-on self-test (POST) Tests of system hardware that runs from firmware when a computer starts up. (7)

PowerShell A Windows CLI scripting environment for advanced users and administrators. (7)

Power User menu A Windows 8 menu that opens when you use the WINDOWS KEY+X shortcut. This menu contains many handy utilities. (5)

predictive notification A feature of Cortana by which it provides a notice or other information in anticipation of a need. (6)

private browsing A security feature available in browsers that allows you to browse the Web without saving any history on the local computer of the sites visited. (10)

private IP address An address from one of three ranges of IP addresses designated for use only on private networks and not to be used on the Internet. The private IP address ranges are 10.0.0.0 through 10.255.255.255, 172.16.0.0 through 172.31.255.255, and 192.168.0.0 through 192.168.255.255. (10)

processes Components of a program that are active in memory. (1)

processor See *microprocessor*. (1)

Program Compatibility Troubleshooter A wizard that you run from Help and Support to set compatibility options for an older application that will "trick" the older program into thinking that the OS is actually the earlier version of Windows required by the application (such as Windows XP). (4)

protocol In the computer technology and networking world a set of rules, usually formalized in a standard published by one of many standards organizations. This is also the term for the software that implements a certain set of rules. (10)

protocol stack A group of bundled programs based on networking protocols and designed to work together. (10)

public IP addresses IP addresses assigned to hosts on the Internet. (10)

Quick link The name for the shortcut on the new Windows 10 Start menu. (6)

random-access memory (RAM) Memory in a computer that acts as the main memory for holding active programs. (1)

ransomware A type of malware that threatens to do damage or lock a user out of a computer unless the user pays a "ransom." (2)

read only memory basic input output system (ROM BIOS) The original system-level PC firmware replaced in recent years by firmware that complies with a newer standard. See *Unified Extensible Firmware Interface (UEFI)*. (1)

recovery key A code generated by OS X when it encrypts the start disk with FileVault. (8)

Red Hat Enterprise Linux (RHEL) Red Hat's commercially available version of Linux. (9)

registry A database of all configuration settings in Windows. (7)

remote access VPN A connection between an individual computer or mobile device using a VPN over a WAN connection. (10)

Remote Desktop client A feature in some editions of Windows that allows a Windows computer to connect to a Remote Desktop host on a remote computer. (5)

Remote Desktop host A feature in some editions of Windows that allows a Windows computer to host incoming Remote Desktop sessions. (5)

remote wipe A feature that allows someone to delete the contents of a mobile device over the Internet. (11)

restore point A snapshot of Windows, its configuration, and all installed programs. If your computer has nonfatal problems after you have made a change, you can use System Restore to roll it back to a restore point. (4)

root account In Linux, an all-powerful account that is used only when absolutely necessary to do advanced tasks. Ubuntu Linux comes with this account disabled in such a way that no one can log in directly with the account, but there is a way to use it temporarily whenever you need it for tasks, such as creating or deleting users. (9)

root key In the Windows registry, each of the top five folders is a root key, sometimes called a subtree in Microsoft documentation. Each of these root keys is the top of a hierarchical structure containing folders called keys. (7)

rootkit Malware that hides itself from detection by anti-malware programs, by concealing itself within the OS code or any other program running on the computer. (2)

router A network device that sits between networks and directs (routes) traffic to destinations beyond the local network. (10)

Safe Mode A start-up mode in which Windows starts without using all of the drivers and components that would normally be loaded. Use Safe Mode when your Windows computer will not start normally. (7)

Safe Mode with Command Prompt A start-up mode in which Windows starts without using all of the drivers and components that would normally be loaded and opens an Administrator Command Prompt window against a black background with the words "Safe Mode" in the four corners of the screen. Use Safe Mode when your Windows computer will not start normally. (7)

sandboxed A feature in OS X that isolates an app so that it cannot access any code or device it is not authorized to access. (8)

scareware A vector technique that uses threatening messages, such as a message offering to fix problems it claims to find and asking for payment. Or it may state that you must complete a survey or it will delete critical files. (2)

screen rotation A feature of mobile operating systems that takes advantage of the built-in hardware accelerometer by rotating the image on the screen to accommodate the position and allow you to read the screen. (1)

Search bar A bar that opens on the right of the screen in Windows 8.*x* after you click or tap the Search charm on the Charms bar. It contains a search box for entering key words to search for all types of data in many locations. (5)

secret key A special code that can be used to decrypt encrypted data. (2)

Second-Level Address Translation (SLAT) A feature found in many newer Intel and AMD CPUs and required by some hypervisors. (3)

Secure Boot A UEFI firmware feature that loads only trusted operating system bootloaders. This is one of the UEFI security features required on computers that come with Windows 8 preinstalled. (7)

Secure HTTP (HTTPS) A form of the HTTP protocol that supports encryption of the communications. HTTPS uses the Secure Sockets Layer (SSL) security protocol. (2)

Secure Sockets Layer (SSL) A security protocol for encrypting network data. (2)

Secure Virtual Memory An OS X feature that encrypts the swap file. (8)

security An operating system function that provides password-protected authentication of the user before allowing access to the local computer. (1)

security account In a security accounts database, a security account is a listing of information about a user, group, or computer. A user or computer account used for authentication; both user and group accounts are used for authorization with assigned permissions. (2)

security ID (SID) A unique string of numbers preceded by *S-1-5* that identifies a security principal in a Windows security accounts database. (7)

semantic zoom A feature in the Windows 8 Metro-style GUI that shrinks objects on the screen. (5)

server A computer that plays one or more of several important roles on a network. In all of these roles, the server provides services to other computers (clients). (1)

server virtualization When a single machine hosts multiple servers, each of which performs tasks independently from the others as separate physical machines would. (3)

Service Set ID (SSID) A network name that identifies a Wi-Fi network. (11)

Settings bar In Windows 8 and Windows 10 a bar containing charms that opens various settings utilities. It opens on the right of the screen when you swipe from the bottom right or use the Windows key+I shortcut. (5)

share A connecting point to which network clients with the correct permissions may connect. It is visible as a folder over the network, but it is a separate entity from the disk folder to which it points. (10)

Shared folder A folder created by OS X in each user's Home folder. It is accessible to other users without restriction. (8)

Sharing Only account In OS X, an account that allows a user to log in remotely and access shared folders, but that does not have a Home folder and cannot be used to log in locally on that computer. (8)

shell The operating system component that provides the character-mode user interface—processing commands and issuing error messages and other limited feedback. (8)

shell command A command entered through a CLI shell. (8)

shortcut An icon that represents a link to an object, such as a file or program. Activating a shortcut (by clicking on it) is a quick way to access an object or to start a program from any location without having to find the actual location of the object on your computer. (4)

shoulder surfing The gathering of information by reading information on a screen as a user works on the device. (2)

Sleep A Windows power down option that leaves the computer in a very-low-power mode in which the system state and user session (applications and data) are saved in RAM, but the screen turns off. (7)

site-to-site VPN A VPN connection between two networks. (10)

smartphone A cell phone that also connects to the Internet and runs a variety of apps for entertainment, education, and work. (1)

SmartScreen A feature introduced in Internet Explorer 9 that prevents the downloading of suspicious programs during Web browsing. It was expanded in Windows 8 so that it is no longer limited just to the Internet Explorer browser and is now called *Windows SmartScreen*. (5)

Snap A feature of Windows 8 that allows two apps to share the screen with a vertical division between them. (5)

social engineering The use of persuasion techniques to gain the confidence of individuals—for both good and bad purposes. People with malicious intent use social engineering to persuade someone to reveal confidential information or to obtain something else of value. (2)

social media A service (Internet-based or other) that provides a place where people can interact in online communities, sharing information in various forms. (2)

social networking The use of social media. (2)

social networking site A website that provides space where members can communicate with one another and share details of their business or personal lives. (2)

solid-state drive (SSD) A storage device that uses integrated circuits, which can be written to and read from much faster than conventional hard disk drives and optical drives. (1)

source code The uncompiled text program statements that can be viewed and edited with a text editor or special program software. (9)

Spaces An OS X feature in which a space is a virtual screen; OS X supports up to 16 Spaces. Use Spaces for separating categories of files, such as those for work, play, and school projects. (8)

spam Unsolicited email. This includes email from a legitimate source selling a real service or product, but if you did not give permission to send such information to you, it is spam. (2)

spam filter Software designed to combat spam by examining incoming email messages and filtering out those that have characteristics of spam, including certain identified keywords. (2)

spear phishing Targeted phishing attacks that often target high-value individuals. (2)

spim An acronym for Spam over Instant Messaging; the perpetrators are called spimmers. (2)

Split View A feature introduced in OS X 10.11 El Capitan that allows two full-screen apps to share the screen. (8)

Spotlight A Mac OS X search utility that, much like Search in Windows, is a live search, so it starts presenting results as soon as you start typing. (8)

spyware A category of software that runs surreptitiously on a user's computer, gathers information without permission from the user, and then sends that information to the people or organizations that requested the information. (2)

Standard account In OS X, an account type that can only access files in that user's Home folder and the Shared folder and is denied access to higher-level system settings. (8)

standard user account An account for an "ordinary" user without administrator status. (2)

Start button A button on the Windows 7 taskbar that opens the Start menu. In Windows 8.1 the Start button returns you to the Start screen. It also displays in the Start screen when a mouse is pointed at the bottom left corner. In Windows 10 the Start button is on the taskbar, as it was before Windows 8. The Start button opens a Start menu. (5)

Start screen The Windows 8 home screen that contains rectangular tiles that you tap with a finger (on touch screens) or click with a mouse to launch the related apps. These tiles replace the old desktop shortcuts and are called live tiles. (5)

Startup Repair A Windows recovery tool that will scan for problems with missing or damaged system files and attempt to replace the problem files. (4)

static IP address An IP address that is manually configured for a host and can, therefore, be considered semipermanent—that is, it stays with the device until someone takes action to change it. (10)

storage virtualization Utilizing multiple networked hard drives as a single logical drive. (3)

subkey In the Windows registry, a key that exists within another key. (7)

subnet mask An important IP configuration parameter as critical as the address itself, because it takes what looks like a single address and divides it into two addresses by masking off part of the address. (10)

Subscriber Identity Module (SIM) An integrated circuit card that, when inserted into a mobile device, programs it for a customer's use on a cellular network. (11)

Switcher A black bar containing thumbnail images of all active apps that slides out of the left edge of the screen after a mouse drag from edge corner. (5)

switch users A feature of most operating systems that allows the currently logged-on users to leave their apps and data open in memory, switching away so that another user can log in to a separate session. (9)

synchronize To match the contents of two locations, sometimes in both directions, so that the contents match. (11)

System Image Recovery A Windows recovery tool that will let you restore a complete PC Image backup, provided you created one. (4)

system-on-a-chip (SoC) A term used to describe a microchip containing all or most of the electronic circuitry for a small computing device, such as a smartphone. (1)

System Preferences The OS X equivalent of the Windows Control Panel. (8)

System Recovery Command Prompt A command prompt accessed by starting a computer from the Windows 7 disc and navigating through the menus to the Recovery Options screen and select Command Prompt. (7)

System Restore A recovery tool that creates restore points, which are snapshots of Windows, its configuration, and all installed programs. If your computer has nonfatal problems after you have made a change, you can use System Restore to roll it back to a restore point. (4)

tablet A mobile computing device with a touch screen, usually no integrated keyboard, and is larger than a smartphone and more portable than a laptop. (1)

Tablet mode Beginning in Windows 10, the mode for displaying the desktop and applications when no keyboard is attached to a device. (6)

task management An operating system function in multitasking OSs that controls the focus. (1)

Task Manager A program for removing errant programs. This Windows utility allows you to see the state of the individual processes and programs running on the computer and to stop one of them, if necessary. (4)

Task view A feature of Windows 10 that lets the user quickly view all open apps. (6)

TCP/IP A suite of protocols that work together to allow both similar and dissimilar computers to communicate. This protocol suite is needed to access the Internet and is the most common protocol suite used on private intranets. It gets its name from two of its many protocols: Transmission Control Protocol (TCP) and Internet Protocol (IP)—the core protocols of TCP/IP. (10)

Terminal A window in the OS X GUI that provides a command-line interface (CLI) for entering UNIX shell commands. The default Terminal shell is BASH. (8)

terminal client Software on a computer that establishes a connection to a terminal server. (3)

terminal services Software running on servers to which user connect from their desktop PCs using terminal client software. (3)

terminal window A window in a Linux GUI that provides a command-line interface (CLI) for entering Linux shell commands. (9)

tethering A. feature that allows you to share your smartphone's cellular data connection with a single computer. The actual connection to the computer, laptop, or tablet can be via USB cable, Wi-Fi, or Bluetooth. Tethering mode turns your phone into a cellular modem. (11)

thin client A minimally configured network computer. (3)

third-party cookie A cookie that originates with a domain name beyond the one shown in the URL for the current Web page. (2)

thumbnail A small graphic image representing a larger object, such as an open app or screen. (5)

Time Machine An OS X backup utility that automatically backs up files to a dedicated drive that is always available when the computer is turned on. (8)

token A physical device that can be used in authentication, either alone or together with a user name and password. (2)

Touch ID A feature in iPhone 5s and newer incorporating a fingerprint scanner into the Home button for authentication. (11)

touch mouse A mouse pointing device that responds to touch gestures on the surface of the mouse, in addition to the typical mouse features. (5)

touchpad A pointing device that responds to finger touch gestures. They are in most laptops and come as separate wireless and USB devices. (5)

Transmission Control Protocol (TCP) The protocol responsible for the accurate delivery of messages, verifying and resending pieces that fail to make the trip from source to destination. Several other protocols act as subprotocols, helping TCP accomplish this. (10)

Trojan horse A program that is installed and activated on a computer by appearing to be something harmless, which the user innocently installs. This is a common way that a virus or a worm can infect a computer. (2)

Trusted Boot A Windows 8 feature that examines each of the system files loaded during the boot process before it is loaded into memory. (7)

two-step verification A security measure used by Microsoft and others (sometimes with different names) that requires, in addition to your credentials, you to enter a numeric code sent to your smartphone or other device, identified in your account information. (6)

Type I hypervisor A hypervisor that can run directly on a computer without an underlying host operating system—sometimes called a bare-metal hypervisor. (3)

Type II hypervisor A Type II hypervisor requires a host operating system. (3)

Ubuntu A group of Linux distributions supported by a company named Canonical. (9)

Unified Extensible Firmware Interface (UEFI) A system firmware standard that replaced the three-decades-old ROM BIOS. (1)

Universal app A type of app, introduced in Windows 10, that adapts to the screen size and type so that it displays in a usable fashion on all Windows 10 devices. (6)

Upgrade An installation of an OS that installs directly into the folders in which a previous version of was installed, preserving all your preferences and data. (4)

user account A record in an accounts database that represents a single person and that is used for authentication. (2)

User Account Control (UAC) A security feature that prevents unauthorized changes to Windows. A user logged on with a privileged account with administrative rights only has the privileges of a standard account until the user (or a malicious program) attempts to do something that requires higher privileges. (2)

user interface (UI) The software layer, sometimes called the shell, through which the user communicates with the OS. (1)

user right In Windows, the privilege to perform a system-wide function, such as access the computer from the network, log on locally, log on to a computer from the network, back up files, change the system time, or load and unload device drivers. (2)

User tile A small image representing the user. A user tile appears in various places in Windows: at the top of the Start menu in Windows 7 and Windows 10 and on the top right of the Start screen in Windows 8.x. Beginning in Windows 8, click or tap the User tile to open User settings. (6)

value entry A setting within a Windows registry key. (7)

vector A mode of malware infection, such as email, code on websites, Trojan horses, searching out unprotected computers, sneakernet, back doors, rootkits, pop-up downloads, drive-by downloads, war driving, and bluesnarfing. (2)

version A unique level of an operating system or other software. (1)

Virtual Desktop A feature introduced in Windows 10 that supports multiple unique instances of the desktop. (6)

virtual desktop infrastructure (VDI) Hosting and managing multiple virtual desktops on network servers. (3)

virtual keyboard An onscreen image of a keyboard with labeled keys that you can tap. (1)

virtual machine (VM) A software simulation of a computer. (3)

virtual machine monitor (VMM) Another name for hypervisor. A software layer that emulates the necessary hardware for an operating system to run in. (3)

virtual memory A system of memory management in which the OS moves programs and data in and out of memory as needed. (1)

virtual private network (VPN) A virtual tunnel created between two end points over a real network or internetwork. This is done by encapsulating the packets. Other security methods are also usually applied, such as encryption of the data and encrypted authentication. When set up in combination with properly configured firewalls, a VPN is the safest way to connect two private networks over the Internet. (10)

virtual reality (VR) When a virtual environment includes three-dimensional images and involves other senses, giving the participant a feeling of actually being present in that time and space. (3)

virtual world An online simulated communal environment within which users, often using an animated computer-generated human (avatar), can interact with one another and create and use various objects. (3)

virtualization The creation of an environment that seems real, but isn't. (3)

virus In the broadest sense, a virus is the term used for all malware, as it is a program that is installed and activated on a computer without the knowledge or permission of the user. The intent is often damage or theft. (2)

Wallet The Apple app (previously named Passbook) that holds credit and debit card data for use with Apple Pay. (11)

war driving The act of moving through a neighborhood in a vehicle or on foot, using a with a Wi-Fi sensor in order to exploit open hotspots, areas where a Wi-Fi network connects to the Internet without the use of security to keep out intruders. (2)

warm boot Restarting a computer without a power-down and power-up cycle. (5)

Web A shortened version of the term World Wide Web (WWW). (9)

Web-based installer An online installer, available through the Microsoft website for upgrading to Windows 8. (5)

Web browser A special type of client software used to navigate the Web. Examples include Firefox, Chrome, Safari, and Internet Explorer. (10)

Web mail A generic term for Web-based email services such as Hotmail, Gmail, and Yahoo! that keep your messages stored on the Internet, allowing you to access them via a Web browser from any computer. (10)

Web Note A feature of Microsoft Edge that allows the user to draw and make notes on a Web page and save a copy of the notated page. (6)

white hat hacker A hacker who is not a cybercriminal. (2)

wide area network (WAN) A network that covers a very large geographic area (miles). (10)

Wi-Fi network A wireless LAN (WLAN) that complies with IEEE 802.11 standards. (10)

wildcard A symbol that replaces any character or string of characters as a parameter in a CLI command. (9)

Windows 8 One of two Windows 8 editions designed for the traditional Intel/AMD computer architecture. This edition is comparable to Windows 7 Home or Home Premium editions, containing features the typical home user would need. (5)

Windows 8 Pro Comparable to Windows 7 Professional and Windows 7 Ultimate, this edition is aimed at individuals with more advanced needs, at home or in a small office. (5)

Windows 8.1 An update to Windows 8 released in late 2013. (5)

Windows 8.1 Pro The Windows 8.1 edition for advanced users and professionals. (5)

Windows 8.1 Pro for Students The discounted edition of Windows 8.1 Pro for students. (5)

Windows 10 Home Edition The basic consumer edition of Windows 10. (6)

Windows 10 Mobile The edition of Windows 10 for smartphones and tablets with screens eight inches or smaller. (6)

Windows 10 Pro The Windows 10 edition for professional users. (6)

Windows Aero Microsoft's name for a group of GUI desktop features and visual themes introduced in Windows Vista. (4)

Windows Defender A free built-in antispyware product in Windows 7. Beginning in Windows 8, this is an improved product with added capabilities that make it a multifunction security program. (4)

Windows Easy Transfer (WET) A utility that will transfer your data, email, and settings for the Windows desktop and your applications from an old installation of Windows to Windows 7. (4)

Windows Explorer The primary tool for copying, moving, renaming, and deleting files in Windows. (4)

Windows Flip A feature of Windows that is activated when you press and hold the ALT KEY while tapping the TAB KEY. It displays a rectangle across the middle of the screen that shows all running apps, including individual Desktop apps. (5)

Windows Hello A Windows 10 biometric sign-in feature that uses fingerprint scanning, facial recognition, or iris scanning. It requires special hardware. (6)

WINDOWS KEY (⊞) A key located near the bottom left of most keyboards that displays a Windows logo and is used in combination with other keys to create keyboard shortcuts. (5)

Windows Memory Diagnostic Tool A Windows recovery tool that tests the system's RAM because RAM problems can prevent Windows from starting. (4)

Windows Preinstallation Environment (Windows PE) A scaled-down Windows operating system. It has limited drivers for basic hardware and support for the NTFS file system, TCP/IP, certain chipsets, mass storage devices, and 32-bit and 64-bit programs. Windows PE supports the Windows Setup GUI, collecting configuration information. (4)

Windows Recovery Environment (Windows RE) A powerful group of Windows diagnostics and repair tools that runs in the Windows Preinstallation Environment (Windows PE). (7)

Windows RT A Windows 8 edition that does not run on the traditional Intel/AMD computer architecture, but comes preinstalled on tablets based on the ARM processor architecture. (5)

Windows RT 8.1 The Windows RT update. (5)

Windows setup The traditional program for installing and upgrading Windows. (5)

Windows SmartScreen A feature based on the SmartScreen feature of Internet Explorer 9. No longer just part of the Internet Explorer browser, it runs at the OS level so that it protects against malicious downloads from any source, such as browsers, email, and even your local network or locally attached drives. SmartScreen uses special sensing features, as well as an online service to determine if software is malicious. (5)

Windows Update A Windows program that can automatically connect to the Microsoft site and download and install updates. (4)

Windows XP Mode Introduced in Windows 7; Windows Virtual PC with a free and legal Windows XP VM preinstalled. (3)

wireless LAN (WLAN) A local area network using one of the standards referred to as Wi-Fi (for wireless fidelity). The Wi-Fi standards of the Institute of Electrical and Electronics Engineers (IEEE) include 802.11a, 802.11b, 802.11g, 802.11n, and 802.11ac. The distance covered by a WLAN is measured in a few hundred feet rather than miles. (10)

wireless wide area network (WWAN) A digital wireless network that extends over a large geographical area. (10)

World Wide Web (WWW) The graphical Internet consisting of a vast array of documents located on millions of specialized servers worldwide. (9)

worm A self-replicating computer virus. (2)

X Window See *X Window System*. (9)

X Window System The program code used as the basis for many GUIs for Linux or UNIX. (9)

Xbox Game bar A bar that displays as part of the Xbox app. It contains buttons for working with Xbox. (6)

zero-day exploit An exploit that a software vulnerability in an operating system or application that is unknown to the publisher of the targeted software. (2)

zombie An individual computer in a botnet. (2)

Photo Credits

Chapter 1

Opener: © Xavier Arnau/Getty Images; p. 2: © Denis Rozhnovsky/Alamy; p. 4 (top): © Philip Sowels/Future Publish/REX/Newscom; p. 4 (bottom): © Studio Works/Alamy; p. 10 (top left): © Apic/Getty Images; p. 10 (bottom left): Reprinted with permission of Alcatel-Lucent USA Inc.; p. 10 (top right): © Xerox/Getty Images; p. 10 (bottom right): © Mark Richards/Zuma/Newscom; p. 11 (top left): © Editorial Image, LLC/Alamy; p. 11 (bottom left), p. 11 (top middle): © SSPL/Getty Images; p. 11 (top right): © DB Apple/picture-alliance/dpa/Newscom; p. 11 (bottom right): © Microsoft/ZUMApress/Newscom; p. 12 (top left): © Time & Life Pictures/Getty Images; p. 12 (top right): © Howard Kingsnorth/Getty Images; p. 12 (bottom right): © Bettmann/Corbis; p. 13 (top left): © INTERFOTO/Alamy; p. 13 (top right): © imago stock&people/Newscom; p. 14, p. 17 (top left): © SSPL/Getty Images; p. 17 (top right): © Bloomberg via Getty Images; p. 18, p. 19: Source: Apple Inc.; p. 20 (top left): © Tony Avelar/AFP/Getty Images; p. 20 (top right): Source: Apple Inc.; p. 20 (bottom right): © Simon Lees/PC Plus Magazine via Getty Images; p. 21 (top left): © FocusDigital/Alamy; p. 21 (top right): © Jens Kalaene/dpa/picture-alliance/Newscom; p. 22 (top left), p. 22 (top right), p. 22 (bottom left): Source: Apple Inc.; p. 22 (bottom right): © Rex Features via AP Images.

Chapter 2

Opener: © Chad Baker/Ryan McVay/Getty Images; p. 41: © Carol and Mike Werner/Alamy; p. 44: © Zmeel Photography/iStock/Getty Images p. 50: © Troy Aossey/Getty Images; p. 51: © Image Source/Getty Images; p. 52: © R and R Images/Getty Images; p. 53: © Comstock Images/Getty Images; p. 54: © artpartner.de/Alamy.

Chapter 3

Page 87: © Bill Johnson/The Denver Post via Getty Images.

Chapter 4

Opener: © Eloy Alonso/Reuters/Landov.

Chapter 5

Page 166: © Jane Holcombe.

Chapter 6

Opener: © Press Association via AP Images; p. 218: Microsoft.

Chapter 7

Opener: © Synergee/iStock/Getty Images.

Chapter 8

Opener: © Ryan Emberley/Invision for Apple/AP Images.

Chapter 9

Opener: © Image Source/Corbis.

Chapter 10

Opener: © Yuriy Panyukov/Alamy; p. 410: © PSL Images/Alamy Stock Photo.

Appendix A

Opener: © Reuters/Corbis.

Index

Note: Page numbers followed by *f* or *t* represent figures or tables, respectively.

Satellite connections, 404–405
    satellite Internet connection
        costs, 405
    satellite Internet connection
        latency, 405
    satellite Internet connection
        speeds, 404–405
Satellite Software International (SSI), 13
SAV extensions, 265
Sbin directory, 373
Scareware, 42
Screen resolution, 179
Screen rotation, 32–33
Script kiddies, 54
Search tool, Linux GUI, 361–362
Second-Level Address Translation
    (SLAT), 100
Secret key, 72
Secure Boot, 276–277
Secure HTTP (HTTPS), 72
Secure Sockets Layer (SSL), 72
Secure Virtual Memory, 332–333
Securing a Linux Desktop
    changing User passwords, 379
    creating a User Account in a GUI,
        376–378
    file and folder permissions,
        380–381
    managing users, 376–379
    root account, 376
    working with directories, 381–382
Securing mobile devices, 455–460
    locator applications, 457–460
    lock screens, 456–457
    operating system patches and
        security updates, 455–456
    software for, 455
Security, 10–11, 33, 39–79
    defenses, 54–74
    mobile computing, 74
    in OS X, 330–335
    physical, 74
    policies, 55–56, 56f
    software, 56–57, 56f
    threats, 40–54
    troubleshooting, 74–76
    Windows 7, 135
    Windows 8.1, 198–202
    Windows 10, 254–257
Security accounts, 66–69
Security certificate, 72
SECURITY hive, 267
Security ID (SID), 269
Security policies, 55–56, 56f
Security software, 56–57, 56f, 125
Servers, 5. *See also* Internet servers
Server virtualization, 86
Service Set ID (SSID), 444
Services.exe, 276
Settings bar, 180
Share, 422

Shared folder, 334
Sharing Only account, 335
Shell, 340, 353
Shell command, 341–342, 353
Shell command system, 369–376
    changing current directory,
        373–374
    displaying contents of a file, 374
    for the Linux File System, 372
    listing contents of a specified
        directory, 372–373
    managing user accounts, 378–379
    relative path, 374
    wildcards, 374–375
Shortcuts
    desktop, 128, 128f
Shoulder surfing, 50
Shutting down a Linux computer, 368
Signing in, to Windows 8.1, 166–167
Simple Mail Transfer Protocol (SMTP), 449
Site-to-site VPN, 406
64-bit operating system, 9
Slackware kernels, 351
Sleep, 273
Smartphone, 4
    connectivity of, 31–32
    operating systems for, 4–5
SmartScreen, 201–202
Snap, 186, 197
Sneakernet, 42
SoC. *See* System-on-a-chip (SoC)
Social engineering, 46–49
Social media, 40, 41
Social networking, 40
Social networking site, 40
SOFTWARE hive, 267
Software versions, 14
Solid-state drive (SSD), 8
Sony, 12
Sophos, 441
Source code, 351
Spaces, 327
Spam, 46
Spam filter, 60
Spear phishing, 48
Spim, 46
Split View, 328, 328f
Spotlight, 316
Spyware, 45
SSD. *See* Solid-state drive (SSD)
Standard account, 334
Standard user account, 67
Start button, 178, 178f
Start menus, Windows 10, 224–225, 225f,
    243–244
Start screen, Windows 8.1, 178, 178f, 185,
    186f, 187–191
Startup
    modifying, 277–281
    troubleshooting with modified,
        288–290

    Windows 7, 274–276
Startup Repair, 136
Static IP address, 393
Storage virtualization, 86
Subkey, 267
Subnet mask, 394
Subscriber Identity Module (SIM), 444
Sudo (Superuser Do) command, 378
Sun Microsystems, 16
Suspending a Linux GUI, 368
Switch Users, 150, 368
Synchronization of mobile devices,
    452–455
    with Android devices, 453
    configuring iOS using iTunes,
        454–455
    connecting mobile devices for
        syncing, 453
    iOS Device with a Mac
        or PC, 453
    in Windows Phone, 455
Synchronous DSL (SDSL), 402
System Configuration Utility
    (MSCONFIG), 297–298, 297f
SYSTEM hive, 267
System Image Recovery, 136, 241
System-on-a-chip (SoC), 4
System Preferences, 324, 324f
System Recovery Command
    Prompt, 289
System Restore, 136

T

Tablet mode, 242–243, 243f
Tablets, 5
Task management, 7–8
Task Manager, 136
Task view, 251, 251f
TCP/IP, 13, 388
TCP/IP protocol suite
    understanding, 388
Terminal (OS X), 340–343
Terminal client, 87
Terminal services, 87
Terminal window in Linux, 368–369
Test Linux case sensitivity, 369
Tethering, 446
Theft
    hardware, 51
    identity, 49
    mobile computing, 74
Thin client, 87
Third-party cookie, 51
32-bit operating system, 9
Threats, security
    accidents/mistakes/disasters, 52
    defenses against, 54–74
    hardware theft, 51
    identity theft, 49
    malware, 40–46